6346

Centennial International Exhibition,
MELBOURNE, 1888.

QUEENSLAND: A SKETCH

BY

H. COURTENAY LUCK, F.R.G.S.

(Issued under the Authority of the Queensland Commissioners.)

Executive Commissioners :

JOHN FENWICK, Esq., J.P.
The Honorable THOMAS MACDONALD-PATERSON, M.L.C.
FRANCIS REID MURPHY, Esq., M.L.A.

Executive Commissioners in Queensland :

F. M. BAILEY, Esq., F.L.S.
C. W. de VIS, Esq., M.A.
JOHN FENWICK, Esq., J.P.
P. R. GORDON, Esq., J.P.
Hon. A. C. GREGORY, C.M.G., M.L.C.
GEORGE GRIMES, Esq., J.P.
JOHN LITTLE, Esq., J.P.
JAMES TOLSON, Esq., J.P.

Secretary :

H. COURTENAY LUCK, F.R.G.S.

CONTENTS.

L
7

QUEENSLAND: A SKETCH.

I.—Introductory and General.

In December. 1823, Surveyor-General Oxley, acting on the information of two castaways, first entered the magnificent river to which he gave the name of the Brisbane. The foundation of Queensland's settlement may be dated from that day. It will not be necessary in this short description to enter minutely into the history of the early settlement of the colony, which for many years remained an integral portion of that of New South Wales. So little seems to have been thought of its future importance that the authorities in 1825 established a penal establishment at the mouth of the river, and it was not until 1840 that the Act of Legislature was passed which abolished transportation to Botany Bay, and that steps were taken to remove this foul excrescence from these fair shores. The first ship bringing free immigrants was the Artemisia, followed quickly by the Fortitude, which was the earliest vessel bringing settlers under Dr. Lang's scheme, and the now populous Fortitude Valley marks the spot which was chosen as the home of the first free pioneers of Queensland.

The year 1859 is memorable as that in which the colony was considered sufficiently important to be granted the inestimable boon of self-government, and from this date commences its real progress, to which the increase of population will afford us some index.

According to the first official figures the population of Queensland in 1860 was 28,056. The estimated number on the 31st December, 1887, was, in round figures, 367,000, of whom 215,000 were males, and 152,000 females.

The colony is situated between the parallels of 10° 40'—29° southern latitude. and 138°—153° 13' east longitude, and within these limits contains an area of 668,224 square miles, with a seaboard of about 2500 miles. On all sides of this immense area are seen evidences of the energy and vitality of the people. Vessels of all sizes swarm along the coast. Railways render easy communication with the principal inland towns and bring rich freights to the coast, and the traveller can now journey by rail uninterruptedly from Brisbane to Sydney, Melbourne and Adelaide. The whole colony is dotted with towns— centres of energy—while the fruits of the indomitable industry of the miner, the pastoralist and the agriculturist, are seen in all directions.

Within the large area covered by the colony there is necessarily a great diversity of climate. Speaking generally, the rainy season throughout the colony occurs in the months of January and February. In the tropical portion there is a well-defined "rainy season," extending from January to March. In the south the rains are more generally distributed over the year. The winter is generally dry and bracing, more especially upon the highland plains west of the coastal range ; indeed, for at least eight months of the twelve the climate of Queensland is most lively and exhilarating, and closely approaches that of Madeira. The total rainfall in 1887 at Brisbane was 81 inches ; at Cooktown, 75 inches ; Warwick, 32 inches : Stanhorpe, 35 inches: Geraldton, 155 inches; Rockhampton, 45 inches; Normanton, 37 inches ; and Townsville, 56 inches.

The mean shade temperature of Brisbane in 1887 ranged from 76° in January to 56° in June. The climate, on the whole, is remarkably healthy, and as the manner of life among the people is brought more in unison with its demands, is shown to be fully as salubrious as that of any other portion of the Australian continent. No part of the colony is unsuited to the European constitution. In the inland plains more especially the climate shows its effect in the physique of the people, and the hearty manner in which athletic exercises are pursued by the younger portion of the community is strong evidence of its invigorating character.

The advance of Queensland is due in great measure firstly to its pastoral and latterly to its mineral resources. Running along the eastern coast, and at a distance varying from 20 to 100 miles from the sea, is the backbone, or great dividing range of mountains. Between this range and the sea is found a belt of rich alluvial soil. well watered by many fine streams, while undulating plains stretch beyond the range westward. The coastal districts are devoted almost entirely to agriculture and timber getting. Beyond, the pastoralist and miner share, with the agriculturist, the produce of the soil.

As the timber getter removed with his axe the giants of the forest, clearing the dense scrub found in his way. he was closely followed by the agriculturist, and sugar. maize. tobacco, cotton, took the place of the stately pine and noble cedar.

Another impetus was the discovery of gold in the range districts, attracting thousands into the colony to better their fortune, and to help forward its progress—which bearing in mind its early history may be said to be almost unparalleled in British Colonization.

Brisbane, the capital city, has now (1888) within its five mile radius a population of 75,000, three times the number of the inhabitants of the whole of Queensland at the date of its separation from New South Wales in 1859. The town is situated on both banks of the river of the same name, and about 12 miles from its mouth. The chief public buildings, banks, newspaper offices, and principal places of business have hitherto been situated on the north side of the river, but recently separate municipal government has been granted to South Brisbane, which bids fair, ere long, to rival in importance its older sister on the north.

On his first visit to the town the stranger will probably be struck with the substantial buildings which everywhere meet the eye. The Queensland National Bank—a most imposing edifice of freestone—will bear comparison with any institution of similar nature in the old country; while the offices of the Australian Mutual Provident Society, the "Courier" Buildings, and many other edifices throughout the city bear witness to the commercial enterprise of its business men, and the magnitude of their operations. The new Government offices, now nearly completed, add another to the massive and elegant buildings of the city.

Sawmills, foundries, shipbuilding yards, and factories of all kinds line the river banks. or are dotted about the city. The wharfs scarcely accommodate the number of vessels of all countries and of the largest sizes, which there discharge their cargoes in the heart of Brisbane. The river is one of the best for commerce in the Australian colonies. A commodious dry dock renders easy repairs to all but the largest vessels.

Among the other important towns along the coast may be mentioned :- -Rockhampton, on the Fitzroy River ; Maryborough on the Mary ; Townsville ; and Mackay, on the Pioneer. Bowen, Cairns, Cooktown, Port Douglas, Bundaberg, Gladstone and Normanton, are other seaport towns rendering easy access to the interior, and which have an important future before them.

The most important inland towns are, Ipswich, one of the oldest and more populous, situated on the Bremer river, 25 miles from Brisbane ; Toowoomba. Warwick. which with other towns are all connected with the capital by rail ; Gympie, the first mining field, with railway communication with Maryborough, and which will shortly be connected in a similar manner with Brisbane ; Mount Perry, the centre of the copper district, within a few miles by rail

of Bundaberg ; Charters Towers, with railway outlet to Towns
ville; Herberton, the rich tin and silver mining district, now
being connected by rail with Cairns, and many other towns, of
which want of space precludes mention here.

The Government of Queensland is vested in a Governor
(appointed by the Crown) and a Ministry chosen from the Legislature, which consists of two Houses—the Legislative Council
and the Legislative Assembly. The former consists of members
nominated by the Governor for life; the latter is elective. The
franchise is framed almost on the basis of manhood suffrage,
every male of the full age of twenty-one years, and being of sound
mind, having a voice in the selection of members of the Assembly.
The colony is also represented in the Federal Council of Australasia The executive business of the country is carried on by
seven responsible ministers, who preside over the various Government departments.

The colony is divided into a number of divisions, each placed
under the control of an elected Divisional Board, consisting of
three or more members. These Boards levy rates and maintain
and control the public highways, bridges, ferries, wharfs, wells,
and other public works within their respective districts. An
endowment is paid by the Government to each Board in proportion
to the amount collected by rates. The wonderful progress of the
colony since the initiation of this system of local self-government
is the best evidence that can be offered as to its wisdom. The
large towns are all incorporated as municipal councils, having
duties similar to the Divisional Boards.

The administration of justice is in the hands of a Chief Justice,
three Puisne, and three District Court Judges. Besides these
Police Magistrates are appointed in every large town, while
Justices of the Peace are found throughout the colony. The
Gold Warden or Minerals Commissioner, who is also generally
a Police Magistrate, is the chief officer on each mineral field.
Bearing in mind the large extent of territory, and its scattered
population, crime cannot be said to be prevalent in Queensland,
although there are several penal stations, the most important
being St. Helena—an island in Moreton Bay.

Reformatories are located in various towns, and, thanks to the
system adopted for the reclamation of juvenile criminals, have
been successful in making numbers of lads good and useful members of society.

The railway system of the colony is being rapidly extended ;
1865 miles are now open for traffic, while a further 600 miles are
authorised or in course of construction. Communication is now
established between Brisbane and Charleville on the western line,
Wallangarra on the southern line, where the Queensland system

connects with that of New South Wales, and thus with those of Victoria and South Australia. Various branch lines exist or are being constructed, bringing the produce of their districts into the towns. The precipitous coastal range was the great obstacle with which the railway engineer had to contend in opening communication with the interior. Steep gradients, sharp curves, cuttings and tunnelings, had to be encountered, fearful gorges spanned, but the difficulty was surmounted, and the result is a triumph of engineering skill and enterprise. The line passes through magnificent scenery, and reaches, near Toowoomba, a height of 2,600 feet. The rolling stock used on the railways is almost entirely made in the colony, either in the government workshops or private establishments.

The other railway systems have been already mentioned The beauties of the scenery through which many of the lines pass, and the wonderful resources which they tap, may be expected to attract the tourist in search of new sights, as well as the commercial man seeking to extend his business or invest his capital.

While offering no serious engineering difficulties the question of the supply of water for Brisbane has engaged considerable attention. It is now obtained from the Enoggera and Goldcreek reservoirs, situated in a range of hills a few miles from the city. In order to obviate any danger of drought, and to meet the rapid increase in the population it is proposed to tap the head of the Brisbane River.

No expense has been spared to render the water supply of Brisbane and other large towns thoroughly efficient. The recent drought, from which all portions of the colony suffered, forced the attention of the pastoralist to the importance of securing a continuous water supply. In most cases shallow boring has brought large stores of excellent water to the surface. Under the supervision of the hydraulic department boring operations in search of water have been carried on in various parts of the colony.

At Blackall a 6 inch bore, carried to a depth of 1663 feet yields 12000 gallons per hour; the temperature of the water being 119° F and the pressure 63lb to the square inch. If pipes could be taken into the air, the water would rise to over 600 feet from the surface. the formation passed through is Ocean mud, the water being struck in the Sandstone at Barcaldine at a depth of 645 feet, 7000 gallons are yielded hourly, the temperature of the water being 101° F., the formation being similar to the Blackall bore. Another bore has also been made 21 miles from Barcaldine, on the route of the Central Railway to the Thompson; these also being flowing bores.

The Telegraphic system is rapidly extending, and by its means the furthermost corner of the colony is now in quick communication with the capital. The length of line now reaches 8,772 miles, with 15,677 miles of wire, worked from 293 stations. Queensland is connected by telegraph with all the colonies, and by means of the South Australian overland line, with the whole civilized world. Ten words, exclusive of sender's name and recipient's address, may be sent to any part of the colony for one shilling.

The Postal system is worked by 716 post and receiving offices, and the routes cover 25,494 miles. The postage on inland letters is two pence. One penny is charged on letters posted in Brisbane or other towns, and addressed to the suburbs.

The development of ocean and coastal steam communication has been rapid. The British India Steam Navigation Company's line runs direct between Brisbane and London, carrying monthly mails, while intermediate boats, richly freighted with the products of the colony, afford the merchant and shipper the means of transporting their wares to the markets of the world. The coastal service is supplied by vessels of the Australasian United Steam Navigation Co., Q S. S. Co., and W. Howard Smith & Sons, besides many smaller crafts owned by private firms.

Great improvements have been made within recent years in the harbors and rivers of the colony, and the coast of Queensland is now the best lighted in Australia. Rivers have been dredged, and the largest steamships now ascend the Brisbane river, discharging their cargoes at the various wharfs of the city. Large sums of money have been profitably expended in works designed to render the navigation of Queensland waters more secure, and the facilities thus rendered have borne fruit in the increased trade which naturally followed. The tonnage of ships entering Queensland ports for the year 1860 was 84,000. The total inward tonnage of 2147 vessels in 1887 was 1,642,024, and the total outward tonnage of 2183 vessels was 1,631.956.

The press literature of the colony is large and varied. Each town possesses one or more newspapers, some of high class, and managed with ability and enterprise. No · is it only in this branch of literature that Queensland can hold her own. In its ranks are writers favorably known among literati, and whose writings are highly appreciated not only in the colony but elsewhere.

While athletic sports and games are well patronised, well supported musical and scientific institutions evince the artistic and intellectual aspirations of Queenslanders. Two excellent social clubs flourish, while the Johnsonian Club, sacred to art, literature and science, and resembling in character the London Savage Club, to which it is affiliated, will bear the palm in comparison with any club of a similar character in the colonies.

The various Friendly Societies, Good Templars, Rechabites. Salvationists. Oddfellows, &c., have their organisations and meeting-houses, while the Freemasons of all three constitutions—English, Scotch and Irish. are a numerous and powerful body. The best companies perform in the theatres of Brisbane, and attract large and appreciative audiences, while the high class performances of the Brisbane Musical Union and Brisbane Liedertafel fill to excess the large hall of the Brisbane Exhibition.

Holidays are numerous. and are the occasion and opportunity for all manner of picnics. racing and athletic sports, &c.

The Brisbane Carnival is the week in which the Exhibition of the National Agricultural and Industrial Association of Queensland is held. This takes place in August, and is eagerly looked forward to and attended by all classes of persons from every portion of the colony, while business is almost entirely suspended.

The trades societies are influential and well managed bodies, and are well supported by the mechanic, artizan and laborer. The business-like manner in which the Trades Congress was conducted during the present year in Brisbane was warmly and favorably commented upon.

Religious bodies have in Queensland no connection with the State. The various denominations carry on their operations with energy, tolerance and success, the ministers and laymen gladly uniting to promote every charitable object.

The Dunwich Benevolent Asylum provides for the aged and infirm poor, while the orphanages undertake the care and education of a large number of children. Hospitals exist in every town, and with other philanthropic institutions are well supported by every class of the community.

By the popularity of the Volunteer system a considerable number of men have been enrolled in the various corps. The Queensland Scottish and the Queensland Irish especially are fine bodies of men. The colony also owns two gunboats, torpedo and other boats. and the Naval Brigade is an efficient and popular branch of the service. The whole force is gathered together at Easter for training in camp. During recent years greater attention has been paid to the defence of the colony. and the results are apparent in the increased smartness and military bearing of the men. Nor is the Queensland youth forgotten in this respect. Cadet corps are attached to the various Grammar schools, and are popular with the boys, many of whom, later on, join the regular Defence Force.

There is no idle class in Queensland. All are workers. The thrifty amongst them are generally the owners of the allotment on which their house is built, or are saving in the Government Savings Bank with the object of becoming their own landlords. The working man manages his own friendly societies, most of which are on a sound financial footing.   All having a voice in the affairs of the colony, take an intelligent interest in them.   Many of our relations in the old country would be pleasantly astonished could they see the wide streets crowded with tram, bus, or cab ; the crowds of well-dressed. orderly and comfortable-looking artizans, with their wives and families ; the brilliant shops and general appearance of independence and prosperity. Probably the general mass of the people of Queensland are as happy and are better paid, better fed, and better clothed than in any country outside Australia.   Long may Queensland remain thus pre-eminent !

II.—Education.

QUEENSLAND may well be proud of her educational system.   One of the first Acts passed by the Legislature, after separation from New South Wales, provided for the primary education of the youth of the colony—framed on the basis of the Irish National School system.   Under this Act schools were divided into two classes—the vested and non-vested.   The former were unsectarian in their character, but the reading of the Scriptures formed part of their syllabus, and while the enforcement of moral duties by selections from the New Testament was permitted, the inculcation of any denominational tenets was strictly and absolutely forbidden.

These schools were managed by a Government Board of Education, under the presidency of a political minister.   The control of expenditure, appointment of teachers, and general administration of the Education Act was committed to this Board.   The salaries of the teachers were at first supplemented by school fees, but this system was afterwards abolished. the teachers receiving increased stipends from the revenue in lieu of fees.   Education in Queensland became free.

The non-vested schools were established and controlled by the Anglican and Roman Catholic Churches, who provided buildings and teachers, whose salaries, however, together with books, were provided by the State.   Religious instruction was permitted in these schools.   Both vested and non-vested schools were subject to Government inspection.   This system continued in force until 1875, when the present system was instituted.   The new Act provided that State aid to all non-vested schools should cease in 1880, and since that date such schools have ceased to exist.

An Act of 1860 provided liberally for the establishment of Grammar Schools, the Governor-in-Council being empowered to make a grant from the public revenue of twice the amount raised by public subscription (such grant not exceeding £2000), for the purpose of erecting buildings.

Where the public have subscribed £2000, and fees to the amount of £500 are guaranteed for three years, the Governor-in-Council may authorise the expenditure of £1000 per annum from the general revenue, to defray the stipends of teachers and the necessary school expenditure. A portion of this latter grant may be reserved for providing scholarships or exhibitions at any British or Australian University

With the approval of the Legislature, Grammar schools may be permanently endowed with Crown land to the value of £2000.

The Act of 1875 provides that State education in Queensland should be FREE, SECULAR, and COMPULSORY.

The inhabitants of any locality requiring a State school, must, before a school can be erected, raise amongst themselves a sum equal to one-fifth of the estimated cost of erecting and furnishing the building. This amount must be paid to the credit of the Minister for Education, and application made to him for the establishment of a school, the prayer being granted or refused by the Governor in-Council as the circumstances of the case may require.

The Act provides that for secular instruction four hours daily shall be set apart'; but, with the exception of infant schools, five hours secular instruction are given, under regulations issued by the authority of the Governor-in-Council Religious instruction may, however, be given in the school buildings, but after school hours, to children willing to receive it, but this permission is by no means freely used, and but little success has attended the privilege. Children look upon it as extra school work, and absent themselves accordingly from an attendance which is absolutely voluntary. School teachers are prohibited from acting in any position approaching that of a minister of religion.

The third great principle of the Act, requiring compulsory attendance, is honored more in the breach than the observance. The clause can only be enforced in districts proclaimed by the Governor-in-Council, and as no such proclamation has ever been made, this portion of the Act remains practically a dead letter. Attention, however, has of late been earnestly drawn to the necessity of enforcing these provisions of the Act, and to preserve the rising youth of the colony from ignorance, if not from crime, it is to be hoped that the compulsory clause of the Act may be no longer permitted to remain inoperative—a fruitful cause of

" larrikinism." The parent of every child between the ages of six and twelve years is, by these clauses, compelled to cause such child to attend a State school not less than sixty days in each half-year. Any parent neglecting or refusing to comply with this condition, except with valid excuse, is liable to a fine of 20s. for the first offence, and £5 for the second or subsequent offence, or in default, may be imprisoned for seven or thirty days respectively. The only valid excuses permitted are, first, that the child is being efficiently taught elsewhere ; second, sickness, fear of infection. or some unavoidable cause ; third, distance of over two miles from school ; fourth, that the child has been educated up to the prescribed standard.

State schools are divided into two classes—State school proper and Provisional schools. The former are those provided and maintained at the Government expense, as previously mentioned, and are furnished with materials for school work—text-books, apparatus for teaching and necessaries, the parents having to furnish only the minor requisites. Such schools can be established only on satisfying the Minister of Education that an attendance of thirty children is probable. Should the attendance fall below twenty-five. the school may be closed.

The syllabus includes instruction in reading, writing, arithmetic, English grammar, geography, history, elementary mechanics. object lessons, drill, and gymnastics, and vocal music ; girls being taught domestic economy and needlework.

These branches of instruction are all efficiently taught. and the diligent lad will find himself on quitting school fairly armed for the battle of life, while his training will, if he be inclined to follow up his education at one of the Grammar Schools, fit him for entrance upon the curriculum there.

Where districts are but sparsely populated, or where occasions warrant, Provisional schools are established, at which an average attendance of not less than twelve children is necessary. A teacher may have two or more schools of this nature under his charge, in which case the average attendance must not be less than six. For neglected children Provisional schools may be opened in the evening or other suitable time, at which twelve is fixed as the minimum average attendance.

Although the teachers in Provisional schools are not classified under the Education Act, the State defrays the cost of their salaries. towards which, however, local contributions are expected but seldom realised. The buildings have to be provided at the expense of the district, and, when warranted, the Provisional schools are transferred into State schools. At the end of 1887, 306 State and 221 Provisional schools were open in the colony, officered by 675 male and 796 female teachers.

The teachers may be classed as head, assistant. and pupil teachers. Of head teachers there are 383 males and 130 females ; of assistants. 122 males, 282 females ; of pupil teachers, 170 males, 381 females. Their training is mainly carried on in the colony, and for efficiency they will bear very strict comparison with any teaching staff.

The standard of education which teachers must reach is high, and the rejected candidates are every year sufficiently numerous to indicate the severity and impartiality of the examination.

The incomes of head teachers vary from £400 to £200 per annum, inclusive of fees and salary, rent being allowed to head teachers where no residence is attached to the school. Female head teachers receive somewhat less than these amounts. The assistant teachers pay ranges from £102 to £250, and from £72 to £150, for males and females respectively ; while male pupil teachers receive from £40 to £70, and females £20 to £50 per annum.

The scholars enrolled numbered, in 1887, 63,704, of whom 33,650 were boys, and 30,054 girls. The mean quarterly enrolment was 25.961 boys and 23,457 girls, and average daily attendance 19,155 boys, and 16,164 girls

Bearing in mind the large territory over which population is scattered, these figures speak well for education in Queensland.

Besides the State Schools there are many private schools of high character situated in towns throughout the colony. The Roman Catholics. while sustaining many schools of their own without pecuniary State aid, and in no way subject to the State, voluntarily placed themselves under Government inspection. and maintain a high standard of education amongst their youth.

Every year 120 scholarships are competed for in the State Schools, of which ninety are for boys and thirty for girls These scholarships entitle the winners to free education for three years at any Queensland Grammar school. The candidates must be under 14 years of age on the 31st of December in the year of examination, and must for six months prior to examination have been regular in their attendance either at a State school or one under Government inspection, the latter provision enabling pupils of Roman Catholic schools to compete. Candidates must also have been pupils in the school for at least eighteen months.

Simultaneous examinations are held throughout the colony, the subjects being those requisite for children of the fourth class. The examinations being over. the papers are forwarded to the Education Department, whose inspectors examine them and adjudicate.

Examinations for three competitive exhibitions to Universities are annually held, the professors of Sydney University preparing and examining the papers. All students under nineteen years of age are eligible as candidates, and the exhibition is worth £100 per annum for three years, the winner having to enter upon his studies at some approved university, and continue thereat as students for the whole term.

The number of youths who, having by their industry at the State school passed by scholarship to the Grammar school, and thence by exhibition to the University, and whose doings thereat have gained them honorable distinction, is a gratifying proof of the thoroughness of the Queensland educational system, and does honor to the institutions in which they trained.

The Department of Public Instruction is under the control of a Minister for Education, under whom the permanent head is the Under Secretary—at present Mr. J. G. Anderson, M.A., the able former coadjutor of Mr. Randall M'Donnell, in his efforts in placing the educational system of the early years in working order. Besides the Under Secretary there is a general inspector and district inspectors, to each of whom a district is assigned. Then come the school committees, who have charge of the school premises, and who, while having no authority over the teachers, are expected to take a lively interest in all that concerns the attendance, discipline, and effectiveness of the school.

The total cost of State education in 1887 amounted to £224,558, State schools costing £173,852, provisional schools £16,084. Building and furnishing amounted to £36,824, and, without taking the value of sites into consideration, school property to the amount of £295,277 is held by the Department. State education in 1887, including all charges, costs £5 7s. 6½d. per child. The grammar schools were subsidised to the extent of £10,000. Exhibitions and scholarships cost £3,010, technical education £600, museums £2,383, and orphanages £18,788.

The wonderful progress of the colony since its separation from New South Wales may well be a source of pride to Queensland, but of nothing should she be prouder than of her noble educational institutions, which, founded so well in the past, must eventually place her foremost in the ranks of civilization. And this sketch of Queensland education would be incomplete without reference to the labors of Chief Justice Sir Charles Lilley, Sir Arthur Palmer, Sir Samuel Griffith, and the late Hon. T. B. Stephens, who, with many other public spirited men, have made our primary and grammar schools the institutions they have become.

During 1887, renewed efforts were made for the establishment of a Queensland University, and at the present time there is every prospect that this—the fitting cap of the Queensland educational system—will before long become a successfully accomplished fact, when it will no longer be necessary for our students to finish their education at foreign institutions before taking that place in the community to which their industry has entitled them.

III.—The Pastoral Industry.

AT the time of the separation of the colony from New South Wales, in 1859, it was estimated that its live stock numbered 23,504 horses, 432,890 cattle, and 3,166,802 sheep. The progress which has since been made in the pastoral industry of Queensland will be shown in the following lines, the information in which has been supplied by Mr. P. R. Gordon, the Chief Inspector of Stock.

Of the total area of the colony, 427,838,080 acres, about seven per cent. only, had on the 31st December, 1887, been alienated from the Crown. A large proportion of the alienated, and the greater portion of the unalienated lands are either held or are available for pastoral purposes.

With the exception of portions of alienated lands on the coast. and on the eastern edge of the Darling Downs, the stock are fed almost entirely upon indigenous grasses.

The "Mitchell Grass" (Astrebla elymoides) is especially a most valuable fodder grass, and extends over a large area of country available for settlement. Unlike ordinary grass, the stalks of the Mitchell grass are perennial, and bud out afresh at each joint after every shower of rain, and it has, therefore, received the suggestive name of the "squatters stand by."

In the excepted portions lucerne (Medicago sativa) or the Californian prairie grass (Bromus unioloides) are cultivated, chiefly for the purpose of fattening store cattle and sheep for the metropolitan market. On some of the rich alluvial flats in the Moreton district forty sheep to the acre have been fattened on these grasses during favorable summer months.

In a colony of such a vast area as Queensland, the variations in topographical features, geological formations, temperature and climate, must necessarily be considerable. These conditions exercise a potent influence on the pasture and on stock. The rank natural vegetation along the coast watershed, and in the northern latitudes, affords excellent pasturage for cattle and horses, but is totally unsuited for sheep, while the salinous herbage in the drier climate of the interior affords sheep pasture which is not excelled and is scarcely equalled in any other country, and is also admirably adapted for cattle, &c. A grazing farm of 20,000 acres, if of good unimproved indigenous pasture will carry in average seasons throughout the year 8000 sheep, or about 1300 cattle.

Where the land is favorably situated for the conservation of water, by the damming of natural watercourses or the excavation of tanks, or where underground supplies can be tapped by sinking or boring, the grazing capabilities of the country can be greatly increased. In many districts supplies of underground water are reached at a depth of from 25 to 40 feet, and raised for the use of stock by inexpensive windmills. It is frequently the case in Queensland, as in other colonies, that some of the best pasture lands are long distances from rivers and watercourses, and are therefore only available for occupation during wet seasons. Where water is procured by sinking, such lands are made permanently available.

The average clip of merino wool per sheep is from 6 lbs. to 8 lbs., and the wages of shearers from 3s. 6d. to 4s. per score. The annual increase of lambs from a flock of breeding ewes ranges from sixty to eighty, and under favourable circumstances, ninety per cent. Good breeding ewes can be purchased, at the present time, at 10s. ; and superior flock rams at from £2 to £3.

Where a grazing farm is situated so as to command a ready market for fat stock, it may be worked to greater profit by purchasing and fattening store stock instead of breeding. Store sheep can be purchased after shearing at prices that will leave a fair margin of profit when sold as fat, and the same remark will apply to store cattle. Or it may be found more profitable to combine breeding with the purchase and fattening of store stock.

Circumstances will determine the description of sheep most suitable for particular localities. Thus on rich soils, with a good average rainfall, a strong, heavy, lustrous description of combing wool will give the best return ; while on thin soil, and on broken or hilly country, a high-class fine clothing wool can be grown to best advantage. If the land is convenient to railway communication, and other circumstances are favourable, the breeding of crossbred sheep may be found more profitable than that of merinos. A cross between the English Lincoln and the merino produces a very valuable sheep, for which there is a great demand at the present time for fattening on the cultivated grasses of the coast and Darling Downs. This cross matures early, and realises, when fat, 75 per cent. higher prices than the merino. The wool is a beautiful long lustrous staple, much sought after by English manufacturers, and commands at the present time as much per lb. as a medium description of merino, while the fleece is considerably heavier than the latter.

The lands immediately to the west of the main coast range, and for a considerable distance inland, are admirably adapted to the growth of fine merino wool, and here the highest quality of combing merino wool is successfully grown. Further to the westward, on the extensive plains in the interior, although the herbage affords more nutritious pasturage, and the sheep, in consequence, attain a greater weight of carcase, the more arid nature of the climate is not so favourable to the secretion of the yolk, and, as a consequence, the wool, although sound in staple and of vigorous growth, is not so free and silky, and therefore not so well adapted for combing purposes as that grown in the more easterly districts, but constitutes a superior wool for clothing purposes.

Of each of the two varieties of sheep in the colony—merino and coarse-wooled—there are several sub-varieties or classes. The merinos may be classed as fine and medium clothing wool, and fine, medium, and strong combing wool, the last named being principally restricted to the richer pasturage and comparatively humid climate of the Downs country, immediately west of main coast range. The number of sheep in the colony on 31st December, 1887, was 12,927,000.

Probably in no other part of the world does the farmer's live stock enjoy such an immunity from disease as in Queensland. Scab in sheep has never existed in this colony, foot rot may be said to be unknown, and with the exception of a few sheep, kept on the coast watershed, fluke has no existence.

The few occasional cases of catarrhal fever have been promptly stamped out by the destruction of the infected flock, the owners being compensated from a fund accruing, under the " Diseases in Sheep Act," from small annual contributions (five shillings per 1000 sheep) to cover the cost of inspection and prevention of disease.

In seasons of severe drought, when there is little nutrition in grass or herbage, considerable losses have occurred in some portions of the colony, from the presence of intestinal worms, but such cases are unknown where feed is abundant, and in districts where the herbage is of a saline nature.

Pleuro-pneumonia, which, on its first introduction—23 years ago—occasioned considerable loss in cattle, has now, by acclimatization, assumed such a mild type that the losses from it are trivial, more especially where inoculation has been resorted to. Anthrax, splenic apoplexy (Cumberland disease) occasionally appears, but its ravages are by no means serious, and are confined to certain districts of limited extent.

A few cases of tuberculosis appear in the herds in the coast districts, but the climate and system of grazing in the open air, summer and winter, are evidently inimical to pulmonary diseases in stock of all kinds.

The devastation of the pastures caused by the increase in the number of marsupials, led to the passing of an Act for their destruction. Stockowners may assess themselves to a limited extent, and the amount thus levied is subsidised by an equal amount from the Government ; and from the fund thus accruing bonuses are paid for all scalps of marsupials presented. The pest has by this means been considerably reduced. It is a matter for regret that comparatively few skins have been preserved. The variety of forms in which these skins can be utilised, leads to the hope that some means will be adopted to prevent the loss of millions of valuable skins throughout the Australian colonies.

Horses.

The horses in the colony number 306,000, and may be classed as follows :—Saddle horses, 56 per cent., light harness horses, 39 per cent., heavy draught, 4 per cent., and blood or thoroughbred horses, 1 per cent. There is a steady demand for good horses within the colony. Heavy draughts command remunerative prices for heavy dray work and sugar plantations, and there is a constant demand for good weight-carrying saddle horses, for Indian cavalry remounts.

The blood stock are bred principally for racing purposes, although the sires in use for hack breeding are, as a rule, drawn from thoroughbred studs. Prices range from £30 to £500.

Saddle horses range in price from £5 to £50. They are capable of great endurance, and stand from 14·2 to 15·3 hands high.

Light-harness horses may be described as the produce of well-bred, clean-legged sires, from active farm mares. But a superior class of light-harness horse is now being raised by the use of Cleveland bays, roadsters and Norfolk trotters, of which there are some very superior imported animals in the colony. Prices range from £10 to £50.

The heavy draught stock are principally composed of the Clydesdale, Shire horse, and Suffolk punch breeds. Many first-class sires have been imported at great expense. Prices for working horses of this class vary from £25 to £60, and for superior sires up to £500.

Cattle.

By far the larger proportion of general herds of cattle are of Durham or Shorthorn origin. About 2 per cent. are graded Herefords, and a small proportion of Devons crosses.

There are a large number of superior stud pedigree herds of Shorthorns, Herefords, and a few of Devons, Ayrshires, Alderney and Brittany, and Aberdeen Angus polled. Some of the Shorthorns and Herefords are of the most fashionable blood procurable. It is the general impression that, on account of their superior hardiness, Herefords and Devons are best adapted to the coast and mountainous districts, although the Shorthorns thrive well in all parts of the colony. Some valuable pedigree herds of Shorthorns have been established far into the interior. All breeds of cattle have, however, answered so well in Queensland that preference for one herd over another would appear to be mere matter of fancy.

The Aberdeen-Angus polled cattle afford abundant proof of the favourable nature of the Queensland climate and pasturage. Natives of a rigorous and moist climate, they thrive and fatten exceedingly well in the colony, with the thermometer frequently reaching 100° F.

Of dairy breeds of cattle the Ayrshires are as yet the leading breed, but there are now several small herds of the Channel Island breeds. The native Durhams, however, when selected and bred with that special object in view, have hitherto held their own as dairy cattle with any other variety.

The natural increase of cattle from a breeding herd ranges from 60 to 90 per cent. ; the general average over the whole of the colonies has been estimated by the Government statistican of New South Wales at 72 per cent.

In normal seasons the price of store cattle $2\frac{1}{2}$ to 3 years old averages about £3 per head, and the price of fat cattle in the metropolitan markets at the present time, is from £4 10s. to £6 ; superior herd bulls, £10 to £15. The number of cattle in the colony on the 31st December, 1887, was 4,474,000.

The value of exports connected with the pastoral industry may be here given, amounting as follows for the year 1887 :—

		£
Hides	... ...	84,000
Skins	. . ..	17,086
Tallow	... ...	99,094
Wool (clean, 15,309,357 lbs)	...	1,060,712
,, (greasy, 32,273,575 lbs)	...	1,307,999

Fencing.

The Crown Lands Act provides that grazing farms shall be enclosed with a fence within three years from the date of first occupation.

Formerly sheep were shepherded in flocks of from one to two thousand in all the Australian colonies. This practice has been abandoned for many years, and shepherding is now a rare exception to the general rule. The benefits of grazing sheep at large, within fences, are many ; among the principal of which may be mentioned increased growth and quality of wool, saving in wages, and a more healthy condition of the sheep. These, together with the greater number of sheep carried per acre, are sufficient to recoup the cost of fencing in a very few years.

The cost of fencing will vary with the description of fence adopted and the quality of the timber available. The best description of fence is wire with hardwood split or sawn posts. For sheep five wires are sufficient. The cost of No. 8 wire delivered in Brisbane is, at the present time, £12 per ton. A ton of this wire measures 11,400 yards, nearly 6½ miles. Smaller wire is slightly dearer, but has the advantage of greater length per ton— thus No. 9 is £12 5s. per ton, of 13,600 yards (or 7¾ miles) ; and No. 10, £13 per ton, equal to 16,380 yards, or over 9¼ miles.

For cattle three wires—the centre one being of barbed wire —are sufficient. Barbed wire, thick set, gives 4 cwt., and long-set 3½ cwt. per mile.

Subdivision fences of same material need not be so high as boundary fences. With these the posts are usually a considerably longer distance apart, the wires in the interspaces being kept in place by battens, which, however, are not sunk in the ground. A fair estimate of the cost of such subdivison fences, with timber and railway carriage available, may be stated at from £16 to £21 per mile. Where the land is not open plain, cheap but efficient rustic subdivision fences may be constructed by unskilled bush labour.

The system of compulsory registration of brands of cattle and horses, introduced in 1872, is the most complete yet adopted by any other country or colony, both as a protection against theft and for the recovery of stray or stolen stock. Each brand is restricted to two letters and one numeral. The changes that can thus be rung are almost unlimited, so that each owner in the colony is allotted a distinct brand. A " Brands Directory" is published annually, containing the names and addresses of all brand owners, in alphabetical and numerical order. A certain order of branding being obligatory. the present owner of the animal is easily dis-covered by the last brand imprinted in that order. The Brands Directory may be seen in the Queensland Court.

The severe drought through which the colony recently passed served at any rate to draw earnest attention to the importance of securing a permanent supply of water ; and, as mentioned in earlier pages, efforts have been made to tap the immense natural reservoirs of fresh water, which have been shown to exist beneath the surface of our widely extending plains. The success which has attended these operations, will, no doubt, lead to trials at other places, and will tend greatly to lessen the disastrous effects which the visitations of drought have had upon the pastoral industry.

IV.—The Minerals of Queensland.

FOR richness and variety of its mineral resources, Queensland stands pre-eminent, and yet, probably, not a tithe of its wealth has been discovered. Indeed, in a large measure, the great value of its mineral deposits has induced waste, which improved appliances and processes would have prevented, and which would have been brought into operation had there been greater difficulty in extracting the treasures which the earth was so willing to yield in abundance. But where the miner could make his "pile" so easily by the rude appliances available, it was useless to talk to him of scientific methods. The formation of large companies, however, gave an impetus to systematic mining, and care is now taken to realise as far as practicable, the riches found beneath the surface.

In the following pages space will not permit of more than a brief reference to a subject with which a volume might be filled.

An examination of the contents of the Queensland Mineral Court will, however, give an idea of the wonderful resources of the colony, and a more detailed notice than can here be given, will be found in the Special Catalogue which the Commissioners have published, descriptive of the mineral exhibits.

Coal.

The Ipswich district was the portion of the colony in which coal for commercial purposes was first raised. It is, however, found abundantly at Maryborough, Bowen, and other northern portions of the colony, as well as on the Darling Downs. Mr. Tenison Woods considers the coal resources of Queensland " equal, if not superior, to any other colony, and will raise her shores to be in the end the grand coal emporium of the Southern hemisphere." Indeed the resources of Queensland as regards coal may be said to be inexhaustible. The railways of the colony, and many of the large ocean-going and coastal steamers now obtain their supplies from the Queensland mines, and, with the increase of facilities for transit and shipment, a great future may be predicted for coal fields.

The upper strata of the coalfields in the neighbourhood of Ipswich consists of a sandstone resting on shales, intersected by thin bands of ironstone, of which some is sufficiently rich for smelting. while the decomposed shales furnish an excellent clay for pottery and brick. The coal from the lower beds furnishes an excellent coke, largely used in the foundries.

The Burrum Field, connected by rail with Maryborough, its port town, 18 miles distant, is about 100 square miles in extent, and possesses several workable seams of coal, very free from intervening veins of shale. The coal is fully equal to that of Newcastle, New South Wales, as regards hardness, quantity of ashes and sulphur, and heating power.

The other discovered coal fields of the colony are being developed and their proximity, in most cases, to seaport towns, will enable them to contribute their quota of coal to the market. The quantity of coal raised in 1887 was 238,813 tons, of the value of £97,460.

Gold.

The year 1858 demonstrated the fact that Queensland was henceforth to be considered a gold-producing country. The first rush to the Canoona field, about 20 miles from Rockhampton, was due to exaggerated rumours of immense wealth of gold deposits, and ended most disastrously to those who were attracted by the reports. Many miners, however, remained, and discovered other goldfields in the vicinity, while Canoona is still also worked. Gold mining in Queensland made but little progress until the year 1868. Previous to that date but 119,384 ounces had been produced, in value £451,039. Since that year 5,487,758 oz., of a value of £19,173,958, have been yielded by Queensland mines. In 1887 the yield of gold in Queensland was 425,923 ounces.

Gympie, discovered in 1868 by a miner named Nash, occupies a foremost place among Queensland goldfields. Operations are here conducted on a large scale, and that a large area of gold-bearing rock is still untouched in this field is shown by the fact that mines of great depth are profitably worked. The returns of gold from Gympie to the end of 1887 were 1,323,480 ounces, valued at £4,632,177.

Several minor fields are established in the vicinity of Gympie, such as Kilkivan, &c., &c., but the gold-bearing ore, although rich in gold, being of a refractory nature, the progress of development of the fields is slow.

The other fields of Southern Queensland are Eidswold, the development of which gives promise of a brilliant future; those situate in the neighbourhood of Warwick, and in which recently the gold mining has been revived; and the Mount Perry District.

In Central Queensland the most notable goldfields are Rockhampton (in which the wonderful Mount Morgan is situated), Port Curtis, Peak Downs, and Nebo.

In the Rockhampton district are (besides Mount Morgan) Canoona, Queensland's oldest field ; Rosewood, Morinish, and Crocodile Creek, from all which good stone is still raised. Inclusive of Mount Morgan, these fields in 1887 yielded 85,305 ounces, valued at £349,750.

The richness of the Mount Morgan gold mine has become almost proverbial. In this the gold is found in a very pure and exceedingly finely divided state. The erection of chlorination works at the mine will enable the company to carry on their operations with but little waste. Mr. Jack, the Government geologist, is of opinion that Mount Morgan was in former geological ages a hot spring or geyser, the water of which held gold in solution, which afterwards was precipitated and consolidated with other mineral matter thrown up by this spring into a ferruginous stone. There are, however, other theories as to its formation, upon which it is not necessary here to speculate.

Gladstone is the seaport town of the Port Curtis area, comprising the Calliope, Cania, Norton, Boyne, and Kroombit field.

Peak Downs and Nebo are smaller goldfields in the central districts.

The total yield in 1887 of the fields in the Port Curtis district, Cloncurry, Calliope, Clermont, Normanby, and small fields, which in the returns of the Mines department are grouped together, was 14,499 ounces, valued at £40,746.

In Northern Queensland, the most noticeable goldfields are Charters Towers, Ravenswood, Etheridge, Woolgar, Gilberton, Hodgkinson, the Palmer, and the more lately discovered Croydon. These fields excel in their richness and extent, and differ in character from those of Southern Queensland, being barren of fossils, and the rocks in the neighborhood of the veins are granitic.

Charters Towers is 85 miles from the port of Townsville, its outlet by rail. On this reef nearly 500 distinct reefs are proved auriferous. Since its discovery, 1,611,977 ounces have been raised to 31st December, 1887, of the value of £5,319,524. In 1887, the yield was 151,377 ounces, value £499,544.

Ravenswood is also connected by rail with Townsville, and the ore is extremely rich in gold, although of a very refractory nature, which makes it difficult to treat remuneratively. The amount of gold raised in 1887 was 10,390 ounces, valued at £35,326, and making a total to end of 1887 of 327,215 ounces, value £1,112,531.

The Etheridge is another goldfield, producing ore of great richness, and less difficult to treat as that of Ravenswood. The development of the field has hitherto been greatly retarded by its distance from the coast and want of railway communication, which latter will, it is expected, before very long be rectified. The yield of the Etheridge, Woolgar, and Gilberton fields in 1887 was 21,036 ounces, valued at £63,108, and making a total to 31st December, 1887, of 341,579 ounces, of a value of £1,024,637.

Croydon, the most recently discovered goldfield, is situated about 120 miles due east of Normanton, its seaport town, and this town will ere long be connected to the field by rail. The rich finds made since its discovery in 1885 have caused it to become one of the largest and most important goldfields in Northern Queensland. The total yield to end of 1887 has been 33,932 ounces, of a value of £90,763 This field is still in its infancy, but its resources are rapidly being developed, and now support a large and increasing population.

The Hodgkinson is situated about seventy miles from Cairns. Thornborough is the head town. The output of gold to 31st December, 1887, from this field and the Mulgrave, was 218,053 ounces, valued at £803,161, of which 2,400 ounces were yielded in 1887.

The Palmer is the most extensive alluvial field in the colony, and is in course of being connected by rail with Cooktown, 120 miles distant. To the end of 1887 1,272,172 ounces. valued at £4,897,862, had been obtained from this field, the year 1887 having credit for 6,981 ounces.

Copper.

Copper occurs in its metallic state in various parts of Queensland, but is principally met with in combination with sulphur.

Mount Perry is the most important source of this ore in the Burnett district, other fields being the Normanby, Woolca, Boolboonda, Edina, &c.

The mineral is also found at Port Downs, 250 miles from Rockhampton.

Cloncurry, however, possesses the most important copper deposits. rivalling in extent and richness the Lake Superior mines in North America. The ore is extremely rich, but the field is greatly handicapped by its position. The railway will, however, be shortly constructed to Normanton, about 200 miles distant, when convenience of transport and the extreme richness of the deposits will enable them to be more remuneratively worked.

The total output of copper ore up to end of 1887 reached 55,695 tons, valued at £1,932,999.

Tin.

Tin was first found in 1872 near the boundaries of New South Wales and Queensland, the township which sprung up being named Stanthorpe. The large quantities of stream tin produced for some time after its discovery, and the trifling expense of working it, enabled many to realise fortunes.

The Herberton tin field is difficult of access owing to the precipitous chain of mountains lying between it and the sea. Railway communication is now, however, being established with Cairns. On this field tin is found in reefs as well as in the alluvial deposits. The minerals exhibited in the Queensland Court by the Herberton local committee, and the trophy shown by Messrs. J. Moffat and Co., are evidence of the great wealth of this field. Tin is also found at Ravenswood, and on the Palmer River, &c.

60,876 tons of tin ore had been raised to the end of 1887, of a value £3,297,485. In 1887 the output was 3,279 tons, valued at £217,339.

Silver and Lead.

Silver and lead are found at Ravenswood and at Herberton. The Queensland ores are of great richness, and are found in large quantities. Smelting works are erected at Ravenswood, and their erection has given an additional impetus to the mining industry.

At Herberton many mines are worked for silver bearing galena, which is generally very rich in silver, and smelting works are established on the field. Silver is also found at Stanthorpe.

Among other minerals which exist in Queensland may be mentioned antimony, found in the Burnett and Thornborough districts, and at Neardie ; Manganese, found in many places, and in large deposits at Gladstone. Iron, plentiful in all parts of the colony. Chromic iron, found at Ipswich ; Cobalt ore, at Kilkivan ; Quicksilver at Kilkivan ; Bismuth, at Cloncurry ; Molybdænum, at Stanthope and other places ; Wolfram, at Stanthorpe and Herberton ; Plumbago, at Tiaro ; Marble and Limestone in many places, but chiefly at Warwick, Gladstone, Rockhampton, Mackay, and various small islants off the coast ; Soda is found in large tracks in the interior ; Building stones and Clays suitable for Bricks and Pottery are found abundantly in many parts of Queensland.

The gems of the colony comprise agates ; opals, which the expert who officially reported upon gems exhibited at the Colonial and Indian Exhibition in 1886, considered that "the Queensland opals rivalled if not surpassed those of Hungary" in their great lustre, brilliancy, and colour, and which are found of large size ; while diamonds, rubies and sapphires have been found at Stanthorpe. Pearls are obtained from the pearl fisheries of North Queensland.

Mineral springs, both hot and cold, exist in Queensland. At Helidon, is situated the spring from which the popular Helidon

Spa Water is produced. The temperature of the spring is 73° F, specific gravity 1 0076, while the analysis gives the following result :—

Bicarbonate Soda	... ...	221.36 grains per gallon.
,, Potash	... ...	2.34	,, ,,
,, Lithium	... ...	1.81	,, ,,
,, Calcium	... ...	10.65	,, ,,
,, Magnesium	...	1.82	,, ,,
,, Rubidium (traces in the spectroscope)		
Chloride of Sodium	...	45.08 grains per gallon.
Silica	...	2 13	,, ,,
Ammonia and Iron	...	3.23	,, ,,
		291.42	,, ,,

Other boiling springs exist in various parts of the colony, notably at the Etheridge, the Herberton district, &c., the spring at Woodleigh being used with considerable effect in rheumatic complaints.

V.—Commerce and Manufacturing Industries.

Banks.

A LARGE number of banks are established in the colony, and have branches in all the chief towns. The Bank of New South Wales, the Union Bank, the Bank of Australasia, and the Australian Joint Stock Bank, were the earliest to commence operations in Queensland. The business of these and other institutions of a similar nature has expanded proportionately with the rapid growth of the colony, and is now conducted in buildings of vast magnitude. Besides those above-mentioned, the following corporations carry on operations within the colony, viz :—The Commercial Bank of Sydney, Queensland National Bank, London Chartered Bank of Australia, Mercantile Bank of Sydney, Commercial Bank of Australasia, Royal Bank of Queensland, and, recently established, the Bank of North Queensland, with headquarters at Townsville.

The vigour, thrift, and prosperity of the colony are well exemplified in the returns showing the business of the Government Savings Bank, which has 116 branches throughout the colony, and in which the sum of £1,426,018 stood at the credit of 39,780 depositors on the 31st March, 1888.

The total imports for the year 1887 amounted to £5,821,611, and the exports to £6,453,945.

Manufacturing Industries.

Queensland is essentially a country for the industrious; the idler meets with no encouragement. Men commencing life with skill and energy as their only capital have found in the colony a ready market, and have become wealthy capitalists and large employers of labour. The vast resources of the colony offered a fair field for profitable investment, of which the man of means was not slow to avail himself.

First, perhaps, in importance amongst the Queensland industries may be mentioned the mechanical. Several large foundries and iron works are established throughout the colony. Commencing with Brisbane, the oldest foundry in Queensland is that now owned by the firm of Smith, Forrester and Co. Started originally by a working man named Cameron, it gradually increased in importance, and passing through the hands of various owners finally reached those of the present proprietors.

The firm now employs about 200 men, and includes a ship-building branch.

Messrs. Sutton and Co.'s establishment turns out machinery of all descriptions and steamers of moderate dimensions, and is another example of what may be done in Queensland by energy and perseverance, from small beginnings. Sugar mills and railway rolling stock are also constructed by this firm. Other large employers of skilled mechanical labor are Evans, Anderson and Co., Harvey, Sargeant and Co., Shillito and Co. of Ipswich, and many other shops. In Ipswich, Toowoomba, Bundaberg, Mackay and Townsville, busy workshops are in operation, and resound with the whirr of machinery and the hum of men. In Maryborough the great firms of J. Walker and Co. and Tooth and Co. turn out work which would be creditable to the great shops of England. These factories are intended to meet the special requirements of colonial industry.

Brass and copper foundries also exist, the chief establishment being that of Messrs. J. Hipwood and Co. The galvanized iron work of Messrs. W. Keith and Co. is so satisfactory that it is displacing in a great measure the imported articles. Specimens of this work may be seen in the Queensland Court.

Galvanized iron workers and plumbers have establishments in every town, and carry on their operations successfully.

Saddlery and harness making is also an important industry. Both the workmen and the work are of the best. Large establishments, giving employment to a number of well paid hands, exist in all the chief towns. Specimens of their handicraft may be seen in the Queensland Court.

The bootmaking trade is extensive, and in this the establishment of Mr. James Hunter is remarkable for its vastness, employing 450 hands, with an output stated to be about 60,000 per week, distributed not only in Queensland but in other colonies.

Cabinet-making is well established, and the work turned out would do credit to any city in the world. As may be seen by a reference to the collection of timbers exhibited by the Commissioners, and other exhibitors in the Queensland Court, the colony possesses woods eminently suitable for all purposes, from that of heavy railway work to that for the finest cabinet work, and when the beauty of grain becomes better known their utility will be availed of to a much greater extent.

The woods of the colony are described at length in the catalogue of the Commissioner's exhibit. and need not be further referred to here. Saw mills and the timber industry generally gives employment to a large number throughout the colony.

The development of the coach-building trades proves that the refinements and luxuries of life are not absent from our social condition. The earliest establishment was that now owned by Mr. A. M'Lean, whose business is now of a more mixed nature, and includes the manufacture of agricultural implements, in which his success is well known in Queensland. Messrs. J. M'Nab and Son are also well known in the colony, and jealously maintains his reputation for turning out first-class work. of which specimens may be seen in the Queensland court There are other establishments throughout the colony employing many hands, and although of a different character, the Queensland Railway Carriage Company's works are too important to be omitted from this sketch. This company, whose shops are situated at Nundah, employs a large number of men, and turns out work unexcelled elsewhere. Other establishments of similar character exist at Ipswich, &c., &c.

The potteries of the colonies are represented in the Queensland Court by the Dinmore Brick and Tile Co., the Waterstown Brick and Tile Co., the Queensland Brick and Tile Co., Messrs. James Campbell and Sons, and other firms, producing articles in every way equal to the imported.

The firm of F. W. Wilson and Co. is pre-eminent in the manufacture of biscuits, and is an establishment of which Queensland may well be proud. Fruit preserving and the manufacture of confectionery are successfully carried on, the principal houses being W. H. Russell and Co., Rankin and Morrow, T. Spilsbury, Dyason Bros., Peacock and Co., B. Skinner (who also makes the manufacture of soup and articles for invalids a speciality), and other firms.

As a sugar-growing colony, it will be readily understood that there is an extensive distillery business in Queensland, and brewing also is a highly flourishing industry.

Ipswich has shown that the woollen manufacture can be profitably pursued in the colony, and the Queensland Woollen Manufacturing Company has, by the excellence of its cloth and variety of patterns, secured a trade which good management is constantly increasing.

It will be seen by the preceding brief remarks that the development of manufacturing industry has so far been satisfactory. With the increase of population, and to satisfy the demands of that increase, the capitalist and laborer have found, and will continue to find, an enlarged and growing outlet for their wares. The evidences of prosperity, the fruits of industry and perseverance, properly applied, are seen in all directions, in improved buildings and many other ways, and in no country probably is there a brighter future in store for the wealth producer than in Queensland.

VI.—The Sugar Industry.

ALTHOUGH the fact that sugar could be profitably grown in the Australian colonies had been much earlier demonstrated, it was not until the years 1847 to 1850 that any real attention was given to its cultivation, and that cane was grown on the Brisbane River and Moreton Bay lands. The first sugar was made in 1852, from Queensland canes grown in the Botanical Gardens.

Public interest was now awakened, and in the following years a decided impetus was given to the industry; cuttings of many varieties of cane were introduced by the Acclimatization Society, and the smaller farmers experimented on its production. The first Sugar Companies were formed in 1864 in Brisbane, Maryborough, and Mackay—the last named having since become the sugar capital of Queensland.

The first official returns show that in 1867 there were six mills at work, which produced 168 tons of sugar and 13,100 gallons of molasses. The development of the industry was now rapid; in 1872 operations were being conducted at 65 mills, crushing 5000 acres sugar cane, yielding 6,266 tons of sugar, and 357,614 gallons molasses. Capitalists were not slow to see the vast sugar-producing capabilities of the colony, and large sums were now invested in the industry; the best methods of growing and manufacturing became better understood, and the cultivation of sugar throve for some years. It was, however, destined to receive a severe check; a disease, locally misnamed "rust," attacked the cane, causing fearful havoc. The planters, however, fought a determined fight against the enemy, and although a panic was created amongst those who had capital in the occupation, and by foreclosing upon the pioneers great hardship was caused, the planters, nevertheless, conquered the disease.

It was found that the annual varieties of a hardier nature, and thinner in the cane, withstood the disease, the rust-stricken cane was extinguished, and the hardier varieties substituted. Economy became the order of the day, capitalists took heart in the future of the industry, and it was shown that sugar growing could be carried on as lucratively as ever.

From 1879 onwards investment in sugar lands, sugar mills, and sugar refineries, amounted almost to a mania. Suitable land was taken up in all directions. Gigantic refineries and stupendous mills were erected by companies with immense capitals. The sugar centres developed into thriving towns, and a general sense of wonderful and seemingly permanent prosperity prevailed.

But again troubles overtook the planter The labour difficulty increased proportionately with the growth of the industry, and following on two successive dry seasons the working expenses were doubled or trebled, while the incoming returns were decreased.

The physique of the imported " Kanaka " labourer deteriorated. The mortality on some of the plantations was great, while high wages were paid to the white laborers who were employed. Many of the pioneer planters, when the prosperity of the industry was at its climax, sold out, realizing large fortunes. Inexperienced men took their places, the price of sugar began to fall, while the European market was swamped by the bounty fed beet sugar of France and Germany.

Nevertheless the planters looked the matter boldly in the face, and saw that cane sugar, of infinitely better quality, could be produced as cheaply in Queensland as the inferior beet sugar in Europe. Stricter economy was exercised in the management of the estates, working expenses were considerably reduced, more cane was grown per acre, and better and less wasteful method of manufacturing were adopted. Still the difficulty of obtaining reliable labor increased, and the Legislature decreed that the recruiting of labor from the South Sea Islands must cease in 1890.

While many think that sugar cannot be profitably and successfully cultivated by white labor in the tropical zones, there are others who, with equal confidence, maintain the contrary opinion, and that the industry will become more permanently established by more divided management by small farmers, who should dispose of their cane to the mill owner. The Legislature, falling in with this idea, and in order to allow the small farmer to become more independent of the large mill-owner working with cheaper black labor, while at the same time giving him greater interest in the work, voted the sum of £50,000 for the erection of mills, worked upon the co-operative principle, and under the management of the farmers, subject to approved regulations.

Notwithstanding, however, all the troubles through which the planter has passed, the importance of the industry and the output of sugar has steadily increased. In the year 1886-7 there were 160 mills in operation, 36,104 acres of cane were crushed, yielding 56,859 tons of sugar and 1,510,308 gallons of mollasses. Ten Rum distilleries also depend on the plantations, and distilled 97,375 gallons of rum, for which a ready sale was found.

Sugar is successfully cultivated along the whole coastal district of Queensland, from the New South Wales border to Cooktown—1300 miles. In the southern portion of the colony, small farmers, with small mills, are generally scattered at intervals. In the middle districts, gigantic refineries, with an underground system of pipes, drawing the cane juice from the small farmer, undertake the manufacture of the sugar ; while in the North the establishment of immense mills, at an enormous expenditure of money, and employing hundreds of laborers, has been the system adopted.

At Nerang Creek, entering the Pacific about 45 miles south of Brisbane, the cultivation of sugar was early started, the fertile alluvial soil well suiting the cane. Dairy farming, however, is now taking the place of sugar in this locality, and the area of land under cane decreases yearly. At Coomera River, a few miles nearer the metropolis, the cultivation has been carried on with much greater energy and success. The soil, once covered by dense scrub, has, by the constant decay of the latter, become extremely fertile, is friable and of great depth.

The subdivision of cane growing, and its manufacture among a number of small farmers is prevalent in the Logan and Albert Rivers district. The mills are none of large capability, and the necessity of improved appliances if the industry is to be profitably carried on, has only recently been seen. Many of the mills in this district are proprietary, *i.e.*, are owned by a company of four to eight farmers, each of whom cuts and tops his own cane, and has it crushed in turn. The work is done by the farmer, his wife, sons and daughters, so that the outlay for manual labour is reduced to a minimum, and with modern appliances for manufacture, a greater profit would be secured both to the mill owner and to the small farmer, who, having no mill of his own, has now to dispose of his cane to the proprietary mills.

The proximity of this district to the capital, however, has raised the value of sugar properties for other purposes, and together with the development of the saw mill and timber industries, brick fields, dairy farming, &c., &c., is making the land too valuable for sugar-growing purposes, which are gradually being relinquished.

The next sugar district is that of the Pine River, then Mooloolah and Maroochie, and the Buderum tableland, all to the north of Brisbane, and worked by small farmers.

Maryborough is the chief town of the district next in order. Here the sugar industry was early established. The sugar manufacture is carried on by Messrs. Cran and Co., at their immense refinery, Yengarie, the juice of the cane being supplied by the farmers, each of whom must have his own crushing machinery. The refinery is fitted with the most modern appliances, and is colossal in extent. The farmer has to cut, cart and crush his own cane, while the juice previously charged with lime to prevent acidity, is either conveyed to Yengarie in trucks, carts, or punts, or by the network of underground pipes by means of power-ful pumps. Pacific Islanders are employed in this district, but occupation is also found for a large staff of ploughmen, mechanics, and skilled white labour.

Proceeding northwards, the Burnett River is reached, with Bundaberg as its centre. Soil and climate are here admirably adapted for sugar growing. Millaquin, the gigantic refinery, per-forms duties similar to that at Yengarie, and is supplied with juice in the same manner. In this district great progress has been made in the industry, which is as flourishing as in any portion of the colony.

Rockhampton, the centre of the next sugar-growing district, is chiefly noticeable as being situated in a comparatively dry belt of country. There is a mill at Yeppoon.

Mackay, the sugar metropolis, is situated in the tropical district of the colony, and here the industry has attained its greatest development. Immense sums of money have been expended in the district, of which this town is the seaport, in the cultivation of the cane and manufacture of sugar. Every modern appliance is found in the mills, all of great capabilities, and situated upon large private estates, and which require an immense area of cane for their maintenance. The farmers also dispose of their crops to these mills, which latter, however, rely primarily on the cane grown upon the estate to which they are attached. On these estates there are miles of railway and the modern powerful steam ploughs, while at night the mills are lighted by electricity to enable the hundreds of laborers to feed the rollers with cane.

Notwithstanding the depression which existed, following on the years of prosperity prior to 1883, the confidence of those who have invested their capital in sugar remains unabated, and the output of sugar will continue to increase. It is in this district, as before

stated, that the central mill system under Goverment aid is first
tried—an experiment watched with great interest by all classes of
the community.

The Burdekin River district, next engages attention.   The
debris, washed down in the course of ages, from the immense
district drained by this river,   has formed a high and dry level
delta, which the planter quickly discovered and utilised for the
successful growing of sugar cane—the soil being of great depth and
fertility, level, and easy to cultivate.

The supply of underground water, at little depth, being practically inexhaustible, irrigation has been adopted, for notwithstanding its position within the tropics, the district is a dry one—
the average rainfall being about 30 inches. The undulating
contour of much of the lands adapts it for the flow of water, which is
pumped into furrows between the canes by powerful engines
driving large centrifugal pumps.   The results of irrigation are
most satisfactorily seen in the increased yield of sugar, and the
prospect of sugar growing in this district appears most cheering.

On the banks of the Herbert River sugar cane has been grown
for many years past.   Unlike the district previously mentioned,
the tropical rains are here copious, the high mountain ranges,
approaching the coast and attracting the water-laden clouds from
the sea. On the Lower Herbert the soil is a rich vegetable
mould. The mills erected here are of immense capacity, and the
plantations have been managed with great energy and skill.   The
Colonial Sugar Company has here (as at Mackay) a gigantic
establishment, miles of railway connect the mill with the farms,
and the mills at night are illuminated by means of electricity.

At the Johnstone River, and in the Cairns district, the rainfall
reaches its maximum intensity.   The mountain range is here
close to the sea, and from its influence the district is one of
tropical luxuriance, and having soil unsurpassed for fertility, is
the delight of the botanist.

The town of Geraldton is the centre of the district, and
many mills, fitted with the best and most modern machinery, are
now in full operation. The idea that first-class sugars could not
be produced from cane in this district has been dissipated. The
cane, though luxuriant in growth, is extremely healthy, and the
yield of sugar per acre exceeds that of any other district of the
colony.

At Cairns also similar success has attended the establishment
of the sugar industry. At Hambledon especially the plantations
and mills will, in their perfection of machinery and arrange-
ments, compare favorably with any in the colony. Capital has
been most freely spent, and the cultivation of the cane on this
plantation has been attended with the most signal success.

At Port Douglas and the Bloomfield River, &c., mills have been erected, and the conditions under which sugar is produced resemble those of the preceding districts.

The inexhaustible fertility of the tropical scrub soils of the colony, the immense area available, freedom from drought, and wonderful adaptability for the growth of the cane, point to the probability of a grand future for the sugar industry of Queensland, and when the labor difficulty is overcome, as ere long it must be, it may safely be predicted that that probability will develop into a substantial realisation.

VII.—Agriculture and Horticulture.

THE diversity of climate necessarily found over a large area o the colony of Queensland, permits the growth within its borders of plants of both temperate and tropical climes, and in the following lines it is proposed to glance very briefly at a few of the more important agricultural crops which are produced with profit to the grower, and also at others for which the Queensland climate is most admirably adapted, but the cultivation of which has not hitherto been attempted on any large scale.

The sugar and pastoral industries have been elsewhere referred to at some length, and need not, therefore, be further treated of here. The consideration of the climate is necessarily an important factor in treating of the agricultural capabilities of the colony, and a glance of its general features is given in preceding pages.

The soil which best repays the labor and skill of the cultivator is that found on the alluvial river flats, and which, before the advent of the settler, had been covered with dense " scrub " or jungle. This land is necessarily in great demand, and by far the greater portion has been alienated from the Crown, immense areas, however, being in the hands of capitalists, who hold them as a speculation, and do not attempt their cultivation.

These lands are amazingly fertile and productive, and are eminently adapted for sugar cane, maize, sweet potatoes, English potatoes, lucerne, tobacco, &c., &c., all of which yield heavy crops with a minimum of labor. This rich soil is often many feet in depth, formed from that washed down from volcanic hills and deposited on the flats, and supplemented by decay of ages of subsequent vegetation.

The forest lands are of larger extent, but generally somewhat inferior in quality of soil. Nevertheless, much of the more lightly timbered land, having soils of volcanic origin, are wonderfully deep and fertile, and vary in color from black to dark chocolate and red. These latter soils are admirably adapted for cereals, lucerne, maize, grasses, &c., &c. There are other forest lands of a sandy nature, which, though poor in quality, are often, by their proximity to markets, rendered profitable both for grazing and agricultural purposes, while the indigenous timber yields a handsome return for labor, independent of the increased value of the land from its being cleared.

Of the agricultural capabilities of the inland plains of the far west very little experience has been obtained. They consist of two descriptious of soil—a clay on which grows luxuriant and fattening herbage, and a soil of a much inferior nature upon which the useless grass termed spinifex grows.

The success which has attended the water boring operations of the Hydraulic Department will, by encouraging irrigation upon the first of the above soils, make much of this fertile land available for the use of the agriculturist.

The other varieties of soil met with are those of the table lands, Silurian Hills, Roma Sand, and Sandy Sea shore. The first of these is wonderfully fertile, and is of a deep red or chocolate color, and originally covered by thick scrub, whose decaying vegetation adds to the richness of the soil. At Roma the sandy loam has been proved to be unsurpassed for the growth of the vine, and latterly cereals of excellent quality have been produced upon it. The third of the soils under consideration is perhaps the poorest found in the coastal districts, and consists of a thin film of loam covering poor gravel, often with silurian rock near the surface. This soil, however, trenched and manured, grows fruit and ornamental trees luxuriantly, while in the flats or gullies in their neighbourhood the soils are much used for market gardening purposes. In the tropical portions of the colony the sandy seashore soils will provide cocoanuts, pineapples, and the mango, in great profusion, and several plantations for the growth of these now exist.

The Darling Downs district to the west of Brisbane is the centre of arable farming, and here the soil is of a volcanic origin, black, chocolate, or red in color, and generally of a clayey nature on the plains, but crumbling with the action of the sun after rains. Here wheat, oats, barley, and rye are grown. Sown from April to June, they are reaped from September to November.

The "rust" fungus is the great trouble to the wheat grower here, and so far no remedy has been discovered which will eradicate this pest. Experiments have been made with varieties of wheat obtained from India, America and elsewhere, but hitherto with but partial success.

For green crops lucerne is found most suitable, and this thrives well on any of the deep rich soils, where also root crops, such as turnips, mangolds and potatoes, produce heavy yields.

In the coastal, scrub land districts, maize takes the place of wheat, and yields enormous crops. Harvests of this crop vary from 40 to 80 bushels to the acre, while the land on which it is grown is often merely "tickled with the hoe"—maize generally being the first crop grown by the new settler—and in the Northern districts two crops of it can be produced in one year.

The sweet potatoe is another most useful plant, either as food for man or beast, both root and tops contributing to its universal use—the latter for table use being as good as spinach. In the North two crops of this plant can be cultivated yearly, a yield of from 8 to 20 tons of roots and an equal weight of tops, being produced per acre.

Millet and Sorghum are also produced, but to a more limited extent, and are used for seed and fodder, which they produce in great quantity, while maturing in three to four months.

In the southern portions of the colony arrowroot grows readily upon scrub lands, and also upon arable lands when well tilled. Pure water is necessary for the manufacture of the farina, but the machinery required is of a simple and inexpensive character.

Among the admirable series of pamphlets published by the Lands Department, that on " Arrowroot," by Mr. Samuel Grimes, one of the pioneers of this industry, affords an ample guide to the growth and manufacture of this useful food.

Tobacco of capital quality grows in every part of the colony, but requires considerable labour for picking and curing the leaves. There is great demand for the leaf, which finds a ready sale.   The labour of children is much utilized in the growth of this article, which is chiefly carried on by the German farmer.   The same remarks apply also to cotton, which grows easily and produces in abundance.

Rice is another prolific crop more especially in the north— where it is the product of excellent quality.   Queensland has been proved to be, in its soil and climate, admirably suited for the growth of coffee—more especially on the scrub soil hills.   The cultivation of the tea plant has also been experimentally conducted with success.

The Acclimatization Society of Brisbane has done much to introduce and to disseminate information upon the cultivation of many plants of economic value—and with the increase of population and greater knowledge of the adaptability of the soil and climate for the growth of these plants, the attention of our farmers will, no doubt, be given to their profitable production.

The bee keeping industry has, withing the last few years, been considerably extended in Queensland, and many of the establishments devoted to it are conducted upon the most improved and scientific methods. The Beekeepers' Association of Brisbane issues a monthly journal, and by papers and otherwise disseminates much useful knowledge as to the best systems, &c., adapted to the colony. The eucalyptus forest affords a perennial harvest for the bees, which need never be idle.

The Mulberry grows well in the colony, and being the staple food for the silk worm, the production of silk on a profitable scale is merely a question of time, as silk of best quality has been produced and manufactured, although only on a small scale.

Dairy farming is another most profitable source of employment, and one which is constantly expanding. The price of butter is high, and the demand far in excess of the supply. The dairyman has only recently realised the importance of the proper and systematic conduct of the dairy, and many establishments are now turning out butter of first-class quality all the year round, and with the choice of fodder which the dairyman commands for winter feed, he has every facility for the production of a superior article, while by the continued addition to the population of the towns he has the advantage of an ever-increasing market. Very little has yet been done in the manufacture of cheese. There is no doubt, however, that a profitable industry could be established in this article.

Pigs are at present comparatively few in number, but breeding has occupied considerable attention, and ere long we may expect an immense increase, as suitable food is readily obtainable.

The extent of the capability of Queensland for horticultural purposes is as yet unknown, but from what has actually been accomplished in the acclimatization of the fruits, vegetables, and flowers of both temperate and tropical climes, there would seem to be hardly any limit to its range.

Most of the annual temperate horticultural products can be grown in the southern districts of the colony, and most successfully so in Darling Downs. There are seen all the fruits, vegetables, and flowers, which are such favorites with the English speaking people, as reminiscent of the old country, and with irrigation, there is undoubtedly an immense field for their most profitable growth.

Among fruits are found apple, pear, plum, peach, apricot, nectarine medlar, mulberry, grape, fig. almond, quince, cherry, chestnut, walnut, filbert, olive, passion fruit, granadilla, pomegranate, persimmon, loquat, lemon, orange, lime and shaddock. &c. &c.

Viticulture is most successfully pursued in this region, and wine making is an industry increasing yearly in importance, which, with greater knowledge of the requirements of soil and climate, may be anticipated to rank as one of the foremost sources of Queensland wealth.

All the British vegetables are successfully cultivated on the Downs, and although in the neigbourhood of the towns market gardening is almost monopolised by the Chinaman, it is merely a question of time for the Australian gardener to find in it a profitable and increasing source of income.

In flowers, Southern Queensland produces all the British favorites in every variety, the rose especially attaining to great perfection, but lilac, honeysuckle, holly, ivy, jasmine, pansies, violets, chrysanthemums, and many of the others grow luxuriantly.

In the sub-tropical portions and in the coastal districts the banana, pine apple, mango, orange, lime, lemon, are at home ; while among vegetables the sweet potato, yams, and many others, afford variety for the table.

In the more northern districts there is a large extent of country in which all tropical fruits flourish to perfection, including the banana, cocoanut and date palms, pine apple, mango, Jack fruit, orange, custard apples, &c.

Ginger, pepper, nutmegs, &c., are indigenous, and the climate and soil are well suited for the growth of vanilla, cinnamon, allspice, &c. Many of these are already acclimatised, but in this region the cultivation of vegetables beyond sweet potatoes, yams, &c., is very limited. The flowers of Northern Queensland are gorgeous in their bloom and foliage. All plants which require protection in the south grow here in the open, while indigenous orchids are found in great variety.

For the agriculturist generally Queensland affords a field for attaining ease, and possibly even affluence within a limited term. The climate is genial and pleasant. The winter is sufficiently cool to make his work enjoyable. He is not debarred from work by frost or snow—flowers and fruits which elsewhere require the lasshouse to bring to perfection grow here in profusion to decorate and adorn his house. The settlement of a small yeomanry is encouraged by all parties. The farmer on his own freehold is thus his own master, subject to no landlord. The facilities for educating his family enable him to bring them up intelligently, while its increase gives him no anxiety for the future. In short, Queensland may be described as very little short of an earthly paradise for the farmer.

VIII.—Fauna and Flora.

In a brief sketch of this nature it would be impossible to do more than summarise the important nature of the Queensland flora and fauna, and indeed a large portion of the colony is as yet quite unexplored, both as regards the plant and the animal world, and in the rich scrubs especially the botanist and timber getter will find a rich harvest awaiting them.

The indigenous woods of Queensland are of great beauty, utility, and variety. In the Commissioner's collection are shown over 500 specimens, and did time and opportunity permit it would be possible to largely supplement this list, which Mr. F. M. Bailey, F.L.S., the Government botanist, and one of the Commissioners has. in the special catalogue published in connection with the exhibit, described in a popular manner.

As the indigenous woods are better known, the variety of purposes for which they can be utilized is more fully appreciated, and they are brought more and more into use by the builder and cabinet maker. The collection of woods shown at the Colonial and Indian Exhibition in London tended greatly to this end, and was much admired. It behoves the Legislature to adopt means to prevent the waste of the vast heritage which the colony possesses in her forests, and under the judicious regulations and fostering care of a Department of Forestry, an inexhaustible source of revenue will be found in this industry.

The barks of many of the Queensland trees and shrubs furnish excellent tanning material, particularly those of the gums Acacia. The fruits of many other trees contain oil in abundance, while the foliage of many are rich in essential oils of delightful fragrance and high medicinal virtue, similar properties being also found in the barks of several trees and in many herbaceous plants ; and all of which are sought after by the druggist all over the world.

Large numbers of the native plants yield excellent fibres, whilst from others rich dyes of brilliant colour are obtained. The bee keeper finds the Queensland flora well suited to his occupation, our trees flowering all the year round, affording ample work for the bee and profit for the master.

No country has richer pasture than Queensland. Three-fourths of the grasses found in Australia occur in Queensland, and among them are found mixed a large number of nutritious herbs which in no small degree contribute to the excellence of the pasture. In the Queensland Court will be found a collection of some of the grasses of the colony, all of which are described in Mr. F. M. Bailey's catalogue of grasses.

Those in search of the beautiful in plant life, will find in the undergrowth of ferns, in the gigantic trees festooned with immense and superb climbers, and in the brilliant and showy foliage of many of the Queensland trees, ample opportunity for the gratification of the eye and brain.

Queensland presents a large field for the naturalist : in every direction new forms are met with, affording pleasure by their novelty. Most of the inhabitants of the animal world of Australia are found in the colony, amongst them being, of course, the kangaroo, wallaby, with their varieties, opossum, native bear, wild cat, bandicoot, ant eater, platypus, dingo, beaver rat, flying fox, &c. Many of these animals possess skins admirably adapted to the use of the currier, but which are at present turned to little or no account. None of the Queensland animals can be said to be dangerous to man, although several often cause havoc in the shepherd's flock and in the poultry yard.

Among birds, about 600 varieties are found in Queensland, often rich and gorgeous in plumage, curious in shape, and peculiar in habit ; birds of all sizes, from the gigantic cassowary and emu, to the wren, some weird, some beautiful in note. Among them may be noted the wedge-tailed eagle, falcon, hawks, kestrel, owl, night jars, swifts, swallows, bee eater, king-fisher, diamond bird, magpie, flycatchers, robins, lyrebird, wren, finches, crow, honey eater, parrots and cockatoos, emu, cassowary, pigeon, bustard, plover, curlew, swan, wild duck, and many others, of which space forbids mention here.

As in other parts of Australia, reptiles are found, some of them being dangerous to life. Amongst the largest is the carpet snake ; a common species is the green snake, brown tree snake, &c. ; amongst those of a venomous description are the black snake and brown snake, and death adder. Alligators are met with in the northern portions of the colony only. Large lizards, iguanuas, &c., are also seen.

The Queensland seas have as yet not been utilized to the extent which the rich hauls which have occasionally been made would cause one to expect. Fish of large size and most delicate in flavour are found along the coast, and as means are adopted for their proper transport to the towns, and for their disposal, they will, no doubt, afford a profitable source of industry to the fisherman, and of nutritious food to the people.

The Dugong is found in the Queensland waters, the flesh of which is cured and sold in various forms. Turtles are also utilized for soup, &c., &c.

Speaking, generally, the riches the colony possesses in its animals. &c., are but little developed—a state of things which time will alter.

IX.—Land Selection in Queensland.

THE following circular has been issued by the Public Lands
Department :—

The conditions under which country lands may be acquired for
settlement are substantially as follows :—

GRAZING FARMS.—Surveyed areas of land being the resumed
portions of runs (large areas leased to Crown tenants for long
periods) are proclaimed open for selection over a great extent of
Queensland territory, within accessible distance of the eastern
seaboard on leases for a term of thirty years, in which intending
settlers can obtain grazing farms of any area up to 20,000 acres,
at their option, at a minimum rent of three farthings an acre,
the rent generally ranging from three farthings to two pence.
This rent is subject to re-assessment by the Land Board after the
first ten years, and subsequently at intervals of five years, but
the rent cannot be increased at any re-assessment to more than
50 per cent. above that for the period immediately preceding.
The land must be continuously occupied either by the lessee or
by his agent or bailiff, and must be fenced in within three years
from the date of selection.   These grazing farms cannot be made
freehold, but the leasehold may be sold, subdivided or mortgaged,
or, with the consent of the Land Board, sublet.

AGRICULTURAL FARMS.—The freehold of agricultural farms
may be secured on terms which it is believed are more liberal
than those obtaining in any other British colony, under the
following conditions :—

The best lands on lines of railway, near centres of population
and on navigable waters, are set apart and surveyed as farms,
with the necessary roads and reserves, the area of the farms
being from 20 to 1,280 acres.   A transferable lease of the farm,
with right of purchase, is issued for a term of fifty years, at an
annual rent varying from threepence per acre to higher rates,
seldom exceeding one shilling, according to the quality and
sittuation of the land, its natural supply of water, &c.   The
selector (who must be eighteen years of age at the time of
selection) must occupy the farm continuously either by himself or
his bailiff or agent, and must within five years fence in the land,
or expend an equivalent sum in other substantial improvements.
The rent is subject to periodical re-assessment, as in the case of
grazing farms.

ACQUISITION OF FREEHOLD.—The freehold of these farms may
be acquired at a price fixed when the land is thrown open for

selection, and being not less than twenty shillings per acre, generally ranging from twenty to twenty-five or thirty shillings.

In order to secure the freehold there must be ten years' personal and continuous *bonâ fide* residence by the lessee or two or more successive lessees, but any lessee may transfer to any other person who is qualified to be a selector.

In effect, these farms are sold to *bonâ fide* selectors on credit, the rent amounting to something like $2\frac{1}{2}$ per cent on the purchasing price ; all rent paid during the period of personal residence being counted as part payment of the purchase money.

The purchase of the freehold may be made at period of the lease after ten years' continuous residence, but if not made within the first twelve years the price is subject to increase in proportion to the increase of rent (if any).

FIFTY YEARS' LEASE.—If the lessee is indisposed to purchase, he may continue to hold the land on lease for the whole period of fifty years, the condition of occupation being performed by the residence either of the lessee or his bailiff or agent.

SMALL FARM FREEHOLDS AT TWO SHILLINGS AND SIXPENCE PER ACRE.—Small farm freeholds or homesteads may be secured in five years in areas not exceeding 160 acres, or smaller areas if desired, at two shillings and sixpence an acre, on a system of deferred payments, extending over the period of five years, at the rate of sixpence per acre per annum.

CONDITIONS TO SECURE FREEHOLD OF HOMESTEADS.—The selector must reside personally on the land during the five years, and must make improvements on it before the end of the five years of a total value equal to not less than ten shillings an acre. Thus, on a farm of 160 acres there must be work done in fencing, clearing, building, or otherwise, of not less than the total value of £80, by the end of the five years ; or, on an 80-acre farm, £40 ; on a 40-acre farm, £20, &c.

When such work is done by the farmer himself there will thus be no actual outlay of money. On the performance of these conditions the selector may claim a grant of the land on payment of the deed fee, amounting on a farm of 160 acres, to £1 10s. The survey-fee on such area, 160 acres, amounts to £7 7s. 6d. ; this must also be paid, but may be paid in five equal annual instalments of £1 9s. 6d. each ; the fees on smaller areas are proportionately less.

FREE GIFTS OF LAND : Land Orders, £20.—Attention is specially directed to what amounts to a free gift of agricultural land in favor of persons of European extraction paying their own passages or those of their families in full to Queensland from Europe, the United States of America, or any British possession other than the Australasian colonies. A wife, child, step-child, or grand-child is reckoned as one of the family. To persons thus paying their passages in full, land-orders are issued of the value of twenty pounds sterling (£20) for each person of twelve years and upwards, and of ten pounds (£10) for each child between the age of twelve months and twelve years of age. These land-orders are available to their full nominal value in payment of the rent of agricultural or grazing farms held by the head of the family or the person in respect to whose passage the land-order is issued, and when used in agricultural areas they amount to a free gift of land, as follows :—

SINGLE LAND ORDER.—A single person, eighteen years of age, holding one land order, value £20, may select in any agricultural area 160 acres of land. The annual rent of sixpence an acre required to be paid for five years to secure the freehold amounts to £20, and the £20 land order, being available to its full nominal value for this purpose, suffices for the payment of the whole rent, and thus secures the fee-simple of the land as a free gift, except the amount of £8 17s. 6d. to be paid for the survey and deed-fees.

The head of a family, say of eight persons, counting seven adults, including the father and mother, paying their passages in full would receive land-orders as follows :—

	£
Father	20
Mother	20
Two children of eighteen years or over	40
Two children of twelve years or over	40
Two children between twelve months and twelve years ...	20
	£140

USE OF LAND ORDERS : RENT.—In such a case the head of a family could obtain either one land-order of the value of one hundred and forty pounds (£140), or separate land-orders, of an equal aggregate amount, in respect of each person. In either case the land-order or land-orders would be sufficient for the payment of the rent of a farm or 1,120 acres for a period of five years at sixpence* an acre a year.

The provisions of the Act relating to homesteads are intended to assist in the settlement of men of small means. If a selector desires to obtain a larger area than 160 acres, he must take up the remainder at some place not adjoining the homestead, and must perform the conditions of occupation of the other farm or farms by an agent or bailiff.

---

* Agricultural land may be obained at threepence an acre, but for tillage-farms, the better lands at about sixpence an acre are much to be preferred.

SEPARATE HOMESTEADS.—In families where there are children of the age of eighteen years or over, a separate farm of 160 acres may be taken up by each such person, so that each may secure the freehold at the end of five years, as already described ; but it must be remembered that the *bonâ fide* personal residence of the selector (*i.e.*, in the case supposed, the child) is required for five years on each separate homestead, as well as an expenditure at the rate of ten shillings per acre within that period.

LAND ORDERS PAY RENT OF GRAZING FARMS.—Land-orders are also available to their full nominal value in payment of the rent of grazing-farms.

For instance, the rent of a grazing-farm of 2,560 acres at twopence (2d.)* an acre being £21 6s. 8d., the land-order given for a family counting as seven adults would pay the rent for more than six years and a half.

APPLICATION FOR LAND ORDERS.—Persons intending to proceed from Great Britain to Queensland, and to pay their own passages in full, are advised to make application to the Agent-General for the Colony, No 1, Westminster Chambers, Victoria Street, London, S.W., for land-orders ; but it should be remembered that these are not transferable, and can be of no use to anyone who does not settle on the land and fulfil the conditions as above described.

Full paying passengers from the United States of America, any European State, or any British possession can obtain the land-orders in the colony. All persons holding land-orders are desired, on arrival at the principal port (Brisbane), to apply at once to the Department of Agriculture, which is under the control of the Minister for Lands ; or, if they arrive at any other Queensland port, to the Immigration Officer or Land-Agent, from whom they can obtain all necessary information to assist them in the selection of land.

VILLAGE SETTLEMENT.—Special provision is made for the settlement of little communities, so that the settlers may live together for mutual protection and convenience, in townships on freehold town allotments, with farms of eighty acres contiguous or in close proximity to their residences.

Land of the best description is now being surveyed in the most suitable localities for carrying out this village settlement, and land-orders are available for taking up and paying for the land in these townships. This scheme, it is believed, will be specially attractive to persons paying their own passages in full, and coming to Queensland from Europe and the United States of America.

---

*The rent may exceed this in some cases, and is often less.

FREEHOLDS—ANNUAL PAYMENTS OF SIXPENCE AN ACRE
SECURE FREEHOLDS—IMPROVEMENTS—TOWNSHIP ALLOTMENTS
ONE ACRE.—In these agricultural townships the payments on
account of rent are the same as on the homesteads before described—namely, five annual payments of sixpence an acre each,
to secure the freehold ; the conditions of continuous *bond fide*
personal residence and of improvements being as before stated ;
but one-fifth part of the required improvements on the farms may
be made on the town allotments, which contain an area of not
more than one acre. The townships, not exceeding two square
miles in area, will provide space for churches, schools, and other
requirements suitable for small communities of people. so that
mutual assistance and protection may be,secured.

SELECTORS MUST BE BRITISH SUBJECTS.—It should be added
that a selector, if an alien, must become a British subject by
naturalisation (to which no obstacles are offered except in the case
of Asiatics) before he can acquire the freehold of his farm.

STATE FREE SCHOOLS.—There is no State-church in Queensland, all denominations being placed on one common platform.
State schools are established in almost every part of the colony
where there are as many as thirty or forty children.

TRAINED TEACHERS—Primary and Grammar Schools.—Well
trained male and female teachers are appointed by the State, and
a good English education may be obtained in any of the State
schools free of any charge. Grammar schools are liberally
endowed by the Government, and scholarships are given annually,
by competitive examination, to pupils of the primary schools,
entitling them to three years' free education in a Grammar school.
Three exhibitions, tenable for three years, are also annually
offered to students desirous of proceeding to any of the Universities of Australasia and Great Britain.

The Queensland Parliament has recently authorised the establishment of a Department of Agriculture and the appointment of
an Inspector in Agricultural Science.

HENRY JORDAN.

Department of Public Lands,
  Brisbane, December, 1887.

IX.—Barron Falls in Flood Time.

BY A. MESTON.

MY first description of these famous falls was written when the river was down to its lowest level. The present article describes the falls during the highest flood in the Barron for seven years. Byron says that no picture can give us an idea of the ocean, and no word painting can give a clear outline of the unimaginable scene at the Barron Falls on the first three days of the present year. I find the blacks have two names for this tremendous cataract—" Biboohra" and " Kamerunga." They appear to avoid the locality, as during visits extending over four years I have not seen a myall near the falls, nor the track of any on the gravel beds of the river. I am not yet on terms of intimacy that would enable me to learn any legends they may have regarding the falls, but shall acquire that interesting information when my relations with the dark sons of the forest are less "strained" than they have been in the past. The actual height of the falls is now ascertained to be about 600ft., or 436ft. higher than Niagara. From the edge of the precipice the river falls 900 feet in half a mile. The Herberton railway will pass right along the top, and the finest view of the whole falls will be seen from the carriage windows. That view in flood time will have no rival in the known world.

"Stand back," said the dying Raphael, as the first glories of the world of spirits appeared to the parting soul, "Stand back until I sketch that heavenly scene !" And, standing by the Barron Falls on the second day of the new year, I, too, felt disposed to say, Stand back until I sketch that mighty picture, hung there on the primal rocks among the everlasting mountains, like an immortal replica by Raphaelistic Nature, from some divine original in the picture gallery of God ! Before me was a torrent of water 300 yards wide and about 60ft. deep, rushing resistlessly along at the rate of twenty miles an hour, tumbling in a solid wall suddenly over the edge of the enormous precipice, launched clear out into space, and descending for over 600ft. into the " waste wild anarchy of chaos, dark and deep," yawning abysmal in the depths below. I look up the river, and see it come sweeping round the bend, divided into three streams that rush together like wild horses as they enter the straight in the dread finish of their last race. They come with the sound of a tempestuous ocean dashing its surges through dark passages in the caverned rocks. Weird Fancy pictures them as the rivers that roll through the gloomy realms of Pluto. Imagination hears the sorrowful wail of Acheron, the lamentation of sad Cocytus, and the hoarse roaring of infernal Phlegethon, " whose waves of torrent fire inflame with rage." They roll over the cliff, strike the first ledge of rock, and the water is dashed into foam and mist, rolling billows of vapour projected with terrific force in vast fantastic forms down the entrance of the Titanic avenue of the river beneath, and clouds of spray float away upwards for 1000 feet, and condense, and drip in showers of emerald dew-drops from the trees on the slopes of the mountains.

The currents of air created by the cataract waved the branches of trees hundreds of feet overhead, as if they were swaying in the contending winds of a storm.

The thunder of the waters was awful. The rocks shook beneath you like a mighty steamer trembling with the vibrations of the screw. The very soul within you recoils appalled before the inconceivable grandeur of that tremendous scene. Those falls stand alone among cataracts like Chimborazo among the mountains.

Eternity itself is throned there on those dark rocks among the wild whirlwind of waters, and speaks to you in solemn tones of the Past, the Present, and the Evermore. You stand voiceless, " mute, motionless, aghast," in that immortal Presence.

The human tongue has no utterance for the thoughts within you. They are not dead those black rocks, those vast columns of descending waters ! They tell you of

Vastness and Age and Memories of Eld,
Darkness and Desolation and dim Night.

Once only in each year do the flood waters of the tropic rains sweep the total surface of the bed rock. The wear of that brief period on the adamantine formation is imperceptible. How long, therefore, has the river occupied in cutting down 1000 feet into the solid rock ? You must look back through the shadowy vista of hundreds of thousands of years that bridge the period of time intervening between us and the dim morning of the world ! The Night of Time hides for ever the birthday of that cataract. Empires have risen and fallen, barbarisms become civilizations, races of men flourished and died, religions triumphed and disappeared into eternal oblivion, thousands of plants and animals vanished for ever, the face of nature changed its aspect in the long wear and waste of centuries, and still those waters rolled down that precipice with a wail of lamentation over a dead Past, like the voice of a lone spirit in the agony of unspeakable despair.

The gulf has a weird and fearful fascination. You feel a mad impulse to leap out into vacancy—to launch out, as Lucifer did. into the wide womb of uncreated Night, and disappear for ever into that yawning chasm, from the vast depths of which rise the sheeted columns of vapor—

> White and sulphury,
> Like foam from the roused ocean of deep hell,
> Whose every wave breaks on a living shore.

At intervals there are deafening explosions, like the discharge of enormous cannon, and the waves of spray roll out like cannon smoke, and recoil upon themselves with the force of the impetus, to be swallowed up in the downward driven current, and finally swept into the abyss. Imagine some Titantic race battling with the demons ! There is a rock fortress 600ft. high, with huge cannon projecting from a hundred embrasures, discharging a continuous shower of projectiles, " winged with red lightning and impetuous rage," into the ranks of the advancing foe ! Terrible beyond conception is the diapason of that cannonade !

On the left of the main falls is the circular pool 200ft. in depth, whose sides slope inward from the top, with a narrow outlet not 20ft. wide at the bottom. Into this frightful cauldron poured a vast body of water from the main river. It fell clear down, struck the surface of the pool as if it were solid rock, dashed itself into vapour, and threw a dense shower of spray far up the face of the opposite rock, from whence it descended in a thousand little rivulets of silver that sparkled like a flood of moonlight on the dark surges of the midnight main. On the left came down a torrent that poured itself out from the dense scrub overhead. That, too, fell clear down on to the pool below in a sheet of glorious spray. Around the face of the rocks grew beautiful and tiny orchids and ferns, and innumerable little plants looking serenely down with their green faces into the awful maelstrom underneath, indescribably beautiful, amid the war of wind and waters—

> Resembling. mid the torture of the scene,
> Hope watching Madness, with unalterable mien.

And gorgeous blue-winged butterflies emerged from the crevices of the rocks, fluttered slowly down until the spray caught them, and vanished like a flash of light into the vortex of remorseless waters, like lost spirits drawn in where the firmament of the Miltonian Hell spouted its cataracts of fire, until caught in the descending flames and swept down into the Infinite Abyss, nameless in dark oblivion there to dwell. From the still pools up the river came magnificent blue and pink and scarlet lilies, with superb fan-like green leaves attached. On one of them was a splendid butterfly, floating along like the Indian Cupid in the Nelumbo flower, down the swift current of the Sacred River.

Swift and painless death for all life once closed in the pitiless embrace of that deadly surge, cleaving the azure with the rapidity of light! One step from where you now stand and you have passed the confluence of the two infinitudes—eternity is before you, and this world with all its madness is behind you; your body is dashed to atoms among those jagged and savage rocks; the spectral winds play your death march on their Æolian harp of pines; the giant cannons fire in volleying thunder their last salute; the cataract wraps its white foam shroud around you; and the mighty mountains, thrown on the primary rocks, stand there aloft in the majesty of eternal silence and immensity as your everlasting monuments! What was the pyramid-piled grave of the Egyptian king compared to this? A tomb here more worthy of divine Cleora than the old Leucadian steep. This is the home of Poesy, first-born of the gods, and Romance, the parent of golden dreams. Alas! that the cold hand of science has dragged the Naiad's from the waters, and hurled the dryads and hamadryads from the woods!

Twilight is descending, and I gaze once more into that awful realm of swimming shadows and enormous shapes, with fearful chasms, rolling billows of foam, vast cloud-like vapours, descending columns of yellow water like liquid fire, opalescent and irridescent, fantastic rocks, scarred and rent by Æons of ages, towering mountains, crowned by mournful pines, showers of spray and wandering mist, mingled with the roar and rush and howl of immeasurable waters, plunging in their death agonies into the "fathomless and thundering abyss," in unutterable sublimity of unfettered chaos and illimitable madness. Alas! after all I have only proved how impotent is language to give more than a vague and shadow outline of that mighty picture hung there on the sullen rocks among the grand old mountains as a presentation picture to Australia from the Art Gallery of the Eternal.—*Brisbane Courier.*

MELBOURNE:

KEMP AND BOYCE, PRINTERS,

RUSSELL STREET.

Centennial International Exhibition,

MELBOURNE, 1888.

⚓ CATALOGUE

OF THE

EXHIBITS

IN THE

QUEENSLAND COURT.

Executive Commissioners:

THE HONOURABLE THOMAS MACDONALD-PATERSON, M.L.C.

JOHN FENWICK, Esq., J.P.

Executive Commissioners in Queensland:

F. M. BAILEY, Esq., F.L.S.

C. W. DE VIS, Esq., M.A.

JOHN FENWICK, Esq., J.P.

P. R. GORDON, Esq., J.P.

Hon. A. C. GREGORY, C.M.G., M.L.C.

GEORGE GRIMES, Esq., J.P.

JOHN LITTLE, Esq., J.P.

JAMES TOLSON, Esq., J.P.

Secretary:

H. COURTENAY LUCK, F.R.G.S.

BRISBANE:

WARWICK AND SAPSFORD, PRINTERS, BOOKBINDERS, ETC., ADELAIDE STREET.

MDCCCLXXXVIII.

A BRIEF SKETCH OF THE COLONY.

QUEENSLAND, in point of organisation, the youngest colony of the Australasian group, is situated between the parallels 10° 40′—29° South latitude, and 138°—153° 30′ East longitude, and contains within these limits an area of 668,224 square miles, with a population, on the 31st December, 1887, estimated in round numbers at 367,000, of whom 215,000 were males and 152,000 females.

A glance at the contents of the Queensland Court will well illustrate the varied character of the resources and vast capabilities of the Colony.

Climate.

Within the large area covered by the Colony there is necessarily a great diversity of climate. Speaking generally, the rainy season throughout the colony occurs in the months of January and February. In the tropical portion there is a well-defined "rainy season," extending from January to March. In the south, the rains are more generally distributed over the year. The winter is generally dry and bracing, more especially upon the highland plains west of the coastal range; indeed, for at least eight months of the twelve, the climate of Queensland is most lively and exhilarating, and closely approaches that of Madeira. The total rainfall in 1887 at Brisbane was 81 inches; at Cooktown, 75 inches; Warwick, 33 inches; Stanthorpe, 36 inches; Geraldton, 155 inches; Rockhampton, 45 inches; Townsville, 56 inches; and Normanton, 37 inches.

The mean shade temperature of Brisbane in 1887 ranged from 76° F. in January to 56° F. in June. The climate, on the whole, is remarkably healthy, and as the manner of life among the people is brought more in unison with its demands, is shown to be fully as salubrious as that of any other portion of the Australian continent. No part of the Colony is unsuited to the European constitution. In the inland plains more especially, the climate shows its effect in the physique of the people, and the hearty manner in which athletic exercises are pursued by the younger portion of the community is strong evidence of its invigorating character.

Mining.

The great importance of this industry, and the rich and varied character of the mineral products of the Colony will be at once apparent on glancing at the display in the Queensland Court.

The chief goldfields are Gympie, Charters Towers, Ravenswood, Palmer, Etheridge and Woolgar, Hodgkinson, and Croydon, while Mount Morgan has probably a world-wide celebrity. There are also many smaller fields, of which the Crocodile, near Rockhampton, is perhaps one of the most noticeable. The yield of gold in 1887 from all fields amounted to 432,120 ounces, of the value of £1,512,420.

It was not until the year 1868 that the importance of the gold discovery was fully realised. Since that year the total output to 31st December, 1887, has been 5,487,758 ounces, valued at £19,173,958. Prior to 1868, 119,384 ounces only had been raised, of the value of £451,039.

Tin and Silver are found in abundance at Herberton, Stanthorpe, and at Ravenswood; Copper at Peak Downs, Cloncurry, and Mount Perry, &c.; Galena, Antimony, Lead, Cobalt, Chrome Iron, Plumbago, and Manganese, are found in various parts in payable quantities, as also Building Stones, Marble, &c., of admirable quality.

The Queensland Opals displayed in London in 1886 were greatly admired by experts.

The Coal deposits of the Colony are large, and are rapidly being developed. The chief source at present of this most useful mineral is in the Ipswich district, but it is also found in abundance in the Maryborough, Bowen, and other Northern portions, and on the Darling Downs.

The seagoing steamers are now largely supplied from Queensland mines, and as facilities for transit and shipment increase, the Coal mining industry bids fair to become one of immense importance.

The total output for 1887 was 238,814 tons, valued at £97,460.

Agriculture.

The chief centre of arable farming is the Darling Downs district. The soil here is of volcanic origin, and varies in colour from black to chocolate and red. Here may be grown Wheat, Oats, Barley, and Rye. Roots also are regular crops on the Downs. Turnips,

Mangolds, Potatoes, &c., in fair seasons, produce heavy yields. In the coastal district the crop taking the place of Wheat is Maize. This grows with great rapidity, and yields enormous crops for a minimum of labour. The Sweet Potatoe is a prolific and perhaps one of the most useful plants cultivated in the Colony; cows produce excellent Milk and Butter when fed with these roots, pigs fatten readily, and fowls thrive well, while by many Queenslanders they are considered to be superior to the ordinary Potatoe for table use. Millet and Sorghum are also grown by the coast farmer to a limited extent.

The period of the year at which the Exhibition opens, and the short time which the Commissioners have had at their disposal, has prevented as good a display of Cereals as they could have desired. Efforts, however, will be made for a special display of Agricultural products during the Exhibition.

In the Southern portions of the colony Arrowroot is a standard product with farmers, and many exhibits of this useful food may be seen in the Queensland Court.

The production of Silk is an industry which the future will develop, the climate being admirably adapted for the cultivation of the mulberry, the principal food of the worm.

Tobacco of good quality may be grown in any part of the Colony. Competent judges pronounce the Queensland product to be fully equal to the real Virginia leaf, and at present the demand for the leaf for manufacture exceeds the supply. There are several factories in successful operation, and the development of this industry appears to be most satisfactory.

Cotton grows easily and produces abundantly, but the labour required renders it at present unprofitable. Rice is grown in various localities along the coast, and Coffee of excellent quality is also produced. The cultivation of the Tea Plant has been experimentally conducted with success.

As population increases and farmers adapt themselves to the conditions of their surroundings, all these products will no doubt afford a source of profitable employment. Bee-farming has, within recent years, occupied considerable attention, and the Beekeepers' Association of Brisbane is doing much to disseminate knowledge of methods of management adapted to the Colony.

Horticulture.

Market Gardening has hitherto been much neglected, and is at present chiefly in the hands of the Chinaman. As the entry of this race in the Colony becomes practically prohibited, the industry will fall more into the hands of the white gardener, to whose skill and labour a handsome return will be yielded.

The fruits of temperate climes are successfully grown in the Southern portions of the colony, and especially upon the Darling Downs. Here in season may be seen the Apple, Pear, Plum, Grape, Apricot, Mulberry, Cherry, Chestnut, Peach, Medlar, Quince, Fig, Walnut, Filbert, Strawberry, Nectarine, Almond, Passion Fruit, Granadilla, Persimmon, Pomegranate, Orange, Lemon, Lime, Shaddock, &c. The Olive also flourishes, but has not been cultivated to any extent. In the coastal and more Northern districts the Pineapple, Banana, Mango, Guava, Custard Apple, and many other fruits yield large crops; while in the North are also produced the Jack Fruit, Cocoanut and Date Palms, Papaw, and all fruit common to the tropics. Ginger, Pepper, and Nutmeg are also grown, and the vegetation of this portion of the Colony is singularly rich and varied.

The Vine is successfully cultivated in the Southern districts, where also flourish all vegetables of temperate climes. In this region may be seen the favourite British flowers, while in the Northern districts the crotons and other showy tropical plants display their gaudy magnificence of bloom.

The large number of economic plants in the Conservatory are an evidence of the vast resources of Queensland soil and climate. As these are fully described in a separate special catalogue they need not here be further referred to.

Pastoral Industry.

The grazing capabilities of the vast inland plains early became manifest. The first wool ship from Brisbane to London sailed in 1851. The statistics for 1887 show that in the latter year the export of wool reached 47,482,926 lbs., of which 15,209,351 lbs. were clean wool, value £1,060,712, and 32,273,578 lbs. were greasy, valued at £1,307,999. Besides 12,927,000 sheep, 306,000 horses and 4,474,000 cattle are pastured in the Colony; while pigs number 74,000.

The total area of the Colony is 427,838,000 acres, of which 295,265,280 acres are held under lease or license for pastoral purposes, in addition to a large proportion of the alienated or "conditionally purchased" land.

Sugar.

The Sugar industry is one of the most important in the Colony. No special facilities were offered to colonists to embark their enterprise and capital in the cultivation of sugar until 1864, in April of which year the first sugar companies were formed in Brisbane, Maryborough, and Mackay. The low price of sugar ruling during the last few years, combined with the labour difficulty, gave a check to the industry from which it has hardly yet recovered. Nevertheless, the export in 1887 reached in amount 837,953 cwt., of a value of £758,362.

In order to encourage the small settler and to enable him to become independent of the large mill-owner and black labour, an experiment is being made in the Mackay district to work upon the co-operative principle, and the Legislative Assembly, falling in with the idea, has voted the sum of £50,000 for the erection of central mills, worked by the farmers under certain approved regulations. The whole coast district, from the New South Wales boundary to Cooktown, a distance of 1,300 miles, is dotted at intervals with plantations for the cultivation of sugar, varying in size from the small mills and farms, so numerous in the Southern portions of the Colony, to the gigantic refineries of the Central districts and the large estates and mills of the North, in which tens of thousands of pounds have been invested.

Woods.

The wealth of the Colony in this direction is well exemplified by the Commissioners' exhibit, which has been prepared rather to point out that Queensland possesses, in her indigenous vegetation, woods suitable for all and every description of work. The Queensland Court has been fitted throughout with bunya bunya pine (*Araucaria Bidwillii*), a wood only found in Queensland.

The woods of the Colony are of great variety and value, and, as they become better known, cannot fail to be appreciated. It is to be hoped that under the care of a Department of Forestry, the now immense timber resources of Queensland will be conserved, and there is no room for doubt that, with proper management and judicious regulations, there is in this industry to be found an inexhaustible source of revenue.

Manufactures.

The chief wealth of the colony has hitherto been derived from its raw products, and it is only recently that manufactures to any extent have been entered upon. The exhibits, however, are evidence of the latent wealth which enterprise and capital may be expected to develop, thus benefiting all classes of the community. Nevertheless, various manufactures are already carried on in 1,125 establishments. At Ipswich the Woollen Company has now for some time been in successful operation, while the machine and metal manufactures, printing establishments, coach, carriage, railway carriage and smelting works, foundries, ship-building yards, boot factories, refineries, breweries, distilleries, and works connected with the preservation of food, &c., bear witness to the energy and enterprise of their founders.

The imports for 1887 amounted to £5,821,611 and the exports to £6,453,945.

Banks and Thrift.

The vigour and prosperity of this young Colony are well exemplified in the returns of Banking business, which on the 31st March, 1888, showed that £9,014,150 stood at deposit irrespective of the sum of £1,426,018 at the credit of 39,780 depositors in the Government Savings Bank, which has 116 branches throughout the Colony. Lately several Deposit Banks have been established in Brisbane, and have been largely supported by the smaller capitalists.

Railways.

The total length of Railways constructed and open (May, 1888) is 1,865 miles, while a further length of 600 miles is under construction or authorised. It is chiefly in reproductive works of this character that the public debt has been contracted.

Post and Telegraph System.

The Telegraph system comprises 8,772 miles of line, and 15,677 miles of wire, worked by 293 stations.

Postal routes cover 25,494 miles, worked from 716 post and receiving offices.

Harbors and Rivers.

During recent years great improvements have been effected in the Harbors and Rivers of Queensland, designed to facilitate trade and to render navigation in its waters more secure. The Queensland coast is the best lighted in Australia. Many of the rivers have been dredged, and steam vessels of the largest size can now ascend the Brisbane River, and discharge their cargoes in the heart of the city. In 1887 the total number of vessels entered inwards was 2,147, of a tonnage of 1,642,024. Outward vessels numbered 2,183, of a tonnage of 1,631,956.

Towns.

Along the extended coast line of Queensland are situated many large seaport towns which afford easy access to the interior.

Brisbane, the seat of Government, situate on the river of the same name, has within its five mile radius a population, according to the 1886 census, of 73,649; the municipality of Maryborough, on the River Mary, had a population of 9,281; Rockhampton, on the Fitzroy, 10,793; Townsville, 7,860; and other towns are Ipswich, 7,576; Toowoomba, 6,270; Warwick, Roma, Stanthorpe, Dalby, &c. (all in railway communication with Brisbane); Gympie, the earliest mining town, connected by rail with Maryborough, as it will shortly be with Brisbane also; Mackay, the centre of the sugar industry; Charters Towers, reached by rail from the port of Townsville; Herberton, the large tin mining centre, in course of being connected by rail with the port of Cairns; and Normanton, the natural outlet of the far Northern district.

Education.

As evidence that in the search for wealth the development of the intellectual faculties of the rising generation has received tha attention which its importance demands, it may be stated that the Education Department has under its control 519 " State schools," the distribution of which is clearly shown in the large map in the Queensland Court. 63,704 children are enrolled as attending these schools, of whom 33,650 are boys and 30,054 girls. The teaching staff numbers 1,471. Annual examinations are held and scholarships awarded by which the State provides three years education in one of the grammar schools of the colony, and in each of these latter exhibitions are annually competed for, enabling the clever and industrious lad to finish his studies at some recognised University. Education is free, secular, and, nominally, compulsory, but little has hitherto been done to make the latter effective. Credit must be awarded to Sir Charles Lilley, the present Chief Justice, for the successful establishment of these principles, which Queensland was the first to practically introduce. Altogether it may with safety be affirmed that the educational system of Queensland will compare most favourably with that of any portion. of Her Majesty's dominions—affording, as it does, the opportunity for any child possessed of the necessary intelligence and industry to pass from the lowest to the highest rung of the educational ladder. Besides the State schools, numerous private schools of high character are found in each of the larger towns—and recently steps have been taken to initiate the establishment of a University, a fitting cap to an educational system of which every Queenslander is justly proud.

Social.

Under the influence of the genial climate it will be readily understood that the chief amusements of the people are of an outdoor character. Athletic sports and games of all kinds are well patronised, while the various musical and scientific societies evince the artistic and intellectual aspirations of Queenslanders. Schools of Art (libraries), subsidised by the Government in proportion to the amount subscribed by the public, are to be found in every town in the Colony, and efforts are being made for the establishment of a free library for Brisbane, a vote for the purpose having been passed by the Assembly. The Queensland Museum in Brisbane was, in 1887, visited by 99,735 persons.

The Trades Societies are well supported by the artisan, mechanic, and labourer, and the business-like and practical manner in which they conducted the Trades Congress at Brisbane in 1888, universally elicited warm encomiums. '

Queenslanders are essentially a clubable race, as witness the various social, scientific, and philanthropic societies in active operation throughout the Colony. Hospitals, partly supported by the public and partly by Government subsidy, are found in all the chief towns.

The large area of public land affords ample opportunity for the successful establishment of Village Settlement, while the prospects of the agriculturist are further brightened by the magnificent discovery of a seemingly unlimited supply of underground water, which, by their operations at Barcaldine and other places in the Western districts, the Hydraulic Department has shown to be available for purposes of irrigation.

In conclusion, it may with safety be asserted that in Queensland may be found climate to suit all constitutions; and unlimited scope for energy, experience, or capital, and should the exhibits in the Queensland Court be the means of inducing those possessing either of these qualifications to cast in their lot with the Queensland people, they will find in the Colony every welcome and encouragement extended to them for its profitable employment.

H. COURTENAY LUCK.

CLASSIFICATION OF EXHIBITS.

Group I.—WORKS OF ART.

Class 1.—Oil Paintings.
Class 2.—Various Paintings, Drawings, &c.
Class 3.—Sculpture and Die-Sinking.
Class 4.—Architectural and Engineering Drawings and Models.
Class 5.—Engravings and Lithographs.

Group II.—EDUCATION and INSTRUCTION;

Apparatus and Processes of the Liberal Arts.

Class 6.—Education of Children, Primary Instruction, Instruction of Adults.
Class 7.—Organisation and Appliances for Secondary Instruction.
Class 8.—Organisation, Methods, and Appliances for Superior Instruction.
Class 9.—Printing, Books, &c.
Class 10.—Stationery, Bookbinding, Painting and Drawing Materials.
Class 11.—General Application of the Arts of Drawing and Modelling.
Class 12.—Photographic Proofs and Apparatus.
Class 13.—Musical Instruments
Class 14.—Mathematical and Philosophical Instruments.
Class 15.—Maps, and Geographical and Cosmographical Apparatus, Meteorology.

Group III.—FURNITURE and ACCESSORIES.

Class 16.—Furniture.
Class 17.—Upholsterers' and Decorators' Work.
Class 18.—Carpets, Tapestry, and other Stuffs for Furniture.
Class 19.—Paperhangings.
Class 20.—Cutlery.
Class 21.—Goldsmiths' and Silversmiths' Work.
Class 22.—Bronzes and Various Art Castings and Repoussé Work.
Class 23.—Clocks and Watches.
Class 24.—Perfumery.
Class 25.—Leather Work, Fancy Articles, and Basket Work.

Group IV.—FICTILE MANUFACTURES; GLASS, POTTERY, &c.

Class 26.—Crystal Glass and Stained Glass.
Class 27.—Pottery, Bricks, &c.

Group V.—TEXTILE FABRICS, CLOTHING, and ACCESSORIES.

Class 28.—Cotton Thread and Fabrics.
Class 29.—Thread and Fabrics of Flax, Hemp, Jute, &c.
Class 30.—Worsted Yarn and Fabrics.

Class 31.—Woollen Yarn and Fabrics.
Class 32.—Silk and Silk Fabrics.
Class 33.—Shawls.
Class 34.—Lace, Net, Embroidery, and Trimmings.
Class 35.—Hosiery and Underclothing and Accessories of Clothing.
Class 36.—Clothing for Both Sexes.
Class 37.—Jewellery and Precious Stones.
Class 38.—Portable Weapons and Shooting and Hunting Equipments.
Class 39.—Travelling Apparatus and Camp Equipage.
Class 40.—Toys.

Group VI.—RAW and MANUFACTURED PROCESSES and PRODUCTS.

Class 41.—Products of the Cultivation of Forests, and of the Trades appertaining thereto; Tanning Barks.
Class 42.—Products of Hunting, Shooting, Fishing and Spontaneous Products, Machines and Instruments connected therewith.
Class 43.—Agricultural Products, not used for food.
Class 44.—Chemical and Pharmaceutical Products.
Class 45.—Chemical Processes for Bleaching, Dyeing, Printing, and Dressing.
Class 46.— Leather and Skins.

Group VII.—MACHINERY.

Apparatus and Processes used in the Mechanical Industries.

Class 47.—Agricultural Implements and Processes used in the Cultivation of Fields and Forests.
Class 48.—Apparatus and Processes used in Agricultural Works, and in Works for the preparation of Food, Irrigation of Land, &c.
Class 49.—Implements, Models, and Plans connected with Irrigation of Land.
Class 50.—Apparatus used in Chemistry, Pharmacy, and Tanning.
Class 51.—Machines and Apparatus in general.
Class 52—Machine Tools.
Class 53.—Apparatus and Processes used in Spinning and Rope-making.
Class 54.—Apparatus and Processes used in Weaving.
Class 55.—Apparatus and Processes for Sewing and Making-up Clothing.
Class 56.—Apparatus and Processes used in the Manufacture of Furniture and Objects for Dwellings.
Class 57.—Apparatus and Processes used in Paper-making, Dyeing, and Printing.
Class 58.—Machines, Instruments, and Processes used in various works.
Class 59.—Carriages and Wheelwrights' Work.
Class 60.—Harness and Saddlery.
Class 61.—Railway Apparatus.
Class 62.—Electric, Pneumatic, and other Apparatus and Processes.
Class 63.—Apparatus and Processes of Civil Engineering, Public Works, and Architecture.
Class 64.—Navigation and Life Saving.
Class 65.—Materials and Apparatus for Military Purposes.

Group VIII.—ALIMENTARY PRODUCTS.

Class 66.—Cereals, Farinaceous Products, and Products derived from them.
Class 67.—Bread and Pastry.
Class 68.—Fatty Substances used as Food, Milk, and Eggs.

Class 69.—Meat and Fish.
Class 70.—Vegetables and Fruit.
Class 71.—Condiments and Stimulants, Sugar and Confectionery.
Class 72.—Fermented and Distilled Drinks.

Group IX.—SANITATION, MEDICINE, HYGIENE, and PUBLIC RELIEF.

Class 73.—Sanitary Appliances, Surgical Instruments, Plans, Models, &c.
Class 74.—Apparatus and Process for Heating and Lighting.

Group X.—AGRICULTURE and ASSOCIATED INDUSTRIES.

Class 75.—Specimens of Farm Buildings and Agricultural Works.

Group XI.—HORTICULTURE.

Class 76.—Conservatories and Horticultural Apparatus.
Class 77.—Flowers and Ornamental Plants.
Class 78.—Vegetables.
Class 79.—Fruit and Fruit Trees.
Class 80.—Seeds and Saplings of Forest Trees.
Class 81.—Plants for Conservatories.

Group XII.—MINING INDUSTRIES.—Machinery and Products.

Class 82.—Apparatus and Processes of the Art of Mining and Metallurgy.
Class 83.—Mining and Metallurgy.

ADDENDA.—Late Entries.

Appendix A.

Catalogue of the Exhibits from New Guinea, shown by the Special Commissioner for New Guinea, Hon. John Douglas, C.M.G.

Appendix B.

Sketch of the Economic Plants of Queensland.

Appendix C.

Catalogue of Queensland Grasses.

Appendix D.

Catalogue of the Indigenous Woods shown in the Queensland Court.

Appendix E.

Catalogue of the Minerals shown in the Queensland Court.

CATALOGUE OF EXHIBITS

IN THE

QUEENSLAND COURT.

Group I.—Works of Art.

Class 1—Oil Paintings.

Aplin, Louisa, Glen Aplin, Stanthorpe—
  1 Oil Painting from nature.

Barlow, Fred. W., The Grange, Toowoomba—
  2 Oil Painting.

Bowkett, Dr. (painted by the late Miss Bowkett), Herberton—
  3 "Orchid: *Oberonia palmicola*.'   .
  4 "Views of Herberton."

Clarke, J. A., Norfolk Road, South Brisbane—
  5 "View of Quart Pot Creek, Stanthorpe."
  6 "Study of a Coleus."

Fristrom, Oscar, Adelaide Street, Brisbane—
  7 "King Sandy," a Queensland aboriginal.
  8 "An Ancient Greek."
  9 "A Brown Study," a Queensland aboriginal.

Jenner, Walter, Taringa, Brisbane—
  10 "The Arched Rock, coast of Durham."
  11 "Boomers at Brighton."
  12 "Land's End, Cornwall," "Lingering Light."
  13 "Seaford Beach and Chalk Cliffs, County Sussex."
  14 "White Cliffs of Albion, Dover."
  15 "The Old Man of Hoy."

Kitson, H. A., Custom House, Mackay—
  16 "View of Mackay and District from Mount Bassett."
  17 "View of Pioneer River and Town of Mackay."

Rayment, Robert S., Adelaide Street, Brisbane—
  18 "A Cloudy Morning," Milton Reach, Brisbane River.
  19 "Brisbane at Sunset."

Rielly, Isa, care of Mrs. Dyson Aplin, Glen Aplin, Stanthorpe—
  20 Oil Painting from nature.

Class 2—Various Paintings, Drawings, Etc.

Austin, William, Spring Hill, Brisbane—

    21   "Arrival of the First Gold Escort in Melbourne, 1852."

    22   "Evening on the North Quay, Brisbane."

Barlow, Fred. W., The Grange, Toowoomba—

    23   Water-colour.

Clarkson, Mrs., Mackay—

    24   Water-colour drawings of Tropical Fruits.

Dewing, Miss Nellie, Skew Street, Brisbane—

    25   Poonah Painting.

    26   Crystal Ivory Type Painting.

Mohr, Otto, Whynot Street, South Brisbane—

    27   Three Water-colour "Illuminations for Addresses," &c.

    28   "Study of Still Life."

    29   Copy of the first three lines of a Mongol Letter, in the Uigar character, sent by Arzhun Khan to Philip the Fair in 1289.

Perkins, George J., Gaythorn, Mackay—

    30   "Bruce," head of dog   A Study in Sepia.

    31   "Original Ode to Australian Pioneers."   Illumination.

Rayment, Robert S., Adelaide Street, Brisbane—

    32   "The Acclimatisation Gardens, Brisbane," water-colour.

    33   "Quart Pot Creek, Stanthorpe," water-colour.

    34   "The Afterglow, Brisbane River," water-colour.

Rice, Lionel K., Mackay—

    35   Four Water-colour Drawings.

CLASS 3.—*No entry.*

Class 4—Architectural and Engineering Drawings and Models.

Buckeridge, John H., architect, Courier Buildings, Brisbane—

    36   Designs for proposed Hotel for Mr. W. Kellett.

    37   Designs submitted in competition for Madrid Exhibition, 1880.

    38   Design for Church.

Clarke, J. J., architect, Queen Street, Brisbane.

    39   View of Public Offices, Brisbane.

    40   View of River Frontage of Public Offices, Brisbane.

    41   View of proposed Town Hall, Brisbane.

    42   Various Public Buildings.

Colonial Architect's Branch, Department of Public Works, Brisbane—

    43   Collection of Drawings of Public Buildings in Queensland.

Gailey, Richard, architect, Queen|Street, Brisbane—

44 Collection of Architectural Designs and Photographs.

London Chartered Bank of Australia, Brisbane—

45 View of the London Chartered Bank, Brisbane.

Oakden, Addison, & Kemp, architects, Queen Street, Brisbane—

46 Photographs of various Buildings, designed by exhibitors, erected or in course of erection in Queensland.

47 Drawing of Villa Residence for R. J. Gray, Esq.

48 Drawing of the Wesleyan Church, Brisbane.

49 Drawing of the Secretary's Residence, Queensland National Association, Bowen Park, Brisbane.

Ports and Harbours Department, Brisbane—

50 Model of Pile Lighthouse, Brisbane River Bar.

51 Model of Lighthouse, Cape Bowling Green.

Stombuco, A., & Son, Queen Street, Brisbane—

52 Sketches of H.I.M. Opera House, Brisbane, and other architectural designs.

Class 5—Engravings and Lithographs.

Mohr, Otto, Whynot Street, South Brisbane—

53 Photo-lithography.

Taylor, John, F S.Sc., Ashwell Schoolhouse, Rosewood—

54 "Portrait of General Sir Thomas Makdougall Brisbane, G.C.B," &c., Governor of New South Wales from 1821 to 1825. Steel Engraving.

55 Book containing view of Brisbane, Ayrshire, the ancient seat of the Brisbane family, from which the City of Brisbane, Queensland, is named.

Group II.—Education and Instruction, Apparatus and Processes of the Liberal Arts.

Class 6—Education of Children, Primary Instruction, Instruction of Adults.

A.—Work by Pupils.

56 Blackstone Primary State School.

57 Bundamba State School.

58 Bundaberg State School.

59 Burnside State School.

60 Caboolture State School.

61 Clifton Homestead Area State School.

B

62   Coningsby (Mackay) State School.
63   Dalrymple Creek (Allora) State School.
64   Dingo (Rockhampton) Provisional School
65   Emu Creek State School.
66   Flat Top (Mackay) Provisional School
67   Freestone Creek (Lower) State School
68   Glenvale (Toowoomba) State School
69   Halifax State School.
70   Herberton State School.
71   Howard State School.
72   Ipswich East State School.
73   Ipswich Central Girls' State School.
74   Kangaroo Point Girls' State School.
75   Laidley State School.
76   Merritt's Creek (Toowoomba) State School.
77   Monkland State School.
78   Newtown (Ipswich) State School.
79   Oakey Creek State School.
80   Ramsay State School.
81   Ravenswood State School.
82   Rockhampton Boys' Central State School.
83   Rosewood State School.
84   Sandgate State School.
85   Sugarloaf State School.
86   Toowoomba East State School.
87   Yengarie State School.
88   Yeulba State School.

B.—Appliances for Teaching, &c.

Taylor, John, F.S.Sc., London, Ashwell Schoolhouse, Rosewood—

89   Sample of School Diagrams used in the Ashwell School,
        as roughly drawn by exhibitor with coloured chalks
        on carbonised paper, adapted to meet the require-
        ments of each class.
90   Rough Plaster Models, as used in the Ashwell School, to
        illustrate lessons in elementary geography classes.
91   Relief Map of Spain and Portugal, vertical scale ten
        times the horizontal.
92   Section of a Glacier, showing the carving of icebergs.

C.—Special.

Merenlender, Julius, Georgetown, Etheridge River—

93   Hebrew Poetry.

CLASS 7.—*No entry.*

Class 8—Organisation, Methods, and Appliances for Superior Instruction.

Cutton Bros., Bicton Clump Point, Cardwell—

94   Articles of Aboriginal Manufacture, consisting of Blanket made from the bark of the Banyan Tree, Dilly Bags, and Necklace.

Harvey, William E., care of Harvey, Sargeant & Co., Alice Street, Brisbane—

95   An Improved Easel for Artists, working with a Ratche and Lever. The Easel can be raised or lowered by one hand at pleasure. It is provided with sliding tray for brushes, &c., and a desk for small pictures, the latter being fixed to the tray by means of a sliding pivot, and can he taken off with ease; can be set to any angle by a quadrant and thumb screw.

New Guinea Special Commissioner (Hon. John Douglas, C.M.G.)—

96   Ethnographical Collection from New Guinea.

Queensland Museum Trustees, Brisbane—

97   Ethnographical Collection from New Guinea.

Class 9—Printing, Books.

Hews, R. S., & Co., Elizabeth Street, Brisbane—

98   Specimens of Printing.

McKellar, Daniel, Elizabeth Street, Brisbane—

99   Chromo-lithographic Printing.

Registrar-General, Brisbane—

100   " Census of Queensland, 1886."   2 vols.
101   " Statistical Register of Queensland for the year 1886."
102   " Statistical Register of Queensland for the year 1887."

Queensland Commissioners, Brisbane—

103   "All range Queensland Register."
104   Bailey's " Synopsis of the Queensland Flora."
105   Bailey's " Supplement to Synopsis."
106   Bailey's " Fern World."
107   Bernays's " Cultural Industries."
108   Bound Acts of the Queensland Legislature.
109   " Brands Directory."
110   " Brisbane Directory."
111   Brunton Stephens's Works.
112   Coote's " History of Queensland."
113   Gordon and Bailey's " Plants Reported Injurious to Stock."
114   Gregory's " Journal of Australian Exploration."
115   Justices Act and Offenders Probation Act.
116   " Queensland: Its Resources and Institutions."

117 Queensland Statutes. 6 vols.
118 Russell's "History of Queensland."
119 The following Newspapers and Journals published in
       the Colony will be kept filed in the Queensland
       Court :—

BARCALDINE: *Western Champion.*

BEENLEIGH : *Logan Witness.*

BOWEN : *Port Denison Times.*

BRISBANE : *Courier.*
          Telegraph.
          Observer.
          Queenslander.
          Week.
          Queensland Government Gazette.
          Southern World.
          Nord Australische Zeitung.
          The Planter and Farmer.
          Queensland Mercantile Gazette.
          Figaro.
          Boomerang.
          Joy Bells.
          Australian Christian World.
          Queensland Freeman.
          Queensland Law Journal.

BUNDABERG : *Star.*
           Bundaberg and Mount Perry Mail.
           Reporter.
           Blue Ribbon Signal.

CAIRNS : *Post.*
        Chronicle.

CHARLEVILLE : *Times.*

CHARTERS TOWERS : *Northern Miner.*
                 Times.
                 Mining Record.
                 Herald.

CLERMONT : *Peak Downs Telegram.*

COOKTOWN : *Courier.*
          Independent.

CROYDON : *Golden Age.*
         Mining News.
         Miner.

CUNNAMULLA : *Express.*

DALBY : *Herald.*

GLADSTONE : *Observor.*

GOONDIWINDI : *McIntyre Herald.*

GYMPIE : *Times.*
        Miner.

HERBERTON: *Advertiser.*
　　　　　Wild River Times.
HUGHENDEN: *Ensign.*
IPSWICH: *Queensland Times.*
　　　　Advocate.
MACKAY: *Mercury.*
　　　Standard.
　　　Banner.
MARYBOROUGH: *Chronicle.* `
　　　　　　Wide Bay and Burnett News.
　　　　　　The Colonist.
　　　　　　Howard and Isis Advocate.
MOUNT MORGAN: *Chronicle.*
NORMANTON: *Carpentaria Times.*
　　　　　　Norman Chronicle.
PORT DOUGLAS: *Chronicle.*
　　　　　Times.
RAVENSWOOD: *Mining Journal.*
ROCKHAMPTON: *Morning Bulletin.*
　　　　　　Northern Argus.
　　　　　　Capricornian.
ROCKHAMPTON, NORTH: *Times.*
ROMA: *Western Star.*
SANDGATE: *Directory.*
　　　　Moreton Mail.
SOUTHPORT: *Southern Queensland Bulletin.*
: T. GEORGE: *Standard.*
STANTHORPE: *Border Post.*
THARGOMINDAH: *Herald.*
TOOWOOMBA: *Darling Downs Gazette.*
　　　　　Chronicle.
　　　　　Darling Downs Zeitung.
TOWNSVILLE: *Herald.*
　　　　　Bulletin.
　　　　　North Queensland Telegraph.
　　　　　North Queensland Sentinel.
WARWICK: *Argus.*
　　　　Examiner and Times.
WINTON: *Herald.*

CLASS 10.—*No entry.*

Class 11—General Application of the Arts of Drawing and Modelling.

Benson, Norman, North Quay, Brisbane—

　120　Cardboard Designs.

Class 12—Photographic Proofs and Apparatus.

Buderus & Shaw, Mackay—
   121   Views of Mackay and District.

Charters Towers Committee—
   122   Collection of Photographs, in frame made of local woods,
         by Mr. Benjamin Toll.

Ching, John Lionel, & Co., Dugong Fisheries, Queensland—
   123   Photographs.

Curtis, L. E., Bundaberg—
   124   Views of Bundaberg and District.

King, G. H. M., Mackay—
   125   Collection of Photographs.

Lomer, A., & Co., Queen Street, Brisbane—
   126   Collection of Photographic Views and Portraits.

Long & Robertson, Habana, Mackay—
   127   Collection of Photographs.

Lundager, J. H., Rockhampton—
   128   Collection of Photographs.
   129   Photographs of Mount Morgan.

Mohr, Otto, Whynot Street, South Brisbane—
   130   Photographic Miniature Reproduction.

New Guinea Special Commissioner (Hon. John. Douglas, C.M.G.)—
   131   Photographs of New Guinea, taken by J. W. Lindt, Esq.

Poulsen, Poul C., Queen Street, Brisbane—
   132   Collection of Photographic Views of Brisbane, Mary-
         borough, Gympie, and Bundaberg.

Queensland Commissioners—
   133   Collection of Photographs of Charters Towers, Brisbane,
         &c., &c.

Railway Department, Chief Engineer for Southern and Central Divisions—
   134   Photographs of Queensland Railway Works.

Reckitt & Mills, Mount Britton, Mackay—
   135   Collection of Photographs.

Strüver, F., Pine Creek, Darling Downs—
   136   Coloured Photographs, representing scenery, buildings,
         improvements, &c., on Pine Creek Station.

CLASS 13.—*No entry.*

Class 14—Mathematical and Philosophical Instruments.

Wragge, Clement, Government Meteorologist, Post and Telegraph Department, Brisbane—

137 Equipment of a Climatological Station, comprising Stevenson's enlarged double-louvred thermometer screen, dry and wet bulb thermometers, maximum and minimum self-registering thermometers, Wragge's "Tropic" rain-gauge, with measuring glass.

138 Wragge's Earth Thermometer Tubes, with thermometer complete, for ascertaining temperature of the ground at depths from 1 to 12 feet, and greater depths; used at observatories of the 1st and 2nd orders in Queensland.

139 Electric Thermometers and Hygrometers, in double-louvred screen, attached to clock, with battery complete; self-registering at any time that may be desired; used at the 1st order meteorological observatories in Queensland, principally for securing 3 a.m. records.

Class 15—Maps and Geographical and Cosmographical Apparatus.

McKellar, Daniel, Elizabeth Street, Brisbane—

140 Map of Brisbane and Suburbs.

Meteorological Department, Brisbane (Clement Wragge, Government Meteorologist)—

141 Forms of Monthly Meteorological Registers employed at stations of the 1st and 2nd order.

142 Forms of Monthly Meteorological Registers employed at Climatological Stations.

143 Forms of Daily Meteorological Registers, &c., exhibited regularly at the Post and Telegraph Office, Brisbane.

144 The Weather of Australasia.

145 The Weather of Queensland.

146 The Weather of East Australia.

147 The Weather of Brisbane.

148 The Weather of Moreton Bay.

149 The Weather Chart of Australasia as supplied to scientific institutions, libraries, learned institutions, &c. Sent post free to subscribers in any part of the Empire at £2 2s. per annum.

150 Small Weather Chart of Australasia (rough sketch for forecasting purposes).

151 Forecasts for all Australia, Tasmania, and New Zealand, issued at 5 p.m. daily.

152 Meteograms showing graphic records of atmospheric pressure, temperature, and humidity by self-recording instruments at the Brisbane Observatory.
153 Small Rainfall Map of Queensland, showing amount of precipitation during 1887.
154 Large Rainfall Map of Queensland, showing amount of precipitation during 1887.
155 Map showing positions of the principal Meteorological Observatories in Queensland.
156 Map showing Prevailing Winds, 1887.
157 Map showing Cloud Areas, 1887.
158 Specimen of Monthly Report of the "Brisbane Observatory."
159 Specimen of Weekly Synopsis, "The Climate of Brisbane."
160 Specimen Monthly "Rainfall of Queensland."
161 Official Accounts of the operations of the Meteorological Branch.

Mines Department—
162 Geological Map of Queensland.
163 Map showing Mineral Areas of Queensland.
164 Map of Gympie.
165 Map of Charters Towers.

Post and Telegraph Department, Brisbane—
166 Map of Queensland, showing Post and Telegraph routes.

Public Instruction Department—
167 Map of Queensland, showing the position of the State Schools of the Colony.

Public Lands Department—
168 General Map of Queensland.

Railway Department, Brisbane, Chief Engineers' Branch—
169 Map of Queensland Railways.

Registrar-General's Department, Brisbane—
170 A Map of the Colony, showing the density of population as ascertained by the census of 1886, and various diagrams of population.

Group III.—Furniture and Accessories.
Class 16—Furniture.
Chubb, Charles F., Ipswich—
171 Occasional Table, made by John Hucker, of Ipswich, from Bunya - Bunya timber, grown from seed sown in exhibitor's garden in 1864, felled in 1878; circumference at butt, 45 inches; height, 60 feet. The dark portions of the table are made from a scrub vine.

Keith, W., & Co., Elizabeth Street, Brisbane—
172 Durham Coal Scoop.
173 Durham Waterloo Coal Scoop.
174 Helmet Coal Scoop.
175 Slop Pail
176 Well Bucket.

Lupton, Walter, Albert Street, Brisbane—
177 Improved Double-oven Portable Kitchen Range.
178 Double-door Fire Proof Safe.
179 Improved Single-oven and Boiler Portable Kitchen Range.

Mitton, T., 80 George Street, Brisbane—
180 Brass Mounted Fender.
181 Gravel Screen.
182 Two Mitton's Patent Curled Wire Door Mats.
183 Woven Wire Mattress, common quality.
184 Woven Wire Mattress, best quality, with roller ends and castings.

Class 17—Upholsterers' and Decorators' Work.

Francis, Mrs. A. M., Barcaldine—
185 Hand-painted Calico Windows, for bush use.

CLASSES 18 to 23.—*No entries.*

Class 24—Perfumery.

Sweeney, E. C., & Co., Townsville—
186 The New Magic Florentine Powder, and other articles.

Class 25—Leather Work, Fancy Articles, and Basket Work.

Queensland Commissioners—
187 Basket Work.

Rawson, E. S., Mackay—
188 Fancy articles made from Bamboo.

———

Group IV.—Fictile Manufactures, Glass, Pottery, Etc.

CLASS 26.—*No entry.*

Class 27—Pottery.

Agnew & Rumble, Sandhurst Pottery, Dinmore—
189 Collection of Rockingham and Majolica Caneware, Bakers' Dishes, Milk Dishes, &c., &c.

Brown, Peter, Ipswich—

190   Pressed Bricks.

Campbell, James, & Sons, Creek Street, Brisbane—

191   Red and Cream Terra-cottaware, comprising Vases, Water Bottles, Butter Coolers, Garden Tiles and Edging, Terra-cotta for Buildings.

192   Fire Bricks, Building Bricks, Socketted Stoneware, Sewerage Pipes, Urinals, Garden Tiles, Chimneys, &c., &c.

Dinmore Brick and Tile Company Ltd., Brisbane—

193   An Assortment of Potteryware, comprising Churns, Breadcrocks, Chicken Fountains, Jars, Barrels, Jugs, &c.

194   Building Bricks, &c.

North Rockhampton Brick and Tile Company Ltd., Rockhampton—

195   Pressed Bricks.

Nöthling, Julius, Beenleigh—

196   Bricks, hand made.

Petrie, John, & Sons, Brisbane—

197   Red and White Building Bricks.

Queensland Brick and Tile Company Ltd., Brisbane—

198   Building Bricks, various.

Rogers, R. H., & Company, Ipswich—

199   Enamelled Bricks.

200   Glazed Potteryware.

201   Garden Pots, &c., &c.

Waterstown Brick and Tile Company Ltd., Brisbane—

20   Granite Bricks.

Group V.—Textile Fabrics, Clothing, and Accessories.

CLASSES 28 AND 29.—*No entries.*

Class 30—Worsted Yarn and Fabrics.

Queensland Woollen Manufacturing Company Ltd., Ipswich—

203   Worsted Cloths and Clothing.

Class 31—Woollen Yarn and Fabrics.

Queensland Woollen Manufacturing Company Ltd., Ipswich—

204   Woollen Cloths and Clothing.

Class 32—Silk and Silk Fabrics.

Chubb, Charles Frederick, Ipswich—
205   Silk Cocoons.
206   Scarf manufactured at Coventry from Silk grown and sent home by exhibitor.

CLASS 33.—*No entry.*

Class 34—Lace, Net, Embroidery, and Trimmings.

De Jersey, Madame, Margaret Street, Brisbane—
207   Mourning Crepe Flowers.
Shearing, Mrs. Elizabeth, Argyle Street, Windsor Road, Red Hill—
208   Crochet-worked Quilt.

Class 35—Hosiery and Underclothing and Accessories of Clothing.

Parker, Thomas, Queensland Woollen Company Ltd , Ipswich—
209   Improved appliance for supporting Trousers, known as " Parker's Self-adjusting Trousers Belt."

Class 36—Clothing for both Sexes.

Queensland Woollen Manufacturing Company Ltd., Ipswich—
210   Worsted and Woollen Clothing.

Class 37—Jewellery and Precious Stones.

Clarke, James, Thursday Island.
211   Pearl Jewellery.
Cregan, John M., Queen Street, Brisbane—
212   Engraving on Precious Stones, and Clockwork.
Stürzebecher, Ernest, Thursday Island—
213   Collection of Queensland Pearls from Torres Straits.

CLASS 38.—*No entry.*

Class 39—Travelling Apparatus and Camp Equipage.

Lade, N., Queen Street, Brisbane—
214   Portmanteaus

Class 40—Toys.

Sweeney, E. C., & Co., Townsville—
215   The Mocking Bird, or Prairie Whistler.

Group VI.—Raw and Manufactured Pro. cesses and Products.

(NOTE.—For Commissioners' Collection of Queensland Woods see Appendix D.)

Class 41—Products of the Cultivation of Forests and the Trades appertaining thereto.

Bailey, F. M., F.L.S., Government Botanist, Brisbane—

216   Queensland Gums.

Burns, Philp & Co., Cairns—

217   Log of Cedar from scrubs of the Upper Barron River, and which came over the Barron Falls (900 feet high) during wet season, 1888.

Fairlie, James, & Sons, Maryborough—

218   One Cedar Plank.

219   Collection of Joinery, comprising :—Three Cedar Doors, One Pine Door, Pair of French Lights, Two Pairs of Sashes, Mouldings, Turnery and Fretwork, &c.

Gordon, A., & Co., Allora—

220   Plank of Cedar (*Cedrela toona*).

221   Plank of *Orites excelsa*.

222   Plank of *Echinocarpus Woolsii*.

223   Plank of *Sideroxylon australis*.

224   Plank of *Dysoxylon Fraserianum* (Pencil Cedar).

225   Plank of a Laurel (probably *Helicia ferruginea.*)

Green, James, Roma—

226   Cypress Pine.   Three pieces.

Grimley, Samuel, Bunya Mountain Saw Mills—

227   Collection of Fancy Timbers.

228   Collection of Timbers in Commercial Forms and Sizes.

229   Section of Bunya Pine Tree.

Herberton Committee—

230   Plank of Cedar.

Hannam, Willoughby, Cairns—

231   Collection of Timbers from the Cairns District.

M'Intosh & Dunnigan, Killarney, Warwick—

232   Pine Slab.

233   Beech Slab.

234   Teak Slab.

235   Mahogany Slab.

Pettigrew, Wm., & Sons, William Street, Brisbane—

236   Collection of Fret Work, comprising: Door Panels, Circular Ventilators for Ceilings, Porch Panels, Facia Boards for Gable Ends, Wall Brackets, Name Plate.

Queensland Commissioners, Brisbane—

237 Tanning Barks, comprising :—

Acacia aulacocarpa (Hickory Wattle).
Acacia complanata (Flat-branched Wattle).
Acacia Cunninghamii (Black Wattle).
Acacia decurrens (Green Wattle).
Acacia falcata (Boomerang-leaved Wattle).
Acacia implexa (Creek Wattle).
Acacia linifolia (Narrow-leaved Wattle).
Acacia longifolia (Long-leaved Creek Wattle.)
Acacia penninervis (Black Wood Wattle).

Stubbersfield Brothers, Gatton—

238 Iron Bark, in plank, planed, tongued, grooved and beaded.

239 Spotted Gum, in plank, planed, tongued, grooved and beaded.

240 Red Gum, in plank, planed, tongued, grooved and beaded.

241 Nut Wood, in plank, planed, tongued, grooved and beaded.

242 Rose Wood, in plank, planed.

243 Blood Wood, in plank, rough and planed.

244 Bastard Mahogany, rough and planed.

245 Brigalow, rough and planed.

Walker, Henry Bleasdale, Town Clerk, Charters Towers—

246 An amateur's collection of Queensland timbers dressed and prepared by the Exhibitor, comprising 102 pieces, the greater number being gathered in Northern Queensland, chiefly from the Charters Towers District.

Class 42—Products of Hunting, Shooting, Fishing, and Spontaneous Products; Machines and Instruments connected therewith.

Burns, Philp & Co., Limited, Thursday Island and Brisbane—

247 Marine Trophy of mother-of-pearl shells, clam and other shells, and various marine products.

248 Beche-de-mer.

249 Turtle Shell.

250 Copra.

251 Pearl Shell, polished, painted, and carved.

252 New Guinea Products, comprising gum copal, sago flour, rattans, blackwood, &c., &c.

Ching, John Lionel, & Co., Townsville—

253 Products of the Dugong (*Halicore australis*), comprising oil, ointment, fœtus, skull, skin, leather, rib-bones, tusks, &c.,

354 Dugong Cutlery, &c.

Cregan, J. M., Queen Street, Brisbane—

255   Collection of Queensland Birds, stuffed.

Dewar, Daniel, St. Helen's, Mackay—

256   Two pairs Dugong Tusks.   Two Dugong Hides.   Dugong Oil.

Field, Henry, Mirani, Mackay—

257   Stuffed Alligator from the Pioneer River.

Heron, Mrs. Eliza, Bowen—

258   Coral.

New Guinea Special Commissioner (Hon. John Douglas, C.M.G.)—

259   Collection of New Guinea Birds stuffed; see separate catalogue of New Guinea exhibits.

Petersen, Louis E., 190 Mary Street, South Melbourne—

260   Collection of 200 Queensland Butterflies, &c.

Queensland Commissioners, Brisbane—

261   Collection of Queensland Birds, in aviary.
262   Marine Collection of Algæ, Coral, Shells, &c., from Thursday Island.

Queensland Museum Trustees, Brisbane—

263   Collection of New Guinea Birds, stuffed.

Class 43—Agricultural Products not used for Food.

NOTE.—Efforts will be made for a special display of Agricultural Products, Wool, &c., of 1888. The Commissioners were not able to secure in time wool from the 1887 clip.

Bailey, F. M, F.L.S., Government Botanist, Brisbane—

264   Collection of Queensland Grasses, described in a separate catalogue.   See Appendix C.
265   Kopak (*Bombax malabaricum.*)   See Bailey's " Economic Plants," page 16, Appendix B.
265A   Lawyer Cane.

Belcher, John William, Welltown Station, Goondiwindi—

266   Bale of Merino Wool, scoured by pot-stick.

Clazy, Main & Smith, Runcorn Bone Mills, Runcorn, Brisbane—

267   Bone-dust.

Greenup Bros., Richmond Tobacco Factory, Texas—

268   Tobacco Leaf, grown at Texas.
269   Tobacco made solely from Texas leaf.

Gunn, Donald, Pikedale, Stanthorpe—

270   Wool.

Hocker, J. H., Kangaroo Point Factory, Brisbane—

271　Case of Manufactured Tobacco.

272　One thousand Cigars.

273　Leaf Tobacco.

Hutchinson, A., Gympie—

274　Oaten and Lucerne Hay.

Lindeman, Sidney A., Abbotsford, Kolan, Bundaberg—

275　Tobacco.

McPherson, Alexander, Brisbane—

276　Queensland Fibres, comprising the following :—

(This list does not by any means exhaust the number of fibres that might be collected in the whole of Queensland. With three exceptions, the whole of the following were grown within three miles of Brisbane.)

ABUTILON, *Gærtn.*—Chinese Lantern Flower.—Order MAL-VACEÆ—Tribe *Malveæ.*

(1) A. OXYCARPUM, *F.v.M., Flora Austr.* I. 204.　*Sida oxycarpa, Fragm.* II. 12.

A tall velvety erect branching shrub of from 3 to 8 feet; found through Queensland; also in North Australia, Western Australia, and New South Wales.

This genus produces good fibre, which is easily prepared, same as flax, by means of water retting.

ACACIA, *Willd.*—Order LEGUMINOSÆ—Tribe *Acacieæ.*

(2) A. AULACOCARPA, *A. Cunn.; Benth.* in *Hook. Lond. Journ.* I. 378; *Flora Austr.* II. 410.

The Queensland Hickory Wattle. Often a tall tree ; the bark very rugged when old; the foliage ash-coloured; flowers in spikes, pale colored.

(3) A. COMPLANATA, *A. Cunn.; Benth.* in *Hook. Lond. Journ.* I. 369; *A. anceps*, Hook., Tc. Pl. t. 167, not of Dl.

A tall shrub or small tree, with flat branches, and fragrant deep yellow flowers in globular heads. Common in Queensland; also in New South Wales.

(4) A. LINIFOLIA, *Willd.; Flora Austr.* II. 371.

A tall slender graceful shrub or small tree; flowers light yellow in globular heads. Common in South Queensland and New South Wales.

Many of the Acacias produce tough fibre. Prepared by beating with a wooden mallet on a block of timber.

AGAVE, *Linn.*—Order AMARYLLIDEÆ—Tribe *Agaveæ.*

(5) A. AUGUSTIFOLIA.

A long narrow-leaved kind.

(6) A. AMERICANA, *Linn.*

The common American Aloe.

(7) A. AMERICANA, *var. variegata.*

The common variegated kind.

(8) A. AMERICANA, *var. striata.*

A striped kind.

All the Agaves produce good fibre, useful for rope making and other purposes; they can be prepared by water retting.

(9) A. CELSII, *Hook.* (*Littœa Celsii,* Hook.)

A species with very broad short leaves. Fibre strong, stiff; suitable for brushes.

(10) A. GLAUCESCENS, *Otto.*

A short-leaved Aloe.

The fibre of this is also strong and stiff, and might be found similarly useful for brush making.

(11) A. RIGIDA.

A dwarf kind—very rigid—producing a strong stiff fibre. The fibres of all the Aloes can be prepared by means of water retting.

ALPINIA, *Linn.*—Order SCITAMINEÆ.—Tribe *Zingibereœ.*

(12) A. CÆRULEA, *Benth.* Native Ginger Plant. (*Hellenia cœrulea,* R. Br. Prod.)

This is a very common plant in Queensland scrubs, both North and South, and also in the northern parts of New South Wales. It attains the height of 6 to 8 feet, and bears a terminal panicle of small white flowers, which are succeeded by blue fruit, the shell of which is dry and brittle, but the closely packed seeds are each surrounded by a thick pulpy substance, which is eaten by the natives. Probably might suit for paper making.

(13) A. NUTANS, *Rose.*—Indian Shell-flower.

This plant, which is largely grown in gardens for the sake of its lovely flowers, attains the height of 6 or 8 feet. Fibre good.

ANANAS, *Adans.*—Order BROMELIACEÆ—Tribe *Bromelieœ.*

(14) A. SATIVA, *Mill.* The cultivated Pineapple.

This well-known plant, so largely grown for the sake of its fruit, was originally found in Peru. The fibre is much used in Japan and China in the manufacture of delicate fabrics.

(15) A. SATIVA, *Mill.* Var., with smooth leaves.

ARCHONTOPHŒNIX, *W. & D.*—Order PALMÆ—Tribe *Areceœ.*

(16) A. CUNNINGHAMII, *W. & D.* (*Ptychosperma Cunninghamii*)

BAMBUSA, *Schreb.*—Order GRAMINEÆ—Tribe *Bambuseœ.*

(17) B. VULGARIS, *Wendl.* Common Bamboo.

This bamboo has been reduced by machinery to a state of pulp and imported to England for the purpose of papermaking. In

China the natives have a means of reducing it to a fine fibre from which they make articles of clothing.

BŒHMERIA, *Jacq.*—Order UrticaceÆ—Tribe *Urticeæ*.

(18) B. nivea, *Hook. and Arn.* China-grass or Reea-fibre plant.

> This useful fibre plant is found in a wild state in India, China and the Indian Islands, and used in the manufacture of the best fabrics, as well as for ropes and canvas.
>
> The China-grass fibre cannot be prepared by means of water retting. The plant grows to perfection, and would produce three crops during the season in the neighbourhood of Brisbane. It is cut like willows, and shoots a new crop from the roots.

BROMELIA, *Linn.*—Order BromeliaceÆ—Tribe *Bromelieæ*.

(19) B. sylvestris, *Willd.* The Brazilian Wild Pine.

> A large plant with long leaves, bordered with very sharp prickles. Produces a well-known strong fibre.

CLADIUM, *R Br.*—Order CyperaceÆ—Tribe *Rhynchosporeæ*.

(20) C. articulatum, *R. Br.* (Baumea loculata, Bœck.)

> A tall rush-like sedge, the stems of which are prominently marked with transverse septa. Met with through Australia and New Zealand.

CALOTROPIS, *R. Br.*—Order AsclepiadeÆ—Tribe *Cynancheæ*.

(21) C. gigantea, *R. Br.* The Indian "Yercum" or Madar-fibre plant.

> This handsome flowering shrub, in India, where it is a common weed, is greatly prized on account of the great strength and silky texture of its fibre. In India it is used for bowstrings, and fishing nets and lines.

CANNA, *Linn.*—Order ScitamineÆ—Tribe *Canneæ*.

(22) C. glauca, *Linn.* A yellow-flowered Indian Shot of the West Indies.

CARYOTA, *Linn.*—Order PalmÆ—Tribe *Areceæ*.

(23) C. urens, *Linn.* The Wine Palm of the East Indies, the leaves of which furnish the "Kittul" fibre. The stem gives sago.

COMMERSONIA *Forst.*—Order SterculiaceÆ—Tribe *Buett-nerieæ*.

(24) C. echinata. *Forst.* The Brown Kurryjong.

> The fibre obtained from the bark of this tree was at one time largely used by the natives for making fishing lines and nets.
>
> Besides N. S. Wales and Queensland, the tree is common to New Guinea, the Indian Archipelago and the Pacific Islands.

CORCHORUS, *Linn.*—Order TiliaceÆ—Tribe *Tilieæ*.

c

(25) C. CAPSULARIS, *Linn.* Jute or Gunny Fibre plant.

> This tall annual plant is extensively cultivated in India for the sake of its fibre which is used for making rice bags, carpets, ropes, while the refuse from the fibre may be converted into paper.

(26) C. CUNNINGHAMII, *F.v.M., Fragm.* III. 8; *Flora Austr.* I. 276.

> A tall, erect annual, common in Queensland scrubs and margins of rivers.
> The stems from which the sample was obtained were only a poor aftergrowth, but if carefully grown, an excellent fibre might be obtained.

(27) C. OLITORIUS, *Linn.* Jute or Gunny Fibre plant.

> This is another annual plant which, like the last, is grown in India for the sake of its fibre, when young the plants are also used as a pot-herb.
> The two varieties of Jute (*Corchorus capsularis* and *olitorius*) have been grown to perfection near Brisbane, where both varieties grow to the height of 14 feet. They come to maturity at the end of 6 months if sown during October. The produce per acre would be about 2,500 lbs. It takes 3 or 4 weeks of water-retting in preparing the fibre.

CORDYLINE, *Comm.*—Palm Lily—Order LILIACEÆ—Tribe *Dracæneæ.*

(28) C. FERREA, var.

CYPERUS, *Linn.*—Order CYPERACEÆ—Tribe *Scirpeæ.*

(29) C. ALTERNIFOLIUS, *Linn.*

> A Madagascar sedge, the variegated forms of which are often seen in garden culture.

(30) C. PAPYRUS, *Linn.*

> The Nile papyrus, or paper reed, which was used by the ancients for making paper.

DIANELLA, *Lam.*—Blue Berry. — Order LILIACEÆ — Tribe *Asphodeleæ.*

(31) D ENSIFOLIA, Red. Lit., t 1. (*D. nemorosa,* Jacq.)

DOMBEYA, *Cav.*—Order STERCULIACEÆ—Tribe *Dombeyeæ.*

(32) D. MASTERSII, *Hook.*

> A shrub of the Isle of Bourbon.

(33) D. MOLLIS, *Hook.*

> A Madagascar shrub.

(34) D. NATALENSIS, *Sond.*

> A Natal shrub.
> The Dombeyas produce a large quantity of useful fibre; the plant grows to perfection near Brisbane.

DORYANTHES, *Correa.*—Order AMARYLLIDEÆ—Tribe *Agaveæ.*

(35) D. EXCELSA, *var. Palmeri.* Queensland Spear Lily.

DRACÆNA, *Linn.*—Order LILIACEÆ—Tribe *Dracæneæ.*

(36) D. DRACO, *Linn.* Teneriffe Dragon Tree.

ENTADA, *Adams.*—Order LEGUMINOSÆ—Tribe *Adenantereæ.*

(37) E. SCANDENS, *Benth.* in *Hook. Journ. Bot.* IV. 332; *Flora Austr.* II. 298.

> *Mimosa scandens* of Linnæus. The Match-box Bean. This gigantic climber is common to the tropical coasts of both the New and Old World. The beans attain to a great length, and the seeds are converted into articles of ornament, and in some parts are considered to possess medicinal virtue.
>
> The woody part of the plant consists entirely of fibre, so that a single plant of large size would produce many hundred-weight of fibre.

URENA, *Linn*—Order MALVACEÆ—Tribe *Ureneæ.*

(38) U. LOBATA, *Linn.*

> The Bun-kara of Bengal, where it is said to be a good substitute for flax.

FICUS, *Linn.*—Order URTICACEÆ—Tribe *Artocarpeæ.*

(39) F. BENGALENSIS, *Linn.* (*F. Indica,* Roxb.) The Banyan.

> This is an excellent shade tree, a single tree affording, according to some writers, shade under a vertical sun to as many as 20,000 men. The fibre is prepared from the young adventitious roots thrown out from the branches, which ultimately form the pillar-like stems for which this tree is famed.

(40) F. MACROPHYLLA, *Desf.* The Large-leaved Moreton Bay Fig.

> This is a favourite tree for planting for shade purposes. The rather large purple fruit is somewhat sweet and juicy. The tree is met with in New South Wales and many localities in Queensland.

(41) F. PLATYPODA, *A. Cunn.*

> There are many forms of this species in Queensland — many planted as shade trees, for which purpose they are admirably suited.
>
> Sheets of the inner bark are used by the natives as a substitute for blankets. It is possible to reduce this fibre to a state that it might be spun into a yarn; and, if reduced to a pulp, it would make a very tough useful paper.

FURCRÆA *Vent.* (FOURCROYA).—Order AMARYLLIDEÆ—Tribe *Agaveæ.*

(42) F. CUBENSIS, *Hav.* (*Agave cubensis,* Jacq.)

> This is very like *F. gigantea*; the leaves differ, however, from that species, in that their edges are armed with regularly hooked brown prickles throughout their entire length.

(43) F. GIGANTEA, *Vent.* (*Agave fœtida*, Linn., var. *Willematiana Rœm.*)

The common form met with in Australian gardens, which is usually furnished with prickles on the margins of the lower half of the leaf.

All Fourcroyas produce a large quantity of good fibre, suitable for rope making. The fibre takes from 3 to 4 weeks of water-retting. The plants attain a large size.

GUAZUMA, *Plum.*—Order STERCULIACEÆ.—Tribe *Buettnerieæ.*

(44) G. TOMENTOSA, *H. B. and K.*

A West India Tree. In the East Indies, where the tree is commonly planted, the wood is used by coachmakers for panels; a strong fibre is also prepared from the young shoots, and the leaves used as cattle fodder.

HIBISCUS, *Linn.*—Order MALVACEÆ.—Tribe *Hibisceæ.*

(45) H. ELATUS, *Swartz.* (*Paritium elatum.*) The Mountain Mahoe, or Cuba Bast Tree.

A West Indian tree.

(46) H. HETEROPHYLLUS, *Vent.* Native Rosella.

At one time the roots and young plants of this shrub were used for food by the natives.

(47) H. MUTABILIS, *Linn.* (*H. sinensis*, Mill.) The Changing Rose.

This shrub is a native of China, but now largely cultivated in most warm countries.

(48) H. ROSA-SINENSIS, *Linn.* Blacking Flower, Shoe Flower, or China rose.

Found in a wild state in many parts of China, where the flowers are used, as in Australia, for decorative purposes, and in India the roots are used medicinally as a substitute for Althæa.

(49) H. SABDARIFFA, *Linn.* Rosella, or Red Sorrel.

This plant is usually cultivated in Queensland as in other warm countries for the sake of the fleshy calices and involucres which surround the seed vessels for jam making, being very wholesome, and of agreeable acid flavour.

The *H. sabdariffa* is an annual plant; it takes nine months in coming to maturity. It produces a large quantity of fibre of a very durable quality. If left in water for five months it will not rot.

(50) H. TILIACEUS, *Linn.* (*Paritium tiliaceum*, St. Hil.)

The Queensland Coast Cotton Tree is an excellent shade tree, and also produces a handsome wood. The bark is largely used in Bengal in the manufacture of rope.

All the varieties of Hibiscus produce good fibres; they grow to perfection near Brisbane. If cultivated for fibre all the shoots should be cut yearly the same as willows are cut for basket making. All the varieties can be prepared by water-retting same as flax. All are suitable for rope-making.

JUNCUS, *Linn.*—Order JUNCACEÆ—Tribe *Eujunceæ.*

(51) J. COMMUNIS, *E. Mey.*

The common Rush; common on swampy land.

KYDIA, *Roxb.*—Order MALVACEÆ—Tribe *Malveæ.*

(52) K. CALYCINA, *Roxb.*

Royle says that the mucilaginous bark of this tree is used in the northern provinces of India to clarify sugar.

LAGUNARIA, *G. Don.*—Order MALVACEÆ—Tribe *Hibisceæ.*

(53) L. PATERSONI, *Don.*

A tree of tropical Queensland.

MALVASTRUM, *A. Gray.*—Order MALVACEÆ—Tribe *Malveæ.*

(54) M. TRICUSPIDATUM, *A. Gray.*

This is a widely-spread weed of warm countries.

MALVAVISCUS, *Dill.*—Order MALVACEÆ—Tribe *Ureneæ.*

(55) M. ARBOREUS, *Cass.* (*Achania Malvaviscus*, Willd.)
An American shrub.

MUSA, *Linn.*—Order SCITAMINEÆ—Tribe *Museæ.*

(56) M. SAPIENTUM, *Linn.* The Banana.

All the varieties produce a good fibre, but if the plants are allowed to bear fruit, the quantity of fibre is reduced, and its quality is inferior.

(57) M. SUPERBA, *Roxb.* The thick-stemmed Banana.

NOLINA, *Mich.*—Order LILIACEÆ—Tribe *Dracæneæ.*

(58) N. RECURVATA, *Lem.* (*Beaucarnea recurvata.*)

A Mexican plant resembling a Dracæna or Yucca.

PANDANUS, *Linn.*—Order PANDANEÆ.

(59) P. PEDUNCULATUS, *R. Br.* Queensland Breadfruit.

(60) P. UTILIS, *Borg.*

A Screw-pine of Madagascar, and considered the most useful of the genus, the fibre being largely in use for bag making.

The aerial roots of this plant are one mass of fine fibre which can be reduced by beating on a block by means of a hardwood mallet.

PHORMIUM, *Forst.*—Order LILIACEÆ—Tribe *Hemerocalleæ.*

(61) P. TENAX, *Forst.* The New Zealand Flax.

RAPHIA, *Beauv.*—Order PALMÆ—Tribe *Lepidocaryeœ.*

(62) R. RUFFIA, *Mart.*

> A Madagascar palm of great beauty. The fibre is worked into mats, fabrics, cloth, hats, &c., &c.
>
> Produces a large quantity of indestructible fibre. It is known to be exposed to the weather on the butt of the tree for fifteen years without the slightest damage to the fibre.

SANSEVIERIA, *Thunb.*—Order HÆMODORACEÆ—Tribe *Ophio-pogoneœ.*

(63) S. CYLINDRICA, *Boj.*, "Ife." The Bowstring Hemp of Zanzibar.

(64) S. QUINEENSIS, *Willd.* The Bowstring Hemp of Guinea.

(65) S. JAVANICA, *Blume.* The Bowstring Hemp of Java.

(66) S. ZEYLANICA, *Willd.* The Bowstring Hemp of Ceylon.

> All Sansevierias produce fine strong fibre. The plants grow to perfection in the public gardens of Brisbane.

SESBANIA, *Pers.*—Order LEGUMINOSÆ—Tribe *Galegeœ.*

(67) S. ACULEATA, *Pers.*

> A tall annual plant found around swamps in Asia, Africa and Australia. In India it is considered to produce excellent fibre, and in Northern Australia the seed are made use of for food by the natives.

SIDA, *Linn.*—Order MALVACEÆ—Tribe *Malveœ.*

(68) S. RHOMBIFOLIA, *Linn.* The Sida retusa, or Sida weed.

> A weed of most warm countries. Large quantities of excellent fibre are obtained from this plant in India. Dr. Royle tells us that a line made from it only ¼ inch in circumference sustained, after exposure to wet and sun for ten days, a weight of 400lbs.
>
> This plant comes to maturity from seed in six months. It takes four weeks water-retting to produce the fibre. The seed is almost indistructible, for one of the samples exhibited was grown from seed kept eight years. By means of suitable machinery it could be spun into a fine yarn if reduced almost to the state of a pulp. The fibre is very light. It would not produce more than 700 lbs. per acre.

STERCULIA, *Linn.*—Order STERCULIACEÆ—Tribe *Sterculieœ.*

(69) S. DISCOLOR, *F.v.M.* (*Brachychiton discolor*, F.v.M.)

> A tall tree of the South Queensland scrubs.
> There are several varieties of Sterculia, all of which produce a strong fibre.

STRELITZIA, *Banks.*

(70) S. AUGUSTA, *Thunb.*

> The majestic bird's-tongue flower of South Africa.

TRACHYCARPUS, *Wendl.*—Order PALMÆ—Tribe *Corypheæ.*

(71) T. EXCELSA, *Wendl.* (*Chamærops.*)

    A Japanese palm.

      The fibre of this palm is used in Japan in rope-making.

(72) T. FORTUNEI, *Wendl.* (*Chamærops.*)

    A palm of North China.

      Ropes made from the fibre of this palm have been found to be very strong, and to last well even when used under water.

XEROTES, *R. Br.*—Order JUNCACEÆ—Tribe *Xeroteæ.*

(73) X. LONGIFOLIA, *R Br.* (*Lomandra longifolia*, Labill.)

    In one or other of its many forms, this plant is met with in all the Australian colonies.

YUCCA, *Linn.*—Order LILIACEÆ—Tribe *Dracæneæ.*

(74) Y. ALOIFOLIA, *Linn.* (*Y. serrulata*, Harv.) Dagger-leaf.

    A Mexican plant.

(75) Y. ALOIFOLIA, *var. variegata.* Striped Dagger-leaf.

(76) Y. FILAMENTOSA, *Linn.* Eve's Thread.

    A plant of Florida.

(77) Y. GLORIOSA, *var. superba, Harv.* Adam's Needle.

    A Florida coast plant.

      All the Yuccas produce good strong fibres by means of wetting, washing, and beating.

Marshall, W. H., Adelaide Street, Brisbane—

    277 Marshall's Exhibition Condiment for Horses, Cattle, &c.

McBryde, John, Richmond Mill, Mackay—

    278 One case Solid Molasses.

Melville, W., Electra, Bundaberg—

    279 Tobacco Leaf, grown by exhibitor in Gin Gin district, Burnett River.

Read, Geo. B., Bloomfield, Texas—

    280 Tobacco Leaf—Broad and Dutch variety.
    281 Tobacco Leaf—Kentucky variety.

Thomas, James, Fairview, Mackay—

    282 Canary Seed.

Class 44—Chemical and Pharmaceutical Products.

Bailey F. M., F.L.S., Government Botanist, Brisbane—

    283 Queensland Gums.
    283A Pituri (*Duboisia Hopwoodii*).

Boldeman, Geo. A., Upper Dawson Road, Rockhampton—

    284 Block of Household Yellow Soap.

Ching, John Lionel, & Co., Maryborough—

285   Oil and Ointment, manufactured from Dugong fat.

Hancock, William, Ipswich—

286   Soap.
287   Tallow Candles.

Helidon Spa Water Co., Brisbane—

288   Natural Mineral Water, from the spouting springs at Helidon.

This water spouts to a height of 20 feet above the ground at the rate of 2000 gallons per hour.

Analysis.

		grs. per gall.
Bicarbonate of sodium		221·36
„ potassium		2·34
„ lithium		1·81
„ calcium		10·65
„ magnesium		1·82
„ rubidium. Traces in the spectroscope.		
Chloride of sodium		48·08
Silica		2·13
Alumina and iron		3·23
		291·42

Sulphates and phosphates. Traces.
Borates only recognisable by the spectroscope after having large quantities of water evaporated.
Iodides, bromides, fluorides. Absent.
Organic substances present only in traces.
Temperature of the water, 60° F.
Specific gravity at 78° F., 1·00766.

Ivison & Co., Charters Towers—

289   Liquid and Solid Compositions for the Prevention and Removal of Incrustation in steam boilers.

Maas, Louis John, Townsville—

290   Six Blocks of Soap.

Queensland Commissioners, Brisbane—

291   Essential Oils, prepared by the Hon. A. C. Gregory, C.M.G., and Mr. K. T. Staiger, as follows:—
Essential Oil of *Melaleuca leucadendron* (Linn.), *var. lancifolium.* Specific gravity at 60° F., 0·917. 320 ounces of oil were obtained from one ton of leaves.
Essential Oil of *Eucalyptus Staigeriana* (F.v.M.) Specific gravity at 72° F., 0·881. 1.200 ounces of oil were obtained from one ton of leaves.
Essential Oil of *Eucalyptus Baileyana* (F.v.M.) Specific gravity at 60° F., 0·890.

Essential Oil of *Eucalyptus haemastoma* (Sm.) Specific gravity at 60° F., 0·880. 672 ounces of oil were obtained from one ton of leaves.

Essential Oil of *Eucalyptus dealbata* (A. Cunn.) Specific gravity at 72° F., 0·871.

Essential Oil of *Eucalyptus microcorys* (F.v.M.) Specific gravity at 60° F., 0·896. 375 ounces were obtained from one ton of leaves.

Essential Oil of *Eucalyptus maculata, var. citriodora.* Specific gravity at 72° F., 0·892.

Essential Oil of *Backhousia citriodora* (F.v.M.) Specific gravity at 72° F., 0·887.

Bailey, F.M., F.L.S., Colonial Botanist—

292 Medicinal Barks, comprising:—

Alstonia constricta (Fever Bark.)

Cryptocarya australis. This bark contains an alkaloid which is thought to be *Curarine.*

Daphnandra aromatica (an aromatic bark from the Johnstone River).

Daphnandra micrantha. The bark contains several alkaloids which are cardiac poisons.

Petalostigma quadriloculare (Bitter Bark).

Watkins, George, Queen Street, Brisbane—

293 *Alstonia constricta.*

294 *Succus hydrocotyle asiatica.*

294A *Duboisia myoporoides.*

Class 45—Chemical Processes for Bleaching, Dyeing, Printing, and Dressing.

Wittgenstein Louis, Brisbane—

295 A New Process of Fellmongering, Woolscouring, and Tanning.

Class 46—Leather and Skins.

Barrett, Patrick, 77 Edward Street, Brisbane—

296 Seven Sides of Sole Leather.

Ching, John Lionel, & Co, Maryborough—

297 Hide and Leather from the Dugong.

Wittgenstein, Louis, Brisbane—

298 Furs, Skins, &c.

Group VII.—Machinery, Apparatus, and Processes used in the Mechanical Industries.

Class 47—Agricultural Implements and Processes used in the Cultivation of Fields and Forests.

Harvey, Sargeant, & Co, Alice Street, Brisbane—
> 299   Corn Sheller.

McLean, Alexander, Elizabeth Street, Brisbane—
> 300   Two-horse Plough.

CLASS 48.—*No entry.*

Class 49—Implements, Models, and Plans connected with Irrigation of Land.

Brisbane Board of Waterworks, Brisbane—
> 301   Model of Pipe Cleaner, with portion of Water-main, showing the opening for introducing and removing the Cleaner from the pipe.

Class 50—Apparatus used in Chemistry, Pharmacy, and Tanning.

Wittgenstein, Louis, Brisbane—
> 302   A New Process of Woolscouring, Fellmongering, and Tanning.

Class 51—Machines and Apparatus in general.

French. Colonel G. A., C.M.G., Brisbane—
> 303   Model of Improved Windmill.

Mitton, T., George Street, Brisbane—
> 304   Galvanised Wire Rat Trap.
> 305   Nest of Five Sieves.

CLASSES 52 TO 58.—*No entries.*

Class 59—Carriage and Wheelwrights' Work

McNab, John, & Son, George Street, Brisbane—
> 306   One Stanhope Dog Cart, four-wheeled, complete, with shafts, brake, and lamps; all made in Queensland except axles and lamps.

Troy, P , Elizabeth Street, Brisbane—
> 307   A Dexter Queen four-wheel buggy, for two persons; panels made of Queensland beech, framework of yellow-wood.

Class 60—Harness and Saddlery.

Jarman, R. E., Queen Street, Brisbane—

308 Secret Roll Seat Jubilee Side-saddle, all over hogskin, with doeskin inlaid seat and safe.

309 Side-saddle, all over hogskin, with doeskin inlaid seat and safe.

310 Gentleman's Saddle, doeskin seat, knee and thigh-pads, hogskin flaps and skirts, being *fac-simile* of saddle presented to H.R.H. the Prince of Wales at the Colonial and Indian Exhibition, London, 1886.

311 Secret Roll Fancy-worked Gentleman's Hogskin Saddle.

312 Gentleman's Best Hogskin Saddle, with doeskin seat.

313 Gentleman's Hogskin Saddle.

314 Gentleman's Light Demi-hogskin Training Saddle.

315 Gentleman's Demi-hogskin Park Saddle.

316 Secret Roll Full Somerset Saddle.

317 Secret Roll Wagga-shaped Demi-hogskin Stock Saddle.

318 Bag Leather Wagga Saddle, with hogskin seat.

319 One Northern Queensland Stock Saddle.

320 Ordinary Best Stock Saddle.

321 Treeless Racing Pad.

322 Set Pair Horse Carriage Harness, with very best hand-plated mounts.

323 Set Pair Horse Concord Buggy Harness.

324 Set Single best Buggy Harness.

Kerr, D., Rockhampton—

325 Stock Saddle, complete with bridle and breast plate, made entirely of Rockhampton-made leather, with the exception of the hogskin seat.

Simon, G., Blumbergville, Ipswich—

326 Set of Pair Horse Buggy Harness.

Class 61—Railway Apparatus.

Batchelder, George, Brisbane –

327 Working Model of Traffic and Dump Car.

CLASS 62.—*No entry*.

Class 63—Apparatus and Processes of Civil Engineering, Public Works, and Architecture.

Harvey, Sargeant & Co., Brisbane—

328 Ornamental and other Castings, designed and executed by exhibitors.

Norris, Charles Sydney, Townsville—

  329 Half Model of 24ft. Centre Board Sailing Boat, for smooth water—scale 1 inch to the foot.

  330 Half Model of English Racing Yacht—scale ½ inch to the foot.

Ricardo, Percy R., Brisbane—

  331 Model of Pole Tool Boring Rig.

Shillito, S., & Son, East Street, Ipswich—

  332 Iron Castings.

Williamson, William, Pilot, Mackay—

  333 Model of Full-rigged Ship under Sail.

CLASSES 64 AND 65.—*No entries.*

Group VIII—Alimentary Products.

Class 66—Cereals, Farinaceous Products, and Products derived from them.

Alford, Henry King, Allora, Darling Downs—

  334 Bag of " Allora Spring Wheat."

  335 Bag of " Talavera Wheat."

  336 Bag of Cape Barley.

  337 Bag of Lammas Wheat.

  338 Bag of Purple Straw Wheat.

  339 Bag of White Lammas Wheat.

Biddles Brothers, Bryrium, Tiaro—

  340 A superior kind of Maize, ripens quickly, and yields a heavy crop.

Carle, Valentine, Sandy Creek, Warwick—

  341 Two bags " Defiance Wheat."

Doherty, William, Pimpama—

  342 Arrowroot in bulk.

Doran, James, Freestone Creek, Warwick—

  343 Two bags Tuscan Wheat.

Grimes, G. and S., Brisbane—

  344 Arrowroot.

Hart, Daniel, Mosman River—

  345 Arrowroot.

Hayes, C., & Co., Warwick—

  346 Two casks of Flour, made by the Steel Roller process, from Wheat grown on the Darling Downs, Queensland.

Henderson, James, Tambourine—

347   Early Amber Sorghum Seed.
348   Giant Honduras Sorghum Seed.
349   Silver Hulled Buckwheat.
350   Gram.

Hutchinson, A., Gympie—

351   Maize in Stalk.
352   Maize in Husk.
353   Maize in Cob.
354   Dressed Maize.

Johnson, John Peter, Rosedale, Daintree River—

355   *Kumala Farina* (Potatoe Flour.)
356   *Kumala Megass*—for Stock-feeding.

Jones, R. O., Port Douglas—

357   Dressed Rice, grown at Port Douglas.
358   Undressed Rice, grown at Port Douglas.

Lahey, F., & Sons, Pimpama—

359   Arrowroot Trophy.
360   Arrowroot in Bulk.

Lahrs, Claus, Yatala—

361   Rice.

Lamb, W. D., Yangan, *via* Warwick—

362   American Maize.

Lewis, Charles, Swan Creek, Warwick—

363   White Tuscan Wheat, grown at Freestone Creek, Darling
      Downs.

Marshall & Slade, Glengallen, Darling Downs—

364   Lucerne Seed.

Mills, George, Nerang Creek—

365   Arrowroot.

Roberts, Thomas, Freestone Creek, Warwick—

366   Two bags Indian Wheat.

Smith, William, Allora—

367   Two bags of Purple Straw Wheat.

Thomas, James, Fairview, Mackay—

368   Rice, grown and dressed at Fairview, Mackay.
369   Rice, undressed, grown at Fairview, Mackay.

Class 67—Bread and Pastry.

Wilson, F. W., & Co., Mary Street, Brisbane—

370   Biscuits—several varieties.

Class 68—Fatty Substances used as Food, Milk and Eggs.

Hutton, J. C., Wickham Street, Brisbane—

    371 Separated Cream Butter.
    372 Bacon—sides and middles.
    373 Hams.
    374 Large Cheese.
    375 Loaf Cheese.

Class 69—Meat and Fish.

Central Queensland Meat Export Company Limited, Fitzroy Meat Works, Rockhampton—

    376 Trophy of Preserved Tinned Meats, comprising—Boiled, roast and spiced beef, boiled, roast and spiced mutton, compressed beef and mutton, luncheon beef, luncheon tongues (smoked and corned), soups, extract of meat, concentrated beef-tea, &c., &c.

Skinner, B., Brisbane—

    377 Preserved Meats, Turtle Soup, Bêche de Mer Soup, Potted Dugong, Stewed Turtle, Turtle Jelly, Ox Tongues, and specialties for invalids.

Class 70—Vegetables and Fruit.

Hutchinson, Abraham, Gympie—

    378 Pumpkins, Peas, Oats, Potatoes, Sweet Potatoes, &c., &c.

Stewart, John Whitehead, Allanton, Daintree, Port Douglas—

    379 Banana Meal.

Swallow & Derham, Cairns—

    380 Banana Meal.

Class 71—Condiments and Stimulants, Sugar and Confectionery.

Adams, Walter, Somerville Plantation, Bundaberg—
    381 Sugars.

Biddles Bros., Bryrium, Tiaro—

    382 Open Pan Sugars—yellow counter—lime process only.
    383 Open Pan Sugar—lime process only.

Bolton, F. W., Farleigh Plantation, Mackay—

    384 Loaf Sugar.
    385 Refined Sugar, $_{0.}^{J.B.L.}$ class.
    386 Refined Sugar, $_{1.}^{J.B.L.}$ class.

Burnett, J. K., Buderum Mountain, Mooloolah—

    387 Coffee Beans.

Carey, John, Killarney, near Warwick—

    388 Honey—1 cwt.

Chubb, Charles Frederick, Ipswich—
- 389 Queensland Olives.
- 390 Cayenne Pepper.
- 391 Coffee Beans.
- 392 Coffee—roasted and ground.

Clarkson, Mrs., The Lagoons, Mackay—
- 393 Tropical Jams and Jellies.

Costello, J. M., Millicent Plantation, Mackay—
- 394 _Coffee, grown, ground, and prepared by exhibitor.
- 395 Coffee Beans.

Cran, Robert, & Co., Maryborough—
- 396 Sugars.

Cran, Robert, & Co., Bundaberg—
- 397 Sugars.

Drysdale Bros. & Co., Lower Burdekin—
- 398 Sugars.

Dyason Bros., Sydney Jam Company, Leichhardt Street, Brisbane—
- 399 Collection of Jams.

Gaylard, John, Windsor Plantation, Bundaberg—
- 400 Collection of Sugars.
- 401 Sugar, No. 1, White.
- 402 Sugar, Large Yellow Crystals.
- 403 Sugar, Small Yellow Crystals.
- 404 Sugar, Large White Brewers' Crystals.
- 405 Sugar, Yellow Counter.
- 406 Sugar, Small White Crystals.
- 407 Sugar Cane, Rappoe variety.

Gibson, Angus, Bingera Plantation, Bundaberg—
- 408 White Refined Sugar, charcoal process, vacuum pans and triple effect; first quality.
- 409 White Refined Sugar, charcoal process, vacuum pans and triple effect; second quality.
- 410 White Refined Sugar, charcoal process, vacuum pans, and triple effect; third quality.

Hart, Daniel, Mosman River—
- 411 Ginger.
- 412 Coffee.

Hooper, J. H., Ipswich—
- 413 Collection Aerated Waters, Syrups, &c.

McBryde, John, Richmond Mill, Mackay—
- 414 Unrefined Sugar, ordinary lime process, open steam evaporating pans and vacuum pans. A. class.

415   Sugar—unrefined seconds. II. class.
416   Unrefined Sugar, sulphur process, open steam evaporating pans and vacuum pans. I. class.

McCready, H., Palmyra Plantation, Mackay—

417   Sugars.

Melbourne-Mackay Sugar Company, Palms Estate, Mackay—

418   First quality Sugar, made by the Icery, Ehrmann, and Bernardt process. A. class.
419   Second quality Sugar, made by the Icery, Ehrmann, and Bernardt process. AA. class.

Neame, F. & A., Macnade Plantation, Dungeness, Herbert River, North Queensland—

420   White Sugar, made by the Icery, Ehrmann, and Bernardt process.

Paget Bros., Nindaroo Plantation, Mackay—

421   Sugar Canes.
422   Sugar Cane Stools.
423   Yellow Sugar.
424   Ration Sugar.

Russell & Co., Victoria Steam Confectionery Works, South Brisbane—

425   Candied Citron Peel, grown and prepared in Queensland.

Skinner, B., Brisbane—

426   Preserved Fruits, consisting of guavas, rosellas, and cape gooseberry, &c.; apple, guava, and other Jams and Jellies.

Smith, Alfred, Victoria Plantation, Mackay—

427   Rosella Wine.

Smith, Thomas Lorimer, Woodlands Plantation, Marburg—

428   Collection of Sugars, all grown and manufactured on Woodlands Plantation.
429   Loaf of Sugar.
430   Golden Syrup.

Swallow & Derham, Hambledon Plantation, Cairns—

431   Sugar Cane—cheribon, rose, and meera varieties.
432   Candied Ginger.
433   Ginger in Syrup.
434   Candied Citron Peel.
435   Candied Lemon Peel.
436   Pine Apples in Syrup.
437   Lemon Peel in Syrup.
438   Pine Apples Candied.
439   Citron Peels in Syrup.
440   Preserved Pine Apples.
441   Preserved Bananas.

442 Sugar, Refined White.
443 Sugar, Unrefined White.
444 Sugar, Grainy Yellow.
445 Sugar, Unrefined Grainy White.
446 Sugar, Ration.
447 Sugar, Brewers' Crystals.

Wood Bros.!& Boyd, Ripple Creek, Herbert River—

448 No. 1 White Sugar.
449 No. 2 Sugar.
450 No. 3 Sugar.

Young, A. H. & E., Bundaberg—

451 Sugars.

Class 72—Fermented and Distilled Drinks.

Alcorn, John, Ontario Vineyard, Peak Mountain—

452 *White Sherry.*—Vintage—February, 1887; full bodied;
age of vine—5 years; northern aspect; soil—red ironstone with limestone pebbles; six acres under cultivation; cultivated with horses and digging fork;
trellised with wire; this wine is fermented with a
little sugar.

453 *Queensland Port.*—Made from the Espar grape, fermented
with a small quantity of sugar. Full bodied; dark
red colour; age of vine—8 years; northern aspect;
soil—red ironstone with limestone pebbles; six acres
under cultivation; cultivated with horses and digging
fork; trellised with wire.

Bassett, S. S., Romavilla Vineyard, Roma, Maranoa—

454 *Amontillado.*—Golden colour; natural wine; medium
character; made from the white Salverino grape; age
of vine—10 years; slightly westerly in aspect;
soil—sandy; twelve acres under cultivation; cultivated with plough and cultivator; trained on stakes.

455 *Burgundy.*—Red colour; natural wine; light in character;
made from Black Cluster grape; vintage—February,
1885; age of vine—6 years; sandy soil; forty-five
acres under cultivation, and ten acres not yet bearing;
cultivated with plough and cultivator; trained on
stakes.

456 *Hermitage.*—Red colour; natural wine; made from the
Hermitage grape; vintage—1884; age of vine—10
years; sandy soil; four acres under cultivation;
cultivated by plough and cultivator; trained partly
on trellised and partly on stake; being a wild grower
it is easier to work it on the trellis.

D

Beh, Mrs. David, Summit Hill Vineyard, Middle Ridge, Toowoomba—

457   *Australian Claret.*—Red colour; natural wine; full bodied; made from the Morocco Prince grape; vintage—1885; age of vine—5 years; easterly aspect; soil—red, volcanic; three acres under cultivation; 2,000 feet above sea level; trained on stakes.

458   *Verdeilho.*—White colour; made from the Verdeilho grape; vintage -1886; natural wine; full bodied; age of vine—5 years; easterly aspect; soil—red, volcanic; two acres under cultivation; trained on stakes.

459   *Reisling.*—White colour; made from the Reisling grape; vintage—1886; natural wine; full bodied; age of vine—5 years; easterly aspect; soil—red, volcanic; two acres under cultivation; trained on stakes.

Clifton & Co., Anchor Brewery, Charters Towers—

460   *Bottled Stout.*—Hops chiefly Colonial; Queensland sugar; malt partly Colonial and partly English.

461   *Bulk Stout.*—Hops chiefly Colonial; Queensland sugar; malt partly Colonial and partly English.

462   *Bottled Ale.*—Hops chiefly Colonial; Queensland sugar; malt partly Colonial and partly English.

463   *Bulk Ale.*—Hops chiefly Colonial; Queensland sugar; malt partly Colonial and partly English.

Dick, James, Reside Vineyard, Ipswich—

464   *White Wine*—Light character; fermented with a small quantity of sugar; made from the Sherry and ——— grape; vintage—1886; age of vine—7 years; south-westerly aspect; cultivated with horse hoe and plough; two acres under cultivation; trained on three wires.

465   *Red Wine.*—Made from the Espar grape; fermented with a small quantity of sugar; full bodied; vintage—1886; age of vine—7 and 11 years; south-westerly aspect; two acres under cultivation; cultivated with horse hoe and plough; trained on three wires.

466   *Red Wine.*—Made from the Espar grape; fermented with a small quantity of sugar; light character; vintage—1886; age of vine—7 to 11 years; south-westerly aspect; cultivated with horse hoe and plough; trained on three wires.

Herzer, Henry, Saxony Gardens Vineyard, Middle Ridge, Toowoomba—

467   *Red Wine.*—Made from the Black Sponge grape; natural wine; full bodied; vintage—1884; age of vine—16 years; westerly aspect; heavy red soil; two acres under cultivation; cultivated with the hoe; not trenched.

468 *White Wine.*—Made from the White Sherry grape; natural wine; light character; vintage—1885; age of vine—16 years; westerly aspect; heavy red soil; two acres under cultivation; cultivated with the hoe; not trenched.

Hooper, John Henry, Ipswich—

469 Cordials, &c., &c.

Kircher, Jacob, Assmanshausen Vineyard, Sandy Creek, Warwick—

470 *Assmanshausen.*—Red wine; made from the Blac Spanish grape; natural wine; light character; strength in proof spirit—20 per cent.; vintage—1887; age of vine—16 years; easterly aspect; soil—sandy loam; ten acres under cultivation; cultivated with plough, horse and hand hoes; trained on short trellis.

471 *Verdeilho.*—White wine; made from the Verdeilho grape; natural wine; light character; strength in proof spirit—about 23 per cent; vintage—1886; age vine—16 years; easterly aspect; soil—sandy loam; ten acres under cultivation; cultivated with plough, horse and hand hoes; trained on short trellis.

472 *Assmanshausen.*—Red wine; made from the Black Spanish grape; natural wine; light character; strength in proof spirit—about 22 per cent.; vintage—1886; age of vine—16 years; easterly aspect; soil—sandy loam; ten acres under cultivation; cultivated with plough, horse hoe, and hand hoe; trained on short trellis.

Lambert, G. S., Daisyvale Vineyard, Indooroopilly, Brisbane—

473 *Madeira.*—White wine; made from Verdeilho grape; natural wine; full bodied; vintage—1885; age of vine—10 years; north-easterly aspect; soil—gravelly, subsoil of clay; two acres under cultivation; hand cultivated; trellised on wires.

474 *Madeira.*—White wine; made from the Verdeilho grape; natural wine; light character; vintage—1886; age of vine—10 years; north-easterly aspect; soil—gravelly, subsoil of clay; two acres under cultivation; hand cultivated; trellised on wires.

475 *Red Hermitage.*—Made from the Red Hermitage grape; natural wine; full bodied; vintage—1886; age of vine—7 years; north-easterly aspect; soil—gravelly, subsoil of clay; three acres under cultivation; cultivated by hand; trellised on wires.

476 *Claret.*—Red wine; made from Red Espar grape; natural wine; light character; vintage—1886; age of vine—10 years; northerly aspect; soil—black loam and

limestone; ten acres under cultivation; horse and
hand cultivated; self-supporting.

477 *White Hermitage.*—Made from the White Hermitage
grape; natural wine; light character; vintage—1885;
age of vine—8 years; north-easterly aspect; soil—
gravelly, subsoil of red clay; three acres under cultivation; hand cultivated; trellised on wires.

Lanfear, Nicol, & Co., West End Brewery, South Brisbane—

478   Bottled Stout.
479   Bottled Ale.

North Queensland Brewery Company Limited, Townsville—

480   Bottled Ale.
481   Bottled Malt Ale, 12 months old.
482   Bottled Stout.
483   Ale in bulk.
484   Stout in bulk.

Queensland Brewery Company Limited, Brisbane—

485   Bottled Ale.
486   Bottled Stout.
487   Ale in bulk.
488   Stout in bulk.

Roggenkamp, C., Warwick—

489   *Red Wine*; vintage—1886.

Smith, Thomas Lorimer, Woodlands Plantation, Marburg—

490   *Queensland Rum,* made at Woodlands.

Waldron, Alfred, Dairy Farm Vineyard, Roma, Maranoa—

491   *Port.*—Red Wine; made from the Black Cluster grape
natural wine; full bodied; vintage—February, 1888
age of vine—3 years; south-easterly aspect; sandy
soil; forty acres under cultivation; ploughed;
trellised.

Walker, Frederick George, Sherwood Orangery, Coomera River—

492   *Golden Orange Wine.*—Made July, 1885; natural wine;
strength in proof spirit—23·9 per cent.; eighteen
acres under cultivation; soil—alluvial, 20 feet deep.

Group IX.—Sanitation,
Medicine, Hygiene and Public Relief.
Class 73—Sanitary Appliances, Surgical Instru-
ments, Plans and Models.

Davis, Henry Lee, Queen Street, Brisbane—

493 Davis's "Patent Diaphragmoptics," an invention for attach-
ment to spectacles.

CLASS 74.—*No entry.*

Group X.—Agricultural and Associated Industries.

Class 75—Specimens of Farm Buildings and Agricultural Works, &c., &c.

Darling Downs and Western Land Company, Jimbour, Darling Downs—

494 A Section of Soil from the Darling Downs.

Department of Public Lands, Brisbane—

495 Sections of Soils from various localities in the Colony.

Keith, W., & Co., Elizabeth Street, Brisbane—

496 Troughing.

Skinner, Thomas, Museum, Brisbane—

497 Electric Incubator.

Group XI.—Horticulture.

CLASS 76—*No entry.*

Class 77—Flowers and Ornamental Plants.

In Conservatory, see Class 81.

Class 78—Vegetables.

Efforts will be made for a special display of Perishable Exhibits of this nature (taken from the coming crops) during the Exhibition.

Class 79—Fruit and Fruit Trees.

Queensland Commissioners, Brisbane—

498 Queensland Fruits, in spirits and dry—

(1) ABERIA CAFFRA, or "Kai Apple" of Natal and Caffraria. This is an African fruit, sometimes used for preserve making; but the best use of the plant is doubtless for forming a live hedge. Off plants in one of our parks.

(2) ACORNS (*Quercus pedunculatus*). Grown by Messrs. Hockings and Co.

(3) AMOMUM DALLACHYI. The arillus surrounding the seed has a pleasant flavour, somewhat resembling the pulp in which the seed of a passion fruit is embedded. Head of fruits collected at Cairns by T. E. White, of Brisbane.

(4) APPLES. Hockings' greening and others. Grown by A. J. Hockings, Brisbane River.

(5) APPLES. Grown by Sam. Young, Killarney, near Warwick.

(6) APPLES. Mobb's Royal russet, Ribstone pippins, striped and red dessert. Grown by Stanthorpe.

(7) BANANAS. Cavendish, coloured, common; Dacca, Fiji, Ladies' Fingers, sugar. Grown by Messrs. Swallow and Derham, Cairns; J. W. Steuart, Port Douglas; John Williams, Mount Cotton, Brisbane.

(8) BRAZILIAN CHERRY (*Eugenia uniflora*). From Brisbane gardens.

(9) BRINGAL or EGG FRUIT (*Solanum melongena*). From M. Rigby; grown by Thomas Melrose, near Cleveland.

(10) BUNYA BUNYA SEED. (*Araucaria Bidwilli*). From Messrs. Hockings and Co.

(11) CALABASH of the West Indies (*Crescentia cujute*). Grown by J. O. Bourne, Brisbane.

(12) CAPE CHESTNUT (*Calodendron capense*). From Bowen Park.

(13) CARAMBA (*Averrhoa carambola*). From Bowen Park.

(14) CHALTA FRUIT (*Dillenia indica*). From Bowen Park.

(15) CHESTNUTS, Spanish (*Castanea sativa*). From Mr. M. Rigby; grown by W. J. McDowell, Everton Park, Enoggera.

(16) COCOA NUTS (*Cocos nucifera*). Grown by J. Armitage, Eimeo, and J. G. Barnes, Mackay.

(17) CUSTARD APPLES, Cherimoyer (*Anona cherimolia*). Grown by

(18) CUSTARD APPLES, Sweet Sop (*Anona squamosa*). Grown by

(19) DATE PLUM (*Diospyros kaki*) seedless, a very superior variety; Zinge, Nino, Die die, Maru, Oval seedless, and Kayayune. Grown by A. Williams, Greenhills Nursery, 8-Mile Plains.

(20) DAVIDSON'S PLUM (*Davidsonia pruriens*). The large fruit, Mulgrave River; the smaller fruits grown by Messrs. Hockings and Co., Brisbane River.

(21) ENDEAVOUR RIVER PEAR (*Eugenia eucalyptoides*). Grown by Messrs. Hockings and Co, Brisbane River. When fresh this is a very beautiful pear-shaped fruit, about $1\frac{1}{4}$ inches long, and of a rosy red colour, and rather nice flavoured.

(22) ELÆAGNUS ARGENTEA. From Brisbane Gardens.

(23) FLACOURTIA CATAPHRACTA, *Roxb.* Grown by E. Hudson, Albion.

(24) GARCINIA LIVINGSTONEI, a small fruit of tropical Africa off tree in Bowen Park.

(25) GRANADILLA, large fruited (*Passiflora quadrangularis, var. macrocarpa*). Grown at St. Helena, Moreton Bay, by Wm. Townley, and by John Cameron, Doobarvah.

(26) GRAPES, white (*Vitis vinifera*), and Black Isabella (*Vitis labrusca*). Grown by Mr. Pullen, Upper Kedron.

(27) GRAPES, black. Grown by Andrew Blackher, Sandy Creek, near Warwick

(28) GREWIA ASIATICA. From Bowen Park.

(29) GUAVA (*Psidium guava*), and other yellow fruited kinds, from Mrs. Chas. Coxen, Bulimba, near Brisbane.

(30) JACK FRUIT (*Artocarpus integrifolia*). From Brisbane Gardens.

(31) LONGAN (*Euphoria longana*). From Bowen Park; sample from a late crop only about one-fourth the usual size.

(32) MARKERS NUT (*Semecarpus anacardium*). Grown in Brisbane.

(33) MANGO (*Mangifera indica*), Malda, Kysapatee, Batavce, Alfonso, Strawberry, Bombay, and De Cruze's favourite. Grown by A. Williams

(34) MONSTERA DELICIOSA. A Mexican fruit. Grown at Bowen Park.

(35) PEACH—"Yellow Mundi" (*Prunus persica*). Grown by H. A. C. Teitzel, Warwick

(36) PEAR (*Pyrus chinensis*). Grown by Messrs. Hockings & Co., Brisbane River.

(37) PINE APPLE (*Ananas satica*), common, smooth leaved. Grown by

(38) PLUM (*Prunus domestica*). Grown by　　　Stanthorpe, and John Brown, Killarney, near Warwick.

(39) QUEENSLAND NUT (*Macadamia ternifolia*). From Bowen Park.

(40) QUINCE (*Pyrus cydonia*). Grown by Geo. J. Wickham, Lagoon Creek, near Warwick

(41) ROSELLA (*Hibiscus sabdariffa*) The calyxes and involucres used for jam making.

(42) SEPISTAN or SEBESTEN (*Cordia myxa, var. latifolia*). From Bowen Park; a late crop, about one-half the usual size.

(43) TAMARIND (*Tamarindus indica*). Off tree at Gracemere, Rockhampton.

(44) TOMATOES (*Lycopersicum esculentum*). Grown by D. O'Connor, Brisbane.

(45) TREE TOMATO (*Cyphomandra betacea*). From Bowen Park.

(46) WALNUT, black (*Juglans nigra*). From Bowen Park.

(47) WHAMPEE (*Clausena wampi*) From Bowen Park; very poor fruit; about one-half the usual size.

NOTE.—Many other fruits could have been shown, only their season was over before the formation of this exhibit was begun. It has also had to be got together hurriedly, and, therefore, the fruits in many cases are far below their average sizes.

Stewart, J. W., Allanton, Daintree, Port Douglas—

499   Bananas.

Swallow & Derham, Hambledon Plantation, Cairns—

500   Bananas.
501   Pine Apples.

CLASS 80—*No entry.*

Class 81—Plants for Conservatories.

A.—Economic Plants.

For a description of these, see separate Catalogue.

B.—Ornamental Plants.

Queensland Commissioners, Brisbane—

502   Ornamental Plants.

Swallow & Derham, Hambledon Plantation, Cairns—

503   Tree Ferns.

Group XIII—Mining Industries, Machinery, and Products.

Class 82—Apparatus and Processes of the Art of Mining and Metallurgy.

Class 83—Mining and Metallurgy.

For description of Exhibits in Group XII., Classes 82 and 83, see special Mineral Catalogue.

ADDENDA

AND

GENERAL INDEX.

ADDENDA,

WITH NAMES OF EXHIBITORS ALPHABETICALLY ARRANGED.

Allan, William, Braeside, Mourilyan Harbour—

504　Ten balls India-rubber, from trees three and four years old.

505　Two parcels Arabian Coffee (1st and 2nd class), from trees two and three years old.

Australasian United Steam Navigation Company, Limited—

506　Large Picture, representing the Brisbane River, and improvements during recent years.

507　Four Paintings of A. U. S. N. Co.'s steamers, "Barcoo," "Maranoa," "Shamrock."

508　Two Models of A. U. S. N. Co.'s steamers.

Blase, Johann, Cabinet-maker, Barcaldine—

509　Table made of Queensland woods (with the exception of sixteen small black pieces in the centre circle, which are ebony). This table contains over one thousand seven hundred different pieces, and about sixty different descriptions of timber. The greater part of these woods have been gathered between Pine Hill and Jericho.

Bowen Municipality—

510　Coal exhibit from Pelican Creek, 60 miles south-west of Bowen.

Brown, Peter, Ipswich—

511　Freestone from Murphy's Creek, Ipswich district.

Burkitt, H., Cooktown—

512　A collection of Bêche de Mer.

Chisholm, James R., Colbrook Station, Hughenden.

513　Coal

Commissioners, Queensland—

514　Building Stone from near D. Martin's half-way house, between Gympie and Noosa.

Department of Public Instruction—

515　Examination Papers.

516　School Books.

517 Appliances.
518 Photos of Buildings and Furniture.

Fraser & Company, Quay-street, Rockhampton—
519 Bale of scoured Combing Wool, from Aramac Station.
520 Bale of scoured Combing Wool, from Coeena Station, Peak Downs.
521 Bale of scoured Clothing Wool, from Aramac Station.

Grieve, William, Glencoe, Warwick—
522 Two Blocks of Marble.

Hunt, Ernest Samuel—
523 Three Samples of Freestone, from Hunt's Quarries, Grantham ; two being for building, monumental, and general purposes.

Hutchinson, A., Gympie—
524 Two Hams (Cumberland cut).

Ivison & Co., Charters Towers—
525 Specimens of Incrustation removed from two steam boilers by Ross's Composition.

Johnson, John P., Rosedale Estate, Daintree River—
526 One Plank Red Cedar.
527 Two Pieces Hickory.
528 Two Pieces Bean Tree.

Lade, N., Brisbane—
529 One Pack Saddle, with all strapping, and One Pair Leather Bags complete.

Parry-Okeden, W. E., Immigration Agent for Queensland, and Emigration Officer for Port of Brisbane.
530 Photographs of New Immigration Depôt and Offices at Kangaroo Point, Brisbane.

Pearson, J., Helidon—
531 Two Blocks Building Stone from Helidon.

Peillon de Lyon, Joseph, Turbot Street, Brisbane—
532 Portable Patent Fence, proof against rabbits, fowls, dogs, kangaroos, wallabies, &c.

Petrie, John, & Son—
533 Block of Granite from Enoggera.
534 Block of Freestone from Breakfast Creek Quarry.
535 White Building Bricks from Petrie's Brickworks, Albion.

Phippard Bros. & Co.—

    536 Freestone used in the erection of new public offices, Brisbane, from Murphy's Creek (top) and Highfields (bottom block).

Pink, James, The Bagdens, Wellington Point—

    537 Pine Apple Plants.
    538 Banana Plants.

Queensland Commissioners, Brisbane—

    539 Brisbane Town Hall plans (two).
    540 Living Specimens of Ceratodus.
    541 Collection of Live Birds.
    542 Collection of Native Weapons from Sandown, Palmer River District:—8 single-pointed Spears—2 two-barbed (bamboo), 3 iron and bamboo, 2 one-barb (bamboo), 1 all wood; 1 double-pointed spear, iron and wood; 6 four-pointed spears—4 wood and bamboo, 2 barbed (iron and bamboo).
    543 Ginger.

Queensland Museum Trustees, Brisbane—

    544 Two Dugongs
    545 Collection of Food Fish, comprising the following species :—

FAMILY—PERCIDÆ.

    (1) Giant Perch, Pseudolates cavifrons, *All.* and *Macl.*; Fitzroy River
    (2) Rock Cod, Serranus undulatostriatus, *Peters*; Moreton Bay
    (3) Rock Cod, Serranus fuscoguttatus, *Rupp.*; Keppel Bay
    (4) Rock Cod, Serranus viridipinnis, *De V.*; Flat Rock, Moreton Bay
    (5) Surveyor, Serranus geometricus, *De V.*; Flat Rock, Moreton Bay
    (6) Rock Cod, Serranus Gilberti, *Rich.*; Noosa
    (7) Spotted Wirrah, Plectropoma maculatum, *Bl.*; Murray Island
    (8) Genyoroge rubicunda, *De V.*; Murray Island
    (9) Hussar, Genyoroge amabilis, *De V.*; Flat Rock
    (10) Queen Fish, Genyoroge regia, *De V.*; Flat Rock
    (11) Mesoprion Johnii; Rockingham Bay
    (12) Epaulette Fish, Glaucosoma scapulare, *Ram.*; Flat Rock
    (13) Murray Cod, Oligorus macquariensis, *Cuv.* and *Val.*; Goondiwindi
    (14) Groper, Oligorus terræ-reginæ, *Ram.*; Moreton Bay

(15) Groper, Oligorus goliath, *De V.*; Moreton Bay
(16) Purple Groper, Homalogrystes luctuosus, *De V.*; Flat Rock
(17) Golden Perch, Clenolates ambiguus, *Rich.*; Goondiwindi
(18) Haswell's Perch, Dules Haswelli, *Macl.*; Brisbane River
(19) Dules productus, *De V.*; Cape York
(20) Dules sp.; Pine River
(21) Pristipoma hasta, *Bl.*; Moreton Bay
(22) Lobotes anctorum, *Cuv.* and *Val.*; Moreton Bay
(23) Bream, Gerres filamentosus; Moreton Bay
(24) Deep-bellied Bream, Gerres profundus, *Macl.*; Cardwell

FAMILY—SQUAMIPINNES.

(25) Quarter-gallery Fish, Scatophagus ætate-varians, *De V.*; Moreton Bay
(26) Scatophagus quadratus, *De V.*

FAMILY—SPARIDÆ.

(27) Black Fish, Girella simplex, *Rich.*; Murray Island
(28) Black Fish, Girella mentalis, *De V.*; Moreton Bay
(29) Sea Bream, Lethrinus ornatus, *De V.*
(30) Emperor, Lethrinus imperialis, *De V.*
(31) Schnapper, Pagrus unicolor, *Cuv.* and *Val.*; Flat Rock
(32) Tarwhine, Chrysophrys sarba, *Forsk.*; Wide Bay
(33) Black Bream, Chrysophrys australis, *Gunth.*; Moreton Bay

FAMILY—SCORPÆNIDÆ.

(34) Red Rock Cod, Scorpæna cruenta, *Rich.*; Flat Rock
(35) Bull-rout, Centropogon robustus, *Gunth.*; Brisbane River

FAMILY—TEUTHIDÆ.

(36) Yellow Trevally, Teuthis flava, *De V.*; Moreton Bay
(37) Spotted Trevally, Teuthis albo-punctata, *Schleg*; Murray Island

FAMILY—CYRTIDÆ.

(37*) Neopempheris Ramsayi, *Macl.*; Rockhampton

FAMILY—POLYNEMIDÆ.

(38) Tassel Fish, Polynemus macrochir, *Gth.*; Maryborough

(39) Blind Tassel Fish, Polynemus cæcus, *Macl.*; Cardwell

FAMILY—SCIÆNIDÆ.

(40) Jew Fish, Corvina axillaris, *De V.*; Moreton Bay

FAMILY—CARANGIDÆ.

(41) White Trevally, Caranx nobilis, *Macl.*; Moreton Bay

(42) Caranx edentulus, *All.* and *Macl.*; Cardwell
(43) Caranx armatus, *Cuv.* and *Val.*; Cardwell
(44) Caranx gallus, *Linn.*; Murray Island
(45) Caranx civis, *De V.*; North Coast
(46) Yellow-tail, Seriola grandis, *Castn.*; Moreton Bay
(47) Chorinemus tooloo, *Cuv.* and *Val.*; Moreton Bay
(48) Chorinemus lysan, *Forsk.*; Cardwell
(49) Tailor (Skip Jack), Temnodon saltator, *Bl.*; Moreton Bay
(50) Trachynotus Baillonii, *Cuv.* and *Val.*

FAMILY—SCOMBRIDÆ.

(51) Bonita, Thynnus M'Coyi, *Cast.*; Moreton Bay
(52) Commerson's Horse Mackerel, Cymbium Commersonii, *Lacep.*; Southport

FAMILY—TRACHININA.

(53) Whiting, Sillago ciliata, *Cuv.* and *Val.*; Moreton Bay

FAMILY—COTTINA.

(54) Flat-head, Platycephalus insidiator, *Forsk.*; Moreton Bay
(55) Flat-head, Platycephalus fuscus, *Cuv.* and *Val.*; Moreton Bay

FAMILY—GOBIIDÆ.

(56) Loter, Eleotris aporos, *Blk.*
(56*) Loter, Eleotris crescens, *De V.*; Rockhampton

FAMILY—SPHRÆNIDÆ.

(57*) Pike, Sphræna dentata, *De V.*; Moreton Bay
(57) Mullet, Mugil peronii, *Cuv.* and *Val.*
(58) Northern Mullet, Mugil waigiensis, *Q.* and *G.*; Cardwell
(59) Sea Mullet, Mugil dobula, *Gth.*; Moreton Bay

FAMILY—LABRIDÆ.

(60) Parrot Fish, Chærops venustus, *De. V.*; Flat Rock
(61)   Do   do   graphicus   do   do

(62) Parrot Fish, Cossyphus aurifer   do   do
(63)   Do   do   latro   do   do

FAMILY—PLEURONECTIDÆ.

(64) Pleuronectes moretoniensis, *De V.*
(65) Flounder, Neorhombus Queenslandiæ, *DeV.*; Brisbane
(66) Fitzroy River Sole, Synaptura Fitzroyensis, *De V.*;
      Fitzroy River
(67) Lemon Sole, Plagusia unicolor, *Macl.*; Moreton Bay

FAMILY—SILURIDÆ.

(68) Tandan, Copidoglanis tandanus, *Mitch.*; Fitzroy
      River
(69) Smooth Cat-fish, Copidoglanis levis, *De V.*; (*loc. ?*)
(70) Cat-fish, Copidoglanis labiosus, *De V.*; Cardwell
(71) Sea Cat-fish, Arius thalassinus, *Rupp.*; Rockingham
      Bay

FAMILY—SCOPELIDÆ.

(72) Saurida undosquamis, *Rich.*

FAMILY—SCOMBRESOCIDÆ.

(74) Sea Pike, Belone Staigeri, *Castn.*
(75)   Do   do   vorax, *De V.*
(76)   Do   do   melanotus, *Blk.*
(77)   Do   do   tyrannus, *Blk.*
(78) Silver Gar, Hemirhamphus argenteus, *Benn.*; Card-
      well
(79) Gar, Hemirhamphus Quoyi, *Cuv.* and *Val.*; Moreton
      Bay

FAMILY—OSTEOGLOSSIDÆ.

(81) Barramundi, Osteoglossum Leichhardti, *Gth.*; Daw-
      son River

FAMILY—CLUPEIDÆ.

(82) Anchovy, Engraulis nasuta, *Castn.*; Cardwell
(83) Bony Bream, Chatoessus Erebi, *Rich.*; Brisbane
      River
(84) Ox-eye, Megalops cyprinoides, *Broun.*; Cardwell
(85) Albula conorhynchus; North Coast
(86) Milk-fish, Chanos salmoneus, *Bl.*; Southport

FAMILY—MURÆNIDÆ.

(87) Pike Eel, Murænesox cinereus, *Bl.*

FAMILY—GANOIDEÆ.

(88) Ceratodus, Ceratodus Forsteri, *Krefft*; Burnett River

Queensland Museum Trustees, Brisbane—

546 Kangaroo
547 Emu
548 Cassowary
549 Group of rare Mammals from Northern Queensland including :—

   (1) Toolah, Phalangista Archeri, *Collet.*
   (2)   Do   do
   (3)   Do   do
   (4) Mongan, Phalangista Herbertensis, *Collet.*
   (5)   Do   do   do
   (6)   Do   do   *Young.*
   (7) Brown Mongan, Phalangista mongan, *De Vis.*
   (8)   Do   do   do
   (9) Yabby, Hemibelideus lemuroides, *Collet.*
  (10)   Do   do   do
  (11) Boongarry, or Lumholtz's Tree Kangaroo, Dendrolagus Lumholtzii, *Collet.*
  (12)   Do   do   do
  (13) Bennett's Tree Kangaroo, Dendrolagus Bennettii, *De Vis.*
  (14) Rufescent Tree Kangaroo, Dendrolagus rufescens, *De Vis.*
  (15) Striped Phalanger, Dactylopsila trivirgata.
  (16) Cuscus, Cuscus maculatus, *variety.*
  (17) Muscaline, Hypsiprymnodon moschatus, *Ramsay.*

550 Twenty shades containing Queensland Birds

Rockhampton Fire Clay Co., Mount Hay, 24 miles south of Rockhampton, per F. M. Byerley, Esq.—

551 Fire Clay.
552 Samples of Rocks found associated with fire clay.

Rockhampton Local Committee—

553 Two Blocks of Stone from Stanwell Quarries.

Rockhampton Natural History Society, Rockhampton—

554 One Basket Sponge from Pine Island, Percy Group

Rockhampton School of Arts—

555 Specimens of Polished Marble.

Rowan, Mrs., 29 Queen Street, Melbourne—

556 Collection of Oil Paintings of Queensland Flowers and Orchids

Rowe, William, Flinders Street, Townsville—

557 Views of Townsville

Simmonds, J. H., Stoneworks, Roma-street, Brisbane—

    558   Twenty-nine Specimens of Queensland Marbles.
    559   Do   do   Building Stone.

Smith, R. H., M.L.A., Bowen—

    560   Collection of Native Weapons and Implements used by Queensland Blacks, Bowen and Cardwell districts

        (1)   Two-handed Sword, straight.
        (2)   Do   do
        (3)   Do   do
        (4)   Do   do
        (5)   Do   do
        (6)   Do   curved.
        (6*)   Do   do
        (7)   Nulla Nulla, head rough, carved in relief.
        (8)   Do   do   do
        (9)   Do   do   do
        (10)   Do   do   do
        (11)   Nulla Nulla, head partly rough, carved in relief.
        (12)   Do   quite smooth
        (13)   Do   smooth, with single row of iron nails
        (14)   Wooden Shield, with oblique grooves on face.
        (15)   Do   plain on face
        (16)   Do   with curved pattern around border.
        (17)   Boomerang with incised pattern on one face.
        (18)   Do   do   do
        (19)   Do   do   do
        (20)   Do   do   do
        (21)   Do   do   do
        (22)   Do   quite plain.
        (23)   Do   do
        (24)   Do   do
        (25)   Do   do
        (26)   Do   with linear grooves on one face.
        (27)   Do   do   do

Thorsborne, A., Fernside, Beenleigh—

    561   Soda Water

Timbury, A. Jefferies, Chemist, Gladstone—

    562   Sample of Oil distilled from the leaves of the Citron-scented Eucalyptus
    563   Leaves of the Citron-scented Eucalyptus

Yatala Saccheureka and Sugar Factors—

    564   One Bag Saccheureka (Horse and Cattle Food).

INDEX

TO

GENERAL CATALOGUE AND ADDENDA.

QUEENSLAND COMMISSION.

Centennial International Exhibition, Melbourne, 1888

COLLECTIONS

FROM

BRITISH NEW GUINEA.

EXHIBITED BY

HER MAJESTY'S SPECIAL COMMISSIONER.

IN CHARGE OF J. W. LINDT, Esq.,

COMMISSIONER FOR NEW GUINEA EXHIBITS.

BRISBANE:

WARWICK AND SAPSFORD, PRINTERS, BOOKBINDERS, ETC., ADELAIDE STREET.

MDCCCLXXXVIII.

CATALOGUE

OF

NEW GUINEA EXHIBITS.

I. Ethnological Exhibits.

Label Nos.	Articles.	Locality.

Weapons of War and Chase.

Label Nos.	Articles.	Locality.
1	One Stone Club (star)	Koiari District
2-8	Seven Do (disc)	Kappa Kappa
9	One Spear (half-made)	East End
10-49	Forty Spears (various)	Do
50-57	Seven Bows and 47 Arrows	Motu Motu
50* & 51* } 57*	Two Bows and 85 Arrows (various) ...	Maat
58-76	Nineteen Swordsticks	East End
77-82	Six Man-catchers	Hula
83	One Shield (plaited)	Kappa Kappa
84-85	Two Shields (large wooden)	West End
86-88	Three do (small)	East End
89	One Drum	Kerepunu
90	Do	Basilisk I.
91	One Mouthpiece (for war)	Cape Rodney
92	Do do	East End
93	One War Knife (bamboo)	Hula
94	One Dagger (bird bone)	Motu Motu
95-96	Two Spears (fishing)	East End
97-98	Four Nets do	Do
99-102	One do (withdrawn)	Do
103	One do (fishing)	Do
104-5	Two do (do small)	Do
106	One Fish-trap (model)	Do

For Personal Wear and Ornament.

(For Woman).

Label Nos.	Articles.	Locality.
107-121	Fifteen Skirts (dancing)	Motu Motu and Kab. di
122	One do (of Sago and Pandanus) ...	Hula
123-5	Three do	Milne Bay, E. End
126-8	Three Mourning Strings of Beads (worn in coils round body)	Cape Rodney
129-30	Two Strings of Mourning Beads	East End
131-32	Do do do	Do
133-138	Six Bags (general utility)	Kabadi and Kerepunu

Label Nos.	Articles.	Locality.
	(FOR MEN).	
139-40	Two Loin Bands ...	Hula
141	One Girdle, sinnet (in parcel)...	East End
142-5	Four Suits (Mourning), with Girdle, Armlets, and Brow Fillet	Cape Rodney
146	One Brow Peak	Do
147	One Brow Ornament	Do
148-9	Two Mourning Fillets	Motu Motu
149*	One Brow Fillet (Coix seeds)	Maat
150	One Brow Fillet	East End
151	One Girdle	Do
151*-4*	Four Body Ornaments (bands of Coix seeds)	Maat
152-4	Three Neck Ornaments	Cape Rodney
155-6	Two do (shell, with circlet of N.G money)	Do
157	One Neck Ornament (boar's tusks) ...	Do
158	Do do (and imitation) ...	Do
159	Do do (alligator's teeth) ...	Do
160	One Necklace (small shell)	Do
161-4	Four do (ordinary)	Do
165-7	One Necklace (dog's tooth and shell) ...	Hula
168	One Do	Dora
168*	One Necklace (wallaby teeth)	Maat
169	One Breast Ornament	East End
170	One Necklace (black bead)	Do
171-2	Two Do (with boar's tusk)	Do
173	One Brow Fillet	Do
174	One Breast Ornament	Do
175	One Necklace (red shell and tusk)	Do
176	One Do (small shell)	Do
177	One Do (cassowary quill)	Do
178	One Do (New Guinea money)... ...	Do
179-80	Two Do (cassowary quill)	Do
181	One Do (New Guinea money)... ...	Do
182	One Breast Ornament	Do
183-5	Three Head Combs	Motu Motu
186	One Do do	West
189	Three Do do	East End
190	One Do do	Do
191	One Do do	Do
192-5	Four Do do (feather tipped) ...	Do
196	Earrings (turtle shell, contains 136 rings) ...	Do
197	One Nose Ornament	Do
198-201	Four Armlets (opaque shells)	Cape Rodney
202-10	Nine Do do do	General
211-13	Three Do do do	Do
214-7	Four Do pearly do	East End
218-26	Nine Do do do	Do
227-30	Four Armlets (pearly)	Do
231-2	Two Do (grass plaited)...	Do
233-4	Two Do do do	Cape Rodney
235-6	Two Do do do	Do
237-9	Three Do (cowrie)	East End
240	One Do (and leg shells)	Do

Label Nos.	Articles.	Locality.
241	One Armlet (cane)	East End
242-3	Two Do do	Cape Rodney
244-5	Two Leglets (cowrie)	Do
246-7	Two Leglets (cowrie, worn below the knee)...	Do
248	One Head-dress (bird of paradise)	Cape Rodney
248*-9*	Two Do do do	Maat
249-53	Five Do (cassowary)	Koiari
254	One Do (parrot)	Kabadi
255-7	Three Do (cassowary)...	Motu Motu
257*-63*	Seven Do do	Maat
258	One Do (dog's tooth and shell) ...	Dora
259-64	Six Do do	East End
265-9	Five Do (bird of paradise) ...	Do
270	One Do (cuscus tail)	Do
271	One Do (parrot and fowl)	Do
272	One Gourd (for lime)	Do
273-4	Two Do (plain)	Do
275	One Do (large)	Do
276-81	Six Do (with sticks ; two with bags)	Do
282	One Do	Do
283-4	Two Do	Do
285-6	Two Spatula, bone (for lime, to eat with betel nut)	Do
287-90	Four Spatula (wood)	Do
291-9	Nine do do	Do
300	One do (bone)	Do
301	One do (turtleshell)	Do
302	One do (bone)	Do
303	One do (wood)	Do
304-5	Two do do	Do
306-9	Four do do	Do
310	One Mortar (wood), for crushing betel-nut...	Do
311-13	Three Hatchets (for shoulder) ...	Do
314	One do do	D.
315	One do (large)...	Do

Implements and Household Objects.

316-27	Twelve Paddles	East End
328	One Canoe Outrigger	Do
329-32	Four do Ornament for	Do
333	One Carved Prow	Do
334	One do Fittings	Do
335	One do do	Do
336	One do do	Do
337-43	Seven Sago Sticks	Do
344-6	Three do	Do
347-57	Eleven do	Do
358	One Digging Stick (for gardens)	Do
359	One Cloth Beater	Do
360	One do	Aroma
361	One do	...
362	One Handle of Tomahawk	East End
363	One Alarm Shell	Do
364	One do	Do

Label Nos.	Articles.	Locality.
365	One Pillow (wooden)	East End
366	One do do	Do
367-71	Five Baskets (oval and round)	Cape Rodney
372-6	Five do do	East End
377	One do do	Do
378	One do (cylindrical)	Do
379-82	Four do (oval and round)	Do
383	One do do	Do
384-5	Two do do	Do
386	One Bowl (earthen)	Do
387-9	Three Bowls (wood)	Do
390	One Cocoanut Cup	Do
391-3	Three do	Aroma
394	One do	Motu Motu
395	Ore do	East End
396-7	Two do	Do
398-403	Six Cocoanut Dippers	Motu Motu
404-6	Three do	Do
407-9	Three do	East End
410	One Mouth Organ	Kerepuna
411-3	Four Do do	East End
414-6	Three Dancing Whistles	Do
417-27	Eleven Adzes (stone, for cutting out canoes, &c.)	Kappa Kappa
427*	Two pieces of Wood to show workmanship effected by stone tools	From old Sogare Canoe lying on beach at Baigoo
428	One Flint Knife in Sheath	West End ;
429-31	Three Meshes (net making)	East End
432-4	Three Turtle Shells (net making)	Do
435-8	Four Pipes (bamboo)	Cape Rodney
439	One Pipe (bamboo, with rattle)	Do
440	One Pipe (ingeniously mended)	Do
441-55	Fifteen Pipes	East End
456	One Sample Fibre for cordage	Do
457	Hank of Cord	Do
458	Do	Do
459	One Sample Fibre (used for making fine nets)	Do
460-1	Two Hanks of Sinnet	Do
462	One Pandanus Mat	Do
463-4	Two do	Do
465	One do	Do
466-7	Two do	Do
468	One do (half made with quill needle and strip of leaf material attached)	Do

Miscellaneous.

469	One Nautilus Shell (offered for sale in thousands by natives boarding vessels)...	East End
470-1	Two Pearl Shells, black tip (also offered as as above)	Do .
472-3	Two Shells (used in making opaque armlets)	Do
474-5	Two Shells (used in making nacreous armlets)	Do

II. Photographs of New Guinea Natives, Scenery, etc.

I. DWELLINGS—

1 Koiari Village; inland from Bootless Inlet. No. 36.*

2 Koiari Chiefs, in front of dwellings; village of Sadera Makera. No. 32.

3 Two Dwellings, with natives; village of Koitapu, Port Moresby. No. 17.

4 Dwellings and Native Women; Motu Motu, Port Moresby. No. 5.

II. NATIVE HOUSES—

5 Native House; Kamali, inland from Hula. No. 7.

6 Same house, from different point of view, with group of natives No. 71.

7 Lateral View of Houses at Kamali, with large group of natives. No. 70 or 40 (?).

8 Houses, with group of natives and Polynesian teacher in foreground. No. 81.

III. TREE DWELLINGS, Etc.—

9 Tree Dwelling, at Koiari. No. 36.

10 Tree Dwellings, stages for disposal of dead, and group of natives; Suan, Stacey Island. No. 102.

11 Chief's House, with spire, ordinary dwellings, and natives; Kalo, Kemp Welch River. No. 77.

12 Native Girls and Papau Tree; Motu Motu, Port Moresby. No. 8.

IV. SEPULTURE—

13 House in which dead bodies are placed, and other houses; Kalo, Kemp Welch River. No. 75.

14 House in which dead bodies are placed, group of natives, and cocoanut palms; Kalo, Kemp Welch River. No. 75.

15 Platform for disposition of dead, fish net, and group of natives. No. 95.

16 Platform for disposition of dead, natives, and block of conglomerate; South Cape. No. 95.

V. LAKE DWELLINGS—

17 Lake Dwellings, Elevala Island, as viewed from Mission House, Port Moresby. No. 1.

---

* These numbers refer to Lindt's original list of New Guinea Photographs.

18 Lake Dwellings, including chief's house; Tupuselei.
    No 59.

19 Lake Dwellings; Tupuselei. No. 60.

20 Village of Tupuselei, lake dwellings. No. 55.

VI. MOTU NATIVES, WITH POTTERY—

21 Motu Woman Carrying Water; Port Moresby. No. 2.

22 Motu Children at Well; Port Moresby. No. 9.

23 Motu Girls Carrying Water; Port Moresby. No. 8.

24 Feasting Stage, Pottery and Natives; Ukaukana, Kabadi
    District. No. 38.

VIII. BUSH SCENES, WITH NATIVES—

25 European Camp, with impromptu bush shelter and group of
    natives (men) in the foreground; Badeba Creek, Laloki
    River. No. 26.

26 European Camp, with natives; Badeba Creek, Laloki River.
    No. 25.

27 Natives Cooking in the Bush; Badeba Creek, Laloki River.
    No. 12.

28 Bush Scene, four natives; on the track between Kamali and
    Babaga (Hula). No. 78.

IX. BUSH SCENES, WITH NATIVES—

29 Group of Natives; near the crossing; Ka Kalo Creek, Kapa
    Kapa. No. 68.

30 Group of Men, natives and Europeans; Port Moresby.
    No. 13.

31 Ka Kalo Creek, Kapa Kapa District; group of natives in
    foreground. No. 66.

32 Coast Scene from the Mainland, with a native in fore-
    ground; near Tupuselei. No 62.

X. RIVER SCENES, WITH AND WITHOUT NATIVES—

33 Scene on Laloki River, with native man and boy in fore-
    ground. No. 30.

34 Scene on Laloki River, with natives in foreground.

35 Laloki River Rapids, from Badeba Creek.

36 A Reach in the Laloki River, near Badoba River.

XI. TROPICAL VEGETATION—

37 Track through Scrub, near Kerepunu. No. 84.

38 Blocks of Conglomerate Rock, rapids on Laloki River, near
    Mount Ventura. No. 38.

39 Cocoanut Grove, near Hood Lagoon. No. 85.

40 Tropical Vegetation, as established in the Brisbane Botanical Gardens. No. 122.

XII. BUSH SCENES, WITH NATIVES—

41 Group of Native Women at Well; Kokiuna, Port Moresby. No. 15.

42 Motu Women and Children carrying water, returning from well; Kokiuna, Port Moresby. No. 42.

43 Native climbing up Cocoa-nut Tree, near Kerepuna. No. 79.

44 Farm Peak and Stacey Island (South Cape), from the shore; two natives in foreground. No. 103.

XIII. NATIVE BOATING—

45 Lakoti, or sailing boat, on beach at Teste Island.

46 Lakoti under sail; Port Moresby.

47 Fleet of Lakotis, a trial trip; Port Moresby.

48 Boat at sea; Tupuselei in the distance.

XIV. BOATING—

49 Two boats with Natives; Mairy Pass, South Cape. No. 104.

50 Boat with Natives; Bertha Lagoon, South Cape. No. 94.

51 Canoe with Natives; Farm Bay, South Cape. No. 91.

52 Two Canoes, with Natives, from Sebaoli. No. 92.

XV. MISCELLANEOUS—

53 Mangrove Vegetation, near Kaili. No. 42.

54 Group of Native Chiefs, from Garia and Saroa, on board s.s. Governor Blackall.

55 Native Woman, Koiari Village. No. 14.

56 Group of Natives at rear of houses, a street scene; Hanuabada, Port Moresby. No. 51.

XVI. THE MISSIONARIES IN NEW GUINEA—

57 Missionary Teacher surrounded by Christian congregation; scene at Kalo. No.

58 Church erected by Missionaries, with ruins of Native edifice, and group of Natives; (loc. ?) No. 56.

59 Native Teachers, Kabade district. No. 41.

60 Teachers from Hula, Kalo, Kerepunu, and Aroma. No. 82.

III.—Two Cases of Stuffed Birds.

CASE No. I.—

PARROTS, &c.

1　Cyclopsittacus diophthalmus *H. et. G.*
2　Geoffroyus cyanicollis, *Müll.*
3　Eclectus pectoralis, *P.L.S. Müll.* (male).
4　　　Do　　　do　　　(female).
5　Dasyptilus Pesqueti, *Less.*; Pesquet's Parrot.
6　Lorius lory, *Linn.*
7　　　Do
8　Trichoglossus coccineifrons, *G. R. Gr.*

HORNBILLS.

9　Rhytidoceros plicatus, *Linn.*; Hornbill

BEE EATERS.

10　Merops ornatus, *Lath.*

KINGFISHERS.

11　Alcyone Lessonii, *Cass.*
12　Tanysiptera galeata, *G. R. Gr.*
13　　　Do　　　do
14　　　Do　　　do
15　Tanysiptera dannæ, *Sharpe.*
16　　　Do　　　do
17　　　Do　　　do
18　Cynalcyon Macleayi, *J. et. S.*
19　Sauropatis saurophaga, *Gld.*
20　　　Do　　　do
21　　　Do　　　do
22　Sauromarptis gaudichaudii, *Q. et G.*

DOLLAR BIRDS.

23　Eurystomus pacificus, *Lath.;* Dollar Bird.

FLYCATCHERS.

24　Rhipidura rufifrons, *Lath.*

THICK-HEADS.

25　Pachycephala collaris, *Ramsay.*

Sun Birds.

26 Hermotinia prosperina, *Wall.*

27   Do   do   do

28 Cyrtostomus frenatus, *S. Mull.* (male).

29   Do   do   do   (female).

Honey Eaters.

30 Xanthotis filigera, *Gld.*

Pittas.

31 Pitta novæ-guineæ, *Mull. et Schleg.*

32   Do   do   do

33 Pitta Mackloti, *Temm.*

34   Do   do

35 Eupetes castanotus, *Salv.*

36   Do   do

Sturnidæ.

37 Melanopyrrhus orientalis, *Schleg.*

Paradise Birds.

38 Manucodia chalybeata, *Penn.*

39   Do   atra, *Less.*

40 Parotia sexpennis, *Bodd.*; 6-plumed Bird of Paradise.

41   Do   do   do   do   do   do

42   Do   do   do   do   do   do

43   Do   do   do   do   do   do

44   Do   do   do   do   do   do

45 Lophorhma superba, *Penn.*; Superb Paradise Bird.

46   Do   do   do   do   do

47 Drepanornis Albertisii, *Sclat*; D'Albertis Paradise Bird.

48 Craspedophora magnifica, *Vieill.*; Rifle Bird (male).

49 Seleucides nigricans, *Shaw.*; 12-wired Bird of Paradise (female).

50 Seleucides nigricans, *Shaw*; 12-wired Bird of Paradise (male).

51   Do   do   do   do   do

52 Paradisea Raggiana, *Sclat*; Raggi's Paradise Bird (male).

53   Do   do   do   do   do

54   Do   do   do   do   do

55 Paradisea decora, *Ram.?*; (male)

56 Diphyllodes chrysoptera, *Gld.* ; Magnificent Paradise Bird!!
57 Cicinnurus regius, *Linn.* ; King Bird of Paradise (male).
58   Do   do   do   do   do
59   Do   do   do   do   (female).

PIGEONS.

60 Ptilopus zonurus, *Salv.*
61   Do   miqueli, *Rosenb.* (male).
62   Do   do   do   do
63 Carpophaga rhodinolœma, *Sclat.*
64   Do   rufiventris, *Salv.*
65   Do   do   do
66 Janthoœnas albigularis, *Tem.*
67 Henicophaps albifrons, *G. R. Gr.* (female).
68 Otidiphaps cervicalis, *Ram.*
69 Goura Sclateri, *Salvad.*
70   Do   do

CASE No. II.—

BIRDS OF PREY.

1 Machærorham phusalcinus, *Western.*
2 Hypotriorchis severus, *Horsf.*
3 Circus sp.

PARROTS.

4 Microglossus aterrimus, *Gm;* Great Palm Cockatoo.
5 Geoffroyus sp.
6 Eclectus pectoralis, *P. L. S. Müll.* (male).
7   Do   do   do   (female).
8 Eos fuscata, *Blyth.*
9   Do   do
10 Trichoglossus massena, *Bp.*

HORNBILLS.

11 Rhytidoceros plicatus, *Penn.*

KINGFISHERS.

12 Clytoceyx rex, *Sharpe.*
13 Tanysiptera galeata, *G. R. Gr.*
14   Do   do   do
15   Do   do   do

16 Tanysiptera salvadoriana, *Ram.*
17   Do   do   do
18   Do   do   do
19   Do   danaæ, *Sharpe.*
20 Cynalcyon Macleayi, *J. et S.*
21   Do   do   do
22   Do   do   do
23 Sauropatis saurophaga, *Gld.*
24 Melidora macrorhina.

DOLLAR BIRDS.

25 Eurystomus pacificus, *Lath*

SWIFTS.

26 Macropteryx mystacea, *Less.*

FLYCATCHERS.

27 Monarcha inornatus, *Garn.*
28 Pœcilodryas placens, *Ram.*
29   Do   do
30 Pœcilodryas albifacies, *Mus.* (male)
31   Do   do   (female)

CROW SHRIKES.

32 Rhectes dichrous, *Bp.*
33   Do   do
34   Do   do

THICK-HEADS.

35 Pachycephala collaris, *Ram.*

SILVER EYES.

86 Zosterops longirostris, *Ram.*
37   Do   do

PITTAS.

38 Pitta novæ-guineæ. *Müll et Schleg.*
39   Do   do   do
40 Pitta mackloti, *Temm.*

STARLING FAMILY.

41 Calornis metallica, *Temm.*
42 Mino dumonti, *Less.*
43   Do   do

PARADISE BIRDS.

44 Manucodia chalybeata, *Penn.*
45   Do   Comriei, *Sclater.*
46   Do   Keraudrenii (female)
47   Do   atra, *Less.*
48 Parotia sexpennis, *Bodd.*; Six-plumed Bird of Paradise.
49   Do   do   do   do   do
50 Lophorina superba, *Penn.*; Superb Bird of Paradise.
51   Do   do   do   do   do
52 Craspedophora magnifica, *Vieill.* (male).
53   Do   do   do
54 Paradisea Raggiana, *Sclat.*; Raggi's Paradise Bird.
55   Do   do   do   do
56 Paradisea minor, *Shaw* (male).
57   Do   decora (female).
58 Cicinnurus regius, *Linn.*; King Bird of Paradise.
59   Do   do   do   do
60   Do   do   do   do
61   Do   do   do   do
62 Amblyornis subalaris, *Sharpe*; Orange-headed Bird of Para-
        dise (male).

PIGEONS.

63 Ptilopus bellus, *Sclat.* (male).
64   do   do   (female).
65 Carpophaga rhodinolæma, *Sclat.*
66   Do   zoeæ, *Less.*
67   Do   ruficauda.
68 Myristicivora spilorrhæa, *G. R. Gr.*; Nutmeg Pigeon.
69   Do   do   do   do   do
70 Philogænas rufigula, *Pucher. et Jacq.*
71 Henicophaps albifrons, *G. R. Gr.* (male).
72 Entrigon terrestris, *G. R. Gr.*
73 Otidiphaps cervicalis, *Ram.*
74 Goura Sclateri, *Salvad.*
75   Do   do
76 Gallus sp. (said to be indigenous).
77   Do   do   do

IV.—A New Guinea Mammal.

CUSCUS MACULATUS.

V.—New Guinea Products.

1   Sample of Gum (Copal).

2   Sample of Gum (Eleine).

3   Sample Native Fibre, suitable for rope-making.

4   *a* Native Fishing Net.
   b Fibre from which net is made.   From Kerepuna.
   c Plant from which fibre is obtained.

5   Spice Barks from Louisiade Archipelago.

6   Bundle of Rattans from South Cape.

7   " Ebony " timber from South Cape.

8   Fifty-three varieties of New Guinea Timbers from St. Joseph and other rivers, in the vicinity of Hall Sound.

9   Bag of Sago Flour, manufactured at Messrs. Burns, Philp & Co.'s trading station, Motu Motu, from native sago palm.

10 Sample Bag of Cobra, manufactured at Messrs. Burns, Philp & Co.'s trading station, Motu Motu, from native cocoanut.

11 Samples of Sponges from China Straits.

                   —*Exhibited by* Messrs. BURNS, PHILP & CO.

QUEENSLAND COMMISSION.

Centennial International Exhibition, Melbourne, 1888.

A SKETCH

OF THE

ECONOMIC PLANTS OF QUEENSLAND.

BY

FREDK. MANSON BAILEY, F.L.S.,

COLONIAL BOTANIST.

BRISBANE:

BY AUTHORITY: JAMES C. BEAL, GOVERNMENT PRINTER.

1888.

PREFACE.

THE Commissioners for the Centennial Exhibition, being desirous of exhibiting live specimens of as many as possible of the economic plants of the colony, considered it would be further useful if a descriptive catalogue accompanied them, in which could be enumerated, not only such plants as were sent, but all the plants of an economic character at present in the colony.

In accordance with the above I have compiled such a catalogue, giving a brief sketch of the plants, their uses, and mode of propagation. The information given may be relied upon as trustworthy, as in all cases it has been gathered from the highest authorities.

It may be fairly hoped that, besides the present Exhibition purpose, this little pamphlet will prove useful to cultivators of the soil throughout the colony. Our numerous pasture grasses and timber trees are not included, as these form separate works.

March, 1888.   F. M. B.

ECONOMIC PLANTS.

ABERIA, *Hochst.*—Order BIXINEÆ—Tribe *Flacourtieæ.*

A. CAFFRA, *Hook.* The Kai Apple of Natal and Caffraria. A large shrub or small tree, furnished with strong, straight, long spines and rather small obovate leaves. The fruit is round, 1 inch or more in diameter, lemon-coloured, of an agreeable subacid flavour, considered by some a desirable fruit for preserves; in an unripe state it is used for pickling. For preserves the ripe fruit is recommended to be used in combination with pumpkin or pie-melon. The plant is one of the best known for hedge-making, for which purpose it must be raised from seed, as it does not strike readily from cuttings.

ABROMA, *Jacq.*—Order STERCULIACEÆ—Tribe *Buettnerieæ.*

A. AUGUSTA, *Linn.* A tall plant; has been introduced and may be seen now and again in our gardens, but it has not yet been grown in Queensland for its fibre, which is said to be strong and easily obtained. In India it is known as "Devil's Cotton." Our indigenous species, so abundant on the tropical coast—*A. fastuosa*, R. Br.—also yields a good fibre. It may be here remarked that in growing plants for fibre they should be sown thickly, that the plants may grow erect and with few branches, that a long clean fibre may be obtained. Propagated by seed.

ABSINTHIUM VULGARE, *Lam.* (See *"Artemisia."*)

ACACIA, *Willd.*—Order LEGUMINOSÆ—Tribe *Acacieæ.*

A. ARABICA, *Willd.* (The *Mimosa arabica* of Lamarck and Roxburgh.) A small tree of India and Africa; in India known under the name of "Babul." Branches slender, bearing stipulary thorns and bipinnate leaves of about 5 pairs of pinnæ, having glands between the first and last pairs; leaflets glabrous, from 15 to 20 to each pinna; flowers in globular heads; pods compressed, thickish. This is one of the plants producing the article known as "gum arabic." The bark, which is used for dyeing and tanning, is powerfully astringent and used as a tonic internally; externally a strong decoction of it is a useful astringent application to ulcers. The wood is very durable if well seasoned, and in India is used extensively for wheels, well-curbs, sugar and oil presses, and boat-building. Sapwood large, whitish; heartwood pinkish white, turning reddish brown on exposure, hard, mottled with dark streaks; weight per cubic foot about 54 lbs. Propagated by seed. With acacia and similar hard seeds it is better to steep them a short time in boiling water before sowing, to crack the hard enamel-like coat of the seed.

A. DECURRENS, *Willd.* Called in Queensland Green Wattle; is the one of which the bark is principally used by Queensland tanners. **A.** FARNESIANA, *Willd.*, and the DOORNBOOM of South Africa (*A. horrida,* Willd.), are utilised in hedge-making. Propagated by seed.

ACER, *Linn.*—Order SAPINDACEÆ—Suborder *Acerineæ.*

A. SACCHARINUM, *Wangenheim.* The Sugar or Bird's-eye Maple. A medium-sized tree, with 3 to 5-lobed leaves, remotely toothed and slightly hairy beneath, deciduous, the flowers appearing with the leaves; wings of fruit nearly erect. This useful North American tree furnishes a handsome cabinet-wood, and is also used for axle-trees and spokes. It yields an abundant supply of a saccharine fluid, which is converted in its native country into maple sugar. According to some writers, as much as 33 lbs. of sugar have been obtained from a single tree in one season. A tree of ordinary size is said to yield from 15 to 30 gallons of sap, from which are made from 2 to 4 lbs. of sugar. The tree is not injured by the operation, but continues to flourish after having been annually tapped for forty years. The bird's-eye maple wood is obtained from old knotted trees. The tree is not suitable for planting in Queensland, except in the southern parts. Propagated by seed.

ACHRAS, *Linn.*—Order SAPOTACEÆ.

A. SAPOTA, *Linn.* The Sapodilla Plum or Nispero of the West Indies and neighbouring continent. A large tree, abounding in thick, white, tenacious milk. Leaves oblong, acute at each end, coriaceous, about 4 or 5 in. long; flowers whitish, axillary; fruit variable in size and form, globose, oval, or ovate; the rind rough, brittle, dull-brown; flesh dirty-white, soft, and sweet; seeds dark, shining, very bitter. The fruit is only eatable when it begins to blett (like the common Medlar); in that state it is considered to equal the pine-apple in flavour. The bark is a powerful astringent, and has been used with success as a substitute for cinchona. The seeds, stripped of their skins, are said to be considered by the people of Martinique powerfully diuretic: six seeds pounded in a mortar, with a glass of wine or water, form a draught which is given daily at a single dose in dysury, strangury, and similar disorders. If the dose, however, is much increased, severe pains, and even danger, are brought on. Propagated by seed.

ADHATODA, *Nees.*—Order ACANTHACEÆ—Tribe *Justicieæ.*

A. VASICA, *Nees.* The *Justicia Adhatoda* of Linnæus. A robust and showy shrub of our gardens, which has considerable reputation all over India as an expectorant and antispasmodic, and is largely prescribed in consumption and other chest affections attended with cough and hectic fever. Propagated by cuttings.

ÆGLE, *Correa.*—Order RUTACEÆ—Tribe *Aurantieæ.*

Æ. MARMELOS, *Corr.* (*Feronia pellucida,* Roth.; *Cratæva Marmelos,* Linn.) The Bael or Bela tree. A common East Indian tree of small size, with a thick, soft, grey bark and yellowish hard wood weighing about 57 lbs. to the cubic foot. Leaves usually of 3 oblong-lanceolate leaflets; flowers white, in terminal panicles; fruit somewhat ovoid or pear-shaped, the shell hard, pulp mucilaginous, seeds woolly. This is a sacred tree amongst the Hindus, its leaves being used in the worship of Siva. In ancient Sanskrit poems it is frequently alluded to as an emblem of increase and fertility. Hindu physicians regard the unripe or half-ripe fruit as astringent, digestive, and stomachic, and prescribe it in diarrhœa and dysentery. The ripe fruit is considered aromatic, cooling, and laxative. A thick sherbet of the ripe fruit has a reputation amongst Europeans as an agreeable laxative; the dose is a tumbler-full. The root-bark is used as a remedy in hypochondriasis, melancholia, and palpitation of the heart. A perfume is distilled from the flowers, and a yellow dye may be obtained from the rind of the fruit. The tree fruits in Tropical Queensland, but so far has not borne fruit in our Southern gardens. The best mode of propagation is by seed.

Æ. SEPIARIA, *DC.* (See "*Citrus.*")

ÆSCHYNOMENE, *Linn.*—Order LEGUMINOSÆ—Tribe *Hedysareæ.*

Æ. ASPERA, *Linn.* The Solah or Shola plant of India. A large erect, or floating, or trailing plant with pinnate leaves of numerous linear obtuse leaflets, and axillary racemes of a few brownish flowers succeeded by pods composed of from 4 to 7 prickly articles. A few years ago a quantity of this plant was grown at Bowen Park, and the seed as usual distributed. In India the pith is much used for the manufacture of hats, bottle-cases, and similar articles. Propagated by seed.

AFRICAN BOWSTRING HEMP. (See "*Sansevieria cylindrica,* Boj.")

AFRICAN RUBBER. (See "*Landolphia florida,* Benth.," and "*L. Kirkii,* Dyer.")

AFRICAN SHEEP-FODDER BUSH. (See "*Pentzia virgata,* Less.")

AGAVE, *Linn.*—Order AMARYLLIDEÆ—Tribe *Agaveæ.*

A. AMERICANA, *Linn.* The American Aloe. This and other species of the genus furnish the strong Pita fibre used in rope-making. The sap can be converted into alcohol, and thus the "tulque" beverage is prepared from the young flower-stem. All the species thrive in Queensland. Propagated by seed or suckers.

AILANTHUS, *Desf.*—Order SIMARUBEÆ.

A. GLANDULOSUS, *Desf.* The Tree of the Gods. Does not succeed well on the coast lands so far as observed, but on the South-western Downs in places it has run from garden culture and become naturalised.

The tree is deserving of notice, from the foliage being the food of a silkworm (*Attacus Cynthia*). The wood is also hard and durable. Propagated by seed or cuttings of the roots.

ALEURITES, *Forst.*– Order EUPHORBIACEÆ—Tribe *Crotoneæ*.

A CORDATA, *Muell. Arg.* (*Elæococca vernicia*, Spreng.) A tall tree of Japan. In general appearance this tree resembles the Candle-nut, and it bears also a somewhat similar fruit. The leaves, however, are larger than that tree, are more cordate or heart-shaped, and have not the mealy pubescence. The wood is said to be of some beauty, and durable; from the seeds also an oil is obtained which serves as a varnish. In Queensland this tree is planted for shade, and thrives well. Propagated by seed.

A. MOLUCCANA, *Willd.* (*Jatropha moluccana*, Linn.; *A. triloba*, Forst.) This tree, which is well known by the name of Candle-nut, attains a large size in many of the coast scrubs of Tropical Queensland; it is also widely spread over the Eastern Archipelago, the islands of the South Pacific, and New Guinea. The wood is soft and light; leaves and young branchlets clothed with a more or less dense mealy substance, which gives to the foliage of the tree, when viewed from a little distance, a remarkable silvery appearance. Leaves ovate-lanceolate on old trees, 3 to 7-lobed on young plants; flowers in broad terminal panicles; fruit 2 to 4 in. diameter, containing from 1 to 3 or even more round seeds. These seeds, when dried, are stuck on a reed and used by Polynesians as a substitute for candles. They may also be eaten, but, if not quite ripe, are apt to make one very ill; in taste they resemble somewhat the walnut. They yield a large proportion of pure palatable oil, used as a drying oil for paint—in Ceylon called kekuni oil—which in England is considered worth about £20 per imperial tun. The cake, after the oil has been expressed, is esteemed as a food for cattle. The root of the tree affords a brown dye. The tree is very hardy, and commonly planted as a shade tree in Queensland; no use, however, is made of the fruit which it produces in great abundance. Propagated by seed.

ALLIGATOR APPLE. (See "*Anona palustris*, Linn.")

ALLIGATOR PEAR. (See "*Persea gratissima*, Gærtn.")

ALLIUM, *Linn.*—Order LILIACEÆ—Tribe *Allieæ*.

A. CEPA, *Linn.* The Onion. This plant crops well in many parts of Southern Queensland. The same may be said of *A. porrum*, Linn. (the Leek), *A. Ascalonicum*, Linn. (the Shallot), and *A. sativum*, Bauh. (the Garlic). Propagated by seed.

ALLSPICE. (See "*Pimenta communis*, Lindl.")

ALMOND. (See "*Prunus*.")

ALOE, *Linn.*—Order LILIACEÆ—Tribe *Aloineæ.*

A. VULGARIS, *Bauhin.* (The *A. vera* of Linnæus, and *A. Barbadensis* of Miller.) Is in many gardens, where, with other medicinal kinds, it is grown for ornament. Plants of this genus thrive well in the colony. Propagated by seed or suckers.

ALSTONIA, *R. Br.*—Order APOCYNACEÆ—Tribe *Plumerieæ.*

A. CONSTRICTA, *F. v. M.* Bitter-bark or Fever-bark. This is a tall slender tree, with glossy leaves (or, in the form *mollis*, hairy leaves), which are borne on long stalks; they are opposite or in threes, and of a narrow lanceolate form, 3 to 5 in. long; flowers terminal in the forks of the branchlets, white; seed-pods or follicles 4 to 10 in. long, very narrow; seeds pubescent with long hairs at the upper end. A tincture made with 3 ounces of the bark of this tree to a pint of proof spirit is in use by medical men in Queensland in the earlier stages of typhoid fever, with considerable success; the dose 5 to 10 drops. The powder in grain dose, made up with extract of liquorice, is also said to form a convenient pill. The tree is most conveniently propagated by seed. The wood is of a pale-yellow colour, close in the grain, but warps in drying; the variety or species *A. mollis* is the better wood of the two and might be used in cabinet-work.

A. SCHOLARIS, *R. Br.* Dita-bark tree. Found in India, Burmah, and Tropical Africa; also in New Guinea and Australia. This tree attains a large size in the Queensland tropical scrubs. The bark is often thick and spongy and of a greyish colour; the branches. like the leaves, are often in whorls; leaves 5 to 7 in each whorl, whitish on the under side, and 4 to 6 m. long; flowers rather small. white, in large spreading terminal panicles; fruit 2 long horn-like follicles often a foot long; seeds hairy at each end, the hair longer than the seeds. The wood is soft, close in the grain, light-coloured, and from our sample does not seem to warp or be attacked by insects; in Burmah it is used for school-boards, on which the children trace their letters in sand, as in the Lancastrian system. In India the bark is considered astringent, tonic, anthelmintic, and antiperiodic. Indian physicians report that equal doses of ditain and of standard quinine sulphate have had the same medicinal effect, but that the ditain leaves none of the disagreeable secondary symptoms, such as deafness, sleeplessness, and feverish excitement, which are the usual concomitants of large quinine doses; the ditain is said to attain its effect swiftly, surely, and infallibly. Although a large tree, it flowers well as a large shrub in the South Queensland gardens, but has not yet fruited. Propagated by seed.

AMATUNGULA PLUM. (See *"Carissa."*)

AMORPHOPHALLUS, *Blume.*—Order AROIDEÆ—Tribe *Pythonieæ.*

A. CAMPANULATUS, *Bl.* (*Tacca phallifera*, Bl.; *Arum campanulatum*, Roxb.; *Candarum Roxburghii*, Schott.) An East Indian plant,

known under the name of Talinga potato. Rootstock large, flattened
on the upper surface; leaf decompound, the petiole rough wi h warts
or scales, appearing and developing after the bloom; the spathe
spreading so as fully to expose the thick fleshy spadix; the male
flowers placed above the female ones. One of the most fœtid flowers
known, so perfectly resembling carrion as to induce flies to cover the
club of the spadix with their eggs. In India the rootstocks are
peeled and cut into segments, and sold under the name of "madan-
mast." These have a mucilaginous taste, and are supposed to have
restorative powers, and thus are in great request. The plant is largely
cultivated, and used as a vegetable; under cultivation much of its
acridity is said to be lost. Propagated by rootstock.

AMERICAN SUMACH. (See "*Cæsalpinia coriaria*, Willd.")

AMYGDALUS. (See "*Prunus*.")

ANANAS, *Adans.*—Order BROMELIACEÆ—Tribe *Bromelieœ*.

A. SATIVA, *Mill.* The cultivated Pineapple. This well-known
fruit is supposed to have been originally found in Peru, and from
thence has been taken and cultivated in most countries, either in the
open ground, as in Queensland, or under glass, as in Europe. The
varieties are numerous. Leaves long, thin, numerous from the base,
their edges prickly or smooth; flowers in a dense spike, the axis
growing out into a leafy crown, the spike becoming a fleshy fruit by
the cohesions, into a single cone-like mass, of the ovaria and floral
envelopes. The Jack-fruit, Bread-fruit, and Mulberry have similar
fruits. Besides producing one of the most delicious of fruits, from
the foliage excellent fibre may be obtained. Really the most important
use of this plant, its fibre. is lost sight of in the colony. It is soft,
silky, and pliant, and much used in Japan, China, and India in the
manutacture of the most delicate fabrics, as well as fishing-lines and
ropes. Propagated by divisions and from the crowns.

ANONA, *Linn.*—Order ANONACEÆ—Tribe *Xylopieœ*.

A. CHERIMOLIA, 'l (*A. tripetala*, Bot. Mag. 2011.) Cherimoyer.
This is a fruit of tropical and sub-tropical South America. A rather
straggling small tree. the leaves rather large, ovate, not dotted, finely
silky on the under side; fruit somewhat heart-shaped and scaly on the
exterior, but containing a delicious pulp Grown for the sake of its
fruit in Queensland gardens. Propagated by seed.

A. PALUSTRIS, *Linn.* Alligator Apple. A West Indian marsh
or seashore small tree, with oblong, pointed, glabrous leaves; flowers
yellow with red at the centre; fruit about 2 in diameter, yellowish;
pulp golden-yellow, seeds yellow. The fruit has a grateful smell but
a very disagreeable flavour, and is considered narcotic and poisonous.
The wood, which is very light, is used by the negroes as a substitute for
cork, for stopping up the mouths of their calabashes. This tree fruits
freely in South Queensland gardens. Propagated by seed.

A. SQUAMOSA, *Linn.* The Custard Apple or Sweetsop. A small tree of the Malay Islands, with an erect short trunk and thin grey bark ; the wood soft, close-grained, of about 46 lbs. to the cubic foot ; leaves lanceolate, smooth, with pellucid dots ; fruit ovate, covered with projecting scales ; rind thick, enclosing a luscious pulp ; the seeds are dark-brown, polished, with two lateral ridges ; these, with the leaves and immature fruit, contain an acrid principle which is destructive to insect life. Grown in the Queensland gardens for its fruit. Propagated by seed.

ANTHEMIS, *Linn.*—Order COMPOSITÆ—Tribe *Anthemideæ.*

A. NOBILIS, *Linn.* The Chamomile. This plant thrives in the cooler districts, where it may be utilised for edging for garden walks. Propagated by division.

ANTIARIS, *Lesch.*—Order URTICACEÆ—Tribe *Artocarpeæ.*

A. TOXICARIA, *Lesch.* The Upas-tree. This is a large tree of the islands of the Indian Archipelago, particularly Java and Celebes. The leaves are deciduous, oblong-oval, more or less rough, with a shortly acuminate apex and obliquely cordate base ; flowers monœcious ; male receptacle flattish, peltate ; peduncles from 1 to 4 together, axillary ; peduncles of the female flowers solitary in the axils below the males ; fruit an oval purple drupe, enclosing a sweet greenish-yellow pulp and a single nut with a thin fragile shell, the kernel of which is said to be given in colic, dysentery, and diarrhœa, the dose being the third or fourth part of a kernel once or twice a day. The inner bark is sometimes used in making coarse stuff for clothing, but persons clad in it are said if exposed to rain to be affected with an intolerable itching. The deleterous quality of this tree is said to reside in the gum. Doubtless the products of this tree, in proper hands, will sooner or later prove of medicinal value, but most exaggerated accounts have been published of its properties. Propagated by seed or cuttings.

ANTIDESMA, *Linn.*—Order EUPHORBIACEÆ—Tribe *Phyllantheæ.*

A. DALLACHYANUM, *Baill.* Herbert River Cherry. A small tree with pubescent ovate-lanceolate leaves, 2 to 6 in. long, on stalks of about ¼-in long ; flowers inconspicuous, the males often paniculate, the females in long racemes ; fruit nearly globular, mottled, rosy, or nearly white, ½ to 1 in. diameter, of a fine sharp acid flavour. Jelly made from this fruit is equal to that from the European red currant. Trees of this desirable fruit produce abundantly in the South Queensland gardens. Propagated by seed.

APIUM, *Linn.*—Order UMBELLIFERÆ—Tribe *Ammineæ.*

A. GRAVEOLENS. *Linn.* The Celery. When wild, growing in wet meadows and in ditches, it is acrid and poisonous ; when cultivated in dry ground, and partially blanched, it is the Celery so well known as a salad. This culinary vegetable is grown to as great perfection in Queensland as in Europe. Propagated by seed.

A. Petroselinum, *Linn.* (See "*Carum Petroselinum,* Benth.")

Apple, English. (See "*Pyrus.*")

Apricot. (See "*Prunus.*")

ARACHIS, *Linn.*—Order Leguminosæ—Tribe *Hedysareæ.*

A. hypogæa, *Linn.* Earth-nut, Pea-nut, or Ground-nut. An annual papilionaceous plant of Brazil ; has at times been grown both for its seeds and as a fodder. It yields a good crop, and has so taken to our soil as to have in a few localities become naturalised. This curious plant after flowering forces its young pods underground, where they ripen. It is extensively grown in many warm climates as an article of food, and for the sake of its oil, which is largely used by perfumers in the preparation of pomades and cold cream, also for soap-making, burning, &c. Propagated by seed.

Arduina grandiflora, *E. Meyer.* (See "*Carissa.*")

ARGEMONE, *Linn.*—Order Papaveraceæ—Tribe *Eupapavereæ.*

A. mexicana, *Linn.* Devil's Fig or Prickly Poppy. This is a plant of American origin, but now naturalised in most warm countries. It may readily be known by its glaucous, prickly, thistle-like foliage and bright poppy-like yellow flowers, the buds of which are erect, and the sepals mounted by 3 horn-like processes; petals 6; capsules prickly, oblong, containing numerous pitted dark-brown seeds; sap of plant yellow. It is one of the plants spoken of as poisonous to stock in New South Wales. In the Concan, the juice with milk is given in leprosy. The oil of the seeds, in doses of from 30 to 60 minims, is a valuable aperient in dysentery and other affections of the intestinal canal, and it is thought that the smallness of the dose required to produce an aperient action, and the absence of any disagreeable taste, may cause it to take the place of castor oil for that purpose. Propagated by seed.

Aralia papyrifera, *Hook.* (See "*Fatsia.*")

ARGANIA, *Ræm.* and *Schult.*—Order Sapotaceæ.

A. sideroxylon, *Ræm.* and *Schult.* Argan-tree of North Africa; was introduced a few years ago, but found not to thrive. There are at present but an isolated plant or so to be seen. Propagated by seed.

Arnotto. (See "*Bixa Orellana,* Linn.")

Arrowhead. (See "*Sagittaria sinensis,* Linn.")

Arrowroot, Purple (See "*Canna edulis,* Ker.")

Arrowroot, White. (See "*Maranta arundinacea,* Linn.")

ARTEMISIA, *Linn.*—Order Composit.æ—Tribe *Anthemideæ.*

A. Absinthium, *Linn.* (*Absinthium vulgare,* Lam.) The Worm-wood. This European herb is grown in Queensland and used in domestic medicine as elsewhere. Also A. Abrotanum, *Linn.* (the Southernwood), and A. Dracunculus, *Linn.* (the Tarragon), but this latter is rare. Propagated by cuttings and seed.

Artichoke, Common. (See "*Cynara Scolymus,* Linn.")

Artichoke, Jerusalem. (See "*Helianthus tuberosus,* Linn.")

ARTOCARPUS, *Forst.*—Order Urticaceæ—Tribe *Artocarpeæ.*

A. incisa, *Linn.* The Breadfruit-tree of South Sea Islands. A tree of moderate size, the branchlets ringed by the marks from where the stipules were attached; leaves large, rough, divided into lobes; fruit round, about 6 in. diameter, the exterior marked with hexagonal knobs, or smooth. There are several varieties of this fruit; the best are said to contain no seeds. The islanders peel the fruit, extract the centre, and dry the remainder, which they pack singly in leaves for future use. The viscid milky sap of the tree is used for caulking canoes. The bark is fabricated into a coarse cloth. The tree is too tender to stand the climate of Southern Queensland, but succeeds well in the tropics. Propagated by seed or cuttings.

A. integrifolia, *Linn.* The Jackfruit-tree. A large East Indian tree with a thick, blackish, cracked bark; wood yellow, but darkening by age and exposure; leaves ovate-oblong, rough, 4 to 6 in. long, usually entire, but on the young plants often lobed, on short stalks; stipules broad; the male inflorescence usually on the young branches, cylindric, 3 or 4 in. long; the female on the same branches or more often on the thicker branches or stem, or ultimately on the roots. There are several varieties of this tree, the fruit of some being very much superior to others. It is of an oval or oblong form and muricated on the rind, often growing to an enormous size; the inner pulp very sweet and a favourite fruit of some persons. The seeds can be roasted and eaten like chestnuts. The tree ripens fruit well in South Queensland gardens. Propagated by seed or cuttings.

ASPARAGUS, *Linn.*—Order Liliaceæ—Tribe *Asparageæ.*

A. officinalis, *Linn.* The well-known Asparagus. This excellent vegetable is seldom grown for market, on account of its requiring more attention than some other culinary vegetables, but it is to be seen in many private gardens, where it thrives well. Propagated by seed.

Asthma Plant. (See "*Euphorbia pilulifera,* Linn.")

Attacus Cynthia. (See "*Ailanthus.*")

AVENA, *Linn.*—Order Gramineæ—Tribe *Aveneæ.*

A. sativa, *Linn.* The cultivated Oat; is largely cultivated for hay and green fodder, and also for the corn, on the Downs, where large crops are often obtained. Propagated by seed.

AVERRHOA, *Linn.*—Order GERANIACEÆ—Tribe *Oxalideæ.*

A. CARAMBOLA, *Linn.* Tamara-tonga of the Malays. A small densely branched tree, largely grown in Indian gardens, but of which the native country is unknown; leaves alternate, pinnate, with 2 to 5 pairs and an odd terminal leaflet, pubescent, acute, lanceolate, and glaucous on the under side; flowers axillary, variegated white and purple; fruit about 3 in. long, with 5 almost winglike angles. The fruit contain an acid watery pulp, and are good when candied or made into syrup. They also make good pickles, and the juice is of use to remove iron-moulds from linen. The leaves are also said to be used for dyeing. The plant fruits well as a shrub in the Southern Queensland gardens. Propagated by seed or cuttings in sand under glass.

AVOCADA or ALLIGATOR PEAR. (See " *Persea gratissima,* Gærtn.")

BACKHOUSIA, *Hook. et Harv.*—Order MYRTACEÆ—Tribe *Leptospermeæ.*

B. CITRIODORA, *F. v. M.* This is a small tree of the South Queensland scrubs. The wood is close in grain and of a light-pink colour. The foliage is very rich in essential oil, having a fragrance closely resembling that of the Sweet Verbena (*Lippia citriodora,* Kunth.) It may here be pointed out that besides the *Backhousia* there are many others of our indigenous trees which would pay for cultivating with a view to obtaining the essential oil from their foliage; for instance, several *Melaleucas* and Eucalypts, these will all bear pruning back, and thus produce a larger quantity of leaves, flowers, and seed annually. Propagated by seed.

BAEL or BELA TREE. (See "*Ægle Marmelos,* Corr.")

BALM. (See "*Melissa.*")

BALSAM OF PERU. (See "*Myrospermum Pereiræ,* Klotz.")

BAMBUSA, *Schreb.*—Order GRAMINEÆ—Tribe *Bambuseæ.*

B. VULGARIS, *Wendl.* This and other species of Bamboo thrive well in Queensland, but are only grown for ornament. Propagated by division of the rootstock or cuttings.

BANANA. (See " *Musa.*")

BANYAN TREE. (See "*Ficus bengalensis,* Linn.")

BARBADOES FLOWER FENCE. (See "*Cæsalpinia pulcherrima,* Sw.")

BARBAREA, *R. Br.*—Order CRUCIFERÆ—Tribe *Arabideæ.*

B. VULGARIS, *R. Br.* (*Erysimum Barbarea,* Linn.) Belleisle or Land Cress. This little wholesome salad herb thrives in Queensland, but is not often grown for market on account of Water Cress being much more productive. Propagated by seed.

BAUHINIA, *Linn.*—Order LEGUMINOSÆ—Tribe *Bauhinieæ.*

B. VARIEGATA, *Linn.* Oxhoof-tree. This is a moderate-sized deciduous tree, of the East Indies, Burmah, and China. It has a grey bark which often opens in vertical cracks; the wood is of a grey colour and moderately hard; leaves rather broader than long, deeply cordate, the obtuse lobes reaching a quarter or more down; flowers variegated with red and yellow (one form, *B. v. candida*), white; pod about 6 in. long. The bark is described as astringent, attenuant, and tonic, and useful to check diarrhœa; it is also used for tanning and dyeing. The buds of the flowers are eaten as vegetables when prepared with animal food. Wood used for agricultural implements; weight per cubic foot about 42 lbs. Thrives in Queensland, but only grown for ornament. Propagated by seed.

BAYBERRY or WAX MYRTLE. (See "*Myrica cerifera*, Linn.")
BELLEISLE CRESS. (See "*Barbarea.*")
BENTHAMIA FRAGIFERA, *Lindl.* (See "*Cornus capitata*, Wall.")

BERTHOLLETIA, *Humb. et Bonpl.*—Order MYRTACEÆ—Tribe *Lecythideæ.*

B. EXCELSA, *H. et B.* Brazil-nuts. A tall tree of Tropical America. Leaves alternate without pellucid dots, bright-green, often 2 ft. long and 6 in. wide; the flowers have a 2-parted deciduous calyx, 6 unequal cream-coloured petals, and numerous stamens united into a broad hood-shaped mass, those at the base being fertile and the upper ones sterile; the fruit is nearly round and about 6 in. diameter, having an extremely hard shell about ½-in. thick, and containing from 18 to 24 triangular wrinkled seeds. These are what are known as Brazil-nuts; they are sometimes called Para-nuts. An oil used by watchmakers is obtained by pressure from these seeds, and the bark is used as a substitute for oakum for caulking ships. The plant will doubtless thrive in Queensland, but as yet there are no established trees. Propagated by seed.

BETA, *Linn.*—Order CHENOPODIACEÆ—Tribe *Chenopodieæ.*

B. VULGARIS, *Linn.* Both the Common Beet and Mangolds thrive well in Queensland. The first is grown as a culinary vegetable, and the latter by a few persons for cattle fodder. Propagated by seed.

BEVILAQUA. (See "*Hydrocotyle asiatica*, Linn.")
BITTER BARK. (See "*Alstonia constricta*, F. v. M.")
BITTER CASSAVA. (See "*Manihot utilissima*, Pohl.")

BIXA, *Linn.*—Order BIXINEÆ—Tribe *Bixeæ.*

B. ORELLANA, *Linn.* Arnotto or Anatto. A tall shrub or small tree of Tropical America, with somewhat heart-shaped leaves which taper into points; leafstalk long; flowers of a pinkish colour, in terminal panicles; fruit a heart-shaped, bristly, 2-valved capsule; seeds angular, covered with an orange-red pulp or pellicle, which is the substance called arnotto in commerce, chiefly used for staining cheese and in the preparation of chocolate. A simple method of obtaining the colouring matter is said to be by removing the pulp with the seeds and soaking this mass in cold or warm water, which should be constantly stirred. After a while the water and separated seeds are strained off, and the precipitate or arnotto dried in the shade. This colouring matter is considered astringent and slightly purgative. When an alcoholic extract is treated with sodium carbonate, a sodium compound of bixin is formed, crystallising in leaflets having a coppery lustre, and from this salt the colouring matter (bixin) may be obtained in a crystalline form. The seeds are cordial, astringent, and febrifuge. Propagated by seed, which it produces abundantly in most parts of Queensland.

BLACK PEPPER.   (See "*Piper nigrum*, Linn.")

BLACK WALNUT.   (See "*Juglans nigra*, Linn.")

BLACKBERRY.   (See "*Rubus.*")

BŒHMERIA, *Jacq.*—Order URTICACEÆ—Tribe *Urticeæ.*

B. NIVEA, *Hook. et Arn.* China-grass, or Rheea-fibre plant. This is found in China, India, and the Indian Islands. It is an herbaceous perennial 3 or 4 ft. in height, with ovate serrate leaves, rough above, snowy-white beneath. The flowers are produced in slender drooping spikes, the sexes distinct. The fibre of the bark is that known as Rheea fibre. This plant is said in India to produce three cuttings a year. The fibre is of different degrees of fineness, according to the age of the plant and the part of the bark from which it is taken; the inner bark of young quickly grown stems yields the beautifully fine delicate fibre from which the best fabrics are manufactured, while the outer portion affords a coarse fibre for rope and canvas. From experiments which have been made it seems to possess nearly double the strength of Russian hemp. Thrives well in most parts of Queensland. Propagated by division.

BOMBAX, *Linn.*—Order MALVACEÆ—Tribe *Bombaceæ.*

B. MALABARICUM, *DC.* Cotton-tree. A large Indian tree, also indigenous in Northern Queensland. The trunk is covered with short conical prickles; the leaves, which are deciduous, are composed of from 5 to 7 leaflets placed at the end of a rather long stalk; flowers large, red, on short stalks at the ends of the branches when the tree is destitute of leaves; capsule large, oblong, containing obovoid seeds enveloped in silky wool or cotton. This latter is in India employed to stuff pillows and in making quilts, and the wood is used for planking, packing-cases, tea-boxes, and although not very durable is said to last tolerably well under water, so is employed in lining wells. Mahometan writers state that the young roots have restorative, astringent, and alterative properties. The gum is also considered astringent, and used in diarrhœa, dysentery, and menorrhagia. Propagated by seed

BOWSTRING HEMP, AFRICAN. (See "*Sansevieria cylindrica*, Boj.")
BOWWOOD or OSAGE ORANGE. (See "*Maclura aurantiaca*, Nutt.")

BRASSICA, *Linn.*—Order CRUCIFERÆ—Tribe *Brassiceæ.*

B. ALBA, *Visiani.* (The *Sinapsis alba* of Linnæus.) White Mustard. *B. oleracea*, Linn.—under which is included the many kinds of Cabbage, Broccoli, Cauliflower, Brussels Sprouts, Kail, and Kohlrabi—is grown in as great variety and perfection in all parts of Queensland as these culinary vegetables are elsewhere. Propagated by seed.

BRAZILIAN CHERRY. (See "*Eugenia uniflora*, Linn.")
BRAZIL NUTS. (See "*Bertholletia excelsa*, H. and B.")
BREADFRUIT TREE. (See "*Artocarpus incisa*, Linn.")
BRINGALS. (See "*Solanum Melongena*, Linn.")
BROAD BEANS. (See "*Vicia Faba*, Linn.")

BROMELIA, *Linn.*—Order BROMELIACEÆ—Tribe *Bromelieæ.*

B. SYLVESTRIS, *Willd.* The Brazilian Wild Pine. This plant somewhat resembles the Pineapple, only the leaves are longer and more rigid and the marginal prickles are stronger. The inflorescence is much more lax than in the Pine. The principal use of this plant is the supply of valuable fibre which is obtained from its leaves. Propagated by offshoots.

BROUSSONETIA.—Order URTICACEÆ—Tribe *Moreæ.*

B. PAPYRIFERA, *Vent.* Paper Mulberry. This is a small tree resembling the smaller-leaved Mulberries. The young branches are clothed with short soft hairs; the leaves are ovate in outline, entire or variously lobed, edges toothed; fruit like a mulberry, insipid. In Japan this plant is cultivated for the sake of the young shoots, which are used in the manufacture of paper. The South Sea Islanders also make their tapa cloth from this tree. Propagated by seed or cuttings.

BUCKWHEAT. (See "*Fagopyrum esculentum*, Mœnch.")
BULLRUSH. (See "*Typha angustifolia*.")
CABBAGE. (See "*Brassica*.")

CÆSALPINIA, *Linn.*—Order LEGUMINOSÆ—Tribe *Eucæsalpinieæ.*

C. CORIARIA, *Willd.* Divi-divi, Dibi-diba, or American Sumach. A small tree of the sea-shores of Central America. Leaves small, bipinnate; pinnæ 6 to 7 pairs; leaflets 15 to 20 pairs, dotted with rows of black dots, linear, obtuse; flowers small; pods flattened, about

B

2 in. long, ¼-in. wide. The chief value of this plant is the pods, which are employed for tanning purposes. They are stated to contain as much as 50 per cent. of tannin, and they are exported from the West Indies into Great Britain for tanning purposes. It is regarded as the most powerful and quickly acting tanning material in India, and is therefore largely cultivated there. Mercantile price of the pods is from £8 to £13 per ton. Trees flower freely every year in South Queensland, but for profit should be planted in the more northern parts of the colony. Two other species of this genus—*C. Gilliesii*, Wall., of the La Plata States, and *C. pulcherrima*, Sw. (the Barbadoes Flower Fence), which adorn our gardens—are useful for forming live fences. Propagated by seed.

CAFFRE THORN. (See "*Lycium afrum*, Linn.")

CAJANUS, *DC.*—Order LEGUMINOSÆ—Tribe *Phaseoleæ.*

C. INDICUS, *Spreng.* The Pigeon Pea of India. A shrub often seen in Queensland, the seed of which are much esteemed by the natives in India. The green plant is a good cattle fodder, and the stalks are used for making charcoal for gunpowder manufacture. Propagated by seed.

CAJEPUT OIL. (See "*Melaleuca leucadendron*, Linn.")

CALABASH TREE. (See "*Crescentia Cujete*, Linn.")

CALODENDRON, *Thunb.*—Order RUTACEÆ—Tribe *Diosmeæ.*

C. CAPENSE, *Thunb.* (*Pallasia capensis*, Houtt ; *Dictamnus capensis*, Linn. f.) Cape Chestnut. A large handsome tree of the eastern districts of South Africa and Caffreland. Branches opposite or in threes; leaves 4 or 5 in. long, with prominent parallel nerves; flowers very showy, in terminal panicles; petals white, sprinkled with purplish glands, reflexed, and about 1½ in. long; capsule hard, containing black, shiny, nut-like seeds, which are said to have somewhat the flavour of chestnuts, and are used for necklaces and other ornaments. The tree succeeds well in the South Queensland gardens, and is highly prized for its beauty and the shade it affords. Propagated by seed or cuttings.

CALOTROPIS, *R. Br.*—Order ASCLEPIADEÆ—Tribe *Cynancheæ.*

C. GIGANTEA, *R. Br.* The Indian Madar-fibre plant. The *Yercum* of Southern India. This is a large shrub, with broad oval leaves of a silvery-grey colour, 6 or more inches long; the flowers are of a rosy-purple colour, and somewhat bell-shaped. The shrub is one of beauty as well as utility, and therefore commonly met with in gardens. Its inner bark gives a valuable fibre of a silky texture, which is strong, and is used in India for bowstrings, fishing lines and nets, on account of its being durable in water. This fibre has been found to bear 552 lbs. against 407 lbs. borne by Sunn hemp (the fibre of *Crotalaria juncea*) and 224 lbs. borne by coir. The silky hair of the seeds is made into thread in Borneo, but it is difficult to spin; but mixed with one-fifth of cotton in Madras it has been made into a good wearing cloth. A kind of gutta-percha has been obtained from the milky juice. The milky juice is applied to carious teeth for relief of pain. The bark in powder is used in cases of lepra, syphilis, and hectic fever. The drug is emetic and a substitute for ipecacuanha. Propagated by seed or cuttings.

CAMELLIA, Linn.—Order TERNSTROMIACEÆ—Tribe *Gordonieæ.*

C. THEA, *Link.* (*Thea chinensis,* Sims.) The Chinese and Assam Tea shrub. This is a shrubby plant with ovate or lanceolate leaves, the edges of which are serrated; flowers white, of 5 or 6 sepals and 6 to 9 petals, borne in the axils of the leaves; capsule 3-lobed. All the kinds of tea are produced from varieties of this species. The tea of commerce consists of the young leaves, heated, curled, and sweated. The plant to be productive requires a rich alluvial soil, plenty of water, but good drainage. Declivities are best adapted and mostly chosen for Congo, Pekoe, and Souchong, while Bohea is often grown in flat countries. Propagated by seed.

CAMPHOR. (See "*Cinnamomum camphora,* Nees.")

CANDLENUT. (See "*Aleurites moluccana,* Willd.")

CANNA.—Order SCITAMINEÆ—Tribe *Canneæ.*

C. EDULIS, *Ker.* Purple Arrowroot. An herbaceous plant with a globose knotty rhizome; stems 5 or 7 feet high; leaves large, ovate-lanceolate, stem-clasping; flowers red; capsule thin, 3-celled, containing many round black seeds, which are said to germinate after being kept for many years. This plant is largely grown for the manufacture of arrowroot, for which there is a large export. Propagated by divisions.

CANNABIS, *Linn.*—Order URTICACEÆ—Tribe *Cannabineæ.*

C. SATIVA, *Linn.* The Hemp-plant. May be seen growing now and again as a garden plant, and it thrives well, but up to the present has not been planted for profit. Propagated by seed.

CAPE CHESTNUT. (See "*Calodendron capense,* Thunb.")

CAPPARIS, *Linn.*—Order CAPPARIDEÆ.

C. SPINOSA, *Linn.* The Caper-shrub. A few years ago fine thriving plants of Caper might be seen in the Brisbane Botanic Gardens. Propagated by seed, or by the very young shoots when about 1 in. long in sand and charcoal.

CAPSICUM, *Linn.*—Order SOLANACEÆ—Tribe *Solaneæ.*

C. FRUTESCENS, *Linn.* The Red Pepper or Chilly shrub has become naturalised in the Queensland scrubs. *C. baccatum,* Linn. (the Bird's-eye Pepper), *C. grossum,* Willd. (the Bell Pepper), and many other species or varieties, are abundant in our gardens, and from the quantity of fruit they bear one would think that it should pay to manufacture Cayenne pepper in the colony, or dry the fruit for exporting to Europe as is done both in the East and West Indies. Propagated by seed or cuttings.

CARAWAY SEED. (See *"Carum carui*, Linn.")

CARICA, *Linn.*—Order PASSIFLORACEÆ—Tribe *Papayaceæ.*

C. PAPAYA, *Linn.* (*Papaya vulgaris*, Lam.; *Papaya carica*, Gærtn.) The Papaw-tree. A soft-wooded tree of 20 or 30 ft., of South America, but cultivated in most countries where the climate suits. Leaves on long stalks, palmately divided into 7 or more acute sinuate lobes; flowers very fragrant, white, on the male trees in long raceme-like panicles, often with a few female flowers which produce fruit at the ends of the branches; flowers of female tree close to the stem in the axils of the leaves; fruit large, succulent, resembling a melon in flavour, somewhat pear-shaped; seed pungent. The young fruit are an excellent substitute for vegetable marrow. The tree is supposed to have the power of rendering meat which is suspended under it tender. A large number of medicinal virtues are ascribed to the tree. Propagated by seed.

CARISSA, *Linn.*—Order APOCYNACEÆ—Tribe *Carisseæ.*

C. GRANDIFLORA, *A. DC.* (*Arduina grandiflora*, E. Meyer.) Amatungula or Natal Plum; is both cultivated as a fruit and hedge plant. Propagated by seed.

C. CARANDAS, *Linn.*, is also in cultivation, and serves the same purposes. Propagation by seed.

CARUM, *Linn.*—Order UMBELLIFERÆ—Tribe *Ammineæ.*

C. PETROSELINUM, *Benth.* (*Apium Petroselinum*, Linn.; *Petroselinum sativum*, Hoffm.) The Garden Parsley. Commonly grown for domestic use. The fruit or seeds are said to be a deadly poison to parrots. Propagated by seed.

C. CARUI, *Linn.* The Caraway plant. This also thrives, but is seldom cultivated. Propagated by seed.

CAROB. (See *"Ceratonia siliqua*, Linn.")
CAROLINA JASMINE. (See *"Gelsemium nitidum*, Mich.")
CAROLINEA ALBA, *Lodd.* (See *"Pachira alba*, Walp.")
CASSAVA, BITTER. (See *"Manihot utilissima*, Pohl.")
CASSAVA, SWEET. (See *"Manihot Aipi*, Pohl.")

CASSIA, *Linn.*—Order LEGUMINOSÆ—Tribe *Cassieæ.*

C. ACUTIFOLIA, *Delile.*, C. ANGUSTIFOLIA, *Vahl*, and C. OBOVATA, *Colla.*, have been grown in Queensland, but no plants are available for this exhibit. Their adaptability for the climate was amply proved by Mr. Walter Hill twenty years ago, when he had plots of sennas and numerous other plants of economic value grown in the Brisbane Botanic Gardens. Propagated by seed.

C. FISTULA, *Linn.* (*Cathartocarpus fistula*, Pers.) Pudding-pipe tree. Indian Laburnum. This is a tree of moderate size, the bark smooth on the young trees, rough on the older ones; leaves pinnate, of about 5 pairs of ovate leaflets; flowers yellow, very showy, in long drooping racemes; pods cylindric, 1¼ to 2 ft. long and ¾ to 1 in. diameter; seeds numerous, each in a separate cell, immersed in a dark sweetish pulp. This pulp is considered a valuable laxative. The root is said to possess purgative properties. The bark is used for dyeing and tanning; the wood is said to be very durable. In Queensland the plant thrives well, but is only planted for ornament. Propagated by seed.

CASTANEA, *Gærtn*—Order CUPULIFERÆ—Tribe *Quercineæ.*

C. SATIVA, *Mill.* (*C. vesca*, Gærtn.) The Sweet or Spanish Chestnut; fruits well on the Downs, but does not mature very good fruit on coast land. Propagated by seed.

CASTILLOA, *Cervant.*—Order URTICACEÆ—Tribe *Artocarpeæ.*

C. ELASTICA, *Cerv.* The Guatemala and West Indian Rubber plant. This is a lofty tree, with a trunk often more than 3 ft. diameter. Branchlets pubescent; leaves oblong, lanceolate, often cordate at the base, attaining 18 in. length and 7 in. width on some trees; stipules large, deciduous. A tree with a trunk of 20 to 30 ft. to its branches, and about 4 ft. diameter of stem, is expected to yield 20 gallons of milk, each gallon of which is said to give 2 lbs. of rubber, and to be, when carefully and judiciously tapped, the most remunerative of rubbers. The tree requires a rich soil and good drainage, with plenty of water. Propagated by seed or cuttings. A cutting is found to root more readily if a shield of old wood is left at its base.

CASTOR OIL PLANT. (See "*Ricinus communis*, Linn.")
CATHARTOCARPUS FISTULA, *Pers.* (See "*Cassia.*")
CATS-TAIL. (See "*Typha angustifolia.*")
CAUSTIC CREEPER. (See "*Euphorbia Drummondii*, Bois.")
CAULIFLOWER. (See "*Brassica.*")
CEARA RUBBER. (See "*Manihot Glaziovii*, Muell. Arg.")
CEDAR, RED. (See "*Cedrela Toona*, Roxb.")

CEDRELA, *Linn.*—Order MELIACEÆ—Tribe *Cedreleæ.*

C. ODORATA, *Linn.* Honduras or Jamaica Cedar. A tall tree; leaves pinnate; leaflets variable, broad or narrow, on long or short stalks, 11 to 17; panicle drooping, about 1 ft. long; flowers pale-yellow ; petals pubescent ; capsule ovoid, somewhat ribbed. This tree produces a useful reddish fragrant wood, always in request in Europe for furniture and indoor work. Propagated by seed.

C. TOONA, *Roxb.* Red Cedar of Australia. The Toon-tree of India. A very large and valuable deciduous tree. The leaves are pinnate, composed of from 11 to 17 leaflets. The flowers are white, small, and borne on drooping panicles ; seed capsules about 1 in. long. The wood is highly prized both here and in Europe, and is the principal wood used in the colonies for furniture. The flowers may be used for dyeing red or yellow. The bark is astringent and has been used as a febrifuge. Propagated by seed.

CELERY. (See "*Apium graveolens*, Linn.")
CERASUS. (See "*Prunus.*")

CERATONIA, *Linn.*—Order LEGUMINOSÆ—Tribe *Cassieæ*.

C. SILIQUA, *Linn.* St. John's Bread, Carob-beans, or Locust-pods. This is a small tree found on the borders of the Mediterranean. It has pinnate leaves composed of a few pairs of blunt leaflets. The flowers are inconspicuous in short racemes. Pods about 6 in. long, 1 in. broad, thick and curved ; they contain a large amount of saccharine matter, and are employed in the south of Europe for feeding horses, pigs, &c. Wood hard, of a pinkish colour. Propagated by seed.

CHALTA. (See "*Dillenia indica*, Linn.")
CHAMOMILE. (See "*Anthemis nobilis*, Linn.")
CHESTNUT, SWEET or SPANISH. (See "*Castanea.*")
CHERIMOYER. (See "*Anona cherimolia*, Mill.")
CHERRY. (See "*Prunus.*")
CHERRY, BRAZILIAN. (See "*Eugenia uniflora*, Linn.")
CHERRY, HERBERT RIVER. (See "*Antidesma Dallachyana*, Baill.")
CHICORY. (See "*Cichorium Intybus*, Linn.")
CHINA or JAPAN RAISINS. (See "*Hovenia dulcis*, Thunb.")
CHINESE SUGAR CANE. (See "*Sorghum saccharatum*, Pers.")
CHINESE TALLOW TREE. (See "*Excœcaria sebifera*, Muell. Arg.")
CHINESE VARNISH TREE. (See "*Aleurites cordata*, Muell. Arg.")

CHLOROXYLON, *DC.*—Order MELIACEÆ—Tribe *Cedreleæ*.

C. SWIETENIA, *Linn.* East Indian Satinwood. A fine tree of Ceylon and the Coromandel coast and other parts of India. The leaves are pinnate, and the leaflets of a pale colour, ovate in form, with pellucid dots or oil-cells ; flowers white, in large panicles. This tree produces the handsome Indian satinwood and also a resin valuable for varnishes. Propagated by seed.

CHRYSOPHYLLUM.—Order SAPOTACEÆ.

C. CAINITO, *Linn.* The Star-apple of the West Indies. A small tree with oval or oblong leaves, golden-silky or silvery on the under side, the veins numerous, the transverse ones parallel, on short stalks; flowers axillary, calyx rusty, 5 or 4-parted.; corolla yellowish, 5 or 4-parted; fruit large, globose; seeds compressed. The fruit of this tree is much liked in the West Indies, and the tree will likely fruit in Queensland in tropical localities, but so far is not a success near Brisbane. Propagated by seed.

CICCA DISTICHA, *Linn.* (See "*Phyllanthus.*")

CICHORIUM, *Linn.*—Order COMPOSITÆ—Tribe *Cichoriaceæ.*

C. INTYBUS, *Linn.* Chicory or Succory. A European waste lands and roadside plant, with rough branching stems of 2 to 3 ft. high, the leaves pinnatifid and coarsely toothed; flower-heads blue. The thick fleshy roots are cultivated in Europe as a substitute for or for mixing with coffee, the flavour of which it is said to improve. The plant has not been grown commercially in Queensland, but it has been noticed in a few gardens and appears to suit the climate. Propagated by seed.

C. ENDIVIA, *Linn.* The Garden Endive; used from very early times as a culinary vegetable. Is grown by a few market-gardeners, but one seldom sees it nicely blanched, except in private gardens. Propagated by seed.

CICER, *Linn.*—Order LEGUMINOSÆ—Tribe *Vicieæ.*

C. ARIETINUM, *Linn.* The Gram. This annual pulse has been found to thrive in the colony, but has not been cultivated to any extent. It is, however, a valuable stable-food, and in India it is also extensively used for human food. Propagated by seed.

CINCHONA, *Linn.*—Order RUBIACEÆ—Tribe *Cinchoneæ.*

C. CALISAYA, *Wedd.* Yellow-bark. A lofty tree of Curabaya, Peru, with a thick bark, longitudinal and transversely fissured; leaves oblong to obovate-lanceolate, shining above, pale beneath, stalk short, variable as to size; stipules oblong, obtuse; panicles large; peduncles tomentose. square; flowers numerous, rosy-red; corolla-tube about ½-in. long, tomentose; capsule ovoid. This species is said to be one of the richest yielders of quinin, and produces, besides, cinchonidin. It furnishes the yellow bark and also partly the crown bark of commerce. Propagated by seed.

C. SUCCIRUBRA, *Pav.* Red-bark. A small erect tree with ovate leaves 4 to 9 in. long and 2½ to 6 in. broad, on stalks of about 1 in.; flowers rosy, in terminal panicles; corolla-tube about ½-in. long, the 5 lobes of limb with hairy margins.; capsule oblong, gaping at the base. This produces what is known as *Cascarilla colorada*, or Red-bark of English commerce. This is the species generally cultivated on the mountains of Bengal, and has been found hardy in Lower Gippsland, Victoria. Many localities in Tropical Queensland are well suited for the growth of Cinchona-trees. They require deep rich soil with plenty of rainfall, and above all good drainage. Much of the hilly country about Cairns is admirably adapted for their growth. Propagated by seed.

CINNAMOMUM, *Blume.*—Order LAURINEÆ—Tribe *Perseaceæ.*

C. CAMPHORA, *Nees.* (*Camphora officinalis*, Nees; *Laurus camphora*, Linn.; *Laurus camphorifera*, Kœmph.) Camphor-tree of China and Japan. A beautiful compact evergreen tree; leaves glossy, ovate, 2 or 3 in. long; flowers minute; fruit like a glossy black berry, about the size of a pea. The wood is pervaded by camphor, hence resists the attack of insects. The camphor is obtained by means of dry distillation. For ornamental planting no tree is better than this in Brisbane; always clean in its growth and affording a fine shade, and will thrive in almost any situation. Propagated by seed.

C. ZEYLANICUM, *Nees.* (*Laurus Cinnamomum*, Linn.) The Cinnamon of Ceylon. Branches angular; leaves ovate-oblong, tapering to an obtuse point, 3-nerved and reticulate; flowers hoary; fruit like a blackberry. The bark of this tree furnishes the best cinnamon of commerce. The tree thrives pretty well in some localities near Brisbane, but, to be grown for profit, should have a tropical climate, say about the Barron River. Propagated by seed.

CITRON-SCENTED GUM TREE. (See "*Eucalyptus maculata* var. *citriodora.*")

CITRUS, *Linn.*—Order RUTACEÆ—Tribe *Aurantieæ.*

Plants of this genus, as the Orange, Lime, Lemon, Shaddock, and Citron, crop very heavily and the fruits are of good flavour in all parts of Queensland.

C. TRIFOLIATA, *Linn.* (*C. trifolia*, Thunb.; *Ægle sepiaria*, DC.) Is in use by some nurserymen as a stock for the other kinds to be grafted upon. It also forms an excellent hedge. Propagated by layers, cuttings, and seed.

CLAUSENA, *Burm.*—Order RUTACEÆ—Tribe *Aurantieæ.*

C. WAMPI, *Oliver.* (*Cookia punctata*, Retz.) The Whampee of the Chinese. A small tree having the branches, leaf-stalks, and inflorescence covered by minute asperities. The leaves are composed of from 7 to 9 obliquely ovate leaflets about 3 or 4 in. long; flowers in broad spreading panicles; fruit a berry of a brownish colour and grape-like flavour, globular and over 1 in. diameter when well grown. Fruits abundantly about Brisbane. Propagated by seed.

CLEOME, *Linn.*—Order CAPPARIDEÆ—Tribe *Cleomeæ.*

C. PUNGENS, *Willd.* Spider-flower. This plant, which is highly spoken of by bee-keepers, has been sown for bees, and in some parts it has become naturalised. Propagated by seed.

CLOVER, WHITE or DUTCH. (See "*Trifolium repens*, Linn.")

COCA. (See "*Eythroxylon coca*, Lam.")

COCCULUS. (See "*Jateorhiza.*")

COCHLEARIA, *Linn.*—Order CRUCIFERÆ.—Tribe *Alyssineæ.*

C. ARMORACIA, *Linn.* The Horse-radish; produces good roots. Propagated by seed or division of root.

COCOA PLANT. (See "*Theobroma cacao*, Linn.")

COCOS, *Linn.*—Order PALMÆ—Tribe *Cocoineæ.*

C. NUCIFERA, *Linn.* Cocoa-nut. A graceful pinnate-leaved palm of tropical sea-coasts, with a trunk attaining 100 feet in height and 2 feet in diameter. The leaves will often measure 18 feet in length, and are usually curved. These leaves are used for thatching, and the net of fibres at their base is made into bags and paper, and in Ceylon for toddy-straining. The wood of the outer part of the stem is that known as "porcupine-wood," and used for walking-sticks and fancy work. The fibre surrounding the nut is "coir" fibre, and used in rope and mat making; and from the kernels is obtained a large quantity of the well-known cocoa-nut oil which is used in the manufacture of soap, candles, &c. This useful tree has been met with in a wild state in a few localities along the Queensland tropical coast, and plantations have also been formed, and are thriving, and producing good crops of fruit. Propagated by planting the nuts.

COFFEA, *Linn.*—Order RUBIACEÆ—Tribe *Ixoreæ.*

C. ARABICA, *Linn.* Coffee-shrub. A small tree or large shrub of Tropical Africa, of erect growth. Leaves oblong-lanceolate, wavy, shining on the upper surface, pale on the under side; stipules subulate; flowers 5-merous, sweet-scented, white, tubular, with a 5-cleft limb; berries oval, reddish-purple, containing 2 seeds. No part of the world is better adapted for the cultivation of coffee; and doubtless before very long there will be plantations formed in North Queensland. The hills about Cairns, which have a deep rich soil, are admirably suited for this plant. Propagated by seed.

C. LIBERICA, *Bull. et Hiern.* Liberian Coffee. This species has a much more robust habit than *C. arabica*, produces larger beans, and is said to thrive at a lower elevation. The leaves vary from 5 to 12 in. long and from 2 to 4 in. wide. The flowers differ from *C. arabica* in being 6 or 7-merous. The coffee is considered by some of inferior quality. Propagated by seed.

COIX, *Linn.*—Order GRAMINEÆ—Tribe *Maydeæ*.

C. LACHRYMA, *Linn.* Job's-tears. This is a tall leafy grass, with monœcious flowers, of the East Indies, Japan. It produces a large quantity of coarse fodder. The seeds of the common kind are very hard, resembling small cowrie shells, and often used as ornaments; but Dr. Hooker says that a kind cultivated in the Khasia Hills has a soft shell and sweet kernel. These seeds are used for food also in other parts. Propagated by seeds and division.

COLOCASIA, *Schott.*—Order AROIDEÆ.

C. ANTIQUORUM, *Schott.* The Taro of the South Sea Islands. Often grown for ornament, and the islanders on some plantations in Northern Queensland cultivate it for food. Propagated by division.

COOKIA PUNCTATA, *Retz.* (See "*Clausena Wampi*, Oliver.")

CORCHORUS.—Order TILIACEÆ—Tribe *Tilieæ*.

C. CAPSULARIS, *Linn.*, of India and Japan, and C. OLITORIUS, *Linn.*, of South Asia and North Australia. Annual erect-growing plants, which in India are cultivated for their fibre, known as jute, and used in making rice and sugar bags in India. The fibre is also largely used in Europe in the manufacture of carpets and other fabrics. Both plants thrive admirably in Queensland, and some excellent fibre has been made and exhibited at various exhibitions. Propagated by seed.

CORDIA, *Linn.*—Order BORAGINEÆ—Tribe *Cordieæ*.

C. MYXA, *Linn.*, var. LATIFOLIA. The broad-leaved Sepistan or Sebesten. The word "Sepistan" is an abbreviation of "sag-pestan," which means in Persian "dog's dugs." This is a small tree, with roundish or somewhat heart-shaped repand leaves, 3-nerved. The flowers are borne in terminal panicles, and succeeded by pale straw-coloured plum-like fruit; when ripe they contain a large quantity of clear, very clammy pulp. In India the natives pickle the fruit. Medicinally, the dried fruit is valued on account of its mucilaginous nature and demulcent properties. It is much used in coughs and chest affections, also in irritation of the urinary passages; in larger quantities it is given in bilious affections as a laxative. The wood, although soft, is strong, and useful for many purposes. Propagated by seed.

CORK OAK. (See "*Quercus suber*, Linn.")

CORNUS, *Linn.*—Order CORNACEÆ.

C. CAPITATA, *Wall.* (*Benthamia fragifera*, Lindl.) A small deciduous tree of Northern India, with thin greyish bark; leaves opposite, lanceolate; fruits small, growing together, and forming a large berry resembling those of the Strawberry-tree *Arbutus*; red when ripe. The tree when in bloom is handsome, from the large cream-coloured involucres. The fruit is eaten, and made into preserves. Propagated by seed or cuttings.

CORYLUS, *Linn.*—Order CUPULIFERÆ—Tribe *Coryleæ.*

C. AVELLANA, *Linn.* The Hazel and Filbert fruit well on the Darling Downs and similar places. Propagated by seed, and the superior kinds by grafting upon the seedlings.

COTTON PLANT. (See "*Gossypium.*")
COTTON TREE, QUEENSLAND. (See "*Hibiscus tiliaceus*, Linn.'')
COTTON TREE, SILK. (See "*Bombax malabaricum*, DC.," and "*Eriodendron anfractuosum*, DC.")

CRATÆGUS, *Linn.*—Order ROSACEÆ—Tribe *Pomeæ.*

C. OXYACANTHA, *Linn.* The Hawthorn or Whitethorn. This suits for hedges in the cooler parts of the colony, but is not suited for such purposes near Brisbane or in the North. The same may be said of *C. pyracantha*, Pers. (Fiery Thorn), an evergreen species. Propagated by seed.

CRATÆVA MARMELOS, *Linn.* (See "*Ægle Marmelos*, Corr.")

CRESCENTIA, *Linn.*—Order BIGNONIACEÆ—Tribe *Crescentieæ.*

C. CUJETE, *Linn.* Calabash-tree of West Indies. This is a small tree, the leaves in clusters of 5, lanceolate, expanding more or less at the base, 4 to 6 in. long; flowers large, variegated with green, purple, red, and yellow; fruit globular or oval, with a very hard woody shell. This is utilised by the natives of the parts of South America where the plant grows wild, in forming into many articles of domestic economy, as for cups, water-bottles, &c. The pulp is considered purgative, and thought beneficial in diseases of the chest. The wood is light, tough, and pliable. The tree stands the Brisbane climate, and has fruited in one or more places, but is better suited for the tropical parts of the colony. Propagated by seed or cuttings.

CRESS, COMMON GARDEN. (See "*Lepidium sativum*, Linn.")
CRESS, LAND. (See "*Barbarea.*")
CRESS, WATER. (See "*Nasturtium officinale*, R. Br.")

CROTALARIA, *Linn.*—Order LEGUMINOSÆ—Tribe *Genisteæ.*

C. JUNCEA, *Linn.* The Sunn-hemp. This plant has been grown, and excellent fibre made from its stalks, but as yet no one has gone in for fibre cultivation. This and many more species are indigenous to Queensland; all give a good fibre. Propagated by seed.

CROTON, *Linn.*—Order EUPHORBIACEÆ—Tribe *Crotoneæ.*

C. TIGLIUM, *Linn.* The Purging Croton. This is a small tree of India and Burmah. Leaves ovate, acute, and 3 to 5-nerved at the base, with glandular serratures; 2 glands at the base, the surface with minute stellate hairs; racemes terminal, erect; flowers downy;

capsules oblong, obtusely triangular; testa of seed dark. These seeds are considered one of the most drastic purgatives known. Ten to twenty seeds are said to be enough to kill a horse. Propagated by seed.

CROTON OIL SHRUB. (See "*Croton Tiglium*, Linn.")

CRYPTOSTEGIA, *R. Br.*—Order ASCLEPIADEÆ—Tribe *Periplocea*.

C. GRANDIFLORA, *R. Br.* (*Nerium grandiflorum*, Roxb.) India-rubber vine. This is a tall climbing plant with opposite elliptic leaves, brownish on the under side; flowers showy-white inside, purplish outside, funnel-shaped, with a corona of 5 bipartite scales; fruit divaricate follicles, which are acutely triquetrous, 1 in. wide at the base and tapering to a point, often the two spreading to 6 or 8 in. wide. The milky sap of this climber contains caoutchouc, and has in India been converted into good rubber. Propagated by seed.

CUBA-BAST. (See "*Hibiscus elatus*, Sw.")
CUCUMBER. (See "*Cucumis*.")

CUCUMIS, *Linn.*; CITRULLUS, *Schrad.*; CUCURBITA, *Linn.*—
Order CUCURBITACEÆ.

CUCUMIS, CITRULLUS, and CUCURBITA, the genera in which are placed the Cucumber, Melon, Water-melon, and Pumpkin, are largely represented in Queensland, and produce crops equal to those of any other part of the world. Propagated by seed.

CUMFREY, PRICKLY. (See "*Symphytum asperrimum*, Sims.")

CURCUMA, *Linn.*—Order SCITAMINEÆ—Tribe *Zingiberea*.

C. LONGA, *Roxb.* (*Amomum Curcuma*, Murr.) This plant, the Turmeric of commerce, requires the same cultivation as Ginger, and has been successfully grown in Queensland. The juice of the fresh rootstock is considered anthelmintic. In India, turmeric, which is prepared from the old rootstock, is regarded as an important bitter aromatic stimulant and tonic, and is employed in debilitated states of the stomach, intermittent fevers, and dropsy. Turmeric paper is unsized paper steeped in tincture of turmeric and dried by exposure to the air. It is employed as a test for alkalies, which render it reddish or brownish. Propagated by division of rhizome.

CURRANT, ENGLISH. (See "*Ribes*.")
CUSTARD APPLE. (See "*Anona squamosa*, Linn.")
CYDONIA. (See "*Pyrus*.")

CYNARA, *Linn.*—Order COMPOSITÆ—Tribe *Cynaroidea*.

C. SCOLYMUS, *Linn.* The Common Artichoke, grown mostly in private gardens. It thrives well, but is not ready of sale in Queensland.

CYPERUS, *Linn.*—Order CYPERACRÆ—Tribe *Scirpeæ*.

C. ESCULENTUS, *Linn.* Chufa or Ground Almond. This is a sedge somewhat resembling the pest known by the name of Nutgrass. The knotty rhizomes are edible, and are said to contain 27 per cent. of starch, 17 per cent. of oil, and 12 per cent. of saccharine substance. They are eaten either raw or cooked. The oil is said to surpass in excellence of taste all others used for culinary purposes. Propagated by the tubers.

C. PAPYRUS, *Linn.* (*Papyrus antiquorum.*) This was used by the ancients for making a substitute for our writing-paper; but at the present time it is used for ornamental more than useful purposes. Propagated by division.

CYPHOMANDRA, *Sendtn.*—Order SOLANACEÆ.

(This genus only differs from *Solanum* in the form of anther and connectivum.)

C. BETACEA, *Sendtn.* (*Pionandra betacea*, Hook.; *Solanum betaceum*, Cav.) This Beet-leaved Nightshade forms a large soft-wooded shrub, often quickly attaining the height of from 6 to 10 feet, and spreading in proportion. The leaves are ovate in form, 6 to 9 in. long and 3 to 5 in. in width, on spotted petioles of about 1 or 2 in. The flowers are borne in racemes or raceme-like panicles, and are somewhat rosy in colour; fruit egg-like, 1 to 2 in. long. In Lima and Buenos Ayres they are used as tomatoes. This shrub has only just begun to fruit in our gardens, but most probably in a very few years it will be found naturalised in our scrubs, for birds and animals eating the fruit of the shrubs in cultivation will carry and deposit the seed far and wide, the same as they have done with other *Solanums*. Propagated by seed.

DALBERGIA, *Linn. f.*—Order LEGUMINOSÆ—Tribe *Dalbergieæ*.

D. SISSOO, *Roxb.* The Sissoo of East India. This is a large deciduous tree, with pinnate leaves; leaflets 3 to 5, alternate, orbicular, or obcordate, with a short sudden acumination, slightly wavy on the margin, when young pubescent; panicles of flowers axillary, composed of several short second spikes or racemes, the flowers nearly or quite sessile, yellowish-white; pod linear, lanceolate, 2-seeded A valuable timber tree; the wood is very durable, and does not warp or split; is used in India for felloes and naves of wheels, for which it is said to be unsurpassed by any other wood. This tree is largely planted in India for timber. It thrives well in Queensland. Propagated by seed.

DANDELION. (See "*Taraxacum dens-leonis*, Hall.")
DATE PALM. (See "*Phœnix dactylifera*, Linn.")
DATE PLUM. (See "*Diospyros Kaki*, Linn.")

DAUCUS, *Linn.*—Order UMBELLIFERÆ—Tribe *Caucalineæ*.
D. CAROTA, *Linn.* The Carrot. Crops well in Queensland.

DAVIDSON'S PLUM. (See "*Davidsonia pruriens*, F. v. M.")

DAVIDSONIA, *F. v. M.*—Order SAXIFRAGEÆ—Tribe *Escalloniæ*.

D. PRURIENS, *F. v. M.* Davidson's Plum. This is a very graceful erect tree of Tropical Queensland. All parts more or less hairy; the large irregularly pinnate leaves very beautiful; flower in a long pendulent raceme-like panicle; fruit oval, size of a goose-egg, clothed with short stiff hairs, which are easily rubbed off the ripe fruit; pulp abundant, of a rich purple colour, and sharp. One of the best culinary fruits of the colony. Wood dark-coloured, close-grained, and tough. Propagated by seed.

DEVIL'S COTTON. (See "*Abroma augusta*, Linn.")
DEVIL'S FIG. (See "*Argemone*.")
DILL. (See "*Peucedanum*.")

DILLENIA, *Linn.*—Order DILLENIACEÆ—Tribe *Dilleniæ*.
D. INDICA, *Linn.* (*D. speciosa*, Thunb.) The Chalta-tree. A large evergreen East Indian tree, with a red bark and oblong, serrated, rough leaves; flowers large, solitary, very showy, white; fruit globose, with the enclosing fleshy calyx 4 to 6 in. diameter; the enclosing calyx, as well as the fruit, edible, acid. The wood is said to be durable under water in India. The tree grows and fruits fairly well in the Brisbane gardens, but seems to require a more tropical climate. Propagated by seed.

DIOSCOREA, *Linn.*—Order DIOSCOREACEÆ.
D. ALATA, *Linn.* The Uvi Yam. Found in cultivation in India and the South Sea Islands. The climbing stems are more or less winged, of 4 angles, but not prickly as in the one called the China Yam. The tubers grow to a large size, and are eaten baked or boiled. Propagated by crowns.

DIOSPYROS, *Linn.*—Order EBENACEÆ.
D. KAKI, *Linn.* Date Plum. A deciduous tree of China and Japan, with ovate, oblong, rather downy leaves varying much in size. Many varieties of this delicious fruit are now grown in Queensland; the best are considered those that are seedless. In shape the fruit is round but flattish, several inches in diameter, of a brownish colour, outside the semi-transparent pulp yellowish, varying in flavour according to variety. The superior varieties are propagated by grafting upon seedlings of the inferior kind or on roots.

DIPLOGLOTTIS, *Hook. f.*—Order SAPINDACEÆ.
D. CUNNINGHAMII, *Hook. f.* Queensland Tamarind. A large tree with a brownish smooth bark; wood light-coloured, close-grained,

very tough; leaves and young growth densely clothed with rusty hairs; leaves pinnate, very large, the leaflets oblong, 6 to 8 in. and often nearly 1 ft. long; flower in a straggling panicle; capsule of 2 or 3 round lobes, enclosing round seeds, each surrounded by a fleshy amber-coloured sweet aril, which latter is often collected and made into a preserve. Propagated by seed.

DIPLOTHEMIUM, *Mart.*—Order PALMÆ—Tribe *Cocoineæ.*

D. MARITIMUM, *Mart.* Wine Palm. Foliage pinnate, somewhat glaucous, the leaves gracefully curved; panicles of fruit large; fruit globular, about 1 in. diameter of a sharp acid flavour. The tree bears an abundance of fruit, of which little use is made. Propagated by seed.

DIPSACUS, *Linn.*—Order DIPSACEÆ.

D. FULLONUM, *Linn.* The Fuller's Teazel. May be seen growing in gardens now and again, and certainly thrives well; but it is not cultivated for use, although the use of it has not yet been superseded by machinery. Propagated by seed.

DITA BARK. (See "*Alstonia scholaris*, R. Br.")
DIVI DIVI. (See "*Cæsalpinia coriaria*, Willd.")

DOLICHOS, *Linn.*—Order LEGUMINOSÆ—Tribe *Phaseoleæ.*

D. LABLAB, *Linn.* Grown for ornament but seldom used for culinary purposes. Propagated by seed.

D. SINENSIS, *Linn.* (See "*Vigna.*")
DOORNBOOM. (See "*Acacia horrida*, Willd.")

DUBOISIA, *R. Br.*— Order SOLANACEÆ—Tribe *Salpiglossidæ.*

D. MYOPOROIDES, *R. Br.* A small tree, the bark corky; leaves narrow oblong, light-grey, 2 to 4 in. long; flowers small, white. in loose spreading panicles; fruit a juicy black berry. The juice of the leaves and fruit acts rapidly on the iris and accommodation of the eye, producing a widely dilated pupil in twenty minutes. This was introduced into practice some years ago by Dr. Bancroft, of Brisbane, and is at present largely used. Propagated by seed.

D. HOPWOODII, *F. v. M.* The Pituri of the natives of Cooper's Creek. This shrub contains an alkaloid analogous to nicotine, and hence forms an article of commerce amongst the natives of the interior, who use dried portions of it as a masticatory. Propagated by seed.

DURANTA, *Linn.*—Order VERBENACEÆ.

D. PLUMIERI, *Linn.* A tall, sharp-thorned shrub of South America. It has opposite serrated ovate leaves, and pretty lilac flowers borne in racemes in the upper axils of the shoots, thus forming terminal panicles; fruit yellow, said to be poisonous. This shrub, which grows very quickly, is the one most generally used in hedge-making. Propagated by cuttings or seed; in planting a hedge, cuttings are more generally used than rooted plants.

EARTH NUT. (See "*Arachis hypogæa*, Linn.")

EGG PLANT. (See "*Solanum Melongena*, Linn.")

ELDER BERRY. (See "*Sambucus*.")

ELÆOCOCCA VERNICIA, *Spreng.* (See "*Aleurites cordata*, Muell. Arg.")

EMBLICA. (See "*Phyllanthus*.")

ENDIVE. (See "*Cichorium Endivia*, Linn.")

ERIOBOTRYA JAPONICA, *Lindl.* (See "*Photinia*.")

ERIODENDRON.—Order MALVACEÆ—Tribe *Bombaceæ*.

E. ANFRACTUOSUM, *DC.* (*Bombax pentandra*, Linn.) The White Cotton tree of India. An erect deciduous tree with prickly stem resembling a *Bombax* but differing in staminal column, being 5-cleft, each branch bearing 2 or 3 anthers, that of *Bombax* being divided at top into an indefinite number of filaments bearing anthers; branches spreading horizontally; leaves digitate, of 5 to 8 leaflets, glaucous beneath and sometimes serrulate towards the point; flowers white, anthers anfractuose (spirally twisted), whence the name; capsule oblong with the seeds embedded in silky cotton. The cotton of the capsules is the "kapok" of commerce, and is used for stuffing pillows, &c. Propagated by seed.

ERVUM LENS, *Linn.* (See "*Lens esculenta*, Mœnch.")

ERYTHROXYLON, *Linn.*—Order LINEÆ—Tribe *Erythroxyleæ*.

E. COCA, *Lam.* The Coca or Spadic plant of Peru. This is a tall graceful shrub with virgate branches. The leaves are oval, 1 or 2 in. long, of a pale-green and thin texture; the axillary flowers small, whitish; fruit a small drupe. The leaves of this shrub are universally chewed by the Indians. It is said that after partaking of their morning meal they stuff a loose handful of leaves into their mouths with a little calcined lime, adding a few fresh leaves during the day. The effect is said to be stimulating, enabling them to work hard on little food. This Coca-bush is extensively cultivated by them; the annual produce is estimated at about 30,000,000 lbs. The leaves are also infused and used as tea. The active principle has been brought into use in Europe as an anæsthetic in superficial surgical operations. The shrub thrives and fruits well in the Brisbane district, and will likely soon be largely cultivated, especially in the more northern parts of the colony. Propagated by seed or cuttings.

EUCALYPTUS, *L' Her.*—Order MYRTACEÆ—Tribe *Leptospermeæ.*

E. MACULATA, var. CITRIODORA, *Hook.* The Citron-scented Spotted Gum-tree. This tree only differs from the Spotted Gum-tree in the foliage being strongly citron-scented; it has the same white, clean, dimpled bark which has got for it the name of spotted gum; is also a tall tree with usually a scanty amount of foliage, and the flowers and fruit, were it not for the peculiar fragrance, could not be distinguished one from the other. The timber is likewise excellent for wheelwright's work. The foliage is rich in essential oil of quite a citron scent. The tree would likely pay if planted for distillation; the trees could be kept well cut back, by which a far greater amount of foliage would be produced and a continual supply obtained. For this purpose, *E. Baileyana*, F. v. M., which produces a strong pungent essential oil, well adapted for medicinal purposes; *E. hæmastoma*, Sm., which produces a peppermint-scented oil; and *E. microcorys*, F. v. M., are well worthy of attention. Propagated best in all cases by seed.

E. STAIGERIANA, *F. v. M.; Bail. in Syn. Ql. Fl.* Lemon-scented Ironbark of the Palmer. This is a small tree of irregular growth, the wood hard, of a red colour, but the logs often pipy; bark dark, rugged. Leaves vary like others of the Gums, but differ from them in the delightful fragrance of their essential oil, which closely resembles that of lemons. One ton of the dry leaves will yield about 1,300 oz. of oil. The tree thrives in the southern parts of Queensland, flowering well as a tall shrub, and would likely pay if planted for the sake of its foliage for distillation. Propagated by seed.

EUCHLÆNA, *Schrad.*—Order GRAMINEÆ—Tribe *Maydeæ.*

E. LUXURIANS, *Ascherson.* (*Reeana luxurians*, Durien.) The Teosinté. This is a very tall branching fodder grass; numerous stems spring from the same root, attaining a height of 12 or more feet, from the knots of which spring numerous shoots, thus producing a large amount of fodder. The plant should have a good soil, and is better suited for the tropical than the southern parts of Queensland, although it thrives fairly well about Brisbane. Propagated by seed.

EUGENIA, *Lindl.*—Order MYRTACEÆ—Tribe *Myrteæ.*

E. JAMBOS, *Linn.* (*Jambosa vulgaris*, DC., *Myrtus Jambos*, Kunth.) The Rose Apple. A tree of moderate size, in garden culture generally forming a wide-spreading shrub; the leaves 4 to 8 in. long, narrow-lanceolate; flowers white, in terminal racemes, very large and showy; berry white, globose, crowned by the 4 persistent calyx-lobes, often 1½ to 2 in. diameter, of a nice flavour, and with a scent of roses, but not much used as a fruit. Propagated by seed.

E. PIMENTA, *DC.* (See *"Pimenta communis*, Lindl.")

C

E. UNIFLORA, *Linn*. (*E. Michelli*, Lam.) Brazilian Cherry. A tall glabrous shrub, with bluntish, ovate-lanceolate, glossy leaves; the flowers small, on long slender stalks; fruit a flattish lobed berry, of about 1 in. diameter, bright-red, very juicy, used as a fruit, and by some considered to possess medicinal virtues. Propagated by seed.

EUPHORBIA, *Linn*.—Order EUPHORBIACEÆ—Tribe *Euphorbieæ*.

E. PILULIFERA, *Linn*. Asthma-plant. A small hairy herb, from 8 to 18 in. high, often of a reddish colour, with opposite ovate-lanceolate leaves of 1 or 2 in. in length; stipules small; flowers in dense globular heads in the axils of the leaves. This common tropical weed is constantly used in the form of a tea by persons suffering from asthma, and is said to give instant relief. For this purpose the whole plant is gathered while in flower and fruit and most carefully dried, for if allowed to mould it is apt to do more harm than good. The tea should be of the same strength as ordinary tea, and a wineglassful for a dose. Propagated by seed.

E. DRUMMONDII, *Bois.*, has also lately been said to possess medicinal virtues. This is the Caustic Creeper so poisonous to sheep. Propagated by seed.

EUPHORIA, *Juss*.—Order SAPINDACEÆ—Tribe *Sapindeæ*.

E. LONGANA, *Lam*. (*Nephelium Longana*, Camp.; *Scytalia Longana*, Roxb.) The Longan of the East Indies, China, and Burmah. This is a pinnate-leaved tree of small size; leaflets 4 to 10, oblong, rather prominently veined and wavy; fruit reddish-purple, globose, ⅜ to ½ in. diameter, rough or at length smooth. The fruit, which consists of a fleshy aril, is wholesome, but far inferior to the Lichi. Propagated by seed.

EXCÆCARIA, *Linn*.—Order EUPHORBIACEÆ—Tribe *Crotoneæ*.

E. SEBIFERA, *Muell. Arg*. (*Stillingia sebifera*, Mich.; *Sapium sebiferum*, Roxb.; *Carumbium sebiferum*, Kurz.; *Sapium sinensis*, Baill.) The Chinese Tallow-tree. A moderate-sized tree with grey bark, the leaves on long stalks, roundish ovate, with 2 glands at the base, and taper-pointed, of a grey colour; flowers yellow, very small in erect spikes; fruit globose, ellipsoid; seeds coated with a fatty substance, which yields the tallow used by the Chinese. The combustion of candles made from this material is said to yield a thicker smoke and a dimmer light, and to consume much more rapidly, than those made from animal tallow. The wood of the Tallow-tree is white and close-grained, and well fitted for printing-blocks; and the leaves give a dye. Propagated by seed or portions of the root.

FAGOPYRUM, *Gærtn*.—Order POLYGONACEÆ.

F. ESCULENTUM, *Mœnch*. The Buckwheat. This is grown as a fodder plant, but not to any extent, although it thrives very well. Propagated by seed.

FATSIA, *Dcne.*—Order ARALIACEÆ—Series *Panaceæ.*

F. PAPYRIFERA, *Benth.* (*Aralia papyrifera*, Hook.) The Rice-paper plant of the island of Formosa. A tall soft-wooded shrub sending up numerous young plants from the roots; leaves on long stalks, cordate, with 5 to 7 acute serrated lobes, when young covered with a dense down, the upper surface glabrous when fully grown; flowers small in numerous capitate umbels, forming a very large terminal panicle. In Queensland often planted for ornamental purposes. The Chinese rice-paper is made from the pith of this plant. Propagated by suckers.

FENNEL. (See "*Fœniculatum.*")
FERONIA PELLUCIDA, *Roth.* (See "*Ægle Marmelos*, Corr.")
FEVER BARK. (See "*Alstonia constricta*, F. v. M.")

FICUS, *Linn.*—Order URTICACEÆ.—Tribe *Artocarpeæ.*

F. BENGALENSIS, *Linn.* (*F. indica*, Roxb.) The Banyan. This is a large evergreen East Indian tree with wide-spreading horizontal branches from which descend roots which, reaching the ground, form additional stems to the tree, thus forming an extensive shade. The leaves are large, thick, bluntly ovate, downy when young. The fruit is about 1 in. diameter, borne in pairs, on very short stalks, or stalkless. The seeds of the fruit are considered cooling and tonic. The white glutinous juice is applied as a remedy for toothache, and to the soles of the feet when cracked and inflamed. The bark is given as a tonic. The leaves, after they have turned yellow, are given with roasted rice in decoction as a diaphoretic. The wood, which is grey and moderately hard, is of little value, but being durable under water is used in India for well-curbs. In Queensland the tree thrives well, and is planted for shade. Propagated by seed or cuttings.

F. SYCAMORUS, *Linn.* The Mulberry Fig or Sycamore Fig. This forms an excellent shade tree, and produces a large quantity of fruit, which is used as food by the Arabs. The wood although light is said to be almost imperishable. Propagated by seed or cuttings.

F. CARICA, *Linn.* The ordinary Fig. Produces good crops in the cooler parts of Queensland, but the fruit is often destroyed by the fly. The Bay-leaves found with imported figs are placed there as a preventive of the ravages of the grub which so often destroys this fruit. The Fig is said to be the Teenah, the first tree mentioned in the Scriptures. Propagated by cuttings.

F. ELASTICA, *Blume.* The India-rubber Fig or Caoutchouc tree. A large East Indian tree, where, like the Banyan, it throws down aërial roots from its branches. The bark is grey or reddish-brown; the leaves oblong, pointed, glossy, and with numerous parallel fine lateral veins; stipules long, purplish-red; fruit in pairs, oblong, ½ to nearly 1 in. long, purple when ripe. The tree is tapped by means of slanting notches made in the stem, aërial roots, and roots,

about 12 in. apart.   The milk is allowed to collect and coagulate in
these notches for two or three days, after which time the hard india-
rubber in each notch is easily collected by being pulled out in a strip.
The milky juice is estimated to contain one-third its weight of caoutchouc. The tree will not bear yearly tapping; once in three years is as
much as it will stand; if tapped yearly it is liable to die off.   There
are but few plants of this beautiful tree in Queensland, but these are
thriving. Propagated by seed or cuttings.

F. RELIGIOSA, *Linn.*   The Peepul or Poplar-leaved Fig.   A large
East Indian tree with grey bark; the leaves on long stalks, ovate,
cordate, with very long points; fruit in pairs, stalkless, small, depressed-globular; wood greyish white, moderately hard.   The tree is
sacred in India, and therefore seldom cut for the wood.   One writer
says that the dried fruits, pulverised and taken in water for fourteen
days together, removes asthma; another, that the leaves and young
shoots are purgative.   The tree is largely planted in Queensland for
ornament, and thrives admirably.   Propagated by seed or cuttings.

FIG. (See "*Ficus Carica*, Linn.")
FILBERT. (See "*Corylus.*")

FLACOURTIA, *Comm.*—Order BIXINEÆ—Tribe *Flacourtieæ.*

F. CATAPHRACTA, *Roxb.*   A small tree of India and Burmah, armed
with large multiple thorns; leaves oval-oblong, acuminate, and
serrate; flowers small, of separate sexes; fruit about 1 in. diameter,
globose, purplish, and pleasant-flavoured.   The plant forms a very
strong hedge. Medicinally the fruit is recommended as useful in
bilious conditions. This tree thrives excellently in Queensland. Propagated by seed.

F. SEPIARIA, *Roxb.*   A very thorny shrub of India.   Leaves
obovate, coriaceous, serrated; flowers axillary, solitary; berry small,
globular, with from 4 to 8 seeds.   These berries are eatable, and the
plant is useful for forming hedges; but as yet not used for that purpose in Queensland.   Propagated by seed.

FLAX or LINSEED.   (See "*Linum usitatissimum*, Linn.")

FŒNICULUM, *Adans.*—Order UMBELLIFERÆ—Tribe *Seselineæ.*

F. OFFICINALE, *Allioni.*   The Fennel.   Is not uncommon in gardens.
Propagated by seed.

FOURCROYA.   (See "*Furcræa.*")

FRAGARIA, *Linn.*—Order ROSACEÆ—Tribe *Potentilleæ.*

F. VESCA, *Linn.*   Strawberry.   The market is well supplied with
this favourite fruit, of which many excellent kinds are grown.
Propagated by the runners.

FRANCHIPANIER or PAGODA TREE. (See *"Plumeria acuminata,* Ait.")

FRENCH BEAN. (See *"Phaseolus."*)

FRENCH HONEYSUCKLE. (See *"Hedysarum coronarium,* Linn.")

FURCRÆA, *Vent.* (FOURCROYA).—Order AMARYLLIDEÆ—Tribe *Agaveæ.*

F. GIGANTEA, *Vent.* (*Agave fœtida,* Linn.) A large Aloe-like plant with long, green, lanceolate leaves, often with prickles near the middle; flowering but once; flower-stem 20 to 30 ft. high, of very quick growth; flower yellowish, succeeded by bulbills, not seed-pods. An excellent strong fibre may be obtained from this South American plant; it thrives well on any soil in Queensland. Propagated by the bulbills from flower-stem.

GARCINIA, *Linn.*—Order GUTTIFERÆ—Tribe *Garcinieæ.*

G. LIVINGSTONEI, *T. Andr.* A small tree of Tropical Africa, with a thick trunk, opposite or ternate oblong, slightly emarginate, coriaceous leaves of a dark green, 2 to 4 in. long; flowers on the old wood often densely clustered; fruit a somewhat flattened pear-shaped or oval berry about 1 to 1¼ in. diameter, the scanty flesh of a pleasant flavour; outer skin orange-coloured; seeds 2. So far as proved in Brisbane gardens, scarcely worth cultivating as a fruit; but the dark-green foliage, bright-coloured fruit, and compact growth make it a favourite tree for ornamental planting. Propagated by seed.

GARLIC. (See *"Allium sativum,* Bauh.")

GELSEMIUM, *Juss.*—Order LOGANIACEÆ—Tribe *Gelsemiæ.*

G. NITIDUM, *Mich.* Carolina Jasmine. An evergreen climber of the Southern States of America, with opposite, lanceolate, shining leaves; flowers in the axils, sweet-scented, with a funnel-shaped 5-cleft corolla. This beautiful plant is considered to possess valuable medicinal properties, and to be especially useful in cases of neuralgia, rheumatics, and fever. Propagated by seed, layers, or cuttings.

GERMAN MILLET. (See *"Setaria italica,* Beauv.")

GINGELLY OIL PLANT. (See *"Sesamum indicum,* Linn.")

GINGER. (See *"Zingiber officinalis,* Roxb.")

GLYCYRRHIZA, *Linn.*—Order LEGUMINOSÆ.—Tribe *Galegeæ.*

G. GLABRA, *Linn.* The Liquorice-plant. In some localities this plant produces good root, but it is very little grown. Propagated by divisions of the roots.

GOOSEBERRY, CAPE. (See *"Physalis."*)

GOOSEBERRY, ENGLISH. (See *"Ribes."*)

GOSSYPIUM, *Linn.*—Order MALVACEÆ.—Tribe *Hibiseeæ.*

G. RELIGIOSUM, *Linn.* (*G. peruvianum*, Cav.) Kidney Cotton, Peruvian or Brazilian Cotton A South American plant, said to be the tallest of cottons. The leaves are more deeply lobed than others, the petals yellow, and the seeds closely connected in oblong masses. The cotton is of a very long staple, white, silky, and easily separated from the seeds. Other species grown in the colony are:— *G. Barbadense*, Linn. (the Sea Island cotton), which has also long lobed leaves and yellow petals, but the seeds of which are black and disconnected. The cotton of this is very long, and of a silky lustre. *G. herbaceum*, Linn., of tropical and subtropical Asia, with short lobed leaves, yellow petals, and disconnected grey-velvety seeds; staple long. A variety of this furnishes that known as Nankin cotton. And *G. hirsutum*, Linn. (the Upland or Short-staple cotton), the seeds of which are disconnected and of a brownish-green colour. Cotton-root bark is used medicinally in similar cases to those in which ergot is employed. The seed is made into a tea for dysentery in America. The seed also yields a useful oil, obtained by pressure. The oil-cake can be used like most substances of similar kinds for stock-feeding Propagated by seed.

GRAM. (See *"Cicer arietinum,* Linn.")

GRANADILLA. (See *"Passiflora quadrangularis,* Linn.")

GRAPE VINE. (See *"Vitis."*)

GRASS-CLOTH. (See *"Bœhmeria nivea,* H. et Arn.")

GREASE NUT. (See *"Hernandia bivalvis,* Benth.")

GREVILLEA, *R. Br.*—Order PROTEACEÆ.—Tribe *Grevilleeæ.*

G. ROBUSTA, *A. Cunn.* Silky Oak, or Tuggan-tuggan of the natives in some localities. This is a tall erect tree, semi-deciduous, with a rugged dark bark and much divided fern-like foliage; flowers, which appear just about as the old leaves are falling and the young ones coming on, are of a rich orange colour. The tree is a great favourite for ornamental planting The wood is also highly prized for cooper's and cabinet-maker's work. Besides this, the tree is an excellent one to plant for bees. Propagated by seed.

GREWIA, *Linn.*—Order TILIACEÆ.—Tribe *Grewieæ.*

G. ASIATICA, *Linn.* (*G. subinæqualis*, DC.) A small tree with rounded coarsely and irregularly t othed leaves, obliquely cordate, 5-nerved; flowers about ¾-in. diameter with yellow linear petals; drupe globose, 1 or 2-lobed, pil se, of a pleasant acid flavour. These fruits are commonly used in India for flavouring sherbets. The fruit of *G. polygama*, Roxb., a wide-spread species very common in Queensland, is used by the natives for food, and the bark for making into twine. Most species produce good fibre. Propagated by seed.

GROUND ALMOND. (See "*Cyperus esculentus*, Linn.")
GROUND NUT. (See "*Arachis hypogæa*, Linn.")
GUAVA. (See "*Psidium*.")

GUAZUMA, *Plum.*—Order STERCULIACEÆ—Tribe *Buettnerieæ*.

G. TOMENTOSA, *H. B. et K.* A West Indian tree, but commonly planted in the East Indies for its beauty and use. A moderate-sized tree, the leaves alternate, ovate or oblong, unequal at the base, toothed, acuminate at the apex, stellately puberulous on the upper side, tomentose beneath; petals yellow, with 2 purple awns at the apex. The fruit is filled with mucilage, which is agreeable to the taste. Wood used in India for making furniture, and by coachmakers for panels. The fibre from the young shoots is said to be strong. A decoction of the inner bark is very glutinous, and has been employed to clarify sugar. Propagated by seed and cuttings.

HÆMATOXYLON, *Linn.*—Order LEGUMINOSÆ—Tribe
Eucæsalpinieæ.

H. CAMPEACHIANUM, *Linn.* The Logwood-tree. This is a tree of medium size belonging to Central America, common about the Bay of Campeachy, hence its name. It has pinnate leaves, the small leaflets being very blunt; flowers yellow, small, in short racemes; pod flat, tapering to each end and containing 2 seeds. This well-known dye-wood is largely used by calico-printers and cloth-dyers. The tree thrives well in Queensland and affords an excellent shade, and is often planted for that purpose. Propagated by seed.

HARICOT BEAN. (See "*Phaseolus*.")

HARPULLIA, *Roxb.*—Order SAPINDACEÆ—Tribe *Sapindeæ*.

H. PENDULA, *Planch.* Queensland Tulipwood. A moderately large tree with wide-spreading branches; leaves pinnate, of from 3 to 6 oval leaflets, usually pale-green; flowers in drooping panicles succeeded by orange-coloured membranous capsules of 2 or 3 lobes, each containing a round black seed. This is an excellent shade tree, very hardy, adapting itself to various soils. It produces also a beautifully figured wood, much prized by cabinet-makers. Propagated by seed, which must be sown as soon as ripe.

HAWTHORN or WHITETHORN. (See "*Cratægus*.")
HAZEL NUT. (See "*Corylus*.")

HEDYSARUM, *Linn.*—Order LEGUMINOSÆ—Tribe *Hedysareæ*.

H. CORONARIUM, *Linn.* French Honeysuckle or Soola Clover. This South Europe fodder plant has been tried, but only found to thrive in the cooler parts of the colony, and even there is not a favourite fodder plant. Propagated by seed.

HELEOCHARIS, R. Br.—Order CYPERACEÆ—Tribe *Scirpeæ*.

H. TUBEROSA, *Ræm. et Schult.* (*Matai* or *Petsi*.) A Chinese Rush or Sedge found in ponds, which produces wholesome edible tubers. Propagated by tubers.

HELIANTHUS, *Linn.*—Order COMPOSITÆ—Tribe *Helianthoideæ*.

H. ANNUUS, *Linn.* (the Sunflower), is in cultivation for the sake of its seeds for fowls, and H. TUBEROSUS, *Linn.* (the Jerusalem Artichoke), for its tubers, but to no great extent. Propagated, the first by seed, the other by tubers.

HELICIA TERNIFOLIA, F. v. M. (See "*Macadamia.*")
HEMP. (See "*Cannabis sativa*, Linn.")
HEMP, QUEENSLAND. (See "*Sida rhombifolia*, Linn.")
HENNA. (See "*Lawsonia alba*, Lam.")
HERBERT RIVER CHERRY. (See "*Antidesma Dallachyana*, Baill.")

HERNANDIA, *Linn.*—Order LAURINEÆ—Tribe *Hernandieæ*.

H. BIVALVIS, *Benth.* The Cudgerie or Grease Nut. This is a tall tree with a smooth bark, common in South Queensland scrubs. The leaves are glossy-green, ovate, and on young plants slightly peltate ; flowers white, in loose terminal panicles, very fragrant ; fruit a black ribbed nut, enclosed in 2 red valves, thus appearing like large bell-peppers. The kernels of the nuts contain over 64 per cent. of oil. The wood is light and soft. Propagated by seed.

HEVEA, *Aubl.*—Order EUPHORBIACEÆ—Tribe *Crotoneæ*.

H. BRAZILIENSIS (SIPHONIA), *Muell. Arg.* The Para Rubber. This is a large tree with alternate 3-foliolate leaves ; leaflets lanceolate, petiolulate ; capsule large, with a somewhat fleshy exocarp. The rubber, which is supposed to be the best exported from Para, in Brazil, is there obtained during the dry season by making deep horizontal incisions near the base of the trunk, and then a vertical one extending up the trunk, with others at short distances in an oblique direction. The milky sap is caught in clay cups placed below the incisions. To grow these trees for the caoutchouc, a situation should be chosen within the tropics where the land is rich. Propagated by seed or cuttings.

HIBISCUS, *Linn.*—Order MALVACEÆ—Tribe *Hibisceæ*.

H. ELATUS, *Sw.* (*Paritium elatum.*) The Mountain Mahoe or Cuba-bast tree. This forms a fine shade-giving tree. The leaves are cordate with rather long points, a good deal like those of *H. tiliaceus*. The flowers are large and in the morning of a pale primrose colour, and become orange-coloured and deep-red as the day advances. The timber is said to be of a greenish blue and to be useful for cabinet-work. The lace-like inner bark furnishes the well-known Cuba bast. Fine specimens of this tree are in our public gardens. Propagated by seed and cuttings.

H. ESCULENTUS, *Linn.* The Ochro, Bandakai, or Gobbo. Commonly grown as a culinary vegetable, the mucilaginous capsules and seeds being used. Propagated by seed.

H. SABDARIFFA, *Linn.* The Rosella. This is an annual plant of from 3 to 6 ft. high and spreading. The leaves are of various forms, some undivided, others palmately divided into 3 or 5 lanceolate serrated lobes; flowers pale with centre dark, involucre fleshy, usually red and of a sharp pleasant acid flavour; this latter part is separated and made into jam. From the stems excellent fibre may be obtained. Propagated by seed.

H. TILIACEUS, *Linn.* (*Paritium tiliaceum*, St. Hil.) The Queensland Coast Cotton-tree. A small tree of the coast. Leaves orbicular-cordate, white on the under side; flowers large, yellow with dark centre. From the bark of this tree a useful strong fibre is obtained which in Bengal is largely used in the manufacture of ropes. It also furnishes a pretty wood for cabinet-work. Propagated by seed or cuttings.

HOG PLUM. (See "*Spondias dulcis*, Forst.")

HONDURAS or JAMAICA CEDAR. (See "*Cedrela odorata*, Linn.")

HOP PLANT. (See "*Humulus Lupulus.*")

HORDIUM, *Linn.*—Order GRAMINEÆ—Tribe *Hordeeæ.*

H. DISTICHON, *Linn.* The English Barley produces heavy crops on the Downs, and H. VULGARE is often grown for fodder in other parts of the colony. Propagated by seed.

HOREHOUND. (See "*Marrubium vulgare*, Linn.")

HORSERADISH, COMMON. (See "*Cochlearia Armoracia*, Linn.")

HORSERADISH TREE. (See "*Moringa pterygosperma*, Gærtn.")

HOVENIA, *Thunb.*—Order RHAMNEÆ.

H. DULCIS, *Thunb.* China or Japan Raisin-tree. A tree of medium size with alternate, cordate, serrated leaves; the flowers in terminal forked panicles, small, but the stalks under the pea-like fruit become enlarged and pulpy, with somewhat the flavour of dates. Propagated by seed.

HUMULUS, *Linn.*—Order URTICACEÆ—Tribe *Cannabineæ.*

H. LUPULUS, *Linn.* European Hop-plant. This well-known climbing perennial has been proved to thrive in Queensland about Brisbane, so it is not improbable that before long persons may turn their attention to its profitable cultivation. Propagated by division of roots.

HUNGARIAN GRASS. (See "*Setaria italica*, Beauv.")

HYDROCOTYLE, *Linn.*—Order UMBELLIFERÆ—Tribe *Hydrocotyleæ.*

H. ASIATICA, *Linn.* Asiatic Pennywort ; Bevilaqua of the French. A creeping-stemmed herbaceous plant often met with in damp spots. Leaves reniform, crenated, with about 7 nerves, on long stalks ; the umbels of flowers on usually much shorter stalks than the leaves. The medicinal virtues of this plant have been highly spoken of by many medical men. Propagated by division and seed.

HYMENODICTYON, *Wall.*—Order RUBIACEÆ.—Tribe *Cinchoneæ.*

H. EXCELSUM, *Wall.* (*Cinchona excelsa,* Roxb.) A large deciduous East Indian tree with oblong pubescent leaves and cordate stipules ; the floral leaves coloured, bullate ; panicies of flowers terminal and axillary ; flowers greenish, small, funnel-shaped, 5-parted. The inner bark is bitter and astringent, and is used as a febrifuge, and for tanning, and the wood is also used in India in the manufacture of toys, grain-measures, and other articles. Propagated by seed.

ILEX, *Linn*—Order ILICINEÆ.

I. PARAGUAYENSIS, *St Hil.* The Paraguay Tea-plant or Maté. A small evergreen tree or large shrub, with dark-green, ovate, serrated leaves 3 or 4 in. long ; flowers small, fruit a small berry. The leaves of this plant occupy the same important position in South America as the Chinese tea does with us. It is said to have an agreeable, slightly aromatic odour, and slightly bitter taste, and to be refreshing and restorative. The plant thrives admirably in Queensland. Propagated by seed, cuttings, or layers.

ILLICIUM, *Linn.*—Order MAGNOLIACEÆ—Tribe *Wintereæ.*

I. ANISATUM, *Linn.* Star or Chinese Anise. This is a glabrous evergreen shrub of China and Japan. The leaves are obovate, obtuse, smooth, firm, and fleshy ; flowers usually lateral, nodding ; fruit consisting usually of a number of follicles arranged in the form of a star. The whole plant has a pleasant aromatic flavour of anise. The starry fruits are used in medicine and as a condiment. Propagated by seed, which is produced in abundance by the plants in Queensland.

INDIAN CRESS OR NASTURTION. (See "*Tropæolum.*")
INDIAN RUBBER. (See "*Ficus elastica,* Blume.")
INDIAN SATINWOOD. (See "*Chloroxylon swietenia,* Linn.")
INDIAN TULIP TREE. (See "*Thespesia populnea,* Corr.")
INDIGO. (See "*Indigofera tinctoria,* Linn.")

INDIGOFERA, *Linn.*—Order LEGUMINOSÆ—Tribe *Galegeæ.*

I. TINCTORIA, *Linn* The Common Indigo-plant. This is a spreading bush of 2 or 3 ft. in height, common in the warmest parts of Asia. Branches pubescent, leaves pinnate ; leaflets oblong, cuneate at the base; racemes of flowers shorter than the leaves; flowers small, of a dull colour; pod straight, cylindrical, many-seeded. When planted on rich soil this plant does well in Queensland; indeed, in some parts it has strayed from cultivation and become naturalised. Besides producing a valuable dye, indigo has some reputation as a medicine. The Hindus prescribe it in whooping-cough and affections of the lungs and kidneys. Indigo is applied to the bites and stings of venomous insects and reptiles to relieve the pain; also to burns and scalds. Propagated by seed.

IPOMŒA, *Linn.*—Order CONVOLVULACEÆ—Tribe *Convolvuleæ.*

I. BATATAS, *Poir.* (*Batatas edulis,* Choisy.) Sweet Potato. The well-known trailing plant, with more or less lobed leaves, flowers usually of a pale colour. The rootstock is one of the most valuable products grown in Queensland. The vine makes excellent fodder for stock, and the tubers are a most nutritious food both for man and beast. Propagated by cuttings of the vine.

I. HEDERACEA, *Jacq.* (*I. Nil,* Roth.; *Pharbitis Nil* and *P. hederacea,* Chois.) A lobe-leaved Morning Glory; is often seen in our gardens. The seeds of this twining annual, called in India "Kálá-dánah," are a safe and effectual cathartic, according to most writers on Indian plants. The plant is also found indigenous in Northern Queensland. Propagated by seed.

> JACK FRUIT. (See "*Artocarpus integrifolia,* Linn.")
> JAMAICA or HONDURAS CEDAR. (See "*Cedrela odorata,* Linn.")
> JANIPHA MANIHOT, *Kunth.* (See "*Manihot utilissima,* Pohl.")
> JAPAN WAX PLANT. (See "*Rhus succedanea,* Linn.")
> JASMINE, CAROLINA. (See "*Gelsemium nitidum,* Mich.")

JATEORHIZA, *Miers.*—Order MENISPERMACEÆ—Tribe *Tinosporeæ.*

J. PALMATA, *Miers.* (*Cocculus palmatus.*) Kalumb or Calumba. This is a palmate-leaved climber of Mozambique, which sends up its annual stems like the Hop-plant, which die back to the rootstock again. Flower minute, in straggling panicles. The drug, which consists of round or oval transverse slices of the root, is considered stimulating, and employed in cases of indigestion dependent upon languor and want of tone in the stomach, and attended by nausea and flatulence. It has likewise the effect of alleviating vomiting. Propagated by divisions of the root.

JATROPHA, *Linn.*—Order EUPHORBIACEÆ—Tribe *Crotonia.*

J. CURCAS, *Linn.* Angular-leaved Physic-nut. This is a large shrub or small tree, with broadly cordate, 5-angled, smooth leaves; the flowers are usually in terminal panicles, the male at the ends of the ramification, the female ones in their divisions; fruit globular, ½ to 1 in. diameter, 3-seeded. The seeds are collected in the Philippine

Islands for the purpose of expressing the oil. It is said the Chinese form a varnish by boiling the oil with oxide of iron. A number of cases of poisoning have occurred from persons eating the seeds entire, but it is said that if the embryo is wholly removed, four or five of the seeds may be used as a purgative without producing either vomiting or griping. Propagated by seed.

JATROPHA. (See "*Aleurites* and *Manihot*.")
JATROPHA MANIHOT, *Linn.* (See "*Manihot utilissima*, Pohl.")
JATROPHA MOLUCCANA, *Linn.* (See "*Aleurites moluccana*, Willd.")
JOB'S TEARS. (See "*Coix lachryma*, Linn.")
JONESIA ASOCA, *Roxb.* (See "*Saraca indica*, Miq.")

JUGLANS, *Linn.*—Order JUGLANDEÆ.

J. NIGRA, *Linn.* Black Walnut. This is a tall-growing erect tree of the Western States of North America. It has more numerous toothed leaflets than the Common Walnut, and a more persistent bark; nut spherical, corrugated, edible, but not equal to the Common Walnut; wood purplish-brown, turning dark with age, strong, tough, not liable to warp or split, and said not to be attacked by insects; seed contain more oil than other kinds. Propagated by seed, which the tree at Bowen Park bears in abundance.

JUGLANS REGIA, *Linn.* The European Walnut; fruits well on the Darling Downs. Propagated by seed.

JUJUBE. (See "*Zizyphus jujuba*, Lam.")
JUSTICIA ADHATODA, *Linn.* (See "*Adhatoda Vasica*, Nees.")
JUTE. (See "*Corchorus*.")
KAI APPLE. (See "*Aberia caffra*, Hook.")
KALA-DANAH. (See "*Ipomœa hederacea*, Jacq.")
KALUMB ROOT. (See "*Jateorhiza palmata*, Miers.")
KAMALA TREE. (See "*Mallotus philippinensis*, Muell. Arg.")

KIGELIA, *DC.*—Order BIGNONIACEÆ.—Tribe *Crescentieæ*.

K. PINNATA, *DC.* Sacred tree of Nubia. A large pinnate-leaved tree of Abyssinia. The flower-panicles very long, hanging down from the branches; flowers large, lobed, of a dull-purple colour; fruit oblong, over 1 ft. long and 4 or 5 in. thick, filled inside with a hard fleshy pulp, and traversed by woody fibres; seeds roundish. The fruits, cut in half and slightly roasted, are employed as an outward application in rheumatic and other complaints. Propagated by seed.

KYDIA, *Roxb.*—Order MALVACEÆ.—Tribe *Malveæ*.

K. CALYCINA, *Roxb.* A small tree with palmately nerved entire or lobed leaves, covered with a close short stellate tomentum; flowers in panicles, pale-yellow; bracteoles 4, persistent and enlarging under the fruit. The bark is mucilaginous, and used in parts of India to clarify sugar. A strong fibre is also prepared from it. Propagated by seed or cuttings.

LACTUCA, *Linn.*—Order COMPOSITÆ—Tribe *Cichoriaceæ.*

L. SATIVA, *Linn.* The Garden Lettuce. Grown to perfection in Queensland. Propagated by seed.

LANDOLPHIA, *Beauv.*—Order APOCYNACEÆ—Tribe *Carisseæ.*

L. FLORIDA, *Benth.* (*L. comorensis*, Benth.; *Vahea comorensis*, Boj.; *Willughbeia cordata*, Klotz.) A large woody climber of Tropical Africa, bearing tendrils and ovate-oblong obtuse or acute leaves with prominent lateral nerves; flowers in pedunculate cymes, white and fragrant; corolla-tube slender, about 1 in. long, hairy inside; segments of limb linear-oblong. The fruit has a sweet acidulous pulp. In some districts it is said that the natives, in collecting the juice, make a cut into the bark and collect the juice upon their arm, going from stem to stem until the arm is covered, when, beginning at the elbow, they roll the caoutchouc back towards the hand till it comes off in the form of a ring. Should be planted in Tropical Queensland, the winter cold of the southern parts of the colony being too great for it. Propagated by seed or cuttings.

LAURUS, *Linn.*—Order LAURINEÆ—Tribe *Litseaceæ.*

L. NOBILIS, *Linn.* The Sweet Bay, or the Warrior's Laurel of the ancients. This is a small tree of Asia Minor. Its leaves are lanceolate, with an agreeable aromatic slightly bitter taste; its flowers yellowish, and its fruit succulent and about the size of a small cherry. The leaves are in much request for flavouring by cooks, and for this purpose they have an advantage over many others, being perfectly safe. They are also placed in boxes of dried figs to prevent the fruit from being destroyed by grubs; but this seems useless, as one often finds the fruit so packed destroyed. From the fruit is expressed a butter-like substance known as "oil of bays," which has been used as an external stimulant. This tree thrives well in the cooler parts of Queensland, as on the Darling Downs, but makes a very poor growth near Brisbane. Propagated by layers or seed.

L. CAMPHORA and L. CINNAMOMUM. (See "*Cinnamomum.*")

LAVANDULA, *Linn.*—Order LABIATÆ—Tribe *Ocimoideæ.*

L. VERA, *DC.* (*L. Spica*, Linn.; *L. angustifolia*, Mœnch; *L. officinalis*, Vill.) The Common Lavender, from which oil of lavender is obtained by distillation, and also spirit of lavender, which is prepared by distilling lavender flowers with rectified spirit, a sufficient quantity of water being added to prevent empyreuma.

L. Spica, *DC.* (the *L. Spica (B.)* of Linn.; *L. latifolia,* Vill.) The French Lavender. This yields the oil of spike used by painters on porcelain, and in the preparation of varnishes for artists.

L. Stœchas, *Linn.* The Topped Lavender. A South Europe and North African undershrub. This has long been employed by the Arabs as a medicinal plant. It is said to be the best known plant for binding loose sand. It is also one of the best bee plants; a writer estimates that annually, from an acre of this, 1 ton of the finest flavoured honey can be obtained.

All these Lavenders thrive better in the cooler parts of Queensland, and are propagated by seed or cuttings.

LAWSONIA, *Linn.*—Order Lythrarieæ—Tribe *Lythreæ.*

L. alba, *Lam.* (*L. spinosa,* Linn.; *L. inermis,* Roxb.) The Henna shrub, also called Egyptian Privet. This forms a shrub of 5 to 10 ft., with opposite ovate-lanceolate leaves about 1 in. long; flowers small, in terminal panicles; fruit the size of peppercorns, 4-grooved. The whole plant of a light colour. The decoction of the leaves is of a deep-orange colour. The use of Henna for dyeing the hands and feet is common among Mahometans in Asia and Africa. An ointment made from the leaves is spoken of as having valuable healing properties, and a decoction of them is used as an astringent gargle. When old the plants become more thorny, whence Linnæus' name of "*L. spinosa.*" It may be utilised in hedge-making. Propagated by seed or cuttings.

Leek. (See "*Allium porrum,* Linn.")
Leng, Ling, or Links of China. (See "*Trapa bicornis,* Linn. f.")

LENS, *Greu.* and *Godr.*—Order Leguminosæ—Tribe *Vicieæ.*

L. esculenta, *Mœnch.* (*Ervum Lens,* Linn.) The Lentil. This plant is grown for fodder by a few farmers. Propagated by seed, and should have a calcareous soil.

Lentil. (See "*Lens.*")

LEPIDIUM, *Linn.*—Order Cruciferæ—Tribe *Lepidineæ.*

L. sativum, *Linn.* The Garden Cress. Often grown in private gardens, but seldom for sale. Propagated by seed.

Lemon-scented Ironbark. (See "*Eucalyptus Staigeriana,* F. v. M.")
Lettuce. (See "*Lactuca.*")
Linseed. (See "*Linum.*")

LINUM, *Linn.*—Order Lineæ.

L. usitatissimum, *Linn.* Flax or Linseed. Crops well, but is little cultivated. Propagated by seed.

LITCHI. (See "*Nephelium Litchi*, Camb.")
LOGWOOD. (See "*Hæmatoxylon campeachianum*, Linn.")
LOQUAT. (See "*Photinia japonica*, Lindl.")
LONGAN. (See "*Euphoria Longana*, Lam.")
LUCERNE. (See "*Medicago sativa*, Linn.")

LUFFA, *Cav.*—Order CUCURBITACEÆ—Tribe *Cucumerineæ*.

L. ÆGYPTIACA, *Mill.*, and L. ACUTANGULA, *Roxb.*, are often grown in our gardens, but the fruits are seldom utilised. When very young they are used in India as a vegetable, but more often the vascular network of the ripe or nearly ripe fruit is used as a bath-brush or sponge, also for common scrubbing-brushes, and numerous other useful purposes. Samples of these vegetable sponges may be seen in all chemists' shops. Propagated by seed.

LYCIUM, *Linn.*—Order SOLANACEÆ—Tribe *Atropeæ*.

L. AFRUM, *Linn.* The Caffre-thorn. This has not been found to succeed as a hedge except in the cooler parts of the colony. Propagated by seed.

LYCOPERSICUM, *Mill.*—Order SOLANACEÆ.

L. ESCULENTUM, *Mill.* The Tomato. Largely grown for the market, and in great variety. A small variety is naturalised in the scrubs, and springs up in plenty at every clearing. Propagated by seed.

MACADAMIA, *F. v. M.*—Order PROTEACEÆ—Tribe *Grevilleæ*.

M. TERNIFOLIA, *F. v. M.* (*Helicia ternifolia*, F. v. M.) Queensland Nut. A tall tree of South Queensland and New South Wales. The leaves usually in threes, about 4 to 6 in. long, and on young trees bordered by sharp teeth, entire on old trees; flowers white, in long racemes; fruit globose, often over 1 in. diameter, containing 1 smooth globose or 2 half-round nuts. Besides the nuts, which are fine-flavoured, the wood of this tree is valuable for cabinet-work, being close in the grain and very prettily marked. The tree readily adapts itself to a variety of soils, and therefore should be planted for timber. Propagated by seed.

MACLURA, *Nutt.*—Order URTICACEÆ—Tribe *Moreæ*.

M. AURANTIACA, *Nutt.* Osage Orange or Bow-wood. Is utilised as a hedge plant, and thrives remarkably well. Propagated by seed.

MAHOGANY. (See "*Swietenia Mahagoni*, Linn.")
MAIZE or CORN. (See "*Zea Mays*, Linn.")

MALLOTUS, *Lour.*—Order EUPHORBIACEÆ—Tribe *Crotoneæ.*

M. PHILIPPINENSIS, *Muell. Arg.* (*Rottlera tinctoria*, Roxb.) The Kamála-tree. A tree of medium size, with, when old, a rugged bark; the leaves on long stalks, various as to form, 3 to 6 in. long, with 3 prominent nerves, oval, and pale-coloured on the under side; the fruit-capsules 3-lobed, about ¼ to ½ in. diameter, covered with a red mealy substance which is the kamála used for obtaining an orange-coloured dye, and as an anthelmintic remedy. The Hindu silk-dyers obtain the dye by boiling the kamála with carbonate of soda. Like lycopodium, kamála is inflammable, and resists admixture with water. The tree is very plentiful in Queensland. Propagated by seed.

MANGIFERA, *Linn.*—Order ANACARDIACEÆ—Tribe *Anacardieæ.*

M. INDICA, *Linn.* Mango. An evergreen Indian tree of medium height. The leaves are harsh, alternate, lanceolate, often 1 ft. long when fully grown, but often delicately tinted when young; flowers in terminal panicles; drupe very various in shape and size, also in flavour. The mango is considered the most delicious fruit of India, and is of a more or less kidney form and yellowish colour, and very wholesome. They may be used when unripe for pickling. The kernels of the seeds are said to contain much nourishment, and may be used boiled for food. Unripe mangoes, peeled and cut from the stones and dried in the sun, form the well-known ámchúr or ambok, so largely used in India as an article of diet. Several excellent varieties are cultivated in the colony. Propagated by seed, upon which the better sorts are often grafted.

MANGO. (See "*Mangifera indica,* Linn.")

MANIHOT, *Adans.*—Order EUPHORBIACEÆ—Tribe *Crotoneæ.*

M. GLAZIONI, *Muell. Arg.*—The Ceara Rubber-tree. This is said to form a good-sized tree in its native country, and to be found on rocky granite soil. The root is thick and tuber-like, somewhat like Tapioca-plant; leaves on longish footstalks, 3-lobed; fruit hard. One of the most valuable of rubbers on account of its thriving on dry poor soil. Propagated by seed or cuttings.

M. UTILISSIMA, *Pohl.* (*Jatropha Manihot*, Linn.; *Janipha Manihot*, Kunth.) The Bitter Cassava, Mandioc-plant, or Tapioca-plant of Tropical South America. A woody shrub of 6 or 8 ft. high, with spreading branches; leaves stalked, palmate, divided nearly to the base into about 5 lanceolate attenuate lobes, glaucous on the under side, with often coloured midribs; panicles axillary or terminal; flowers small, reddish, 5-parted; capsule ovate, triangular, tre-coccous; seeds elliptical, blackish. The tubers attain a length of 2 or 3 ft. without the central fibres of the sweet cassava, and can be converted into bread or cakes, the volatile poison of the milky sap being destroyed through pressing of the grated root in the first instance, and the remaining acridity is expelled by the heating process. The starch heated in a moist state furnishes the tapioca. Has been successfully cultivated in Queensland, and good tapioca and cassava bread made. Propagated by seed or strong cuttings of the woody stems.

M. AIPI, *Pohl.* Sweet Cassava is a somewhat similar plant. The roots, however, are reddish and harmless, so can be used without the above preparation; in fact, they only require the boiling of other culinary esculents. Ligneous tough fibres are found through the whole axis of the tubers; this is wanting in the tubers of Bitter Cassava. Propagated by cuttings of the woody stems.

MAPLE. (See *"Acer."*)

MARANTA, *Linn.*—Order SCITAMINEÆ—Tribe *Maranteæ.*

M. ARUNDINACEA, *Linn.* (*M. indica,* Tussac.) A Barbadoes herbaceous plant of 2 or 3 ft. in height; leaves with long sheaths, hairy, blade ovate-lanceolate; panicle terminal, with long sheathing bracts at the ramifications; corolla white, fruit globular. It is from the tubers of this plant that the white arrowroot is obtained, but, not being so productive as the purple, it is seldom grown in Queensland for manufacture. These tubers were supposed to be powerfully alexipharmic, and reputed to possess the property of counteracting the effects of poisoned arrows, whence it is said the name of "Arrowroot" was given. Propagated by division of the roots.

MARJORAM. (See *"Origanum."*)
MARKING NUT. (See *"Semecarpus Anacardium,* Linn.")

MARRUBIUM, *Linn.*—Order LABIATÆ—Tribe *Stachydeæ.*

M. VULGARE, *Linn.* The White Horehound, once a popular remedy for asthmatic complaints, is a naturalised weed in Southern Queensland. Propagated by seed or cuttings.

MATAI or PETSI. (See *"Heleocharis tuberosa,* R. and S.")

MEDICAGO, *Linn.*—Order LEGUMINOSÆ—Tribe *Trifolieæ.*

M. SATIVA, *Linn.* The Lucerne. Largely cultivated for fodder. Propagated by seed.

MEDLAR. (See *"Pyrus germanica,* B. and H.")

MELALEUCA, *Linn.*—Order MYRTACEÆ—Tribe *Leptospermeæ.*

M. LEUCADENDRON, *Linn.* Broad-leaved Tea-tree or Paper-barked Tea-tree. There are several varieties of this tree; some attain to a large size, and others have very broad leaves. They are mostly found growing on wet land. The foliage abounds in essential oil, similar if not identical with that known in commerce as "Cajeput." Propagated by seed.

D .

MELISSA, *Linn.*—Order LABIATÆ—Tribe *Satureineæ.*

M. OFFICINALIS, *Linn.* The Balm-herb. This perennial herb may now and again be seen in market gardens growing luxuriantly, but, although a good bee plant, is not largely cultivated. Propagated by seed or division.

MELON, SWEET or ROCK. (See *"Cucumis."*)
MELON, WATER. (See *"Citrullus."*)

MENTHA, *Linn.*—Order LABIATÆ—Tribe *Satureineæ.*

M. PIPERITA, *Linn.* This perennial herb, from which is obtained by distillation the well-known peppermint oil of commerce, grows well and may often be seen in our gardens, but as yet no attempt has been made at cultivating this and similar plants for distillation. *M. viridis*, Linn. (the Spear-Mint) is grown with the other domestic herbs by market gardeners, and at one time Mr. W. Hill had the common Pennyroyal (*M. Pulegium*, Linn.) growing well at the Botanic Gardens. This plant requires a damp soil. Propagated by division.

M. SATUREIOIDES, *R. Br. Prod.; Flora Austr.* v. 84. (*Micromeria satureioides*, Benth.) The Brisbane Pennyroyal. This is a very common plant in Queensland; on hard stony spots it may often be seen to form a dense turf. This herb has long been used as a medicine by bushmen. It yields by distillation a good-flavoured oil, which may be found to possess medicinal properties. A small sample tried, yielded about 7 oz. from 1 cwt. of the fresh plant. Propagated by seed or division.

MESPILUS GERMANICA, *Linn.* (See *"Pyrus germanica,* Hook.")
MIMOSA. (See *"Acacia."*)
MINT. (See *"Mentha."*)

MORINGA, *Juss.*—Order MORINGEÆ.

M. PTERYGOSPERMA, *Gærtn.* (*Guilandina Moringa,* Linn.; *Hyperanthera Moringa,* Vahl.) Horseradish-tree. A medium-sized tree, with a corky thick bark; the leaves 2 to 3-pinnate; flowers white, in loose panicles, of 5 nearly equal petals; pods long, 1 ft. or more; these are eaten as a vegetable and also pickled. The root has a strong flavour of horseradish, and is used in medicine as a vesicant. A decoction of the rootbark is used as a fomentation to relieve spasm. The seeds are rich in oil; they were formerly known as "Ben-nuts," from which the oil of ben was extracted. Propagated by seed.

MORUS, *Linn.*—Order URTICACEÆ—Tribe *Moreæ.*

All the species of Mulberry thrive in Queensland, and silkworm culture has often been started, but little progress made, owing to the high price of labour. Propagated by cuttings.

MONSTERA, *Adans.*—Order AROIDEÆ—Tribe *Calleæ*.

M. DELICIOSA, *Leib.* A short stout climbing plant of South America, with very large perforated leaves; spatha of flower light-buff, large; fruit cylindrical, very sweet when fully ripe, and by some considered of delicious flavour. Requires a sheltered locality and rich soil. Propagated by cuttings or seed.

MULBERRY. (See *"Morus."*)
MULBERRY, PAPER. (See *"Broussonetia papyrifera,* Vent.")
MURRAY DOWN. (See *"Typha angustifolia."*)
MUNDAR FIBRE. (See *"Calotropis gigantea,* R. Br.")

MUSA, *Linn.*—Order SCITAMINEÆ—Tribe *Museæ*.

M. SAPIENTUM, *Linn.* (the Tall Banana), of which there are several varieties, and M. CAVENDISHII, *Lamb.* (the Dwarf Banana), are largely and profitably grown for home consumption and export. Propagation by offshoots.

MYRICA, *Linn.*—Order MYRICACEÆ.

M. CERIFERA, *Linn.* Wax Myrtle or Bayberry of North America. A small shrub with lanceolate often serrated leaves; male flowers in short catkins; female flowers on different shrubs from the male, the flowers also smaller, and are succeeded by clusters or aggregations of small globular fruits resembling berries, which at first are green but finally become nearly white. They consist of a hard stone studded on the outside with small black grains over which is a crust of dry white wax. This gives to the fruit a granulated appearance. This wax may be collected and used as beeswax. Propagated by suckers; only male plants are in Queensland.

MYRISTICA, *Linn.*—Order MYRISTACEÆ.

M. FRAGRANS, *Houtt.* (*M. moschata,* Thunb.; *M. officinalis,* Linn.) The Nutmeg-tree belonging to the Indian Archipelago. Leaves ovate, elliptical, acute at the base, acuminate at the apex, with about 8 or 9 lateral nerves on each side; peduncles above the axils, the males few-flowered, female flowers solitary, pedicels nearly as long as peduncle; bracteole under the flower broadly ovate, flowers nodding; fruit ovoid-globose, drooping; aril laciniated, red, aromatic, covering the seed. This tree is said to begin to bear at about eight years of age, and to be productive until sixty or more. The mace is the aril of the nut, and prepared by only just sun-drying, but the nuts have to be smoked by slow wood fires for some months before they are ready for exporting. Propagated by seed.

MYROSPERMUM, *Jacq.*—Order LEGUMINOSÆ—Tribe *Sophoreæ*.

M. PEREIRÆ, *Klotz.* Balsam of Peru. A tree of South America with pinnate leaves; the leaflets ovate-lanceolate, 2 or 3 in. long, the number various, the pellucid dots linear; flowers white in axillary racemes, the stamens free or nearly so and falling off with the petals; pod about 2 in. long (samaroid), containing seed at the apex, the rest flattened and wing-like. From this tree is obtained the fragrant bitter aromatic balsam, called Balsam of Peru, having stimulant, tonic, expectorant properties, and at one time employed in chronic asthma, &c. Propagated by seed.

MYRTUS PIMENTA, *Linn.* (See "*Pimenta communis*, Lindl.")

NASTURTION. (See "*Tropæolum.*")

NASTURTIUM, *R. Br.*—Order CRUCIFERÆ—Tribe *Arabideæ.*

N. OFFICINALE, *R. Br.* The well-known Water Cress; grown by market gardeners for sale; but in many mountain streams of Southern Queensland this excellent aquatic salad plant has become naturalised. Propagated by division and seed.

NECTARINE. (See "*Prunus.*")

NEPHELIUM, *Linn.*—Order SAPINDACEÆ.

N. LITCHI, *Camb.* The Litchi, Litschi, Lichi, Leechee, or Litji is a Chinese fruit, often imported in a dry state. The tree is of medium size, with pinnate leaves; the leaflets pale-coloured on the under side, oblong or lanceolate in shape, and 2 or 3 in. long; flowers small, in panicles; the fruit globose, 1 to 1½ in. diameter, the thin brittle shell reddish and rough with wart-like protuberances; the part eaten is the aril which surrounds the seed, which is white and nearly transparent and very sweet when fully ripe; seeds globose. The whole fruit is dried, although only the sweet aril is eaten. This tree is largely cultivated in India for its fruit. It thrives well in Queensland, even about Brisbane, but is better suited to the North. Propagated by seed, and the better kinds by grafting upon the seedlings.

N. LONGANA, *Camp.* (See "*Euphoria.*")

NEW ZEALAND FLAX. (See "*Phormium tenax*, Forst.")

NEW ZEALAND SPINACH. (See "*Tetragonia expansa*, Murray.")

NICOTIANA, *Linn.*—Order SOLANACEÆ—Tribe *Cestrineæ.*

N. TABACUM, *Linn.* The ordinary Tobacco-plant. Profitably cultivated in many parts of Queensland, and a ready market found for the leaf at the several manufactories. Propagated by seed.

NISPERO. (See "*Achras sapota*, Linn.")

NUTMEG. (See "*Myristica fragrans*, Houtt.")

NUX-VOMICA. (See "*Strychnos nux-vomica*, Linn.")

NYCTANTHES, *Linn.*—Order OLEACEÆ—Tribe *Jasmineæ.*

N. ARBOR-TRISTIS, *Linn.* Tree of Sadness. A small Indian tree, the shoots 4-angular, leaves opposite on short stalks, ovate-acuminate; flowers in terminal panicles, very fragrant, white with orange-coloured eye and tube; they expand in the evening, and fall to the ground in the early morning, when they are collected and used as a perfume or for obtaining a dye. Propagated by seed and cuttings.

OAK, ENGLISH. (See *"Quercus."*)

OAT. (See *"Avena."*)

OLEA, *Linn.*—Order OLEACEÆ—Tribe *Oleineæ*.

O. EUROPÆA, *Linn.* The European Olive. This is a well-known small tree with opposite, lanceolate, usually stiff leaves, and axillary racemes of small white flowers, which are succeeded by oval or round drupes. As yet it has not been planted for profit in Queensland; however, it might be planted with advantage in the cooler districts. Propagated by seed; the superior by grafting on seedlings or by truncheons.

OLIVE. (See *"Olea europæa,* Linn."*)

ONION. (See *"Allium cepa,* Linn."*)

ORIGANUM, *Linn.*—Order LABIATÆ—Tribe *Satureineæ*.

O. MAJORANA, *Linn.* (the Knotted or Sweet Marjoram), and O. VULGARE, *Linn.* (the Common or Pot Marjoram), are grown with other herbs by market gardeners. Propagated by division.

ORYZA, *Linn.*—Order GRAMINEÆ—Tribe *Oryzeæ*.

O. SATIVA, *Linn.* The Common Rice-plant. An annual or perennial grass, with long rough leaves; panicles terminal, drooping from the weight of corn, but erect at first; glumes awned or awnless. Found indigenous in Northern Queensland, with dark grain, and very long awns. Many varieties of rice have been introduced into Queensland, and excellent crops have been obtained, both in the North and South. Propagated by seed.

OSAGE ORANGE. (See *"Maclura."*)

OTAHEITEAN APPLE. (See *"Spondias dulcis,* Forst."*)

PACHIRA, *Aubl.*—Order MALVACEÆ—Tribe *Bombaceæ*.

A. ALBA, *Walp.* (*Carolinea alba,* Lodd.) Brazilian Silk Cotton tree. A small branching deciduous tree, with unarmed stem; bark grey; leaves on long footstalks, of 7 petiolulate, elliptical-lanceolate, glabrous leaflets; peduncles stout; flowers large and showy; the petals strap-like, of a cream colour on the inside, and glabrous, the outside clothed with a dense felt of brown hairs; the filaments forked, very numerous. This is spoken of as the most useful tree of New Grenada; the inner bark furnishing the whole country with cordage, which is both strong and durable. The tree thrives well in Queensland. Propagated by seed or cuttings.

PAGODA TREE. (See *"Plumeria acuminata,* Ait."*)

PANDANUS, *Linn.*—Order PANDANEÆ.

P. UTILIS, *Bory.* A Madagascar tree, said to attain the height of 60 ft. Its leaves are long, erect, with sharp red prickles on the edges; the fruit-heads are globular, about 1 ft. in diameter, borne on long stalks; each head will contain about 100 drupes of from 3 to 8 cells. The plant is cultivated at the Mauritius for the sake of its leaves, from which material is obtained for making sugar-bags, &c. Propagated by seed.

PANICUM. (See "*Setaria.*")

PAPAVER, *Linn.*—Order PAPAVERACEÆ.

P. SOMNIFERUM, *Linn.* The Opium Poppy. Has only as yet been grown in a few gardens. It, however, when given an opportunity, thrives, and will likely sooner or later be cultivated for profit. Propagated by seed.

PAPAW TREE. (See "*Carica papaya*, Linn.")

PAPER MULBERRY. (See "*Broussonetia papyrifera*, Vent.")

PAPYRUS. (See "*Cyperus papyrus*, Linn.")

PARAGUAY TEA. (See "*Ilex paraguayensis*, St. Hil.")

PARA RUBBER. (See "*Hevea braziliensis*, Muell. Arg.")

PARITIUM ELATUM. (See "*Hibiscus.*")

PARKINSONIA, *Linn.*—Order LEGUMINOSÆ—Tribe *Eucæsalpinieæ.*

P. ACULEATA, *Linn.* This tall, thorny, leguminous shrub of America, called in Jamaica "Jerusalem Thorn," and in the French West Indian Islands "Genet épineux," grows strongly, and is utilised in hedge-making. Propagated by seed.

PARSLEY. (See "*Carum Petroselinum*, Benth.")

PARSNIP. (See "*Peucedanum.*")

PASSIFLORA, *Linn.*—Order PASSIFLOREÆ.

P. EDULIS, *Sims* (the Small Passion-fruit), P. QUADRANGULARIS, *Linn.* (the Granadilla), and the larger form of this species, P. MACROCARPA, *Masters*, are all cultivated for their fruits. This latter has attained the weight of 8 lbs.

P. LAURIFOLIA, *Linn.* (*P. tinifolia*, Jussieu.) The Water Lemon of the West Indies. This plant is grown in some gardens, but requires the warmth of the tropics to fruit well. Propagated by seed and cuttings.

Passion Fruit. (See "*Passiflora*.")

Pastinaca. (See "*Peucedanum*.")

Patchouli. (See "*Pogostemon Patchouli*.")

Pea, Common Garden. (See "*Pisum sativum*, Linn.")

Peach. (See "*Prunus*.")

Pea Nut. (See "*Arachis hypogæa*, Linn.")

Pear, Alligator. (See "*Persea gratissima*, Gærtn.")

Pear, Common. (See "*Pyrus communis*, Linn.")

Peepul. (See "*Ficus religiosa*, Linn.")

PENNISETUM, *Pers.*—Order Gramineæ—Tribe *Paniaceæ*.

P. thyphoideum, *Rich.* (The *Penicillaria spicata* of Willdenow.) Has been frequently introduced as a fodder-plant, but it is not equal to others, so is but little grown. Propagated by seed.

PENTZIA, *Thunb.*—Order Compositæ—Tribe *Anthemideæ*.

P. virgata, *Less.* South African Fodder-bush. This is a much-branched, rigid little bush, more or less hoary, spreading, and of about 1 or 2 feet high; the flower-heads are yellow, about ½-in. diameter. It has been introduced as a sheep fodder, but, like most South African plants, does not take kindly to the Queensland climate. Propagated by seed or cuttings.

Pepper, Black. (See "*Piper nigrum*, Linn.")

PERESKIA, *Mill.*—Order Cacteæ—Tribe *Opuntieæ*.

P. aculeata, *Mill.* The Barbadoes Gooseberry; often mixed with other plants to form live fences. Produces flowers in abundance, and has been highly praised as a bee plant. P. Bleo is equally valuable for the same purpose. Propagated by seed or cuttings.

PERSEA, *Gærtn.*—Order Laurineæ—Tribe *Perseaceæ*.

P. gratissima, *Gærtn.* (*Laurus Persea*, Linn.) The Alligator or Avocado Pear, also called Vegetable Marrow and Midshipman's Butter. Tree of medium size, found in Brazil, Mexico, and Peru. The branches and inflorescence are pubescent; the leaves alternate, elliptical-oblong, 4 to 7 in. long, of a pale colour; fruit pear-shaped, with a smooth brownish-green or purplish skin, the pulp firm and considered delicious by some. Will only thrive in the tropics. Propagated by seed.

Persica. (See "*Prunus*.")

Peruvian Bark. (See "*Cinchona*.")

Peruvian Pepper Tree. (See "*Schinus molle*, Linn.")

PEUCEDANUM, *Linn.*—Order UMBELLIFERÆ—Tribe *Peucedaneæ.*

P. GRAVEOLENS, *Benth.* (*Anethum graveolens,* Linn.) The Dill, a plant much resembling the Fennel, may be met with now and again in garden culture, the fruits of which were at one time much used in domestic medicine.

P. SATIVUM, *Benth.* (*Pastinaca sativa,* Linn.) The Parsnip. Grown by market-gardeners as a culinary vegetable, but not by farmers for fodder. It is said to be excellent fodder for dairy cows, increasing the supply of milk, and as the plant gives a good crop in Queensland it ought to be grown by dairymen. Propagated by seed.

PHALARIS, *Linn.*—Order GRAMINEÆ—Tribe *Phalarideæ.*

P. CANARIENSIS, *Linn.* The Canary-grass. Yields good crops on the Downs, and forms a good fodder on the coast lands.

PHARBITIS. (See "*Ipomæa.*")

PHASEOLUS, *Linn.*—Order LEGUMINOSÆ—Tribe *Phaseoleæ.*

P. COCCINEUS, *Kniphof.* (*P. multiflorus,* Willd.), the well-known Scarlet Runner, and P. VULGARIS, *Linn.* (Haricot or French Bean), are largely grown for culinary purposes. Propagated by seed.

PHŒNIX, *Linn.*—Order PALMÆ—Tribe *Phœniceæ.*

P. DACTYLIFERA, *Linn.* The Date Palm. This tree is said to attain the height of 60 ft., and to live and bear its fruit for over 200 years. The graceful pinnate foliage causes it always to be a favourite in the garden. In Queensland it is planted for its fruit, and is likely to prove one of the most profitable to grow. *P. sylvestris,* Roxb., also thrives well, and may at some future date be cultivated for both sugar and fibre. Propagated by seed.

PHORMIUM, *Forst.*—Order LILIACEÆ—Tribe *Hemerocalleæ.*

P. TENAX, *Forst.* The New Zealand Flax. This swamp plant has long sword-shaped leaves, which shortly clasp the stem at the base. The flower stem attains a height of 10 to 14 ft., bearing brownish flowers, rich in honey. Although a most useful plant in its own and other cool climates, it is not likely to be much planted in Queensland; for as a rule New Zealand plants do but poorly here, and the present is no exception. Propagated by seed and division.

PHOTINIA, *Linn.*—Order ROSACEÆ—Tribe *Pomeæ.*

P. JAPONICA (ERIOBOTRYA), *Lindl.* (*Cratægus Bibas,* Lour.) The Loquat. This tree is said to attain a large size in its native country, Japan; the leaves are large, oblong, rugose, and with the young shoots often covered by a woolly tomentum. The oval fruit is used in a raw or cooked state, and when the trees are attended to the fruit is large and juicy, but when neglected, as so many are in Queensland, it is worthless. Propagated by seed, or the best varieties by grafting on seedling plants.

PHYLLANTHUS, *Linn.*—Order EUPHORBIACEÆ—Tribe *Phyllantheæ.*

P. DISTICHA, *Muell. Arg.* (*Cicca disticha*, Linn.) Country Gooseberry of India. A small tree with long slender branchlets, resembling pinnate leaves, oval; stipules minute; flowers in axils of the leaves; fruit round, about the size of a gooseberry, green, and about 5-furrowed. In India they are used in various ways. The Europeans make of them pickles and preserves. The fruit is very acid. The seeds are said to be cathartic, and a decoction of the leaves sudorific and diaphoretic. Propagated by seed.

P. EMBLICA, *Linn.* (*Emblica officinalis*, Gærtn.) Another useful Indian tree; also growing in Queensland gardens, but the fruit is not used. In India a sherbet of the fruit, sweetened with sugar or honey, is a favourite cooling drink for sick people; it is said to be diuretic. Propagated by seed.

PHYSALIS, *Linn.*—Order SOLANACEÆ.

P. PERUVIANA, *Linn.* Well known as the Cape Gooseberry. Springs up at almost every clearing, and from these places rather than from cultivated plants the fruit is gathered for sale. Propagated by seed.

PHYSIC NUT. (See "*Jatropha curcas*, Linn.")

PIMENTA, *Lindl.*—Order MYRTACEÆ—Tribe *Myrteæ.*

P. COMMUNIS, *Lindl.* (*P. vulgaris*, W. and A.; *Myrtus Pimenta*, Linn.; *Eugenia Pimenta*, DC.) The Allspice-tree or Jamaica Pepper. A tree; the branchlets compressed, somewhat 4-angled; leaves oblong or oblong-lanceolate; flowers in cymes, calyx 4-lobed, petals 4 or 5; fruit globose. For commerce the fruit is gathered when nearly ripe, as it is found at that period to contain the best essential oil. Will thrive in Northern Queensland. Propagated by seed.

PINE APPLE. (See "*Ananas sativa*, Mill.)
PIONANDRA BETACEA, *Hook.* (See "*Cyphomandra.*")

PIPER, *Linn.*—Order PIPERACEÆ.

P. NIGRUM, *Linn.* Black Pepper. A climbing plant of the Malabar forests, somewhat resembling Ivy. Leaves somewhat cordate, pale on the under side, 7 to 9-nerved; flowers in spikes shorter than the leaves; berries red when ripe. "Black pepper" consists of the dried unripe berries; "white pepper" is the ripe fruit deprived of its rind by macerating. This useful plant thrives well in Queensland. Propagated by seed or cuttings.

PISUM, *Linn.*—Order LEGUMINOSÆ—Tribe *Vicieæ.*

P. SATIVUM, *Linn.* The Common Pea. One of the most common culinary vegetables of Queensland. Propagated by seed.

PITHECOLOBIUM, *Mart.*—Order LEGUMINOSÆ—Tribe *Ingeæ.*

P. DULCP, *Benth.* (*Inga dulcis,* Willd.; *Mimosa dulcis,* Roxb.) A small tree with straggling thorny branches; the leaves consist of 2 pinnæ, each with 2 leaflets; flowers in globular heads, very pale, nearly white; pods twisted and swollen over the seeds; seeds enclosed in a white pellucid aril, which is edible but far from being agreeable. This plant may be utilised in hedge-making. Propagated by seed.

PITA FIBRE. (See "*Agave americana,* Linn.")

PLUM. (See "*Prunus.*")

PLUMERIA, *Linn.*—Order APOCYNACEÆ—Tribe *Plumerieæ.*

P. ACUMINATA, *Ait.* (*P. acutifolia,* Poir.; *P. obtusifolia,* Lour.; *Flos convolutus,* Rumph.) The Franchipanier or Pagoda tree. A small tree with thick obtuse branches, leafy at the ends; leaves oblong, acute at both ends; flower white, very showy and fragrant; follicles cylindric, about 5 in. long. The trivial name is said to be from the French, "Franchipane," coagulated milk, alluding to the milky sap. Flowers useful to the perfumer. Propagated by seeds or cuttings.

POGOSTEMON, *Desf.*—Order LABIATÆ—Tribe *Satureineæ.*

P. PATCHOULI, *Pellet.* The Patchouly or Pucha-pat. An undershrub of 2 or 3 feet, pubescent; leaves stalked, rhomboid-ovate, crenate; flowers in terminal and axillary spikes, white with red stamens, the calyx hairy as well as the filaments The volatile oil is obtained by distillation. The "Sachets de Patchouli" consist of the herb coarsely powdered, mixed with cotton-root and folded in paper. These are placed in drawers to drive away insects. Propagated by seed or cuttings.

POLYGALA, *Linn.*—Order POLYGALEÆ.

P. SENEGA, *Linn.* The Senega or Snake Root. This plant is found in North Carolina and Kentucky in dry rocky woods. The roots are thick and woody, stems about 6 in. high, the base clothed with small, oval, scale-like leaves; the other leaves 1 or 2 in long and about ¼-in. wide; spikes of flowers dense, about 1 or 2 in. long; flowers greenish-white. The roots are supposed to possess medicinal virtues. Propagated by seed or cuttings.

POMEGRANATE. (See "*Punica granatum,* Linn.")

POPLAR-LEAVED FIG. (See "*Ficus religiosa,* Linn.")

PRICKLY POPPY. (See "*Argemone.*")

PROSOPIS, *Linn.*—Order LEGUMINOSÆ—Tribe *Adenantherea.*

P. JULIFLORA, *DC.*, and others of this genus, are growing in our gardens, having been introduced as fodders; but while we can grow so many plants of superior merit, they are not likely to be used. Propagated by seed.

PSIDIUM, *Linn.*—Order MYRTACEÆ—Tribe *Myrteæ.*

P. GUAVA, *Raddi.* The Large Apple or Pear Guava thrives so well that in several localities it has become naturalised. P. CATTLE-YANUM, *Sabine* (the Purple or Strawberry Guava), also bears prolifically, and there are several other varieties of this fruit grown in Queensland. All make excellent preserves. Propagated by seed.

PUDDING-PIPE TREE. (See "*Cassia fistula*, Linn.")

PULQUE. (See "*Agave americana*, Linn.")

PUNICA, *Linn.*—Order LYTHRARIEÆ.

P. GRANATUM, *Linn.* Pomegranate. *Malum punicum; Rimmon* of the Hebrews. A tall shrub or small tree, with opposite oblong-lanceolate leaves; the flowers large, nearly stalkless, scarlet; fruit globose, crowned by the thick calyx lobes; seed covered with a pellucid pulp, of an agreeable acid flavour. The rind of the fruit is a strong astringent, and was at one time employed in dyeing; it was also used by the Romans in tanning leather and in forming gargles. The young plants are cut down and sent from Algeria to England for making into walking-sticks. The plant is sometimes utilised in forming live fences. Propagated by seed or cuttings.

PRUNUS, *Linn.*—Order ROSACEÆ—Tribe *Pruneæ.*

P. AMYGDALUS, *Hook.* (The *Amygdalus communis* of Linnæus.) The Almond; crops well on the Downs.

P. CERASIFERA, *Ehrhart.* (The *P. myrobalanus* of Desf.) The Cherry-Plum. In favourable seasons this tree will bear a few fruit in the Brisbane district, but on the Darling Downs it crops as well as in the southern colonies. Propagated by seed, or root-cuttings upon which approved kinds are worked by budding or grafting.

P. PERSICA, *Hook.* (the *Amygdalus Persica* of Linnæus, the Peach and Nectarine), P. DOMESTICA, *Linn.* (the Plum), P. CERASUS, *Linn.* (the Cherry), and P. ARMENIACA, *Linn.* (the Apricot), fruit well on the Downs, and many varieties succeed well on the coast lands, especially some varieties of American plums and China peaches. Propagated by seed, or root-cuttings upon which are budded or grafted the approved kinds.

PUMPKIN. (See "*Cucurbita.*")

PYRUS, *Linn.*—Order ROSACEÆ—Tribe *Pomeæ.*

P. MALUS, *Linn.* (the Apple), P. COMMUNIS, Linn. (the Pear),
P. CYDONIA, Linn. (the Quince), and P. GERMANICA, Hook. (the
Medlar), all thrive well on the Downs, and a few kinds are found to
fruit fairly on the coast lands. Propagated by seed, or cuttings of the
roots upon which the better varieties are grafted.

QUEENSLAND COTTON TREE. (See "*Hibiscus tiliaceus,* Linn.")
QUEENSLAND HEMP. (See "*Sida rhombifolia,* Linn.")
QUEENSLAND NUT. (See "*Macadamia ternifolia,* F. v. M.")

QUERCUS, *Linn.*—Order CUPULIFERÆ—Tribe *Quercineæ.*

Q. PEDUNCULATA, *Willd.* The English Oak. Thrives and fruits
well in the Brisbane district, and all parts of Southern Queensland.
The plant exhibited in the collection is one raised from acorns ripened in
Brisbane. Many other oaks are doing well in the colony, and amongst
them *Q. suber,* Linn. (the Cork Oak). Propagated by seed.

QUINCE. (See "*Pyrus Cydonia,* Linn.")
RAMEE. (See "*Bœhmeria nivea,* H. and Arn.")

RAPHANUS, *Linn.*—Order CRUCIFERÆ—Tribe *Raphaneæ.*
R. SATIVUS, *Linn.* The Radish. Very plentiful.

RASPBERRY. (See "*Rubus Idæus,* Linn.")
RED CEDAR. (See "*Cedrela Toona,* Roxb.")
REEANA LUXURIANS, *Duri.* (See "*Euchlœna.*")
REEDMACE. (See "*Typha angustifolia.*")
RHEA. (See "*Bœhmeria nivea,* H. and Arn.")

RHEUM, *Linn.*—Order POLYGONACEÆ—Tribe *Rumiceæ.*

R. RHAPONTICUM, *Linn.* The Garden Rhubarb. Grown to
perfection in Queensland, the stalks being very tender and juicy.
Propagated by seed.

RHINACANTHUS, *Nees.*—Order ACANTHACEÆ—Tribe *Justicieæ.*

R. COMMUNIS, *Nees.* (*Justicia nasuta,* Linn.) The Naga-mulli
or Jasmine of the Cobra-di-capello of India; so called, Roxburgh
says, on account of the roots being used for the bite of poisonous
snakes. This shrub is common in our gardens, where it is a favourite
for its pretty white flowers and general neat appearance. It is
generally used in India as a remedy for ringworm; but latterly, Dr.
Dymock says, under the name of "Tong-pang-chong," it has found
considerable favour in Europe as a remedy for chronic eczema and
some other skin affections of a similar character, an extract of the
plant being considered the best preparation. Propagated by seed or
cuttings.

RHUS, *Linn.*—Order ANACARDIACEÆ—Tribe *Anacardieæ.*

R. SEMIALATA, *Murray.* (*R. buckiamela*, Roxb.; *R. javanica*, Linn.) A China, Japan, and East Indian tree of moderate size. The bark rough, with vertical furrows; leaves pinnate, the petiole usually winged above; leaflets 4 to 6 pairs, sessile, toothed, pubescent beneath; panicle long as leaves; drupe $\frac{1}{8}$-in. diameter, orbicular, compressed, red, shining, acid. This tree produces a kind of nutgalls. The wood is tough and durable. Propagated by seed or suckers.

R. SUCCEDANEA, *Linn.* (*R. acuminata*, DC.) Japan Wax-tree. An East Indian deciduous small tree with a thin bark; leaves pinnate, of 3 to 6 pairs of oblong-elliptic or ovate-lanceolate leaflets, with tail-like apex; flowers in slender panicles; drupes $\frac{1}{4}$-in. diameter, gibbous, stone compressed. The crushed drupes, steamed and pressed, furnish about 15 per cent. of wax, which consists mainly of palmatin and palmitic acid. Propagated by seed.

RHODOMYRTUS, *DC.*—Order MYRTACEÆ—Tribe *Myrteæ.*

This is a moderate-sized Tropical Queensland tree, with large, oval-oblong, thin-textured leaves 6 to 10 inches long, with prominent veins; flowers rather large, about 3 together. The fruit is about 1 in. long, juicy, and useful for jam-making. The wood is of a light-grey colour, hard and tough. Propagated by seed.

RIBES, *Linn.*—Order SAXIFRAGEÆ—Tribe *Ribesieæ.*

R. GROSSULARIA, *Linn.* (the Gooseberry), R. NIGRUM, Linn. (Black Currant), and R. RUBRUM, *Linn.* (the Red Currant), will all succeed on the Downs, but not on the coast lands. Propagated by cuttings.

RICE. (See "*Oryza sativa*, Linn.")
RICE PAPER PLANT. (See "*Fatsia papyrifera*, Dcne.")

RICINUS, *Linn.*—Order EUPHORBIACEÆ—Tribe *Crotoneæ.*

R. COMMUNIS, *Linn.* The Castor Oil plant has become naturalised in many parts of Queensland, and large quantities of seed might be collected from wild plants; amongst these may be seen many varieties differing in colour of foliage and size of fruit. Propagated by seed.

ROSE APPLE. (See "*Eugenia Jambos*, Linn.")
ROSELLA. (See "*Hibiscus sabdariffa*, Linn.")
ROSEMARY. (See "*Rosmarinus officinalis*, Linn.")

ROSMARINUS, *Linn.*—Order LABIATÆ—Tribe *Monardeæ.*

R. OFFICINALIS, *Linn.* The Rosemary. This forms a pretty edging for garden walks in the cooler parts of the colony, and may at some future time be grown for its essential oil, which is used in perfumery. Propagated by seed or cuttings.

ROTTLERA TINCTORIA, *Roxb.* (See "*Mallotus.*")

RUBIA, *Linn.*—Order RUBIACEÆ—Tribe *Galieæ.*

R. CORDIFOLIA, *Linn.* (*R. Munqista*, Roxb.; *R. javana*, DC.; *R. alata*, Wall.; *R. secunda*, Moore Cat.) A climbing perennial with leaves in whorls of 4, ovate-cordate, acute, 3 to 7-nerved; the whole plant very rough; flowers in terminal cymes, white, minute. This plant in India produces a kind of madder. *R. tinctoria*, Linn., the Common Madder, was grown by Mr..W. Hill some years ago in the Brisbane Botanic Gardens, but it did not thrive so well as *R. cordifolia* is at present doing at Bowen Park. Propagated by seed and cuttings.

RUBUS, *Linn.*—Order ROSACEÆ—Tribe *Rubeæ.*

R. IDÆUS, *Linn.* The Raspberry fruits on the Downs, but has not been a success on the coast lands; but if hybridised with our native species (*R. rosæfolius*, Sm.), a hardy fruitful kind might probably be obtained; the wild one fruits well but is wanting in flavour. A few American Blackberries bear abundance of rich juicy fruit around Brisbane; one of the most prolific is that known as Lawton's Blackberry. Propagated by suckers or layers.

RUE. (See *"Ruta graveolens*, Linn.")

RUTA, *Linn.*—Order RUTACEÆ—Tribe *Ruteæ.*

R. GRAVEOLENS, *Linn.* The Rue-plant, which at one time was much used in domestic medicine. It is an active irritant whether applied externally or taken internally. Propagated by cuttings.

RYE. (See *"Secale cereale*, Linn.")

SACCHARUM, *Linn.*—Order GRAMINEÆ—Tribe *Andropogoneæ.*

S. OFFICINARUM, *Linn.* The Common Sugar-cane. Largely cultivated in the colony, and sugar forms one of the chief exports. Propagated by cuttings.

SAGE. (See *"Salvia officinalis*, Linn.")

SAGITTARIA, *Linn.*—Order ALISMACEÆ.

S. SINENSIS, *Sims.* (*S. sagittifolia*, Lour., or the Chinese Arrowhead.) Forms edible rhizomes, which are used for food in China. This plant may probably sooner or later become naturalised in the swamps. Propagated by divisions.

SALIX, *Linn.*—Order SALICINEÆ.

WILLOWS grow well, and on wet land in the more southern parts of the colony might profitably be planted for basket-work.

SALVIA, *Linn.*—Order LABIATÆ—Tribe *Monardeæ.*

S. OFFICINALIS, *Linn.* The Garden Sage. Grown with other herbs by market gardeners.

SAMBUCUS, *Linn.*—Order CAPRIFOLIACEÆ—Tribe *Sambuceæ.*

S. NIGRA, *Linn.* The Elder grows and fruits well on the downs of Southern Queensland.

SANDALWOOD. (See *"Santalum album,* Linn.")

SANSEVIERIA, *Thunb.*—Order HÆMODORACEÆ—Tribe *Ophiopogoneæ.*

S. CYLINDRICA, *Boj.* (*S. angolensis,* Wellw.) Ifé; Tercte-leaved Bowstring Hemp. This plant has long, erect, stout, terete leaves, which arise in tufts from a creeping rhizome; scape below the flowers about 1 ft. long, flower-racemes also about 1 ft. long; flowers white and pink, stamens much exserted. At Angola excellent fibre is produced from this plant. *S. zeylanica,* Willd., and several other species are in our gardens and grow very rapidly; thus are well adapted for cultivating for fibre. Propagated by division.

SANTALUM, *Linn.*—Order SANTALACEÆ.

S. ALBUM, *Linn.* Indian Sandalwood. This forms a round-headed small tree. Leaves opposite, foot-stalks short, oblong, entire, of a glaucous colour on the under side; flowers in axillary or terminal panicles, yellowish at first; berry round, black when ripe. This furnishes the fragrant wood of commerce. The sandal oil is obtained by slow distillation from the heartwood and roots. Propagated by seed.

SAPODILLA PLUM. (See *"Achras sapota,* Linn.")

SARACA, *Linn.*—Order LEGUMINOSÆ—Tribe *Amherstieæ.*

S. INDICA, *Miq.* (*Jonesia Asoca,* Roxb.) An East Indian small tree of great beauty. Leaves drooping, pinnate; leaflets lanceolate, about 6 pairs; flowers in dense large clusters, scarlet; ripe pods cimeter-shaped. The bark is used medicinally by the Hindu physicians. Propagated by seed or cuttings.

SARSAPARILLA. (See *"Smilax."*)

SCARLET RUNNERS. (See *"Phaseolus."*)

SCHINUS, *Linn.*—Order ANACARDIACEÆ—Tribe *Anarcardieæ.*

S. MOLLE, *Linn.* Peruvian Pepper or Mastic tree. Molli or Molle of the Peruvians, An evergreen small tree with pinnate leaves, the leaflets entire or serrated, lanceolate; flowers small in terminal or axillary panicles; berries pink, somewhat pungent, and used as a condiment. The tree thrives well in Queensland, and is often used in ornamental planting. Propagated by seed.

SEBESTAN FRUIT. (See *"Cordia Myxa,* var. *latifolia."*)

SECALE, *Linn.*—Order Gramineæ—Tribe *Hordeæ.*

S. cereale, *Linn.* The Rye. On the coast lands this is sometimes grown for fodder, but on the Downs it is cultivated for both fodder and grain. Propagated by seed.

SEMECARPUS, *Linn f.*—Order Anacardiaceæ—Tribe *Anacardieæ.*

S. Anacardium, *Linn. f.* Marking-nut of India. Tree of medium size with rugged bark; the leaves oblong to ovate-lanceolate, the veins prominent and pale on the under side, 4 to 8 in. long; flowers small, in pyramidal terminal panicles; fruit somewhat reniform, seated upon a yellowish or red succulent base. This latter part is edible either raw or roasted, but the nut contains a corrosive juice which is poisonous. The root-bark is very thick and contains a large quantity of acrid juice similar to that found in the pericarp; this dries into a black varnish. The tree is not uncommon on the coast of Tropical Queensland, and grows and fruits well about Brisbane. Propagated by seed.

Senegal or Snake Root. (See "*Polygala senega,* Linn.")

Senna Plant. (See "*Cassia obovata,* Coll.")

SESAMUM, *Linn.*—Order Pedalineæ—Tribe *Sesameæ.*

S. indicum, *Linn.* Til or Gingelly Oil plant. This plant is cultivated in India for the oil which is obtained from its seeds. Since its introduction about twenty years ago the plant has become naturalised. Propagated by seed.

SESBANIA, *Pers.*—Order Leguminosæ—Tribe *Galegeæ.*

S. aculeata, *Pers.* A tall rapid-growing annual, often found as a weed in cultivation on rich damp land, and indigenous about the margins of rivers and swamps in Queensland. It has long, narrow, pinnate leaves, and drooping racemes of yellowish flowers, which are succeeded by long narrow pods containing oblong beans; these, in the interior, are used as food by the natives. This plant yields an excellent fibre, and in India is grown for that purpose. Propagated by seed.

SETARIA, *Beauv.*—Order Gramineæ—Tribe *Paniceæ.*

S. italica, *Beauv.* (*Panicum italicum,* Linn.; *P. germanicum,* Roth.) Italian Millet, Hungarian Grass, or German Millet, known as Panicum in Queensland. A tall, leafy, annual Indian grass of very quick growth. The panicles are often nodding by the weight of grain. In India this grass is held in high esteem for its grain, which is used especially by the Brahmins for cakes and porridge; boiled with milk it makes a pleasant light diet for invalids. As a green fodder it is equal to any, and the grain is one of the best for poultry. In America it is cut when in flower for forage. On good soil if the ground be moist, it will be ready for mowing 60 days from being sown, and produce from 2 to 4 tons of hay per acre. Propagated by seed.

SHALLOT. (See "*Allium Ascalonica*, Linn.")

SIDA, *Linn.*—Order MALVACEÆ—Tribe *Malveæ*.

S. RHOMBIFOLIA, *Linn. Sida retusa* or Sida-weed. A tall quick-growing undershrub, attaining on rich land the height of 8 to 12 ft. in a season. Leaves very various when on healthy plants, ovate-lanceolate, obtuse, cuneate towards the base; flowers on pedicels often as long as the leaves, yellow, opening in the middle of the day; fruit-carpels about 10. This is a pest in cultivation; but from its stems a very fine fibre is obtainable in Queensland. Large quantities of this fibre are obtained in India for the European market. Propagated by seed.

SIDA WEED or QUEENSLAND HEMP. (See "*Sida rhombifolia*, Linn.")

SILK COTTON TREES. (See "*Bombax*" and "*Eriodendron*.")

SILKY OAK. (See "*Grevillea robusta*, A. Cunn.")

SISSOO. (See "*Dalbergia Sissoo*, Linn. f.")

SMILAX, *Linn.*—Order LILIACEÆ—Tribe *Smilaceæ*.

SARSAPARILLAS. Many of the medicinal species of this genus are in our gardens in a most neglected state. Propagated by division or seed.

SNAKE ROOT. (See "*Polygala senega*, Linn.")

SOLANUM, *Linn.*—Order SOLANACEÆ.

S. MAGLIA, *Schlecht.* Has been grown in the Botanic Gardens, and found to crop well, but no further experiments have been made. Propagated by tubers.

S. MELONGENA, *Linn.* The Egg-plant, called also Aubergines, Bringals, or Begoons. These grow like weeds, but are not in much demand as culinary vegetables. S. TUBEROSUM, *Linn.*, the well-known Potato, crops well at two periods of the year in all parts of Southern Queensland. Propagated by seed.

SORGHUM, *Pers.*—Order GRAMINEÆ—Tribe *Andropogoneæ*.

SORGHUMS of several kinds are largely grown for fodder. Great Honduras, Johnstone-grass, Imphee, and Black Sorghum are some of the names under which they are known by farmers. Propagated by seed.

E

SPADIC PLANT OF PERU. (See "*Erythroxylon Coca*, Lam.")
SPINACH. (See "*Spinacia oleracea*, Linn.")

SPINACIA, *Linn.*—Order CHENOPODIACEÆ—Tribe *Atriplicæ.*

S. OLERACEA, *Linn.* The Garden Spinach or Spinage. A vegetable very seldom grown for sale, although it thrives very well. Propagated by seed.

SPONDIAS, *Linn.*—Order ANACARDIACEÆ—Tribe *Spondieæ.*

S. DULCIS, *Forst.* Hog Plum, Otaheitean Apple, Vi Apple, Wi Apple. A tall tree with a smooth whitish bark and pinnate leaves, glabrous, with dark-green ovate leaflets, serrated on the edge; fruit oval, sometimes large and weighing over 2 lbs. These have a nice fragrance and flavour, and in Viti are said to be used as food. Propagated by seed.

STAR ANISE. (See "*Illicium anisatum*, Linn.")
STAR APPLE. (See "*Chrysophyllum Cainito*, Linn.")
STILLINGIA SEBIFERA, *Mich.* (See "*Excœcaria.*")

STROPHANTHUS, *DC.*—Order APOCYNACEÆ—Tribe *Echitideæ.*

S. KOMBE, *Oliver.* A woody climber of Tropical Africa; shoots hairy, compressed at the nodes; leaves about 3 in. long, 2 in. broad, scabrous, hairy above but more densely so beneath; pedicels hairy, about as long as calyx; calyx-lobes ½-in. long; corolla puberulous, lobes of corolla elongated to 2 in.; follicles 1 ft. or more long, terminating in a subpeltate disk of about ⅓-in. diameter. A new and valuable medicine has lately been obtained from this plant, which has been useful in pulmonary œdema, pneumonia, &c. Propagated by seed.

STRYCHNOS, *Linn.*—Order LOGANIACEÆ—Tribe *Euloganieæ.*

S. NUX-VOMICA, *Linn.* (*S. ligustrina*, Blume; *S. colubrina*, W. and Wight.) Nux-vomica. A small Indian tree, with a close-grained light-coloured wood; the leaves ovate, 5-nerved, glabrous, about 3 in. long, 2 in. wide; cymes of flowers terminal; flowers small; fruit globose, about 1 in. diameter. The fruit of this tree is highly poisonous; the seeds contain the two poisons, strychnia and brucia. The pulp of the fruit is said by some to be innocuous, while others consider it poisonous. Propagated by seed.

SUGAR CANE. (See "*Saccharum officinarum*, Linn.")
SUGAR MAPLE. (See "*Acer saccharinum*, Wang.")
SUNFLOWER. (See "*Helianthus.*")
SUNN HEMP. (See "*Crotalaria.*")
SWEET POTATO. (See "*Ipomœa Batatas*, Poir.")
SWEET SOP. (See "*Anona squamosa*, Linn.")

SWIETENIA, *Linn.*—Order MELIACEÆ—Tribe *Cedreleæ*.

S. MAHAGONI, *Linn.* Mahogany-tree. A large West Indian timber tree, with pinnate glabrous leaves; the leaflets about from 6 to 10, ovate-lanceolate; panicles of flowers axillary; petals twisted; capsule woolly, seeds with a terminal oblong wing. This valuable tree is largely planted in the East Indies. It thrives well in Queensland, and should be planted for its wood. Propagated by seed.

SYMPHYTUM, *Linn.*—Order BORAGINEÆ—Tribe *Borageæ*.

S. ASPERRIMUM, *Sims.* Prickly Cumfrey. This large, leafy, herbaceous plant was introduced some years ago as a′ fodder, for which, however, it has not proved a success. Where the soil is good enough to grow Cumfrey, far more profitable fodders can be grown in Queensland. Propagated by seed or division.

TACCA, *Forst.*—Order TACCACEÆ.

T. PHALLIFERA, *Blume.* (See "*Amorphophallus campanulatus*, Bl.")

T. PINNATIFIDA, *Forst.* This plant, which is plentiful on sandy land in Tropical Queensland, is the one from which the main supply of the Fiji arrowroot is prepared. This arrowroot is particularly recommended in cases of dysentery and diarrhœa. Propagated by seed or roots.

TALINGA POTATO. (See "*Amorphophallus campanulatus*, Bl.")

TAMARIND, INDIAN. (See "*Tamarindus indica*, Linn.")

TAMARIND, QUEENSLAND. (See "*Diploglottis Cunninghamii*, Hook.")

TAMARINDUS, *Linn.*—Order LEGUMINOSÆ—Tribe *Amherstieæ*.

T. INDICA, *Linn.* Tamarind-tree. This is a large evergreen Indian tree. The bark is rough, and the wood hard and durable; the leaves are glabrous and pale-coloured, composed of from 10 to 20 pairs of oblong-linear leaflets about ½-in. long; the stipules are small and deciduous; flowers yellow, in loose short racemes; bracts deciduous; pod thick, about 3 to 6 in. long and 1 in. broad. The pulp of the pods is used in medicine as a laxative, and also made into preserves. The leaves are used in curries; and the seeds, ground into powder and mixed with gum, give a strong cement. The tree thrives both North and South in Queensland. Propagated by seed.

TANACETUM, *Linn.*—Order COMPOSITÆ—Tribe *Anthemideæ*.

T. VULGARE, *Linn.* The Common Tansy grows well in Queensland, and is cultivated with other domestic herbs. Propagated by seed or division.

TANSY. (See "*Tanacetum.*")

TAPIOCA PLANT. (See "*Manihot utilissima*, Pohl.")

TARAXACUM, *Hall.*—Order Composite**—Tribe** *Cichoriaceæ.*

T. dens-leonis, *Hall.* The Dandelion is grown now and again for medicinal purposes, but on the coast land does not thrive very well. Propagated by seed or roots.

Taro. (See "*Colocasia.*")

Tea Plant, China. (See "*Camellia Thea*, Link.")

Tea Plant, Paraguay. (See "*Ilex paraguayensis*, St Hil.")

Teak. (See "*Tectona grandis*, Linn.")

Teazel. (See "*Dipsacus fullonum*, Linn.")

TECTONA, *Linn. f.*—Order Verbenaceæ**—Tribe** *Viticeæ.*

T. grandis, *Linn. f.* Teak-tree of India. A large deciduous tree, with a thick grey bark; the young shoots 4-angled; leaves opposite, oval, very large, rough above, downy beneath; panicle terminal, flowers white, fruit 4-celled. The wood is one of the best in India; it does not split, crack, or alter its shape when once seasoned, and is said not to be attacked by the white ant. From the leaves is obtained a red dye. The wood gives an oil which is used medicinally, and as a substitute for linseed oil, and as a varnish. The tree thrives well in Queensland. Propagated by seed.

Teosinte. (See "*Euchlœna luxurians*, Achers.")

TETRAGONA, *Linn.*—Order Ficoideæ.

T. expansa, *Murray.* The New Zealand Spinach. This is met with on the Queensland coast and around swamps in a wild state, and, as in other countries, used as a culinary vegetable. Propagated by seed.

Thea chinensis, *Sims.* The Tea-plant. (See "*Camellia.*")

THEOBROMA, *Linn.*—Order Sterculiaceæ.**—Tribe** *Buettnericeæ.*

T. cacao, *Linn.* The Cocoa or Chocolate tree. A small tree of Tropical America, with oblong acuminate entire leaves, with about 10 pairs of lateral nerves; flowers on the branches and stems; the calyx somewhat rosy, the petals yellowish; fruit 10-ribbed, 5-celled, 3 to 6 in. long, containing numerous rather large seeds. From these the well-known cocoa is prepared. Has fruited in Queensland, and should be planted for its commercial produce in Tropical Queensland. The hills about Cairns are recommended. Propagated by seed.

THESPESIA, *Correa.*—Order Malvaceæ**—Tribe** *Hibisceæ.*

T. populnea, *Corr.* The Tulip-tree of India; has a very wide range, being found in Western Africa, South America, and the islands of the Pacific, besides Tropical Queensland and New Guinea. It forms a lofty tree and affords excellent shade. The large hibiscus-like flowers are yellow with purple centre. The bark yields a strong fibre, and is used in Demerara for making coffee-bags and cordage. The wood has a pretty grain and is useful for cabinet-work, gunstocks, &c. The capsules yield a yellow dye, and the seeds a thick deep-red coloured oil. Propagated by seed or cuttings.

THYME. (See *"Thymus vulgaris*, Linn.")

THYMUS, *Linn.*—Order LABIATÆ—Tribe *Satureineæ*.

T. VULGARIS, *Linn.* The Common Garden Thyme is grown with other herbs by market gardeners. The Lemon Thyme is often used in the cooler parts of the colony for an edging for garden-walks. Propagated by cuttings.

TOMATO. (See *"Lycopersicum esculentum*, Mill.")

TRAPA, *Linn.*—Order ONAGRARIEÆ.

T. BICORNIS, *Linn. f.* The Leng, Ling, or Links of China have been grown in waterholes near Brisbane, but as yet do not seem likely to become naturalised. Probably the plant is kept back by water animals eating the nuts. Propagated by seed.

TREE OF THE GODS. (See *"Ailanthus.*")

TREE OF SADNESS. (See *"Nyctanthes arbor-tristis*, Linn.")

TREE, TOMATO. (See *"Cyphomandra tebacea*, Sendt.")

TRIFOLIUM, *Linn.*—Order LEGUMINOSÆ—Tribe *Trifolieæ*.

T REPENS, *Linn.* The White or Dutch Clover has become naturalised in the cooler parts of the colony, and is also commonly grown for fodder This is also an excellent bee-plant. Propagated by seed.

TRITICUM, *Linn.*—Order GRAMINEÆ—Tribe *Hordeeæ*.

T. VULGARE, *Villars*, which is considered to include all the cultivated wheats, has proved, under proper cultivation, to be well suited for the Downs, and several Indian varieties have proved suitable for coast lands. Wheat has been known to produce a crop even far into Tropical Queensland. Propagated by seed.

TROPÆOLUM, *Linn.*—Order GERANIACEÆ—Tribe *Pelargonieæ*.

T. MAJUS, *Linn.* The Indian Cress or Nasturtion, so frequently pickled as a substitute for Capers, does remarkably well in Queensland, and may frequently be seen in our flower-gardens, where the rich colouring of their blooms makes them especial favourites. Propagated by seed.

TULIP TREE, INDIAN. (See *"Thespesia populnea*, Corr.")

TULIP-WOOD, QUEENSLAND. (See *"Harpullia pendula*, Planch.")

TYPHA, *Linn.*—Order TYPHACEÆ.

T. ANGUSTIFOLIA, *Linn.* The Bullrush, Reedmace, or Cats-tail is plentiful in most of the still waters in Southern Queensland, but has not been utilised, although a few years ago a trade was carried on in the southern colonies, collecting the spikes of inflorescence, which were used in stuffing pillows, &c., under the name of "Murray down." The rootstocks contain much starch, and can be used for food. The leaves, both in Europe and India, are employed in making mats and baskets. Propagated by division of rhizome and seed.

UPAS TREE. (See "*Antiaris toxicaria.*")

VANILLA, *Plum.*—Order ORCHIDEÆ—Tribe *Neottieæ.*

V. AROMATICA, *Sw.*, and V. PLANIFOLIA, *Andr.* The Vanilla of commerce is the dried capsules of these climbing plants. They thrive well in Queensland, but only in the tropical parts. Propagated by cuttings.

VI APPLE. (See "*Spondias dulcis,* Forst.")

VICIA, *Linn.*—Order LEGUMINOSÆ—Tribe *Vicieæ.*

V. FABA, *Linn.* The Broad Bean. Grown by the market gardeners for culinary purposes, but the variety known as the Horse Bean is seldom grown as a field crop. Our farmers perhaps overlook the value of this plant for a rotation crop. V. SATIVA, *Linn.*, is grown for fodder. Propagated by seed.

VIGNA, *Savi.*—Order LEGUMINOSÆ—Tribe *Phaseoleæ.*

V. SINENSIS, *Endl.* (Linnæus' *Dolichos sinensis.*) Represented by the varieties *V. sesquipedalis* and *V. melanophthalma.* The first of these, which has been called German Bean, may be known by its long pods and (when ripe) red seeds. The pods of the latter are shorter, and the ripe seeds white with a black or dark eye. When boiled, these are of a much softer nature than the common French beans. Propagated by seed.

VITIS, *Linn.*—Order AMPELIDEÆ.

V. VINIFERA, *Linn.* The Common Grape. Largely grown both for the table and wine. There are also many varieties of the American *V. Labrusca,* Linn., and *V. vulpina,* Linn., in cultivation, which are favourites with some on account of their not being so liable to the oidium disease. Propagated by cuttings.

WALNUT. (See "*Juglans.*")
WATER CRESS. (See "*Nasturtium officinale,* R. Br.")
WATER LEMON. (See "*Passiflora laurifolia,* Linn.")
WATER MELON. (See "*Citrullus.*")

WAX, JAPAN. (See *"Rhus succedanea*, Linn.")

WAX MYRTLE, or BAYBERRY. (See *"Myrica cerifera*, Linn.")

WEST INDIAN and GUATEMALA RUBBER. (See *"Castelloa elastica,* Cerv."*)

WHAMPEE. (See *"Clausena Wampi*, Oliver.")

WHEAT. (See *"Triticum."*)

WHITE THORN. (See *"Cratægus."*)

WI APPLE. (See *"Spondias dulcis*, Forst.")

WILLOW. (See *"Salix."*)

WILLUGHBEIA CORDATA, *Klotz.* (See *"Landolphia."*)

WINE PALM. (See *"Diplothemum maritimum*, Mart."*)

WITHANIA, *Pauq.*—Order SOLANACEÆ—Tribe *Solaneæ.*

W. SOMNIFERA, *Dun.* (*Physalis somnifera.*) A soft-wooded shrub of 2 or 3 ft.; the stems flexuose; leaves ovate, entire, in pairs, pubescent like the stems; flowers axillary, yellowish; berry red, about the size of a pea, covered with the somewhat angular inflated calyx. The fruit are employed in the coagulation of milk in making butter. The root is said to act medicinally much like that of Podophyllum. Propagated by seed.

YAMS. (See *"Dioscorea."*)

YERCUM FIBRE. (See *"Calotropis gigantea*, R. Br.")

YUCCA, *Linn.*—Order LILIACEÆ—Tribe *Dracæneæ.*

Y. ALOIFOLIA, *Linn.*, Y. GLORIOSA, *Linn.*, and several other kinds are common plants of our gardens; they will grow on any rocky poor soil. Some day they may be planted for their fibre, which is similar to that obtained from the *Agaves* and *Furcræas.* Propagated by seed or divisions of the roots.

ZEA, *Willd.*—Order GRAMINEÆ—Tribe *Maydeæ.*

Z. MAYS, *Linn.* The Maize or Corn. Largely and profitably grown. Besides the many uses as food, &c., to which the grain is put, and the green plant as fodder, the silky tassel (the stigmata) is used, it is said, with good effect in decoction in diseases of the bladder. The drug is called *"Stigmata Maidis,"* and is said to be of undoubted value in pystitis and cystitis. Propagated by seed.

ZINGIBER, *Adans.*—Order SCITAMINEÆ—Tribe *Zingibereæ.*

Z. OFFICINALIS, *Rosc.* The Ginger of commerce. Stems from creeping rhizome 1 to 3 ft. high, clothed by the sheathing bases of the grass-like leaves; flowers in a somewhat cone-like spike arising from the rhizome, the flowers closely protected by bracts; filaments prolonged beyond the anther in the form of a long beak. There are several varieties of Ginger in the colony which, with very little care, yield a good crop. Propagated by division of rhizomes.

ZIZYPHUS, *Juss.*—Order RHAMNEÆ—Tribe *Zizypheœ.*

Z. JUJUBA, *Lam.* Jujube. A small deciduous tree with short stipular prickles, sometimes wanting; leaves ovate or nearly orbicular, obtuse, 1 to 3 in. long, entire or toothed, 3-nerved, glabrous above, covered underneath, as well as the petioles and branchlets, with a close white or rusty tomentum; cymes small, flowers small; drupe globular, about ¾-in. diameter. Fruit eatable; the bark may be used in tanning, and the plant forms a strong hedge. Propagated by seeds or cuttings of the roots.

ADDITIONS AND CORRECTIONS TO ECONOMIC PLANTS.

ALEPPO SENNA. (See "*Cassia obovata,* Colla.")

BABUL. (See "*Acacia.*")

CARROT. (See "*Daucus.*")

ENDEAVOUR RIVER PEAR. (See "*Eugenia eucalyptoides,* F. v. M.")

EUGENIA, *Lindl.* ·

E. EUCALYPTOIDES, *F. v. M.*, Fragm. iv. 55; Flora Austr. iii. 285. (*Jambosa eucalyptoides,* F. v. M., Fragm. i. 226.) The Endeavour River Pear. A tall shrub or small tree, the branches drooping; leaves long, narrow. Flowers rather large and showy, borne in cymes at the ends of the branches. Fruit usually pear-shaped, about 1½ in. long, rosy-red and white, very beautiful and of agreeable flavour. This tree, apart from its usefulness as a fruit, is well worthy of cultivation for its beauty, and when better known will be in great demand for ornamental planting. At present the only tree in cultivation is at Hockings's Nursery, South Brisbane. The tree is found on the borders of rivers from the Victoria River in North Australia to the Endeavour River in Queensland. Propagated by seed.

FUNARIA, *Linn.*—ORDER PAPAVERACEÆ—Sub-order *Funarieœ.*

F. OFFICINALIS, *Linn.* The Common Fumitory. This is a delicate annual weed, of a pale-green colour, of weak trailing habit, the leaves much divided and the segments generally 3-lobed. Flowers in racemes of 1 to 2 in. long, the petals oblong, closed so as to form a tubular corolla, with dark-coloured tips; the nuts nearly globular. This introduced weed of some of our gardens may rank as of economic importance, as we find it mentioned by medical writers as possessing laxative and diuretic properties, and said to have been found useful in cases of dyspepsia depending upon torpidity of the liver, and in scrofulous skin affections. Dose—2 oz. of the decoction (1 oz. to 1 pint) three times a day.—*Dymock* in Veg. Mat. Med. W. India, 53.

INDIGOFERA.

I. ANIL, *Linn.* The West Indian Indigo. A shrub of a few feet in height, more or less clothed with a light pubescence. The leaves have from 3 to 7 pairs of leaflets. The flowers are borne in dense rather short racemes, and the seed-pods are sickle-shaped, bearing from 3 to 6 seeds. This plant is said to yield excellent indigo. It thrives well in all parts of Queensland. Propagated by seed.

MANGOLD or MANGOL WURZEL. (See "*Beta.*")

MECCA SENNA. (See "*Cassia angustifolia,* Vahl.")

PARITIUM. (See "*Hibiscus.*")

POTATO. (See "*Solanum.*")

RHODOMYRTUS, page 61.—Under generic name add R. MACROCARPA, *Benth.*

SHOLA OR SOLAH. (See "*Æschynomene.*")

STIGMATA MAIDIS. (See "*Zea Mays.*")

TENNEVELLY SENNA. (See "*Cassia acutifolia,* Delile.")

TREE TOMATO, page 69.—For *tebacea* read *betacea.*

WEST INDIAN INDIGO. (See "*Indigofera Anil,* Linn.")

By Authority: JAMES O. BEAL, Government Printer, Brisbane.

F

QUEENSLAND COMMISSION.

Centennial International Exhibition, Melbourne, 1888

---◆---

A FEW QUEENSLAND GRASSES

WITH

SHORT NOTES, RANGE OF EACH SPECIES,
&c., &c.

BY

FREDK. MANSON BAILEY, F.L.S.,

COLONIAL BOTANIST.

BRISBANE:
WARWICK AND SAPSFORD, PRINTERS, BOOKBINDERS, ETC., ADELAIDE STREET.

MDCCCLXXXVIII.

PREFACE.

To PERSONS used to preparing botanical specimens it may not be necessary to point out that grasses, like all other plants, require that a specimen for identification should show flower or fruit, both if possible, but in an exhibit of grasses like the present, such specimens give but a poor idea of the rich luxuriance of the Queensland pasture. Most of the kinds in this exhibit, at certain periods of their growth, produce an abundant bottom leafy growth, but if such portions alone were shown it would be almost impossible to distinguish one kind from another, yet it is this leafy part of the plant which is of the greatest importance to the pastoralist. Therefore, for information regarding the value or properties of the various species, the inquirer is referred to the brief notices after each name in this Catalogue, where also will be found all the local names procurable, many scientific synonyms, and the range of each kind both within and beyond Australia. It may be here noted that the grasses of Australia number about 360 kinds, of which three-fourths are met with in Queensland. Growing with these are a large number of nutritious herbs, and it is doubtless owing to this admixture of herbage that Queensland holds her unrivalled position as a pastoral country.

F. M. B.

June, 1888.

A FEW QUEENSLAND GRASSES.

ACRATHERUM. (See *Arundinella.*)

ÆGOPOGON. (See *Amphipogon.*)

1 AGROPYRUM SCABRUM, *Beauv.* (*Festuca scabra*, Labill; *Triticum scabrum*, R. Br.)

This is a rather harsh grass when in seed, but during winter and early spring supplies a large quantity of feed. On poor land its height would be about a foot, but on good land it attains 3 or 4 feet; cut when in flower it makes good hay; the seeds are not injurious. This grass is met with in Tasmania, New Zealand, and all the Australian Colonies. In New Zealand it often has a bluish tinge, and hence has received from the settlers the names of blue tussac grass and blue oat grass, neither of which is suitable to the grass as seen in Australia.

AGROSTIS. (See *Deyeuxia, Dichelachne, Echinopogon,* and *Sporobolus.*)

AIRA. (See *Eriachne.*)

2 ALOPECURUS GENICULATUS, *Linn.* (*A. australis*, Nees.) The Knee-jointed Foxtail or Water Foxtail Grass.

This rather weak grass is valuable as producing on the South Western Downs a quantity of herbage during the winter when many other grasses are at a standstill. It has a wide range, being common in the temperate regions of the northern hemisphere, New Zealand, Tasmania, and all the Australian Colonies.

ANATHERUM. (See *Chrysopogon.*)

3 AMPHIPOGON STRICTUS, *R. Br.* (*Ægopogon strictus*, Beauv.)

This is an erect grass, of which there are several varieties, none of them, however, affording much herbage. It is met with in the south-western parts of Queensland and all the other Australian Colonies.

4 ANDROPOGON BOMBYCINUS, *R. Br.*

This is a somewhat dry harsh grass of two or three feet in height, usually met with on dry stony hill sides in Queensland; the white woolly spikelets give a peculiar appearance to the panicle, and the bases of the stalks are quite aromatic. It seems to be only cropped by stock in its early growth. This grass is met with in Central Australia, N. S. Wales, South and Western Australia.

5 ANDROPOGON ERIANTHOIDES, *F. v. M.* Satin-top or Blue Grass.

One of the very best Queensland grasses; it forms a close turf of rich succulent herbage, the stems attain a height of four or five feet, bearing glossy, silky-white inflorescences; the leaves have a somewhat bluish tinge, thus this grass is in some localities known as "Blue Grass." Stock are apt to eat it out they are so fond of it, but when given a chance it seeds freely and spreads also from its shortly creeping rootstock. Queensland and New South Wales.

6 ANDROPOGON FRAGILIS, *R. Br.*

This is a delicate little grass, very leafy, and much branched; affords a fair pasture; only met with in the tropical parts of Queensland and Northern Australia.

7 ANDROPOGON INTERMEDIUS, *R. Br.* (*A. inundatus*, F. v. M.)

A large tufted grass producing usually a quantity of coarse herbage, but readily eaten by all stock; commonly to be met with on springy land and the borders of rivers in Queensland, both north and south, and also in several of the other Australian Colonies.

8 ANDROPOGON LACHNATHERUS, *Benth.* (*A. procerus*, F. v. M.)

During the early part of summer this grass affords a fair amount of herbage, after which it sends up a number of flattened wiry stems, the greater parts of which is occupied with the branching dry inflorescence, which is seldom touched by stock. Met with in Queensland and New South Wales.

9 ANDROPOGON PERTUSUS, *Willd.*

A rather tall grass, common on open pasture land, affording a fair quantity of herbage for the greater part of the year. Besides Queensland and New South Wales this grass is widely spread in tropical Asia.

10 ANDROPOGON REFRACTUS, *R. Br.* By some called Kangaroo Grass.

A very abundant grass in Southern Queensland. It gives a large amount of herbage, and is one of the best for hay, but can only be depended upon for summer feed, as little is seen of it during the winter months in the south, although in the tropics it grows the year through. Has been met with in Victoria and is also plentiful in Japan.

11 ANDROPOGON SERICEUS, *R. Br.* The Blue Grass of Queensland.

This is looked upon as the best of all the indigenous grasses. Is generally found growing upon rich land, furnishing excellent pasture and hay. It seeds freely, and is of very rapid growth. Met with in Central Australia, Western Australia, New South Wales and throughout Queensland.

12 ANDROPOGON SERICEUS, *var.* POLYSTACHYUS, *Benth.*, *Flora Austr.* vii., 530 Tassel Blue Grass.

This is also a good pasture grass, differing from the former in its greater size and larger head of spikes. A tropical grass.

ANDROPOGON. (*See Sorghum, Rottboellia, Ischæmum, Heteropogon, Elionurus, Chrysopogon.*)

13 ANTHISTIRIA AVENACEA, *F. v. M.* (*A. basisericea*, F. v. M.) The Tall Oat Grass of the Darling Downs.

This is one of the best fodder grasses of Australia; it is only met with on good rich open land. Besides its tall stems it produces a large quantity of good leafy feed at the base. Found on Darling Downs and similar places in Queensland, New South Wales, and Central Australia.

14 ANTHISTIRIA CILIATA, *Linn.* (*A. australis*, R. Br.; *A. cæspitosa*, Anders; *A. cuspidata*, Anders.) The common Kangaroo Grass.

This grass enjoys a world-wide reputation. There are many forms of the species, having such slight differences as one being of a deep-green, another glaucous, and some much more hairy than others; but all are equally good fodders. Found and well-known throughout Australia, New Guinea, and also tropical Asia and Africa.

15 ANTHISTIRIA FRONDOSA, *R. Rr.*

Very like *A. ciliata*, but with broader leaves, and generally a coarser plant. Found at the Etheridge in Queensland, and from thence to Port Darwin.

16 ANTHISTIRIA MEMBRANACEA, **Lindl.** (*Iseilema Mitchelli*, Anders.) The Landsborough Grass, Red Gulf Grass, and Barcoo Grass.

A grass well worthy of extensive cultivation both for feeding or hay, of rapid growth when under cultivation, the stems long and weak, forming an entangled mass one to two feet deep. This grass is very brittle, thus it is much broken by stock, but it is said that stock are so partial to it that they often lick up the broken pieces off the ground. Found in Queensland and Central Australia.

ANTHOXANTHUM. (See *Dichelachne*.)

17 ARISTIDA ARENARIA, *Gaudich.* (*Arthratherum arenarium*, Nees; *Aristida contorta*, F. v. M.)

A grass usually met with on poor, sandy or sour land. In winter and the early spring months it gives a fair feed, but it soon becomes wiry and useless from its troublesome awns and sharp seeds. More or less common throughout Australia.

18 ARISTIDA HYGROMETRICA. *R. Br.*

A poor grass with regard to fodder, as most of the plant is occupied by its inflorescence; principally noticeable for its long three-branched awns. Common on Gulf country where the land is poor or sandy.

19 ARISTIDA LEPTOPODA, *Benth.* Three Awned Spear Grass.

A Downs grass, affording good pasture prior to flowering, when the large spreading wiry panicles and sharp seeds cause it to be avoided by stock. Found in South Queensland and New South Wales.

20 ARISTIDA RAMOSA, *R. Br.* Three Awned Spear Grass.

A dry wiry grey grass, often met with on rocky land, and during the winter months affording some pasture, but in summer bearing too much seed and flower stalks to be much use as feed. Found in Queensland, New South Wales, and New Guinea.

21 ARISTIDA STIPOIDES, *R. Br.*

A very poor grass, of a dry wiry nature, and bearing troublesome awns. Met with on Gulf country and in Central Australia.

22 ARISTIDA VAGANS, *Cav.* Wandering Three Awned Spear Grass.

A common grass about Brisbane, especially on dry rocky parts, where it affords good pasture, growing through the year and forming a good leafy bottom. The awns of this are shorter and less troublesome than some others of the genus. Met with in Queensland and New South Wales.

ARTHRATHERUM.   (See *Aristida.*)

23 ARTHRAXON CILIARE, *Beauv.*; var. *australe*, Benth, in *Flora Austr.*, vii.,524. (*Batratherum echinatum*, Nees; *Andropogon echinatus*, Heyne.)

Stems straggling, much branched and leafy, with broad leaves, seems to be well relished by cattle. Only, so far as at present known, met with in New England in New South Wales, and Toowoomba in Queensland.

ASPRELLA.   (See *Leersia.*)

24 ASTREBLA ELYMOIDES, *Bail et. F. v. M.*   Mitchell Grass.

This is a weak straggling grass, sprouting at the joints after every shower of rain, and affording a large amount of excellent fodder. So far as at present known peculiar to Queensland, and a great favourite with stockholders.

25 ASTREBLA PECTINATA, *F. v. M.* (*Danthonia pectinata*, Lindl., and when very coarse it constitutes the *D. triticoides* of Lindley; *A. triticoides*, F. v. M.)   Mitchell Grass.

A tall erect coarse grass, sprouting at the joints of the stems, and affording a large quantity of fodder, suitable for cattle. The seeds of this genus are large and separate like wheat, free from the chaff, and are in the interior largely used by the natives for food. Met with in Queensland and Central Australia.

26 ARUNDINELLA NEPALENSIS, *Trin.* (*Acratherum miliaceum*, Link.)

A tall erect dry grass; met with usually on poor land, such as ironbark ridges; affording, however, better fodder when in the tropics and on better soil. Found throughout Queensland and North Australia, and widely spread over the hills of tropical Asia and South Africa.

ARUNDO.   (See *Phragmites.*)

AUSTRALIAN OATS.   *Ceratochloa unioloides.*

AVENA   (See *Deyeuxia.*)

BAMBOO GRASS.   *Stipa verticillata.*

BARCOO GRASS.   *Anthistiria membranacea.*

BARLEY GRASS OF AYRSHIRE DOWNS.   *Panicum decompositum.*

BARLEY GRASS.   *Bromus arenarius.*

BARNYARD GRASS.   *Panicum crus-galli.*

BERMUDA GRASS.   *Cynodon dactylon.*

BARRON RIVER TUSSAC GRASS.   *Rottboellia ophiuroides.*

BLADY GRASS   *Imperata arundinacea.*

BLUE GRASS.   *Andropogon sericeus.*

BLUE STAR-GRASS.   *Chloris ventricosa.*

27 BRIZA minor, *Linn*. (*B. virens*, Linn.) Small Quaking Grass.

The species of this genus are prized usually for their beauty, but nevertheless, the one under notice affords by no means a bad pasture during the latter end of winter and beginning of summer. The plant is widely spread in Australia, Africa and America.

Brome Grass (sand). *Bromus arenarius*.

28 BROMUS arenarius, *Labill*. (*B. australis*, R. Br.) Barley Grass.

The Australian or Sand Brome Grass. In New Zealand called Sea-side Brome Grass from its being so frequently found on coast sand. In Queensland often called Oat Grass. It is a winter or early spring grass, and is considered a good kind by many of our sheep farmers, especially on the inland plains. This grass is found in most parts of Australia and New Zealand, and probably in Japan. (*B. japonica*, Thunb.)

Bromus. (See *Ceratochloa*.)

Brown-top Grass. *Pollinia fulva*.

Buffalo Grass. *Stenotaphrum americanum*.

Bunch Spear Grass. *Heteropogon contortus*.

Burr Grass (scrub). *Cenchrus australis*.

Burr Grass (small). *Tragus racemosus*.

Calamagrostis. (See *Deyeuxia*.)

Cane Grass. *Leptochloa subdigitata*.

29 CENCHRUS australis, *B. Br*. Scrub or Hillside Burr-grass.

A very abundant scrub grass, growing in tufts, the leaves long, rough, and very numerous, which, when young or in times of scarcity, are eaten by stock; whole hillsides on the ranges may often be seen covered by this grass, both in New South Wales and Queensland.

30 CENCHRUS elymoides, *F. v. M.*

This grass has the same habit as the last, differing only in a botanical sense. Johnstone River.

31 CENTOTHECA lappacea, *Desv*.

This is a tall rough-leaved grass, found in the scrubs of tropical Queensland, but, like the Cenchrus, has little to recommend it as fodder; it has a wide range, being found in New Guinea and many other tropical countries.

32 CERATOCHLOA unioloides, *D.C.* (*Festuca unioloides*, Willd.; *Bromus unioloides*, H. B. et. K.; *B. Willdenowii*, Kunth.; *Ceratochloa festucoides*, Beauv.)

In America it is known by the name of *Bromus Schraderi*, Kunth., or Australian oats, Schrader's grass, and Rescue grass; in Australia it is known as Prairie grass. This excellent winter grass has become natura-lised in many localities in Queensland and the other Australian colonies. Baron Mueller mentions having gathered specimens of it as far back as 1847, on the mountains of St. Vincent's Gulf. No grass gives better

B

satisfaction or is so largely cultivated in Queensland than this. It gives a rich nutritious fodder through the winter and early spring months, and is also a good kind for hay; on loose soil, however, it is apt to be pulled up by animals grazing on it. Its natural habitat is Central America.

33 CHIONACHNE CYATHOPODA, *F. v. M.* (*Sclerachne cyathopoda* F. v. M.)

This is a tall grass found by the margins of swamps and rivers in Northern Queensland, where it produces a large quantity of good coarse fodder. Besides Queensland, this grass is met with in New Guinea.

34 CHLORIS DIVARICATA, *R. Br.* Star Grass or Dog's-tooth Star Grass.

This grass is not in favour with some pastoralists, but, nevertheless, it provides a pasture for sheep during winter and the early months of summer when feed is usually scarce. It makes a very fair quantity of leafy growth prior to seeding.

35 CHLORIS TRUNCATA, *R. Br.*

This is a tall good pasture grass either for sheep or cattle. It may often be seen in large quantities on rich river flats. It also makes excellent hay. Found in Southern Queensland and New South Wales.

36 CHLORIS SCARIOSA, *F. v. M.* Rockhampton Star Grass.

A beautiful grass but of little value for pasture; worthy of garden cultivation. Rather common about Rockhampton.

37 CHLORIS VENTRICOSA, *R. Br.* (*C. sclerantha* Lindl.) Blue Star Grass.

A good pasture grass, and also useful for hay. Plentiful in New South Wales and South Queensland.

38 CHRYSOPOGON GRYLLUS, *Trin.* (*Andropogon Gryllus*, Linn.; *Holcus Gryllus*, R. Br.)

A fine pasture grass; makes a good quantity of succulent leafy bottom, independent of the flowering stems, which are not numerous from each tuft. Common throughout Queensland and Central Australia.

39 CHRYSOPOGON PARVIFLORUS, *) enth.* (*Holcus parviflorus*, R. Br.; *Andropogon micranthus*, Kunth.; *Anatherum parviflorum*, Spreng ; *Sorghum parviflorum*, Beauv. ; *Andropogon violascens*, Nees. ; *Holcus cœrulescens*, Gaudich.; *Chrysopogon violascens*, Trin.; *Andropogon montanus*, Roxb.; *Chrysopogon montanus*, Trin.) Scented Golden Beard.

This is a tall rough grass, usually forming large tussacs of coarse fodder, freely eaten by stock when young but rejected when old. It is one of those requiring to be burnt off once a year. Very common in Queensland and New South Wales.

40 CHRYSOPOGON PARVIFLORUS, *Benth.*, var. *flavescens.*

This form has the same habit but differs in the colour of the inflorescence, the former being dark, somewhat purplish, while this is of a lovely pale yellow colour. All the varieties are easily known by the peculiar fragrance of the panicle on being rubbed. Found on the Darling Downs.

41 CHRYSOPOGON PARVIFLORUS; var. *spicigera*, Benth.

This is a much more delicate grass than the common form, and better suited for pasture, as it does not form dense tussacs. Met with in several parts of Queensland and New South Wales.

CINNA. (See *Echinopogon*.)

COAST COUCH GRASS. *Zoysia pungens*.

COAST GRASS. *Imperata arundinacea*.

COCKATOO GRASS. *Panicum semialatum*.

COMET GRASS. *Perotis rara*.

COOLIBAR GRASS. *Panicum trachyrrhachis*.

CORIDOCHLOA. (See *Panicum semialatum*.)

COUCH GRASS (common). *Cynodon dactylon*.

COUCH GRASS (mountain). *Micraira subulifolia*.

COUCH GRASS OF THE COAST. *Zoysia pungens*.

CROW-FOOT GRASS. *Eleusine indica*.

CRAB GRASS. *Eleusine indica*.

CRAB GRASS OF SOUTHERN STATES OF AMERICA. *Panicum sanguinale*.

42 CYNODON CONVERGENS, *F. v. M.* The Northern Couch Grass.

This has a somewhat similar habit to the common Couch, but is more harsh, and does not spread and cover the land so quickly, but forms a good pasture. Found on the Gulf country of Northern Queensland.

43 CYNODON DACTYLON, *Pers.* (*Panicum dactylon*, Linn.) The Common Couch Grass, Bermuda Grass or Durba Grass of India.

Is a very productive grass, will thrive where the soil is hard from being much trodden. An American writer says: "As a permanent pasture grass, I know of no other that I consider so valuable as this, after having grown it for thirty-five years." It makes a good hay, and may be mown three or more times a year. It is an excellent lawn grass, and useful for binding banks and drifts. Animals also thrive on its running underground stems. This grass is also used medicinally in India.

CYNOSURUS. (See *Eleusine*.)

DACTYLOCTENIUM. (See *Eleusine*.)

DANTHONIA. (See *Astrebla, Anisopogon*.)

44 DANTHONIA LONGIFOLIA, *R. Br.*

A long-leaved good pasture grass, especially on rich land. Met with in Southern Queensland and the southern colonies.

45 DANTHONIA PALLIDA, *R. Br.* White Topped Grass.

Very general on Downs country; affording good pasture in most parts of Australia.

46 DANTHONIA PILOSA, *R. Br.*

An excellent pasture grass, and like others of this genus, a good seed-bearer, therefore not as likely to be lost by over stocking the land as with many other grasses. Found on the Downs country in Queensland, and in many other parts of Southern Australia, and also New Zealand.

47 DANTHONIA RACEMOSA, *R. Br.*

A common Downs grass, affording excellent sheep pasture, seeds freely, and makes a good close turf. Found on the Darling Downs, Queensland, and through the southern colonies.

48 DANTHONIA SEMIANNULARIS, *R. Br.* (*Arundo semiannularis,* Labill.; *D. varia,* Nees.; *D. setacea,* Hook.; *D. eriantha,* Lindl.) New Zealand Oat Grass.

A grass of two or three feet, excellent for pasture or hay, considered one of the most nutritious of the native grasses, producing feed during winter and early in spring. Spread through the southern colonies of Australia and New Zealand, but in Queensland confined to the cooler most southern parts.

DEYEUXIA. (See *Anisopogon.*)

49 DEYEUXIA FORSTERI, *Kunth.* (*Agrostis Fosteri,* Rœm and Schult; *A. æmula,* R. Br.; *A. retrofracta,* Willd; *Lachnagrostis retrofracta,* Trin.; *L. Willdenowii,* Trin.; *Calamagrostis æmula,* and *C. Willdonowii,* Steud.; *Agrostis debilis,* Poir.; *A. Solandri,* F. v. M.)

This is a quick-growing grass, springing up with the slightest shower of rain, especially during winter, but at the approach of summer its light panicles break off and are seen blown about in all directions. One or other of its several forms may be met with throughout southern Australia and New Zealand.

50 DEYEUXIA QUADRISETA, *Benth.* (*Avena quadriseta,* Labill.; *Agrostis quadriseta,* R. Br.)

An erect stiff grass, met with in Queensland on granite country; a fair cattle grass, at times making a good bottom, but the cane-like stem seldom touched by stock. Found at Stanthorpe in Queensland, and throughout the southern colonies.

DIASTEMANTHE. (See *Stenotaphrum.*)

51 DICHELACHNE CRINITA, *Hook.* (*Anthoxanthum crinitum,* Linn, f.; *Agrostis crinita,* R. Br.; *Muchlenbergia crinita,* Trin.; *M. mollicoma,* Nees.; *Dichelachne Hookeriana, D. Forsteriana, D. comata,* and *D. longiseta,* Trin.) The long hair Plume Grass.

This is a quick-growing excellent pasture grass, and also makes good hay; it has the advantage over most others of producing good feed all the year round, for the least rain starts it into growth. It is found, and is a favourite grass all over Australia and New Zealand.

DIGITARIA. (See *Panicum sanguinale.*)

52 DIMERIA TENERA, *Trin.* (*D. psilobasis,* F. v. M.)

This is a small delicate grass, found on damp sandy land in a few localities of tropical Queensland and Port Darwin, its only recommendation being that of growing where better species would scarcely afford superior pasture; the same species is widely spread over India.

53 DIPLACHNE FUSCA, *Beauv.* (*Festuca fusca*, Linn.; *Leptochloa fusca*, Kunth.; *Triodia ambigua*, R. Br.; *Uralepis fusca* and *U. Drummondii*, Steud.

An annual succulent grass, often met with in brackish swamps, where it affords a good fodder, greedily devoured by stock. In similar localities it is also found throughout Australia.

54 DIPLACHNE LOLIIFORMIS, *F. v. M.* (*Festuca* or *Leptochloa loliiformis*, F. v. M.)

A small erect close-growing grass, of little value as fodder. Found usually on rocks or hard poor soil in central and tropical Australia.

DUTCH MILLET. *Paspalum scrobiculatum.*

DOG'S-TOOTH STAR GRASS. *Chloris divaricata.*

DURBA GRASS. *Cynodon dactylon.*

EARLY SPRING GRASS. *Eriochloa annulata.*

ECHINOCHLOA. (See *Panicum crus-galli.*)

55 ECHINOPOGON OVATUS, *Beauv.* (*Agrostis ovata*, Forst.; *Cinna ovata*, Kunth.; *Echinopogon Sieberi*, Steud.) Rough-bearded Grass.

A rough annual grass and often met with on hill sides, valuable as affording a winter herbage, which, however, is wanting in nutrition. The species is widely spread over Australia and New Zealand.

56 ECTROSIA GULLIVERI, *F. v. M.*

This is a rather dry annual grass, not affording much feed, but found on dry land where it is seldom one meets with good pasture. A Norman and Gilbert Rivers grass.

57 ECTROSIA LEPORINA, *R. Br.* Hare's-tail Grass.

This is a rather slender tufty dry grass, but superior as a fodder to *E. Gulliveri*; it often attains the height of two feet, will thrive on dry land. Found throughout Queensland and North Australia.

EHRHARTA. (See *Microlæna.*)

58 ELEUSINE ÆGYPTIACA, *Pers.* (*Cynosurus ægyptius*, Linn.; *Dactyloctenium ægyptiacum*, Willd.; *Eleusine cruciata*, Lam.; *E. radulans*, R. Br.; *Dactyloctenium radulans*, Beauv.) The Small Crow-foot Grass.

This is a tufty or shortly creeping grass, which forms during summer a fair amount of feed, relished by stock It is common in Queensland, New Guinea, and also frequently met with in other warm countries

59 ELEUSINE INDICA, *Gærtn.* (*E. marginata*, Lindl.) Yard Grass, Crow-foot, Crab Grass, Wire Grass.

This is a strong-growing succulent summer grass, producing a large quantity of feed. It is a common grass of warm climates, and generally considered nutritious. In America it is said to be a good grazing, soiling, and hay grass.

60 ELIONURUS citreus, *Munro*. (*Andropogon citreus*, R. Br.)

This is a tall river or swamp-side grass, affording by no means a bad fodder, it has also an agreeable fragrance of lemons. Found in many parts of Queensland.

ERAGROSTIS. (See *Leptochloa*.)

61 ERAGROTIS Brownii, *Nees*. (*Poa polymorpha*, R. Br.; *Megastachya polymorpha*, Beauv.; *Poa Brownii*, Kunth.) All this genus are known under the local name of Love Grasses from their beauty.

This is a very variable but excellent pasture grass; grows more or less all the year through. The herbage is sweet and nutritious; it also is a good kind for hay. Found in the Queensland pastures throughout, and in many other parts of Australia.

62 ERAGROSTIS Brownii, *Nees*; var. *interrupta*, Benth. (*Poa interrupta*, R. Br.; *Eragrostis interrupta*, Steud.)

This is a very tall or long straggling often hoary form, met with along the coast. Very harsh, and of little value as a fodder, but useful for binding the coast sands and affording a bite for stock in such localities.

63 ERAGROSTIS Brownii, *Nees*; var. *patens*, Benth. Spreading Love Grass.

Only differing from the common form in having wide-spreading panicles; a good pasture grass. Found from north and south Queensland to Victoria.

64 ERAGROSTIS chætophylla, *Steud*. (*E. setifolia*, Nees.; *Poa diandra*, F. v. M.) Bristle Love Grass.

A densely tufted and very pretty grass, but of too wiry a nature to be of much service for pasture. An inland species met with in many parts of Australia.

65 ERAGROSTIS diandra, *Steud*. (*Poa diandra*, R. Br.; *P. interrupta*, Sieb.)

An erect grass, very like *E. Brownii*—perhaps only one of its many forms—the panicle never spreading but remaining always spike-like; excellent for pasture and hay. Met with more or less abundance throughout Australia.

65A ERAGROSTIS falcata, *Gaudich*. (*Poa falcata*, Gaudich.)

A rather harsh, slender, tufted grass, about one foot high, with narrow leaves, most of the plant consisting of the numerous flower-stalks. Only a moderate pasture grass, an abundant seed-bearer. Found on the inland plains of New South Wales and Queensland, reaching across to Western Australia.

66 ERAGROSTIS leptostachya, *Steud*. (*Poa leptostachya*, R. Br.)

A little tufty grass often found on dry ridges, where it affords much sweet feed, although short. Abundant on the high land about Brisbane, reaching almost to the Darling Downs; also in many localities in New South Wales.

67 ERAGROSTIS PILOSA, *Beauv. (Poa pilosa*, Linn.; *P. verticillata*, Cav.; *P. parviflora* and *P. pellucida*, R. Br.; *Eragrostis parviflora*, Trin.; *E. pellucida*, Steud.; *Poa tenella*, Seib.)

This is a most prolific annual grass, springing up with the slightest rain and affording a large amount of sweet feed for the greater part of the year. A common weed of warm countries.

68 ERAGROSTIS TENELLA, *Beauv.*; *Benth. Fl. Hongk.*, 431; and *Fl. Austr.*, VII. 643. (*Poa tenella*, Linn.)

A small delicate erect tufted grass, forming excellent pasture and hay Common on the inland plains of northern Queensland, also in central and north Australia, and widely spread through eastern tropical Asia.

69 ERIACHNE CILIATA, *R. Br.* (*Aira ciliata*, Spreng.)

A small hairy grass of little value for pasture. Found in several parts of tropical Queensland and northern Australia.

70 ERIACHNE OBTUSA, *R. Br.*

This is a fairly good pasture grass suitable for sheep, it is variable as to height but generally branches much from the base, and before seeding makes a good leafy bottom. Found in the interior and throughout the inland parts of Queensland.

71 ERIACHNE SQUARROSA, *R. Br.* (*Aira squarrosa*, Spreng.)

This is an inferior grass to *E. obtusa* on account of the long awns to the seeds, but before sending up its flowering stems it affords fair pasture. Met with in several parts of tropical Queensland.

ERIANTHUS. (See *Pollinia.*)

72 ERIOCHLOA ANNULATA, *Kunth.* (*Paspalum annulatum*, Flügge.) Early Spring Grass.

A quick-growing grass, furnishing feed most of the year round; will suit itself to almost any kind of soil, differing from the next but very slightly, of a lively green colour, not glaucous. Found in New South Wales and Queensland in Australia, and widely in tropical Asia.

73 ERIOCHLOA PUNCTATA, *Hamilt.* (*Panicum helopus*, Milium; *punctatum*, Linn., R. Br., Prod.; *Paspalum punctatum*, Flügge)

A fine pasture grass, of a glaucous colour, always in growth, sweet and nutritious, excellent for hay. Found on every kind of soil, and widely spread as the former, being common in the tropics of both the new and the old world—throughout Queensland, New Guinea, and New South Wales.

74 FESTUCA BROMOIDES, *Linn.* (*F. plebeia*, R. Br.)

A rather dry slender tufted grass, found usually on poor dry soil, of little value for pasture. Met with in all the colonies, but not to the north of Brisbane, also common in temperate regions of the northern hemisphere.

FESTUCA. (See *Diplachne, Agropyrum, Ceratochloa.*)

FOX-TAIL (swamp). *Pennisetum compressum.*

GOLDEN-BEARD. *Chrysopogon parviflorus.*

GUINEA GRASS.   *Panicum maximum.*

GYMNOTHRIX.   (See *Pennisetum.*)

75 HEMARTHRIA COMPRESSA, *R. Br.*   (*H. uncinata*, R. Br.)   Mackay Sugar Grass.

> This is a rather harsh wiry grass, the flattish stems often extending the length of five or six feet. It affords a course fodder around swamps and the margins of rivers, which is of value during very dry seasons. The flattened running stems are very sweet, and as the water dries up in the swamps, these are greedily eaten by stock; horses are said to leave all else for these stems. It is common to all parts of Australia.

76 HETERACHNE BROWNII, *Benth.* (*Poa abortiva*, R. Br.)

> A rather poor pasture grass met with on the Gulf country, seldom over a foot in height, and not forming much leafy feed, except when on good land. Most of the plant is occupied with the thick oval or globose spikes of inflorescence.

77 HETEROPOGON CONTORTUS, *Rœm and Schult.* (*Andropogon contortus*, Linn.; *Heteropogon hirtus*, Pers.; *Andropogon striatus*, R. Br.)   The Bunch Spear Grass.

> A strong-growing leafy grass, affording plenty of herbage, suitable for a cattle-run, but the numerous sharp seeds cause it to be a most injurious grass on a sheep-run. Common in the coast lands of Queensland to Port Darwin; also not uncommon in the tropics of both the new and old world.

78 HETEROPOGON INSIGNIS, *Thu.* (*Andropogon triticeus* R. Br.)   Tall Spear Grass.

> A very tall tropical grass, the flower stems often from six to twelve feet high, and, cane-like, completely hiding the cattle. It, however, produces a quantity of leaf at the bottom, which affords good fodder, and it is therefore a good cattle grass. The spear-like seeds are troublesome if not really dangerous to man and beast. Found on the coast lands of tropical Queensland, North Australia, also in Timor and Ceylon.

HARE'S-TAIL GRASS.   *Ectrosia leporina.*

HOLCUS.   (See *Sorghum, Chrysopogon.*)

HOLOGAMIUM.   (See *Ischæmum.*)
HYMENACHNE MYURUS.   (See *Panicum myurus.*)

79 IMPERATA ARUNDINACEA, *Cyrillo.*   Blady Grass or Coast Grass.

> This broad and long leaved tough grass, is found wherever the land is at all wet and springy, and after being burnt off the young growth affords by no means a bad feed, but if the old leaves are left standing no stock will touch it. The running rhizomes are useful for binding sand. Found throughout Australia and most other warm countries.

80 ISACHNE AUSTRALIS, *R. Br.* (*Panicum atrovirens*, Trin.; *P. antipodum*, Spreng.)

> This is a good grass for wet pasture; it is of rapid growth and bears abundance of seed, and is a general favourite with pastoralists. Found in many other parts of Australia besides Queensland, also in New Zealand and tropical Asia to south China.

81 ISACHNE ᴍʏᴏꜱᴏᴛɪꜱ, *Nees.* (*Panicum myosotis*, Steud.)

Like the last, this grass is only met with in wet situations; it is of a somewhat creeping habit, and produces a fair quantity of good fodder. In Queensland, met with near the Johnstone and other tropical rivers, also in the Malayan Archipelago and South China.

82 ISCHÆMUM ᴀᴜꜱᴛʀᴀʟᴇ, *R. Br.* (*Andropogon cryptatherus.* Steud.)

This grass is only met with on damp land, often with Blady Grass; and, like that species, is of little use unless the land is closely fed, or the old growth burnt off. Like that kind it has a deep running rhizome, and is thus enabled to stand a length of dry weather, and continue to afford a bite for stock after many others have given up. Found throughout Queensland, New South Wales and northern Australia.

83 ISCHÆMUM ʟᴀxᴜᴍ, *R. Br.* (*Andropogon nervosus*, Rottb.; *Hologamium nervosum*, Nees.) Rat's Tail Ischæmum.

This is a coarse grass often met with at the base of hills. Before seeding it affords a fair pasture for cattle; but not adapted for sheep. The species is widely spread in Queensland, and extends also to tropical Asia and Africa.

84 ISCHÆMUM ᴘᴇᴄᴛɪɴᴀᴛᴜᴍ, *Trin.* (*Andropogon falcatus*, Steud.)

This is a very close-growing grass, forming on even dry stony ridges a close turf. It is common in Queensland, and also met with in Ceylon and the Indian Peninsula.

85 ISCHÆMUM ᴛʀɪᴛɪᴄᴇᴜᴍ, *R. Br.* (*Andropogon triticiformis*, Steud.) Wheat Grass.

A coarse erect grass, the stems arising from a running underground stem. The leaves are broader and the flower-spikes larger than in *I. australe*; but, like that grass, is of little value for fodder. A common coast grass in Queensland and the northern coast of New South Wales.

Iꜱᴄʜᴀᴍᴜᴍ. (See *Rottbœllia.*)

Iꜱᴇɪʟᴇᴍᴀ. (See *Anthistiria.*)

Kᴀɴɢᴀʀᴏᴏ Gʀᴀꜱꜱ, (common). *Anthistiria ciliata.*

Kᴀɴɢᴀʀᴏᴏ Gʀᴀꜱꜱ *Andropogon refractus.*

Lᴀɴᴅꜱʙᴏʀᴏᴜɢʜ Gʀᴀꜱꜱ. *Anthistiria membranacea.*

Lᴀᴄʜɴᴀɢʀᴏꜱᴛɪꜱ. (See *Deyeuxia.*)

Lᴀᴘᴘᴀɢᴏ. (See *Tragus.*)

86 LEERSIA ʜᴇxᴀɴᴅʀᴀ, *Swartz.* (*L. australis*, B. Br.; *Asprella australis*, Rœm. and Schult; *Leersia mexicana*, Kunth.) Rice Grass.

This is a prolific quick-growing grass, always met with in or near water; stock are particularly fond of it. In the Philippine Islands this grass is said to be cultivated for fodder, receiving all the attention of rice. Found in most warm countries.

87 LEPTASPIS Bᴀɴᴋꜱɪɪ, *R. Br.* (*Pharus Banksii*, Spreng.)

The erect stems, one to two feet high, with flat broad leaves and loose panicle, the branches of which are thread-like, with bladdery globular flowers, somewhat unlike a grass. Found in swamps, where it forms pretty green tufts; scarcely plentiful enough to be of great service for fodder. From Rockingham Bay to Cape York.

88 LEPTOCHLOA chinensis, *Nees.* (*Poa chinensis*, Kœn; *Leptochloa tenerrima*, Rœm. and Schult; *Poa decipiens*, R. Br.; *Eragrostis decipiens*, Steud.)

A rather tall feathery grey-coloured grass, usually found on the margins of rivers, producing a large quantity of fodder, relished by stock; the panicle is very delicate and drooping. Found throughout Queensland, also in New South Wales and many warm countries.

89 LEPTOCHLOA subdigitata, *Trin.* (*Poa digitata*, R. Br.; *Eleusine digitata*, Spreng; *E. polystachya*, F. v. M.) Cane Grass.

A tall tussac grass, with numerous erect branching leafy stems, usually met with around dams and river banks, and affording a large supply of coarse herbage. A common inland grass of most parts of Australia.

Leptochloa. (See *Diplachne.*)

90 LEPTURUS repens, *R. Br.*

This is a creeping grass, useful for binding the coast sands; it is the principal grass on some of the islands off the tropical coast; is cropped by cattle, but too harsh for fodder generally. Met with on the islands of the South Pacific.

Love Grass. *Eragrostis.*

91 MANISURIS granularis, *Swartz.*

This is a dwarf branching grass, leafy and bearing much seed, usually met with on dry poor land. It is widely spread over warm countries, and besides its use as a fodder, in India it was at one time classed as a medicinal plant. It is not common in Queensland, but is met with in a few localities.

Meadow Rice Grass. *Microlæna stipoides.*

Megastachya. (See *Eragrostis Brownii.*)

92 MICRAIRA subulifolia, *F. v. M.* Mountain Couch.

A creeping grass, found growing on rocks, forming a fine dense springy turf. Glasshouse Mountains and mountains, Rockingham Bay.

93 MICROLÆNA stipoides, *R. Br.* (*Ehrharta stipoides*, Labill *Microlæna Gunii*, Hook.) Meadow Rice Grass of New Zealand.

This is an excellent grass for winter pasture, and it often keeps up a growth during the greater part of summer, and considered by all a good fattening grass. Found throughout extra-tropical Australia and New Zealand.

Milium. (See *Eriochloa.*)

Mitchell Grass. *Astrebla.*

Muchlenbergia. (See *Dichelachne.*)

Mulga Grass. *Neurachne Mitchelliana.*

94 NEURACHNE Mitchelliana, *Nees*.

Mulga Grass, so called from often being, in the Maranoa, found under mulga trees. It has somewhat of a creeping habit, and is liked by stockholders on account of its affording feed on poor land and under the shade of trees. Met with in similar situations in New South Wales.

New Zealand Oat Grass. *Danthonia semiannularis*.

Oat Grass of Darling Downs. *Anthistiria avenacea*.

95 OPLISMENUS compositus, *Beauv*. (*Panicum compositum*, Linn., Trin. Spec. Gram.; F. v. M. *Fragm.* VIII.; *Orthopogon compositus*, R. Br., Prod.)

This first form is the *O. æmulus*, R. Br., Prod., a hairy, shade-loving grass, seldom eaten by stock, but useful for forming a green swarth under trees. The leaves are broad, and often prettily variegated. Found abundantly in the scrubs of Queensland and New South Wales, and common in most warm countries.

96 OPLISMENUS compositus, *Beauv*., var. *imbecillis*.

This is the nearly glabrous form, and represents R. Brown's *Orthopogon flaccidus* and *O. imbecillis*; also the *Oplismenus flaccidus* and *O. imbecillis* of Kunth, and the *Panicum imbecille*, Trin., Spec., Gram. It is very similar in habit to the last, usually, however, with much narrower and darker leaves. The range is the same. Some writers speak well of it, but certainly it is not readily eaten by stock in Queensland.

97 OPLISMENUS compositus, var. *setarius*. (*O. setarius*, Rœm. et Schult.; *Panicum setarium*, Lam.)

This is altogether smaller than the two preceding kinds. It forms a rather more dense close turf, is of a pleasing green colour, is not admired much by stockowners, but nevertheless is useful as being one of the few grasses found to thrive under the shade of trees, and in such situations will be found useful for ornamental planting. Found in Victoria and New South Wales, and as far north as Keppel Bay.

Oplismenus. (See *Panicum crus-galli*)

Ornithocephalochloa. (See *Thuarea*.)

Orthopogon. (See *Oplismenus*.)

98 ORYZA sativa, *Linn*. Wild Rice.

This the normal rice is met with in abundance in some of the Gulf country swamps, and considered by stock holders as excellent fodder. Common in India, the Rice of commerce is the produce of cultivated varieties of this grass.

99 PANICUM argenteum, *R. Br*.

A tufty grass with numerous leafy stems of about one foot or more in height, softly pubescent; the silvery-white seeds of this grass are very conspicuous. In the Gulf country, where it abounds, it is considered a good pasture grass.

100 PANICUM Baileyi, *Benth*.

This is very near *P. parviflorum* in general appearance, and, like that species, a good pasture or hay grass; it attains the height of from two to four feet and is plentifully supplied with leaves. The panicle is composed of a few filiform branches, the small spikelets more or less hairy.

Is usually met with on good soil, Brisbane River to Port Curtis, but so far as at present known peculiar to Queensland.

101 PANICUM CRUS-GALLI, *Linn.* (*Oplismenus crus-galli*, Kunth.; *Echinochloa crus-galli*, Beauv.) Barn-yard Grass.

This is a fine strong succulent grass, sending up many leafy stems two to eight feet high from the same root, on damp land; worth cultivating to cut for green fodder; usually the panicle are strongly bearded, but if fed close, the panicles then formed are often beardless. This grass is highly thought of in America. One writer says that it gives five tons of hay per acre without care or cultivation, and that on the Mississippi hundreds of acres are annually mowed on single farms. A common grass of hot or temperate climates abundant in Queensland.

102 PANICUM DECOMPOSITUM, *R. Br.* (*P. proliferum*, F. v. M.; *P amabile Balansa*, *P. lævinode*, Lindl.) The Barley Grass of Ayrshire Downs and a few other places. Native name on Cloncurry, "Tindil."

A common glabrous grass of Downs country excellent for pastur , often found also on damp swampy land, then a much stouter and more succulent grass, but always a desirable fodder. Met with throughout Australia. "The seeds used by the natives for food."—*E. Palmer.*

103 PANICUM DISTACHYUM, *Linn.* (*P. subquadriparum*, Trin.)

An excellent grass for either pasture or hay, and would pay for cultivating for the latter as it is relished by stock and yields a heavy crop, for this latter purpose it might be profitably mixed with the Landsborougn grass. Met with as far south as the Brisbane River, but more common in tropical Queensland, and said to be widely distributed over India and the Malayan Archipelago.

103A PANICUM DIVARICATISSIMUM, *R. Br.*, *Prod.*; *Flora Austr.*, *VII.*, *467.*

A common grass on downs country; it produces a large amount of pasture, and plenty of seed. There are several varieties of it, one or other being met with throughout New South Wales and South Australia.

104 PANICUM EFFUSUM, *R. Br.* (*P. capillare*, Gronov., F. v. M.)

A fine pasture grass, producing a good deal of leafy bottom before seeding. Whole plant hairy, and found on all kinds of soil throughout Queensland, and also in most of the other colonies.

105 PANICUM FLAVIDUM, *Retz.* (*P. brizoides*, Jacq. f.) The Warrego Summer Grass.

Said to be the best fattening grass of the district. It grows to the height of two or more feet, forms a good quantity of leafy feed, and when in seed the stalks are loaded nearly from top to bottom with grain. Not often met with on coast lands, but plentiful on the other side of the range; also in north Australia and India.

106 PANICUM FLAVIDUM, *Retz.*, var. *tenuior*, Benth; *Flora Austr.*

A small grass, the stems often prostrate from the weight of seed. It forms a good pasture, as besides the seed it gives a large quantity of leaves. Very common about Brisbane,. and in many other parts of Queensland; also in New South Wales.

107 PANICUM FOLIOSUM, *R. Br.*

A handsome broad-leaved grass, found usually on broken land, the borders of scrubs and river sides, or amongst rocks. Of straggling habit, the whole plant clothed with short hairs ; does not bear feeding off, for stock destroy it by pulling it up by the roots, it has so slight a hold of the ground. A Queensland species, and near the Queensland border in New South Wales.

108 PANICUM GRACILE, *R. Br.*

This grass is usually met with on the side of hills where the land is fairly rich, and then it will often form rather large tufts, very leafy and producing but little seed. Although the leaves are narrow and somewhat harsh, stock are said to be fond of it. The plant is very variable in aspect, but one or other of its variaties is met with in all the Australian colonies.

109 PANICUM INDICUM, *Linn.* (*P. phleoides*, R. Br., and *P. arcuatum*, R. Br.)

An erect thin wiry grass, with a spike-like inflorescence. Of little value as a pasture except in low damp localities, where better kinds are seldom found. Found in New South Wales, common throughout Queensland, tropical Asia and Africa.

110 PANICUM LACHNOPHYLLUM, *Benth.*

An erect-stemmed harsh grass, found usually on dry land ; forms but poor feed. The leaves short and whole plant hairy. A Queensland species.

111 PANICUM LEUCOPHŒUM, *H. B. et R.* (*P. villosum*, R. Br.; *P. Brownii*, Rœm et Schult.; *P. glareœ*, F. v. M.; *P. laniflorun*, Nees.)

An erect-growing leafy grass of from one to three feet; when on poor land somewhat dry and wiry, but on good soil forms very fair pasture; pretty generally distributed over Australia, also in tropical America and Africa. E. Palmer says that the Cloncurry natives obtain a fibre from this grass which they form into twine.

112 PANICUM MACRACTINIUM, *Benth.*

This conspicuous grass forms, prior to sending up its flower stems, a good tuft of leafy bottom, thus affording good pasture. Found in plenty upon Downs country in Queensland.

113 PANICUM MAXIMUM, *Jacq.* (*P. jumentorum*, Pers.) The Guinea Grass.

A tall grass of tropical Africa, which has become naturalized in many localities in Queensland. It is extensively cultivated for fodder; produces heavy crops, and is rich in nutritive materials.

114 PANICUM MELANANTHUM, *F. v. M.*

A tall grass producing a fair amount of fodder, usually met with on damp land during the summer months in Southern Queensland, and thence through New South Wales into Victoria.

115 PANICUM MYOSUROIDES, *R. Br.* (*P. angustum*, Trin.)

A very delicate erect grass found on swampy land in the tropical parts of Australia, where it affords a light pasture. It is said to be also met with in many parts of Asia and Africa.

116 PANICUM MYURUS, *Lam.* (*Hymenachne myurus*, Beauv.; *Panicum interruptum*, Willd.)

This is a tall grass, always growing in or near water, and in such localities produces good fodder. So far as at present known Cairns is its only Australian habitat, but it is not uncommon in the tropical parts of both the new and old world.

117 PANICUM PARVIFLORUM, *R. Br.*

There are several forms of this fine pasture grass. It forms a good leafy bottom, grows for the greater part of the year, and is found on all kinds of soil throughout Queensland and New South Wales.

118 PANICUM PARVIFLORUM, var. *pilosa.*, Benth. in *Flora Austr.*, VII., 471.

A good pasture and hay grass, only differing from the last in being hairy. Common about Brisbane.

119 PANICUM PYGMÆUM, *R. Br.*

A small hairy creeping grass, of little value as a fodder, but will grow under the shade of trees and on dry land; therefore useful for covering otherwise bare spots. Found in many parts of Queensland, and a few places in New South Wales.

120 PANICUM RARUM, *R. Br.*

A dwarf grass of rather wiry habit; the greater part of the plant occupied by the inflorescence. Met with on poor land at the Etheridge and a few other Northern localities; also on the islands of the north coast.

121 PANICUM SANGUINALE, *Linn.* (*Digitaria sanguinalis*, Scop.) Common Crab Grass of the Southern States of America.

The common summer grass of Queensland. A troublesome garden weed during wet in summer. Gives a large amount of fodder, and is good for hay; for this latter purpose it is highly spoken of in America, where it is said that horses are so fond of the hay that they leave all other for it. A wide-spread weed, being found in most warm countries.

122 PANICUM SEMIALATUM, *R. Br.* (*Urochloa semialata*, Kunth.; *Coridochloa semialata*, Nees.) Cockatoo Grass.

Dr. Lumholtz found this grass, in North Queensland, to furnish the principal food of white cockatoos. An excellent pasture grass, producing a large amount of leafy bottom, although the hard cane-like stems are refused by stock. This species has a wide range, in Australia being found throughout Queensland, in New South Wales and New Guinea, through tropical Asia, and extending to South China.

123 PANICUM TENERIFFÆ, *R. Br.*; var. *rosea.* (*Tricholæna rosea*, Nees.) Known in Queensland as Red Natal Grass.

This excellent South African fodder grass was introduced some years ago by the Queensland Acclimatisation Society, and it has taken so kindly to the climate that it has become naturalised in many localities, and is highly esteemed by agriculturists. Stock are fond of it; it makes excellent hay; and produces abundance of seed, which, being carried about by winds, is thus sown far and wide.

124 PANICUM TRACHYRHACHIS, *Benth.* (*P. virgatum*, Linn., F. v. M.) Coolibar Grass. Native name on Cloncurry, "Oo-kin."

A tall species, with erect stout stem, with large panicle. This is one of the principal grasses of downs country, especially on low spots. It furnishes a large quantity of good though coarse fodder. Met with from the Darling Downs to Port Darwin. "Fibre of the leaves used by the natives on the Mitchell for making twine."—*E. Palmer.*

125 PANICUM TRICHOIDES, *Sw.*

This is a soft hairy grass of little value as fodder. Met with on some of the ranges in tropical Queensland, its light leafy stems forming intricate masses. Also found at Port Darwin.

126 PANICUM UNCINULATUM, *R. Br.*

This is a grass usually met with in mountain scrubs, also amongst brigalow; it forms large tufts or tussacs, and furnishes in many places the principal scrub fodder both in New South Wales and Queensand.

PANICUM. (See *Setaria, Paspalum, Isachne, Eriochloa Cynodon.*)

127 PAPPOPHORUM NIGRICANS, *R. Br.* (*P. pallidum*, R. Br.; *P. purpurascens* and *P. gracile*, R. Br.; *P. cœrulescens*, Gaudich; *P. flavescens*, Lindl.; *P. virens*, Lindl.; *P. commune*, F. v. M.)

This is an erect grass, and, although rather wiry in appearance, furnishes a good quantity of feed and bears close cropping; there are many forms of it, some of which would be worthy of cultivation as ornamental grasses. One or other form is met with in all parts of Australia.

128 PASPALUM BREVIFOLIUM, *Flügge.* (*Panicum tenuifolium*, R. Br.)

A small grass having a creeping underground stem from which leafy tufts are sent up, the broad tender foliage affording good but short early summer feed, the flowering stems very slender and from one to two feet high. This is a widely spread grass in tropical Asia, Queensland, and New South Wales.

129 PASPALUM DISTICHUM, *Linn.*

This broad-leaved creeping grass has been introduced and become naturalized in many wet localities, many south Queensland swamps being now over run with it. It is the common grass of our town gutters, is a much more rank grass than the Australian form found in coast swamps, and will not stand the least salt water. During summer this is an excellent fodder. Widely spread over tropical countries.

130 PASPALUM DISTICHUM, *Linn.*, var. *littorale.* Sea-side Millet.

This has the same running underground stems as the introduced grass, but differs in its narrower leaves, erect stems, and being only met with in coast swamps, where it forms a most nutritious pasture. These two varieties keep their distinctive characters when grown side by side on damp land, or near fresh water swamps, but this latter thrives best in brackish swamps.

131 PASPALUM MINUTIFLORUM, *Steud.*

This is a tall erect grass from a creeping underground stem, very near *P. brevifolium*, of which it might be called the autumnal form, having somewhat the appearance of *Panicum parviflorum* or at times *P. sanguinale*, only perfectly glabrous. It gives good pasture and produces plenty of seed ; is usually met with on damp land about Brisbane, but is found in the tropical parts of Queensland, and tropical Asia.

132 PASPALUM SCROBICULATUM, *Linn.* (*P. orbiculare*, Forst. ; *P. polystachyum*, and *P. pubescens*, R. Br. ; *P. metabolon*, Steud.) Ditch Millet.

A very coarse grass often met with on wet land ; when closely cut or fed down, freely eaten by stock, but if allowed to stand and become old refused, except by very hungry cattle. A grass of most tropical and sub-tropical countries.

PASPALUM. (See *Eriochloa*.)

133 PENNISETUM ARNHEMICUM, *F. v. M.*

A little known grass, but seems of little value for pastoral purposes, on account of its numerous bristly spikes Found by Mr. F. T. C. Wildash on the Gilbert River, also common in Northern Australia.

134 PENNISETUM COMPRESSUM, *R. Br.* (*Setaria compressa*, Kunth. ; *Gymnothrix compressa*, Brongn.) Swamp Fox-tail Grass.

This swamp tussac grass forms large tufts in most of the Queensland swamps, which, during long droughts, afford a coarse fodder for stock. Found in similar localities in New South Wales.

PENNISETUM. (See *Setaria*.)

135 PEROTIS RARA, *R. Br.* Comet Grass.

A small decumbent grass, affording excellent sheep pasture in open country, growing quick after showers ; the seeds, though sharp, are not very troublesome. Widely spread over tropical Queensland and common also in other tropical countries.

PHARUS. (See *Leptaspis*.)

136 PHRAGMITES COMMUNIS, *Trin.* (*Arundo phragmites*, Linn.)

This is the common Reed so abundant on the margins of rivers and in swamps ; it is useful as affording food for stocks during dry seasons. In the tropics, especially at the Barron River, although the plant is equal in size to the southern one, it is much more tender, and has a greater tendency to sprout at the joints, and therefore a better fodder. This grass is met with in all parts of the world. "The natives make their reed-spears from the stems of this grass ; using the stems of *Sesbania ægyptiaca* or peabush, called by them 'Ngeen-jerry,' for the sharp woody point."—*E. Palmer.*

PIGEON GRASS OF AMERICA. *Setaria glauca*.
PLUME GRASS. *Dichelachne crinita*.

137 POA CÆSPITOSA, *Forst.* (*P. australis*, *P. lævis*, *P. plebeia*, *P. affinis*, R. Br.) Tussac Poa or Weeping Polly Grass.

A most variable grass as to size, sometimes forming large tussac-like tufts, at other times it may have but a delicate growth. It is, however, a valuable pasture grass, and readily eaten by all kinds of stock. It is usually met with on good land, and, in one or other form, in all the colonies, including New Zealand.

138 POA CÆSPITOSA, *Forst.*, var. *latifolia.*

This is a tall luxuriant grass, well worthy of cultivation; its broad leaves and large panicles of flowers reminds one of the Guinea grass. It seems to be naturally a mountain grass, as its only known Queensland habitat is the top of the Mount Mistake range, and in New South Wales it has been gathered at the Illawarra and Munyong Mountains.

POA. (See *Leptochloa, Heterachne, Eragrostis.*)

139 POGONATHERUM SACCHAROIDEUM, *Beauv.* (*P. crinitum,* Trin.; *P. refractum*, Nees.)

A beautiful grass, about one or two feet high, of rather tufty habit, very leafy, and from all appearances not a bad cattle grass, but the rather numerous awns might prove troublesome to sheep. The plant, however, is worthy of garden culture. The only so far known Australian habitat is the Johnstone, but it is not uncommon in India, the Malayan Archipelago, China, and Japan.

139A POLLINIA ARTICULATA, *Trin.* (*Erianthus articulatus*, F. v. M. ; *Pogonatherum contortus*, Brougn.)

A small annual wiry delicate grass, of little value as a pasture species. Widely spread over tropical Queensland, North Australia, and the Malayan Archipelago.

140 POLLINIA FULVA, *Benth.* (*Saccharum fulvum*, R. Br.; *Erianthus fulvus*, Kunth.) Brown Top or Sugar Grass.

A tall grass, usually met with on wet land. Produces a good deal of sweet fodder, much relished by stock; thus often closely cropped. The rich brown silky spikes of flowers have procured for it the one local name, and its sweetness the other. Met with through Australia.

141 POLLINIA IRRITANS, *Benth.* (*Saccharum irritans*, R. Br.; *Erianthus irritans*, Kunth.)

Previous to ripening its seed, this grass affords good feed, but the sharp seeds, when ripe, are very troublesome to sheep. Found throughout tropical Queensland.

PRAIRIE GRASS. *Ceratochloa unioloides.*

PUNGENT COUCH GRASS. *Zoysia pungens.*

QUAKING GRASS. *Briza.*

RAT'S-TAIL GRASS. *Ischæmum laxum.*

RAT'S-TAIL GRASS. *Sporobolus indicus.*

RED GRASS (Gulf). *Anthistiria membranacea.*

RED NATAL GRASS. *Panicum Teneriffæ*, var. *rosea.*

REED (Common). *Phragmites communis.*

RESCUE GRASS. *Ceratochloa unioloides.*

C

Rice Grass.   *Leersia hexandra.*

Rice (Wild).   *Oryza sativa.*

142 ROTTBOELLIA formosa, *R. Br.*

A small grass, of little value as a pasture kind. Met with on coast lands of tropical Queensland and North Australia.

143 ROTTBOELLIA ophiuroides, *Benth.*   (*Ischæmum rottboellioides,*
R. Br.; *Andropogon rottboellioides,* Steud.) Barron River
Tussac Grass.

This tall branching grass produces fodder of good quality, and equal in amount to the best sorghum. It is often met with on the banks of the rivers in tropical Queensland in large tussacs, but where stock can get at it, is closely cropped.

Saccharum.   (See *Pollinia.*)

Satin Top or Blue Grass.   *Andropogon erianthoides.*

Scented Golden Beard Grass.   *Chrysopogon parviflorus.*

Schrader's Grass.   *Ceratochloa unioloides.*

Sclerachne.   (See *Chionachne.*)

Scrub or Hillside Burr Grass.   *Cenchrus australis.*

Seaside Millet.   *Paspalum distichum littorale.*

144 SETARIA glauca, *Beauv.* (*Panicum glaucum,* Linn.; *Pennisetum glaucum,* R. Br.)   In America called Pigeon Grass.

In tropical Queensland this is represented by a form seldom over one foot in height, but in southern Queensland it forms a rich fodder grass of two to three feet, and bears an abundance of seed even though closely fed. It is met with in most parts of Queensland, central and southern Australia, New Guinea, and, in fact, most parts of the globe.

145 SETARIA macrostachya *H. B.* and *K.* (*Panicum macrostachyum,*
Nees ; *Panicum italicum,* R. Br. and F. v. M.; not the
Panicum italicum, Linn.)

This grass has a much broader leaf than *S. glauca,* and more spread-ing panicles. Naturally it is met with in rich scrubs, from whence it has been brought and sown on open lands with good results, proving itself worthy of field culture either for cutting for green fodder or for grazing. Besides Queensland this grass is found in New Guinea and many other parts.

Setaria.   (See *Pennisetum.*)

146 SORGHUM plumosum, *Beauv.* (*Holcus plumosus,* R. Br.;
Andropogon australis, Spreng.)

This is a coarse grass similar to the last, but more widely spread in Australia, being met with as far south as the Snowy River in Victoria. It is not liked by the sheepfarmers, but for a cattle run it is a very good grass.

SORGHUM. (See *Chrysopogon.*)

147 SPINIFEX HIRSUTUS, *Labill.* (*S. sericeus*, R. Br.) Spiny Rolling Grass.

This is a hard coarse coast grass, highly valuable probably for binding the loose coarse coast sand by its long creeping stems, which root at the joints, but of little value as a fodder. It has a very peculiar inflorescence, which is often gathered for ornamental purposes. The male and female flowers are borne on different plants, and are very dissimilar in appearance. Common on coast sands all round Australia and New Zealand.

SPINIFEX (Warrego.) *Triodia Mitchellii.*

SPINY ROLLING GRASS. *Spinifex hirsutus.*

148 SPOROBOLUS ACTINOCLADUS, *F. v. M.* (*Vilfa* or *Agrostis actinoclada*, F. v. M.)

A delicate pasture grass not of so tufty a habit as most others of the genus; gives a good quantity of herbage and seed. Found on the inland plains, tropical Queensland.

149 SPOROBOLUS DIANDER, *Beauv.* (*Vilfa erosa*, Trin.)

This grass is always met with on good land, especially on river flats, where it forms clumps of deep green feed much relished by stock when young, but, like others of this genus, if allowed to become old is refused by most animals on account of its extreme toughness. Besides Australia this species is widely spread over India.

150 SPOROBOLUS INDICUS, *R. Br.* Rat's-tail Grass. Cloncurry native name, " Jil-crow-berry."

This is a tufty grass which cattle and horses are fond of when it is frequently cut or grazed down ; but if allowed to remain untouched long, they will not eat it unless very hungry, as it becomes tough and unpalatable. This is a very wide spread tropical grass. The seeds used for food by the natives according to E. Palmer.

151 SPOROBOLUS INDICUS, *R. Br.*, var. *elongatus.* (*S. elongatus*, R. Br.; *S. tenacissimus*, Beauv.)

Véry like the last but with narrower leaves, and longer and looser panicle, and not quite so tufty; a good pasture and hay grass, but rather tough except when young ; grows quickly, therefore the closer cropped the better. A very wide-spread form.

152 SPOROBOLUS LINDLEYI, *Benth.* (*S. pallidus*, Lindl.; *Vilfa Lindleyi*, Steud ; *S. subtilis*, F. v. M., not of Kunth.) Cloncurry native name, " Yak-ka-berry."

A very pretty meadow grass producing a fair quantity of tender herbage and an abundant supply of seed. Met with on the inland plains. " Seeds collected for food by the natives."—*E. Palmer.*

153 SPOROBOLUS virginicus, *Kunth.* *(Agrostis virginica*, Linn.; *Vilfa virginica*, Beauv.*)*

A creeping grass, sending up erect leafy stems from its underground running rhizome, common on the salt marshes of Queensland, where it affords a very fattening pasture. Two forms are shown both from Moreton Bay, one much more robust than the other. This grass is widely spread over the warmer regions of the world.

Star Grass. *Chloris divaricata.*

154 STENOTAPHRUM americanum, *Schrank.* *(S. glabrum*, Trin.; *Rottboellia compressa*, Beauv.; *Diastemanthe platystachys*, Steud.*)* Buffalo Grass.

Naturally this is a c ast grass, but in Queensland it thrives everywhere, and has become naturalised in many localities even on the tops of some of the ranges. For binding banks no better kind could be found, and some speak highly of it as a fodder. It is met with near the sea in tropical regions both of the new and old world.

155 STIPA aristiglumis, *F. v. M.*

This is a strong growing grass, producing a large quantity of excellent fodder; indeed it is one of the very best species found on the Downs; the seed also are not so troublesome as some others of the genus. Met with in Victoria, New South Wales, and Queensland.

156 STIPA setacea, *R. Br.* The Common Spear-Grass of the southern colonies.

This is an excellent grass prior to seeding when it is very troublesome to sheep. Only met with in the most southern parts of Queenlsand, but abundant in all the other colonies.

157 STIPA verticillata, *Nees.* *(S. micrantha*, R. Br.; *Streptachne verticillata*, Trin.; *Stipa ramosissima*, Nees; *Streptachne ramosissima*, Trin.; also *Urachne ramosissima*, Trin.)* Bamboo Grass.

A tall tufty grass, often met with in scrubs and on the sides of hills. The stems are often four or five feet high, strong and numerous, and at the joints are produced large dense tufts of leaves. Horses are particularly fond of this grass. Found in Queensland and New South Wales.

Streptachne. (See *Stipa.*)

Sugar Grass of Mackay. *Hemarthria compressa,*

Sugar Grass. *Pollinia fulva.*

Summer Grass. *Panicum sanguinale.*

Summer Grass of Warrego. *Panicum flavidum.*

Swamp Foxtail. *Pennisetum compressum.*

Tall Spear Grass. *Heteropogon insignis.*

Three-awned Spear Grass. *Aristida.*

Tassel Blue Grass. *Andropogon sericeus*, var. *polystachyus.*

158 THUAREA sarmentosa, *Pers.* (*T. latifolia, T. media,* and *T. involuta,* R. Br.; *Ornithocephalochloa arenicola,* Kurz.)

This grass is found on the sandy beach of tropical Australia, and similar places in other tropical countries, its long running stem and short tufts of foliage affording a bite where little else would grow; but perhaps the most economic use of the plant is as a binder of drift sand.

159 TRAGUS racemosus, *Desf.* (*Lippago racemosa,* Willd.) Small Burr Grass.

A small annual grass, often met with on dry stony knolls, where in winter and early spring it produces a fair amount of feed. Although a burr grass, this is said to do no harm to the wool. A weed of most tropical and temperate regions.

Tricholæna rosea. (See *Panicum Teneriffæ,* var. *rosea.*)

160 TRIODIA Mitchellii, *Benth.* (*T. pungens,* Lindl.) The Warrego Spinifex.

A very handsome tufty grass, four or five feet high; of little use for feed except after being burnt off, when the young growth is greedily eaten by stock. Found in the small brigalow scrubs of the Maranoa.

Triodia. (See *Diplachne.*)

161 TRIRAPHIS mollis, *R. Br.*

This is a rather wiry grass, found on poor land, the most conspicuous part of which being its rather large, long, dense panicle. When met with on good soil, however, it produces a very fair amount of feed. Widely spread through Australia.

Triticum. (See *Agropyrum.*)

Tussac Poa. *Poa cæspitosa.*

Uralepis. (See *Diplachne.*)

Urochloa. (See *Panicum semialatum.*)

Vilfa. (See *Sporobolus.*)

Warrego Summer Grass. *Panicum flavidum.*

Warrego Spinifex. *Triodia Mitchellii*

Water or Knee-jointed Foxtail Grass. *Alopecurus geniculatus.*

Weeping-polly Grass. (*Poa cæspitosa.*)

Wheat Grass. *Ischæmum triticeum.*

Wild Rice. *Oryza sativa.*

Wire Grass. *Eleusine indica.*

Yard Grass. *Eleusine indica.*

162 ZOYSIA PUNGENS, *Willd.* (*Rottboellia uniflora*, A. Cunn.)
Pungent Conch Grass or Coast Couch Grass.

This is a common grass in maritime sands of tropical and eastern Asia, also on the coast lands north and south in Australia and New Zealand. It forms a compact turf, and affords a large supply of herbage, and, if not found indigenous, should be introduced in sandy districts near the sea, where, from the saline nature of the soil, other herbage would hardly thrive. Stock are particularly fond of this grass and thus crop it down closely.

Case Nº1, wood 408, Nº2, 411, Nº3, 412, Nº4, 409, & Nº5, 410.

Carved. Case 1&2 .....
{ 80
3... 244
4... 245
5... 266

Pillar . Case 1 .....
{ 239
2... 210
3... 548
4... 366
5... 404

Case 1 & 2 .....
{ 134
3... 140ª
4... 403

Carved. Case 1 & 2 .....
{ 264
3... 43
4... 250
5... 355

Pilasters. Case 1 .....
{ 128ª
2... 67
3... 164
4... 16
5... 331

A11 131.
" 159ª

A11 112.
" 163C
" 115ª

Case 1 & 2, 12.
" 5,4&5 148.
A11 125.

Panels. Case 1 405
" 2 406
" 3 161
" 4 105
" 5 183

Case 1 & 2. 45ª.
" 3, 4, & 5. 132C

C. Madsen. Del.

QUEENSLAND COMMISSION.

Centennial International Exhibition, Melbourne, 1888

QUEENSLAND WOODS

WITH A

BRIEF POPULAR DESCRIPTION

OF

THE TREES, THEIR DISTRIBUTION, QUALITIES,
USES OF TIMBER, &c., &c.

BY

FREDK. MANSON BAILEY, F.L.S.,

COLONIAL BOTANIST.

BRISBANE:

WARWICK AND SAPSFORD, PRINTERS, BOOKBINDERS, ETC., ADELAIDE STREET.

MDCCCLXXXVIII.

PREFACE.

— ◆◆ —

IN PREPARING this second descriptive catalogue of Queensland woods, an opportunity has been taken to correct a few errors occurring in a former catalogue, printed for the Colonial and Indian Exhibition. A large amount of additional information has also been given as to the uses of the various trees, with more local and native names, and further references to works where detailed descriptions may be found and where plates may be consulted.

The present exhibit contains 538 kinds of wood, probably little more than one-half of what might be collected in Queensland did time allow, for no country in the world has a greater variety of useful and beautiful woods.

The remarks on the practical characteristics of each sample of wood have been supplied by Mr. CARL MADSEN, of Messrs. Pettigrew's establishment, where the entire exhibit has been prepared.

F. M. B.

June, 1888.

INDEX.

QUEENSLAND WOODS.

Class 1.—DICOTYLEDONS.

Order DILLENIACEÆ.

WORMIA, *Rottb.*

1—W. ALATA, *R. Br.* in DC. Syst. Veg., i., 434; Flora Austr., i., 16. A tree of moderate size, with a thick, papery, loose bark of a reddish colour. The leaves large, oval or oblong, with more or less winged stalks. Flowers large, yellow, the petals soon falling away. —On the tropical coast; often met with on the borders of the coast swamps of Queensland; flowering in January. The tree also inhabits New Guinea.

B.P.V.—Wood of a dark colour; cut one way it shows a pretty red "clash," differing in colour but somewhat resembling that of English Oak. It is close in grain and easy to work; a good cabinet-maker's wood.

Order ANONACEÆ.

POLYALTHIA, *Blume.*

3—P. NITIDISSIMA, *Benth.*, Flora Austr., i., 51; Fragm. xii., 126. A small glabrous tree with elliptical or almost lanceolate leaves, two or three inches long, narrowed to a short foot stalk, smooth and shiny, the fine netted veins not numerous. Peduncle solitary, axillary, with two or three small bracts near the base. Sepals short and broad. Petals linear. Stamens short and closely packed. Carpels globular or ovoid, one-seeded on short stalks. Found in tropical Queensland.

B.V.—Wood of a dark-grey colour, close-grained, nicely marked, and with a strong spice-like fragrance when fresh cut.

EUPOMATIA, *R. Br.*

3A—E. LAURINA, *R. Br.* in Flind. Voy., ii., 597, t. 2; Flora Austr., i., 54. A tall shrub with rather large, glossy, laurel-like, deep-green leaves, flowers in the exits of the leaves large and showy; blooming in November and December. Fruits resembling a medlar in form. Generally to be met with in Queensland scrubs, and also in those of New South Wales.

B.V.—Wood of a light colour, close-grained, and prettily marked.

B

Order CAPPARIDEÆ.

CAPPARIS, *Linn.*

4—C. NOBILIS, *F. v. M.*, Flora Austr., i., 95. Native Pomegranate. A small tree, the stem usually of a crooked irregular growth. Leaves oblong, the young plants and at times the branches of the trees prickly. Flowers showy-white, but very fragile, in December. Fruit round, one to two inches in diameter, eaten by the natives. Found commonly in the scrubs of Queensland, and also in those of the northern portion of New South Wales.

R.P.V.—Wood of a light or whitish colour, close-grained, firm, and likely to prove useful for carving.

6—C. MITCHELLI, *Lindl.* in Mitch. Three Exped., i., 315; Flora Austr., i. 96; *Busbeckia Mitchelli*, F. v. M., Pl. Vict. i., 53, t. Suppl. 4. Pomegranate; native name on Cloncurry, "Karn-doo-thal." A small tree with a very dense head of foliage; the leaves oblong and velvety, the shoots furnished with short often hooked prickles. Flowers white, showy, very fragile. Fruit one to two inches in diameter, the rind unevenly waled, the pulp eaten by the natives. This is another fruit called Native Pomegranate. An inland tree often found growing in clumps in open country, in North Australia, Queensland, New South Wales, and South Australia.

B.P.V.—Wood whitish, close-grained, hard; suitable for engraving, carving, and similar purposes.

Order BIXINEÆ.

COCHLOSPERMUM, *Kunth.*

7—C. GREGORII, *F. v. M.*, Fragm., i., 74; Flora Austr., i., 106. A small tree, the leaves divided into about seven narrow lobes. Flower-panicles not much branched. Fruit in a pear-shaped capsule, the seeds enveloped in wool. Tropical Queensland.

B.P.V.—Wood of a dark colour, soft and spongy. The log from which the samples were worked was received from the Endeavour River, as *C. Gregorii*, but the specimens were not sufficient to determine the species; but it most probably is *C. Gilliveræi*, Benth.

SCOLOPIA, *Schreb.*

7A—S. BROWNII, *F. v. M.*, Fragm., iii., 11; Flora Austr., i., 107. A small glabrous tree, with oval or oblong lanceolate leaves, one to three inches long on stalks, the margin entire or slightly toothed. Racemes of flowers about two inches long. Fruit a small berry. Met with in Queensland from Mackay to Cape York, also in the northern parts of New South Wales.

B.V.—Wood pinkish, dar ening towards the centre, close grained and tough.

Order PITTOSPOREÆ.

PITTOSPORUM. *Banks.*

8—P. RHOMBIFOLIUM, *A. Cunn.*, in Hook. Ic. Pl. t. 621; Flora Austr., i., 110. A small tree, with dense head affording good shade. Leaves glossy rhomboid-oval, irregularly toothed, two to four inches long. Flowers small white, borne in terminal panicles. Fruit small, pear-shaped, orange colour. Found in South Queensland along the borders of rivers, also in New South Wales.

B.P.V.—Wood whitish, close-grained and tough, rather hard, suitable for carving and engraving.

9—P. UNDULATUM, *Vent.*, Hort. Cels. t. 76; Flora Austr., i., 111. F. v. M., Pl. Vict., i., 71 and 224. Called mock orange in New South Wales. A tree of medium size, with umbrageous head. Leaves glossy with wavy margins, three to six inches long. Flower fragrant, white, in terminal umbels or cymes. Capsules nearly globular, ¼ inch in diameter, valves coriaceous, seeds numerous. In many South Queensland scrubs, more frequent in New South Wales and Victoria.

B.V.—Wood light coloured, close in grain and tough.

10 –P. FERRUGINEUM, *Ait.*, Hort. Kew, ed. 2, ii., 27; Flora Austr., i., 112; Vict. Nat., April, 1885. A small tree more or less clothed with a rusty tomentum The leaves about three or four inches long, ovate or almost lanceolate. Flowers rather small, in terminal panicles. Capsules nearly globular, about ¼ inch in diameter. Common in tropical Queensland, New Guinea, and extending over the Malayan Peninsula.

B.P.V.—Wood of a light-grey colour, close-grained and tough.

11—P. PHILLYRÆOIDES, *DC.*, Prod , 347; Flora Austr., i , 112. In South Australia called in some localities Butter Bush, in others Willow Tree, but the most general local name there is Poison-berry Tree. A small tree with usually drooping branches and long narrow leaves. Flowers fragrant Fruit about the size of a cherry, opening in two valves showing a mass of sticky seeds. In South Australia during long droughts this small tree has proved a valuable fodder. Common to all the colonies, in the interior. In Queensland it is usually met with in brigalow scrubs.

B.V.—Wood close-grained, light in colour, and very hard.

HYMENOSPORUM, *F. v. M.*

12—H. FLAVUM, *F. v. M.*, Fragm. ii., 77; Flora Austr., i., 114; *Pittosporum flavum*, Hook., Bot. Mag. t., 4799. A tall erect tree often flowering as a shrub, glabrous or the young growth, and underside of leaves hoary—pubescent, oblanceolate, entire acuminate, much narrowed towards the short foot-stalk, three to six inches long. Panicle terminal, loose, bracts linear or lanceolate. Flowers fragrant, large, yellow, the petals easily detached. Petals silky tomentose, the claw often one inch long, and the spreading blade ½ inch long ; capsule more or less flattened, often over one inch broad; seeds closely packed, winged. Common on ranges of Southern Queensland and New South Wales.

B.P.V.—Wood whitish close in grain and tough.

BURSARIA, *Cav.*

13—B. INCANA, *Lindl.* in Mitch. Trop. Austr., 224; Flora Austr., i., 115. Native Olive. A small erect tree with olive-like leaves, usually hoary-white and two or more inches long. Flowers white, small, in terminal panicles. This tree is frequently met with in the interior and in the Gulf country, and is not uncommon on the Main Range and Darling Downs.

B.P.V.—Wood of a white or light colour; seems suitable for engraving and similar purposes.

CITRIOBATUS, *A. Cunn.*

13A—C. MULTIFLORUS, *A. Cunn.* in Loud. Hort. Brit, i., 585. Rockhampton native name Kary. Usually a small thorny bush, but at times growing into a small tree. Leaves toothed, small, nearly orbicular, or if long then wedge-shaped, but seldom over ½-inch long. Flowers small in the axils of the leaves, succeeded by small round berries of an orange colour. The shrub is found in South Australia, New South Wales and Extratropical Queensland.

B.V.—Wood close in the grain and very tough; light coloured.

14—C. PAUCIFLORUS, *A. Cunn.* in Loud. Hort. Brit., i., 585 ' *Ixiosporus spinescens,* F. v. M.; Fragm., ii., 76. Usually a larger plant than the last, with fewer flowers and much larger fruit, this latter of a softer nature and often one inch in diameter. Tropical Queensland and North Australia; sometimes but very rarely met with out of the tropics.

B.V.—Wood close-grained, of a light uniform yellowish colour, and hard.

Order GUTTIFERÆ.

CALOPHYLLUM, *Linn.*

16—C. INOPHYLLUM, *Linn; W. et Arn.,* Prod., i., 103. The Alexandrian Laurel or Domba Tree. A tall tree, the bark longitudinally and often tranversely cracked, forming squares of a yellowish colour. Leaves cblong, large, marked with fine parallel tranverse veins. Flowers white. Fruit globular, over one inch diameter. Tropical Queensland coast, New Guinea, and several places in India. The tree also inhabits South India, Burmah, and Andaman Islands, where the wood is used for masts, spars, railway sleepers, and the oil expressed from the fruit is used both medicinally and for burning. This oil is known in Ceylon as " Domba oil."

The following analysis of the fruit is by Mr. K. T. Staiger, F.L.S.:—Shells, 62·5 per cent.; kernels, 37·5 per cent. Greenish-yellow oil, 43 per cent.; dry residue, 27 per cent.; moisture, 30 per cent. Ashes of whole kernels, 1·66 per cent.; ashes of exhausted residue, 6·15 per cent. Mr. Staiger finds the green oil on saponification gives a bright-yellow soap, the green pigment of the oil having changed into a bright yellow.

B.P.V.—Wood of a reddish colour and pretty wavy figure, strong and durable; a useful wood for the joiner and cabinet-maker.

16A—C. TOMENTOSUM, *Wight; Hook*, Fl. Ind., i., 274; Fragm., ix., 174. Keena or Poon Spar Tree. A tall tree, the bark longitudinally cracked, the young shoots and fruits somewhat downy. Leaves with strong mid-rib and fine, thread-like, numerous, parallel, tranverse veins, tapering towards each end. Fruit in spikes shorter than the leaves. Queensland habitat, from Rockingham Bay to the Endeavour River ;· also in India.

This yields the Poon spars of commerce. It is used for bridgework in Iudia, where the seeds are also said to give an oil.

B.V.P.—Wood of a red colour, strong and durable; also a useful wood for the joiner and cabinet-maker.

Order MALVACEÆ.

HIBISCUS, *Linn.*

17—H. HETEROPHYLLUS, *Vent.*, Hort. Malm., t. 103; Flora Austr., i., 212. Wild Rosella. A tall shrub or small tree, the branches and foliage rough or prickly, the leaves entire or divided into two or more finger-like lobes. Flowers large, white with a purple centre. Common in most Queensland scrubs and borders of rivers, also in New South Wales.

B.V.—Wood of a pale yellow colour and open grain, smooth and tough ; suitable, probably, for making musical instruments, as it is a good conductor of sound.

19—H. TILIACEUS, *Linn.*; *DC.*, Prod. i., 454; Flora Austr., i., 218. *Paritium tiliaceum*, St. Hils Wight, Ic. Pl. t., 7. Cotton-tree; native name, "Talwalpin." A small tree with large roundish leaves, hoary-white on the under side. Flowers large; yellow with crimson centre. Abundant on the Queensland sea-coast, and also the islands of the Pacific, the West Indies, and New Guinea; in fact, on the tropical coasts of both continents.

In Central America the fibre is known as "majagu," and in Bengal as "bola," and being little affected by moisture is therefore selected by surveyors for measuring lines. The Queensland blacks at one time used the roots and young growth of this tree for food. In the West Indies, in times of scarcity of bread-fruit, the mucilaginous bark is said to be sucked for food.

B.P.V.—Wood close-grained, colour invisible green, beautifully marked, easy to work, and takes a good polish ; supposed by some to resemble Pollard Oak.

LAGUNARIA, *G. Don.*

20—L. PATERSONI, *Don.*, Gen. Syst., i., 485; Flora Austr., i., 218. Var. *bracteata.* A small tree, the foliage and shoots covered by close, minute, scurvy scales, the leaves on rather long stalks, oblong, three to four inches long, one inch wide at the base, but tapering towards a blunt point, the upper surface green, the under surface nearly white. Flowers pink, slightly downy outside, on short stalks in a cup of three to five lobes. Found at Bowen and a few other parts of North Queensland.

B.P.V.—Wood firm, close in grain and nearly white, easy to work; would be useful.

BOMBAX, *Linn.*

22—B. MALABARICUM, *DC.*, Prod., i., 479; Flora Austr., i., 223. Wight, Ill. t., 29. Silk-cotton tree. A large tree with the branches in whorls; young branches often covered with short conical prickles, dropping the leaves in winter. Leaves of five to seven leaflets. Flowers large, red, in clusters near the ends of the branches. Seed-capsule oblong, the seeds enveloped in a silky wool. Found at the Endeavour River and North Australia; also throughout India and Burmah.

In India the wood is not considered durable except under water. The cotton which surrounds the seeds is used for stuffing pillows, &c. Dr. Dymock says that according to Mahometan writers the young roots have restorative, astringent, and alterative properties.

B.P.V.—Wood light, coarse-grained, and soft.

Order STERCULIACEÆ.

STERCULIA, *Linn.*

23—S. QUADRIFIDA, *R. Br.* in Benn. Pl. Jav. Rar., 233; Flora Austr., i., 227. A tree of medium size, with oval leaves two to five inches long, covered more or less with star-like hairs; the bunches of greenish flowers near the ends of the branches succeeded by bright red pods containing several oval black seeds, which are excellent eating. Found in the Queensland scrubs, both north and south of Brisbane; also in North Australia and New South Wales.

B.V.—Wood light-grey, close-grained, light and easily worked. The bark yields a useful fibre, and the seeds are edible and of agreeable flavour.

24—S. DISCOLOR, *F. v. M.* in Flora Austr. (*Brachychiton discolor,* F. v. M., Fragm., i., 1) The Sycamore or Hat-tree of New South Wales. A tall smooth-barked tree, with palmate-lobed leaves more or less downy, on rather long stalks. The flowers large, bell-shaped, of a dull-red colour. The seed-pods (follicles) four to six inches long, clothed with rusty close hairs, like the young shoots. This tree, like several of our deciduous trees, does not always shed its leaves in winter; flowers in December.

B.P.V.—Wood soft, coarse grained, and of a light colour.

26—S. ACERIFOLIA, *A. Cunn.* in Loud. Hort. Brit., 392; Flora Austr., i., 229. Flame-tree. A large tree, partly or wholly dropping its leaves in winter, with a smoothish bark, and large more or less lobed leaves on long stalks. Flowers bell-shaped, rich red, in large, drooping, straggling panicles, succeeded by pods four to five inches long. Scrubs of Southern Queensland and New South Wales.

B.P.V.—Wood soft, light, and of a light colour.

27—S. DIVERSIFOLIA, *G. Don.*, Syst., i., 516; Flora Austr., i., 229• (*Brachychiton populneum*, R. Br.) Kurrajong of New South Wales. A tree sometimes large but usually small, with a thick somewhat smooth stem, and glossy variously lobed leaves, the lobes or leaves with long narrow points. Flowers bell-shaped, of a dull-brown colour. Pods two to four inches long, the seeds coated with prickly hairs. Found on downs country and also ranges of Southern Queensland, and in the interior of New South Wales and Victoria.

B.V.—Wood soft, coarse grained, and of a light-yellow colour; easily worked.

28—S. RUPESTRIS, *Benth.* (*Delabechea rupestris*, Lindl.; *Brachychiton Delabechii*, F. v. M.) Narrow-leaved Bottle-tree. When growing in scrubs a tall tree, with stout but not much bottled trunk, when in more open country a dwarf tree, with spreading head and much swelled trunk. Leaves very much dissimilar. Quite entire oblong-linear or lanceolate, three to six inches long, or consisting of from five to nine linear-lanceolate lobes. Flowers bell-shaped, deeply lobed, tomentose. Pods (follicles) ovoid acuminate, about one inch long. This curious tree is met with in many Brigalow and Dead Finish scrubs in Queensland, and in times of long drought the trunks have been the means of saving a large number of cattle. The succulent stem, before giving to stock as fodder, is usually passed through the chaff-cutter. Cattle do well on this food, and are exceedingly fond of it; indeed it is said that they even eagerly gather up the chips as they fly from the axe.

B.—Wood soft and spongy.

TARRIETIA, *Blume.*

29—T. ARGYRODENDRON, *Benth.*, Flora Austr., i., 230. Stave-wood; native name, "Boiong." Black Stave-wood and Iron-wood of New South Wales. A tall tree, the foliage silvery on the under side. Leaves usually of three leaflets. Flowers in panicles, white, small, and numerous. Fruit with a long straight wing. Common to the scrubs of Queensland, both north and south; also in New South Wales.

B.P.V.—Wood of light colour, close-grained, tough and firm; may be used as a substitute for English Beech.

29A—T. TRIFOLIOLATA, *F. v. M.*, Fragm., ix., 43. Stave-wood. A tall tree, the foliage of a coppery colour on the under size. Leaves usually of three leaflets. Flowers small, white, in spreading panicles. Fruit with a long straight wing. Plentiful in the North Queensland scrubs, also here and there in the South and in New South Wales.

B.V.—Wood like the last, but of a darker colour.

29B—T. ARGYRODENDRON is probably a form of *T. trifoliolata*, and not *T. argyrodendron* as on the label. The leaflets are much narrower than usual, and they are rather coppery than silvery on the under side. The specimen was received from the Endeavour River.

B.P.V.—Wood of a light-grey colour, close in the grain, hard and tough useful for making tool handles.

30—T. ACTINOPHYLLA, *Bail.*, Syn. Ql. Flora., i., 37. Stave-wood or Iron-wood of New South Wales. A very large tree, with spreading head of a deed-green dense foliage. Leaves of from three to nine leaflets, measuring from three to nine inches each, radiating from the top of the stalk like the ribs of an umbrella. Flowers white, numerous in long loose panicles. Fruit with a broad straight wing. Found on the ranges of Southern Queensland and Northern New South Wales.

B.P.V.—Wood very tough, of a stringy straight grain resembling English Ash ; will bend better than that wood, which points it out as a suitable wood for chair-making, carriage-work, axe-handles, &c.

HERITIERA, *Dry.*

31—H. LITTORALIS, *Dry.* in Ait. Hort. Kew, iii., 546; Flora Austr., i., 231. Red Mangrove or Looking-glass tree. A tree of often crooked growth, but sometimes attaining a great size. Leaves large, oval, silvery on the under side. Flowers small, numerous in loose panicles. Fruit hard, ovoid, two or three inches long, somewhat boat-shaped, with a sharp keel. Abundant in the swamps of the Queensland tropical coast, also in New Guinea and India.

In India, as in Australia, this tree is found on the coast and in tidal forests, In Bengal it is known by the name of "Sundri," is considered durable, tough, and heavy, and is used extensively in boat-building, buggy-shafts, and furniture.

B.P.V.—Wood firm, close-grained, of a dark colour.

COMMERSONIA, *Forst.*

32—C. ECHINATA, *Forst.; D. C.,* Prod. i., 486; Flora Austr., i., 243. Brown Kurrajong of N.S.W. A small tree, the leaves and young branches often covered by a cottony down. Leaves of the young plants resembling those of the common Mallow in shape, often large; those of the older tree oval, and about three inches long. Fruit dry, round, bristly. Queensland scrubs; also in New South Wales, New Guinea, the Indian Archipelago, and the Pacific Islands

B.P.V.—Wood soft, close-grained, white and light, yields a strong fibre used by the natives for making fishing lines and nets.

Order TILIACEÆ.

ECHINOCARPUS, *Blume.*

32A—E. AUSTRALIS, *Benth.*, Journ. Linn. Soc. v. Suppt. 73; Flora Austr., i., 279; under *Sloanea*, in F. v. M., Census of Austr. Pl. A large glabrous tree with obovate oblong leaves, six inches to one foot long, often sharply and irregularly toothed, tapering much towards the base, but obtuse or slightly cordate at the petiole. Flowers rather large, usually in terminal racemes; capsule opening in four bristly valves. Maroochie in Queensland; also in New South Wales, where the timber is said to be used in cabinet work, and to be soft, durable, and easily wrought, and known there as the "Maiden's blush."

B.P.V.—Wood pinkish, close-grained, light, might serve for flooring boards, also is suitable for lining boards.

33—E. WOOLLSII, *F. v. M.*, Fragm., vi. and viii., under *Sloanea.* A large tree with dense head of dark-green foliage, the leaves thick, three to five inches long and one and a half inches broad, and bordered by somewhat blunt teeth. Flowers small. Capsules two-valved, about $\frac{3}{4}$ inch long, covered with somewhat soft prickles. Only found on mountain ranges Southern Queensland and New South Wales.

B.V.—Wood of a light colour, close-grained and tough, useful for flooring and lining boards. When newly cut with somewhat celery-like scent.

ELÆOCARPUS, *Linn*

33A—E. KIRTONII, *F. v. M. (inedit.)* ; Suppt. Syn. Ql. Fl. White Beech or Kirton wood of the Bunya Mountains. A tall tree, often attaining more than 100 feet in height, the young growth silky. Leaves narrow, from four to eight inches long, toothed, and showing the netted veins very prominently. Drupe ovoid. This tree seems to be only found on high mountains. The only places where it is known in Queensland are the Bunya Mountains and on Mount Mistake; and it was first found in similar situations in New South Wales.

B.P.V.—Wood light-brown colour, fine-grained, suitable for furniture. It somewhat resembles English Sycamore.

33C—E. BANCROFTII, *F. v. M. et Bail.* in Proc Roy Soc. Ql., 1885. A lofty handsome tree, the oval leaves usually somewhat clustered near the ends of the rather stout branchlets. Flowers rather large and profuse, much sought after by various honey-eating birds. Fruit roundish, the stone pitted but smooth, containing a single kernel which is of an agreeable flavour. Scrubs of the Johnstone River, Queensland.

B.P.V.—Wood hard and durable, light with a darker colour in the centre; likely to prove useful for sheaves for blocks.

34—E. OBOVATUS, *G. Don.*, Gen. Syst., i., 559; Flora Austr., i., 281. Native name, "Woolal." Pigeonberry Ash of N.S.W. A medium-sized or small tree, with oval leaves two to four inches long, and small white flowers succeeded by oval blue fruit. This tree is met with in several localities in southern Queensland, New South Wales, North Australia, and also in New Guinea.

B.P.V.—Wood light-coloured, close-grained, firm, and easy to work.

c

35—E. CYANEUS, *Ait.*, Epit. Hort. Kew ; Flora Austr., i., 281. Bot. Mag. t. 1737. Native Olive or White Boree of New South Wales. A small tree or tall shrub, glabrous, the leaves usually lanceolate and three or four inches long, more or less serrated and very prominently veined. Flowers in racemes, shorter or as long as the leaves; petals white or pinkish and much divided. Fruit an oval drupe of a blue colour and one-seeded. Flowering during October, November, and December. Southern Queensland, usually in open country; also in New South Wales and Victoria. Wood considered suitable for wood-engraving in New South Wales.

B.—WOOD close-grained and of whitish colour.

36—E. GRANDIS, *F. v. M.*, Fragm., ii., 81; Flora Austr., i., 281. Brisbane Quandong; Blue Fig of New South Wales. A large tree, the branches almost forming whorls round the stem; leaves long, pointed, and more or less bordered by small teeth. Flowers in large bunches of a dirty-white colour, in May near Brisbane. Fruit round, about one inch in diameter; stone rough; ripe about October near Brisbane. Found in the rich scrubs of Queensland both north and south.

B.P.V.—WOOD of a light colour, grain close ; a tough timber; not much used in Queensland. In New South Wales used as a building timber.

Order LINEÆ.

ERYTHROXYLON, *Linn.*

37—E. AUSTRALE, *F. v. M.* in Trans. Vict. Inst., iii., 22 ; Flora Austr., i., 284. Native name at Rockhampton, Moolkellam. A slender shrub with oblong leaves about one inch long, bearing small flowers in the axils of the leaves, which are succeeded by a small one-seeded drupe; in flower in February, and fruit ripe in April. Found in the brigalow scrubs of Queensland.

Mr. Staiger finds that the leaves do not contain cocaine, but they contain coca-tannic acid, and also a yellow dye-stuff which may prove of value.

B.V.—WOOD red in colour, close in grain, and prettily marked.

Order RUTACEÆ.

BOSISTOA, *F. v. M.*

89—B. SAPINDIFORMIS, *F. v. M.*, Flora Austr., i., 359. The "Towra" of the natives; Union Nut of New South Wales. A small erect tree with large, opposite, rough, pinnate leaves, with from 7 to 11 opposite leaflets, which are often more than eight inches long and bordered by saw-like teeth. Flowers in a terminal panicle, small. The fruit dry, rough outside. Found in the scrubs south of Brisbane and some of the northern scrubs, also in New South Wales.

B.P.V.—WOOD close in the grain, of a yellow colour, liable to split in drying.

MELICOPE, *Forst.*

40—M. NEUROCOCCA, *Benth.*, Flora Austr., i., 360; under *Bouchardatia*, in F. v. M., Census of Austr. Pl. A small tree of rather scanty foliage. Leaves pinnate, of one or two pairs of leaflets and an odd one, the leaflets of unequally sized pairs, two to four inches long, sprinkled with a few hairs. Flowers white, very small, the fruits strongly ribbed, about ¼-inch broad. Found in the range scrubs of southern Queensland; also at Wide Bay and in the northern parts of New South Wales.

B.V.—WOOD very hard and close-grained, of a uniform light yellow colour.

EVODIA, *Forst.*

41—E. MICROCOCCA, *F. v. M*, Fragm., i., 144; Flora Austr., i., 361. A tall tree, with three-leafletted leaves and rather dense small bunches of flowers, the rough little fruits containing shining black seeds. Mountain scrubs, southern Queensland and New South Wales.

B.P.V.—WOOD of a light yellow colour, close in the grain and tough.

42—E. ACCEDENS, *Blume*, Bijdrag. Fragm., ix., 102. Native name, "Bunnec-walwal." A tall tree with a smooth bark, the leaves rather large, of three leaflets. Flowers pink, turning bluish as they die away. Not uncommon in rich scrubs, both north and south, in Queensland; also in New South Wales.

B.P.V.—WOOD very white, light, and soft; a good substitute for the European Lime-tree.

MEDICOSMA, *Hook.*

43—M. CUNNINGHAMI, *J. D. Hook.* in Flora Austr., i., 363; Bot. Mag. 3994. Placed in the genus Evodia by F. v. M. Tree of medium size with smooth bark, but stem often crooked and knarled. Leaves opposite, oblong, the stalk jointed. Flowers rather large, white, woolly. A tree frequently met with in the Queensland scrubs to the south, reaching into New South Wales.

B.P.V.—WOOD of a light-yellow colour, close in the grain; a good cabinet-maker's wood.

ZANTHOXYLUM, *Linn.*

44A—Z. VENEFICUM, *Bail.* in Suppl. to Syn. Queensl., Flora, 11. (So named from its poisonous nature.) Tree medium-sized, glabrous, the branches prickly. Leaves pinnate, with from four to seven opposite oval-oblong leaflets, the base unequal-sided, the principal veins almost transversely spreading and prominent, texture thin. Flowers in a terminal panicle; no fruit seen, and the flowers only in early bud. Johnstone River scrubs.

Dr Thos. L. Bancroft says of this tree that it contains in its bark a poisonous principle as toxic as strychnine, and to whose physiological action it has some resemblance. Res. into the Pharm. of some Queensl. Pl., published at Christchurch, N. Zea., Feb., 1888.

B.P.V.—Wood of a yellow colour, close in grain, and easy to work.

45—Z. BRACHYACANTHUM, *F. v. M.*, Pl. Vict., i , 108; Flora Austr., i., 363. Satinwood. In New South Wales called Thorny Yellow-wood, and Satinwood. A small tree, the stem and branches usually covered by short conical prickles. Leaves deep-green, of from 10 to 13 pairs of leaflets, often glossy. Flowers small, white, in bunches; the small capsules opening and showing the black seeds when ripe (in March). A common tree in the range scrubs of Queensland and in the northern parts of New South Wales.

B.V.—Wood of a glossy yellow colour, superior to the wood used in Europe under the name of Satinwood; a valuable wood for cabinet-work.

GEIJERA, *Schott.*

45A—G. MUELLERI, *Benth.*, Flora Austr., i., 364. A scrub tree of medium size, with dense head of deep-green glossy foliage, which give out a strong fragrance on being rubbed in the hand. Leaves oval. Flowers small, white, in straggling bunches. Queensland, from Brisbane northward. The bark is said to yield a Nankeen dye. W. Hill, Cat. of Woods, 1862.

B.P.V.—Wood with a beautiful dark-clouded heartwood, the rest of a light colour, all hard and close-grained, and would suit well for cutting into veneers for cabinet-work.

46—G. SALICIFOLIA, *Schott.*, Rut., t. 4; Flora Austr., i., 364. Tallow-wood. A moderate-sized tree, with at times the under side of the leaves slightly hoary, the leaves somewhat oblong, three or four inches long. Flowers very small, white. A common Queensland tree, also in New South Wales, where, according to C. Moore's "Woods of New South Wales," ink of good quality has been made from its bark.

B.P.V.—Wood of a light-yellow colour, no dark heartwood; hard, close-grained, and of a somewhat greasy nature, suitable for engraving, skate-rollers and hand-screws.

47—G. PARVIFLORA, *Lindl.*, in Mitch. Trop. Austr, 102; Flora Austr., i., 364. Wilga of New South Wales. A small tree with rough bark and drooping branches, the leaves narrow, three to six inches long, and not more than ¼-inch broad, the midrib prominent. Flowers small, white. Brigalow scrubs north and south in Queensland; also in New South Wales, Victoria, South Australia, and Western Australia.

B.V.—Wood hard and tough,[close in grain, of a yellow colour and agreeable fragrance.

PENTACERAS, *Hook f.*

48. P. AUSTRALIS, *Hook f.*, Flora Austr., i., 365. The Scrub White Cedar of New South Wales. A tree of medium size, with glabrous light-green pinnate] foliage ; footstalk of leaf rather long,

leaflets in opposite pairs with a terminal odd one, 7 to 11—two to four inches long; the oil dots large and numerous. Flowers small, white, in large spreading terminal panicles. Fruit, with wing, over one inch long. New South Wales and south Queensland, often in brigalow scrubs.

B.V.—Wood a light-yellow, close-grained and hard. A useful timber.

ACRONYCHIA, *Forst.*

49—A. BAUERI, *Schott*, Fragm. Rut. t. 3. (*A. Hillii*, F. v. M., Fragm. i., 26.) A small tree, the young growth and inflorescence more or less mealy. Leaves opposite, ovate or obovate, three to five inches long, of a somewhat firm texture. Panicles in the axils of the leaves very short; flowers white. Fruit, nearly globular or four-angled, ½in. or more in diameter. This tree is met with in many of the Queensland and New South Wales scrubs.

B.V.—Wood of a uniform yellow colour, or somewhat darker colour towards the heart, close-grained and hard.

50—A. LÆVIS, *Forst.*, Char. Gen., 53, t. 27; Flora Austr., i., 366. At times a tall tree, with irregularly opposite or alternate oblong leaves, from one and a half to four inches long, jointed on to the footstalk. Flowers greenish white, fruit often angular. A scrub tree frequently met with in Queensland and New South Wales.

B.P.V.—Wood close-grained, hard, and of a light colour.

HALFORDIA, *F. v. M.*

52—H. DRUPIFERA, *F. v. M.*, Fragm. v., 43. A small tree with oblong leaves three or four inches long, and terminal panicle of white flowers, succeeded by oval or oblong purplish berries. Frazer's Island, Queensland.

B.P.V.—Wood of a yellowish colour, close in grain, tough and durable.

52A—Of Colonial and Indian Catalogue see 211 of this.

MICROMELUM, *Blume.*

53—M. PUBESCENS, *Blume*; Oliv. in Journ. Linn. Soc. v., Suppl. 40; Flora Austr., i., 368. A small slender tree, more or less pubescent; leaves pinnate, alternate, of from 9 to 15; ovate leaflets, one to three inches long; corymbs of flowers terminal; berries oval, red. Not an uncommon tree in Queensland scrubs, and also found in tropical Asia and the Eastern Archipelago.

B.—Wood of light colour and close grain.

ATALANTIA, *Corr.*

54—A. GLAUCA, *J. D. Hook.* in B. and H. Gen. Pl., i., 305; Flora Austr., i., 370. Kumquat or Lime of the Downs. Usually a shrub, but growing in some localities into a tree with a knotty stem. Foliage grey, the leaves wedge-shaped, one to two inches long. Flowers fragrant, white. Fruit soft, acid, round, about ½-inch in diameter. Usually found on downs country in Queensland, north and south.

B.P.V.—Wood of a bright yellow, with numerous brown streaks or veins, close-grained and easily worked. From the fruit is made a useful preserve.

CITRUS, *Linn.*

. 55—C. AUSTRALIS, *Planch.* in Hort. Donat., 18; Flora Austr., i., 371. *C. Planchonii*, F. v. M. Native Orange. Usually a small tree, but in some scrubs 60 or more feet high with straight erect trunk, the whole often thorny. Leaves narrow or nearly round, deep-green. Flowers pinkish. Fruit round, from one to nearly two inches in diameter. Brisbane River and ranges about.

B.P.V.—Wood of a light-yellow colour, close-grained, hard and durable, useful for cabinet-work. It might probably serve for engraving. The fruit makes a good preserve.

56—C. AUSTRALASICA, *F. v. M.*, Fragm., i., 26; Flora Austr., i., 371. Finger-lime. A tall thorny shrub with small narrow leaves and white flowers, the fruit having an agreeable acid flavour, two to four inches long and about one inch in diameter.

B.V.—Wood close-grained, of a yellowish colour. The fruit makes very good jam.

Order SIMARUBEÆ.

AILANTHUS, *Desf.*

57—A. IMBERBIFLORA, *F. v. M.*, Fragm., iii , 42; Flora Austr., i., 373. A large tree, the leaves with 15 to 17 narrow-ovate leaflets, the flowers in narrow panicles, fruit with a wing two inches long. In scrubs near Rockhampton, and also at Mount Perry.

B.V.—Wood yellow, porous, soft and light.

CADELLIA, *F. v. M.*

57A—C. MONOSTYLIS, *Benth.*, Flora Austr., i.. 375. *Guilfoylia monostylis*, F. v. M., Fragm., viii., 34. A tall shrub with deep-green narrow-ovate leaves. Flowers small in straggling bunches; fruit oval, like purple plums. Mount Mistake Range.

B.V.—Wood of a yellowish colour, somewhat resembling some kinds of Walnut and Satinwood. It is of a pretty grain, and would be useful for cabinet-work and for toy-making.

Order BURSERACEÆ.

GARUGA, *Roxb.*

57B—G. FLORIBUNDA, *Dcne.* in Nouv. Annal. du Mus., iii., 477; Muell. Census, 25; Flora Austr., i., 377. A tree of medium size, the branches marked with broad scars of the fallen leaves. Leaves of seven or eight pairs of leaflets, crowded at the ends of the branches. The flower-panicle broad, terminating leafless bunches; flowers hoary.

Found at the Endeavour River in Queensland, North Australia, and at Timor.

B.P.V.—Wood tough, close-grained, firm and easy to work, colour grey.

CANARIUM, *Linn.*

58—C. AUSTRALASICUM, *F. v. M.*, Fragm., iii., 15; Flora Austr., i., 377. A tree of medium size, the thick branches showing scars where the fallen leaves were attached; the leaves composed of about seven harsh leaflets, the veining very conspicuous. The flowers are very small, in straggling bunches, succeeded by oval fruits of the size of olives. Found only in the tropics in Queensland, and North Australia.

B.P.V.—Wood of a grey colour, dark towards the centre; works easily, and would suit for lining-boards for houses.

Order MELIACEÆ.

TURRÆA, *Linn.*

59—T. PUBESCENS, *Hellen.; Willd.*, Spec. Pl., ii., 555; Flora Austr., i., 379. A small tree. losing the leaves in winter and often flowering before they appear again. Leaves oval, often hairy, two to four inches long. Flowers showy and fragrant, white, with narrow long petals. Fruit five-celled. Common within the tropics, and also some of the southern scrubs, on ranges in Queensland, and also in New Guinea, India, China, Cochinchina, Philippines, and Java.

R.V.—Wood close-grained and hard, the centre very dark, the outer part somewhat of a bright-yellow colour.

MELIA, *Linn.*

60—M. COMPOSITA, *Willd.; Willd. et Arn.*, Prod., 177; Flora Austr., i., 380. White Cedar. A large tree, but flowering as a shrub; loses its leaves in winter. Leaves mealy, much divided. Flowers blue, fragrant, succeeded by oval yellow berries containing a fluted stone. Abundant in Queensland scrubs, and in those of the northern parts of New South Wales; also in New Guinea, India, Burmah, and China.

B.P.V.—Wood easy to work, of a light-red colour, soft and light.

DYSOXYLON, *Blume.*

61A—D. MUELLERI, *Benth.*, Flora Austr., i., 381; "Kedgy-kedgy," or Pencil Cedar. Turnip-wood of New South Wales. A tall tree, the leaves from one to two feet long, composed of from 11 to 21 narrow oval leaflets, which are from three to six inches long. Flower-panicle nearly one foot long, branched and bearing numerous flowers. Fruit nearly without hairs. Found in scrubs of Southern Queensland and New South Wales.

B.P.V.—Wood of a red colour, prettily marked; a useful wood for the joiner and cabinet-maker. Used in New South Wales for making cigar-boxes.

62—D. RUFUM, *Benth.*, Flora Austr., i., 382. Usually a small tree, with leaves about two feet long, the leaflets three to six inches long, more or less downy, the flower-panicles scarcely branched, the round fruits covered with rigid golden hairs. Scrubs of southern Queensland and New South Wales.

B.V.—WOOD of a light yellow colour, hard and close-grained; the figure-lines small.

63—D. RUFUM, VAR. GLABBESCENS. A large tree, very like the last in the fruit, but the leaves less downy. Rockhampton scrubs.

B.V.—WOOD of a straw colour, coarse in the grain, easy to work.

63A—D. FRASERIANUM, *Benth.*, Flora Austr., i., 381. Pencil Cedar. Rose-wood of New South Wales. A large handsome tree. Leaves of from five to nine leaflets, the leaflets about three to six inches long, and usually having tufts of hairs in the axils of the principal veins on the back or under surface. Fruit somewhat pear-shaped. Mountain scrubs of southern Queensland and New South Wales.

B.P.V.—WOOD of a red colour, close-grained, and easy to work; a useful wood for cabinet-work and lining boards. In New South Wales said to be used in making furniture, ship-building, turnery, and carving.

63B—D. OPPOSITIFOLIUM, *F. v. M.* A medium-sized tree with opposite leaves of about eight leaflets. Flowers in short bunches; ruit about $\frac{1}{2}$in. in diameter. Rockingham Bay to Endeavour River.

B.P.V.—WOOD with a small prettily-marked heartwood, and a large quantity of yellow wood towards the bark; grain close, easily worked, and fragrant; a useful wood for both joiner and cabinet-maker.

AMOORA, *Roxb.*

64—A. NITIDULA, *Benth.*, Flora Austr., i., 383. A tall tree with a dense foliage, the leaves of two or four opposite leaflets about four inches long, of a thick consistency; the panicle of few flowers. Fruit pear-shaped; seeds globular. Scrubs of southern Queensland and New South Wales.

B.P.V.—WOOD of a light colour, close and tough in grain.

OWENIA, *F. v. M.*

66—O. ACIDULA, *F. v. M.* in Hook. Kew Misc., ix,, 303; Flora Austr., i., 385. Sour Plum; Emu Apple. A small tree with a dense head of a lively green foliage, the branches pendulous. Leaves with from 9 to 30 narrow leaflets, about an inch or more long. Flowers in narrow panicles very small. Fruit an inch or more in diameter, reddish and very sour. Frequently met with in the interior in Queensland, New South Wales, and South Australia. Fruit eaten in a raw state but very acid.

B.P.V.—WOOD reddish, close-grained, hard, but very easy to work; useful for cabinet-making and turnery.

67. O. VENOSA, *F. v. M.* in Hook. Kew Misc., ix., 304; Flora Austr., i., 386. Tulip Wood and Sour Plum of New South Wales,

and Crow's Apple in Queensland. Native name near Rockhampton, Pyddhart. A large tree; leaves of from six to eight oblong leaflets, prominently veined and often notched at the end, two to four inches long, the stalk more or less winged. The flowers in long straggling bunches, very small. Fruit round, about one inch in diameter. A common tree in the scrubs of North and South Queensland.

B.P.V.—Wood of a reddish colour, hard, of close grain, very strong and durable; useful for various purposes.

CARAPA, *Aubl.*

68—C. MOLUCCENSIS, *Lam.; D.C.*, Prod., i., 626; Flora Austr., i., 387. A tree of medium size, the bark falling off in scale-like patches, with leaves of usually four leaflets some two or three inches long, the flowers rather small, but the fruit often from three to five inches in diameter, containing large angular seeds. Frequently met with on the tropical coast of Queensland, Northern Australia. A sea-coast tree also of tropical Asia and Africa.

In India and Burmah an oil is said to be obtained from its seeds.

B.P.V.—Wood resembling Red Cedar, of close grain, prettily marked; a good cabinet wood.

CEDRELA, *Linn.*

69—C. TOONA, *Roxb.*, Pl.'Corom., iii., 33, t. 238; Flora Austr., i., 387; Wight, Ic. t. 161; *C. australis*, in F. v. M., Census of Aust. Pl. Red Cedar or Toon tree; native name at Brisbane, "Mamin" and "Mugurpul;" at Wide Bay, "Woota." A very large tree, with spreading head, losing its leaves in the winter; the leaves of from 11 to 17 leaflets, the flowers in long panicles. Seed-capsules about one inch long. A common tree of the Queensland and New South Wales scrubs, bordering rivers and creeks; found also in India and Burmah.

The timber of this tree, which is abundant in India and Burmah, is that known in the English market as Moulmein Cedar. In North-west India, as in Australia, it is used for furniture, carvings, &c.; in Bengal and Assam, in making tea-boxes.

B.P.V.—Wood beautifully grained, of a red colour, easy to work and very durable. The wood most generally in use with cabinet-makers in Queensland.

FLINDERSIA, *R. Br.*

70—F. AUSTRALIS, *R. Br.* in Flind. Voy., ii., 595, t. i.; Flora Austr., i., 388. Sometimes called Crow's Ash. A tree of medium size, frequently if not always losing its leaves in winter. The bark, like that of the Cedar, falling off in irregular-shaped woody patches or scales; the leaves alternate, of three to six oblong leaflets, generally crowded at the ends of the branches; the flowers white, in rather dense bunches. Fruit about three inches long, very rough, not separating into distinct boat-like portions, but opening to near the base, so as to allow of the escapement of the placentas and winged seeds. Of frequent occurrence in range scrubs, Queensland; also in New South Wales.

B.P.V.—Wood yellow, close-grained, very hard, and of great strength and durability; does not rust iron.

71—F. Schottiana, *F. v. M*, Fragm., iii., 25; Flora Austr., i, 388. Ash and Stavewood of New South Wales. A tall tree, stem smoothish, erect. Leaves large, opposite, of from eight to twelve leaflets, which measure from four to six inches long, and more or less covered by soft short down. Flowers numerous in a large spreading panicle. Fruit large, splitting into separate boat-like pieces, the outside covered by prickly processes. River scrubs in both North and South Queensland; also in New South Wales.

Dr. Thos. L. Bancroft found the bark of this and some other Flindersias to contain a poisonous principle.

B.P.V.—Wood of a pale-yellow colour, close-grained and firm; useful for cabinet work.

72—F. Oxleyana, *F. v. M.*, Fragm., i., 65; Flora Austr., i., 389. Common yellow-wood. Usually a tall erect tree having a smooth bark; the leaves crowded at the ends of the branches. Leaves opposite, of from four to ten leaflets, with or without an odd one shortly pointed, and from two to four inches long, often curved. Flowers in a loose panicle. Fruit dividing when ripe into boat-shaped pieces two to four inches long, rough on the back. Scrubs of southern Queensland and New South Wales.

B.P.V.—Wood of a bright-yellow colour, strong and fibrous, used in cabinet-work. It is not readily attacked by the white ant, and is useful for handscrew-making and buggy-shafts.

73—F. maculosa, *Lindl.* (As an *Elæodendron* in Mitch. Trop. Austr., 384; also in part in Flora Austr., i., 389.) Spotted tree or Leopard-wood. A small tree with linear, obtuse, entire, opposite leaves of from one to two inches long, the veins not prominent. Flowers very small in terminal panicles of one to three inches long, and but little branched. Fruit small, rough, about one inch long, dividing into boat-shaped pieces. Cunnamulla, in Queensland.

B.P.V.—Wood bright-yellow, nicely marked, close in grain, and very hard; would suit well for bearings of shafting.

73a—F. Bournjotiana, *F. v. M.*, Fragm., ix., 133. A noble tree, with dense deep-green foliage. Leaves of from one to nine oval leaflets, several inches long; the flowers small, in very spreading panicles. Fruit rough, oblong, about three inches long, breaking up as in most other species. Found first at Cardwell, since in scrubs further north.

B.P.V.—Wood strong, durable, easily worked, of a light colour.

73b—F. Strzeleckiana, *F. v. M.*, Fragm., i., 65, and Flora Austr., i., 389, in part. Spotted tree. A small tree, the bark hard and falling off in patches, leaving light-coloured indentations in the bark. Leaves of one or two pairs of narrow-linear leaflets about one inch in length and not ¼-inch broad, the leaf-stalk winged. Flowers in terminal short panicles. Capsules about one inch long, and when ripe dividing into boat-shaped pieces. Brigalow scrubs, Leichhardt district, Queensland.

B.P.V.—Wood of a yellow colour, close in the grain, hard, strong, and durable.

73c—F. Strzeleckiana, *F. v. M.*, var. *latifolia.* A small tree, the leaves of few leaflets about two or three inches long and nearly one inch broad. Flower in terminal panicle, the capsule about one inch and a-half to two inches long, dividing into separate boat-shaped pieces. Main Range, Queensland.

B.P.V.—Wood hard, close-grained, yellow, strong and durable.

74—F. Bennettiana, *F. v. M.*, Flora Austr., i., 389 ; Fragm., ix., 131, and xi., 135. Bugum bogum, Teak and Bulboro of New South Wales. A large tree, with opposite leaves of from three to five oval leaflets, two to three inches long, or longer on some trees, the stalks angular. Flower panicle large, or at times short. Fruit two to three inches long, rough. Scrubs of South Queensland and New South Wales.

B.V.—Wood hard, fine in the grain, and light in colour.

Order OLACINEÆ.
XIMENIA, *Linn.*

74d—X. americana, *Linn; DC.*, Prod. i , 533; Flora Austr., i., 391. A small crooked-stemmed tree, the branches often furnished with sharp spines. Foliage scanty ; leaves ovate, one to two inches long. Flowers sweet-scented, white : the petals hairy inside with white hairs. Fruit a yellow plum of about one inch in diameter. Found at Clermont, in Queensland ; also in North Australia, and in tropical regions out of Australia, of both the New and Old World.

Roxburgh says that the wood of this is used in India as a substitute for Sandal-wood.

B.P.V.—Wood close-grained, tough, hard, and light in colour. It works like English Box, and might be suitable for engraving.

VILLARESIA, *Ruiz et Pav.*

74e—V. Moorei, *F. v M.*, Flora Austr., i., 395. A tall tree, the leaves deep-green, oblong, three or four inches long, the flowers in little-branched often raceme-like bunches. Fruit damson-like. Bunya Mountains, in Queensland, and Clarence River, New South Wales.

B.P.V.—Wood of a light-grey colour, close-grained and prettily marked. Useful both for the cabinet-maker and joiner.

Order CELASTRINEÆ.
CELASTRUS, *Linn.*

75—C. bilocularis, *F. v. M.*, in Trans. Phil. Inst. Vict., iii., 31 ; Flora Austr., i., 399. A small tree, with oval and slightly pointed leaves, sometimes bordered by teeth. The flowers small, in axillary bunches, capsules two-valved. Found in several parts of southern Queensland.

B.V.—Wood of a light-grey colour, close in the grain, hard and tough.

75A—C. DISPERMUS, *F. v. M.*, Trans. Phil. Inst. Vict., iii , 31 ; Flora Austr., i., 399. A small glabrous tree. Leaves elliptical to broadly lanceolate, and two or three inches long, and much narrowed into a rather long foot-stalk. Flowers in axillary or lateral racemes. The flowers five-merous and the capsules about $\frac{1}{4}$-inch long, and two-celled, or at times three-angled and three-celled.

B.P.V.—Wood of a light colour, close-grained and prettily marked.

76—C. CUNNINGHAMII, *F. v. M.*, in Trans. Phil. Inst. Vict., iii., 30; Flora Austr., i., 399. A small tree, the foliage having a greyish look ; the leaves narrow, one to three inches long, often rigid, the midrib alone prominent. Flowers very small, succeeded by small two-valved capsules, containing one or two seeds. Common in open country, or on the borders of scrubs in North Australia, Queensland, and New South Wales.

B.P.V.—Wood of a pinkish colour, nicely marked; useful for cutting into veneers for cabinet-work.

DENHAMIA, *Meisn.*

77—D. PITTOSPOROIDES, *F. v. M.*, in Trans. Phil. Inst., Vict., iii., 30; Flora Austr., i., 402. A small tree, with hard, narrow, ovoid leaves, the margins of which are more or less toothed, the veins prominent. Flowers minute ; fruit globose, hard, splitting at the top into three divisions to allow the seeds to escape. Met with in brigalow scrubs and open country, both North and South Queensland ; also in New South Wales.

B.P.V.—Wood of a uniform pale-yellow colour, resembling the English Elder; suitable for engraving, pattern-making, and similar uses.

ELÆODENDRON, *Jacq. f.*

78—E. AUSTRALE, *Vent.*, Jard. Malm., t., 117; Flora Austr., i., 402. A medium-sized tree, the leaves usually opposite, ovate, two to four inches long, with often blunt teeth. Flowers very small. Fruit a red, oval, dryish drupe, containing a hard usually one-seeded stone. Found on the borders of scrubs, North Australia, Queensland, and New South Wales.

B.P.V.—Wood of a pinkish colour, close in grain and very tough, but warps a good deal in drying if cut up before it is seasoned; useful for tool-handles.

78A—E. AUSTRALE, VAR. ANGUSTIFOLIA, Flora, Austr., i., 403. A similar tree to the last, differing only in the leaves, being narrow-oblong. South Queensland, and Rockhampton in the North.

B.V.—Wood similar to the last.

79—E. MELANOCARPUM, *F. v. M.*, Fragm., iii., 62; Flora Austr., i., 403. Tree of medium size, deep-green foliage ; the leaves opposite, oval, with broad blunt teeth; the fruit resembling in shape and colour a large damson. Common on the Queensland northern coast, at Mount Perry and other inland localities, and in North Australia.

B.P.V.—Wood tough, of a light colour and fine grain.

SIPHONODON, *Griff.*

80—S. AUSTRALE, *Benth.*, Flora Austr., i., 403. Ivory-wood. A tall tree with straight erect stem, the bark of a light colour. Leaves alternate, pale-green, with few prominent veins, about two to four inches long, tapering towards the foot-stalk. Flowers very small. Fruit round or pear-shaped, pale-yellow, dry and hard, one inch or more in diameter. Found in the dense scrubs both north and south in Queensland, and also in New South Wales.

B.P.V.—Wood white, very close in grain, firm and easily worked; an excellent wood for the cabinet-maker, and probably would suit for engraving.

Order RHAMNEÆ.

VENTILAGO.

81—V. VIMINALIS, *Hook.* in Mitch. Trop. Austr., 369; Flora Austr., i., 411. A small tree, the branches slender and often whitened, the leaves linear but narrowed towards the base, seldom over $\frac{1}{4}$-inch broad, three to five inches long, the midrib prominent, the primary lateral veins few, distant, and almost running parallel with the midrib. Flowers very small in raceme-like panicles. Stamens five, but no petals. This small tree is met with in brigalow scrubs and on open inland downs in Queensland; also in North Australia, New South Wales, and South Australia.

B.V.—Wood very hard and heavy, close-grained, and of a dark-brown colour.

The specimens sent belong to the above plant, but I am afraid the log belonged to some other tree, not having correct samples or description of the wood for comparison; it is worked for exhibit.

ZIZYPHUS, *Juss.*,

82—Z. JUJUBA, *Lam.*, W. and Arn., Prod. 162; Flora Austr., i., 412; Bedd. H. Syl. t. 149. Jujube. A tall moderate-sized deciduous or semi-deciduous tree, with a dark rough bark, with or without stipular prickles. Leaves ovate or nearly orbicular, three-nerved, glabrous above, clothed with a white tomentum beneath. Flowers in compact small cymes. Fruit, a plum-like drupe. Tropical Queensland; also in India, Burmah, etc.

B.P.V.—Wood whitish, close-grained, and hard.

ALPHITONIA, *Reissek.*

84—A. EXCELSA, *Reissek* in Endl. Gen.; Flora Austr., i., 414. Red Ash. Leather Jacket of New South Wales. Native name "Mee-a-mee." A small or in the scrubs a tall tree, the bark very rough on old trees, smooth on the younger trees. Leaves usually three to six

inches long, green on the face but white or rusty underneath. Flowers
dingy-white. Fruit black when ripe, the outer skins cracking off and
showing a mealy substance of a light or dark yellow colour. Widely
spread, often in open country in Northern Australia, Queensland,
and New South Wales; also South Cape, New Guinea.

B.P.V.—Wood near the outside somewhat pinkish, the inner wood dark-
brown or party-coloured throughout, close-grained, very tough, warps in drying,
but probably a useful wood for the cabinet-maker.

EMMENOSPERMUM, *F. v. M*.

84A—E. ALPHITONIOIDES, *F. v. M.*, Fragm. iii, 63; Flora Austr.,
i., 415. Tree of medium size, quite glabrous. Leaves opposite or
nearly so, ovate acuminate, two to three inches long, entire green on
both sides. Flowers in umbel-like cymes, arranged in trichotomous
cymes in the upper axils or terminal. Fruit three or four lines long.
Met with in the northern parts of New South Wales, and several
localities in Queensland.

B.V.—Wood yellow with a small pinkish centre, close-grained, useful for
cabinet-work.

Order AMPELIDEÆ.

VITIS, *Linn.*

85—V. ANTARCTICA, *Benth.*, Flora Austr., i., 447. (*Cissus antarctica*, Vent.; Bot. Mag. t., 2488. *C. glandulosa*, Poir.; *V. Baudiniana*,
F. v. M.; Census of Austr. Plants.) A large climber, often forming
stems a foot in diameter and climbing to the tops of our scrub trees,
the young growth often rusty. Leaves ovate oblong, three or four
inches long, entire or toothed, frequently with glands on the under
side in the axils of the principal veins. Flower cymes dense. Berry
black, globular, at times ½-inch in diameter.

B.—Wood dark brown, coarse-grained.

85A—V. NITENS, *F. v. M.*, Fragm., ii., 73; Flora Austr. i., 448.
A large glabrous climber, the leaves of three ovate thick remotely
toothed leaflets three to five inches long. Flowers in umbel-like
cymes, nearly glabrous, two or three together or solitary on a very
short peduncle; petals four or rarely five, falling off separately;
berries ovoid, sharply acid South Queensland scrubs, climbing to the
tops of the trees; also in New South Wales.

B.—Wood soft and spongy of a brown colour and coarse grain.

86—V. HYPOGLAUCA, *F. v. M.*, Pl. Vict., i., 94; Flora Austr., i.,
450. A tall climber, the leaves composed of usually five oval-pointed
leaflets from three to five inches long and often toothed, white on the
under surface, and placed finger-like on the top of the stalk. Flowers
small, bright-yellow; fruit round, black, of an acid flavour, and about
¼-inch diameter. Met with on river-banks and scrubs in Queensland,
New South Wales, and Victoria.

B.V.—Wood soft and spongy, of a grey colour.

86A—V. STERCULIFOLIA, *F. v. M.*, Flora Austr., i., 450. A tall climber, the leaflets similarly placed but of a coarser nature and not white on the under side. Fruit ovoid. Found in Queensland coast scrubs and also in New South Wales.

B.V.—WOOD light-brown, soft and spongy.

Order SAPINDACEÆ.

DIPLOGLOTTIS, *J. D. Hook.*

88—D. CUNNINGHAMII, *J. D. Hook.* in Benth. and Hook. Gen. Pl., 395; Flora Austr., i., 455; Bot. Mag. t., 4470, under *Cupania.* Native Tamarind. A large tree with a somewhat brownish smooth bark, the young branches densely clothed with rusty hairs, bluntly angular. Leaves often very large and rough, the leaflets oblong, one to eight, often nearly one foot long. Flowers small, in clusters along the branches of a straggling panicle. Fruit of two or three roundish lobes, each containing a round seed which has an amber-coloured inner covering of an agreeable acid flavour. Scrubs of Queensland, and New South Wales.

R.P.V.—WOOD light-coloured except near the centre, close-grained and very tough.

CUPANIA, *Linn.*

88A—C. WADSWORTHII, *F. v. M.*, Census of Austr. Plants, 24; *Harpullia Wadsworthii*, F. v. M., Fragm. iv., 1, t. 26., ix., 89, 197. A small or medium-sized slightly hairy tree, the leaves of few, opposite leaflets, usually only one or two pairs, ovate-cuneate, the apex very blunt and broad as if cut off, from one and a half to over three inches long, and from one to two inches broad at the end, glossy on the upper surface, the primary nerves few and distant, the smaller reticulation rather prominent. Flowers in racemose panicles on rather slender stalks; capsule, two or three valved, the valves coriaceous and slightly silky inside; seeds about one and a half inch long. Found in several localities in tropical Queensland.

B.—WOOD close-grained, tough, with a somewhat pinkish tinge.

89. C. SHIRLEYANA, *Bail.*, 2nd Suppl. Syn. Queensl Flora. A tall shrub or small tree with bright green foliage; leaves pinnate, leaflets serrated, numerous, covering the whole leaf, the largest at the end, the lowest often stipule-like and overlapping the stem Flowers in long slender racemes, fruit oblong, the seeds nearly covered by the arillus. Sankey's Scrub, Logan Road.

B.—WOOD of a yellow colour, close-grained and tough.

90—C. SEMIGLAUCA, *F.v M.*; Flora Austr. i., 457. (*Arytera semiglauca*, F. v. M., in Trans. Vict Inst., iii., 25.) In New South Wales called White Bark and Black Ash. A small tree, the leaves with from two to six oblong-elliptical or almost lanceolate leaflets, from two to four inches long, entire, narrowed into a short footstalk, grey

on the under side. Flowers small, in axillary or terminal panicles;
capsules, four to five lines diameter, with divaricate compressed lobes;
seeds shining, with a thin arillus. Met with in many south Queensland scrubs, bordering upon forest land; also, in New South Wales.

B.V.—Wood of a light pinkish colour, tough, close-grained, very prettily
marked.

91—C. ANACARDIOIDES, *A. Rich.*, Sert. Astrol., 33, t. 13; Flora
Austr., i., 458. Native name "Tuckeroo." A moderate-sized tree
with umbrageous head, the leaves of usually eight obtuse rigid
leaflets. Flowers in straggling bunches, greenish. Fruit of three
roundish lobes. A river-side tree found in North Australia, Queensland, and New South Wales.

B.P.V.—Wood of a light pinkish colour, close-grained and tough; might
serve for making handles for tools.

91A—C. ANACARDIOIDES. Variety with smaller leaves. Main
Range.
B.V.—Wood light-coloured, close-grained, very tough.

93—C. PSEUDORHUS, *A. Rich.*, Sert. Astrol., 34, t. 14; Flora
Austr., i., 459. Tree medium size, bark smooth, the branches and
foliage rusty. Leaves of from 13 to 21 narrow-oval pointed leaflets,
shining on the upper side, more or less hairy underneath.
Flowers small. Capsules densely covered with dark-brown hairs
when ripe, but in an early stage they are quite velvety and of a rich
purplish colour, a pleasing contrast to the dark green foliage.
Generally found bordering rivers, and in coast scrubs in Queensland
and New South Wales.

B.P.V.—Wood of a light colour, grain close, very tough; would be excellent for pick-handles.

94—C. XYLOCARPA, *A. Cunn.* A medium-sized tree, the branchlets
rusty. Leaflets three to six or reduced to two, oblong, two or three
inches long, toothed or entire, with usually small tufts of hairs in the
forks of the principal veins on the back. Flower bunches short;
capsule nearly globular, woody, about ½in. in diameter. Borders of
rivers, and in mountain scrubs in Queensland and New South Wales.

B.P.V.—Wood very tough, of light yellow colour, the grain resembling
Lancewood; would be useful for making tool-handles.

94A—C. NERVOSA, *F. v. M.* in Trans. Vict. Inst., iii., 27; Flora
Austr., i., 459. A tree of moderate size, the young branches but
slightly downy. Leaves of three to six leaflets, three to six inches
long, toothed or entire, with sometimes tufts of hairs in the axils of
the raised primary veins. Flowers in simple racemes of one or two
inches. Capsules nearly globular, smooth outside, hairy inside.
North and south scrubs in Queensland; also in New South Wales.

B.P.V.—Wood, the outer part of a light colour, but the centre dark-brown,
the grain close, very tough and strong.

RATONIA, *DC.*

95—R. PYRIFORMIS, *Benth.*, Flora Austr., i., 461. (Cunningham's specimens gathered at the Hastings River are marked *Cupania laurifolia.*) A fine umbrageous tree, the leaves of from three to six oval smooth leaflets, four to six inches long. Flowers in a straggling panicle, very small; fruit pear-shaped, about ½-inch long. Scrubs of southern Queensland and New South Wales.

B.P.V.—WOOD of a light colour, firm and tough; suitable for axe-handles.

96—R. TENAX, *Benth.*, Flora Austr., i., 461. Usually a small tree. Leaflets of the leaf various as to number and shape, usually two to six, oblong, pale-green; panicles short; fruit pear-shaped, but more or less flattened, more than ½-inch long. River scrubs in Queensland; also in New South Wales.

B.P.V.—WOOD light in colour, dark towards the centre, very tough and close-grained.

ATALAYA, *Blume.*

98—A. HEMIGLAUCA, *F. v. M.*, Flora Austr., i., 463. A small tree, producing abundance of white flowers. The leaves light-grey, of few long narrow lobes, which are often curved, and from two to eight inches long. Fruit with a wing one to one and a-half inch long. North Australia, Queensland, New South Wales, and South Australia. On downs country called Cattle-bush, and frequently felled for fodder during droughty weather.

B.V.—WOOD yellowish, hard, and of a close grain.

NEPHELIUM, *Linn.*

99—N. CONNATUM, *F. v. M.*, Flora Austr., i., 465. (*Sapindus cinereus*, A. Cunn.) Referred to by A. Gray, Bot. Amer. Expl. Exped., i., 258. A coast tree of small size, the foliage dense and of a grey-hue, leaflets two to six, oblong, two to four inches long, and one and a-half to two inches broad. Flowers in a pyramidal panicle. Fruit three or four furrowed, splitting irregularly; seeds black, arillus red. Southern and at a few northern parts of the Queensland coast.

B.V.—WOOD of a light colour, close-grained, very hard and tough.

99A—N. TOMENTOSUM, *F. v. M.*, in Trans. Vict. Inst. ii., 64; Flora Austr., i., 466. A medium-sized tree, clothed with a rust-coloured soft down. Leaves of four to eight oval-oblong leaflets more or less toothed. Flower small, in slightly branched panicles. Fruit softly velvety, of two or three globular lobes. River scrubs of southern Queensland and northern scrubs of New South Wales.

B.P.V.—WOOD of a yellow colour, close-grained and hard.

99B—N. SUBDENTATUM, *F. v. M.*, Flora Austr., i,, 465. A medium-sized tree with smooth bark. The shoots and inflorescence more or less tomentose. Leaflets few, ovate lanceolate, slightly toothed, two to five inches long, glabrous. The panicles short, not at all or

D

only slightly branched. Fruit slightly hoary, the usual two lobes globular and united to the top. Nerang Creek, Queensland, and New South Wales.

B.P.V.—Wood of a light colour, close-grained and tough.

HETERODENDRON, *Desf.*

100A—H. OLEÆFOLIUM, *Desf.* in Meur. Mus., par. iv., t. 3; Flora Austr., i., 469. A small tree, the young shoots minutely downy. Leaves narrow, two to four inches long, rigid. Flowers in a panicle, shorter than the leaves. Fruit of from one to four globular lobes. Usually met with in dry or brigalow scrubs in many parts of Queensland, New South Wales, Victoria, South Australia, and Western Australia.

B.P.V.—Wood, the outer yellow, the inner dark-brown, hard and close-grained, suitable for engraving or any purpose to which Box is applied.

101—H. DIVERSIFOLIUM, *F. v. M.*, Fragm. i., 46; Flora Austr., i., 469. A small erect tree, the branches tomentose or glabrous. Leaves from linear-cuneate to oblong-cuneate, from under one inch to over two inches long, usually pungent-pointed, and with sharp lobes or teeth. Flowers few, in short panicles. Fruit-lobes very divaricate, ovoid, arillus red. Brigalow scrubs.

B.V.—Wood pinkish except the heart-wood, close in grain, hard and tough useful for engraving and many other purposes.

HARPULLIA, *Roxb.*

103—H. HILLII, *F. v. M.*, Trans. Vict. Inst., iii., 26; Flora Austr., i., 470. A moderate-sized tree, the young growth and inflorescence downy, otherwise glabrous. Leaves pinnate, leaflets five to eleven, oval-oblong and obtuse, three to five inches long or more. Panicle shorter than the leaves but little branched. Capsule one and a half inch broad. The turgid lobes hairy inside and slightly downy outside. Queensland coast scrubs, and the northern scrubs of New South Wales.

B.—Wood of a light colour, close grained.

104—H. PENDULA, *Planch.*, in Trans. Vict. Inst., iii., 26; Flora Austr., i., 471 Tulip-wood. A fine tree, the foliage dense, of a light-green colour. Leaves from three to six or more, ovate, three to five inches long; panicle of flowers drooping. Fruit a capsule of usually two papery orange-coloured lobes, each containing a glossy black seed; but by far the greater number of fruits are abortive—that is, the capsule is fully developed, but the seed is wanting. Common in Queensland scrubs north and south, also in New South Wales.

B.P.V.—Wood of a light colour, or in some trees showing a more or less quantity of a beautifully figured and coloured dark wood towards the centre. The outer or light wood is very tough, easily worked, and might suit for engraving purposes; this outer wood is said to be the best in Australia for Lithographers' scrapers.

AKANIA, *J. D. Hook.*

106—A. HILLII, *J. D. Hook.*, in Benth. and Hook. Gen. Pl., i., 409. Turnip-wood. A small, handsome, erect tree, the leaves two or more feet long, composed of long narrow leaflets bordered by sharp teeth, shining on the upper side, the under side showing the netting of the veins, and each mesh enclosing three or four dots. Panicle long, loose; capsule globose, about one inch in diameter, two or three-valved. Southern Queensland scrubs and New South Wales.

B.V.—Wood of a light colour, close grained, and prettily marked; warps much in drying, but the log used was from a young tree.

BLEPHAROCARYA, *F. v. M.*

106A—B. INVOLUCRIGERA, *F. v. M.*, Fragm., xi., 16. A tree with leaves of about seven pairs of leaflets. Fruit in a much divided cup. Mountains about the Endeavour River, Queensland.

B.P.V.—Wood of a light-red colour, of a close grain, soft and easy to work.

DODONÆA, *Linn.*

107—D. TRIQUETRA, *Andr.*, Bot. Rep., t. 230; Flora Austr., i., 474. Hop-bush; native name, "Kinjenga kilamul." A tall shrub with sharp angular branches and long willow-like leaves, the hop-like fruit very abundant. Found in open country and borders of scrubs in South Queensland, New South Wales, and Victoria.

B.P.V.—Wood of a light-colour except near the centre, which is dark; close-grained, hard, tough, and nicely marked.

108—D VISCOSA, *Linn.*, DC., Prod., i., 616; Flora Austr., i., 475. Hop-bush. A small tree shedding its bark in long thin strips, the young shoots often very viscid, the branches somewhat angular. Leaves oblong, the capsule with membranous wings resembling the hop. Found in nearly all parts of Queensland, North Australia, Western Australia, South Australia, Victoria, Tasmania, and New South Wales; also in Tropical America, Africa, and Asia, the Pacific Islands, New Zealand, and New Guinea.

The form growing in India is said to be used for engraving, turning, tool-handles, and walking-sticks. Has a white sapwood and a hard dark-brown heartwood, which is close-grained. The leaves of a form of this species are said to be used in some parts of India as a febrifuge.

B.V.—Wood of a brown colour, close-grained and hard.

Order ANACARDIACEÆ.

RHUS, *Linn.*

109—R. RHODANTHEMA, *F. v. M.* in Journ. Pharm. Soc. Vict. Pl., i., 43; Muell. Census Austr. Pl. Deep or Dark Yellow wood; native name, "Jango-jango." Yellow Cedar of New South Wales. A tall tree, the leaves of from seven to nine leaflets two or three inches long, with often little tufts of hair along the midrib, the leaflets of the young plants very much larger and often bluntly lobed.

Flowers in dense bunches, red; fruit globose, brown and glossy. Queensland scrubs and creek-sides, north and south; also in New South Wales.

B.P.V.—Wood in demand for cabinet work ; the heartwood of a beautiful glossy dark-yellow or bronzed colour; soft and fine-grained.

BUCHANANIA.

109a—B. mangoides, *F. v. M.* Tree, the smaller branches downy, the leaves large, oblong, green on the upper surface, pale on the under side. Flowers small in a terminal panicle.

B.V.—Wood of a pinkish colour, close in grain, tough, and easy to work.

SEMECARPUS, *Linn.*

110—S. anacardium, *Linn ; W. et Arn.*, Prod., 168 ; Flora Austr., i., 491. Australian "Cashew Nut ;" Marking Nut Tree. A tree with oblong leaves six to nine inches long, pale or nearly white on the under side. Flowers in terminal bunches. The fleshy cup on which the fruit is seated is of a bright red colour and eatable. Cairns and northward on the Queensland coast, also in Northern Australia.

In "Gamble's Indian Timbers," page 111, it is stated:—"The wood contains an acrid juice which causes swellings and irritation, and timber-cutters object to felling it. The fruit when ripe is used ; the fleshy cup is eaten, but it is best either dry or roasted. The pericarp contains an acrid juice, which is universally used in India for marking ink and in medicine. The ink is improved by the addition of limewater. The green fruit is pounded and made into birdlime.

B.P.V.—Wood yellow with brown markings, easy to work, strong and tough ; might be used in cabinet-work.

EUROSCHINUS, *J. D. Hook.*

111—E. falcatus, *J. D. Hook.*, in Benth. and Hook. Gen. Pl., i., 422 ; Flora Austr., i., 490. Maiden's-blush Timber. Mostly of small size, but at times a large tree, with a glossy green foliage, with a scent when rubbed in the hand somewhat like celery. Leaves of four to eight leaflets, curved and tapering to the point, two to four inches long. Flowers small, in straggling bunches. Of very frequent occurrence in Queensland, also in New South Wales.

B.P.V.—Wood of a pinkish colour, or quite white, very soft, light, and tough ; perhaps might serve for making oars.

111a—E. falcatus, var. angustifolius, Flora Austr., i., 491. Maiden's Blush. Only differs from the last in the leaves being narrower, and, perhaps, the flowers rather larger.

B.P.V.—Wood perhaps of a deeper pink colour, tough, easy to work, close-grained and light.

SPONDIAS, *Linn.*

112—S pleiogyna, *F. v. M.*, Fragm., iv., 78. (Native name at Rockhampton, " Rancooran ; " at Port Curtis, " Noongi.") Burdekin

Plum or Sweet Plum. A tree of medium size, with spreading head. Leaves of from two to four pairs of leaflets. Flowers small; fruit somewhat globose, with the top flat, one to one and a-half inch in diameter, rich purple. Several localities on the Queensland coast.

Fruit eaten by the natives.

B.P.V.—Wood hard, dark-brown with red markings, resembling American Walnut; the grain pretty close, splits quite straight; an excellent wood for the joiner or cabinet-maker, also suitable for turnery.

Order LEGUMINOSÆ.

JACKSONIA, R. Br.

113—J. SCOPARIA, R. Br. Dogwood. A tall or short broom-like shrub with a greyish foliage, and twigs often covered with small yellow flowers. This shrub is sometimes infested by a curious fungoid blight called Ræstelia polita, Berk. A common plant on open country in Queensland, north and south.

B.V.—Wood yellowish, brown towards the centre.

DAVIESIA, Sm.

114—D. ARBOREA, W. Hill, in Cat. of Woods sent to Melb. Inter. Exhib., 1880. A medium-sized tree, with a dark rugged bark; branchlets slender, angular. Leaves linear-lanceolate, two to four inches long, and about ¼-inch broad. The apex glandular pointed, one-nerved and prominently reticulate. Racemes numerous, often two inches on axil, about one inch long, bearing eight or nine golden-coloured flowers on long slender pedicels; bracts minute; calyx about one line long, with ciliate teeth; petals with dark markings, the standard about three lines long; pod small. Habitat, Logan River district.

In general appearance this tree resembles one of the narrow-leaved Wattles. The above specific name seems first to have been attached to it by Mr. Walter Hill, it was afterwards noticed by the late Rev. B. Scortechini. There is little, however, except size, to separate it from D. corymbosa, Sm.

B.V.—Wood of a pinkish colour, with numerous reddish longitudinal streaks, and beautifully mottled, fragrance peculiarly agreeable; a strong useful cabinet wood.

HOVEA, R. Br.

115—H. ACUTIFOLIA, A. Cunn., in G. Don. Gen. Syst., ii., 126; Flora Austr., ii., 174. A tall shrub, the shoots and under side of the leaves clothed more or less with rusty down, the leaves narrowed towards each end, two or three inches long. Flowers very numerous, in clusters of from two to three in the axils of the leaves, of a pretty purple. Pods black when ripe, oblong, about ½-inch long. On open forest country, southern Queensland to Wide Bay, and also in New South Wales.

B.V.—Wood close-grained, yellow, and firm.

115A—H. LONGIPES, *Benth.*, in Hueg. Enum., 37; Flora Austr., ii., 174. Port Curtis "Yellow-wood." A small tree with a deeply furrowed uneven stem; leaves oval, deep-green, with oblique parallel veins on the upper surface, the under surface covered with a yellowish down; flowers dull-purple. Borders of scrubs, tropical Queensland, and at the Clarence River in New South Wales.

B.P.V.—WOOD of a dark-yellow colour, close-grained and very hard.

ERYTHRINA, *Linn.*

117—E. VESPERTILIO, *Benth.*, in Mitch. Trop. Austr., 218; Flora Austr., ii., 253. Cork-tree. A deciduous tree of medium size, the branches covered with short dark prickles. Leaves of three leaflets, which are lobed so as to give a fanciful resemblance to a bat flying. Flowers pale-pink, the bunches drooping. Pods four or five inches long, containing red beans. Found throughout Queensland and central and northern Australia.

B.P.V.—WOOD of a straw colour, soft and light.

118—E. INDICA, *Lam.*; *DC.*, Prod., ii., 412; Flora Austr., ii., 253; Wight, Ic. Pl., t., 58. Coral-tree. Often a large tree, deciduous, the branches covered with sharp, short, black prickles. Leaves of three leaflets, some of which at times measure as much as eight inches; the southern trees with smaller leaflets. Flowers scarlet, in dense racemes; pods six to nine inches long, containing few red beans. Main Range, South Queensland, and commonly found in the coast scrubs of tropical Queensland; also in New Guinea, India, and Burmah.

In India the wood, although so light—17 to 26 lbs. per cubic foot—is said to be durable and not to warp or split. It is there used for light boxes, toys, scabbards, and trays. The leaves and bark are said to be used in India as a febrifuge.

B.P.V.—WOOD straw-coloured, very light and soft.

DALBERGIA, *Linn.*

118A—D. DENSA, *Benth.*, in Hook. Lond. Journ., ii., 217; Flora Austr., ii., 271. A small tree with smooth shining bark. Leaves of from seven to 15 broadly oblong, very obtuse leaflets, ¾ to one and a-half inch long, hairy on the under side. Flowers in clusters, very small. Pod thin, obtuse, one and a-half to three inches long and about half-an-inch wide. Tropical Queensland and New Guinea.

B.V.—WOOD of a light colour, close grain.

LONCHOCARPUS, *H. B. et K.*

119—L. BLACKII, *Benth.*, Flora Austr., ii., 271. Bloody-Bark. A very large climber, the young branches and foliage rusty. Leaves of from seven to 11 leaflets, about one to one and a-half inch, or sometimes longer. Flowers small, dark-purple, in large dense bunches. Seed-pods very thin, two to five inches long, one-half to three-quarter inch broad. A scrub climber of North and South Queensland, and the northern scrubs of New South Wales.

B.V.—Wood very stringy, dark-brown, and porous. The blood-like sap which flows from the bark when cut, would likely give a dye.

PONGAMIA, *Vent.*

120—P. GLABRA, *Vent.*, in Jard. Malm., t. 28; Flora Austr., ii, 273. A tree of medium size, the leaves of five to seven leaflets, which are ovate and about three inches long. Flowers in racemes about four to five inches long; flowers pink, in pairs Pod one and a-half to two inches long and about one inch broad. Along the sides of rivers and creeks in tropical Queensland, Northern Australia, New Guinea, Southern India, and the Archipelago.

In India the wood is thought to be of little value on account of its being so readily eaten by insects. (This is also the case in Queensland.) It is, however, used for solid cart-wheels. A large quantity of a pale sherry-coloured oil is obtained from the seeds, which, besides being used for burning is considered to possess medicinal virtues, especially in skin diseases and rheumatism, when externally applied. Surgeon-Major Dymock, of Bombay, recommends this oil as a cure in *Pityriasis versicolor*, and says that by rubbing the oil in twice a day, several cases where the disease occurred upon the face, neck, and shoulders were cured in less than a fortnight; he points out also that this oil has the advantage over iodine and Goa powder of not discolouring the part to which it is applied.

B.P.V.—Wood yellow, close-grained, tough, and prettily marked; might be useful for chair-making, as it bears bending.

PODOPETALUM, *F. v. M.*

121A—P. ORMONDI, *F. v. M.*, Melb. Chem. and Drugg., June, 1882. Tree with pinnate leaves, the leaflets large, deep-green. Flowers pink. Endeavour River, Queensland.

B.P.V.—Wood of a pinkish grey colour, strong and firm, easy to work.

CASTANOSPERUM, *A. Cunn.*

122—C. AUSTRALE, *A. Cunn.*, in Hook Bot. Misc., i., 241, t. 51, 52; Flora Austr., ii., 275; Plants Reported Poisonous to Stock in Queensland, p. 29. Bean Tree or Moreton Bay Chestnut. A tall tree with smooth bark and large deep-green leaves, with from 11 to 15 oblong pointed leaflets; the flower bunches shooting out from the branches below the leaves. Flowers at first canary but changing to a rich scarlet. Pods very large, oblong, containing beans resembling chestnuts. A common tree of Queensland scrubs; also found at the Clarence River in New South Wales.

B.P.V. – Wood with usually a large quantity of dark-coloured heartwood, prized by cabinet-makers and turners; the outer wood of a yellow colour. The wood shrinks very much in drying. The foliage is thought to be deleterious to stock, should they browse on it in times of drought.

BARKLYA, *F. v. M.*

123—B. SYRINGIFOLIA, *F. v. M.*, in Journ. Linn Soc., iii., 158, and Fragm., i., 109, t. 3; Flora Austr., ii., 275. A medium-sized tree of great beauty and, like many other Queensland trees, blooming freely as a shrub. Leaves broadly heart-shaped, two to four inches long and broad, with five to seven prominent nerves. Flowers in dense bunches, deep yellow. Pod flat, containing one or two flat seeds. Found in a few of the scrubs of southern Queensland, Wide Bay, and Rockhampton; also in New South Wales.

B.P.V.—Wood blackish grey, close in grain and very tough; suitable for tool handles.

MEZONEURUM, *Desf.*

123A—M. BRACHYCARPUM, *Benth.*, Flora Austr., ii., 278. A tall woody climber, stems with large central pith, usually hollow when old, bark smooth, never corky, prickly and tomentose on the younger growth. Leaves abruptly bipinnate, often exceeding one foot in length, of about eight or ten pairs of pinnæ, about four inches long, with six to ten almost opposite pairs of leaflets, each of which are oblong, and about three-quarters of an inch long, a curved prickle close to the base of each pinna. Flowers brownish yellow, in large spreading terminal panicles. Pods obliquely and broadly ovate, fully two inches long and one and a half broad, containing one flat, round, or reniform blue seed. This species differs from *M. Scortechinii*, F. v. M., in the absence of the corky wings to the stems, in its much larger leaflets, and also much larger pods, the pods of *M. Scortechinii* seldom being over one inch long, one and a half inch wide, of papery texture and lanceolate shape.

B.—Wood close-grained and tough, of a brown colour.

CASSIA, *Linn.*

124—C. BREWSTERI, *F. v. M.*, 4th Ann. Rep., 17; Flora Austr., ii., 282. A small tree, with leaves of two to four pairs of oblong leaflets, notched at the end. Flowers brownish. Pods often over one foot long, thick and flattened, and one inch broad. Clermont and other parts of northern Queensland.

B.V.—Wood pale yellow, close-grained and nicely marked.

124A—C. BREWSTERI, *var.* TOMENTOSA, Flora Austr., ii., 282. Bean Tree of Obum Obum. A tall tree with a deep green foliage, the leaves a foot long, of many oblong leaflets. Pod cylindric, from one to nearly two feet in length, of a bright reddish-brown colour. South Queensland.

B.P.V.—Wood pinkish, close-grained and tough.

BAUHINIA, *Linn.*

125—B. CARRONII, *F. v. M.*, in Trans. Vict. Inst., iii., 49; Flora Austr., ii., 295. Native names, "Pegunny" and "Thalmera." Queensland Ebony. Tree of medium size, the leaves of two rather narrow leaflets, three-quarter to over one inch long. Flowers reddish, the calyx slightly downy. Petals silky outside, some of them very short. Pod, one and a half inch broad and four or five inches long.

Found in the interior of Queensland and New South Wales. "The honey from the flowers is used for food by the natives on the Flinders and Mitchell."—*E. Palmer.*

B.P.V.—Wood light brown, but becoming much darker towards the centre, hard, heavy, close in the grain; suitable for cabinet work.

126—B. Hookeri, *F. v. M.*, in Trans. Vict. Inst., iii., 51 ; Flora Austr., ii., 296. Queensland Ebony. Tree of medium size, with a dense head of foliage. Leaves of two leaflets, which are very obliquely ovate, three quarter to one and a half inch long, and finely five or seven nerved. Flowers large, showy white. Pods broad, over one inch, and wavy, containing a few flat light-brown seeds. Met with in the interior and Rockhampton, and other coast localities; the islands of Torres Straits in Queensland ; also in several places in North Australia.

B.P.V—Wood, the outer of a light brown, the inner dark-brown, nicely marked, hard, heavy, and close-grained ; very suitable for cabinet-work.

AFZELIA, *Sm.*

126a—A. australis, *Bail.*, 2nd Suppl. to Syn. of Queensl. Plants. Johnstone River Teak. A lofty tree, attaining a height of over 100 feet, with an erect trunk over two feet in diameter ; bark covered by rather large lenticellæ, and exfoliating by hard thick oval or oblong patches similar to some *Flindersias* and the Red Cedar; wood very hard and durable, of a reddish-brown. Leaves alternate, glabrous, of two or three pairs of very obtuse nearly orbicular leaflets from three to five inches long and nearly as broad, very unequal-sided at the base, on petiolules of about quarter of an inch, the divergent almost parallel veins joining far within the margin, and forming an intramarginal one, the netted veinlets numerous and somewhat prominent. Flowers pubescent. Calyx-tube ribbed, about quarter of an inch long ; lobes very unequal and much imbricate, sightly longer than the tube. Petal orbicular, undulate, veined, on a claw about as long as the calyx-lobes. Stamens hairy. Ovary stipitate, flat, the edges tomentose. Pod oblong, six to seven inches long and over two inches broad, glabrous, coriaceous, with transverse veins. Seeds dark-brown, three or four, very flat, more or less covered by a mealy substance, oblong or orbicular, about one and a quarter inch in diameter, the short thick funicle expanding into an oblong appressed aril. This tree was found on the Johnstone River by Dr. Thos. L. Bancroft.

(This wood was worked in mistake for *Cynometra* for the Colonial and Indian Exhibition.)

B.P.V.—Wood of a brown colour, rather coarse in grain, hard and heavy, but easy to work, and would be well adapted for house-building work. The sawdust of this Australian tree yields a purplish dye.

CYNOMETRA, *Linn.*

127—C. ramiflora, *Linn.*; *DC.*, Prod., ii., 509 ; Flora Austr., ii., 296. A tree with leaves of usually two pairs of obliquely oblong leaflets, two or three or more inches long. Flowers small. Fruit broad as long, thick, from half to more than one inch long and rough. Frequently met with in the coast swamps of tropical Queensland ; also in the tidal forests of South India and Burmah.

In India the wood of this tree is used for house-building, carts, &c., and the chips are said to give in water a purple dye.

B.P.V.—Wood of a light-brown colour, close-grained and tough.

ERYTHROPHLŒUM, *Afzelius.*

127a—E. Laboucherii, *F. v. M.,* in Flora Austr., ii., 297. Dr. Leichhardt's Leguminous Ironbark ; native name on the Mitchell, "Ah-pill." A medium-sized tree with a very rough furrowed bark. Leaves twice pinnate, the leaflets almost round and from one to two inches in diameter. Flowers minute. Pods about six inches long and one inch broad, containing a few flat nearly round seeds. In Queensland near the Endeavour, Gilbert, Burdekin, and Johnstone Rivers, Torres Straits, and through to North Australia.

Used by the Mitchell natives for making into spear-heads and wommeras.

B.P.V.—Wood red, very hard—the hardest in Australia—close-grained, very durable.

ENTADA, *Adams.*

127b—E. scandens, *Benth.,* in Hook. Journ. Bot. iv., 332; Flora Austr., ii., 298. Match-box Bean. A large woody climber with a pubescence on the infloresence and young growth. Leaves abruptly bipinnate, the pinnæ of the upper pair often converted into tendrils without leaflets. Flower-spikes from one to 12 inches long. Flowers somewhat rigid. Pods two to four feet long, containing from 10 to 30 flattish round seeds often two inches in diameter. This plant so common on the tropical coasts of Queensland, is common within the tropics of both the new and old world. A single plant of this gigantic climber has been said to cover the trees on some acres of ground. The seeds are converted into match-boxes, and in India they are used medicinally, and even used as food ; an infusion of the stem is used in the Philippines with advantage for various affections of the skin.

According to E. Palmer's paper on the plants used for food by the Flinders and Mitchell River natives, these beans are used by them for food after being roasted, pounded and soaked for several hours in water.

B.—Wood very stringy, dark-brown.

ADENANTHERA, *Linn.*

128—A. abrosperma, *F. v. M.,* Fragm., v., 30 ; Syn. Queensl. Flora, 130. Native name on the Mitchell, "Oon doo." A small tree, the branchlets slightly pubescent. Leaves of about four pairs of pinnæ, each two or three inches long, leaflets eight to 12, four to eight inches long, quarter to half an inch broad. Pod brownish, sometimes about five inches long and nearly one inch broad. Seeds very pretty, one-half black, the other half red, slightly compressed. Specimen from Musgrave Electric Telegraph Station.

" Seeds roasted and eaten by the natives."—*E. Palmer.*

V.—Wood of a red colour, close-grained, likely to prove useful.

ACACIA, *Willd.*

128ᴀ—A. FASCICULIFERA, *F. v. M.*, in Flora Austr., ii., 361; F. v. M., Ic. Dec. 4. An erect tree, the branches often drooping, branchlets angular. Leaves four to six inches long, rather more than half an inch broad, thick, the midrib prominent and the margins nerve-like. Flower heads globular, often clustered in the axils of the leaves. Pods long, flat, about half an inch broad. Rockhampton, and thence inland in Queensland; also in some parts of New South Wales.

B.P.V.—Wood of a red colour, very hard, and close in the grain; useful for building purposes.

128ʙ—A. SENTIS, *F. v. M.*, in Journ. Linn. Soc., iii., 128, and Pl· Vic., ii., 18; Flora Austr., ii., 360; F. v. M., Ic. Dec. 4. A small tree, branches hairy when young. Leaves oblong-narrow, one-nerved, about one inch long and seldom quarter of an inch wide, often much less, with usually sharp fine spines at their base. Flowers in small globular heads. Pods flat, half to three-quarters of an inch broad. An interior shrub or small tree within all the colonies; also in Tasmania.

B.V.—Wood close-grained, hard, and nicely marked.

128ᴄ—A. FALCATA, *Willd.*, Spec. Pl., iv., 1053; Flora Austr., ii., 361. A small tree with angular branchlets. Leaves much curved and tapering towards each end; the midrib prominent, much nearer one side than the other, and the lateral veins distant from each other. Flowers in small globular heads, arranged in a loose bunch, pale-coloured. Pod slightly flattened, narrow, purple, about five inches long. Generally found on hill-sides, Queensland, north and south; also in New South Wales.

B.P.V.—Wood near the outside yellow, the rest light-brown, heavy and tough; might be useful for cabinet-work.

129—A. MACRADENIA, *Benth.*, in Mitch. Trop. Austr., 360; Flora Austr., ii., 362; i., F. v. M., Ic. Dec. 5. A small tree with twisted, angular, drooping branches. Leaves curved, narrowed towards each end, the gland near the base long, one-nerved, and six to nearly twelve inches long. Flowers in small globular heads. Pods narrow, three or four inches long, dark-coloured; seeds oval. Inland in Queensland; common in the Leichhardt district, also in New South Wales.

B.V.—Wood close-grained and tough.

130—A. PENNINERVIS, *Sieb.*, in DC. Prod., ii , 452; Flora Austr., ii., 362. Black-wood of New South Wales. A tree usually small, but at times attaining the height of forty feet. Leaves lanceolate, sickle shaped, usually about three or four inches long, one-nerved, with mostly a secondary nerve, which terminates in a marginal gland much below the middle. Flowers pale-yellow in globular heads in loose racemes. Pods flat, four or six inches long, and nearly half-inch broad. Met with in southern Queensland and most of the other Australian colonies.

The bark used for tanning and the wood for cabinet-work in New South Wales.

B.P.V.—WOOD a dark-brown, with a small yellow sapwood, tough, and useful for cabinet-work.

130A—A. PENNINERVIS, VAR. FALCIFORMIS. Differing from the normal form in that the leaves are much broader, and at the marginal gland it often forms a short prominent point. Pod often much broader also. An inland tree or large shrub.

B.V.—WOOD, the sample received unfit to work up.

130B—A. NERIIFOLIA, A. Cunn.; Benth., in Hook. Lond. Journ., i., 357; Flora Austr., ii., 363. A small tree, the branchlets slightly angular and mealy when young. Leaves grey, linear, more or less curved, the small callous point often recurved, about five inches long and ¼-inch broad, one-nerved, and one, two, or three, marginal glands, or wanting. Flowers in small globular heads. Pod flat, straight, a few inches long, and about ¼-inch broad. Open country inland, Stanthorpe in Queensland, also inland in New South Wales and South Australia.

The bark contains 13·91 per cent. of tannin.

B.P.V.—WOOD dark-coloured, prettily marked, close-grained, and tough.

131—A. SALICINA, Lindl., in Mitch. Three Exped., ii., 20; Flora Austr., ii., 367. "Baka" of the Rockhampton natives. Koobah of New South Wales. A small tree with a light-grey foliage, the branches often pendulous. Leaves oblong, narrowed towards the base, four or five inches long and half-inch broad, the midrib at times not very prominent. Flowers pale, in globular heads. Pods straight, thick, one to three inches long; seeds round, funicle, scarlet. According to the late Mons. Thozet this was used by the natives of the Fitzroy River district for poisoning fish in small lagoons. Frequent in inland open country in Queensland, North Australia, Western Australia, New South Wales, South Australia, and Victoria.

B.V.—WOOD dark-coloured, tough, easy to work; would be a useful cabinet wood. The foliage considered good fodder in New South Wales.

132—A. LINIFOLIA, Willd., Sp., Pl., iv., 1051; Flora Austr., ii., 371. A tall straggling shrub, grey or green, the branchlets angular. Leaves narrow-linear, one to two inches long and under ¼-inch broad, with the midrib often hairy, and a small gland above the base. Racemes of globular flower-heads very numerous. Pod linear, flat, about four inches long and ¼-inch broad. Found on creek-sides in Queensland and New South Wales.

B.V.—WOOD of light colour, red in the centre, close-grained and tough.

133—A. PODALYRIÆFOLIA, *A. Cunn.*, in G. Don. Gen. Syst., ii., 405; Flora Austr., ii., 374 Silver Wattle. A tall shrub, more or less mealy, grey, or silvery; the leaves obliquely oblong, about one or one and a half inch long, one-nerved, and with one or two marginal glands. Flower-racemes numerous, bearing small globular heads of flowers. Pods flat, over half-inch broad and about three inches long. On or near ranges, southern Queensland; also New South Wales.

The bark contains 12·40 per cent. of tannin.

B.V.—Wood of a pinkish colour, nicely marked.

133A—A. HOMALOPHYLLA, *A. Cunn.; Benth.*, in Hook. Lond. Journ., 1365; Flora Austr., ii., 383; F. v. M., Ic. Dec. 6. Gidia; on the Cloncurry called "Wong-arrah." Yarran of New South Wales. A small tree, the foliage hoary and the branchlets slightly angular. Leaves narrow-oblong, linear, one to three inches long, and about ¼-inch broad, thick, with parallel nerves. Flowers in globular heads; pods linear, grey like the leaves, slightly curved, and about ¼-inch broad. Western inland Queensland; and in New South Wales, South Australia, and Victoria.

B.V.—Wood dark, close-grained, hard, heavy, and prettily marked.

134—A. PENDULA, *A. Cunn.* in G. Don. Gen. Syst., ii., 404; Flora Austr., ii., 383; F. v. M., Ic. Dec. 6. Weeping Myall. A small tree with an ash-grey foliage, the branchlets slightly angular and drooping. Leaves linear, two or three inches long, with parallel nerves. Flowers in globular heads. Pods flat, nearly half-inch broad, the suture bordered by a very narrow wing. An inland tree in South Queensland, also in New South Wales.

B.P.V.—Wood fragrant, dark, close-grained, hard; much prized by the cabinet-makers and turners.

135—A. STENOPHYLLA, *A. Cunn.; Benth.*, in Hook. Journ., i., 366; Flora Austr., ii., 385; F. v. M., Ic. Dec. 6. Dalby Myall. A small tree with a dark hard bark, the branches angular. Leaves long, linear, often very narrow, nearly one foot long and under ¼-inch broad, with many fine parallel nerves, the flowers in short racemes, bearing few globular heads of flowers. Pods long, necklace-like; seeds ovate. On downs and borders of creeks inland in Queensland, North Australia, New South Wales, Victoria, and South Australia.

B.P.V.—Wood useful for cabinet-work; dark, prettily marked, close-grained and very hard.

136—A. IMPLEXA, *Benth.*, in Hook. Lond. Journ., i., 368; Flora Austr., ii., 389. A glabrous tree of small size, the foliage usually dense Leaves four to six inches long with several slender longitudinal veins. Peduncles few in a very short raceme, bearing each a small dense head of numerous flowers. Pod narrow, linear, much curved and twisted. Seeds ovate-oblong, longitudinal. Found from the Yarra River in Victoria, through New South Wales, to the Burnett and Dawson in Queensland.

B.V.—Wood prettily marked the outer of a light colour, the heartwood greyish-brown; a useful cabinet wood.

137—A. HARPOPHYLLA, *F. v. M.*, in Benth. Flora Austr., ii., 389; F. v. M., Ic. Dec. 6. Brigalow. A tall tree with an upright stem, the bark rough, the branchlets angular. Leaves much curved, tapering towards each end, six to eight inches long, of a deep-green or sometimes quite a grey colour; veins parallel. Flowers in small globular heads. Queensland, south and north, often forming scrubs known in Queensland "as brigalow scrubs."

B.P.V.—Wood brown, close-grained, elastic, scented; a good cabinet wood.

137A—A. EXCELSA, *Benth.*, in Mitch. Trop. Austr., 225; Flora Austr., ii., 390. Ironwood Wattle. Often a tall tree with a rugged bark, the branchlets slightly angular. Leaves oblong, slightly curved, two to three inches long and half an inch or rather more broad, rather thick, with five to seven parallel nerves; the globular heads of flowers on short stalks. Pods straight, flat, about quarter inch broad. Queensland, on downs country inland.

B.P.V.—Wood very hard, dark, close-grained; useful where strength and durability are required.

137B—A. COMPLANATA, *A. Cunn.*; *Benth.*, in Hook. Lond. Journ., i., 369; Flora Austr., ii., 390; *A. anceps*, Hook. Ic. Pl. t., 167, not of DC. A tall shrub or small tree, glabrous; the branchlets bordered by two or three acute angles or wings. Leaves (*Phyllodia*) two to four inches long, half or one inch broad, with from five to nine longitudinal nerves, and a few fine veins between them. Flowers in globular heads on stalks about one inch long, often numerous in the axils of the leaves. Pods curved, four or five inches long, and about two or three lines broad. More or less plentiful from the Clarence River in New South Wales to the Endeavour in Queensland.

B.—Wood of a yellowish colour; close-grained and tough.

138—A. ORARIA, *F. v. M.*; Fragm., xi., 66; Syn. Queensl. Fl., 140; F. v. M., Ic. Dec. 8. A small tree with spreading head, the leaves of a grey colour, somewhat oblong, two or three inches long and about one inch broad. Flowers in globular heads of a pale colour. Pods three or four inches long and about three-quarters of an inch broad, hard, and transversely veined. Found on the tropical beach in Queensland.

B.V.—Wood close-grained, outer whitish. heartwood dark-brown, tough and nicely marked.

138A—A. FLAVESCENS, *A. Cunn.*; *Benth.*, in Hook. Lond. Journ., i., 381; Flora Austr., ii., 391; F. v. M., Ic., Dec. 8. A small tree, the young shoots clothed with a hoary or yellowish mealy down, branchlets angular. Leaves very broad in the middle, tapering each way, four to eight inches long, and from one to three inches broad, with usually three prominent nerves. Flowers in globular heads. Pods curved, flat, three to five inches long and nearly one inch broad. Common on coast lands in tropical Queensland.

The bark contains 10·20 per cent. of tannin.

B.V.—Wood of a brown colour, prettily marked, close-grained and hard.

139—A. LONGIFOLIA, *Willd.*, Spec. Pl., iv. 1052; Flora Austr., ii., 397. A small tree, the branches angular. Leaves oblong, obtuse, five or six inches long, with parallel nerves. Flowers in spikes; pods long, slender. Creek sides in south Queensland, also in New South Wales, Victoria, South Australia, and Tasmania.

The bark contains 12·67 per cent. of tannin.

B.P.V.—Wood towards the outside pale yellow, the inner brown streaked with black; tough and easily worked; a useful cabinet wood.

139A—A. GLAUCESCENS, *Willd.*, Spec. Pl., iv., 1052; Flora Austr., ii., 406 One of the so-called Rosewoods. A tall erect tree, with a thin bark, roughened by small pieces forming little curls all over the stem; branchlets more or less angular. Leaves oblong, narrowed towards both ends, four to six inches long, half an inch or more broad, three to five of the nerves more prominent than the rest. Spikes of flowers often clustered, one to two inches long. North and south in Queensland; also in New South Wales.

B P.V.—Wood with a very narrow quantity of sapwood of a light-yellow colour; all the rest dark, resembling English Walnut and Rosewood; a valuable wood for veneers; more or less fragrant; useful in turnery and cabinet work.

139B—A. GLAUCESCENS, *var.* Ringy Rosewood. This tree seems to differ only in the wood having transverse wavy lines, but no flowers or pods have been sent in with the logs of wood, only the foliage. Queensland (inland).

B.P.V —Only differing from the last in the transverse wavy lines observable in the wood, and which give to a turned stick a ringed-like appearance.

139C—A. DORATOXYLON, *A. Cunn.*, in Field N.S.W., 345; Flora Austr., ii., 403. Mulga. A small tree of a grey hue, the branchlets angular. Leaves linear, slightly curved, with an oblique or recurved point, four to eight inches long and about a quarter inch broad, rather thick, with many parallel nerves, the middle one more prominent than the others. Flowers clustered or solitary. Inland, on downs country in Queensland, New South Wales, South Australia, and Victoria.

B.P.V—Wood dark-brown, with a small yellow sapwood, close-grained, very hard, and prettily marked. In New South Wales used for gates and buggy-poles.

139D—A. TORULOSA, *Benth.*, in Journ. Linn. Soc., iii., 139; Flora Austr., ii., 405. A small tree with angular branchlets. Leaves linear, curved, with an oblique glandular point, four to eight inches long, often over ¼-inch broad, with three to five more prominent than the rest. Spikes of flowers solitary or two or three together. Pods long, necklace-like; seeds oblong. Endeavour River, Queensland, and North Australia.

B.P.V.—WOOD dark-brown, tough and strong.

140—A. CUNNINGHAMII, *Hook.*, K. Pl., t. 165; Flora Austr., ii. 407. Black Wattle; native name, "Kowarkul." In New South Wales called "Bastard Myall." Tree of medium size, the branchlets acutely three-angled, often reddish. Leaves much curved, tapering each way, four to over six inches long and one to one and a half inch broad, with from three to five prominent longitudinal nerves, confluent with the lower margin near the base. Flower-spikes three or more inches long. Pod linear, much twisted and narrow. Wide-spread in Queensland, but forming the largest growth near the coast; also in New South Wales.

The bark contains 9·13 per cent. of tannin.

B.P.V.—WOOD of a dark colour, close-grained, hard, heavy, and prettily marked. Used in New South Wales for turning and cabinet-work.

140B—A. LEPTOCARPA, *A. Cunn.; Benth.*, in Hook. Lond. Journ., i., 376; Flora Austr., ii., 407. A small tree, the leaves curved, narrowed towards each end, four to six inches long, about half-inch broad, three of the nerves more prominent than the others, the finer ones not very close. Flower-spikes about two inches long; pod linear, nearly straight, very narrow. Queensland tropical coast.

B.P.V.—WOOD dark-brown, close-grained, hard and prettily marked, useful for cabinet and turnery work.

140A—A. POLYSTACHYA, *A. Cunn.; Benth.*, in Hook. Lond. Journ., i., 376; Flora Austr., ii., 407. Tree medium sized, branchlets angular at first. Leaves curved, narrowed towards each end, six to ten inches long, one to one and a half inch broad, with three to five very prominent nerves, the others fine and numerous. Flower-spikes one to two inches long, solitary or two or three together. Pod several inches long and half-inch broad. Tropical Queensland coast and North Australia.

The bark contains 7·59 per cent. of tannin.

B.P.V.—WOOD dark-coloured and close-grained, with pretty markings.

141—A. AULACOCARPA, *A. Cunn.; Benth.*, in Hook. Lond. Journ., i., 378; Flora Austr., ii., 410. Native name at Port Curtis, "Dilka." Hickory Wattle. Tree of medium size, the foliage coated with a thin grey wax, giving it a hoary appearance. Leaves narrow to each end, four to six inches long, half to one inch broad, three to five of the parallel veins more prominent than the others and confluent at the lower margin near the base. Flower-spikes two or three inches long, the flowers of a pale colour. Pods oblong, three or four inches long and half-inch broad, with oblique transverse grooves. Common in forest country, Queensland.

B.P.V.—WOOD hard, heavy, tough, and dark-red coloured; useful for cabinet-work.

141A—A. CALYCULATA, *A. Cunn.*; *Benth.*, in Hook. Journ., i., 379; Flora Austr., ii., 410. A small tree, the branchlets flat when young. Leaves two to three inches long and half-inch broad, rather thick, with closely packed parallel veins, a few stronger. Spikes clustered, one-half to one inch long; flowers very small. Pod curved, oblong, flat, thick, hard, and obliquely veined. Tropical coast, Queensland.

B.P.V.—Wood dark-brown, hard, heavy, and close-grained; suitable for turnery and cabinet-work.

141B—A. CRASSICARPA, *A. Cunn.*; *Benth.*, in Hook. Lond. Journ., i., 379; Flora Austr., ii., 410. Tree medium size, grey or hoary. Leaves curved, oblong, narrowed at both ends, five to eight inches long, one to two inches broad, very oblique, with some of the principal nerves confluent with the lower margin near the base. Flower-spikes about one inch long. Pods oblong, flat, thick, hard, obliquely veined, nearly one inch broad and two or three inches long. Coast, tropical Queensland and North Australia.

B.P.V.—Wood prettily marked, hard, and dark-coloured.

142—A. POLYBOTRYA, VAR. FOLIOLOSA, *Benth.*, in Flora Austr., ii., 414. A tall shrub more or less hairy. Leaves twice pinnate; pinnæ four to six pairs, two to three inches long; leaflets 15 to 25, from one-quarter to one-half inch long. Flowers showy, in rather small globular heads, composed in a terminal panicle. Ranges of South Queensland.

B.V.—Wood pinkish, close in grain, hard and beautifully marked; would be a useful wood for the cabinet-maker.

142A—A. DECURRENS, *Willd.*, Spec. Pl., iv., 1072; Flora Austr., ii., 414. Green Wattle. In South Australia called Black Wattle and also Silver Wattle. A small tree with a grey feathery foliage, the branchlets angular. Leaves twice pinnate; pinnæ 8 to 15 pairs, the leaflets very small and numerous. Flowers in terminal or axillary panicles, composed of small globular heads of yellow flowers. Pods three or more inches long and about ½-inch broad; seeds ovate. Open forest country in South Queensland; also in New South Wales, South Australia, Victoria, and Tasmania.

The bark contains 15·08 per cent. of tannin.

B.P.V.—Wood tough, firm, and easy to work; the sapwood white, heart-wood of a pinkish colour; used for tool-handles and staves in New South Wales.

142B—A. DECURRENS. VAR. PAUCIGLANDULOSA, *F. v. M.*, Flora Austr., ii., 415. A medium-sized tree, with beautiful light soft feathery foliage, the young growth golden yellow. Leaflets small, about two lines long; glands few, often only under the last one or two pairs of pinnæ. Brisbane River.

B.V.—Wood of a pinkish colour, close-grained, and nicely marked.

B

143—A. DECURRENS, VAR. LEICHHARDTI, *Benth.*, in Flora Austr., ii., 415. A tall shrub, clothed with spreading hairs, the leaflets very small. Maroochie, Queensland.

B.P.V.—WOOD of a light colour near the outside, but pinkish towards the centre; the grain close and prettily marked.

145—A. BIDWILLI, *Benth.*, in Linneæa, xxvi., 629; Flora Austr., ii., 420. Native name at Cloncurry, "Yadthor." A small tree, the bark corky, light-green foliage, and the branches often prickly and drooping. Leaves twice pinnate; pinnæ 15 to 20 pairs, the leaflets 15 to 25 pairs, oblong, about a line long. The peduncle with a ring-like leaf about the middle, and bearing a globose head of pale-yellow flowers at the end. Pod straight, three to six inches long and half-an inch broad; seeds large, ovate. Often on open forest land in tropical Queensland; also in North Australia.

The roots of the young trees roasted for food, after peeling, by the natives on the Flinders and Mitchell.—*E. Palmer.*

B.P.V.—WOOD light-yellow near the outside, the inner wood dark, close-grained, light and easy to work.

145A—A. BIDWILLI, VAR. MAJOR, *Benth.*, in Flora Austr., ii., 420. A medium-sized tree resembling the last, only so much larger. Gulf country.

B.P.V.—WOOD of a light colour; easy to work.

ALBIZZIA, *Durazz.*

145B—A. TOONA, *Bail.*, in First Suppt. to Syn. Ql. Fl. Acacia Cedar or Mackay Cedar. A large tree with dense head of dark foliage, the young shoots rusty. Leaves feathery, of very numerous small leaflets, more or less downy. Tropical Queensland.

B.P.V.—WOOD of a light colour for several inches in from the bark, the rest resembling Red Cedar; a valuable wood for many purposes.

146—A. BASALTICA, *Benth.*, in Flora Austr., ii., 422. Dead Finish. A small tree, the branches rusty with glandular hairs. Pinnæ one or two pairs; leaflets five to ten pairs, oblong, about quarter of an inch long. Peduncle bearing a dense globular head of flowers. Pod about three or four inches long and nearly half-an-inch broad. An inland tree in Queensland, forming very dense thickets.

B.V.—WOOD towards the bark bright-yellow, the heartwood dark-red, close-grained, hard, and very beautiful; excellent for cabinet-work.

147—A. THOZETIANA, *F. v. M.*, in Flora Austr., ii., 422. A large tree. Leaves small, of one pair of pinnæ and two to four pairs of leaflets, which are from half to one inch long. Peduncles about one inch long, with a globular head of flowers. Pod four to eight inches long and over half-an-inch broad. Seeds flat, orbicular, with a wing-like border. Coast scrubs of tropical Queensland.

B.P.V.—WOOD of a red colour, hard. heavy, and durable, very tough and close in the grain.

148—A. CANESCENS, *Benth.*, Flora Austr., ii., 423. A small tree with a light-coloured corky bark. Leaves twice pinnate, wide-spreading, with two pairs of pinnæ, seldom more; leaflets five to eight pairs, three-quarters to one and a-half inch long. Flower-heads in a terminal panicle. Pods eight to ten inches long and one and a-half to two and a-half broad; seeds arranged along the centre of these thin flat pods. In open forests, tropical Queensland.

B.P.V.—Wood brown, resembling Walnut, nicely marked; very suitable for cabinet-work. Considered by some to resemble Walnut.

148A—A. PROCERA, *Benth.*, in Hook. Lond. Journ., iii., 88; *Hook.*, Fl. Ind., ii., 299; Flora Austr., ii., 422. A large deciduous tree, the bark brownish or greyish, rough with irregular horizontal cracks; the leaves large, with four to six or even more distant pairs of spreading pinnæ, with six to ten pairs of oblong leaflets one to one and a-half inch long and half-an-inch or more broad; pods thin and broad. Thursday and other islands of Torres Straits; also in India.

In India the dark heartwood is considered durable, and is used for sugarcane crushers, rice-pounders, wheels, agricultural implements, bridges, and house posts. It is found to split well, and so used for fencing by tea-planters. It is occasionally used for tea-boxes, and is excellent for charcoal. The tree is of rapid growth, making in thirty years a girth of from four to six feet.

B.P.V.—Wood of a dark colour resembling Walnut; a useful cabinet wood.

PITHECOLOBIUM, *Mart.*

149—P. PRUINOSUM, *Benth.*, in Lond. Journ., iii., 211; Flora Austr., ii., 423. Tree of medium size, the young branches downy. Leaves spreading, irregular as to size, twice pinnate; pinnæ, one or two pairs; leaflets broadly oblong, very irregular as to number and size. Flowers yellowish in globular umbels. Pod several inches long and about a quarter inch broad; seeds, black, glossy, ovate. Queensland coast scrubs; also in New South Wales.

B.V.—Wood of a light yellow colour, becoming brown near the centre; very disagreeably scented when newly cut.

149A—P. TOZERI, *F. v. M.*, in Trimen's Journ. Bot., 10, and in Census of Austr. Pl. A medium-sized tree. Leaves and flowers like the last, only larger, the leaves of a firmer consistency. Coast scrubs in Queensland, also in New South Wales.

B.V.—Wood light yellow, red and nicely marked towards the centre, close in the grain, light and easy to work; possessing a most disagreeable scent when newly cut.

ARCHIDENDRON, *F. v. M.*

150—A. VAILLANTII, *F. v. M.*, Fragm., v., 60; ix., 178. A moderate-sized tree. Leaves very large of one pair of pinnæ; leaflets three or four pairs, ovate, three to seven inches long Flowers purplish in heads. Johnstone River, Queensland.

Dr. T. L. Bancroft has found the bark of this tree to have a hot acrid-tasting principle, which is probably saponine.

B V.—Wood of a red colour, close-grained, strong and durable.

Order ROSACEÆ.

PARINARIUM, *Juss.*

151—P. Nonda, *F. v. M.*, in Flora Austr., ii., 426. A shady tree, more or less downy, the leaves oval, one to three inches long, one to one and a half inch broad, whitish on the under side, with prominent veins. The flowers small in a terminal panicle. Fruit oval, yellow, one and a half inch long, with a dry mealy taste, stone small and rough. This fruit is eaten by the natives. Tropical Queensland and North Australia.

B.P.V.—Wood light yellow colour, cross-grained, very strong.

Order SAXIFRAGEÆ.

ARGOPHYLLUM, *Forst.*

151A—A. Lejourdanii, *F. v. M.*, Fragm., iv., 33; Flora Austr., ii., 437. A tall shrub, the branches silvery-white. Leaves ovate, about four inches long, silvery on the back; flowers and fruit small. Not very common, but met with at distant localities, as Logan River, Mount Perry, and Mount Elliott.

B.V.—Wood yellow, close-grained, and hard.

CUTTSIA, *F. v. M.*

152A—C. viburnea, *F. v. M.*, Fragm., v., 47; *Bail.*, Syn., 150. A tall straggling shrub, the leaves from four to eight inches long, with distant teeth. Flowers in bunches at the ends of the branches. Capsule globular, small. Mountain creeks, southern Queensland.

B.V.—Wood white, close in the grain, and very tough.

DAVIDSONIA, *F. v. M.*

154—D. pruriens, *F. v. M.*, Fragm., vi., 4; *Bail.*, Syn., 152. A slender, erect, small tree, more or less covered with stiff brown hairs. Leaves large, pinnate, the leaflets very irregular as to size, toothed. Flowers in a long drooping panicle. Fruit oval, at first covered with stiff brown hairs, juice purple when ripe, of a sharp acid. On the wild trees this fruit attains the size of goose-eggs, on the cultivated trees near Brisbane the fruit seldom exceeds one and a-half inch in diameter. Tropical Queensland scrubs.

B.P.V.—Wood of a dark-brown colour, close-grained, hard, tough, and durable, useful for tool-handles and mallets.

WEINMANNIA, *Linn.*

155—W. lachnocarpa, *F. v. M.*, Fragm., viii., 7; *Bail.*, Syn., 153. Marara; often also called Scrub Redwood. A large tree with a rough scaly bark. The leaves of three leaflets two to six inches long, and toothed. Flowers small, succeeded by densely woolly capsules of reddish brown. Scrubs of southern Queensland and New South Wales.

B.P.V.—Wood light-pink, close in the grain; might be used for making planes, mallets, and chisel-handles.

Order RHIZOPHOREÆ.

RHIZOPHORA, *Linn.*

156—R. MUCRONATA, *Lam.*; *DC.*, Prod., iii., 32; Flora Austr., ii., 493. Mangrove. A small tree with thick branches and oval leathery leaves three or four inches long, the projecting point at the end generally present, but sometimes worn off. Flowers stiff; segments of calyx four; petals four. Fruit germinating before falling off the tree. A maritime tree, found on the coast from New South Wales to Cape York, and in New Guinea and tropical Africa and Asia.

The bark contains 18·20 per cent. of tannin. In India the wood is considered very durable, extremely hard, and splits and warps but little in seasoning· The bark is also used in tanning.

B.P.V.—Wood of a light-colour, with a reddish centre or heartwood; the grain close, tough.

CERIOPS, *Arn.*

157—C. CANDOLLEANA, *Arn.*, Ann. Nat. Hist., i., 364 Flora Austr., ii., 494. A small evergreen tree growing with mangroves. Leaves broadly oblong, one and a-half to three inches long. The flowers borne in small heads on recurved peduncles in the axils of the leaves. The conical fruit about half-an-inch long. All along the Queensland coast, also the Indian coast and the Archipelago.

In India the bark is used for tanning and the wood for the knees of boats.

B.V.—Wood of a dark-brown colour, close-grained, hard and tough.

BRUGUIERA, *Lam.*

157A—B. PARVIFLORA, *W. et Arn.*, Prod., i., 311. A tropical coast swamp tree of small size, glabrous except the petals. Leaves oblong or broadly lanceolate, two to over three inches long, tapering towards the petiole, which is rather slender and about half-an-inch long. Stipules about one and a-half inch long. Flowers small, pedicellate in a once or twice trichotomous cyme. Calyx-tube prominently ribbed, tapering towards the base; lobes eight, lanceolate, erect, rigid, and scarcely over one and a-half line long. Petals shorter than the calyx-lobes, cleft, with a bristle in the sinus and with three or more at the apex of each of the lobes, the incurved sides hairy where they embrace the stamens. Ovary three-celled, ribbed. Fruit sub-cylindrical, about one inch long, according to Hooker's Flora of British India, but not sent with Queensland specimens. Johnstone River and Mackay, Queensland.

B.—Wood of a light straw-colour, close-grained and hard.

158—B. RHEEDII, *Blume*, Enum. Pl. Jav., 92; Flora Austr., ii., 494. Red Mangrove; native name, "Kowinka." A small tree with hard black bark and deep-green glossy leaves, oblong, three to six inches long, of a leathery consistence. Flowers red, solitary in the axils of the leaves; segments of calyx about 12, the petals shorter and hairy. Fruit germinating before falling from the tree. All round the Queensland coast, and also North Australia, New Guinea, and tropical Asia.

The bark contains 19·48 per cent. of tannin.

B.P.V.—Wood of a light colour, close-grained, tough, and nicely marked; useful for many purposes, especially as axe and pick handles.

CARALLIA, *Roxb.*

159A—C. INTEGERRIMA, *DC.*, Prod., iii., 33; Flora Austr., ii., 495. A medium-sized tree with oblong leaves three to five inches long, the flowers usually borne on the branches below the leaves, each bunch bearing three to five flowers. Fruit succulent, round, about a quarter inch in diameter. Queensland tropical coast, North Australia, India, Burmah, and South China.

In India the wood is used for furniture and cabinet-making, and in Burmah for planking, furniture, and rice-pounders.

B.P.V.—Wood light-coloured, but darkening towards the centre, close in the grain, and easy to work.

Order COMBRETACEÆ.

TERMINALIA, *Linn.*

160—T. PLATYPTERA, *F. v. M.*, Fragm., ii., 151; ix., 160; Flora Austr., ii., 498. A small tree, the young growth often hoary. Leaves obovate-oblong, very obtuse, two or three inches long, prominently netted veined. Flower-spikes longer than the leaves, slender, interrupted. Fruit two-winged, tomentose-pubescent, one to three inches broad, including the horizontally divaricate wings which are quite distinct. Specimen from Musgrave Electric Telegraph Station; also found at Port Darwin.

V.—Wood of a light-yellow colour, close-grained, and hard.

161—T. OBLONGATA, *F. v. M.*, Fragm , ii., 152; Flora Austr., ii., 499. A tree of moderate size, the shoots hoary. Leaves oblong, clustered on the short branchlets, two or three inches long Flowers in slender spikes, two or three inches long. Fruit two-winged, a little over half-inch long. In the tropical Queensland scrubs

B.P.V.—Wood light-coloured, nicely marked; suitable for cabinet-work.

161A—T. BURSARINA, *F. v. M.*, Fragm., ii., 149; Flora Austr., ii., 499. A small creek-side tree, the branches and leaves silky. Leaves from one to one and a-half inch long, oval, showing the netted veins. Flower small, in spike of two or three inches in length. Fruit from three to five lines long, pointed, somewhat ovate and three-angled, the one face broader than the others, and furnished about the centre with a blunt prominent spur. Gulf country, Queensland; also in North Australia.

B.P.V.—Wood of a dark colour, close-grained, hard, and prettily marked; useful for cabinet work.

162—T. MELANOCARPA, *F. v. M.*, Fragm., iii., 92; Flora Austr., ii., 500. A tall tree, the young buds silky. Leaves very obtuse, three or more inches long, the veins prominent on the under side. Flowers in spikes about as long as the leaves, the tube silky-hairy, but few hairs on the other parts of the flowers. Drupe ovoid, compressed. Queensland tropical coast.

B.V.—Wood of a light-yellow colour, close-grained, hard and tough.

163—T SERICOCARPA, *F. v. M.*, Fragm., ix., 159; Syn. Ql. Fl., 160. A tall tree, the branchlets silky. Leaves narrow-ovate, but tapering much towards the base, both sides glossy, the midrib and primary veins fine but prominent, two to four inches long. Flower-spikes longer than the leaves, erect, very delicate. Fruit oblong, silky, flattish, with acute margins, about half-inch long. Tropical coast scrubs, Queensland.

B.P.V.—Wood a light-yellow, with a darker-coloured heartwood, hard and tough; would suit well for chair-making.

163A—T. MUELLERI, *Benth.*, Flora Austr., ii., 500. A tall tree, the young buds silky. Leaves obovate, three or four inches long. Spikes of loose flowers several inches long. Fruit ovoid, bluish, about three-quarters of an inch long, no wing. Scrubs of the tropical Queensland coast.

B.P.V.—Wood yellow, but pinkish towards the centre, tough and light; suitable for axe-handles.

163B—T. PLATYPHYLLA, *F. v. M.*, Fragm., ii., 150; Flora Austr., ii., 502. Native name on the Flinders, "Durin." Tree of medium size, the young growth hoary. Leaves broadly ovate, very obtuse, four to six inches long, generally hoary on both sides Flower-spikes shorter than the leaves. Fruit hoary, ovoid or oblong, often with a more or less elongated beak. Eaten in a raw state, when ripe, by then natives.—*E Palmer*. Gulf country and islands of Torres Straits, Queensland.

B.P.V.—Wood dark-coloured, close in the grain, tough, hard, and prettily marked.

163C—T. PORPHYROCARPA, *F. v. M.*, Flora Austr., ii., 501. A tall tree, the leaves and young shoots hoary. Leaves ovate, two or three inches long, clustered at the ends of the rather thick branches. Flower-spikes rather dense. Fruit ovoid. Scrubs of tropical Queensland.

B.P.V.—Wood of a yellow colour, nicely marked, close-grained, hard, and tough; useful for house-building and cabinet-work.

LUMNITZERA, *Willd.*

164—L. RACEMOSA, *Willd.; DC.*, Prod, iii, 22; Flora Austr., ii., 504. A small tree, the leaves one to two inches long, obtuse and tapering much towards the base, rather fleshy. Flowers white, in

short axillary racemes.   Found amongst the mangroves on the coast
in a few places in southern Queensland, but common in the tropics
in similar situations, in India, East Africa, the Pacific Islands, and
New Guinea.

B.P.V.—WOOD of a pinkish-grey colour. hard, and close in the grain.

MACROPTERANTHES, *F. v. M.*

164A—M. FITZALANI, *F v M.*, Fragm , viii., 160. A moderate-
sized tree, the tips of the shoots silky, and a few hairs showing on the
leaves.   Leaves obovate, one to one and a half inch long, the principal veins rather distant, not very prominent.   Peduncles about half
inch long, bearing two small flowers. Gladstone and Bowen, Queensland.

B.P.V.—WOOD near to the bark yellow, the centre of a dark-grey, very
close-grained and hard; useful in turnery and cabinet-work.

GYROCARPUS, *Jacq.*

165—G. JACQUINI, *Roxb.*, Pl. Corom., i., 2, t. i.; Flora Austr., ii.,
505.   A small deciduous tree, the alternate lobed leaves often over
eight inches in diameter.   Flowers in small globular heads in a
spreading panicle.   Fruit ovoid, with two wings, often four inches or
more long and half-inch broad.   Scrubs near Rockhampton, and
tropical coast scrubs, Queensland, North Australia, New Guinea, and
the tropics of both the New and Old World.

In India the wood is preferred to all others for catamarans.   The seeds
are also made into rosaries and necklaces.

B.P.V.—WOOD very light and soft.

Order MYRTACEÆ.

BÆCKEA, *Linn.*

165A—B. VIRGATA, *Andr.*, Bot. Rep. t., 598; Flora Austr, iii., 81 ;
Bot. Mag., t., 2127. A tall shrub, the leaves linear, one or three
nerved, and from half an inch to one inch long.   The flowers small,
often several together in a loose umbel.   Stamens 5 to 15, none
opposite the centre of the petals; ovary, three-celled; capsule flat-
topped, seeds angular.

B.—WOOD close-grained, nicely marked ; of light colour.

LEPTOSPERMUM, *Forst.*

166—L. FLAVESCENS, *Sm.*, in Trans. Linn. Soc., iii., 262; Flora
Austr., iii., 104. A tall shrub, with or without silky hairs on the
young growth.   Leaves one or three-nerved, about half an inch long.
Flowers solitary, terminating short branchlets.   Capsule prominent
above the calyx-tube.   Abundant in swampy land about Brisbane,
and not scarce in most Queensland swamps north and south ; also in
New South Wales, Victoria, and Tasmania, in the Indian Archipelago
and Malacca.

B.V.—WOOD light coloured, close-grained and tough.

166B—L. MYRTIFOLIUM, *Sieb.* in, DC. Prod., iii., 238; Flora Austr., iii., 108. A tall shrub with slender branches, the leaves seldom over half an inch long, oblong, one or three nerved. Flowers small, solitary in the axils of the leaves; calyx-tube silky, capsule flat-topped. Coast lands in Queensland, New South Wales, and Tasmania.

B.P.V.—WOOD close-grained, tough, and dark in colour.

166C—L. ABNORME, *F. v. M.*, Flora Austr., iii., 109. A tall shrub, or at times quite a small tree, with a deciduous bark; the leaves one to two inches long, with one prominent nerve and one or two faint lateral ones. Flowers numerous, small. Capsule shorter than the tube. Stanthorpe, and in coast swamps up to Cape York in Queensland; also in North Australia, and the Hastings and Severn Rivers in New South Wales.

B.P.V.—WOOD of a dark colour, hard, heavy, and close-grained.

CALLISTEMON, *R. Br.*

167—C. LANCEOLATUS, *DC.*, Prod., iii., 223; Flora Austr., iii., 120. Red Bottle-brush or Water-gum; native name, "Marum." A small tree with a rather rough brown bark and narrow feather-veined leaves, one to three inches long, and attaining in some a quarter inch breadth, usually silky. The flowers in nodding spikes of a pink or deep red colour. Common throughout Queensland in beds of rivers and creeks, and also in New South Wales and eastern Gippsland, Victoria.

B.P.V.—WOOD of a red colour, close in grain, hard and tough; used for ship building and wheelwrights' work.

168—C. SALIGNUS, *DC.*, Prod., iii., 223; Flora Austr., iii., 120. A small tree with a papery bark and feather-veined leaves, two to four inches long, half an inch broad. The flowers yellowish, in spikes two to four inches long. Creek sides and swamps, southern Queensland.

B.P.V.—WOOD of a light colour, close-grained and tough; useful for any purpose where strength and durability are required.

MELALEUCA, *Linn.*

168A—M. SYMPHYOCARPA, *F. v. M.*, in Trans. Phil. Inst. Vict., iii., 44; Flora Austr., 138. A small tree, with oblong alternate leaves, one and a half to nearly three inches long, mostly vertical, many-nerved. Flowers in dense globular heads on the previous year's wood. Islands of the Gulf of Carpentaria.

B.V.—WOOD dark-coloured, close-grained, hard and prettily marked.

168B—M. ANGUSTIFOLIA, *Gœrtn.*, Fruct., i., 172, t. 35; Flora Austr., iii., 139. A small tree with alternate narrow leaves one and a half to two inches long, distinctly five-nerved; the flowers in dense terminal heads. Endeavour River, Queensland.

B.P.V.—Wood of a dark colour, hard and tough. Excellent for posts and piles.

168c—M. ACACIOIDES, *F. v. M.*, Fragm., iii., 116; Flora Austr., iii., 138. A small tree, leaves alternate, oblong, one to two inches long, faintly three or five-nerved, often vertical Flowers small, in dense globular heads. Islands of Torres Straits and North Australia.

B.P.V.—Wood strong, of a dark colour.

169—M. LINARIIFOLIA, *Sm.*, in Trans. Linn. Soc., iii., 278; Flora Austr., iii., 140. A tall tree, with white bark in loose papery layers, the shoots hairy, leaves mostly opposite, linear, acute, three-quarter to one and a half inch long. The flowers in distinct pairs in spikes one inch to one and a half inch long, the stamens in bundles often half an inch long; seed capsules very small, globular. Southern and northern Queensland and New South Wales.

B.P.V.—Wood of a dark red colour, very durable; useful for building stumps and piles for wharves.

169A—M. LEUCADENDRON, *Linn.*, Mant., 105; Flora Austr., iii., 142. Paper-barked Tea-tree. Native name at the Mitchell " Atchoourgo ;" at Port Curtis, "Bethar." A large tree, the bark white, spongy, in thin paper-like layers, the leaves alternate, two to four inches long, broad or narrow, with from three to seven nerves; the flowers yellowish, in interrupted spikes, the axis growing out after flowering into a leafy branch. Johnstone River and other river-sides in tropical Queensland.

In India the oil from the foliage is much used as an external application for rheumatism.

B.P.V.—Wood of a pinkish colour, hard and close-grained, very valuable for underground work and wharf-piles.

170—M. LEUCADENDRON, *Linn.* Var. *lancifolia*, Bail., Syn., 170. Paper-barked Tea-tree. Often a large tree, the bark in thin white layers, the leaves stiff, about three inches long, the end pointed; spikes of greenish-yellow flowers, often two together. Common in the swamps of south Queensland.

One ton of fresh leaves yields 320ozs. of oil similar if not identical with cajeput.

B.P.V.—Wood of a pinkish grey colour, close-grained and firm ; very useful for underground work.

170A—The dark book-block is made from a stump of a tree found at a depth of 28 feet, when excavating for the foundations of the *Courier* buildings in Queen-street, Brisbane, 1887.

171—M. LEUCADENDRON, *Linn.* Var. *saligna*, Bail. Syn., 170. Drooping Paper-barked Tea-tree. A large tree, the bark in white papery layers, the branches long, slender, and drooping like the Weeping Willow. Leaves six or more inches long and about half an inch wide ; the flowers very distant on the spike, and the stamens sometimes stained with red. Swamps and river-sides in tropical Queensland.

B.P.V.—Wood of a light grey colour, very durable, especially in underground work.

172—M. LEUCADENDRON, *Linn.* Var. *Cunninghamii*, Bail. Syn., 171. A small tree, the bark papery; leaves very stiff, large, and broad. Flowers large, yellowish, the spikes about five inches long. Swamps of tropical Queensland.

B.P.V.—Wood hard, of a dark colour, very durable.

172A—M. LEUCADENDRON, *Linn.* Var. *Cunninghamii.* Differs from the last only in its flowers being of a dark-red colour. Thursday and other islands of Torres Straits.

B.P.V.—Wood similar to the last.

One or other forms of *M. leucadendron* are found in North Australia, West Australia, New South Wales, and Queensland, in Australia; also in New Guinea and India, in which latter the oil called "cajeput" is obtained from its foliage.

172B—M. GENISTIFOLIA, *Sm.*, in Trans. Linn. Soc., iii., 277; Flora Austr., iii., 143. A tall tree, with a rough dark-coloured bark, the leaves narrow, about half-an-inch or more long, with about seven nerves; the flowers white, in oblong spikes. Usually along riversides in North and South Queensland, North Australia, and New South Wales.

B.P.V.—Wood of a grey colour, hard, close-grained, and tough.

ANGOPHORA, *Cav.*

174—A. SUBVELUTINA, *F. v. M.*, Fragm., i., 31; Flora Austr., iii., 184. Apple-tree. Tree of a medium size, the bark persistent. Leaves broad and stalkless or with very short stalks, the netted veins prominent, velvety or grey. Flowers in a loose corymb. Generally met with at the foot or on the side of hills in South Queensland and New South Wales.

In New South Wales this wood is much used by wheelwrights.—*C. Moore,* "Woods of New South Wales."

B.P.V.—Wood pinkish-grey, close-grained and tough.

175—A. INTERMEDIA, *DC.*, Prod., iii., 222; Flora Austr., iii., 184. Apple-tree. Tree of medium size, bark and the first leaves like the last species, but changing on the upper branches to leaves like a Gum-tree, long, narrow, and tapering to a point. Flowers also resembling *A. subvelutina.* Interior, also on the coast side of the range in Queensland, and also in New South Wales and Victoria.

In New South Wales used in wheelwright work.—*C. Moore,* "Woods of New South Wales."

B.P.V.—Wood of a grey colour, close-grained and easily worked.

175A—A. WOODSIANA, *Bail.*, Syn. Ql. Fl. Tree resembling *A. intermedia*, but the foliage and flowers and fruit larger. The trunk also is found often with hollows full of liquid gum of a bright-red colour, like that of the Bloodwood (*E. corymbosa*). Eight-mile Plains near Brisbane.

B.P.V.—Wood of a pinkish colour, hard and heavy.

176—A. LANCEOLATA, *Cav.*, Ic., iv., 22, t. 339; Flora Austr., iii., 184. Rusty Gum; native name, "Toolookar." A large tree, the bark deciduous, having somewhat the appearance of Spotted Gum, the bark often stained a rusty-red colour from the gum; the leaves often narrow, willow-like, but at times an inch broad, but tapering towards the point. A very abundant flowering tree, the flowers large in bunches. Common both inland and on the coast, in South Queensland and also in New South Wales.

B.P.V.—Wood of a pinkish colour, hard, heavy.

EUCALYPTUS, *L'Her.*

177—E. PLANCHONIANA, *F. v. M.*, Fragm., xi., 43; and plate in Eucalypt. Decade, 4. Tree of medium size, the bark persistent, more or less fibrous. Leaves thick, curved, and tapering towards the point. Flowers three to seven, large, on the top of a flat stalk. Fruit large, often one inch long and marked with ribs. Eight-mile Plains and other places in Southern Queensland and New South Wales.

B.P.V.—Wood of a grey-colour, hard and heavy, useful for house-building.

177A—E. EUGENIOIDES, *Sieb.*, in Spreng. Cur. poster., 195; *F. v. M.*, Cens. Austr Pl., 57; and plate in Eucalypt. Decade, 10. Stringybark. A tree of moderate size, with a fibrous persistent bark, leaves dark-green, very unequal-sided at the base; fruit nearly globular. Southern Queensland, New South Wales, and Victoria.

B.P.V.—Wood of a pinkish colour, hard and tough; used in house-building, fencing-rails, &c.

178—E. ACMENIOIDES, *Schau.*, in Walp. Rep., ii., 924; Flora Austr., iii., 208; and plate in Baron Mueller's Eucalyptographia, 10th Decade. Stringybark. A moderate-sized tree, with a fibrous persistent bark, the leaves paler on the under side. Fruit almost globular, the valves slightly exserted. Queensland coast country, north and south; also in New South Wales.

B.P.V.—Wood of a grey colour, close in the grain, hard and durable; used in house-building.

179—E. PILULARIS, *Sm.*, in Trans. Linn. Soc., iii., 284; Flora Austr., iii., 208; and plate in Eucalypt. Decade, 3. Blackbutt; native names, "Tcheergun" and Toi." A very large tree, the bark persistent at the base, but falling off in stripes from the upper part of the trunk and branches. Leaves thick, tapering from the base towards the point, and more or less curved. Flower-lid conical. Fruit semiglobose, a quarter to nearly half an inch diameter. Usually a mountain tree, but found also on level country near rivers in South Queensland; also in New South Wales and Victoria.

B.P.V.—Wood of a light-grey colour, hard, tough, and durable; used for house-building, fencing, and other work where strength and durability are required.

180—E. OCHROPHLOIA, *F. v. M.*, Fragm., xi., 36. Paroo Yellow-jacket. A moderate-sized tree, the bark of a light colour, somewhat spongy; the leaves somewhat thick, light coloured. Flower-lid about a quarter inch long; fruit about twice as long. Paroo, Cunnamulla, and other inland places in Queensland and New South Wales.

B.V.—Wood of a brownish colour, hard, heavy, and close-grained.

180A—E. GRACILIS, *F. v. M.*, in Trans. Vict. Inst., i., 35; Fragm., ii., 55; Flora Austr., iii., 211; also *Pl.*, in Muell. Eucalypt; *F. v. M.*, Eucalypt. Decade, 3; and Brown's Forest Flora of South Australia. A small tree with white and grey stem from the patches of bark falling off at irregular times, like that of the Blue and the Grey Gum-trees. The leaves are thick and shiny as in the Paroo Yellow-jacket, green on both sides, the veins hardly discernible from the thickness of the leaves, slightly curved, and about three or four inches long, and narrow; the flower-stalks bearing but a few small flowers. Fruit somewhat jug-shaped, small, but in shape like those of the Common Bloodwood. A small inland tree met with in all the Australian colonies.

B.P.V.—Wood hard, heavy, and close in the grain, of a yellowish-grey colour, tough and durable.

181—E. HÆMASTOMA, *Sm.*, Trans. Linn. Soc., iii., 285; Flora Austr., iii., 212; also plate in Eucalypt. Decade 2. White or Scribbly Gum; native name " Kurra-gurra." A moderate-sized tree, the bark very white, usually showing the serpentine marks left by some small boring insect; the leaves rather broad, and with a peppermint-like scent. Flowers six to eight, on the top of an angular stalk. Fruit quarter-inch in diameter, nearly globose, the top rim often coloured. South Queensland, and nearly if not quite into the tropics, usually on poor land; also in New South Wales, Victoria, and Tasmania.

The fresh leaves yield 672 oz. of oil from one ton. The gum contains 64·51 per cent. of kino tannin.

B.P.V.—Wood of a grey or reddish colour, not durable if exposed.

182—E. MICROCORYS, *F. v. M.*, Fragm , ii., 50; Flora Austr., iii., 212; also plate in Eucalypt. Decade 2. " Tee " of the natives; also called Turpentine and Peppermint. Tallow-wood of New South Wales. A large tree with a reddish fibrous persistent bark. Leaves narrow-ovate, about four inches long, dark-green. Flowers with a yellowish tinge, the buds club-shaped, the cap very small. Fruit about quarter-inch long. A common tree on the hills of southern Queensland; also in New South Wales.

One ton of fresh leaves yields 375 oz. of oil. The gum contains 53·32 per cent. of kino tannin.

B.P.V.—Wood of a grey colour, close-grained, very tough and durable, used for ship and house building purposes; also by the wheelwright for naves, felloes, and spokes.

183—E. POPULIFOLIA, *Hook.*, Ic. Pl., t. 879; Flora Austr., iii., 214; F. v. M., Eucalypt. Dec. 3. Poplar Box. White Box of New South Wales. A small or moderate-sized tree, the bark grey, somewhat spongy, closely persistent. Leaves glossy green, thick, on longish stalks, usually about one and a half inch to three inches broad, but at times much broader. Flowers very small. Found in many places both inland and coast in Queensland, but not on rich land frequently; also in New South Wales.

B.P.V.—Wood of a grey or light-brown colour, very tough and strong, hard to work, but is a handsome wood when polished; used in house building, dray-poles, and ship-building.

184—E. HEMIPHLOIA, *F. v. M.*, Fragm., ii., 62; Flora Austr., iii., 216; also plate in Eucalypt. Decade 5. Gum-topped Box. A tall tree, shedding its bark in long strips. Leaves often broad, thick, and long, tapering to a point. Flowers rather large, several on the top of an angular stalk, lid conical. Fruit oblong, about quarter-inch long. Common in South Queensland, sometimes in the tropical portions; also in New South Wales, South Australia, and Victoria.

B.P.V.—Wood of a yellowish-grey colour, very tough and elastic.

185—E. SIDEROPHLOIA, *Benth.*, Flora Austr., iii., 220; F. v. M., Eucalypt. Dec. 4. Iron-bark; native name, "Tanderoo." A large tree with a blackish, deeply furrowed, thick bark, the leaves narrow-ovate, three to six inches long. Flowers in bunches at or near the ends of the branches. Fruit about quarter of an inch long. South Queensland and New South Wales.

The gum contains 72·13 per cent. of kino tannin, and is totally soluble n water.

B.P.V.—Wood of a grey colour, close-grained, hard, heavy, and very durable; useful for the large beams in buildings, railway sleepers, and other work where strength and durability are required.

185A—E. SIDEROPHLOIA, *Benth.* Var. *rostrata*, Flora Austr., iii., 220. Large-leaved Ironbark. A large tree, the bark black and thick, deeply furrowed, but still separable into layers. Leaves very large, often from two to six inches wide on young trees. About Taylor's Range, in Queensland; also in New South Wales.

B.P.V.—Wood red, close in grain, considered the best of all the Ironbarks for building purposes; it is very hard and heavy.

186—E. MELANOPHLOIA, *F. v. M.*, in Journ. Linn. Soc., iii., 93; Flora Austr., iii., 220. Silver-leaved Ironbark. A crooked-stemmed spreading-headed tree, with opposite, stalkless, broad, silvery leaves, the bark dark and rugged. Flowers and fruit small. On open country, both north and south in Queensland; also in New South Wales.

B.P.V.—Wood towards the outside greyish, the centre red, close in the grain and hard.

187—E. CREBRA, *F. v. M.*, in Journ. Linn. Soc., iii., 87; Flora Austr., iii., 221; also plate in 5th Decade of Eucalypt. Narrow-leaved Ironbark. A small or medium-sized tree, with usually a greyish-coloured rough bark, the leaves long and narrow. Flowers small; fruit also small. A common Queensland tree, north and south; also in New South Wales and North Australia.

B.P.V.—WOOD white near the bark; all the rest of a pinkish grey, close-grained, very tough and durable.

188—E. STAIGERIANA, *F. v. M.*; *Bail.*, in Syn. Ql. Fl., 176. Lemon-scented Ironbark. A small tree with a rugged irregularly fissured bark, the leaves having a greyish hue, narrow usually, but at times broad-ovate, two to five inches long, having a delightful lemon-like fragrance, flowering abundantly as a shrub. Fruit small. Palmer River, Queensland.

One ton of the dry leaves yields 1,290 oz. of oil.

B.P.V.—WOOD of a red colour, hard and durable. The principal value of this tree is in the foliage for oil.

189—E. RAVERETIANA, *F. v. M.*, Fragm., x., 99; F. v. M., Eucalypt. Dec. 1. Thozet's Box or Iron Gum-tree. A large tree with a scaly bark persistent on the trunk. Leaves dark-green, three to five inches long. Flowers very small, in rather large terminal panicles. Fruit minute. Scrubs near Rockhampton, Queensland.

B.P.V.—WOOD of a dark-drab colour speckled with white, close-grained, very hard and tough; valuable for building purposes; would also be useful for cabinet-work.

190—E. MICROTHECA, *F. v. M.*, in Journ. Linn. Soc., iii., 87; Flora Austr., iii., 223; also plate in 10th Decade of Eucalypt. Native names, "Jinbul" or "Kurleah" and "Coolibar." A small tree, the bark somewhat persistent at the base, but deciduous and white on the upper part of the stem; young branchlets reddish, but covered by a grey bloom. Leaves three to six inches long, pale-coloured on both sides. Fruit with the valves exserted. Cunnamulla, in Queensland; also in New South Wales and South Australia.

B.P.V.—WOOD near the outside grey, the rest all of a rich deep-red colour; useful in building and cabinet-work, although perhaps too hard to work for the latter.

190A—E. ROBUSTA, *Sm.*, Bot. Nov. Holl., 40, t., 13; Trans. Linn. Soc., iii., 283; Flora Austr., iii., 228; also plate in 7th Decade of Eucalypt. Swamp Mahogany Gum; native name, "Kimbarra" or "Gnorpin." A large tree with rugged bark. The leaves large, broadly ovate or long and then narrower, very stiff and thick, of a dark-green colour. Flowers large, on a more or less flattened stalk. Fruit often half an inch long. Stradbroke Island and at the Logan River, in Queensland; also in New South Wales.

B.P.V.—WOOD of a deep-red colour, close-grained; a useful building wood.

190B—E. PALLIDIFOLIA, *F. v. M.*, Fragm., iii., 131; Flora Austr., iii., 236. A small tree with smooth ash-coloured bark and foliage.

Leaves oblong, about three inches long, rather thick; the flower-stalk bearing four to six rather small flowers. Fruit nearly globose. Gulf country in Queensland, and North Australia.

B.P.V.—WOOD yellow near the bark, the rest red, hard, close-grained, and prettily mottled.

191—E. BOTRYOIDES, *Sm.*, in Trans. Linn. Soc., iii., 286; Flora Austr., iii., 229; also plate in 4th Decade of Eucalypt. Woolly-butt of some localities. A very large tree, the bark rugged and persistent for a distance up the stem, after which it is white and deciduous. Leaves long, thick, the base broad but tapering towards the point. Flowers on a flattened footstalk. Fruit smooth, a quarter to nearly half an inch long, but narrow. In mountain gullies and river flats in southern Queensland; also in New South Wales, Victoria, and Tasmania.

B.P.V.—WOOD of a red colour, close in grain, hard, tough, and durable; useful in large buildings, wheelwright's work, and in all works where large beams of hardwood are required.

191A—E. DEALBATA, *A. Cunn.*; *Schau.*, in Walp. Rep., ii., 924; Flora Austr., iii., 239. Stanthorpe Messmate. A moderate-sized tree with spreading head and rough persistent bark at the base or on all the trunk; all the younger trees, and often a great part of the foliage of the older ones, of a silvery-grey colour, the leaves often then broadly ovate. Flowers in small bunches at the axil of the leaves on short stalks. Fruit almost globular. Stanthorpe and other inland localities in Queensland, also in New South Wales.

B.P.V.—WOOD of a pinkish colour, only fit for being used in the whole log as it is apt to split, and is usually full of hollows containing gum. The wood of this and similar Eucalypts is very durable when used for underground work.

191B—E. STUARTIANA, *F. v. M.*; F. v. M., Eucalypt., Dec. 4. Stanthorpe Box. A moderate-sized tree with a soft persistent bark, the foliage in a young state perhaps grey like *E. dealbata*, which in many respects this tree resembles. The leaves are on rather long stalks of often a reddish colour, tapering towards the apex and often curved; the flowers small in heads on a rather short stalk, in the axils of the leaves, but the fruiting heads usually below the leaves on account of the shoot growing out and the subtending leaves having fallen. Found on poor land, Stanthorpe, Queensland; also in New South Wales, Victoria, and Tasmania.

B.P.V.—WOOD of a grey colour, hard, tough and durable.

192—E. ROSTRATA, *Schlech.*, Linneæ, xx., 655; Flora Austr., iii., 240; also plate in 4th Decade of Eucalypt Stanthorpe Yellow-jacket. Tree of moderate size with deciduous white bark. Leaves three to six inches long, the flower-buds with a prominent beak. Stanthorpe and other localities in south Queensland.

B.P.V.—WOOD of a dark colour, close-grained, strong and durable if kept dry.

192A—E. EXSERTA, *F.v.M.*, in Journ. Linn. Soc., iii., 85; Flora Austr., iii., 241. A moderate-sized tree, the bark more or less deciduous; the leaves three to six inches long, tapering towards the point. Fruit nearly globular, the valves protruding. Along the banks of inland rivers at Cunnamulla and other places in Queensland.

B.P.V.—Wood of a pinkish colour, hard, tough and durable.

193—E. TERETICORNIS, *Sm.*, Bot. Nov. Holl., 41, and in Trans. Linn. Soc., iii., 284; Flora Austr., iii., 241; F. v. M., Eucalypt., Dec. 9. Blue Gum; native name, "Mungara;" Grey Gum and Bastard Box of New South Wales. A tall handsome tree, the bark deciduous, leaving here and there patches of a bluish hue. Leaves four to six inches long; the flowers with a lid often more than half an inch long, and of nearly white colour. Fruit nearly globular. Common on good land in Queensland, north and south; also in New South Wales and Victoria.

B.P.V.—Wood of a red colour (called Blue Gum from the supposed blue colour of the bark), close-grained, tough and durable; used for building and many other purposes.

194—E. PLATYPHYLLA, *F. v. M.*, in Journ. Linn. Soc., iii., 93; Flora Austr., iii., 242. Broad-leaved Poplar Gum. Usually a tree of moderate size, but sometimes large; both bark and leaves deciduous; the leaves often very large, somewhat heart-shaped or resembling large Poplar leaves, three to ten inches diameter. Tropical Queensland and North Australia, on the islands of the Gulf of Carpentaria and New Guinea.

B.V.—Wood deep-red, subject to gum-veins, hard and close-grained; considered by some very durable as fencing material.

195—E. SALIGNA, *Sm.*, in Trans. Linn. Soc., iii., 285; Flora Austr., iii., 245; also plate in 2nd Decade of Eucalypt. Grey Gum. A tall tree with deciduous rather thick bark of a greyish colour. Leaves three to over six inches long, much narrowing towards the point. Flowers not large, several together upon the top of an angular stalk; flower-lid conical. Southern Queensland, usually plentiful on ridges; also in New South Wales.

B.P.V.—Wood very tough and close grained, of a grey colour, very hard.

196.—E. RESINIFERA, *Sm.*, in White Voy., 231, in Trans. Linn. Soc. iii., 284, and Exot. Bot., t. 84; Flora Austr., iii., 245; also plate in 1st Decade of Eucalypt. "Jimmy Low." Forest Mahogany of N.S.W. Usually a very large tree with a rough, reddish, fibrous bark; the leaves large, straight or curved, and tapering towards the point; the stalk of the flowers more or less flattened. In a few places in South Queensland, perhaps the finest at Maroochie; also in New South Wales.

The gum contains 65·57 per cent. of kino tannin.

B.P.V.—Wood of a rich red colour, from which it is called by some Mahogany; strong and durable; most useful for piles, fencing-posts, and the

F

large beams in buildings. In New South Wales, where it is used for fencing, it has been known to keep sound for 50 years.

196A.—E. CLAVIGERA, *A. Cunn.*, in Walp. Rep. ii, 926; Flora Austr., iii., 250; also plate in 4th Decade of Eucalypt. A tree of moderate size with grey bark, opposite nearly stalkless leaves, and large bunches of flowers on rather long stalklets, club-shaped in the buds. Islands of the Gulf of Carpentaria.

B.V.—WOOD of a dark brown colour, close in the grain, hard and durable.

196B.—E. PHŒNICEA, *F. v. M.*, in Journ. Linn. Soc., iii., 91; Flora Austr., iii., 251; F. v. M., Eucalypt. Dec. 1. Tree of medium size with a smooth bark. Leaves four to six inches, netted. Flowers in bunches below the leaves, the stalklets of each flower rather long. Gulf country, Queensland.

From the fragmentary specimen sent in with the log it is impossible to speak with certainty of this, but it is probably a form of *E. phœnicea*, with fewer flowers in the bunch and whitish stamens.

B.P.V.—WOOD grey for a good distance in, but the centre dark-brown, tough and heavy.

197.—E. TESSELLARIS, *F. v. M.*, in Journ. of Linn. Soc., iii., 88; F.v M. Eucalypt. Dec. 9. Native name at Port Curtis, "Wonkara." Moreton Bay Ash. A very graceful often large tree, with the bark persistent and cracked into squares on the lower part of the trunk, but deciduous on the upper part and branches; the flowers in scanty bunches. Fruit ovoid, more than a quarter inch long, and more fragile than many others. Found throughout the Queensland coast country and North Australia.

B.P.V.—WOOD of a dark-brown colour except near the bark, close-grained, tough and durable, especially that of the northern trees.

198.—E. TESSELLARIS, *F. v. M.* Var. *Dallachyana*, Flora Austr., iii, 251. Usually a small crooked-stemmed tree, without the tessellated bark at the base, but fruit resembling the normal form. Rockhampton.

B.P.V.—WOOD brownish, tough and close-grained.

198A.—E. SETOSA, *Schau.*, in Walp. Rep., ii., 926; Flora Austr., iii., 254; F.v M. Eucalypt. Dec. 6. A small tree, the branchlets and inflorescence often covered with stiff rusty-coloured hairs. Leaves opposite, ovate, stalkless. Fruit nearly globose or pitcher-shaped. Tropical Queensland, islands of the Gulf of Carpentaria, and North Australia.

B.P.V.—WOOD of a dark-brownish colour, subject to gum veins, therefore only fit for using in the whole log; hard, strong, and durable.

199. -E. CORYMBOSA, *Sm*, Nov. Holl., 43, and in Trans. Linn. Soc., iii., 287; Flora Austr., iii., 256; F.v.M. Eucalypt Dec. 5. Bloodwood; native name, "Boona." A tall tree with persistent, spongy, somewhat fibrous bark, the leaves rather thick, tapering towards the apex, three to six inches long, often hispid with glandular hairs when shooting from an old butt. Flowers large; fruit pitcher-

shaped, half to nearly one inch long. The commonest Eucalypt in Queensland; found wide-spread, north and south; also in North Australia and New South Wales.

The gum contains 43·71 per cent. of kino tannin; it contains also a great deal of insoluble matter kinoised, especially catechu and kionoin.—*K. T. Staiger*.

B.P.V.—Wood of a red colour containing large cavities full of gum; a very durable wood if used whole, as for piles, posts, &c.

199A—E. CORYMBOSA, *Sm.* Var. *terminalis*, F. v. M. The foliage of this species or form is of a glaucous colour, and the bark lighter and, though spongy, not so rough as in the normal form. The fruit is somewhat larger and more pitcher-shaped. A tree of the tropical Queensland coast.

B.P.V.—Wood red, subject to large gum-veins.

200—E. TRACHYPHLOIA, *F. v. M.*, Journ. Linn. Soc., iii, 90; Flora Austr., iii., 221. F. v. M , Eucalypt., Dec. 5. White Blood-wood. A moderate-sized tree, with a dense foliage, the bark persistent, spongy-fibrous Leaves four or more inches long. Flowers in terminal panicles. Fruit pitcher-shaped, about quarter inch long. Found on or near the ranges of southern Queensland.

B.P.V.—Wood of a grey colour, hard, heavy, and durable; a useful, strong, tough timber.

201—E. BAILEYANA, *F. v. M.*, Fragm , xi., 37; Syn. Ql. Fl., 181; also plate in 3rd Decade of Eucalypt. Rough Stringybark. A tall tree, the bark very rough and fibrous. Leaves rather thick. Flowers rather small, five to ten on the top of the stalk. Fruit pitcher-shaped, three-celled, the seeds oblong and rather large. Eight-mile Plains, near Brisbane

One ton of fresh leaves yields 322 oz. of oil. For medicinal use, the oil of this species is considered superior to most.

B.P.V.—Wood of a light-grey colour, very tough, suitable for tool-handles and other purposes where toughness is required; the bark yields a strong fibre.

202—E. MACULATA, *J. D. Hook.*, Ic. Pl., t. 619; Flora Austr., iii., 258; also plate in 3rd Decade of Eucalypt. Spotted Gum; native name, "Urara." A fine large handsome tree, the bark deciduous, falling off in patches, leaving an indentation where each piece was peltately attached, thus giving a spotted appearance to the trunk; leaves often very large and coarse. Flowers large. Fruit semi-globose, or almost pitcher-like. Southern Queensland, usually on stony ridges: also in New South Wales.

The gum contains 34·97 per cent. of kino tannin.

B.P.V.—Wood of a light-grey colour, very elastic and durable, valuable in wheelwright and carriage work.

203—E. MACULATA, *Hook.* Var. *citriodora*, Bail., Syn. Queensland Flora, 181. Citron-scented Gum. Only differing from the normal form in the citron-like fragrance of its foliage. Gladstone and Rockhampton.

B.P.V.—Wood of perhaps a darker colour, but very like the last.

TRISTANIA, *R. Br.*

204—T. suaveolens, *Sm.*, in Rees. Cycl, xxxvi.; Flora Austr., iii., 262. Swamp Mahogany; native name, "Boolerchu." Broad-leaved Water Gum of New South Wales. A small or large tree, the bark somewhat fibrous and persistent, the leaves oval, three or more inches long and more or less downy or hoary as well as the young shoots. Flowers in pretty, white, small bunches; the fruit usually under quarter-inch diameter. All over the Queensland coast lands, often in swamps; also in North Australia and New South Wales.

B.P.V.—Wood of a red colour, resembling Spanish Mahogany, hard and close-grained, but best fitted for underground work; extensively used for piles, as it is found to resist the ravages of the teredo longer than any wood as yet tried in this colony.

205—T. suaveolens, *Sm.* Var. *glabrescens*, Syn. Ql. Fl., 182. Native name, "Boobarchoo." This differs from the normal form only in the want of the hoariness of its foliage, the leaves being a bright shiny-green. Found in low, almost swampy, localities, South Queensland.

B.P.V.—Wood similar to the last, and used for the same purposes.

206—T. conferta, *R. Br.*, in Ait. Hort. Kew, ed. 2, iv., 417; Flora Austr., iii., 263. Brisbane Box; native name, "Tubbil-pulla." A fine handsome tree, the bark persistent on the base of the stem, deciduous above and on the branches, of a brownish colour. Leaves crowded at the ends of the branches and often large; the buds are usually protected by large dry scales, which fall as it bursts into fresh growth in the spring. Flowers showy. Fruit hemispherical, quarter to half-inch in diameter. Found north and south on the Queensland ranges; also in New South Wales.

B.P.V.—Wood of a dark-grey colour; hard, tough, and close in the grain; when kept dry very durable. Shrinks very much in drying; used for joists, knees of vessels, and by the wheelwright.

206a—T. exiliflora, *F. v. M.*, Fragm., v., 11; Flora Austr., iii., 264. A medium-sized tree, with smooth bark, the inflorescence slightly hoary; the leaves long, narrow; flowers yellow; fruit obovoid-globular. Tropical Queensland.

B.P.V.—Wood of a dark colour, close in the grain, very tough and elastic; useful for tool-handles.

206b—T. laurina, *R. Br.*, in Ait. Hort. Kew, ed. 2, iv., 417; Flora Austr., iii., 264. Called Beech and Swamp Mahogany in New South Wales. Tree usually of moderate size, but sometimes found very large; the bark smooth or slightly fibrous; the young shoots somewhat angular and often purplish. Leaves long, narrow, and deep-green. Flowers yellow. Found on the borders of rivers in South Queensland, from Maroochie to the border; also in New South Wales and Victoria, in Gippsland.

B.P.V.—Wood of a dark colour, close-grained, very tough and strong; useful for tool-handles.

206c—T. MACROSPERMA, *F. v. M.*, Notes on Papuan Plants, 104. Tree of medium size, the bark somewhat fibrous. Leaves oval, two to three or more inches long, on slender stalks. Flowers in spreading terminal panicle. Capsule oval, three-celled, seeds winged. Probably this species, but no flower seen. Thursday Island, Torres Straits, and New Guinea.

B.P.V.—Wood of a straw colour, close-grained, very hard and tough, stands well in drying, and will likely prove valuable for building purposes. So far as I can determine from the specimens received from Thursday Island, this seems identical with the New Guinea tree.

SYNCARPIA, *Ten.*

207—S. LAURIFOLIA, *Ten.*, in Mem. Soc. Ital. Sc. Moden., xxii., t. 1; Flora Austr., iii., 265. New South Wales Turpentine tree. A tall erect tree with a fissured, fibrous, persistent bark, the leaves being clustered at the ends of the branches so as to appear whorled; smooth on the upper side but more or less hoary beneath, three or four inches long. The flowers in heads of from six to ten flowers. The fruits joined together, forming a head. Southern Queensland, and also in New South Wales.

B.P.V.—Wood of a light colour near the bark, but all the rest dark-brown easy to work, but shrinks and warps much in drying. Used in New South Wales for piles, shipbuilding, railway sleepers, girders, and for all underground work.

208—S. LEPTOPETALA, *F. v. M.*, Fragm., i., 79; Flora Austr., iii., 266. A small tree minutely hoary. Leaves ovate, pointed, two to four inches long. Flowers small, in dense globular heads on slender stalks. A tree of river-side scrubs, southern Queensland and New South Wales.

B.P.V.—Wood of a light colour, close-grained, hard and tough.

209—S. HILLII, *Bail.*, in Proc. Roy. Soc. Ql., i., 86. Turpentine-tree of Fraser's Island; native name, "Peebeen." A large tree, with a thick, fibrous, deeply-fissured bark; the leaves ovate, four to six inches long and two to four broad. Flowers united in heads, usually a whorl of six large flowers and a central one forming the head; the fruiting heads about one and a-half inch across. Frazer's Island, Queensland, is, so far as at present known, its only habitation.

The bark contains 7·68 per cent. of tannin.

B.P.V.—Wood of a dark-pink colour, close in the grain and tough; a useful building wood.

LYSICARPUS, *F. v. M.*

210—L. TERNIFOLIUS, *F. v. M.*, in Trans. Phil. Inst. ii., 68; Flora Austr., iii., 267. Tom Russell's Mahogany. An erect pine-like tree with narrow-linear leaves, opposite or in whorls of three, two to three inches long. Flowers rather small, solitary or in bunches. Usually found on the ranges or in brigalow scrubs in Queensland.

B.P.V.—Wood light-brown, well-marked, hard, heavy, and elastic; suitable for cabinet-work; has been largely used for railway sleepers.

XANTHOSTEMON, *F. v. M.*

211—X. PACHYSPERMUS, *F. v. M. et Bail.* Occasional papers on Queensl. Flora, No. 1. (Name referring to the thick large seeds.) The Yellow-wood of the Johnstone River. A glabrous tree of medium size, the leaves alternate but often crowded at the ends of the shoots, and so close as to appear opposite, petiolate, ovate-lanceolate, at times very obtuse but always much tapered towards the base, three to five inches long, penniveined, with the primary lateral veins rather distant and prominent. Flowers in slender often raceme-like panicles, two or three inches long, in the upper axils, on slender pedicels. Capsules somewhat globose, more than half superior, half to three-quarter inch diameter, opening in three hard valves, rugose on the back. Seeds one or two in each cell, thick, somewhat flattened, three or four lines diameter, with a thin glossy testa.

Hab.: Johnstone River.—*Dr. Thos. L. Bancroft.*

By mistake the wood of this tree is described under *Halfordia scleroxylon* (No. 52a) in the catalogue of the woods sent to the Colonial and Indian Exhibition.

B.P.V.—Wood of a grey colour, fine in the grain, tough and strong.

BACKHOUSIA, *Hook. et Harv.*

212—B. MYRTIFOLIA, *H. et Harv.*, in Bot. Mag., t., 4133; Flora Austr., iii., 269. A small tree, the under side of leaves and young shoots silky-hairy. Leaves narrow-ovate, scented, one or two inches long; the flowers white, myrtle-like. A river-side tree in southern Queensland and New South Wales.

B.P.V.—Wood of a light grey colour, darker in the centre; close in the grain; very hard and tough; said to be used in New South Wales for mallets and tool-handles.

212B.—B. BANCROFTII, *Bail. et F. v M.* Johnstone River or Langdon's Hardwood. A tall handsome tree with a rather thin, grey, scaly bark. Leaves in opposite pairs, ovate; those near the flowers small, but the others from two to four inches long, the midrib and primary veins prominent. Flowers in a more or less spreading terminal panicle, white, the petals dropping, but the sepals persisting and enlarging after flowering, but of unequal size. Fruit a dry capsule, with about twelve seeds. Johnstone River, Queensland.

B.P.V.—Wood of a light-grey colour, hard, close-grained, something like the teak, useful as a building timber; rather darker towards the centre in large trees; splits straight and freely.

213.—B. CITRIODORA, *F. v. M.*, Fragm., i., 78; Flora Austr., iii., 270. A small tree, slightly hoary, with leaves of a verbena-like fragrance, three to five inches long. Flowers numerous, in umbel-like clusters. Maroochie, the Pine River, and some few other localities in southern Queensland.

B.P.V.--Wood close-grained, hard, of a light-pink colour.

OSBORNIA, *F. v. M.*

213A.—O. OCTODONTA, *F. v. M.*, in Fragm., iii., 31; Flora Austr., iii., 272. A bushy shrub, glabrous except the flowers. Leaves obovate-oblong, very obtuse, three-quarters to one and a half inch long, much narrowed towards the stalk. Flowers solitary in the axils between two concave deciduous tomentose bracteoles, or three together at the ends of the branches. Found on the tropical coast amongst the mangroves.

B.V.—Wood of a darkish brown colour, close-grained, and very hard.

RHODOMYRTUS, *DC.*

214.—R. PSIDIOIDES, *Benth.*, Flora Austr., iii., 272; Fragm., ii., t., 13. A small tree, more or less hoary, the leaves three to five inches long, the margins often recurved, and here and there stained red. Flowers rather large, and fruit soft, oval, yellow, the size of a pigeon's egg. Borders of creeks in southern Queensland; also in New South Wales.

B.P.V.—Wood light-coloured, close-grained and tough.

216.—R. MACROCARPA, *Benth.*, Flora Austr., iii., 273. Native Loquat. A tree of moderate size, with oval-oblong leaves of thin texture, six to ten inches long, the veins prominent; the flower-stalks bearing one or three flowers. Fruit cylindrical, one inch long or rather more. Scrubs of tropical Queensland.

B.V.—Wood of a light-grey colour, hard and tough.

MYRTUS, *Linn.*

217.—M. HILLII, *Benth.*, Flora Austr., iii., 275. Scrub Ironwood. A small tree with a smooth, very thin, often reddish bark. Leaves glossy, ovate, pointed, one or two inches long. Flowers small on rather long slender pedicels. Fruit globular, small, containing several seeds. Scrubs of Queensland, north and south.

B.V.—Wood of a light-grey colour, close in the grain, and very hard; warps in drying.

217A.—M. RACEMULOSA, *Benth.*, Flora Austr., iii., 276. A small tree with rather roughish bark. Leaves pointed, ovate, about two inches long, the flowers in a somewhat loose axillary raceme. Fruit globular, containing one or two nearly globular seeds. Scrubs of tropical Queensland.

B.P.V.—Wood of a close grain and tough; warps in drying.

RHODAMNIA, *Jack.*

218A.—R. SESSILIFLORA, *Benth.*, Flora Austr., iii., 277. A medium-sized tree with a somewhat fibrous bark, the branchlets slightly hoary; the leaves narrow-ovate, three to five inches long, rather thin. Flowers often three together in the axils, stalkless. Fruit globular, with one to four seeds. Scrubs of tropical Queensland.

B.P.V.—WOOD of a dark colour, close-gained and tough.

219.—R. TRINERVIA, *Blume*, Mus. Bot., i., 79; Flora Austr., iii., 278; Bot. Mag., t., 3223. The Three-nerved Myrtle. A medium-sized tree, or on the ranges a tall tree, more or less velvety. Leaves ovate-lanceolate, prominently three-nerved from the base, and much reticulate. Peduncles axillary, bearing from one to three small white flowers. Berries globular, purplish, about quarter of an inch in diameter. New South Wales and Queens'and.

B.P.V.—WOOD brown, close-grained, tough, strong, and durable; useful for house building and many other purposes.

220.—R. ARGENTEA, *Benth.*, Flora Austr., iii., 278. White Myrtle of New South Wales. Often a tall tree, more or less silvery. The leaves ovate-lanceolate, silvery white on the under side, triplinerved (the lateral nerves, one on each side, diverging from the midrib a little above the base of the leaf). Flowers usually in trichotomous cymes, small, white. Fruit, a berry, globose, about quarter of an inch in diameter, purplish. Met with in the scrubs of the northern parts of New South Wales and Queensland.

B.P.V.—WOOD dark brown, close-grained, hard, tough, and durable.

EUGENIA, *Linn.*

221.—E. SMITHII, *Poir.*, Dict. Suppl., iii., 126; F. v. M., Vict. Pl., t. 18; Flora Austr., iii., 282; Bot. Mag. t. 5480. Lilly-pilly; native name, "Coochin-coochin." Usually a small tree, the bark somewhat fibrous. Leaves narrow-oval, two or three inches long. Flowers small, in a terminal panicle. Fruit white, stained with purple, round, quarter to half an inch in diameter; ripe about April and May. Many parts of Queensland, as top of Bunya and other mountains, along the borders of creeks, etc., both north and south; North Australia, New South Wales, and Victoria.

B.P.V.—WOOD of a dark colour, close-grained, tough; warps in drying.

222.—E. VENTENATII, *Benth.*, Flora Austr., iii., 283. Water Gum A large spreading-headed tree, the branches often drooping, the oblong leaves four to six inches long, of a lively-green colour, finely veined. Flowers in rather large spreading panicles. Fruit round, greenish-white, about half an inch in diameter, but often larger. Found bordering creeks and rivers in North and South Queensland, also in New South Wales.

Used in New South Wales for boat-building and handles of tools.—
C. Moore, "Woods of New South Wales."

B.P.V.—Wood of a grey colour, soft and easy to work ; might be suitable
r cabinet-work.

222A.—E. LEPTANTHA, *Wight*, Illustr., ii., 15, and Ic., t. 528;
Flora Austr., iii., 283. Tree, the foliage pale, inflorescence hoary.
Leaves oval to oblong on short stalks. Flowers in short bunches on
the previous year's wood at the knots formed by old leaves, the
calyx-tube half an inch long, narrow, club-shaped. Scrubs of tropical
Queensland.

B.P.V.—Wood of a grey colour, close-grained and hard.

222B.—E. LEPTANTHA, *Wight*, Var. A form with small narrow-
lanceolate leaves; a tree of medium size, met with in the scrubs of
the Johnstone River.

B.P.V.—Wood of a grey colour, close-grained, soft, easily worked ; suitable
for flooring-boards of verandahs. Only this form was worked for the Colonial
and Indian Exhibition.

223.—E. JAMBOLANA, *Lam.*, Dict., iii , 198 ; Flora Austr., iii., 283 ;
Wight, Illustr., ii., 16, and Ic. 535, 624. The Jambul of India. A tall
tree, the bark with depressions where the scaly flakes have fallen off, with
the leaves oblong, somewhat stiff, often ending in a blunt point, four to
six inches long and one and a-half to over two inches broad, often glossy.
Flowers rather large, few in forked bunches on the branches below
the leaves. Fruit over one inch in diameter, containing one seed.
Tropical scrubs in Queensland and North Australia ; also in India,
where the wood is considered useful for building purposes, the bark
for tanning and dyeing, and also for medicine in cases of dysentery.
The seeds are recommended as a remedy in diabetes, prescribed in
the form of powder.

B.P.V.—Wood of a flesh colour, close in the grain, stands well in drying ;
suitable for house-building purposes.

224.—E. CORMIFLORA, *F. v. M.*, Fragm., v., 32 ; Flora Austr.,
iii., 284. A tree of moderate size with a somewhat scaly bark, with
a much-knotted belt five or six feet from the ground, and from these
knots it blossoms and fruits. Flowers large, often of a pale-pink
colour. Fruit oval, white on some trees, and two inches long.
Scrubs of tropical Queensland.

B.P.V.—Wood of a dark colour, close-grained and tough. The knobby
inequalities noticeable on the bark of the plank piece are the knots from which
the flowers are produced year after year.

226—E. GRANDIS, *Wight*, Illustr., ii., 17, and Ic., t., 614 ; Flora
Austr., iii., 285. White Apple. A fine tree, the bark pealing off in
very thin skin-like flakes. Leaves thick, oval oblong, four to six
inches long, shiny. Flowers large, terminal or near the ends of the
branches. Fruit globular, white, more than one inch in diameter,
containing one or two large seeds. Tropical Queensland, also in
India.

B.P.V.—Wood light-brown, close-grained, hard and tough; might serve for making staves for rum-casks; suitable also for building purposes.

227—E. suborbicularis, *Benth.*, Flora Austr., iii., 285. A large tree, the bark peeling off in thin skin-like flakes, with broadly obovate leaves, four to six inches long, the parallel divergent veins prominent and joining within the margin, forming a looped intra-marginal one. Flowers large. Tropical Queensland.

B.P.V.—Wood of a dark-grey colour. with peculiar corky concentric rings several inches asunder. The natives of the Johnstone River form their canoes out of the trunk of this tree.

227a—E. Wilsonii, *F. v. M.*, Fragm., v., 12; Flora Austr., iii., 285. Tree of moderate size. Leaves five or six inches long, the transverse veins fine. Flowers large, in terminal bunches, the stamens reddish purple. Fruit ovoid, about one and a half inch long. Tropical Queensland.

B.P.V.—Wood of a uniform dark-brown colour, close-grained, hard, and tough; useful for building purposes, mallets, and other implements.

228—E. myrtifolia, *Sims*, Bot Mag., t. 2230; Flora Austr., iii., 286. Scrub Cherry. A large tree with a somewhat fibrous bark, the leaves oval-oblong or pointed, two to three inches long, the transverse veins prominent. Flowers rather large. Fruit ovoid or oblong, red. Not uncommon in most Queensland scrubs. Trees very large in mountain scrubs; also in New South Wales.

B.P.V.—Wood of a light grey, close in the grain; suitable for tool handles on account of its toughness. The fruit is used for jam and wine making.

BARRINGTONIA, *R. et G. Forst.*

229—B. speciosa, *R. et G. Forst.*, Gen., 76., t. 38; Wight, Ic., t. 547. A rather large tree, the long ovate leaves clustered at the ends of the thick branches. The flowers large in terminal racemes, the stalklets one or two inches long. Calyx of two or three oblong leaves, the petals twice as long as these calyx-leaves. Stamens numerous, red, two to four inches long. Fruit large and four-angled. Found on the tropical Queensland coast, New Guinea, India, the Indian Archipelago, and the Pacific Islands.

B.P.V.—Wood of yellow colour, tough and firm; might be used in cabinet work.

229a—B. racemosa, *Gaudich*, in Freyc. Voy. Bot., and F.v.M., in Fragm., ix., 118. A tree of medium size, leaves large, on short footstalks, acuminate and crenately toothed The flowers white or pale red, in long glabrous racemes, stamens longish, colour of petals. Fruit obtuse, quadrangular, often large. Johnstone River and Rockingham Bay in Queensland; Ceylon, tropical Africa, the East Indies, and several other parts.

B.—Wood close-grained, yellow; but of little value, being too readily eaten by insects.

CAREYA, *Roxb*.

230—C. AUSTRALIS, *F.v.M.*, Fragm., v., 183, and Flora Austr., iii., 289. Native names on the Cloncurry, "Go-onje" and "Guntha-marrah," and on the Mitchell, "Ootcho;" at Rockhampton, "Barror." Usually a stunted, small, crooked tree with a corky bark; the leaves obtuse, tapering into a rather long stalk. Flowers large, terminal, the stamens very long. Fruit ovoid, eaten by the natives. Tropical Queensland coast and North Australia.

B.P.V.—WOOD of a light grey colour, red in the centre, close in the grain and tough; works easily.

Order LYTHRARIEÆ.

LAGERSTRŒMIA, *Linn*.

231—L. ARCHERIANA, *Bail*., in Syn. Ql. Fl., 196. A small tree with a close, thin, smooth bark of a whitish colour. The leaves oblong, three to six inches long, one and a half to two and a half inches wide, downy on the under side. Flowers a lilac-purple, in large panicles. Palmer River, Queensland.

B.V.—WOOD firm, of a brown colour.

Order SAMYDACEÆ.

HOMALIUM, *Jacq*.

232—H. VITIENSE, *Benth*., in Journ. Linn. Soc., iv., 36; Flora Austr., iii., 310. A moderate-sized tree, the leaves broadly ovate, with wavy margins, two to four inches long. Flowers in spikes. Rockhampton scrubs, Queensland; also in New Caledonia and Fiji.

B.P.V.—WOOD white, close in grain; suitable for cabinet-work.

Order ARALIACEÆ.

PANAX, *Linn*.

232A—P. MURRAYI, *F. v. M.*, Fragm., ii., 106; Flora Austr., iii., 381. A very handsome tree, the leaves simply pinnate on young trees five to six feet long, with the leaflets eight to twelve inches long, entire or slightly toothed. Rockingham Bay and Johnstone River in the north, and Mount Mistake Range and Tambourine Mountain in the south of Queensland; also in New South Wales.

B.P.V.—WOOD of a light colour, soft and light; would make good lining-boards.

233—P. ELEGANS, *F. v. M.*, in Trans. Phil. Inst. Vict., ii., 68 Flora Austr., iii., 383. Mowbulan Whitewood; native name at Bunya Mountains, "Greyanger." A tall and sometimes large tree, the foliage generally at the ends of the branches; the leaves very large, wide-spreading, and much divided into ovate leaflets. Flowers in a very large, much-branched, dark-coloured terminal panicle. In all the coast scrubs of Queensland, forming often a large tree in mountain scrubs; also in New South Wales.

B.P.V.—Wood soft, light, and elastic; might suit for cricket-bats, excellent for lining-boards; will likely prove a most useful wood to the musical instrument makers.

BRASSAIA, *Endl.*

235—B. ACTINOPHYLLA, *Endl.*, Nov. Stirp. Dec., 89; Flora Austr., iii., 385. Umbrella-tree. A very handsome small tree, the leaves on long stalks, with 7 to 16 stalked oblong leaflets at the top, each from 6 to 12 inches long. Flowers in small heads along long, erect, stout spikes, the whole inflorescence red. Tropical Queensland.

B.V.—Wood soft, close-grained, dark.

Order CORNACEÆ.

MARLEA, *Roxb.*

237—M. VITIENSIS, *Benth.*, Flora Austr., iii., 386. Var. *tomentosa*. Musk-wood. A moderate-sized tree. The leaves ovate-oblong, more or less velvety, often have a small dimple formed in the axils of the principal veins. Flowers hairy, fruit ovoid. Not uncommon on the borders of rivers, both north and south, in Queensland.

B.P.V.—Wood of a yellow colour towards the bark, the centre black, close in the grain, with a musk-like scent; an excellent wood for cabinet-work.

Order CAPRIFOLIACEÆ.

SAMBUCUS, *Linn.*

238—S. XANTHOCARPUS, *F. v. M.*, in Kew Journ., viii., 145, and in Trans. Phil. Inst. Vict., i., 42; Pl. Vict., t. 29; Flora Austr., iii., 398. Native Elderberry. A tall shrub or small tree, with a light-coloured corky bark and light-green pinnate leaves. Flowers white, berries yellow. Common on the borders of scrubs in South Queensland; also in New South Wales and Victoria.

B.V.—Wood soft, light and pale-coloured.

Order RUBIACEÆ.

SARCOCEPHALUS, *Afz.*

239—S. CORDATUS, *Miq.*, in Flora Ind. Bot., ii., 133; Flora Austr., iii., 402. Leichhardt-tree or Canary-wood. Native name on the Mitchell, "Oolpanje;" on the Cloncurry, "Coobiaby;" at Rockhampton, "Toka." A large tree with a thick, soft, corky bark of a more or less yellowish colour; the opposite leaves very large, with broad stipules at their base. Flowers in globose heads, yellow. Fruit a globular mass. Tropical Queensland, North Australia; widely spread in India, also in the Archipelago, and Tropical Africa.

The wood of this tree is used in Burmah and India for sandals, common furniture, doors, &c., but is considered a poor perishable wood.
B.P.V.—Wood of a dark-yellow colour, close-grained, soft, and having a strong musk-like odour when fresh cut; useful both to the carpenter and cabinet-maker. The wood also furnishes a good dye.

WEBERA, *Schreb.*

239A—W. Dallachiana, *F. v. M.*, Flora Austr., iii., 412. A small tree, leaves oval elliptical or oblong, acuminate, narrowed at the base, six to eight inches long. Flowers very numerous in a terminal trichotomous corymb shorter than the leaves, calyx small, the limb short, cup-shaped, obscurely toothed, corolla-tube slender about five lines long; lobes oblong, not half the length of the tube. Anthers linear. Style very long. Scrubs of tropical Queensland.

B.V.—Wood close-grained and light coloured.

RANDIA, *Linn.*

239B—R. chartacea, *F. v. M.*, Rep. Burdek. Exped., 12; Flora Austr. A tall shrub with most variable shaped leaves, opposite or whorled, from elliptical-oblong to narrow linear and six to ten inches long, obliquely and prominently veined. Flowers white, very fragrant, in terminal clusters. Fruit oblong, reddish when ripe, resembling a large gooseberry. South Queensland and New South Wales.

B.V.—Wood close-grained, hard, tough, and nicely marked.

240—R. Fitzalani, *F. v. M.*, in Flora Austr., iii., 411. A slender-stemmed tree with oblong, glossy, green leaves, often more than six inches long and two or three inches wide. Flowers white, rather large. Fruit oblong or globular, often four inches long and two inches diameter. Scrubs of tropical Queensland.

B.V.—Wood straw-coloured, close in grain, hard and tough.

241—R. densiflora, *Benth.*, in Flora Hongk., 155; Flora Austr., iii., 412. A small tree with oval-oblong leaves, somewhat thick and shining; the flowers crowded in the axils. Berries globular. Tropical Queensland, North Australia, New Guinea, and Hongkong.

B.P.V.—Wood of a light colour, very close in the grain, hard and tough; might prove suitable for wood-stamps.

GARDENIA, *Linn.*

242A—G. Macgillivræi, var. (or perhaps a new species between that and *G. megasperma*, but better specimens must be had before it can be fully determined). The leaves on the shoots received were of a rather thin texture, ovate-lanceolate, with tufts of hairs in the axils of the principal veins, otherwise glabrous; petioles short. Flowers solitary, terminal on a peduncle of one inch or more long. Calyx-tube ribbed, the six lobes nearly as long as the corolla-tube. Corolla-tube one to one and a half inch long, the six lobes about one inch long.

B.P.V.—Wood of a light colour, firm and close in the grain.

GUETTARDA, *Linn.*

244—G. putaminosa, *F. v. M.*, in Fragm., ix., 183; Flora Austr., iii., 419. A small tree, the young parts often silky; the leaves oblong, about one inch long. The flowers in the axils, small. Fruit about quarter inch long. Tropical Queensland.

B.P.V.—Wood of a light-yellowish colour, quite equal to Box; the grain is close, and it may prove suitable for engraving.

TIMONIUS, *Rumph.*

245—T. Rumphii, *DC.*, in Prod., iv., 461; Flora Austr., iii., 417. Native name at Rockhampton, "Kavor Kavor." A tree of moderate size, the bark somewhat fibrous Leaves narrow-ovate, pointed, and with the young shoots often silky. Flowers small; fruit globular, quarter to half inch in diameter. M. Thozet says that the natives are very fond of this fruit. Moreton Bay and Taylor's Range in South Queensland. Common on the borders of rivers in tropical Queensland, North Australia; also in Timor, Amboyna, and Sumatra.

B.P.V.—Wood light in colour and close in grain, suitable for lining-boards; is easily worked, resembling somewhat the English Sycamore.

HODGKINSONIA, *F. v. M.*

246—H. ovatiflora, *F. v. M.*, in Fragm., ii., 132; Flora Austr., iii., 420. A small tree, the branches slender; leaves ovate, two or three inches long; the flower-stalks bearing a few almost delicate globular flowers; the fruit small, nearly globose. Scrubs of southern Queensland and New South Wales.

B.V.—Wood white, close-grained and firm.

PLECTRONIA.

247—P. latifolia, *F. v. M.*, in Flora Austr., iii., 421. A small tree with broad deep-green leaves, the veins distant. Flowers small, white; berries small. Southern Queensland, on the borders of river scrubs; also in New South Wales, South Australia, and West Australia.

B.V.—Wood pink with darker streaks, close-grained and hard; a cabinet-wood.

248—P. odorata, *F. v. M.*, in Fragm., ix., 185. A small tree, the foliage often glossy. Flowers white; fruit globular or double. Scrubs of Queensland; also in North Australia and New South Wales.

B.V.—Wood of a yellow colour, close-grained, tough, and nicely marked; likely to prove useful for cabinet-work.

251—P. vaccinifolia, *J. D. Hook.*; *F. v. M.*, Fragm., ix., 186. A small erect tree with a fluted stem; the leaves very small, almost round. Flowers small, white. Often met with on the borders of scrubs in South Queensland and New South Wales.

B.V.—Wood tough, close in grain, and of a straw colour.

252—P. barbata, *J. D. Hook.* *Canthium coprosmoides*, in Flora Austr., iii., 423. A tree of medium size, with broadly ovate somewhat glossy leaves with distant veins; the small white flowers in the axils of the leaves, hairy about the throat, the berry-like fruit red. On the borders of scrubs in Queensland and New South Wales.

B.P.V.—Wood dark-yellow streaked with a brown colour, very prettily marked or grained; a useful wood for turnery and cabinet-work.

252ᴀ—P. BUXIFOLIA, *Benth.*, Flora Austr., iii., 422. A small tree with deep-green obtuse leaves about one inch long. Flowers small, white; berries small. Range scrubs of southern Queensland.

B.V.—Wood of a light colour, close in grain; useful for turnery and cabinet-work.

IXORA, *Linn.*

253—I. TIMORENSIS, *Dcne.*, in Herb. Tim. Descr, 90; Flora Austr., iii., 415. A small tree, the leaves oblong, four to eight inches long; those immediately under the inflorescence stalkless and somewhat heart-shaped. Flowers white, in a large spreading panicle at the ends of the branches. Tropical Queensland and North Australia; Timor and other islands of the Archipelego.

B.V.—Wood of a light colour, close in grain, hard and tough.

253ᴀ—I. BECKLERII, *Benth.*, Flora Austr., iii., 415. A small tree of south Queensland scrubs, met also as far north as Bundaberg. Leaves glossy, four or five inches long; the flowers white, fragrant, in dense corymbs in the axils of the leaves. Fruit about quarter of an inch in diameter. This tree is also found in the northern scrubs of New South Wales.

B.V.—Wood of a darkish colour, close-grained, and tough.

PAVETTA, *Linn.*

254—P. INDICA, *Linn.* (*Ixora pavetta*, Roxb.) Flora Austr., iii., 414; Wight, Ic., t., 148. A tall shrub or small tree, with opposite lanceolate leaves three to five inches long. Flowers white in terminal corymbs, corolla-tube nearly half an inch long, the lobes spreading, but shorter than the tube. Fruit about quarter of an inch diameter. Common in Queensland scrubs, also spread over India and the Archipelago. The root has some reputation in India as a bitter and aperient.

B.V.—Wood of a light colour, close-grained, and firm.

MORINDA, *Linn.*

255—M. CITRIFOLIA, *Linn.*; DC., Prod., iv., 446; Flora Austr, iii., 423; Wight, Ill. t. 126. (*M. tinctoria*, Roxb.) A tall shrub, with four-angled branches; the leaves large, ovate, 6 to 10 inches long, on short stalks; the flower-heads on short stalks; the fruit a pulpy mass, an inch or more in diameter. Queensland tropical coast, tropical Asia, and the Pacific Islands.

The roots of this, as well as some others of the genus, are used for obtaining a red dye as well as a medicine by the natives of India. The fruit is considered by the Cochin Chinese to be deobstruent and emmenagogue. In Bombay the leaves are used as a healing application to wounds and ulcers, and are administered internally as a tonic and febrifuge.—*Dymock.*

B.V.—Wood of a dark-yellow colour, easy to work; also yields a dye.

255ᴀ—M. JASMINOIDES, *A. Cunn.*; *Hook.*, Bot Mag., t., 3351; Flora Austr., iii., 424. A tall climber, the leaves narrow-ovate, the heads of small flowers on slender stalks. Fruit a globular mass of about one inch diameter. Southern Queensland, New South Wales, and Victoria.

B.V.—Wood yellow, prettily marked.

CŒLOSPERMUM, *Blume*.

256—C. RETICULATUM, *Benth.*, in Flora Austr., iii., 425. Usually a shrub, but at times forming a tree with crooked stem of one foot in diameter, the bark very thick, rough or deeply furrowed, and of a reddish colour. Leaves oval, of a dry nature, and prominently netted. Flowers white, small, the corolla-tube about a quarter of an inch long, the four or five lobes small, the flowers hairy inside. Fruit nearly globular, a little over a quarter inch long. A common plant in tropical Queensland and North Australia.

B.P.V.—Wood of a grey colour; the bark, which is often very thick, produces an excellent dye.

PSYCHOTRIA, *Linn.*

258—P. DAPHNOIDES, *A. Cunn.*; Hook., Bot. Mag., t., 3228; Flora Austr., iii., 428. A tall dark green shrub, leaves obovate or oblong, very obtuse, about one inch to one inch and a half long. Flowers in terminate pedunculate trichotomous cymes. Fruit ovoid, ribbed. Found in scrubs and along the banks of rivers in most parts of Queensland.

B.—Wood close-grained and of light colour.

Order COMPOSITÆ.

CASSINIA, *R. Br.*

258A—C. LÆVIS, *R. Br.*, in Trans. Linn. Soc., xii., 128; Flora Austr., iii., 587. Wild Rosemary. A tall shrub, with narrow linear leaves; the branches and under side of the leaves white. Flower-heads white, in short rather dense panicles Found frequently in hilly parts of southern Queensland; also in New South Wales and South Australia.

B.V.—Wood dark and beautifully marked, close-grained; would be a very valuable wood cut in veneers for cabinet work.

258B—C. SUBTROPICA, *F.v.M.*, Fragm., i., 17; Flora Austr., iii., 588. A tall, erect, tomentose-pubescent branching shrub, of neat and handsome appearance. Leaves obovate, half to three-quarters of an inch long, glossy above, white underneath. Flower-heads small, in numerous terminal panicles. Common on the margins of creeks in southern Queensland as far north as the Pine River.

B.—Wood of a grey colour, close-grained.

Order EPACRIDEÆ.

TROCHOCARPA, *R. Br.*

259—T. LAURINA, *R. Br.*, in Prod., 548; Flora Austr., iv., 166; Bot. Mag., t., 3324. A small tree, the bark often stringy; the leaves one to two inches long, clustered at the ends of the branches; the young growth often a pretty purplish colour; nerves of leaves five to seven. Flowers small, white, in terminal spikes. Fruit purple, depressed globular. Southern Queensland, on the edges of creeks; also in New South Wales.

B.P.V.—Wood of a pinkish colour, close-grained, nicely marked and hard.

LEUCOPOGON, *R. Br.*

259A—L. MELALEUCOIDES, *A. Cunn.*; DC., Prod., vii., 750; Flora Austr., iv., 207. A tall shrub, very twiggy; the leaves oblong-linear, with a sharp point, about half an inch long. Spike of flowers usually terminal, the flowers small, white. South Queensland and New South Wales.

B.V.—Wood of a rather dark colour and nicely marked, hard and close in the grain.

MONOTOCA, *R. Br.*

259B—M. SCOPARIA, *R. Br.*, in Prod., 547; Flora Austr., iv., 230. A bushy shrub of several feet; the leaves oblong, pale on the back, about half an inch long. Flowers small, white, in clusters. Fruit ovoid, small. Southern Queensland, New South Wales, Victoria, and Tasmania.

B.V.—Wood of a pale yellow colour, close-grained, nicely marked, and easily worked.

Order MYRSINEÆ.

MYRSINE, *Linn.*

260.—M. VARIABILIS, *R. Br.*, in Prod., 534; Flora Austr., iv., 275. A small tree, the foliage very variable as to shape and size, sometimes bordered by teeth. Flowers small, very numerous along the branches. Fruit a small berry. Queensland, north and south, often on the sides or tops of ranges; also in New South Wales and Victoria.

B.P.V.—Wood close-grained, light-coloured, and firm.

ÆGICERAS, *Gærtn.*

261.—Æ. MAJUS, *Gærtn.*; *A. DC.*, Prod., viii, 142; Flora Austr., iv., 277; Wight, Illustr., t., 146. River Mangrove. A small tree, leaves thick, very obtuse but tapering into a moderately long stalk, two to four inches long. The flowers white, in pretty, white, loose bunches at the ends of the branchlets. Fruit a little white curved horn. On the beach and borders of tidal rivers in Queensland and North Australia; also in the South Pacific Islands, India, and Burmah.

B.V.—Wood of light colour, close-grained, and easily worked.

G

Order SAPOTACEÆ.

CHRYSOPHYLLUM, *Linn.*

262.—C. PRUNIFERUM, *F. v. M.*, in Fragm., vi., 26 ; Flora Austr., iv. A small tree, the leaves oblong, woolly on the under side. Flowers in axillary clusters ; fruit resembling an Orleans Plum. Scrubs north and south in Queensland, also in New South Wales.

B.P.V.—WOOD of a light-yellow colour, close-grained, hard and tough ; might be suitable for bent-work.

LUCUMA, *Juss.*

263.—L. SERICEA, *Benth. et Hook.*, in Gen. Pl., ii., 654. A small tree, the branches and under side of the leaves silky. Leaves ovate, two or three inches long. Flowers in axillary clusters ; fruit ovoid, about one inch in diameter. Tropical Queensland, North Australia.

B.P.V.—WOOD light-yellow, somewhat resembling Birch, close in the grain and firm ; useful in cabinet-work.

SIDEROXYLON, *Linn.*

264.—S. POHLMANIANUM, *Benth. et Hook.*, in Gen. Pl., ii., 655. A moderate-sized tree, clothed with soft silky hairs. Leaves oblong, four or five inches long, clustered at the ends of the branches ; the flowers clustered on the old wood ; fruit globular. Common in Queensland river scrubs, north and south.

B.V.—WOOD of a bright-yellow, hard and close-grained ; the best of all Queensland woods for engraving work.

264A.—S. LAURIFOLIUM, *F. v. M.*, in Flora Austr., iv., 282. A tall tree with a sweet bark ; the leaves oval-oblong, three or more inches long ; fruit obovoid. Maroochie, Queensland.

B.P.V.—WOOD light-grey towards the outside, brown in the centre ; grain close.

265—S. AUSTRALIS, *Benth. et Hook.*, in Gen. Pl., ii., 655. Scrub Crab or Black Apple. A tall tree, the leaves oblong, three or more inches long. Flowers in axillary clusters ; fruit purple, ovoid, often nearly two inches in diameter. Queensland scrubs, north and south ; also in New South Wales.

B.P.V.—WOOD of a dark colour, close-grained and tough ; useful for building purposes.

265A—S. OBOVATUM, *R. Br.*, Prod., 530 (under *Sersalisia*) ; Flora Austr., iv., 283. Tree of moderate size, the under side of the leaves slightly silky. Leaves three to five inches long. Fruit oblong, often one-seeded. Tropical Queensland.

B.P.V.—WOOD of a yellow colour, hard, and close in the grain.

266—S. MYRSINOIDES, *A. Cunn., Benth.*, in Flora Austr., iv., 283. Nut Apple of New South Wales. A small tree found in mountain and brigalow scrubs, densely leafy, often even on the trunk. Leaves glossy, broadly elliptical, often obtuse and tapering much towards the base, one to two inches long. Flowers in axillary clusters or solitary, about three lines long. Fruit small. Throughout Queensland.

B.P.V.—Wood of a light-yellow colour, close-grained, does not shrink or warp much in drying; useful for cabinet-work.

HORMOGYNE, *A. DC.*

266A—H. COTINIFOLIA, *A. DC.*, Prod., viii., 176; Flora Austr., iv., 284. A small scrub tree, the leaves obovate, and flowers in the axils. Found on the borders of scrubs, Queensland and New South Wales.

B.P.V.—Wood of a dark-yellow colour, close in grain and very hard.

MIMUSOPS, *Linn.*

267—M. PARVIFOLIA, *R. Br.*, Prod., 531; Flora Austr., iv., 284 A small tree, the branchlets and young foliage downy. Leaves paler on the under side when full grown, but not white, about two inches long. The flowers solitary or in twos in the axils of the leaves. Tropical Queensland and North Australia.

B.P.V.—Wood of a pinkish colour, close-grained, firm, and easy to work.

267A—M. BROWNIANA, *Benth.*, Flora Austr., iv., 285. A tree of moderate size, the leaves broad, thick, and white or rusty on the under side. Fruit globular, about one inch in diameter Tropical Queensland.

B.P.V.—Wood red, fine-grained, and works easily.

Order EBENACEÆ.

MABA, *Forst.*

268—M. FASCICULOSA, *F. v. M.*, Fragm., v., 163; Flora Austr., iv., 163. An erect tree with smooth dark-coloured bark; the leaves oval-oblong, dark-green, three to five inches long; the flowers in axillary clusters. Fruit nearly globular, resting in the enlarged cup. Queensland scrubs; also in New South Wales.

B.P.V.—Wood of a light colour, with black specks or streaks, close-grained, strong and elastic; suitable for carving on wood-stamps.

268A—M. RETICULATA, *R. Br.*, Prod., Flora Austr., iv., 291. A small tree, glabrous except the flowers. Leaves obovate-oblong, much netted on the upper side, two or three inches long. Male flowers in short racemes, calyx nearly glabrous, about one line long; corolla silky-pubescent, the tube scarcely so long as the calyx, the lobes a little longer, stamens nine to twelve; female flowers solitary, without stamens or staminodia. Berry globular, calyx somewhat enlarged. Scrubs of northern Queensland.

B.P.V.—Wood of a light colour, with black specks or streaks near the heart, very close in grain, strong, elastic, useful in making carpenter's bench and handscrews.

269—M. GEMINATA, *R. Br.*, Prod., 527; Flora Austr., iv., 291. A small tree, the obtuse leaves from one to two inches long. Fruit in twos or solitary; berries ovoid. Queensland scrubs; also in North Australia.

B.P.V.—Wood light-coloured near the outside, black in the centre, close in grain, hard and tough; the black a good substitute for Ebony.

269A—M. HUMILIS, *R. Br.*, Prod., 527; Flora Austr., iv., 291. Native name on the Cloncurry, "Thankoiu" and "Mogiore." A small tree, the branchlets very dense; leaves half to one inch long, obovate; the fruits often solitary, ovoid. Queensland coast and mountain scrubs; also in North Australia.

Fruit eaten by the natives without cooking.—*E. Palmer.*

B.P.V.—Wood, the outer part light, the centre black, hard, and very tough; a useful cabinet wood.

DIOSPYROS, *Linn.*

269B—D. HEBECARPA, *A. Cunn.*, Flora Austr., iv., 286. A tree of moderate size. Leaves oval-oblong, showing the netted veins, on short stalks, two or three inches long. Berry about three-quarters inch in diameter, covered with short hairs, containing eight seeds. Tropical Queensland coast.

B.P.V.—Wood of a yellow colour, with numerous small black spots, very close in grain and tough.

270A—D. PENTAMERA, *F. v. M.*, Fragm., iv., 82; Flora Austr., iv., 288. Black Myrtle; in New South Wales, Grey Plum. A tall erect smooth-barked tree, the leaves oblong, two or three inches long. Flowers in clusters. The fruits solitary, about half-inch in diameter. Scrubs of southern Queensland and New South Wales.

B.P.V.—Wood close-grained and very tough. Said to be used for tool-handles and flooring boards in New South Wales.

Order STYRACEÆ.

SYMPLOCOS, *Linn.*

271—S. STAWELLII, *F. v. M.*, Fragm., v., 60. A small tree with usually narrow, irregularly-toothed, somewhat dark-green leaves, two to four inches long. Flowers in spikes. Fruit ovoid. Queensland scrub borders; also in New South Wales.

B.V.—Wood white, close-grained; suitable for any purpose to which Box is applied.

271A—S. THWAITESII, *F. v. M.*, Fragm., iii., 22; Flora. Austr., iv., 293 A small tree with glossy green leaves four or five inches long. Flowers in spikes, fruit ovoid. Scrubs north and south in Queensland; also in New South Wales.

B.P.V.—Wood light in colour, fine in grain, and tough.

Order OLEACEÆ.

LINOCIERA, *Sw.*

272—L. RAMIFLORA, *DC.*, Prod., viii., 297; Flora Austr., iv., 301; Wight, Ic. t. 734. (Chionanthus.) A tree of moderate size with a light-coloured bark. Leaves six to nine inches long, dotted; the flowers small, white, in loose panicles, often on the shoots below the leaves. Fruit oval, half-inch long. Common in the coast scrubs of tropical Queensland, New Guinea, Moluccas, and the Philippines.

B.P.V.—WOOD dark grey, somewhat mottled, of close grain, and easy to work.

NOTELÆA, *Vent.*

273—N. LONGIFOLIA, *Vent.*, Choix., t. 25; Flora Austr., iv., 299; in New South Wales called Native Olive. A small tree with a rough bark and stiff prominently-veined body, two to six inches long; the flowers small in axillary racemes. Fruit ovoid, black and bitter. Forest country and borders of creeks, Queensland, north and south; also in New South Wales and Victoria.

B.P.V.—WOOD of a light colour, hard, tough, and close-grained.

274.—N. MICROCARPA, *R. Br.*, Prod., 524; Flora Austr., iv., 300. A small tree, the branches slender. Leaves narrow, two to four inches long, with prominent veins. Flowers very small; fruit small, globular. Open country, north and south Queensland; also in New South Wales.

B.P.V.—WOOD of light colour, dark towards the centre, close-grained and very hard.

OLEA, *Linn.*

275.—O. PANICULATA, *R. Br.*, Prod., 523; Flora Austr., iv., 297. Native name (Bunya Mountains), "Billan-billan." The Ironwood and Marblewood of New South Wales. A tall tree, the bark speckled. Leaves pale-green, on long stalks, pointed-oval, two to five inches long. Flowers small, white, the bunches in the axils of the leaves and at the ends of the shoots; fruit roundish. River-side or most Queensland scrubs; also in New South Wales.

B.P.V.—WOOD of a whitish colour, darkening towards the centre, prettily figured, hard, close-grained, and, when newly cut, of a rose-like fragrance.

Order APOCYNACEÆ.

CARISSA, *Linn.*

276.—C. OVATA, *R. Br.*, Prod.; Flora Austr. iv., 305. "Kunker-berry" of the Cloncurry natives. A tall glabrous spiny shrub. Leaves ovate rhomboidal, half to one inch long. Flowers in small compact axillary cymes, white and fragrant. Fruit oval about three-quarters inch long, black, often eaten and considered to be of agreeable flavour and wholesome. Common in Queensland; also in New South Wales.

Fruit eaten in a raw state by the natives and settlers; quite sweet and wholesome.

B.—Wood close-grained, and of light colour.

ALYXIA, R. Br.

277.—A. RUSCIFOLIA, R. Br., Prod. 470; Bot. Mag., t. 3312; Flora Austr., iv., 308. Swizzle-stick shrub, or Chain-fruit. A tall close-growing shrub or small tree, with the leaves in whorls of three or four, ovate-elliptical with sharp points, obliquely and prominently veined, three-quarters to one and a half inch long. Flowers small, fragrant, in small heads. Fruit of one or two globular articles, quarter inch or rather more in diameter, of an orange colour.

B.—Wood close-grained, and of whitish colour.

CERBERA, Linn.

278—C. ODOLLAM, Gærtn.; A. DC., Prod., viii., 353; Flora Austr., iv., 306. Wight, Ic. t. 441; Bot. Mag., t. 1845. A tall tree with a milky sap, the leaves alternate, tender, narrow, and often nearly one foot long, but usually four to six inches long. Flowers showy, in large terminal panicles, white and yellow, and fragrant. Fruit large. Coast scrubs of tropical Queensland, New Guinea, India, and Burmah.

In India the wood does not seem to be used, but from the seeds an oil used for burning is said to be obtained.

B.P.V.—Wood of a dark-yellow, close in the grain, and firm.

ALSTONIA, R. Br.

280—A. SCHOLARIS, R. Br.; A. DC., Prod., viii., 408; Wight, Ic. t. 422. White or Milkwood. Often a large tree, the bark greyish, the branches whorled like the leaves. Leaves five to seven in each whorl, whitish on the under side, four to six inches long. Flowers rather small, white, in large spreading terminal panicles. Fruit two long, horn-like, narrow pods, containing hairy seeds. Coast scrubs of Queensland, New Guinea, India, and Burmah; also tropical Africa.

In India the wood is used for furniture, scabbards, and coffins; in Burmah for school blackboards, and in Assam and Cachar for tea-boxes. Wood and bark bitter. The latter, which furnishes the ditain of commerce, is considered a valuable remedy in chronic diarrhœa and advanced stages of dysentery. At Mackay used for shingles and palings as it is abundant and easy to split, but is better adapted for indoor-work.

B.P.V.—Wood soft, close-grained, and of light colour.

281—A. VERTICILLOSA, F. v. M., Fragm., vi., 116; Flora Austr., iv., 313. Tree of considerable height, of milky sap. Leaves in whorls of four to seven, narrow, and pale on the inner side, and from three to four inches long; the panicle of flowers bearing more dense clusters than A. scholaris. Tropical coast of Queensland, and North Australia.

B.P.V.—Wood of light colour, soft and easy to work.

281ᴀ—A. ᴠɪʟʟᴏsᴀ, *Blume*; *F. v. M.*, Fragm., vi., 117; Flora Austr., iv., 313. A small tree, the branchlets and under side of the leaves velvety. Leaves in whorls of three, oval-oblong, four to six inches long. Inflorescence terminal, hoary. Fruit double, horn-like, and narrow, 6 to 12 inches long, containing hairy seeds. Tropical Queensland and Java.

B.P.V.—Wood of a light colour, close in grain, works easily, is firm, and would probably suit for staves.

282—A. ᴄᴏɴsᴛʀɪᴄᴛᴀ, *F. v. M.*, Fragm., i., 57; Flora Austr., iv., 314. Fever-bark or Quinine-tree. A slender tall tree, with a rough dark bark; the leaves glossy, on long stalks, three to five inches long. Flowers in loose bunches, small and white. Fruit of two narrow horn-like pods, containing hairy seeds. Common on the inland downs country in Queensland; also in New South Wales.

B.P.V.—Wood of a pale-yellow, close in the grain; warps in drying.

282ᴀ—A. ᴄᴏɴsᴛʀɪᴄᴛᴀ, ᴠᴀʀ. ᴍᴏʟʟɪs, Flora Austr., iv., 315. Bitter-bark or Fever-bark. An erect slender tree, similar to the last, only velvety. Common in Queensland on the borders of creeks.

B.P.V.—Wood white, close-grained; might suit for cabinet work.

TABERNÆMONTANA, *Linn.*

283—T. ᴏʀɪᴇɴᴛᴀʟɪs, ᴠᴀʀ. ᴀɴɢᴜsᴛɪғᴏʟɪᴀ, *Benth.*, Flora Austr., iv., 311. A tall dichotomously-branched shrub or small tree. Leaves oblong, lanceolate, two to four inches long. Flowers white, very fragrant, in pedunculate cymes, usually in the forks of the branches, in flower from September to December. Fruit yellow, two carpels united at the base or distinct, more or less three-angular, one to one and a half inch long, opening along the inner face, and showing the bright-reddish seeds. A very common shrub in Queensland scrubs.

Of one form of this shrub in New South Wales the bark is considered medicinal, and known as "Bitter-bark."

B.—Wood of a uniform yellow, close-grained.

WRIGHTIA, *R. Br.*

284ᴀ—W. sᴀʟɪɢɴᴀ, *F. v. M.*, Flora Austr., iv., 316. *Balfouria saligna*, R. Br., Prod.; Endl. Iconogr., t. 75. Milk-bush. A tall shrub or small tree with long linear leaves three to five inches long. Flowers yellow; pods about six inches long. Gulf country; also on the tropical coast in Queensland and North Australia.

B.P.V.—Wood of a uniform pale-yellow colour, the grain close; might be useful for cabinet-work, carving, and engraving; thought to resemble English Elder.

Order LOGANIACEÆ.

FAGRÆA, *Thunb.*

284ʙ—F. Mᴜᴇʟʟᴇʀɪ, *Benth.*, Flora Austr., iv., 368. A small tree, the leaves three to six inches long, oblong, opposite but crowded at the ends of the branches. Flowers few at the top of the shoot; fruit red. Tropical scrubs, Queensland.

B.P.V.—Wood of a yellow colour, close-grained and hard.

STRYCHNOS, *Linn.*

286—S. psilosperma, *F. v. M.*, Fragm., iv., 44; Flora Austr., iv., 369. In tropical Queensland, a rambling shrub; but on Taylor's Range, near Brisbane, a fine erect small tree of 60 or more feet and armed with slender spines one inch long. Leaves broadly ovate, three to five nerved, one to two inches long; berry globular. Taylor's Range, southern Queensland (a tree), common on the borders of stony scrubs in tropical Queensland.

B.P.V.—Wood light-yellow with numerous white longitudinal streaks, the centre black or dark, the grain close; very hard and tough.

Order BORAGINEÆ.

CORDIA, *Linn.*

287—C. myxa, *Linn.*; *DC.*, Prod., ix., 479; Flora Austr., iv., 386; Wight, Illustr., t., 169. Sebastan Tree, or, according to Dr. Dymock, "Sapistan," which he says is an abbreviation of Sag-pistan, which means in Persian "dogs' dugs." A moderate-sized tree with a dense head of foliage. Leaves broadly ovate on long stalks, entire or lobed, three or five nerved at the base, three or more inches long, rough to the touch. The flowers rather long in straggling bunches, succeeded by oval drupes of a pale yellow colour or turning to a pink, very viscid. In tropical Queensland, found on the borders of scrubs and sides of rivers; common also in India and Burmah.

In India the wood is considered fairly strong, and is used for boat-building, well-curbs, gun-stocks, and canoes; the bark for rope-making and the fruit for eating. Medicinally the dried fruit is valued on account of its mucilaginous nature and demulcent properties; it is much used in coughs and chest affections, also in irritation of the urinary passages; in larger quantities it is given in bilious affections as a laxative.—*Dymock*, Veg. Mat. Med. of Western India.

B.P.V.—Wood of a light-colour, coarse-grained, easy to work, and strong.

EHRETIA, *Linn.*

287a—E. acuminata, *R. Br.*, Prod., 497; Flora Austr., iv., 387. One of the woods called Brown Cedar. A small tree with oval-oblong toothed leaves three to six inches long. Flowers in panicles, terminal, or in the upper axils. Fruit small, globular. In South Queensland, a creek-side tree; also found in New South Wales and Victoria.

B.P.V.—Wood light brown, grain coarse, firm, easy to work; closely resembles English Elm.

Order SOLANACEÆ.

SOLANUM, *Linn.*

289—S. VERBASCIFOLIUM, *Linn.*, Spec. Pl., 184; *Ait.; Dun.*, in DC. Prod., xiii., part i., 114; Flora Austr., iv., 449. A small tree, densely clothed by a woolly substance, the leaves ovate, six to eight inches long. Flowers white, in dense flat bunches at the ends of the branches, or lateral from the growing out of the shoot. Berries about half an inch in diameter, of a yellowish-green. Queensland scrubs, north and south; also in New South Wales, New Guinea, tropical Asia, and America.

B.P.V.—Wood of a yellow colour, easily worked, of a close grain and light.

DUBOISIA, *R. Br.*

290—D. MYOPOROIDES, *R. Br.*, Prod., 448; Flora Austr., iv., 474; Miers, Illustr., t., 87. New South Wales Corkwood. A small tree with a white corky bark; the leaves narrow-oblong, of a grey colour, two to four inches long; the flowers in large spreading panicles, very pale blue or white. Fruit small, globose, black and juicy when ripe. Borders of scrubs, north and south Queensland; also in New South Wales.

B.V.—Wood of a light-yellow colour, light and firm, easy to work, useful for cabinet-work; and Mr. Moore in his pamphlet on "The Woods of New South Wales," says it is excellent for carving and wood-engraving. This plant is the source of the mydriatic drug "duboisine," discovered by Dr. Bancroft, of Brisbane.

Order BIGNONIACEÆ.

DIPLANTHERA, *R. Br.*

292—D. TETRAPHYLLA, *R. Br.*, Prod., 449; Flora Austr., iv., 541. A large tree with thick, soft, somewhat corky bark. Leaves usually in fours round the stem, on very short thick stalks, often two feet long and one foot wide, rough; the flowers in a terminal panicle, yellow, in form like the Foxglove; capsule oblong. Rockingham Bay and northward in Queensland.

B.V.—Wood of a whitish colour, close-grained and firm. The sample shown is of a small tree.

Order ACANTHACEÆ.

GRAPTOPHYLLUM, *Nees.*

293—G. EARLII, *F. v. M.*, Fragm., vi., 87; Flora Austr., iv., 551. A small slender tree, the leaves oblong-acute, with sometimes a few teeth, one to two inches long. Flowers a rich reddish purple, the lips incurved, shorter than the tube; capsule about one inch long. Scrubs on the Fitzroy River, Rockhampton.

B.P.V.—Wood flesh-coloured, becoming brown towards the centre, very hard, tough, and close-grained.

Order MYOPORINEÆ.

MYOPORUM, *Banks et Sol.*

295—M. ACUMINATUM, *R. Br.*, Prod., 515; Flora Austr., v., 3. Native name, "Mee-mee." New South Wales Dogwood. A small tree having a rough corky bark, a dense head of deep-green foliage, and a pretty star-like flower; the leaves alternate on the stem and from two to three inches long, narrow and pointed. Flowers white or stained with purple; the small berries purple. Common in one or other of its forms throughout Australia.

B.P.V.—WOOD of a light colour, firm and easily worked.

EREMOPHILA, *R. Br.*

295A—E. STURTII, *R. Br.*, App. Sturt Exped., 22; Flora Austr., v., 21. Scentless Sandalwood. A small tree, the foliage somewhat hoary, viscid, and having a heavy scent. Leaves narrow-linear, one or more inches long, with a hook at the point. Flowers from the dried specimens appearing to be white stained with purple, hairy. Cunnamulla in Queensland; also at inland localities both in South Australia and New South Wales.

B.V.—WOOD of a grey colour, hard, close-grained, and nicely marked.

296—E. MITCHELLI, *Benth.*, in Mitch. Trop. Austr., 31; Flora Austr., v., 21. Native name at Rockhampton, "Balvora." Scented Sandalwood; one of the New South Wales Rosewoods. A pretty, round-headed, small tree with dense foliage. Leaves narrow, hooked at the point, one-nerved. One to two inches long. Flowers solitary in the axils, the corolla falling and the calyx-segments lengthening out, giving the appearance of a second dry veiny flower. Fruit ovoid. Found in abundance on the inland downs, Queensland and New South Wales.

B.P.V.—WOOD for a short distance in from the bark white, all the rest o a brown colour, hard and close-grained, very fragrant; an excellent wood for cabinet-work.

297—E. BIGNONIÆFLORA, *F. v. M.*, in Proc. Roy. Soc. Tasm., iii., 294; Flora Austr., v., 25. Native name at Rockhampton, "Pombel." A small tree, but the largest of the genus in Queensland; the young growth very viscid. Leaves linear, three to six inches long. Flowers one inch long, enlarging from the base, white and purple. Drupe half-inch or more long. Tropical Queensland, on the borders of scrubs; also in North Australia, New South Wales, and Victoria on the Murray.

B.P.V.—WOOD of a yellowish-brown, close in grain, prettily marked, and ragrant; useful for cabinet-work.

Order VERBENACEÆ.

LANTANA, *Linn.*

297A—L. CAMARA, *Linn.* A tall rambling shrub, attaining in some scrubs the height of 20 or 30 feet; on open forest land spreading much, but seldom over 10 feet high. Branches angular, bearing curved prickles on the angles. Bark on the stems loose and papery. Leaves rough, somewhat heart-shaped, two to four inches long. Flowers of a yellow, orange and reddish colour, in heads of an inch or more diameter. Fruit, juicy black berries. This plant, which is a native of tropical America, is taking possession of all the waste ground and scrubs in the Brisbane district, and is one of the greatest pests introduced. The fruit is often eaten by children, who call them "black currants," but as the berries have been thought to have made some children ill they are considered poisonous by many persons. Some fancy articles having been made from the wood in Brisbane lately, a sample is shown in this collection.

B.V.—Wood of a light-grey colour, close-grained and firm, not unlike the Queensland Beech.

PREMNA, *Linn.*

298—P. OBTUSIFOLIA, *R. Br.*, Prod., 512; Flora Austr., v., 58. A tall shrub, with broadly ovate leaves three to six inches long. Flowers in a terminal panicle, white or greenish. Fruit globose, very small. Tropical coast of Queensland and North Australia.

The form of the pith in the stem of this is most remarkable. The central hollow or pith-tube is ribbed on the inner surface with about 14 prominent and numerous line-like ribs; to these are attached at distances of about three lines thin filmy disks or septæ of a pale-pink colour and tough consistency, which may be removed from the stem readily without injury; those of the stem noticed when thus removed measured eight lines in diameter.

B.V.—Wood brown.

GMELINA, *Linn.*

298A—G. MACROPHYLLA, *Benth.*, Flora Austr., v., 65. A tall tree, the leaves ovate-oblong, eight or ten inches long. Flowers pale-blue, in terminal panicles. Drupe about three-quarter-inch in diameter. Tropical scrubs of Queensland and North Australia.

B.P.V.—Wood close-grained, the outer or sapwood prominently marked, of a pretty purple colour, the rest grey; a useful timber for flooring-boards and planking, the timber closely resembling that of No. 299—the Queensland Beech.

299—G. LEICHHARDTII, *F. v. M.*, Flora Austr., v., 66. Queensland Beech; native name, "Cullonen;" known as White Beech in New South Wales. A tall tree with grey bark, the leaves rough, oval, three to six inches long. Flowers white stained with purple, in terminal panicles. Fruit blue, globose or half-globose, one inch or more in diameter. Coast scrubs of southern Queensland and New South Wales.

B.P.V.—Wood light-grey, close-grained, extensively used for planking for ships' decks and flooring of verandahs; is not readily attacked by the white ant.

VITEX, *Linn.*

299A—V. TRIFOLIA, *Linn; Schau.*, in DC. Prod., xi., 683; Flora Austr., v., 66. A tall or dwarf shrub. Leaves very variable, simple or of three to five leaflets, hence in Egypt it is sometimes called "The Hand of Mary;" often white on both sides. Flowers pale-blue, in terminal panicles. Fruit globular, small, resembling pepper-corns. A common shrub of the Queensland and North Australian coast.

The leaves, root, and fruit are used by some medical men in India, and considered anodyne, diuretic, and emmenagogue.—*Dymock.*

B.V.—Wood a dark-grey colour, firm and close-grained.

300—V. LIGNUM-VITÆ, *A. Cunn.; Schau.*, in DC. Prod., xi., 692. Lignum-vitæ. A tall tree with a thin bark of a greyish colour, the outer often somewhat loose and fibrous. Leaves oval, two to three inches long (often lobed on young plants, and on shoots from an old butt). Flowers dingy; fruit rosy-red, size of a cherry, which the fruit much resembles. Scrubs of Queensland and New South Wales.

B.P.V.—Wood dark, close in the grain, hard and tough, suitable for cabinet-work.

301—V. ACUMINATA, *R. Br.*, Prod., 512; Flora Austr., v., 67. A large tree with a thin smooth bark, the young growth hoary, the leaves of three or sometimes five narrow leaflets. Flowers small; drupe globular. Tropical coast scrubs; also in a few extra-tropical scrubs north of Brisbane, islands of the Gulf of Carpentaria, and North Australia.

B.P.V.—Wood brown, with darker streaks, close-grained; suitable for cabinet-work.

CLERODENDRON, *Linn.*

301A—C. INERME, *R. Br.*, Prod., Flora Austr., v., 61. A tall rambling shrub, either glabrous or pubescent. The leaves on long stalks, ovate, pointed, two or three inches long. Peduncles axillary, bearing a few pedicellate flowers; calyx minutely toothed; corolla-tube about one inch long, the stamens protruding about one inch. Fruit about half an inch long, obovoid, but sometimes much larger and corky. Found along the coast from New South Wales to the Gulf and New Guinea.

B.V.—Wood light-coloured, firm, and close-grained.

302—C. TOMENTOSUM, *R. Br.*, Prod., 510; Flora Austr., v., 62. A small tree, the leaves and young growth more or less velvety. Leaves oval on long stalks, the bunches of bloom terminal; the flower-tubes one inch long, with the stamens protruding for about another half inch; flowers white. Fruit purple or black, resting in the enlarged calyx-cup. Most South Queensland scrubs and frequent on hill-sides; also in New South Wales.

B.V.—Wood of a yellow colour, close-grained, light, and easy to work.

302A—C. FLORIBUNDUM, *R. Br.*, Prod., Flora Austr., v., 63 Native name on the Cloncurry, "Thurkoo." A tall shrub or small tree, glabrous, or the young growth tomentose. Leaves on long stalks, ovate to lanceolate, two to four inches long or more. Flower-cymes loose; calyx about a quarter inch long, with acute lobes; corolla-tube about one inch long; the stamens exserted about one inch. Fruiting calyx expanded over half an inch diameter. Common on the tropical coast of Australia and New Guinea.

Two dried sticks of this plant are used for drills to make fire with.—*E. Palmer.*

B.V.—Wood close-grained and light-coloured.

AVICENNIA, *Linn.*

303—A. OFFICINALIS, *Linn.*; *Schau.*, in DC. Prod., xi., 700; Flora Austr., v., 69; Wight, Ic. t., 1481. White Mangrove; native name, "Tchoonchee." A small tree with a smooth bark and greyish-green foliage. Leaves ovate, two to four inches long, rather thick and often blistered, the under side silky. Flowers small; the fruit resembling a broad bean seed. Great quantities may be seen at the water's edge of tidal rivers, Queensland sea-coast; and also a common sea-coast tree of Asia, Africa, and America.

The fruit is baked or steamed in hollows made in the ground, in which they make fires, then taken out and soaked, and baked in the ashes, by the Gulf natives for food.—*E. Palmer.*

B.P.V.—Wood strong, tough, hard, and durable; useful for many purposes.

Order NYCTAGINEÆ.

PISONIA, *Linn.*

303A—P. ACULEATA, *Linn.*; *Chois.*, in DC. Prod., xiii., ii., 440; Flora Austr., v., 279; Wight, Ic., t., 1763, 1764. A large woody straggling climber, which often forms almost impenetrable masses on the borders of rivers and swamp scrubs; bark thin, light brown, often armed with recurved axillary prickles; leaves opposite, or here and there alternate, two to four inches long and about one and a half inch wide. Flowers diœcious, in small cymes or globular clusters, forming small panicles. Fruit oblong, about half an inch long, five-ribbed, glandular-muricate. Met with around most coast swamps in Queensland and the northern parts of New South Wales; also widely spread in tropical regions of both the new and the old world in similar situations.

B.V.—Wood light-coloured, of coarse grain, very tough.

304—P. BRUNONIANA, *Endl.*, Prod. Fl. Norf., 43; Flora Austr., v., 280. A large tree with obovate or oblong leaves, eight or more inches long, of a somewhat leathery consistence. Fruit with five tuberculate angles. Tropical coast scrubs and river sides; also in New South Wales, New Guinea, New Zealand, and Norfolk Island.

B.P.V.—Wood soft and light, of a light colour.

Order PHYTOLACCACEÆ.

CODONOCARPUS, *A Cunn.*

304A—C. AUSTRALIS, *A. Cunn.*, Herb.; *Moq.*, in DC. Prod., xiii., ii., 39; Flora Austr., v., 148; Hook., Bot. Misc., i., 244, t., 53. Bell-fruit. A small tree, the bark smooth, branches slender, leaves tapering into long narrow points, bright-green. Fruit pear-shaped, separating at maturity into thin wing-like seeds. Found on ranges, and also on the islands along the coast of southern Queensland; also in New South Wales.

B.V.—WOOD soft and spongy, and of a light colour.

Order PIPERACEÆ.

PIPER, *Linn.*

305—P. NOVÆ-HOLLANDIÆ, *Miq.*, in Medd. Akad. Netensk. Amsterd., ser. 2, ii.; Flora Austr., vi., 204. Native Pepper-vine. A climber with stems often a foot in diameter, the younger stems adhering to the stems of trees like Ivy. Leaves deep-green, heart-shaped, on very short stalks, three or four inches long and five to seven nerved. Berries red, ovoid. A common scrub-climber in Queensland and New South Wales.

The ethereal spirituous extract of the wood yields crystals, the nature of which have not been ascertained.

B.V.—WOOD coarse-grained, and pungently scented when newly cut.

Order MYRISTICEÆ.

MYRISTICA, *Linn.*

306—M. INSIPIDA, *R. Br.*, Prod., 400; Flora Austr., v., 281. Native Nutmeg. A moderate-sized tree, the young shoots often rusty. Leaves oval, the under side of a light colour, four to six inches long, the veins prominent. Fruit oval, about one inch long. Tropical Queensland scrubs; also in North Australia.

B.V.—WOOD of a pinkish-grey colour, tough and easily worked.

Order MONIMIACEÆ.

MOLLINEDIA, *Ruiz et Pavon.*

306A—M. HUEGELIANA, *Tul.*, in Ann. Sc., Nat., ser. 4, iii., 45, and in Archiv. Mus., Par. viii., 399; Flora Austr., v., 286; *Wilkiea Huegeliana*, *A. DC.*, Prod., xvi., ii., 669. A small tree, the young growth hoary. Leaves oblong-lanceolate, more or less bordered by teeth, three to six inches long, of a dry harsh nature, strongly veined. Flowers small, in short panicles in the leaf axils; fruit ovoid, about half an inch long, black. Common in the scrubs of southern Queensland, and in the northern parts of New South Wales; also in New Guinea.—*F. v. M. Papuan Plants.*

B.—WOOD light-coloured, close-grained, hard and tough.

307—M. LOXOCARYA, *Benth.*, Flora Austr., v., 286. A small tree, the branches somewhat compressed under the leaves. Leaves elliptical-oblong, four or five inches long, of a leathery consistence, on rather long stalks; the fruiting panicle only about two inches long, the drupes stalkless, ovoid. Scrubs of tropical Queensland.

B.V.—Wood yellowish, close in grain, and prettily marked.

KIBARA, *Endl.*

307A—K. MACROPHYLLA, *Benth.*, Flora Austr., v., 288. A small tree, the leaves on short stalks, oblong-lanceolate, very rigid and glossy, three to eight inches long, usually bordered by pungent teeth. Flowers small, axillary. Fruit ovoid, black and glossy, about three-quarter inch long. In scrubs, Queensland throughout.

B.—Wood light-coloured, close-grained and nicely marked.

308—K. LONGIPES, *Benth.*, in Flora Austr., v., 289 Tree of medium size, with oval, glossy, more or less toothed leaves, four to eight inches long. Drupes ovoid, half-inch long. Tropical Queensland.

B.V.—Wood straw-coloured, close in grain, hard, and nicely marked.

DAPHNANDRA, *Benth.*

308A—D. AROMATICA, *Bail.*, in 1st Suppl. to Syn. Ql. Fl. Tree of moderate size, the bark like Sassafras, and with rather stiff fragrant leaves, three or four inches long. The fruiting perianth-tube black, about one inch long, in very short panicles. Carpels densely hairy, with light-brown glossy hairs. Johnstone River scrubs.

B.P.V.—Wood of a light colour, not unlike pine wood, for which it would form a substitute.

309—D. MICRANTHA, *Benth.*, Flora Austr., v., 285. Called in New South Wales Light Yellow-wood and Satinwood. A tall handsome tree with smooth bark, the young growth often much flattened at the joints. Leaves opposite, petiolate, oval or oblong, the margins bordered by blunt teeth two to four inches long and deep-green. Flower panicle about as long as the leaves. Fruiting perianth tube about one inch long; carpels hairy, with glossy brown hairs. Scrub tree of southern Queensland and New South Wales.

B.P.V.—Wood of a glossy yellow colour, close-grained and firm, stands well in seasoning; useful for cabinet work and carving.

309A—D. REPANDULA, *F. v. M.*, Fragm., x., 105. A tree of moderate size, with rather thin leaves, the margins wavy, four to six inches long; the flowers fringed, in straggling bunches. Fruit about one inch long, the seeds hairy. Scrubs of tropical Queensland.

Dr. T. L. Bancroft has found in the bark of all the Daphnandras several alkaloids, which are respiratory and cardiac poisons, which kill by paralysing the respiration.

B.P.V.—Wood of a light colour, nicely figured, grain close; probably it might serve for engraving. It closely resembles English Holly.

Order LAURINEÆ.

CRYPTOCARYA, *R. Br.*

310—C. Murrayii, *F. v. M.*, Fragm., v., 170; Flora Austr., v. 295. A large tree, the young shoots hairy, leaves oval, six to ten inches long, of a light colour on the under side, except the veins which are rusty. Fruit ovoid or globular, shining. Scrubs of tropical Queensland.

B.P.V.—Wood of a dark colour, hard, and close-grained.

311—C. obovata, *R. Br.*, Prod., 402; Flora Austr., v., 296. Called in New South Wales She-Beech and Sycamore. A tall tree with a thin greyish scented bark, the young shoots and leaves covered with rusty hairs. Leaves oblong, two to four inches long; fruit globular, about half an inch diameter. Queensland scrubs, north and south; also in New South Wales.

B.P.V.—Wood of a light colour, very tough; a useful wood, if not exposed to the weather.

311a—C. obovata, *R. Br.*, var. A broad-leaved form from Mackay.

B.P.V.—Wood of a light colour, close-grained and tough.

312—C. glaucescens, *R. Br.*, Prod , 402; Flora Austr., v., 297. A tall tree, usually without hairs, but sometimes the leaf-stalks slightly hairy. Leaves oval, green on both sides, or slightly white beneath in some forms. Fruit depressed-globular, half an inch or more in diameter. One or other form of this tree met with in most Queensland scrubs; also in North Australia and New South Wales.

B.P.V.—Wood of a light colour, easily worked, and likely to prove useful for many purposes.

313—C. triplinervis, *R. Br.*, in Prod., 402; Flora Austr., v., 297. A tall tree with dark-green foliage, hairy on the under side, the leaves three or four inches long, the three nerves starting from above the base. Panicles of flowers hoary, dense Fruit oval, nearly half an inch long. Common in Queensland scrubs; also in New South Wales.

B.P.V.—Wood of a grey colour, close in the grain, tough.

313a—C. cinnamomifolia, *Benth.*, in Flora Austr., v., 298. Variety with small leaves. A moderate-sized tree with a deep-green foliage, the leaves about two inches long, ovate and three-nerved. Fruit black, globular. Mount Mistake Range, South Queensland.

B.P.V.—Wood of fine grain, easy to work, of a light colour.

314—C. australis, *Benth.*, Flora Austr., v., 229. Queensland Laurel. Usually a small tree or large shrub, with rather narrow, bright, glossy leaves, paler on the under side, one of the lateral veins diverging from the midrib on either side and running parallel with it to the point of the leaf. Flowers greenish, rather small. Fruit about one inch in diameter, rather red or pale yellow. Frequent in Queensland scrubs; also in the northern parts of New South Wales. The bark of this tree, and also *C. triplinervis*, contains an intensely bitter alkaloid, which has been thought by Dr. Thos. Bancroft to be curarine.

B.P.V.—Wood light-coloured, close-grained, easily worked; suitable for lining-boards.

BEILSCHMIEDIA, *Nees.*

315—B. obtusifolia, *Benth. et Hook.*, in Gen. Pl , iii., 1521. Sassafras-tree. A tall tree with light-coloured fragrant bark and foliage. Leaves oblong, rather narrow, four or more inches long. Flowers in a terminal panicle. Scrubs, north and south, in Queensland; also in New South Wales.

This contains a tannin similar or identical with cinchona tannin; the amount, seven and a-half per cent. One ton of the dry bark yields 770 oz. of oil.—*K. T. Staiger.*

B.P.V.—Wood pale-coloured, close in grain, firm, easy to work; suitable for joiners' work.

ENDIANDRA, *R. Br.*

316—E. glauca, *R. Br.*, Prod., 402; Flora Austr., v., 300. A small tree with a thin, hard, smooth bark, the young shoots and inflorescence clothed with a rusty coating of hairs. Leaves oblong, pointed, three to five inches long, white on the under side. Fruit black, oval, half-inch long. Scrubs of tropical Queensland.

B.V.—Wood light-coloured, close-grained, hard and tough.

317 —E. Sieberi, *Nees.*, Sys. Laurin., 194; Flora Austr., v., 301. Native name at Moreton Bay, "Till." A tree of moderate size, the leaves oblong, three or four inches long, green on both sides, showing the netted veins very plainly Fruit oval, about one inch long. South Queensland scrubs; also in New South Wales.

B.P.V.—Wood grey or light-brown, close in the grain; suitable for tool-handles.

317A—E. virens, *F. v. M.*, Fragm., ii., 90. A tree of medium size. Leaves oblong, three or four inches long, or at times more. Fruit black, shiny, and globular, half to one inch in diameter. Often met with on the margins of creeks in South Queensland and New South Wales.

B.P.V.—Wood of a grey colour, close-grained and firm; useful for many purposes.

CINNAMOMUM, *Burm.*

318.—C. Tamala, *Th. Nees.*, Sys. Laurin., 56; Flora Austr., v., 303. Native Cinnamon A large tree with a smooth fragrant bark. Leaves ovate, usually opposite, three to six inches long, the three longitudinal nerves starting from above the base. Scrubs of tropical Queensland; also in India and Burmah.

H

In India the bark is said to be collected and sold under the name of "Taj," and the leaves under the name of "Tezpat, tajpat."

B.P.V.—Wood of a grey colour, close-grained, firm, and strongly scented.

PERSEA, *Gærtn.*

319.—P. BAILEYANA, *F. v. M.* Candle-wood of Frazer's Island. A scrub tree of about 60 feet in height, glabrous except the inflorescence. Leaves opposite or here and there alternate, ovate or ovate-lanceolate, two or three inches long, petiole about half inch long, green on both sides, prominently triplinerved and finely reticulate, most conspicuous on the under side. Inflorescence terminal or in the upper axils forming short trichotomous panicles, or more or less racemose, bearing distant, few flowered clusters. Perianths silky-white on short pedicels, the segments about two lines long. The flowers seen not perfect enough to fully describe, and no fruit seen.

B P.V.—Wood of a dark-grey colour, close-grained, firm, and slightly fragrant.

LITSEA, *Lam.* (including Tetranthera).

320.—L. DEALBATA, *Nees.*, Sys. Laurin., 630; var. *rufa*, Benth., Flora Austr., v., 308. A moderate-sized tree, the young parts clothed with reddish hairs. Leaves oval, three to six inches long, white on the under side; the flowers in close bunches along the branchlets. Fruit globose, purple, about quarter inch in diameter. Frequently met with in the south Queensland scrubs; also in New South Wales.

B.P.V.—Wood of a yellowish colour, with numerous short brown longitudinal streaks; tough and close-grained.

321—L. (TETRANTHERA) LAURIFOLIA, *Jacq.*, Flora Austr., v., 305. A small tree with hoary branchlets and inflorescence. Leaves ovate, four to eight inches long, light coloured on the under side, the primary veins prominent. Flowers clustered or racemose, the peduncles about half-inch long. Fruit globular. Tropical Queensland, North Australia, and India, where the wood is prized and the bark used medicinally. Internally on account of its demulcent properties in diarrhœa and dysentery, and externally as an emollient application to bruises, &c.—*Dymock.*

B.P.V.—Wood of a yellowish-colour, with a small quantity of dark-brown heart wood, close-grained.

321A—L. FERRUGINEA, *Benth.*, in B. and H. Gen. Pl., iii., 161. A tree of moderate size, clothed with rusty short hairs. Leaves three to six inches long, rusty on the under side where the veins are raised. Fruit oval. Scrubs of tropical Queensland.

B.V.—Wood pale-yellow, light, close-grained, and easily marked.

321B—L. FERRUGINEA VAR. LANCEOLATA, *Meissn.*, *Benth.*, Flora Austr., v., 306. A small slender erect tree, the branches rusty, velvety tomentose Leaves on very short stalks, oblong-lanceolate, six to nine inches long, usually rounded at the base, the veins raised and prominent underneath. South Queensland scrubs.

B.—Wood of a grey colour, close-grained.

322 –L. RETICULATA, *Benth.*, in B. and H. Gen. Pl., iii., 161. "Cudgerie" of Bunya Mountains. A large tree with dark-green foliage; the leaves prominently netted-veined on both sides, oblong, three or four inches long, green on both sides. Fruit rather large, plum-like, of a purple-colour. Bunya Mountains in south Queensland; also in the tropical scrubs.

B.P.V.—Wood of a grey colour, close grain, light and easy to work.

HERNANDIA, *Linn.*

324—H. BIVALVIS, *Benth.*, Flora Austr., v., 314. "Cudgerie" or Grease-nut. A tall tree with a smooth bark. Leaves glossy-green, ovate to nearly heart-shaped, peltate on young plants when the plants have thick fleshy roots. Flowers in terminal panicles, fragrant, often in threes, the central flower being female. Fruit a black-ribbed nut, surrounded by two red fleshy leaves, giving the appearance of a large bell pepper. Scrubs of south Queensland.

The shells of the fruit of this tree contain a dye, soluble in soda but not in ether, alcohol, or water. The kernel contains 64·8 per cent. of oil, which is similar to common laurel oil, is of the same consistency, and also the same stearine and narcotic smell.—*K. T. Staiger.*

B.P.V.—Wood of a dark-grey colour, grain close, light and soft; suitable for carriage-brakes, lining-boards, and similar uses.

Order PROTEACEÆ.

PERSOONIA, *Sm.*

325—P. FALCATA, *R. Br.*, in Trans. Linn. Soc., x., 162, and Prod., 373; Flora Austr., v., 385. Native names on the Mitchell, "Nanchee" and "Booral." A small tree, the young shoots silky. Leaves curved, narrow, three to eight inches long. Flowers axillary, but forming leafy racemes by the abortion of the leaves. Tropical Queensland and North Australia.

B P.V.—Wood light with a reddish centre, hard and close-grained.

326—P. MEDIA, *R. Br.*, Prot. Nov., 16; Flora Austr., v., 391. Geebong; native name, "Koombarra." A small tree with silky foliage; the leaves almost elliptical, the point acute, two to four inches long. Flowers axillary, yellow. Fruit oval, half to nearly one inch long. In open coast country, South Queensland, and New South Wales.

B.P.V.—Wood of a light colour, close in grain and firm; might prove useful for tool-handles. It somewhat resembles the English Beech, and may prove as serviceable to musical instrument makers.

MACADAMIA, *F. v. M.*

328 —M. TERNIFOLIA, *F. v. M.*, in Trans. Phil. Inst. Vict., ii., 72; Flora Austr., v., 406. Queensland Nut. A tall tree, the foliage

dense and dark-green. Leaves in whorls of three or four, usually about four to ten inches long, and bordered by sharp teeth. Flowers white, in long racemes. Fruit globose, often more than one inch in diameter, containing a smooth globose nut, or sometimes two half-round nuts. Scrubs of South Queensland and New South Wales.

B.P.V.—Wood of a red colour, close-grained, firm, and prettily marked; will doubtless become a favourite wood with the cabinet-makers.

XYLOMELUM, *Sm.*

339—X. PYRIFORME, *Knight*, Prot., 105; Flora Austr., v., 408. Wooden Pear. A small tree, the young shoots rusty-hairy. Leaves prominently veined, narrow-oval, four to six inches long on some of the branches, armed with prickly teeth. Flowers in woolly spikes. Fruit pear-shaped, opening in two woody valves. Seeds flat with a long wing. Open country, South Queensland and New South Wales.

B.P.V.—Wood dark-red, coarse-grained, prettily figured; suitable for cabinet-work.

330—X. SALICINUM, *A. Cunn.*, in R. Br. Prot. Nov., 31; Flora Austr., v., 408. Wooden Pear. A small tree, the foliage silky; the leaves elliptical, marked by a few undulate prickly teeth, three to five inches long, and narrower than the last. Flower-spikes three to five inches long. Fruit as in the last species, only not so velvety, and usually narrower. Various parts of Queensland, but frequent on the coast.

B.P.V.—Wood of a dark-red colour, close in grain, tough, and durable.

HELICIA, *Lour.*

331—H. PRÆALTA, *F. v. M.*, Fragm., iii., 37; Flora Austr. Long-leaved Nut Tree of New South Wales. A small or in some localities lofty tree, glabrous or the young shoots in inflorescence minutely rusty tomentose, and a rusty mark on the stem just about the leaf axil. Leaves lanceolate, three to twelve inches long and about one to two wide, penniveined and reticulate. Racemes axillary or lateral, three to six inches long; flowers half to three quarters of an inch long. Fruit globular, one to two inches diameter. Found in many Queensland scrubs, usually in the southern parts of the colony, and northern parts of New South Wales, where it is said to be in use for staves, shingles, bullock-yokes, and indoor work.

B.P.V.—Wood of a red colour, nicely marked, close in the grain, tough, strong, and durable; useful for cabinet-work, handles of tools, and other purposes. When newly cut it has a very disagreeable odour.

331A—H. FERRUGINEA, *F. v. M.*, Fragm., iii., 37; Flora Austr., v., 405. A large tree with thick bark, the branchlets clothed with close rusty hairs, which are also found on the principal veins of the leaves. Leaves oblong or nearly lanceolate on the large trees, three or four inches long, and with a few distant teeth on the margins, the leaves larger and more serrated on younger trees; prominently reticulate. Flowers in dense terminal or axillary racemes, the perianths clothed with rusty hairs. Fruit ovate-globular. Found in the northern scrubs of New South Wales, and throughout Queensland; usually in mountain scrubs.

B.P.—Wood of a dark-pink colour, prettily figured, close-grained, and useful for both the cabinet-maker and boat-builder.

331B—H. FERRUGINEA, VAR. A small tree, the branches more or less rusty as well as the inflorescence. Leaves near the 'flowers lanceolate, about eight inches long and two wide; veins prominent. Flower-racemes four or five inches long; flowers white. Johnstone River.

B.V.—Wood of a pinkish colour, nicely marked, close-grained; will be useful to coopers as well as cabinet-makers.

ORITES, *R. Br.*

332—O. EXCELSA, *R. Br.*, Prot. Nov., 32; Flora Austr., v., 411. Sometimes called Silky Oak, and in New South Wales Red Ash. A tall tree, leaves on the flowering branches narrow, entire or slightly toothed, four to six inches long, netted-veined, grey on the under side. Flower-spikes axillary; fruit about one inch long, containing flat-winged seeds. Ranges of South Queensland (Mount Mistake Range); also in New South Wales.

By mistake the wood of *Rhodamnia trinervia* was worked and exhibited under this number at the Colonial and Indian Exhibition.

B.V.—Wood dark towards the centre of the tree, the outer part yellowish and often prettily marked, close-grained, easy to work; a useful wood for the joiner and cabinet-maker.

GREVILLEA, *R. Br.*

332A—G. PINNATIFIDA, *Bail.* (*Kermadecia pinnatifida*, Bail., Queensland Woods, No. 332A, Colonial and Indian Exhibition.) A very handsome erect tree of medium size, the smaller branches angular and velvety, with rusty-brown hairs. Leaves alternate, entire or pinnatifid, those of the barren shoots and young plants often exceeding eighteen inches in length, divided nearly to the midrib into from two to four pairs of opposite, long, norrow-linear, attenuated, somewhat approximate lobes about one inch broad, with or without a terminal odd lobe, the base decurrent on the petiole; the upper surface of a greyish-green, the under surface bright rusty-brown, prominently reticulate, the lateral oblique primary veins joining in an intramarginal one some distance from the edge of the leaf. The leaves near the inflorescence simple and lanceolate, about six inches long. Inflorescence silky-white in a terminal panicle of raceme-like branches three to five inches long, bearing pedicellate flowers, scattered solitary or in clusters of two or more. Bracts linear, two or three lines long, very deciduous. Perianth silky, glabrous inside,

about three or four lines long, the segments very narrow, the limb
globose; ovary stipitate, glabrous; style filiform; stigmatic disk
lateral and somewhat dilated; hypogynous gland broad.   Fruit an
oblong coriaceous follicle, pendulous on the rhachis, about seven lines
long and four lines broad, slightly compressed, bearing the straight
persistent style.   Seeds two, bordered all round by a membranous
wing.   Johnstone River, Queensland.

This fine species is allied to *G. Hilliana*, F. v. M., from which, however, it
differs in having a paniculate inflorescence, the flowers of which are not so
crowded; the fruit is also smaller than that species and not so hard and woody.
Before the fruit was seen it was thought probable that the tree was a new
Kermadecia, under which genus it is provisionally noticed in the Catalogue of
Woods sent to the Colonial and Indian Exhibition.

B.P.V.—WOOD of a pinkish colour, close in grain, and very prettily
marked; useful to coopers and cabinet-makers.

335A—G. POLYSTACHYA, *R. Br.*, in Trans. Linn. Soc., x., 177;
Prod., 380; Flora Austr ,·v., 459. A small tree, the branchlets silky,
the leaves linear, undivided or irregularly into linear segments, six
inches long, the leaf often being one foot long, all silky-white.
Flowers in racemes, forming a terminal panicle, pale-yellow.   Tropical
Queensland and North Australia.

B.P.V.—WOOD red, hard, close-grained, and durable, prettily marked;
suitable for cabinet-work.

336—G. ROBUSTA, *A. Cunn.*, in R. Br. Prot. Nov., 24; Flora Austr.,
v., 459; Bot. Mag. t. 3184.   Silky Oak; native name, "Tuggan-
tuggan." A tall slender tree with a rugged bark, the leaves divided
so as to resemble a fern-frond, the entire leaf from six to twelve
inches long, and nearly as broad.   Flowers orange-coloured in
October, but often again during summer. A good flower for bees.
South Queensland and New South Wales.

B.P.V.—WOOD of a light-pinkish colour, grain close, prettily marked;
used for staves and in cabinet-work.

337—G. STRIATA, *R. Br.*, in Trans. Linn. Soc., x., 177; Prod.
380; Flora Austr., v., 462.   Beefwood.   A slender-branched small
tree, with a dark rugged bark and silky-white foliage.   The leaves
strap-like, six to eighteen inches long and under half-inch wide, with
from two to twelve raised parallel nerves.   Flowers in short spikes.
A tree frequently met with in open country, both in the interior and
on the coast of tropical Queensland; not so common in the more
southern parts of the country.   Also an interior tree in New South
Wales and South Australia.

B.P.V.—WOOD dark-brown, prettily marked, strong, close-grained; useful
for staves and cabinet-work.

338—G. HILLIANA, *F. v. M.*, in Trans. Phil. Inst., Vict., ii., 72;
Flora Austr., v., 463.   Yiel-yiel; Silky oak of New South Wales. A
beautiful tree of about 50 to 60 feet in height, with a rugged bark;
leaves large, entire or deeply lobed, glabrous above, penniveined and

netted-veined, the primary veins confluent in an intramarginal nerve, more or less silvery on the under side. Flowers small, white, in dense cylindrical racemes. Fruit hard, about one inch long Found in the Logan and Albert River scrubs; also in the northern scrubs of New South Wales.

B.V.—Wood dark-brown, with a small sapwood of a lighter colour, close-grained, hard, and prettily marked.

339—G. GIBBOSA, *R. Br.*, in Trans. Linn. Soc., x., 177; Prod., 380; Flora Austr., v., 463. A small tree, the foliage clothed with white, silky, short hairs. Leaves narrow, tapering towards both ends, four or five inches long. Flowers small in a dense spike-like raceme, in November and December. Fruit nearly globular, woody, one to one and a-half inch in diameter, containing one or two very thin winged seeds.

B.P.V.—Wood dark-brown, prettily marked, close-grained, and hard; of a greasy nature, which prevents it showing well when polished.

HAKEA, *Schrad.*

341A—H. PEDUNCULATA, *F. v. M.*, in Melb. Chem., July, 1883. A small tree with dark-coloured rugged bark, and oblong obtuse leaves of two or three inches in length. Endeavour River, Queensland.

B.V.—Wood dark brown, close in the grain, nicely marked, and hard.

CARNARVONIA, *F. v. M.*

342—C. ARALIÆFOLIA, *F. v. M.*, Fragm., vi, 81, t. 55, 56; Flora Austr., v., 410. A moderate-sized tree, with Umbrella-tree-like leaves; leaflets three to five, on the end of a rather long stalk, some of the leaflets again divided; the capsules incurved, pointed, one and a-half inch long, thin; seeds winged. Tropical Queensland scrubs.

B.P.V.—Wood of a red colour, firm, and fine-grained; useful for coopers' and cabinet-makers' work.

DARLINGIA, *F. v. M.*

344—D. SPECTATISSIMA, *F. v. M.*, Fragm., v., 152; Flora Austr., v., 533. A moderate-sized tree. Leaves oblong, entire or lobed, the whole leaf sometimes 18 inches long. Racemes of flowers numerous in the upper axils of the leaves. Capsule one and a-half to two inches long; seeds oblong. Tropical Queensland.

B.P.V.—Wood of a light-brown colour, nicely marked, light and firm; a useful wood for both cooper and cabinet-maker. Does not shrink nor warp much in drying.

CARDWELLIA, *F. v. M.*

345—C. SUBLIMIS, *F.v.M.*, Fragm., v., 24; Flora Austr., v., 538. Gold Spangle-wood. A large tree, the young growth rusty hoary. Leaves of four to ten oblong leaflets, three to eight inches long. Inflorescence a terminal panicle of several racemes, the flowers hoary.

Fruit three or more inches long, one and a half inch broad; seed about three inches long, three quarters of an inch broad. Scrubs of tropical Queensland.

B.P.V.—Wood of a light colour, prettily marked, suitable for cabinet work, wine-casks, and coopers' work; stands well in drying.

STENOCARPUS, *R. Br.*

346—S. sinuatus, *Endl.*, Gen. Pl. Suppl., iv., 88; Flora Austr., v., 539; Bot. Mag., t., 4263, as *S. Cunninghamii*, Hook, not R. Brown. Tulip-flower. A tall handsome tree, with glossy foliage; the leaves on young plants often over a foot long and of several more or less spreading lobes, but usually undivided, and not over six inches long on the adult trees. Flowers in large bunches, scarlet, about April. Fruit spindle-shaped; towards the lower part full of closely packed winged seeds. Scrubs of South Queensland and New South Wales.

B.P.V.—Wood of a light colour, close in grain, tough and firm; suitable for cabinet work, or any work in which English Beech is employed, which this resembles.

347—S. salignus, *R. Br.*, Trans. Linn. Soc., x., 202; Prod., 391; Flora Austr., v., 539; Bot. Reg. t., 441. One of the woods called Silky Oak; called both Beefwood and Silky Oak in New South Wales. A graceful tree of erect growth, the leaves in some forms lobed, but mostly narrow, four or more inches long, one or more inches broad; bunches of flowers in the upper axils. Fruit narrow and several inches long, closely packed with winged seeds. South Queensland ranges or coast; also in New South Wales.

B.P.V.—Wood of a red colour, hard, close-grained, and nicely marked; useful for the finer kinds of coopers' work and cabinet work.

BANKSIA, *Linn. f.*

348—B. integrifolia, *Linn. f.*, Suppl. 127; Flora Austr., v., 554; Bot. Mag., t., 2770. Honeysuckle; native name, "Pomera." Flowering as a shrub, but attaining a good size in some localities; the bark rough and corky. Leaves very variable in shape, some very long, narrow and quite entire, others sharply toothed, but generally white on the under side. Flowers greenish white, or with a yellowish tinge. Cone three to six inches long, and one to two inches in diameter. Common in most parts of Queensland, New South Wales, and Victoria.

B.P.V.—Wood pinkish, close in the grain, and nicely marked; used for shoemakers' lasts, cabinet work, and in boat building.

349—B. dentata, *Linn. f.*, Suppl., 127; Flora Austr., v., 555. A small tree, the bark rough. Leaves white on the under side, four to eight inches long, the edges sharply toothed, broad at the top, and from thence tapering towards the base. The flower spike and fruit longer, but closely resembling those of *B. integrifolia*. Coast of tropical Queensland and New Guinea.

B.V.—Wood of a dark-red colour, hard, close-grained, and prettily marked.

351—B. ÆMULA, *R. Br.*, in Trans. Linn. Soc., x., 210; Prod., 395; Flora Austr., v., 557; Bot. Mag., t., 2671. Native name on Fraser's Island, "Wallum." A small tree; but the stem of this, *B. integrifolia* and *B. dentata* often attain a diameter of one or two feet. Flower-spikes oblong, the flowers with a yellowish-green tinge; cones very large. Islands of Moreton Bay; also in New South Wales, and Gippsland in Victoria.

B.P.V. — Wood deep-red, coarse-grained, prettily marked, shrinks unequally in drying; an excellent wood for the cabinet-maker.

Order THYMELÆACEÆ.

WIKSTRŒMIA, *Endl.*

351A—W. INDICA, *C. A. Meyer*, in Bull. Acad. Sc. Petersh., i. (1843), 357; Flora Austr., vi., 37; Pl. Rep. Pois. to Stock in Qd.,p. 75. A tall shrub, with slender often silky branches, the bark very tough. Leaves ovate, one or two inches long. Flowers few together, yellowish-green, little tubes with short holes at the top; fruit an oval reddish berry. Common on the borders of scrubs in Queensland; also in North Australia and New South Wales; extending to the Indian Archipelago and China.

B.V.—Wood of a yellowish colour, soft and close-grained.

Order ELÆAGNACEÆ.

ELÆAGNUS, *Linn.*

352—E. LATIFOLIA, *Linn*, Flora Austr., vi., 39; Wight, Ic., t., 1856. A large rambling shrub. Leaves ovate-lanceolate, two to four inches long, clothed with silvery scurfy scales. Flowers several together in the leaf axils, or in spikes of a pale colour. Fruit about half-inch long. Found in tropical Queensland, and common in India where it is said the fruit is eaten.

B.—Wood of a yellow colour.

Order SANTALACEÆ.

SANTALUM, *Linn.*

353—S. LANCEOLATUM, *R. Br.*, Prod., 356; Flora Austr., vi., 214. Name on Cloncurry, "Tharra-gibberah." A small slender tree, the branches often drooping. Leaves oblong, two or three inches long. Flowers yellowish. Fruit globular with a circular scar below the summit, of a sweetish taste Met with in all parts of Queensland; also in New South Wales, North, South, and West Australia.

B.P.V.—Wood of a bright-yellow colour, close in grain, firm; useful for cabinet-work.

EXOCARPUS, *Labill.*

355—E. LATIFOLIA, *R. Br.*, Prod., 356; Flora Austr., vi., 228. Scrub Sandalwood or Broad-leaved Cherry. A tall tree with an erect trunk, the bark brown and slightly fibrous. Leaves ovate, stiff, one or two inches long, often very obtuse, with several nerves diverging from the base. Fruit ovoid, on a red fruity stalk. Coast and river scrubs of Queensland, North Australia, New South Wales, New Guinea, the Eastern Archipelago, and Philippine Islands.

B.P.V.—Wood fragrant, dark-coloured, coarse in grain, and hard; useful in cabinet-work.

356—E. CUPRESSIFORMIS, *Labill.*, Voy., i., 155, t. 14 ; Flora Austr., vi., 229. Cypress Cherry ; native name, "Tchimmi-dillen." A small tree resembling a Cypress or *Arbor-vitæ*, the branches drooping. Flowers minute. Fruit globular, on a short pedicle, which after fecundation enlarges, becomes red and succulent, and is eaten under the name of cherry in the southern colonies The tree is met with in all parts of Australia, except perhaps in the north.

B.P.V.—Wood of a pinkish-grey colour, soft, close-grained and light.

Order EUPHORBIACEÆ.

RICINOCARPUS, *Desf.*

357—R. PINIFOLIUS, *Desf.*, in Mem. Mus Par., iii., 459, t. 22 ; Flora Austr., vi., 70. Flowering as a small shrub, but attaining in some localities the height of 30 feet. Leaves crowded, linear, giving the plant a pine-like appearance. Flowers showy, terminal, white. Fruit like small castor oil fruits. Islands of Moreton Bay ; also in New South Wales, Victoria, and Tasmania.

B.P.V.—Wood light-coloured, soft, close in the grain, and works easily.

BRIDELIA, *Willd.*

358—B. EXALTATA, *F. v. M.*, Fragm., iii., 32; Flora Austr., vi., 119. A tree of moderate size, with a somewhat scaly bark, the leaves long-ovate, often obtuse, two to five inches long, often grey on the under side. Fruit globose, shiny-brown, and somewhat succulent. Southern Queensland and New South Wales.

B.P.V.—Wood of a dark-drab colour, hard and close in the grain ; somewhat resembling Walnut, and as suitable for cabinet-work.

358A—B. FAGINEA, *F. v. M.*, in Flora Austr., vi., 120. A small tree, the branches and under side of the leaves sometimes hoary. Leaves ovate, one to two inches long. Fruit globular, small. Queensland, north and south.

B.P.V.—Wood greyish-brown, mottled and becoming darker towards the centre ; an easily-worked wood ; suitable for cabinet-makers.

CLEISTANTHUS, *J. D. Hook.*

359—C. CUNNINGHAMII, *Muell. Arg.*, in DC. Prod., xv., ii., 506 ; Flora Austr., 122. A small tree with very dense head of rather rough foliage. Leaves oval-oblong, one to two inches long, pale on the under side, rather rough. Flowers minute. Fruit depressed-globular, three-lobed, hairy at an early stage. Common on the borders of scrubs throughout Queensland; also in New South Wales.

B.V.—Wood hard, close-grained, and light colour.

PHYLLANTHUS, *Linn.*

361—P. Ferdinandi, *Muell. Arg.*, in Flora, 1865, 379, and in DC. Prod., xvii., 300; Flora Austr., vi., 96. Native name, "Towwar." A moderate-sized tree, with lively green foliage, the branchlets often reddish. Leaves oval-oblong, usually three or four inches long, but at times much longer. Flowers in the axils, or some distance up the stem towards the next leaf, very irregular even on the same tree in this respect. Fruit depressed-globular, a quarter to half an inch in diameter. Along creek-sides throughout Queensland; also in North Australia and New South Wales.

B.P.V.—Wood easy to work, close in the grain, and of a grey colour; warps a good deal in drying.

361A—P. lobocarpus, *Benth.*, Flora Austr., vi., 97. Opher-wood of Fraser's Island. A small tree with a dark rugged bark, splitting lines, the young branches pubescent. Leaves oblong-lanceolate, two or three inches long, green above pale on the under side Stipules minute. Flowers diœcious, the males two or three together on recurved pedicles, the females solitary on longer pedicles. Capsules about four lines diameter, much depressed, more or less deeply divided into six or fewer lobes. Seeds when ripe orange-red. Scrubs of tropical Queensland.

B.P.V.—Wood of a pinkish colour, close-grained, tough and elastic; useful for tool-handles.

BREYNIA, *Forst.*

362—B. oblongifolia, *Muell. Arg.*, in DC. Prod., xv., ii., 440; Flora Austr., vi., 114. A small graceful tree, with a grey-green foliage, the leaves oblong and about one inch long. Fruit globular, red. A common creek-side small tree in Queensland, also in New South Wales.

B.V.—Wood straw-coloured, close-grained, and firm.

PETALOSTIGMA, *F. v. M.*

363.—P. quadriloculare, *F. v. M.*, in Hook. Kew. Journ., ix., 17; Flora Austr., vi., 92. Emu Apple, Crab-tree, or Bitter-bark; native name, "Muntenpin." In New South Wales called both Native Quince and Crab-tree. A small round-headed tree, the shoots and under side of the leaves more or less silky. Leaves oblong or almost round, the upper side often glossy, half to one inch long. Fruit orange colour, about half inch or more in diameter, splitting to pieces when ripe, the seeds like small castor-oil beans A very common tree in open country in Queensland; also in North Australia and New South Wales.

B.P.V. — Wood dark-brown, hard and close-grained, shrinks much in drying; resembling in some degree the English Laburnum.

HEMICYCLIA, *Wight et Arn.*

364.—H. SEPIARIA, *W. & Arn.*, Muell. Arg. in DC., Prod. xv., ii., 487; Flora Austr., vi., 117; var. *oblongifolia.* A tall shrub, the young shoots minutely pubescent, the adult foliage glabrous. Leaves petiolate, ovate-oblong, one or two inches long. Male flowers several together in axillary clusters. Stamens six to eight.

The identity of the tree from which the wood sample was taken is doubtful as to species, as no flowers were seen, but the foliage agree well with specimen gathered in North Australia of the Australian form of *H. sepiaria.*
B.P.V.—Wood greyish, hard, heavy, and close in grain.

365.—H. AUSTRALASICA, *Muell. Arg.* in DC. Prod. xv., ii., 487; Flora Austr., vi., 118. A tree of moderate size, the leaves two or three inches long; the lower ones, or those on young plants, bordered by teeth, holly-like, the upper ones entire. Fruit oval, red, about half inch long, somewhat succulent. River scrubs Queensland, north and south; also at the Clarence River, New South Wales.

B.P.V.—Wood yellow when fresh, changing to a greyish-yellow when dry; grain close, tough and hard.

DISSILIARIA, *F. v. M.*

366.—D. BALOGHIOIDES, *F. v. M.*, in Baill. Adans., vii., 359; Flora Austr., vi, 90. Native name, "Currungul." Teak. A tall tree with somewhat thin glossy leaves two to five inches long, oblong and opposite. Fruit about one inch in diameter, splitting to pieces when ripe; seeds oval, shining. A common tree of south Queensland scrubs.

B.P.V.— Wood hard, close-grained, brown, becoming darker towards the centre of the tree; might be used for any purpose to which the English Apple is put, which this wood is thought to resemble.

ALEURITES, *Forst.*

368.—A. MOLUCCANA, *Willd.*; *Muell. Arg.* in DC. Prod., xv., ii., 723; Flora Austr., vi., 28. Candle-nut. A tall tree with a wide-spreading head, the foliage and young shoots covered by a mealy substance. The leaves on young plants three or more lobed, entire and ovate-rhomboidal on large trees. Flowers in broad terminal panicles; the fruit two inches or more in diameter, seed or nut nearly globular, several in each fruit. Scrubs of tropical Queensland, and New Guinea; spread over the Eastern Archipelago and the islands of the South Pacific.

The fruit of this large tree is said to furnish the principal food of the cassowary.
The oil of the nuts of this tree is known in commerce as Candle-nut or country walnut oil. Mr. Staiger found the nuts to consist of the following :— The dry nuts—shell, 70 per cent.; kernel, 30 per cent. Kernel freed from shell—oil, 54·3 per cent.; amylaceous and nitrogenous substance, 45·7 per cent. This latter gives 10¼ per cent. ashes rich in phosphoric acid.

B.P.V.—Wood of a light colour, soft and light; if cut when full of sap liable to decay.

CROTON, *Linn.*

369—C. INSULARIS, *Baill.*, Adans, ii., 217 ; Flora Austr., vi, 124. Queensland Cascarilla Bark. A small round-headed tree when growing in open country, but in the scrubs a tall erect tree of scanty foliage. Bark rough, fragrant, the leaves ovate, two to four inches long, and with the young shoots silvery, of a red colour when dying off. Flower-racemes three to five inches long. Capsules three-lobed, about quarter-inch in diameter. Common in Queensland, north and south.

B.P.V.—Wood of a yellow colour, close-grained, hard, and very tough.

370—C. PHEBALIOIDES, *F. v. M.*, Flora Austr., vi., 125. A tree with strongly-scented thin grey bark and erect growth, like *C. insularis* also in its silvery appearance ; but the leaves are much narrower and more pointed, about two inches long. Flower-racemes numerous, capsules hairy and rough, about quarter-inch in diameter. Often found in range and river scrubs of north and south Queensland ; also in New South Wales.

B.V.—Wood yellow, close-grained, and tough.

370A—C. PHEBALIOIDES, *F. v. M.*, var. *hirsuta.* An erect tree, the young shoots and leaves covered with longish hairs. Leaves oblong, four or more inches long. differing from the normal form in the larger foliage, which is much more hairy, and in the less silvery appearance. Found in the scrubs of Taylor's Range, near Brisbane, Queensland.

B.P.V.—Wood of a yellow colour, close in the grain, hard and tough.

371—C. VERREAUXII, *Baill.*, Etud. Euph., 357; Flora Austr., vi., 126. A small tree with oblong, narrow, green leaves, turning red or orange before falling, three to five inches long, entire or toothed, not fragrant as those of *C. insularis.* Racemes of flowers numerous. Capsules nearly globular. A common creek-side shrub or tree in Queensland ; also in North Australia and New South Wales.

B.V.—Wood of a yellowish colour, close-grained, and firm.

BALOGHIA, *Endl.*

373—B. LUCIDA, *Endl.*, Prod. Fl. Norf., 84; Flora Austr., vi., 148. Scrub Bloodwood. A large tree, the stem often knotted, and the rough bark stained by the red sap which flows from the least wound. Leaves opposite, deep-green, oblong, three to five inches long, often glossy. Flowers white, very fragrant; capsule with blunt prickles, over half-inch in diameter. Queensland, north and south, but most abundant in range scrubs ; also in New South Wales, Norfolk Island, and New Caledonia.

B.P.V.—Wood of a light-yellow, prettily marked, close in the grain, hard and tough; a useful cabinet-wood; might probably prove suitable for engraving.

CLAOXYLON, *A. Juss.*

375—C. AUSTRALE, *Baill.*, Etud. Euph., 494; Flora Austr., vi., 130. A small tree of straggling growth, more or less covered by a mealy down; the leaves oblong, three to six inches long, and green on both sides, the texture tender, pointed, and the margins toothed. Flowers in short spikes in the axils of the leaves, small, greenish; the capsules about quarter inch broad. Common in Queensland scrubs, north and south; also in New South Wales.

B.V.—Wood of a light-yellow colour, hard and close-grained; useful for cabinet-work.

ALCHORNEA, *Swartz.*

876.—A. ILICIFOLIA, *Muell. Arg.* in Linnæa, xxxiv., 170; DC. Prod. xv., ii., 906; Flora Austr. vi., 136. Queensland Holly. A tall shrub or small tree with glabrous holly-like leaves of a dull-green colour, and prominently netted. The flowers male and female, the males in slender axillary racemes, the females in much shorter racemes; capsules depressed globular, usually three-celled. Common both in New South Wales and Queensland.

B.V.—Wood close-grained, hard and tough, of a yellow colour.

MALLOTUS, *Lour.*

378.—M. CLAOXYLOIDES, *Muell. Arg.* in Linnæa, xxxiv., 192; Flora Austr., vi., 140. A small tree, the rough foliage emitting a strong and rather disagreeable odour. Leaves opposite, the pairs unequal as to size, oval or oblong, three to six inches long, more or less distinctly three-nerved. Flowers greenish, the sexes in different bunches. Capsule something like a castor-oil capsule. A common tree in Queensland scrubs; also in New South Wales.

B.V.—Wood of a bright-yellow colour, close-grained; useful for cabinet-work.

379.—M. PHILIPPINENSIS, *Muell. Arg.* in Linnæa, xxxiv., 296; Flora Austr., iv., 141. Kamela-tree. Native name, "Poodgee-poodgera." A small tree, the inflorescence and foliage more or less rusty. Leaves on long stalks, oval, pale on the under side, often three-nerved, three to six inches long; capsules covered by a red mealy substance. Common in open country throughout Queensland; also in New South Wales, New Guinea, tropical Asia, and south China.

In India the bark is used for tanning, and the red powder surrounding the ripe capsules is used for dying silk. As a purgative and anthelmintic, this red substance is known as "kamela," and is soluble in alcohol but not in water—amount, 3¼ per cent.; the bark of the roots contain a similar dye.

B.P.V.—Wood close-grained, hard, and very tough, of a light-straw colour.

379A.—M. POLYADENUS, *F. v. M*, Fragm., vi., 184; Flora Austr., vi., 142. A small tree, the leaves oblong, covered on the under side with minute glands, three to six inches long. Capsules with the same scale-like glands as the rest of the plant. Tropical Queensland.

B.P.V.—Wood light-yellow outside, changing towards the centre to a brown, close in grain and hard; suitable for mallets, chisel-handles, &c.

380A.—M. DISCOLOR, *F. v. M.*, Flora Austr., vi., 143. A tall tree with light-coloured bark. The leaves on rather long stalks, ovate, about three inches long, three-nerved, white on the under side. The capsules about quarter inch in diameter, covered with a light-yellow mealy substance. Scrubs of south Queensland; also in New South Wales.

The capsules of this give a bright-yellow dye.

B.P.V.—Wood light-yellow, close in grain, and tough.

MACARANGA, *Thou.*

380B.—M. INAMÆNA, *F. v. M.*, Flora Austr., vi., 145. A small tree, the foliage rough. Leaves oblong, green on both sides, three to five inches long, on stalk of about one inch. Flower in spike of four or five inches; capsules two or three-celled, somewhat prickly. Tropical Queensland coast scrubs.

B.P.V.—Wood of a light colour, tough and close-grained.

380C—M. INVOLUCRATA, *Baill.*, Etud. Euph., 432; Flora Austr., vi., 146. Tree, the branches, inflorescence, and under side of the leaves covered by a mealy substance. Leaves broadly ovate. Flower-spikes in axillary panicles; the flowers in dense clusters within a heart-shaped small leaf. Capsule globular, covered by soft processes. Tropical Queensland.

B.V.—Wood very light and soft; might be found serviceable for making splints.

381—M. TANARIUS, *Muell. Arg.* in DC. Prod., xv., ii., 997; Flora Austr., vi., 146. Native name, "Tumkullum." A small tree, the shoots whitish. Leaves very large, almost orbicular, attached to the stalk far in from the margin; nerves about nine, radiating from the top of the stalk; capsule covered with blunt prickles. A common sea-coast shrub or tree in Queensland; also in New South Wales, North Australia, India and the Archipelago, and China.

B.P.V.—Wood of a light colour, soft and close-grained.

HOMALANTHUS, *A. Juss.*

381A—E. POPULIFOLIUS, *Grah.*, in Bot. Mag., t 2780; *F. v. M.*, Fragm., i., 32; Pl. Rep. Pois. to Stock in Qd., p. 87. A small tree with smooth grey foliage, the leaves on long stalks, ovate-triangular, turning red when about to fall; racemes of flowers four or five inches long; capsules smooth. Borders of Queensland scrubs; also in New South Wales and Victoria, the Eastern Archipelago, and islands of the Pacific, at which latter Baron Mueller states it is poisonous to stock.

B.P.V.—Wood soft, of a light colour.

EXCÆCARIA, *Linn.*

382—E. AGALLOCHA, *Linn.; Muell. Arg.* in DC. Prod., xv,. ii., 1220; Flora Austr., vi., 152; Pl. Rep. Pois. to Stock in Qd., p. 87. Milky Mangrove or River Poison-tree. Tree of moderate size with a yellowish free foliage and smooth bark, the sap milky. Leaves oblong, somewhat fleshy, two or three inches long; spikes of flowers (male) three or four inches long, of an orange colour; the female flower in much shorter spikes; capsules about quarter-inch in diameter. Common all around the coast and up tidal rivers in Queensland and North Australia; also in New South Wales, and is a tropical maritime tree of Asia.

In India the wood is considered useful for general carpentering purposes.

At some excavations carried out on the banks of the Brisbane River for the new Gasworks, the workmen came, at a depth of some 20 to 30 feet, upon large masses of fossilised leaves and wood. Many of the leaves and much of the wood have doubtless belonged to trees of this common coast swamp tree.

B.P.V.—WOOD of a light colour and soft, close in the grain, and easy to work.

383—E. DALLACHYANA, *Baill.*, Adans., vi., 324; Flora Austr., vi., 153; Pl. Rep. Pois. to Stock in Qd., p. 91. Scrub Poison-tree A small tree with a dark-green foliage and milky sap; the leaves one to three inches long, bluntly toothed; capsules three-lobed, about quarter-inch diameter. A common scrub tree in Queensland, both north and south.

B.P.V.—WOOD yellow with black heart, close in the grain and very tough; might be found suitable for axe-handles.

384—E. PARVIFOLIA, *Muell. Arg.*, in Flora, 1864, 433, and DC. Prod., xvii., 1221; Flora Austr, vi., 153. Gutta-percha tree or "Jil-leer." A small tree with narrow-oblong leaves, one half to one inch long. Male racemes of flowers one half to one inch long. Gulf country in Queensland; also in North Australia.

B.P.V.—WOOD near the outside yellow, the heart dark and very beautifully marked, close-grained and easily worked; an excellent wood for the cabinet-maker.

Order URTICACEÆ.

CELTIS, *Linn.*

384A—C. PHILIPPINENSIS, *Blanco.*, Fl. Philip., 197; Flora Austr., vi., 156. A small tree with broadly ovate rigid leaves, two or three inches long, three-nerved. Drupes oval. Scrubs of the tropical Queensland coast, extending over the Archipelago to south China.

B.V.—WOOD light-coloured, hard, and close-grained.

TREMA, *Lour.*

385—T. ASPERA, *Blume*, Mus. Bot., ii., 58; Flora Austr., vi., 158; Pl. Rep. Pois. to Stock in Qd., p. 93. Peach-leaf Poison-bush. A small tree with a smooth bark, the leaves narrow-ovate and often very rough, two to four inches long, three-nerved. The flowers in little bunches at the axils of the leaves, very small, succeeded by little round black berries. Very common around the Queensland scrubs, and fully believed to be poisonous to stock; also met with in New South Wales and North Australia.

B.V.—WOOD of a whitish colour, soft and light.

385A—T. ORIENTALIS, *Blume*, Mus. Bot., ii., 62; Flora Austr., vi., 158. Charcoal-tree of India. Usually of larger growth, and having the under side of the leaves of a light colour, otherwise resembling *T. aspera.* Found plentifully in the north but sparingly in the south of Queensland, and at Parramatta in New South Wales; widely spread in East India and the Archipelago.

In parts of India this tree is allowed to grow for shade in coffee plantations. The wood is used for making gunpowder charcoal.

B.P.V.—WOOD of a red colour, soft, and resembling Cedar.

APHANANTHE, *Planch.*

386—A. PHILIPPINENSIS, *Planch.*, in Ann. Sc. Not., ser. 3, x., 337; Flora Austr., vi., 160. A small tree with dense foliage; the leaves rough and bordered by sharp distant teeth, one to three inches long, ovate, or, when long, narrow. Fruit ovoid, about a quarter of an inch long. River sides and the borders of scrubs throughout the coast country of Queensland; also in New South Wales and the Philippine Islands.

B.V.—WOOD close-grained, light in colour; might do for stamps.

MALAISIA, *Blanco.*

387—M. TORTUOSA, *Blanco*, Fl. Felip, 789; Flora Austr., vi., 180. A large rambling or climbing milky-juiced shrub, with rather rough oblong leaves, two to four inches long. Fruit bright red in axillary heads. Common in Queensland scrubs and along river banks; also in New South Wales and 'Port Darwin, and the Indian Archipelago, the Philippines and other islands.

B.V.—WOOD close-grained and tough, parti-coloured, the outer part yellow, the centre brown.

PSEUDOMORUS, *Bureau.*

388—P. BRUNONIANA, *Bureau*, in Ann. Sc. Nat., ser. 5, xi., 372; Flora Austr., vi., 181. A small tree with a close dense foliage, the leaves narrow-ovate, one to four inches long, toothed, very rough; the female flowers in very short heads, but the male in drooping spikes over one inch long. Berries white, sweet-flavoured. Borders of scrubs and margins of rivers, both north and south in Queensland and New South Wales, extending to Norfolk Island and New Caledonia.

B.P.V.—WOOD light-yellow, close-grained, hard and tough.

I

FICUS, *Linn.*

389—F. CUNNINGHAMII, *Miq.*, in Ann. Mus. Lugd. Bot., iii., 286 ; Flora Austr., vi., 165. A large tree, often but not always shedding its leaves in winter. Leaves glossy, light-green, oval-oblong, abruptly pointed, four to nearly six inches long, and two or more inches broad ; the primary veins distant and prominent. Fruit at first white, but turning to a pretty purple, globose, a quarter inch or rather more in diameter, close in pairs in the axils of the leaves. South and north in Queensland.

B.P.V.—WOOD of a light colour, soft and porous.

390—F. PLATYPODA, *A. Cunn.*, var. *petiolaris*, Flora Austr., vi., 169. A moderate sized tree, the leaves glossy, deep-green, on somewhat flattened rather long stalks, four inches long or more, and about two inches or more broad. Fruit on short stalks, globular. North and South Queensland.

B.P.V.—WOOD soft, of a light-yellow colour with a strong fibre.

391—F. MACROPHYLLA, *Desf.*, Pers. Syn. Pl., ii., 609. Flora Austr., vi., 170. The Moreton Bay or large Fig-tree. This is perhaps the largest tree of Queensland, stems may be seen 20 feet in diameter. Leaves often 8 or 10 inches long, and four or five broad, obtusely pointed at the apex, footstalks three or four inches long, stipules three to five inches long. The receptacles or figs globular or pear-shaped, purplish spotted with white, often over one inch diameter, on stalks one inch long. Found throughout Queensland and the northern parts of New South Wales.

B.P.V.—WOOD light-coloured, coarse-grained, soft and light.

452—F. ASPERA, *Forst.*, Prod., 76; Flora Austr., vi., 174. Rough or Purple Fig. Tree of moderate size, dark-coloured bark and very rough foliage. The fruit when ripe dark purple. Scrubs of South Queensland, very common, and New South Wales.

Largely used for food by the Cloncurry and Mitchell River natives.— E. Palmer.

B.P.V.—WOOD yellow-coloured, close-grained.

393—F. HISPIDA, *Linn. f*, Suppl.; Flora Austr., vi., 176; *F. oppositifolia*, Roxb.; Wight, Ic. t., 638. A moderate-sized tree, the young branches hollow. Leaves all opposite, broadly oblong-elliptical, six to ten inches long, and four or five broad ; the primary veins distant, prominent as well as the transverse veinlets, the basal pair very oblique. Receptacles (figs), in pairs in the lower axils or more frequently in leafless clusters or racemes on the old wood, globose or somewhat turbinate, about one-inch diameter. This tree is common in India where the foliage is used for cattle fodder; met with in many parts of tropical Queensland and North Australia.

B.P.V.—WOOD of a light-yellow, coarse-grained and light.

394—F. FASCICULATA, *F. v. M.*, Flora Austr., vi., 177. A large shrub, the young shoots clothed with short stiff hairs. Leaves alternate, ovate or broadly elliptical, shortly acuminate, eight to ten inches long and four or five inches broad, the distant primary veins and transverse reticulations prominent, and often hispid. Figs in pairs, axillary or more frequently on the branches below the leaves, about half-inch diameter, tubercular-scabrous, marked with about six longitudinal ribs. Found in the tropical Queensland scrubs from Rockhampton northward.

B.P.V.—WOOD soft, coarse-grained, and light-coloured.

394A—F. PLEUROCARPA, *F. v. M.*, Fragm., viii., 246; *Bail.*, Syn· Ql. Fl., 490. Johnstone River Ribbed Fig. A tree of moderate size, the leaves oval, pointed, three to five inches long, about two inches broad. Fruit ribbed, two inches or more long, somewhat conical. Johnstone River, Queensland.

B.P.V.—WOOD light, soft, and elastic, with very open pores.

394B—F. CASEARIA, *F. v. M*, Flora Austr., vi., 177. A small tree with broad spreading head, quite glabrous. Leaves alternate, on short stalks, ovate, acuminate, entire, rounded or cuneate at the base, three to six inches long, one and a half to two and a half inches broad, membranous, the principal primary veins distant, the basal oblique pair very small or obsolete Stipules about one inch long, acuminate, deciduous. Figs on stalks of about one quarter inch long, or nearly stalkless, quite glabrous, depressed-globular, about half an inch diameter, with about six longitudinal raised ribs. Met with on the scrub lands of tropical Queensland

B.V.—WOOD light-coloured, close-grained, and firm.

395—F. GLOMERATA, *Willd.*, Spec. Pl., iv., 1148; Flora Austr., 178; Wight, Ic. t., 667. A large spreading-headed tree, the foliage slightly hairy and light in colour. Leaves narrow-ovate, pointed, two to six inches long, with distant veins. Fruit large, in bunches on the tree and thick branches. North and South Queensland; also North Australia and India.

In India the wood is used for well-frames, as it is found, though soft, to last well under water.

B.P.V.—WOOD of a straw colour, coarse in grain, light, soft, and porous.

CUDRANIA, *Trécul.*

396—C. JAVANENSIS, *Tréc.*, in Ann. Sc. Nat., ser. 3, viii., 123; Flora Austr., vi., 179. Cockspur Thorn. A tall rambling shrub with a thick stem; bark corky, yellow, the stems armed with spines about one inch long, often curved. Leaves oblong, one to two inches long; the ripe fruit like a round yellow mulberry. Common on the borders of scrubs in north and south Queensland; also in New South Wales, Java, Burmah, and India.

B.V.—WOOD dark-yellow, close-grained; a desirable cabinet-wood.

LAPORTEA, *Gaudich.*

397—L. GIGAS, *Wedd.*, Monogr. Urt., 129, t. 3 and 4, and in DC. Prod., xvi., i., 82; Flora Austr., vi., 191. Large Stinging-tree. A very large tree, trunk four or five feet or even more in diameter, with a height of over 100 feet, the bark grey; the leaves large somewhat heart-shaped, and over one foot in diameter, covered with soft hairs; the bunches of inflorescence with the pedicles enlarged and fleshy when the fruit comes to maturity. Scrubs, south Queensland and New South Wales.

It may be here noticed that the pain caused by the sting of these plant may be instantly relieved by the milky juice of the lower part of the stem of *Colocasia macrorrhisa*—"Cunjevoi" of the natives—being rubbed on the affected part.

B.P.V.—Wood spongy, brownish, soft.

398—L. PHOTINIPHYLLA, *Wedd.*, Monogr. Urt., 138, and in DC. Prod., xvi., i., 83; Flora Austr., vi., 192. Shiny-leaved Stinging-tree. A large tree with a soft grey bark. The leaves green and shining, ovate, three-nerved, four to six inches long; the ripe nuts with their fleshy stalks forming a white fleshy mass. Queensland scrubs, north and south; also in New South Wales.

B.P.V.—Wood very soft, brownish.

PIPTURUS, *Wedd.*

400—P. ARGENTEUS, *Wedd.*, in DC. Prod., xvi., i., 235; Flora Austr., 185. Native name, "Coomeroo-coomeroo." A small tree, the branches and under side of the leaves hoary-white. Leaves on long often pink stalks, ovate, pointed, three or five-nerved, the edges slightly toothed, three to six inches long. Fruit small, white, edible. Found in most Queensland coast scrubs; also in New South Wales, the Indian Archipelago, and Pacific Islands.

B.P.V.—Wood brown, close-grained, and soft. The bark yields good fibre.

Order CASUARINEÆ.

CASUARINA, *Linn.*

401—C. GLAUCA, *Sieb.*, in Spreng. Syst., iii., 803; Flora Austr., vi., 196. Swamp Oak; native name, "Billa." In New South Wales called "Belar" and "Bull Oak." A moderate-sized tree with a rough bark, the shoots greyish, sheath-teeth pointed, usually ten to twelve. Male spikes about one inch long. Cones subglobose, flat-topped, about half-inch in diameter. Found on the margins of rivers in Queensland, New South Wales, Victoria, and South Australia.

B.P.V.—Wood of a red colour, beautifully marked, close-grained, hard and tough; useful in cabinet-work; used for shingles and staves.

401A.—C. EQUISETIFOLIA, *Forst.*, Char. Gen., 103, t. 52; Flora Austr., vi., 197. Tree of moderate size, with drooping branches of a greyish colour; bark rough, sheath-teeth usually about seven, but varying from six to eight; male spikes about one inch long; cones almost globular, about half inch in diameter, velvety. Tropical Queensland coast, North Australia, New Guinea, East India, and the Archipelago.

This is one of the woods largely planted in India.

B.V.—Wood of a dark colour, coarse-grained, but nicely marked.

402.—C. EQUISETIFOLIA, *Forst.*, var. *incana*; Flora Austr., vi., 197. Native name, " Wunna-wunnarumpa." Tree of moderate size, the young shoots woolly or hoary, and drooping; cones nearly one inch in diameter. Found on the islands of the Queensland coast.

B.P.V.—Wood light-brown, prettily marked, close-grained and very tough

403.—C. SUBEROSA, *Ott. et Dietr.*; Miq.. Rev. Cas. 54, t. 6, and DC. Prod., xvii., ii., 337; Flora Austr., vi., 197. In New South Wales known as River, Black, and Swamp Oak. Often a tall tree, the bark rough but not corky; the sheath-teeth seven or from six to eight; the male spikes slender, several inches long, of a reddish colour. Cones oblong, often flat at each end, and over one inch long. Open country north and south in Queensland, often in forests almost entirely confined to themselves; also in New South Wales, Victoria, and Tasmania.

B.P.V.—Wood dark-brown, prettily marked, coarse in grain, hard and tough; used for bullock-yokes and hurdles. In New South Wales used for mauls, shingles, staves, &c.

404.—C. CUNNINGHAMIANA, *Miq.*, Rev. Cas., 56, t. 6, and in DC. Prod., xvi., ii., 335; Flora Austr., vi., 198. A tall tree with slender branches, sheath-teeth as in *C. suberosa.* Cones under half inch long, nearly globular. River sides, often at inland localities in Queensland; also in New South Wales.

B.P.V.—Wood of a dark colour, close-grained, and prettily marked.

405.—C. INOPHLOIA, *F. v. M. et Bail.*, Melb., Chem., 1882; Bail., Syn. Ql. Fl., 495. Thready-barked Oak. A small tree with a curious bark, loose, and composed of long, flat, thread-like scales; branches slender; sheath-teethed seven to nine, acute; male spikes reddish or purplish, long and slender, the cones about one inch in diameter, of irregular shape. Found on sandy poor land inland, but on both sides of the coast range in Queensland.

B.P.V.—Wood very beautiful, of a reddish colour, but with numerous dark marks, the grain close; a very desirable wood for cabinet-work.

406.—C. TORULOSA, *Ait.*, Hort. Kew, iii., 320; Flora Austr., vi., 200. Forest Oak. Native name, " Koondeeba." A tree of moderate size, the bark corky, and the branches drooping and very slender; sheath-teeth four or perhaps five; male spikes slender, and long cones, globular and oblong, velvety, over one inch in diameter. A common tree on ranges in Queensland ; also in New South Wales and South Australia.

B.P.V.—Wood of a red colour, very nicely marked, close in the grain, and hard ; used for bullock-yokes.

Sub-Class GYMNOSPERMEÆ.

Order CONIFERÆ.

CALLITRIS, *Vent.*

407—C. Parlatorei, *F. v. M.*, in Seemann. Journ. Bot., 267 ; Fragm., v., 186 ; and Flora Austr.. vi., 235.   Stringybark Pine.   An erect tree of moderate size, the bark very stringy.   Cones pyramidal, over six inches long, six-valved.   On ranges of southern Queensland and New South Wales.

B.P.V.—Wood fragrant, of a light straw colour, close-grained, soft, and easily worked ; suitable for cabinet-work or joinery.

408—C. Robusta, *R. Br.*   A tall tree of a grey colour, the cones globular, valves alternately smaller.   An inland Pine of Queensland and all the other Australian colonies.

B.P.V.—Wood fragrant, varies much as to colour from a light to a dark brown, with often pinkish longitudinal streaks, often full of beautiful markings very durable ; in use for piles and sheathing of boats, as it resists to a great degree the attacks of the teredo ; an excellent cabinet-wood.

408a—C. robusta, *R. Br.*, var. *microcarpa* ; Flora Austr., vi , 237. Native name at Brisbane, " Pooragri ;" at Wide Bay, " Coolooli."   A coast Pine, head very dense and dark-green.   Cones globose, half-inch or more in diameter.   Valves very unequal, with the central columella more than usually developed   On the Queensland coast, and also New South Wales.

B.P.V.—Wood of a dark colour, close-grained. fragrant, and durable ; used for piles of wharves, sheathing of boats, resisting attacks of the teredo ; also an excellent cabinet-wood.

408c—C. Rhomboidea, *R. Br.*, in Rich. Conif., 47, t. 18 ; Flora Austr., vi., 238.   Native name, " Brorogery."   Tree of medium size, with slender drooping branches ; the cones clustered ; valves six, alternately smaller, the larger ones dilated at the top, with a little point near the centre.   Islands of Moreton Bay, Queensland ; also in New South Wales, Victoria and South Australia.

B.P.V.—Wood of a light colour, close-grained and durable ; uses same as th last.

408d—C. calcarata, *R. Br.*, in Mem. du Mas. Par., xiii., 74 ; Flora Austr., vi.. 238.   A small tree, branches drooping and angular.

Cones clustered, about half-inch in diameter; valves six, somewhat smooth, and the larger ones little or not dilated upwards, the cone furrowed at the junctions before it opens. Various parts of Queensland, New South Wales, and Victoria.

B.P.V.—Wood of a light colour, fine in the grain and prettily marked; a useful wood for joinery as well as cabinet-making.

PODOCARPUS, *L'Her.*

409—P. ELATA, *R. Br.*; *Mirb.*, in Mem. Mus. Par., xiii., 75; Flora Austr., vi., 247. She-Pine; native name, "Kidneywallum." Native Plum, Deal or Damson of New South Wales. No 101 under *P. spinulosa*, R. Br., in New South Wales Forestry Exhibit at the Jubilee Exhibition, Adelaide. A tall erect tree, with a thin somewhat stringy bark and long linear glossy-green leaves from two to six inches long; male spikes one inch or more long, often two or three together. Fruit oval, resting upon a purple fleshy foot; sometimes this fleshy part is over one inch in diameter. A common tree of coast scrubs in Queensland and New South Wales.

B.P.V.—Wood of a light-yellow colour, close in the grain, strong and durable; used for piles and boat-sheathing, as it fairly resists the attacks of the teredo; excellent for spars and masts of vessels.

AGATHIS, *Salisb.*

410—A. ROBUSTA, *C. Moore* (under *Dammara*), in Trans. Pharm. Soc., Vic., ii., 174; Flora Austr., vi., 244. Dundathu Pine or Kauri Pine. A tall tree with the branches in whorls. Leaves of a deep-green colour, ovate, two to five inches long, and from one to over two inches broad. Cone smooth, oblong. Queensland coast country; usually on ranges.

B.P.V.—Wood of a light-yellow colour, close-grained, soft, and easy to work; largely used by joiners and cabinet-makers.

ARAUCARIA, *Juss.*

411—A. CUNNINGHAMII, *Ait.*, in Sweet's Hort. Brit., 475; Flora Austr., vi., 243. Moreton Bay or Hoop Pine. Native name at Brisbane, "Cumburtu;" Wide Bay, "Coonam." A tall tree, the branches in whorls; leaves narrow, needle-like. Male spikes cylindrical, two or three inches long. Cones ovoid, four or more inches in length, and two or more in diameter. Coast ranges, north and south; also in New South Wales.

B.P.V.—Wood straw-coloured, strong and durable, used extensively for flooring and lining boards in house-building, also by the cabinet-makers. This wood is often very prettily marked; it is said that it lasts well for the bottoms of punts when kept constantly wet.

412—A. BIDWILLI, *Hook.*, Lond. Journ. Bot., ii, 503, t. 18; Flora Austr., vi., 243. Bunya Pine. A fine glossy-green large tree, the branches in whorls. Leaves lance-shaped, one inch or more long. Male spikes three or four inches long. Cones very large. Seeds two inches long; at one time largely used by the natives for food. On the Bunya Range, and Condamine, Dawson, and the Burnett Rivers.

B.P.V.—WOOD light in colour, often very prettily marked, is strong, durable, and easily worked; in use by joiners and cabinet-makers for various kinds of work.

Order CYCADACEÆ.

CYCAS, *Linn.*

413—C. MEDIA, *R. Br.*, Prod., 348; Flora Austr., vi., 249. A fern-like small tree, trunk eight or more feet high, with a crown of pinnate leaves, each leaflet with a prominent midrib. Male flower in a cone covered by a mealy substance; the fruit on broad, notched, abortive leaves. Seeds oval, about one and a half inch long, yellowish. Tropical Queensland and North Australia.

V.—WOOD of outer part stringy, the centre of stem spongy.

Class II.—MONOCOTYLEDONS.

Order LILIACEÆ.

DRACÆNA, *Linn.*

414B—D. ANGUSTIFOLIA, *Roxb.; Baker*, in Journ. Linn. Soc., xiv., 526; Flora Austr., vii., 20. A tall shrub or small slender tree, the stem marked by rings, scars of fallen leaves; the leaves crowning the head of the stem, long and narrow with fine points. Flower-panicle a foot or more long and but little branched, flowers white. Fruit rather pulpy, containing from one to three rather large seeds. Tropical Queensland and North Australia; also New Guinea.

B.V.—WOOD, or the outer hard portions of the stem, of a light colour, the rest very soft and spongy.

CORDYLINE, *Comm.*

414C—C. TERMINALIS, *Kunth; Baker*, in Journ. Linn. Soc., xiv., 539; Flora Austr., vii., 21. The Lily Palm. A small tree, the leaves crowded at the top, one to two feet long, one to four inches broad. Flowers blue, in drooping panicles, succeeded by bright red berries.

B.—WOOD light-coloured.

Order JUNCACEÆ.

XANTHORRHÆA, *Sm.*

414A—X. ARBOREA, *R. Br.*, Prod., 288; Flora Austr., vii., 115. Grass-tree or Black-boy. Trunk ten or more feet high, often thick coated by the bases of old leaves. Leaves forming a dense crown to the stem, long, narrow, grass-like. Flower-spike several feet long, flowers white, seeds black. Found on rocky or sandy poor land in Queensland and New South Wales.

Often burned by bushmen to drive away mosquitos.

B.V.—Wood, or outer hard part of stem, straw-coloured, cross-grained. The centre of the stem contains five per cent. of sugar; the outer part of stem yields the acaroid gums of commerce, which form a polish by merely being dissolved in spirits.

Order PALMÆ.

ARCHONTOPHŒNIX, *Wendl. et D ude.*

418—A. CUNNINGHAMII, *W. et D*, in Linnæa, xxxix., 214; Flora Austr., vii., 141. Native name, "Piccabeen." A tall slender tree, the leaves pinnate, leaflets green on both sides, tapering towards the point, where it is at times toothed. Flowers in large bunches. Fruit ovoid-globose. Common in many parts of south Queensland, and some places in the tropics; also in New South Wales.

B.V.—Wood or outer part of stem very hard and prettily marked.

PTYCHOSPERMA, *Labill.*

419—P. NORMANBYI, *F. v. M.*, Fragm., viii., 235, xi., 56; *Bail.*, Syn. Ql. Fl., 564. Black Palm. A tall tree, dense head of leaves, stem very hard and dark. Leaves six to eight feet long, with long sheathing bases; the stem stout and covered with white mealy hairs, furnished with leaflets to the base, each leaflet divided to the base into usually nine narrow lobes, one to one and a half foot long, which are toothed at the end; the nerves numerous and prominent, the under side white. Fruit ovoid, with conical points, one and a half inch long. Country about the Daintree River, Queensland.

B.P.V.—Wood, or outer part of the stem, very hard and black, beautifully marked; used in the manufacture of walking-sticks.

LICUALA, *Rumph.*

420—L. MUELLERI, *Wendl. et Drude*, in Linnæa, xxxix., 223; Flora Austr., viii., 145. The most beautiful palm of Australia, with erect very tall stem, not plainly scarred by fallen leaves. Leaves almost like a round fan divided into wedge-shaped portions with large saw-like teeth at the end At an early stage these portions are more or less joined for several inches at the top, but they are always free from each other at the base, where they join the stalk. The leaves three to six or more feet in diameter; stalks furnished near the base with short sharp prickles, below which the margins expand into an entire, strong, lace-like sheath, which ends on the opposite side of the stem in a long, entire, thin, narrow, strap-like point This peculiar development at the leaf's base forms a bulb-like mass above the clear part of the stem. Fruit crimson, in large straggling bunches, ovoid or globular, about quarter or three-quarter inch in

K

diameter. Found at Rockingham Bay and Johnstone River, in Queensland.

B.V.—Wood, or the outer hard part of stem, hard, and marked with narrow black lines.

LIVISTONA, *R. Br.*

420A—L. HUMILIS, *R. Br.*, Prod., 268; Flora Austr., vii., 146.   A small tree with crown of palmate leaves; leaves with a radius of one foot and a half, deeply divided into narrow plaited segments tapering to a fine point, with a thread-like bristle between the lobes, the stalk flattened and prickly on the edges; berry ovoid-oblong, in large bunches.   Gulf country, Queensland; and many parts of North Australia

B.V.—Wood, or the outer hard portion of stem, hard and of a light colour, the inner soft.

420B—L. INERMIS, *R. Br.*, Prod., 268; Flora Austr., vii., 146. A small tree with crown of palmate leaves, the stalks slender, without prickles on the edges, or only one or so very small ones near the top. Rockingham Bay, Queensland.

B.P.V.—Wood, or outer part of stem, of a light-grey, streaked by a darker colour.

421—L. AUSTRALIS, *Mart.*, Hist. Nat. Palm., iii., 241; Bot. Mag. t., 6274; Flora Austr., vii., 146.   Common Cabbage Palm.   A tall tree with stout stems and large crown of palmate leaves, five or more feet in diameter, the segments cleft at the top into two narrow lobes; panicle large.   Fruit globose, often nearly one inch in diameter. Coast country from Rockhampton to the southern border in Queensland; also in New South Wales and Victoria.

Formerly the leaves of this palm were largely used in hat-making, the cabbage-tree hat being generally worn. The wood is also used by the natives for making spear-heads.—*E. Palmer.*

B.V.—Wood, or outer part of the stem, moderately hard, of a dark colour, and beautifully marked.

Order PANDANEÆ.

PANDANUS, *Linn.*

422—P. PEDUNCULATUS, *R. Br.*, Prod., 341; Flora Austr., vii., 149. Breadfruit; native name, "Wynnum." Tree of moderate size, emitting strong roots from the stem, several feet from the soil. The leaves several feet long, tapering to a long narrow point, the edges with small sharp prickly teeth. Fruit a large globose head, composed of clusters of drupes which are about two inches long. A sea-side tree, all round the Queensland coast; also in New South Wales.

B.V.—Wood, or the firm outer part of the stem, of a light colour, and prettily marked. Aërial roots and leaves supply good fibre.

Class III.—ACOTYLEDONS.

Order FILICES.

ALSOPHILA, *R. Br.*

424—A. AUSTRALIS, *R. Br.*, Prod., 158; Hook. Spec. Filic I., t., 18; Flora Austr., vii., 710. Common Tree Fern; native name, " Nanga-nanga." A tall tree with stout stem and fine crown of fronds, each six to ten feet long and several feet broad, the stalk often covered by long thin whitish scales. Found in many parts of Queensland · New South Wales, Victoria, and Tasmania.

B.V.—Wood, or the hard outer part of the stem, brown and white in streaks, the brown very hard.

425—A. LEICHHARDTIANA, *F. v. M.*, Fragm.. v., 53, 117; Flora Austr., vii., 711. Prickly Tree Fern. Stem tall, dark, hard, and often free from the bases of old fronds. Fronds four to seven feet long, the stalk prickly with sharp black prickles. Common north and south, in Queensland, also in New South Wales.

B.V.—Wood, or the outer hard portion of stem, black with white streaks the black very hard.

DICKSONIA, *L'Her.*

427—D. YOUNGIÆ, *C. Moore*, in Baker's Syn. Filic., 461; Flora Austr , vii., 713. A tall stout Tree Fern, the crown of the stem and bases of the fronds clothed with long, bright, brown, hairy scales; fronds long and broad. Bunya Mountains and high ranges in Queensland; also in New South Wales.

B.V.—Wood, or outer part of the stem, black streaked with white, the dark very hard.

———————————

537 kinds woods are comprised in this catalogue.

DICOTYLEDONS ...	...	...	...	∴	524
MONOCOTYLEDONS	...	...	...	...	10
ACOTYLEDONS ...	...	...	...	...	3

QUEENSLAND COMMISSION.

Centennial International Exhibition, Melbourne, 1888.

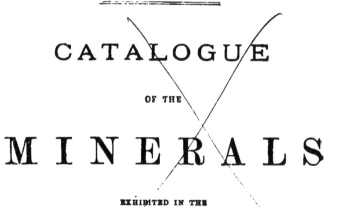

CATALOGUE

OF THE

MINERALS

EXHIBITED IN THE

QUEENSLAND COURT.

BRISBANE:

WARWICK AND SAPSFORD, PRINTERS, BOOKBINDERS, ETC., ADELAIDE STREET

MDCCCLXXXVIII.

PREFACE.

UNDER adverse circumstances the Commissioners have done their best to bring together a series of Mineral exhibits in some degree representing the actual fertility and proportionately sustaining the well-earned reputation of the colony. That they have not succeeded in displaying as they wished the extent of this branch of its material resources—of giving thereby an adequate idea of the enormous superficial range, general distribution, and easy accessibility of its metallic products—is due chiefly to the very limited time and moderate expenditure at their service—chiefly, but not solely, for they are unhappily constrained to say that their efforts have not in all cases been seconded by the mining interest with that readiness which public spirit alone might have prompted. The statement will serve to emphasize the expression of gratitude which the Commissioners, on behalf of the country, feel to be owing to the generality of mining bodies, many of whom have generously contributed to the exposition " specimens " of considerable value.

The minerals, hurriedly collected, have, as a natural consequence, been crudely catalogued. With no time at command for critical examination of the exhibits procured, the adoption of the names and descriptions accompanying them has for the most part been unavoidable. The Commissioners therefore do not hold themselves responsible for inaccuracy, insufficiency, or absence of such details.

The arrangement of the Catalogue is geographical, and to aid the enquirer in ascertaining the locality of any given mine, the whole country is taken as divided into nine portions by arbitrarily chosen lines of latitude and longitude. In each division the chief circles of the industry are named as districts; each district comprehending one or more groups of mines or fields. By help of the Index, it is hoped that the position and surroundings of every claim represented will be discoverable with ease.

At a glance over the divisions which are the chief tributaries to the collection shown, it will be apparent that the profitable employment of the miner is at present almost wholly restricted to the eastern moiety or less of Queensland territory. This is the direct result of geological conditions. Over this area, whether on account of greater age or greater proximity to the sea, or of both combined, the newer rocks have, as a rule, been removed, washed away by the usual denuding agents, and the older and mineralised deposits thus brought within the reach of the shallow sinker; while these metalliferous beds themselves have had to submit gradually to the same destructive operations, and compelled to discharge their metals in one form or another—in the case of gold, enriching by concentration either the decomposed materials on the spot or the alluvial drifts derived from them. Subjected for ages to this treatment in the laboratory of nature, the surface rocks have stored up incalculable wealth for appropriation by the first comer, and render Queensland the most remunerative of fields for the employment of capital prudently invested. The promise of the future is scarcely less than the productiveness of the present.   kill and capital brought to bear on the more refractory ores abundant in the deep sinkings of the seaboard region will continuously maintain and increase our return of the precious and useful metals, and beyond that region we may look below the vast plains of the west.   There is no reason to assume that beneath the secondary rocks of the interior mineralisation is not as prevalent and productive of wealth as in the east.   That wealth waits to reward the future.   On the whole, therefore, it is no exaggeration to say that the mineral riches of Queensland are practically inexhaustible.

In the following Catalogue exhibitors not specified are, in all cases, the Queensland Commissioners.

❖INDEX.❖

QUEENSLAND.

Catalogue of Mineral Exhibits.

SOUTH-EAST DIVISION.*

GYMPIE DISTRICT.

Mount Shamrock Field.

CHOWEY CREEK... ... ... *Allendale Silver Mine*

1 Cinnabar in limestone
2 Oxide ore, from surface to 25ft level
3 Galena and pyrite from lode at 25ft level
4 Foot-wall and hanging-wall, alike, pyritous slate
5 Porphyry dyke running north and south and intersecting lode at right angles

CHOWEY CREEK ... ... *Lady Florence Gold Mining Company*

6 Quartz from No. 1 Reef, molybdenite and mundic
7 Foot-wall, aplite, at 30ft
8 Hanging-wall and country rock, aplite
9 Quartz showing gold with molybdenite and tetradymite. A trial crushing of one ton yielded 1oz. 15dwts.; average width of reef 3ft
10 Quartz and molybdenite from Reef No. 2; width of reef 3ft 6in
11 Surface quartz showing gold, from Reef No. 3, width of reef 3ft 6in
12 Sample of reef No. 4 from surface to 50 feet in depth, width of reef 3ft 6in
13 Surface stone from Reef No. 5, 1ft wide
14   Do   do   No. 6, 10in wide
15   Do   do   No. 7, 18in wide
16   Do   do   No. 8, 24in wide
17   Do   do   No. 9, 36in wide
18   Do   do   No. 10, 22in wide
    All the reefs run east and west, with a southerly underlay

---

*From southern boundary to 25¼ S. lat., and from seaboard to 146 E. long.

B

MOUNT SHAMROCK   ...   ...   *Kent's Knob Gold Mining Company*

21   Lode from centre of claim, surface stone
22   Lode from centre of claim
23   Lode stuff from tunnel on east side of hill
24   Lode at 80ft level
25   Foot-wall with lode stuff, lode deposit in sight about 150ft
         by 250ft
26   Kaolin
27   Bismuth ore

This claim is situated at the junction of Chowey and Didcot Creeks, where there is a permanent supply of water sufficient for any machinery that may be erected.

CHOWEY CREEK...   ...   .   *Jubilee Gold Mining Company*

30   Reef from tunnel No. 2, more than 12in wide, but not
         yet cut through
31   Reef at 52ft level, 20in wide, running north and south
         and dipping west 1 in 6
32   Foot-wall, hanging-wall and country rock, serpentine with
         bismuthite

CHOWEY CREEK   ...   ...   *Mount Shamrock Gold Mining Company.*

40   Lode from surface to 40ft level
41   Bismuth ore from 40ft to 60ft level
42   Mundic ore from 80ft to 100ft level
43   Lode from 60ft to 107ft level
44   Crushing stuff from shaft, all put through and carrying a
         little gold
45   Country rock, porphyry.

CHOWEY CREEK   ...   *No. 1 West, Lord Nelson Gold Mining Company*

50   Surface ore, lode about 5ft wide

CHOWEY CREEK   ...   .   *New Chum Claim*

55   Sample of stone

This claim is situated north from the Lady Florence; the area is 24 men's ground. The present shareholders are exclusively working men, and capital is required to work the claim, which is said to show excellent prospects.

Pride of Gebangle, No. 1 Claim

60   Lode at surface
61   Do   20ft
62   Do   bottom of shaft

Lode of unknown dimensions, the shaft being entirely in lode stuff. The claim adjoins Mount Allen on the south side.

Pride of Gebangle, No. 2 Claim

70 Surface stone
71 Lode at 25ft level

Lode running about east and west and perpendicular; where opened it is 6ft in width.

CHOWEY CREEK .. .. *Lord Nelson Prospecting Claim*

80 Lode No. 1, auriferous stone from tunnel at the foot of mount
81 Lode No. 1, showing gold, from shaft on the hill; width of the lode unknown, no walls having been reached
82 Do No. 2 about 12ft wide, running east and west
83 Do No. 3, 18in wide, running north and south

CHOWEY CREEK ... ... *The Achillea Gold Mining Company*

84 Stone from No. 1 face, lode 15ft wide in face
85 Stone from No. 2 face, face 35ft wide, width of lode unknown
86 Stone from No. 3 face, face 35ft wide
87 Stone from No. 4 face, face 7 to 10ft; in a trial crushing of 10 tons gave 1oz. 16dwts. per ton

The claim is 1200ft x 1200ft, with five acres for machine area. The crushing plant consists of a 5ft Huntingdon roller mill, now being erected.

CHOWEY CREEK... ... *No. 1 South Achillea Gold Mining Company*

88 Lode at surface
89 Do 25ft level

The claim is 400 x 400 yards, the sinking 25ft, all in lode stuff. ·

CHOWEY CREEK ... ... *Mount Toohey P.C. Gold Mining Company*

90 Lode at surface
91 Do 40ft level, shaft No. 1
92 Hanging-wall at 40ft level, porphyry and slate

This lode crops out on the western side of the ridge; it is supposed to run north and south, with a westerly underlay.

CHOWEY CREEK... ... ... *Lady Frances Gold Mining Company*

93 Reef from surface to 11ft in shaft No. 1, ironstone and quartz
94 Reef from surface to 22ft in shaft No. 2, white quartz
95 Foot-wall and country rock, syenite
96 Hanging-wall, syenite

The reef runs east and west, underlaying south about 1 in 7, with an average thickness of about 12in

CHOWEY CREEK   ...   .. *Blyth's Victoria Gold Mining Company*
  97 Mundic from leader at 35ft level, assays 7oz. gold per ton

CHOWEY CREEK   ...   . *Quartz Gold Mining Company*
  98 Quartz-reef 4ft wide at 20ft level, running north-east and south-west, and dipping westerly about 1 in 4
  99 Lode at 30ft level, running north and south

Mount Perry Field.

MOUNT DRAIN   ...   . *Great Freehold, Rocky Creek*
  100 Lode from shaft No. 2 on west side of hill, 29ft from surface, pyritous quartz
  101 Lode from shaft No. 1, ferruginous quartz, decomposed porphyry, magnetite, hornblende
  102 Ore from face No. 1, chalcopyrite, pyrite, magnetite, hornblende rock
  103 Ore from face No 2, magnetite, hæmatite, göthite, hornblende, decomposed porphyry
  104 Auriferous ore from face No. 3, chalcopyrite, magnetite, coarse syenite, decomposed hornblende
  105 Gossan from face No. 4, lode 4ft wide running east and west, dipping south
  106 Lode from face No. 4, chalcopyrite, pyrite, magnetite, hornblende
  107 Auriferous iron ore, from lode 9in thick, 10ft from surface, running east and west, dipping south, assays 9ozs per ton
  108 Mundic from 50ft from surface, lode about 2ft 6in wide, running east and west and nearly vertical, mispickel
  109 Hanging-wall of mundic lode, coarse syenite
  110 Footwall of mundic lode, syenite
  111 Country rock of mundic lode, granulite

MOUNT DRAIN   ...   . *Harper's Hill*
  120 Carbonates of copper, from 4ft to 20ft level, yielding 44ozs silver per ton with traces of gold
  121 Gossan with carbonates, from 20ft level
  122 Oxide ore and chalcopyrite, from 20ft level; lode, 18 to 30in wide, running south-east and north-west; underlaying west about 1 in 8

MOUNT DRAIN   ...   . *Mount Webster Gold Mining Co.*
  130 Gossan from shaft No. 2, 15ft from surface
  131 Carbonates of copper from shaft No. 2, near surface; lode about 12in wide
  132 Mundic stone from shaft No. 1, from 8ft to 22ft levels

133 Surface ironstone from main workings on western side of hill ᴅɪɢɢɪɴɢ

134 Surface stone from shafts Nos. 1 and 2, eastern side of hill

YABROL ... ... *The Mystery Gold Mining Company*

140 Quartz from surface to 20ft level, reef running north-east and south-west, dipping north-west and underlaying 2 in 5, average width 2ft

REID'S CREEK *Reid's Creek and Mount Perry Gold Mining Company*

150 Reef from about 250ft in depth
151 Reef from about 220ft in depth
152 Hanging-wall, syenite
153 Foot-wall, granulite

REID'S CREEK ... ... *California Reef*

160 Reef from 50ft level, pyrite and galena-lode, 4ft to 5ft wide

Welcome, Nos. 3, 4, and 5

170 Reef at 70ft level
171 Reef at 130ft level
172 Foot-wall and country rock, granite decomposed and mineralised

The reef runs about east and west, dips north and under-lays about 1 in 6, its average thickness is 18in., the total depth of shaft is 147ft

REID'S CREEK ... ... *Caledonia Mine*

190 Stone from reef at 70ft level
191 Do do 90ft „
192 Do do 117ft „
193 Hanging-wall, diorite
194 Foot-wall and country rock
195 Concentrated mundic
196 Refuse tailings
197 Stone from reef at 130ft level

The reef runs north and south, dips east with an under-luy of 1 in 4, and average thickness of 20in. The total depth sunk, working with whip and horse, is 168ft. The plant consists of a battery of ten head of stamps, one Wheeler-pan, four Berdan-pans, two percussion-tables, and a roasting furnace for concentrated tailings.

REID'S CREEK ... *No 1 and 2 North Manning Gold Mining Company*

200 Reef from surface to 21ft level
201 Do at 26ft
202 Do at 30ft

203 Foot-wall, a soft schistoze decomposite impregnated with
        copper carbonates
204 Country rock, highly pyritous aplite
205 Lode at 50ft level, very rich bornite

The reef runs north and south, dips west, with an underlay of 1 in 6, and has an average thickness of 30in

Kilkivan Field.

Walter Smith's P.C.

221 Cobaltiferous wad (asbolite); samples in the Queensland
        Museum assayed:—

Cobalt ...	...	...	22·207 per cent.
Nickel ...	...	...	3·510	,,
Iron ...	...	...	29·130	,,
Manganese	...	...	2·360	,,
Copper ...	...	...	0·103	,,

222 Cinnabar in limestone
225 Eclogite, polished
226 Country rock at surface
227 Heavy spar
300 Sample of lode, 3ft in width
301   Do   same lode to the north, 5ft wide
302   Do   do   further north, 10ft wide

The lode runs nearly north and south, with a westerly
dip. All the workings are on the surface.

303 From cross lode 8ft wide, running about east and west,
        with a southerly dip

A trial crushing from the large No. 1 south lode is
in preparation.

Kilkivan Amalgamated Gold Mining Company

310 Quartz from 100ft level

BLACK SNAKE ...   . *Kilkivan Gold and Mineral Company*

320 Kaolin occurring in small masses in the cobalt mine
321 Ferruginous quartz, 30ft. from surface. Lode runs north-
        east and south-west, with an underlay of about 1 in 10,
        and a width of about 2ft
322 Cobalt ore (wad, variety asbolite) in matrix from 60ft.
        level ; lode about 30ft wide
323 Cobalt ore
324 Sample of lode 3ft wide, 40ft from surface, carrying
        gold, silver, and copper
325 Sample of lode 5ft wide, 90 feet from surface
326 Sample of lode 4ft wide, carrying gold, silver and copper

Mount Neurum ...   .   *Perseverance Gold Mining Company*
340 Quartz at 60ft, crushing yield 17dwts per ton, average, 2ft
341 Sample of reef at surface
342 Foot-wall at 20ft, quartz
343 Hanging-wall
344 Foot-wall at 60ft, apparently decomposed porphyry

Kaboonga   ...   .   *Kaboonga Mineral Mining Company*
350 Surface stone, copper, carbonates and cuprite
351 Lode at 20ft level, cuprite and carbonates of copper
352 Stone from near surface, rich in gold
353 Lode at 50ft level, carbonates, chalcopyrite, magnetite
354 Lode at 100ft, No. 3 shaft, chalcopyrite, pyrite
355 Lode at 150ft, No. 2 shaft, chalcopyrite, pyrite, magnetite
356 Bismuth ore at 200ft level
357 Lode and foot-wall, from unsettled country
358 Lode and country rock at 150ft, No. 2 shaft
359 Country rock, serpentine

360 Cinnabar   *Queensland Quicksilver Company*
361   Do
362   Do   in limestone
363   Do
364   Do
365   Do   with azurite
366   Do
367   Do   on calcspar
368   Do   with azurite
369   Do   in limestone
370   Do
371   Do   in limestone
372   Do   with azurite
373   Do
374   Do   in limestone

                 Mount Bouple Plumbago Mine, near Maryborough
380 Plumbago
                         —*Exhibitor:* C. S. A. Drain, Esq.

Eidsvold Field.
                                             Mount Craven
400 Sample of reef-quartz from surface to 30ft
401   Do   do   do   30ft to 70ft, showing gold
402 Hanging-wall of reef
403 Foot-wall of reef, chlorite
404 Formation between reef-walls
412 Bulk samples of reef-quartz
         The reef runs north-west and south-east, underlying 1
     in 10 north-east; average width 20in; area 900 ftx 400ft

Maid of Erin Gold Mining Company

420* Quartz from surface to 18ft level

The reef runs north and south, underlying 1 in 8 east; average width 3ft

421* Quartz with bismuth ochre showing free gold, from tunnel reef 40ft on underlay

This reef runs east and west, underlying 1 in 2 south

Omeo Gold Mining Company, Limited

430 Sample of reef, from surface to 55ft

431   Do   do   from 63ft level

432 Foot-wall, hanging-wall, and country rock

The reef is the same as in the Craven P.C.

Mount Rose reef runs about east and west, dipping southerly and underlaying 1 in 6, with an average thickness of 4ft

Tunnel reef runs about north-west and south-east, with an underlay of 1 in 6 to south-west.

No. 3 West Mount Rose Gold Mining Company, Limited

440 Decomposed syenite from lode at 50ft depth

441 Foot and hanging wall

The reef runs north and south, underlying 1 in 12 east; average width, 18in

No. 2 North Craven Gold Mining Company, Limited

450 Sample of reef from 60ft level

451 Foot-wall, hanging-wall, and country rock.

This reef is the same as that of the Craven P.C.; it underlies 1 in 6, with an average width of 15in

Melbourne P.C. Gold Mining Company, Limited

460 Reef at surface

461 Calcspar from lode about 14ft from surface

462 Gossan, immediately beneath No. 461

463 Decomposed hornblende

464 Foot-wall

465 From lode 18ft from surface

The lode in shaft No. 1 runs north-north-west and south-south-east, dipping south-westerly and underlying 1 in 6; average width about 8in. In shaft No. 2 the lode runs north-north-west and south-south-east, dipping south-westerly and underlying 1 in 6; average width about 8in. These lodes are about 18ft apart and parallel. They are intersected by a leader running north and south and carrying coarse gold.

No. 1 South Mountain Maid Gold Mining Company

470 Reef, from surface to 20ft
471 Quartz, from 65ft
472 Foot-wall, hanging-wall, and country rock
This reef is the same as in the Craven P.C., underlying 1 in 5, with an average thickness of 4ft

Lady Alma Gold Mining Company, Limited

480 Sample of reef
The reef at the 86ft level is 6in wide. It is supposed to over-lie the Stockman Reef.

Caledonia Gold Mining Company, Limited

490 Mundic, galena and mispickel from reef at 50ft level
491 Foot-wall and hanging-wall
This also is the Craven P.C. reef; it underlies 1 in 5. The Company's area is 600ft x 400ft
492 Country rock

The Excelsior Gold Mining Company, Limited

400ᴀ Quartz reef at surface
401ᴀ Foot-wall

No. 1 South Craven Gold Mining Company, Limited

410ᴀ Antimony in quartz, from reef at 12ft to 20ft level
411ᴀ Country rock
Same reef under the same conditions as the Craven P.C. The two companies have recently been amalgamated.

No. 1 North Craven Gold Mining Company, Limited

420ᴀ Sample of reef from surface to 27ft
Same reef as Craven P.C.; under similar conditions with an average width of 12in. Depth of shaft 43ft

Thistle Hill P.C., Gold Mining Company, Limited

430ᴀ Quartz from 30ft to 40ft depth

Stockman P.C. Gold Mining Company, Limited

440ᴀ Sample of quartz from surface
441ᴀ Sample of stone from 200ft level
442ᴀ Foot and hanging walls, syenite

No. 4 West Mount Rose Gold Mining Company, Limited

450ᴀ Quartz from reef at 65ft from the surface, yields by crushing 2oz 6dwts per ton.

No. 1 East Mount Rose Gold Mining Company, Limited

459A Quartz from surface
460A Mundic, blende and mispickel in quartz from 35ft level
461A Same as No. 460A from 60ft level
462A Quartz in tunnel supposed to be the Stockman's reef
463A Country rock in connection with tunnel reef
464A Hanging-wall at 60ft level
465A Foot-wall at 60ft level
466A Country rock, Mt. Rose reef
467A Formation on foot-wall

Heights of Alma Gold Mining Company, Limited

470A No. 1 shaft; sample of reef at 94ft level
471A Reef (quartz) at 50ft level
472A Mundic and mispickel in quartz
473A Reef from surface; iron-stained quartz
  This reef runs north-west and south-east, dipping north-east with an underlay of 1 in 2

Lady Augusta Gold Mining Company, Limited—Block Claim on Stockman Reef.

480A Sample of quartz containing mispickel and mundic from reef at 90ft level
481A Foot-wall at 90ft
482A Hanging-wall and country rock at 90ft
  The reef runs north-west and south-east, dipping north-east 1 in 3; its average width is 10in

The Australian P. C. Gold Mining Company, Limited

490A Gossan
491A Chalcedony from reef at 30ft level
492A Country rock at 30ft level
493A Foot and hanging-walls
  The reef runs east-south-east and west-north-west vertical, averaging 3ft in width.   Total depth of shaft 30ft.

Golden Spur Gold Mining Company, Limited

400B Quartz from reef at 86ft level
401B Formation from between walls of reef
402B Hanging-wall and country rock
403B Reef from surface to 50ft in underlay
404B Sample of reef from underlay shaft 500ft east of vertical shaft
405B Country rock of No. 404B
406B Formation passed through in hanging-wall in connection with No. 404B—" Kaolin "
  The reef runs about east and west, dipping southerly with an underlay of 1 in 3, and an average thickness of 2ft

Mount Rose United P. C. Gold Mining Company, Limited

410B Quartz showing gold

411B Hanging-wall

412B Foot-wall

    The reef runs east and west, dips south with an underlay of 1 in 6, and an average thickness of 3ft.

No. 1 North Policeman Gold Mining Company Limited

420B Sample of reef at 70ft. level

    The reef runs north-west and south-east, dipping northerly with an underlay of 1 in 12, and au average thickness of 18in; 4ft. between the walls. The Company's area is 500ft x 400ft.

Golden Crown Gold Mining Company, Limited

430B Quartz from 90ft level

    This reef runs north-north-west and east-north-east, dipping easterly with an underlay of 1 in 18 and an average thickness of 10in. A trial crushing of 4 tons gave 1oz per ton

Camboon P.C. Gold Mining Company, Limited

490B Hornblendic rock; yield by chlorination, 1oz 12dwt

491B Pyritous stone from surface; yield by chlorination, 8dwt

Gympie Field.

Nos. 7 and 8 Monkland

500   Slate from 523ft level on boundary of eastern crosscut

501   Greenstone, 430ft west of east boundary of eastern crosscut

502   Carbonaceous slate, 389ft level

503   Carbonaceous slate, chiefly quartz, off break

504   Fault rock, 424ft level, 150ft south of main shaft, underlying 1 in 1, or 45° to north-east

505   Black rock, 360ft level; in its vicinity 55 tons gave over 1,000oz of gold

506   Calcareous conglomerate, from south side of break and shaft, 360ft level, fossiliferous

507   Black rock and conglomerate in contact, from near reef, 270ft level

508   Black rock, near Glanmire Reef, 250ft level

509   Coarse-boulder conglomerate, from near " plumbago " break or " slip," 190ft level, fossiliferous

510   Carbonaceous slate, 190ft level; in its vicinity very rich gold was obtained

511   Conglomerate with plagioclase felspar in crystals, 523ft level

512   Quartz from lode 2 to 3ft wide, running north 25° west, underlying 1 in 2 west, 270ft level

513   Quartz, 290ft level

514 Auriferous quartz, 523ft level
515 Fluted chlorite ; in its vicinity heavy gold has been obtained

No. 1 North Great Eastern

520 Carbonaceous limestone, calcareous shale with fossils (spirifera spp), from surface to 160ft
521 Boulder conglomerate from 160ft to 235ft
522 Black slate from a bed 2ft thick, 235ft to 237ft
523 Auriferous quartz with mundic, lode 10in thick, strike north by east, dip westerly, underlay 1 in 3½
524 Boulder conglomerate, altered, 270ft
525 Carbonaceous shale from a bed at 270ft level
526 Limestone and quartz conglomerate, 2ft thick, at about 150ft from surface
527 Mudstone, an altered sediment from bottom of shaft at 275ft, supposed to overlie greenstone

Mr. Rands states that the shaft in this, the most easterly claim on the field, is being sunk to cut the upper or Monkland slates. The claim has been at work for six months with an 18 h.p. nominal engine.

South Ellen Harkins and Wilmot

530 Greenrock from surface to 100ft
531 Conglomerate with purple specks
532 Altered sedimentary rock
533 Purple shale
534 Altered conglomerate
535 Quartz from reef 2ft wide, 518ft level
536 Black rock, 581ft
537 Quartz from reef 8in wide, 625ft level
538 Pyritous black rock or third bed of slate at 629ft
539 Pyritous flinty rock, altered sediment, usually of **great** thickness, at 710ft
540 Spotted conglomerate, 724ft
541 Pyritous conglomerate, occasionally porphyritic

"This claim is situated in the southern portion **of the** field, to the west. The workings are in the lowest **auriferous** beds on the field—i.e., on the same horizon as those in **the** Ellen Harkins, the lowest beds in the Wilmot Extended **and** Golden Crown claims and in the London Two-mile."—**Rands**.

Columbia Smithfield

545   Quartz, 280ft level
545A Fossiliferous slate, 280ft level, aviculopecten sp.
546   Reef at 330ft level
547   Slate   do
548   Do   350ft do

549 Sample from large cross-course, 55ft thick, dipping north, with an underlay of 3 in 4

550 Country rock near cross-course, altered conglomerate

"Situated near the South Ellen Harkins and Wilmot, in the central portion of the field. A large fault with a down throw of 880ft to the north runs east 20° north through the claim."—*Rands*.

Ellen Harkins

551 Greenstone, about 200ft thick

552 Slate or "black rock," 580ft level; near a heavy find of gold

553 Pyritous slate, 800ft level

554 Purple conglomerate, 840ft level

555 Altered sediment, occurring at various levels; samples from 800ft

556 Spotted conglomerate, 826ft level

557 Altered sediment, coarsely mineralised, occurring rarely between spotted and purple conglomerates

558 Quartz from 500ft level

"The workings are in the lowest known auriferous rocks, called the third bed of slate"—*Rands*.

No. 3 North Phœnix

560 Fossiliferous sediment, altered and mineralised, overlying slate at 500ft level

561 Boulder conglomerate, an altered breccia; from 590ft level

562 Gold-bearing rock from 590ft level

563 Gold-bearing quartz from 590ft level

564 Greenstone, 680ft level

565 Gold-bearing rock over 590ft level in stopes

566 Gold-bearing quartz over 590ft level in stopes

567 Fossiliferous slate from 500ft level

"This claim is situated in the middle portion of the field; the workings are in the upper slate beds."—*Rands*.

568 Auriferous quartz from Phœnix, No 1 North Phœnix, Nos. 2 and 3 South Smithfield, Ellen Harkins, and Nos. 3 and 4 North Glanmire

Golden Crown

570 Black slate on March reef, 875ft level

571 Purple conglomerate overlying black slate, 830ft level

572 Altered sediment, probably same as No. 539, alternating with shales, 830ft level

573 Greenstone, about 300ft thick in shaft, considered to be an intrusive sheet

574 Green conglomerate, an altered sediment overlying green-stone

575 Pyritous slate from 240ft level, adjacent to heavy deposits of gold, occasionally fossiliferous (Productus, &c.)

c

576   Calcareous sediment at 240ft level, underlying first bed of slate
577   Auriferous quartz from 830ft level
578   Barren quartz
579   Aviculopecten multiradiatus in black slate at 240ft level
580   Chloritic sediment with gold-bearing quartz, Phœnix reef at 540ft level
581   Boulders from auriferous deposit lying on foot-wall of reef
582   Calcareous sediment in vicinity of gold, Phœnix reef at 460ft level
583   Calcareous chlorite with gold-bearing mundic, averaging 25 dwt. per ton

" This claim is being worked from two shafts, the eastern shaft works the upper or Phœnix beds of slate, the highest in the series of the auriferous beds on Gympie. The western shaft passed through three lower beds known as the first, second, and third beds. The third bed, from which specimens have been taken, is the same as that in the Ellen Harkins, and is the lowest in the field."—*Rands.*

South Phœnix

585   Greenstone, overlying slate, 400ft level
586   Black slate, carbon faced, 450ft level
587   Calcareous clay sediment overlying black rock at 500ft
588   Black rock at 525ft level
589   Coarse conglomerate, 600ft to 800ft
590   Quartz and calcspar forming a barren portion of the reef at 900ft level
591   Purple rock from 900ft to 950ft
592   Sample from large cross-course or fault rock running easterly and westerly and dipping north

No. 1 North Glanmire

600   Quartz from 580ft level, Great Eastern Reef, 30ft below gold-bearing country, averages 3ft in thickness
601   Foot-wall side of reef
602   Calcspar on side of reef
603   Calcareous formation between walls of reef
604   Black slate, 420ft level. gold bearing, Great Eastern Reef
605   Quartz, within 10ft of heavy gold, 560ft level
606   Slate from between walls of No. 5 reef, showing gold freely on partings, 420ft level

" This claim is working the Monkland or upper slates."—*Rands.*

London Two Mile

610   Surface stone near reef
611   Stone close to and underlying No. 610
612   Altered sandstone, underlying No. 611, close to reef
613   Slate from wall of reef at about 60ft

614 Porphyritic formation from between walls of reef
615 Reef from about 60ft, dipping 1 in 1, about 45° west, running approximately north and south
616 Carbonaceous shale from reef on foot-wall
617 Grey conglomerate, at about 130ft, near reef

From shaft 200ft west of underlie shaft

618 Altered breccia from near reef and slate
619 Surface sandstone to about 50ft level
620 Sandstone, underlying No. 619, mineralised
621 Spotted conglomerate at 90ft level
622 Altered sandstone, 100ft level
623 Altered sediment, 130ft level
624 Altered rock, 210ft level
625 Black conglomerate and black rock, 211ft
626 Pyritous rock from bottom of shaft, 220ft line
627 Surface country rock

From deep shaft assisted by Government grant

628 First bed of slate at 150ft level, has yielded very rich gold
629 Auriferous quartz from 150ft level, reef running approximately north and south, dipping west 1 in 10, known as the London reef
630 Calcite and quartz over second bed of slate
631 Second bed of slate at 690ft level, about 40ft thick
632 Barren quartz in slate from very unsettled country at 692ft level
633 Altered sediment under third bed of slate at bottom of shaft, 736ft
634 Formation sometimes auriferous at 140ft
"The London is working beds of shale which are on the same horizon as the second and third beds on Gympie proper, the lower bed being identical with that worked at the Ellen Harkins."—*Rands.*

Milton Extended

640 Black rock on hanging-wall side of reef, 100ft level
641 Quartz from Hamburg reef
642 Second bed of slate at 282ft level, gold-bearing, 80ft east of shaft, formation about 2ft wide
643 Quartz from Hamburg reef at 282ft level, formation 7ft wide
644 Quartz from hanging-wall side of reef
645 Green rock (altered sediment) from foot-wall of Hamburg reef
646 Green conglomerate, carbon-faced, from eastern crosscut, 170ft from shaft
647 Green conglomerate, eastern crosscut, overlying No. 645
648 A much-altered sediment met in sinking at 215ft, in a bed 5ft thick

649   Rock immediately below slate at 282ft level
      "This claim is near the centre of the field, and is work-
ing the first and second beds of slate."—*Rands.*

Great Monkland

Collection of strata formed by the present manager during
                his charge of the sinking.

650   Sinking at 1025ft
651   Do   1030ft
652   Do   1046ft
653   Do   1048ft
653*   Do   1057ft
654   Do   1122ft
655   Do   1148ft
656   Do   1162ft
657   Do   1200ft
658   Do   1210ft
659   Fossil in third bed of slate
660   Calcite at 1272ft
661   Rock at bottom of shaft
      "This claim is the deepest (1276ft) on the field; it re-
ceives the grant from the Government deep-sinking fund."—
Rands.
670   100 bags of gold-bearing quartz from No. 1 North Phœnix,
      No. 3 North Glanmire Nicholls' Lease, North Glan-
      mire, and No. 1 North Glanmire

No. 1 North Phœnix Gold Mining Company

680   Gold specimens
681   Model of the mine, showing workings and country passed
      through
                    —*Exhibitors :* THE COMPANY.

Glastonbury Field.

Without a Friend

700   Country rock from Burgess reef
701   Sandstone bar from Burgess reef
702   Quartz from Burgess reef.   The reef runs north-west and
      south-east, dipping south-west about 1 in 4, with an
      average thickness of 1ft
703   Surface quartz, western reef, average width 6in, crushed
      4¼oz per ton
704   Gold-bearing quartz at 57ft
705   Country rock near reef at 57ft on underlay

Great Western Amalgamated

710   Surface quartz from reef 2ft wide; reef running north-west
      and south-east, with underlay 2 in 5 to the south-west

711 Surface slate
712 Gold-bearing quartz
713 Slate from tunnel at 80ft level
714 Soft dyke cutting reef
715 Gold-bearing leader from tunnel, containing arsenical
      pyrites

Great Tasman

720 Surface quartz, reef running north-west and south-east,
      dipping south-west about 48° or 1 in 1, 20in wide, and
      crushing 8dwts
721 Foot-wall of reef on underlay at 50ft
722 Hanging-wall of reef at 50ft on underlay; the reef is sup-
      posed to be the Western reef
723 Quartz showing gold from tunnel near surface; reef very
      flat; trial crushing 10½dwts
724 Foot-wall of Tasman reef
725 Hanging-wall of Tasman reef
726 Country rock strongly impregnated with manganite

Doran's Claim

730 Gold-bearing quartz, from reef bearing north-west and
      south-east, dipping south-west, underlying 1 in 3,
      averaging 9in in width, and crushing 1oz per ton
731 Foot-wall, sometimes carrying gold
732 Hanging-wall and reef with hanging-wall attached, from
      24ft level

Dryfesdale

735 Pyrolusite
      On the land of Mr. Armstrong, 7 miles west of Gympie

STANTHORPE DISTRICT.

Mineral Exhibit of Stanthorpe Local Committee, London, 1886.

1000 Alluvial tin washdirt
1001 Quartz crystal
1002 Plumbago, 18 miles from Stanthorpe
1003 Plumbago
1004 Tinstone pebbles
1005 Tinstone crystals with quartz, from Mole Tableland
1006 Lode tin, Severn River
1007 Quartz and tinstone from Johnson's new discovery
1008 Tinstone in quartz, Pikedale, 20 miles from Stanthorpe
1009 Auriferous mundic and galena, Pikedale
1010 Country rock, Pikedale
1011 Tinstone with quartz and mica, from the Noble Tin
      Mining Company
1012 Country rock, Lode Creek

1013 Lode tin, Mount Marley
1014 Tinstone with mica
1015   Do   do and quartz
1016   Do   in quartz

Railway Cutting, Stanthorpe Extension

1017 Orthoclase and smoky quartz
1018   Do   do
1019 Smoky quartz

SPRING CREEK ...   . *Slattery Bros' Claim*
    1020 Wash dirt
    1021 Stream tim

—*Exhibitor :* J. C. SLATTERY, ESQ.

CANNON CREEK ... . *Slattery Bros' Claim*
    1022 Wash dirt
    1023 Stream tin

—*Exhibitor :* J. C. SLATTERY, ESQ.

SPRING CREEK ...   . *Sim's Claim*
    1024 Wash dirt
    1025 Stream tin

—*Exhibitor :* J. C. SLATTERY, ESQ.

QUART-POT CREEK ...   . *Hannigan Claim*
    1026 Stream tin

—*Exhibitor :* J. C. SLATTERY, ESQ.

SEVERN RIVER ...   . *Ballandean*
    1027 Stream tin

—*Exhibitor :* F. H. FLETCHER, ESQ.

QUART-POT CREEK ...   . *Miller's Grand Junction Claim*
    1028 Stream tin

—*Exhibitor :* J. C. SLATTERY, ESQ.

SPRING CREEK ...   . *Corrigan's Claim*
    1029 Stream tin

—*Exhibitor :* J. C. SLATTERY, ESQ.

PIKEDALE, *12 miles from Stunthorpe, known as Thirteen-Mile Pikedale*
    1030 Stream tin

—*Exhibitor :* J. C. SLATTERY, ESQ.

Wesley Tin Mining Company, Limited

    1040 Lode tin
    1041 Mundic in quartz

1042 Mica
1043 Country rock

—Exhibitor : THE COMPANY

Welsby's Mine

1044 Rocks in connection with lode

—Exhibitor : J. C. SLATTERY, ESQ.

LODE CREEK ... ... *The Noble Tin Mining Company's Claim*

1045 Tinstone in micaceous rock

—Exhibitor : THE COMPANY

Mount Marley Tin Mining Company

1046 Wolfram in quartz
1047 Tinstone in micaceous rock

—Exhibitor : J. C. SLATTERY, ESQ.

LODE CREEK ... ... *Herding Yard Creek, and Ruby Creek*

1048 Lode tin

Accommodation Creek Railway Cutting

1049 Orthoclase felspar

SPRING CREEK.

1050 Granite and pebbles from tin wash
1051 Quartz crystals ᵇʰ:ᵖᵒᵗ
1052 Quartz and topaz pebbles found associated with tinstone

New Borrowdale Graphite Mine

1058 Graphite
1059 Carbonaceous sandstone
1060 Fireclay

River Tree Silver Company

1061 Stibnite
1062 Silver ore

River Tree P.C.

1063 Silver ore

Silvery Wave

1064 Silver ore

—Exhibitors : MESSRS. ARCHIBALD & HORTON

RIVER TREE ... ... *Mount Fox*

1065 Silver ore

WYLIE CREEK.

1066 Stream tin

GLEN APLIN ... ... *Aplin's Tin Mine*

1070 24 samples of wash-dirt

—Exhibitor : MRS. DYSON

Ballandean

1071   Silver ore (mispickel, with a little galena)
1072   Mispickel, blende and pyrite

—*Exhibitors :* Messrs. F. H. FLETCHER & Co.

JIBBENBAR   ...   .   *Border Chief Silver Mining Company*

1074   Silver ore

—*Exhibitors :* Messrs. F. H. FLETCHER & Co.

JIBBENBAR ...   .   *Jibbenbar Silver Mining Company*

1075   Mispickel in quartz (argentiferous)
1076   Blende in quartz
1077   Blende and mispickel in quartz
1078   Country rock

—*Exhibitors :* THE COMPANY

PIKE'S CREEK   ...   .   { *Jibbenbar Silver Mining Company,*
{ *J. D. Steele, proprietor*

1080   Silver ore at 4ft, from first discovered part of reef
1081   Do   do   8ft
1082   Do   do   12ft
1083   Hanging-wall
1084   Foot-wall

—*Exhibitor :* A. BARTON, ESQ.

KETTLE SWAMP CREEK   ...   .   { *Mineral   Selection* 683,
{ *P. Scully, proprietor*

1085   Various samples of lode tin
Reef runs north-east by north, nearly perpendicular, as
shown in a small cross-cut 4ft deep.   It is situated a mile
from the railway station on a good road ; an unfailing supply
of water is at hand.

—*Exhibitor :* A. BARTON, ESQ.

WARWICK DISTRICT.

THANE'S CREEK ...   .   *Hidden Treasure Reef*

1302   Quartz from 17ft level, with galena and blende
1303   Country rock, grey slate
The reef runs north and south, dips east, and underlays 1
in 16 ; average width, 8in

Gladstone Reef

1304   Quartz from surface to 60ft level showing gold
1305   Do   40ft
1306   Country rock ; wall the same
This reef runs east and west, dips north and underlays 1
in 8 ; it has an average thickness of 9in on surface, 2ft at
60ft level, and 1ft in western shaft

Lone Star

1307 Reef from surface to 10ft
 The reef runs east and west, dips north and underlays 1 in 3; average width, 9in
1307* Manganese ore

Queen Gold Mining Company, Limited

1308 Quartz from surface
1309   Do   120ft level
1310 Hanging-wall, black slate
1811 Foot-wall, schist
 The reef runs north and south, dips north, and is nearly vertical; it has an average width of 15in, and a crushing average of 1oz 1dwt per ton

Providence P.C.

1312 Quartz with galena from reef on surface
1313 Quartz at 20ft, shewing blende and mundic
1314 Country rock
 The reef runs north and south, dips west and underlays 1 in 10; average width about 1 foot

Just-in-Time Reef

1315 Quartz from 30ft level
1316 Country rock, slate
 The reef runs north and south, dips west and underlays about 1 in 2; average width 18 in

TALGAI FIELD   ... *Prince of Wales Gold Mining Company, Limited*

1324 Quartz showing gold from 31ft level
1325 Country rock
 The reef runs north-east and south-west vertically; its average width nearly 3ft; crushings have yielded as high as 12oz per ton

Washpool Reef

1326 Quartz from 55ft level
1327 Country rock on foot-wall
 The reef runs east and west, dips south, underlays 1 in 10, and has an average thickness of 2 feet

Malakoff Gold Mining Company, Limited

1328 Quartz at surface
1329 Quartz at 130ft level
1330 Hanging-wall and foot-wall, black slate
1331 Grey slate from surface

Monte Christo Extended Gold Mining Company, Limited

1332 Quartz from surface to 10ft
 The reef runs east and west, dips south, with an underlay of 1 in 1

Monte Christo Gold Mining Company, Limited

1333 Quartz from 100ft level, east shaft
1334 Quartz from 40ft level, west shaft
1335 Country rock
    The reef runs east and west, dipping south, with an
underlay of 1 in 1, and an average width of 1ft

Queenslander Gold Mining Company, Limited

1336 Quartz from reef of old shaft east of claim
    The reef runs east and west nearly vertically

Big Hill Extended Gold Mining Company, Limited

1337 Quartz from tunnel about 150ft from surface
1338 Quartz with manganese from lode about 3in wide
1339 Red iron oxide from large deposit in tunnel
1340 Formation from tunnel
    The reef runs north-west and south-east, dips north nearly
vertically; total length of tunnel, 564ft

New-Chum Reef

1341 Stone from very large reef in tunnel

Tailor's Reef Gold Mining Company, Limited

1343 Quartz from 22ft level
1344 Country rock, trap
    This reef runs north and south, dips east, and underlays
1 in 1; average width 18in

CANAL CREEK FIELD.

1346 Manganese and limonite
1347 Pyrolusite, massive
1348 Tinstone

—Exhibitor : C. HAYES, ESQ.

MORETON DISTRICT.

MOGGILL CREEK   ...   . *Brookfield*

2700 Manganese ore, said to contain silver
2701 Bar of metal smelted from the above, said to contain
    silver

—Exhibitor : MRS. PACEY

NORTH PINE   ...   . *Lacey's Creek*

2702 Mundic from new rush, prospector's samples, said to carry
    2oz. of gold per ton
2703 Mundic and black slate

—Exhibitors : TRUSTEES OF QUEENSLAND MUSEUM

ENOGGERA ... ... *Mount Pleasant*

    2705 Quartz with mundic

                   —*Exhibitor :* C. BOUEL, ESQ.

ENOGGERA ... ... *Mountain Camp*

    2706 Quartz with mundic and galena

                   —*Exhibitor :* C. BOUEL, ESQ.

IPSWICH.

    2720 Serpentinous country rock
    2721 Country rock
    2722 Chromite

This chromite is found seven miles to the west of Ipswich. Mr. Williams, of Melbourne, kindly furnishes the following report. The serpentine has a strike north-west and south-east, with an underlie to west :—" The chromite is found in pockets in the serpentine, no distinct vein having been yet discovered. These pockets may be the result of the de-grading of the serpentine ; the chromite, from a vein or lode from a higher level of the hill, having also degraded and lodged in the irregularities of the rock at a lower level."

                   —*Exhibitor :* JOHN KNOX, ESQ.

    2723 Chromite

                 —*Exhibitor :* JOHN HARRIS, ESQ.

    2724 Chromite

                 —*Exhibitor :* C. F. CHUBB, ESQ.

EAST-CENTRAL DIVISION.*

RAVENSWOOD DISTRICT AND FIELD.

Ravenswood Gold Mining and Ore Concentrating Works

    4000 Hand-picked gold-bearing mundic
    4001   Do   do   blende

                                         Hector

    4002 Hanging-wall, 85ft level
    4003 " Horse " in reef, 30ft from surface
    4004   Do   do   50ft   do
    4005 Gold-bearing mundic in lode, formation above water level

---

* From 25¼ to 20½ S. lat., and from seaboard to 146 E. long.

4006 Gold-bearing mundic and blende in lode, formation below water level
4007 Gold-bearing blende and mundic
4008 Do do do in quartz
4009 Do blende, mundic, and chalcopyrite; assays, 29oz 18dwts per ton
4010 Calcspar-vein on hanging-wall from 85ft level
4011 Pyrite and quartz-crystals in drusy cavity at 85ft level
4012 Specimen from drusy cavity
4013 Bulk sample of ore; the lode 15in wide
4014 Country rock

London Claim

4015 Pyrite crystals, gold-bearing
4016 Pyrite, gold-bearing, in quartz
4017 Decomposing mundic and chalcopyrite, gold-bearing

Currency Lass

4018 Pyrite, blende, chalcopyrite and galena, gold-bearing
4019 Stibnite, from surface outcrop, 7 miles east of township

Buck Claim

4020 Malachite and black oxide of copper
4021 Blende, pyrite, and mispickel in quartz, gold-bearing

Angleterra Claim

4022 Chalcopyrite and mundic in quartz, gold-bearing
4023 Do do felspathic quartz, gold-bearing
    The claim is on the Buck line of reef, the samples assay 2oz per ton

Ravenswood Gold Smelting Company

4024 Limestone quarried near the township
4025 Same showing dendritic markings of pyrolusite
4026 Ironstone, Mount Right
4027 Do do
4028 Do Ravenswood
4029 Do quarried by company
⎱ Lime and iron-stone used in mundic smelting
4030 Copper matte as produced in original process
4031 Matte, by-product of present process, containing by assay gold, 2½oz; silver, 50oz per ton; copper, 4 per cent
4032 Slag from present process
4033 Matte
4034 Coating adherent to furnace below the water-jacket

SANDY CREEK ... ... *Politician Claim*

4035 Galena and mundic
4036 Do do in quartz
4037 Galena, mundic, and chalcopyrite with quartz, and chalcopyrite with quartz and steatite

4038 Galena, mundic, and chalcopyrite from centre of lode at 100ft level; lode from 2ft to 3ft thick
4038ᴀ Sample from centre of mine, 333ft level
4038ʙ Sample of stone or quartz Do do
4038ᴄ Do   do   275ft do
4038ᴅ Surface stone
4038ᴇ Formation within walls, 350ft level
4038* Stone or quartz
4038** Country rock
4038*** Ore at various depths

     —*Exhibitors :* Messrs. DONALD BROTHERS

          Satisfaction Claim

4039 Brown hæmatite, 12ft from surface
4040 Red hæmatite, surface
   These hæmatites are raised for smelting purposes

           Kay's Claim

4041* Silver-bearing galena, 13ft from surface

        Markham's Silver Lease

4041* Silver-bearing galena from 120ft level; value £22 per ton
4041** Country rock
4042 Calcspar

          New England

4043 Country rock
4044 Mispickel, blende, pyrite, quartz and steatite, gold-bearing
4045 Chalcopyrite, blende and mispickel, with quartz crystals
4046 Do   do   do in minute crystals, with crystals of quartz

          Outsider No. 2

4047 Fine-grained pyrite in quartz
4048 Do   do with adherent country rock
4049 Do   do gold-bearing
   The shaft on this claim has been sunk 50ft

          Wild Irish Girl

4050 Country rock
4051 Mundic and mispickel in felspathic quartz matrix
4052 Do mispickel, and blende in quartz
4053 Do in felspathic quartz
   The ores are gold-bearing but intractable

          Black Jack

4054 Hanging-wall
4055 Iron-stained quartz from 20ft level, containing 3oz free gold per ton
4056 Mundic and chalcopyrite, decomposing
4057 Blende, pyrite and chalcopyrite in quartz, 50ft level

4058   Pyrite and chalcopyrite from centre of lode, very rich
4059   Chalcopyrite, " peacock ore," very rich
4060   Pyrite and chalcopyrite, very rich
4061   Blende and chalcopyrite
4062   " Horse " in lode at 25ft from surface
4063   Same " horse " at 200ft, carrying mundic
4064   Country rock
4065   Marcasite, chalcopyrite, blende and galena from lode

Mr. D. McRea's Claim, Concentrated Gold Ores

4065*   Jigged ore, Black Jack
4065**   From tyes, Melaneur Junction
4065*** Handpick blende, Hector
4065**** Finest jigged ore, Hector

London No. 2

4066   Gold-bearing mundic and chalcopyrite in quartz and
          brown hæmatite

New England Mundic Company, Limited

4066*   Gold-bearing mundic

Hannan's Lease

4067   Gold-bearing pyrite and blende
4068   Gold-bearing pyrite and blende with steatite

Ravenswood Great Extended

4069   Argentiferous galena in felspathic quartz
4070   Argentiferous galena, pyrite and blende in layers alternat-
          ing with country rock
4071   Mundic and blende
4072   Country rock

Ravenswood Silver Mining Company, Limited

4073   Country rock
4074   Surface blow of lode
4075   Galena and mundic in calcite and quartz from foot-wall
4076   Mundic and galena from centre of lode.
4077   Mundic, galena, and quartz crystals
4078   Mundic, chalcopyrite, and blende, with calcspar
4079   Argentiferous galena, surface outcrop.   The lode is
          parallel to the main reef
4080   Galena and carbonates of lead, iron, &c., assays 350oz to
          400oz silver and 4oz gold per ton
4081   Cerussite and decomposing galena, 180oz to 300oz per
          ton
4081*   Argentiferous galena, assaying 66¼% lead, 150oz 8dwts
          16grs silver per ton

—Exhibitors: THE COMPANY

General Grant

4082 Mispickel in quartz, with mundic and chalcopyrite, from 400ft underlie shaft, at about 300ft vertical
4083 Chalcopyrite and blende
4084 Quartz reef crossing lode nearly at right angles
4085 Country rock

Sunset Claim

4086 Mundic and mispickel
4087 Mispickel and chalcopyrite
4088 Chalcopyrite
4089 Chalcopyrite and blende on calcspar
4090 Calcite, foot-wall
4091 Country rock

Jackson's Lease

4092 Ferruginous silver-lead ore, carrying about 5dwt. gold per ton

General Gordon

4093 Argentiferous galena (silver-lead)

Hornung's Lease

4094 Argentiferous galena from main shaft, 70ft from surface

Trieste

4095 Argentiferous galena, decomposed
4096   Do   do   assays over 100oz. silver per ton

Ellen Ross

4097 Galena and chalcopyrite from 80ft level; yields by crushing 4oz. gold per ton

Pyramid Lease

4098 By analysis—

	Per cent.
Zinc	34·23
Lead	42·01
Sulphur	22·80
Iron	1·11
	100·15

—*A. W. Clarke.*

Birthday Gift

4099 Galena, blende, chalcopyrite from 4ft beneath surface; assays 113oz. silver per ton

Bonnie Dundee

4100 Galena and blende, assaying 100oz. silver per ton

Australia Felix

4101   Mundic in quartz from 100ft level, assays 7oz. gold per ton

4102   Mundic and mispickel, assays 18oz. to 20oz. gold per ton

Sellheim River

4103   Fine-grained galena, assays nearly 200oz. silver per ton

4104   Blende, mundic, chalcopyrite, and galena

Outsider No. 1 North

4105   Hanging-wall impregnated with mundic

4106   Gold-bearing mundic from lode formation, assays 9oz gold per ton

4107   Sample from centre of lode, carrying gold and silver with pyrites

4108   Country rock

BOWEN   ...   .   *Happy Valley*

4109   Marcasite in quartz

4110   Magnetic iron ore

—*Exhibitor :* REV. W. F. TUCKER

Comstock Silver Mine

4110*   Argentiferous galena, containing lead 73·5 per cent; silver, 81¾oz per ton, bulk sample

4111   Argentiferous galena, decomposing, containing lead, 33 per cent; silver, 66½oz per ton

4112   Argentiferous ochre, containing 14¼ per cent lead; 19oz 12dwts silver; and 1oz 13dwts gold per ton

—*Exhibitor :* MR. W. R. KING

This claim is 4 miles east of Ravenswood

Saratoga Gold Mining Company, Limited

4120   Refractory mundic ore with blende

—*Exhibitor :* THE COMPANY *per* F. B. WISE

Australia Felix

4130   Quartz showing galena, mundic, and blende; yielding 4oz gold per ton, value £3 5s per oz

4131   Buddlings

—*Exhibitor :* STEPHEN JOHNSON

Fanny Fern

4140   Mundic ore with galena ; yielding 6oz gold per ton

—*Exhibitor :* DR. CUTHBERT

New England Mine

4150 Refractory mundic at 80ft level; assays 10oz gold per ton

—*Exhibitor :* MR. JAMES WILSON

MOUNT WRIGHT ... ... *Moonlight Lease*

4170 Galena, assaying 100oz per ton

—*Exhibitor :* MR. P. MARKHAM

Ravenswood Silver Mining Company

4180 Galena containing 58 per cent lead, 274oz 8dwts silver per ton

4181 Galena containing 75 per cent lead, 169¾oz silver per ton

4182 Galena containing 65 per cent lead, 259oz 3dwt 8grs silver per ton

—*Exhibitor :* THE COMPANY *per* MR. E. J. KING, *Manager*

Ravenswood Gold Company, Black Jack Mine

4190 Refractory mundic and chalcopyrite

—*Exhibitor :* THE COMPANY

SANDY CREEK, 3 miles west of Ravenswood ... { *John Bull Gold Mining Company, Ltd, John Bull Block Mine.*

4200 Auriferous sulphides in quartz

—*Exhibitor :* MR S. F. TRENFIELD

4201 Free auriferous quartz in bulk, 170ft level
4202   Do   do   do

—*Exhibitor :* MR. F. H. WILKINS, *Sec.*

CHARTERS TOWERS DISTRICT AND FIELD.

Eastward Ho

6000 Country rock
6000A Foot-wall showing mundic from 520ft level
6001 Foot-wall showing mundic from 600ft level
6002 Country rock at 520ft
6002* Auriferous quartz from 600ft level
6003   Do   do   with crystals of pyrite
6004   Do   do   with pyrite and galena from 520ft level

Queen's Lease, No. 2, S.W.

6005 Country rock from 370ft level
6006 Mundic and galena in quartz, auriferous
6007 Auriferous galena and mundic, from 250ft level

D

6008   Auriferous galena and mundic, from 250ft level
6009   Do   do   do   370ft level
6010   Dyke traversing reef, which is from 6in to 2ft wide

Alexandra Hill Gold Mining Company

6011   Blende, mundic and chalcopyrite in quartz, from 300ft level
6012   Mundic with mispickel in quartz, from 300ft level
6013   Do   do   510ft level
6014   Galena and chalcopyrite from centre of lode at 320ft level
6015   Mundic and galena in quartz
6016   Galena and mundic
6017   Galena and mundic, from 320ft level
6018   Auriferous quartz, from 420ft level, carrying 3oz 2dwts
       per ton

Mount Devonport, Lower Cape River

6019   Auriferous mica slates
6020   Auriferous mica slates

Upper Cape River

6021   Country rock, auriferous

Queen Lease, No 6, N.E.

6021* Mundic and galena in quartz at 300ft level
6022   Do   do
6023   Finegrained pyrite on coarse galena and pyrite; the fine-
       grained pyrite carrying more gold than the coarser
6024   Pyrite in quartz at the northern level, 300ft

BONNIE DUNDEE   ...   ...   *Bonnie Dundee Gold Mining Company*

6025   Mundic, blende and galena in quartz with steatite
6026   Do   do   do
6027   Pyrite and galena in quartz, 200ft level
6028   Country rock

Day Dawn P.C.

6029   Galena and mundic from 600ft level, carrying 2oz gold
       per ton
6030   Country rock
6031   Galena and mundic from 520ft level
6032   Galena and mundic in quartz
6033   Chalcopyrite in quartz

Day Dawn Block

6034   Hanging-wall, 700ft level
6034* Galena and mundic in quartz
6035   Formation with attached foot-wall, from 740ft level
6036   Auriferous galena and mundic
6037   Foot-wall at 700ft level

Bryan O'Lynn

6038   Granite, with scales of mundic, assaying 1¾ to 2dwt per ton

Continong, on the Burdekin River, 80 miles from Charters Towers

6039   Filigree gold in coppery quartz

Sunburst P.O.

6040   Auriferous mundic
6041   Blende, galena and mundic in quartz from 130ft level
6042   Do   do   do   do   190ft level

Sunburst

6043   Country rock at 130ft level
6044   Mundic in foot-wall
6041* Dyke crossing lode

North Australian-Mosman Gold Mining Company

6042* Auriferous mundic and galena in quartz from 600ft level
6043*   Do   do   do   do   do
6044*   Do   do   do   do   500ft level
6045   Do   do   do   do   480ft level
6046   Country rock at 400ft level
6047   Lode formation with barren mundic
6048   Dyke crossing reef

Old Identity

6049   Mundic, auriferous, from 450ft level
6050   Do   do
6051   Country rock

Black Jack, Broughton

6052   Auriferous blende and mundic in quartz

Occidental, Cape River

6054   Auriferous mundic in quartz, carrying 2ozs gold per ton
6055   Auriferous calcite, carrying about 2dwts per ton

Tunnel Claim, Upper Cape River

6056   Dyke running north-east and south-west, carrying 4dwts gold per ton.

Broughton Consolidated

6057   Auriferous mundic and galena in quartz

Mount Leyshon

6058   Auriferous ironstone
6059   Do   do

Mount Leyshon is the culminating point of the Pyramid Range. The ironstone had probably a similar origin to that of Mount Morgan

—*Exhibitor :* A. G. CHARLTON, ESQ.

Disraeli Syndicate

6060   Formation
6061   Mundic and galena in quartz
6061*   Do   do   do   lower level

Hope Gold Mining Company, Limited, Hope Mine

		Lode.	Mine.	Depth.
6064	Vein quartz	Lady Maria ...	Lady Maria Coy. ...	200ft
6065	Do		Sons of Freedom ...	100ft
6066	Do	Newton Butler	Newton Butler P.C.	50ft
6067	Do	Identity ...	Hit or Miss ...	100ft

—*Exhibitors:* THE COMPANY

Caledonia P.C. Gold Mining Company, Limited

6070   Mundic and galena in quartz at a depth of 185ft; average
       width of reef, 1ft. The last crushing of 70 tons yielded
       4oz 10dwts smelted gold per ton
       The mine is at present let on tribute, and pays well; area,
       12¾ acres

Black Jack Gold Mining Company, Limited

6080   Mundic, with blende and galena in quartz; from the south
       level, at a depth of 300ft from surface; average width
       of reef, 22in; total depth of shaft, 450ft; area of
       ground, 20 acres. £20,625 has been paid in
       dividends since the formation of the Company in 1885

Black Jack Block Gold Mining Company, Limited

6081   Auriferous mundic with blende and galena, from No. 2 level
       south, at a depth of 581ft; average width of reef, 1ft;
       the depth is 491ft vertical, 90ft on the underlie

Day Dawn No. 3 West Gold Mining Company

6090   Auriferous mundic and galena in quartz, at a depth of
       550ft; average width of reef, 24in; depth of shaft,
       600ft. Since September, 1887, £7500 has been paid in
       dividends. A crushing of 300 tons is going through the
       mill, which will yield 4oz and 5oz. per ton

Lubra Gold Mining Company, Limited

7000   Auriferous mundic, with galena and blende at a depth of
       455ft; width of reef, 18in to 24in. The Company's
       ground adjoins the Black Jack P.C. on the south

Swedenborg P.C. Gold Mining Company, Limited

7010   Auriferous mundic, chalcopyrite, galena, and blende, in
       quartz from bottom of underlie shaft at a depth of
       336ft; average width of reef, 18in; supposed yield at

ordinary crushing mill, 5ozs per ton. The present
Company have had no crushing, but the shallow ground
worked by former parties yielded as high as 6ozs per
ton. The reef runs north-west and south-east, and
dips easterly

Great Britain Gold Mining Company, Limited

7020 Auriferous mundic from 227ft level; average yield last
two crushings, 2½ozs per ton; average width of reef,
4ft 6in

St. George, Queen and Victory Grand Junction Gold Mining Company, Limited

7030 Auriferous mundic from 500ft level; width of reef (just
opened out), 24in

Towers Extended P.C. Gold Mining Company, Limited

7040 Sample of stone from a depth of 65ft; average width of
reef, 5ft

Iron Duke Gold Mining Company, Limited

7050 Auriferous mundic at a depth of 200ft; average width of
reef, 15in; depth of shaft, 440ft, with a reef averaging
14in of good quality stone. £1800 has been paid in
dividends by the present Company; area, 13 acres

Mary P.C. Gold Mining Company, Limited

7060 Auriferous mundic from 50ft level underlay; estimated
yield, 3oz per ton; width of reef, 12in; depth of straight
shaft, 225ft; underlay, 150ft—total, 375ft; area, 12
acres
This reef has yielded since its opening over 10,000ozs
of smelted gold, the yield at the mill being 1½oz to 11oz per
ton. The property is t-aversed by the Rainbow Reef.

Lady Maria Gold Mining Company, Limited

7070 Auriferous mundic and galena in quartz at a depth of
350ft on underlie; average width of reef 15in; estimated yield at ordinary crushing mill, 4oz to 5oz per
ton. This reef has yielded about 10,000ozs of gold,
the yield at the mill being from ½oz to 10oz per ton;
depth of shaft 530ft; area, 15 acres. The reef runs
nearly north and south and dips east.

Stockholm Gold Mining Company, Limited

7080 Auriferous mundic, galena and blende in quartz from the
south level at a depth of 300ft; average width of reef,
2ft 6in. The last crushing of 275 tons yielded 465oz.

Sunburst Gold Mining Company, Limited

7090   Auriferous mundic at 240ft level, from a crushing of 90
     tons yielding 4oz per ton

Old Identity P.C. Gold Mining Company, Limited

7100   Auriferous mundic from the foot-wall reef off from the
     660ft level

Day Dawn No. 4A West Gold Mining Company, Limited

7110   Auriferous mundic, with galena from the slope over the
     intermediate level on east side of shaft at a depth of
     400ft, 236ft vertical, 164ft on underlie

Rainbow P.C. Gold Mining Company, Limited

7120   Auriferous mundic, with galena, at a depth of 700ft;
     average width of reef, 2ft; present depth of shaft, 839ft
     The mine is situated near the well-known Day Dawn line
of reef.

7130   A series of polished rock sections.

    —*Exhibitor:* A. W. CLARKE, ESQ., *one of the Government
Lecturers on Mineralogy*

GLADSTONE DISTRICT.

NORTON FIELD   ...   . *No. 1 South Advance*

8000	Auriferous mundic and blende at 210ft			
8001	Do	do	do	200ft
8002	Do	do	do	180ft, in quartz
8003	Do	do	do	180ft, in calcite
8003*	Country rock			
8004	Calcite formation			

No. 2 South Advance

8005	Auriferous mundic
8006	Calcite vein at 215ft
8007	Auriferous mundic, blende and galena, in quartz
8008	Formation, carrying a few dwts of gold per ton
8009	Auriferous mundic, blende and galena
8010	Do do do at 220ft
8011	Country rock

Advance P.C.

8012	Mundic, blende and galena, carrying nearly 3oz gold per ton
8013	Do do do do do
8014	Quartz leader, carrying auriferous mundic and blende
8015	Auriferous galena and mundic, under calcite and over quartz

8016   Blende, galena, and mundic, with calcspar crystals
8017   Hanging-wall
8018   Foot-wall side

Hickey's Reef

8019   Iron pyrites and blende in calcite
8020   Auriferous surface stone, with crystals of fluor spar
8021   Mundic, galena, and blende in quartz
The reef is parallel to the " Who'd a Thought It " reef, 5 or 6 chains north. The shaft is 40ft deep.

" Who'a a Thought It "

8022   Calcspar at 336ft
8023   Quartz leader running parallel with reef at 250ft
8024   Formation main reef, calcspar, mundic, galena, and blende, at 300ft level
8025   Auriferous quartz and calcspar crystals at 120ft
8026   Calcspar and quartz, carrying auriferous mundic, adherent to hanging-wall at 336ft
The reef runs east and west. The main shaft is about 336ft down. One hundred and forty-seven tons stone from a mullocky leader have been crushed for an average of 10oz to the ton; 453 tons for an average of 35oz per ton; $31\frac{1}{2}$ tons of tailings have yielded by treatment at the Pyrites Works, Sandhurst, 135oz 18dwt.

FRAMPTON'S LIMITED MINES   ...   .   *Little Wonder Claim*

8031   Auriferous mundic

Frampton's Shaft

8032   Auriferous spongy silica at 20ft

Frampton United

8033   Auriferous spongy silica
Exhibitor's description:—" This reef is a large mundic vein, and splits in places into three or four veins; they are formed by ' horses' in the throat of the upcast. These specimens are taken from places where the splits take place, and are like pumice-stone, they are so light. I have tried a number of these varieties—for they are of all colours—and they are richer than the main reef. The lighter the specimens the richer the return for gold."
8034   Auriferous spongy silica at 15ft
8034A   Do   do   from west wall of lode
8035   Auriferous mundic and blende at 96ft
8036   Formation at 96ft
8037   Mundic at 65ft
8038   Mundic and blende at 65ft

Martin's Shaft

8039 Auriferous quartz at 25ft
8040 Do   mundic and blende

Never Never Shaft

8041 Mispickel and mundic at 99ft
8042 Do   do   The black~ decomposing
      mundic, the richest in gold
8043 Mispickel and mundic in quartz
8044 Fine-grained mispickel in quartz

Goody's Shaft

8045 Auriferous mundic and blende
8046 Do   do   galena
8047 Do   do   blende
8048 Auriferous ochre, said to be rich in gold

The following are the analyses of auriferous pyrites from this company's claims by Messrs. Johnson, Matthey, and Co.:—

Auriferous Pyrites from Goody's Reef.

Iron	30·60
Lead	8·90
Zinc	6·00
Arsenic	1·55
Copper	0·95
Sulphur	36·00
Alumina	0·40
Siliceous insoluble matter	15·20
Gold, silver, oxygen, and loss	0·40
	100·00

oz.
Produce of gold ... 2·400 ⎫
      „   silver ... 14·700 ⎬ Per ton of 20 cwt. of ore.

Sample from Frampton's Claim.

Iron	25.10
Lead	1·10
Zinc	7·60
Arsenic	6·80
Sulphur	25·70
Copper	0·65
Alumina	0·20
Siliceous insoluble matter	32·60
Gold, silver, oxygen, and loss	0·25
	100·00

oz.
Produce of gold ... 5·500 ⎫
      „   silver ... 4·700 ⎬ Per ton of 20 cwt. of ore.

Sample Auriferous Pyrites from Never Never Claim.

Iron ...	...	...	...	...	...	41·30
Arsenic	...	...	...	...	...	2·10
Copper	...	...	...	...	...	1·20
Lead ..	...	.	...	...	...	0·20
Sulphur	...	...	...	...	...	33·40
Moisture	..	...	...	...	...	1·00
Siliceous insoluble matter	...	...	...	...		17·40
Gold, silver, oxygen, and loss			...	...	...	3·40
						100·00

oz.

Produce of gold ... 3·200 ⎫
   ,,   silver ... 8·500 ⎬ Per ton of 20 cwt. of ore.

This group of properties is held by a company who intend treating the pyrites ores by chlorination or some modification of that process. A good deal of the spongy quartz (50 or 60 tons) was crushed, and the average yield was nearly 4oz. The specimens called spongy silica are indeterminate, as the constituents are variable, but the hollow spaces are not spherical; they have possibly been filled at one time with crystals of minerals that have weathered away, leaving the casts behind, and until more work has been done in the way of developing the mine it is difficult to say exactly what action has taken place.

—*Exhibitor:* MR. GOLD WARDEN MCARTHUR

GLADSTONE · Tipp Stone, 25 miles south-west of

    8049   Jasperoid rock

KROOMBIT FIELD.

    8050   Surface-stone, yield by crushing 4oz gold per ton

CANIA FIELD.

    8051   Auriferous copper oxide

Mr. Gold-Warden McArthur says of these fields that they lie "one on the north and the other on south side of the Dawes Range, respectively, or perhaps, more correctly, they are on the range, and for many miles beyond the limits of the fields the leaders carry copper and gold. They were opened out in 1870. Carriboe Creek, on the Kroombit, turned out great quantities of alluvial gold, and on the Four-mile and Eight-mile Creeks in Cania Gold Field rich claims were worked. The most valuable claims were on Moonlight Gully, Cania, where the majority of the claims averaged each £600 for eighteen months. When the reefs began to be worked, Mount Rose Prospecting Claim and Mount Rose No. 1 came to the front, and for the last six years the Mount Rose No. 1 has been the most paying reef in the district, the shareholders having already netted £3,000 per share. The prospecting claim gave good returns for the first five years, but there is so much copper in the lode at the present depth that it no longer pays to work for gold."

The Gold-Warden goes on to state "that many of the reefs would pay at a depth, but as yet no capital has been expended on prospecting in deep ground." The riches of the field are very great, but there are so many other fields in more accessible neighbourhoods that are paying and absorbing capital, that Cania is lost sight of by miners and capitalists. The mineral collector was unable to visit the district, which is another example of how serious a question to the well-being of a field is its accessibility. The average crushings of clean quartz have been over 2oz per ton.

The surface of the country is very hilly, and the soil is exceedingly rich, being either black or red volcanic. The climate is perfect, the elevation being from 1,500 to 2,000 feet above the sea level. All fruits grown in temperate zones flourish on the Dawes Range slopes; and the water supply is plentiful, as the ranges bring down the rain.

THE TABLELAND DIGGINGS.—Following one of the spurs of the Dawes Range you come on to the "Coast Range," which rises to a great elevation at Mount Fuller's Hat and Mount Buckland—viz., from 2,000ft to 3,000ft high. Between these two mountains there is a tableland of rich black soil, and on the slopes on the coast and Fitzroy River sides there have been great quantities of alluvial gold got. Some gold-bearing leaders have been found, but in the absence of water, no one has attempted reefing. The country is most beautiful, and looks like a rich reefing district; but a constant succession of dry seasons has retarded progress.

CALLIOPE FIELD   ...   .   *Kelly's Gully*

8052   Serpentinous slate, foot-wall
8053   Auriferous quartz at 60ft ⎱ yield by crushing, nearly 2oz
8054   Do   do   20ft ⎰   gold per ton

Theresa

8055   Auriferous quartz at 15ft

Company's Reef

8056   Foot-wall at 150ft
8057   Auriferous quartz at 150ft

This claim was a very important one, but it is abandoned. It is a strong reef of compact quartz, which has turned out a quantity of beautiful "specimens," but the shafts are full of water now and the workings are completely deserted. The specimens were obtained from the hotel proprietor. Mr. Gold-Warden McArthur says of this field that it promised to be the best in the district, but when the miners had sunk below the water-level—50ft—the water charges became too heavy. No proper pumping gear has been erected at all. Claim after claim was abandoned, and at the present time there is not one reef at work.

The soil is black, lightly timbered, and fit to grow anything. The Gold-Warden expresses his belief, after knowing the field for years, that, with pumping gear and machinery, the reefs would be remunerative if prospected to the depth of 100ft.

GLADSTONE TOWN.

    8058 Pyrolusite
    8059   Do   botryoidal
    8060   Do

The strike of the lode is nearly east and west.

Messrs. Johnson, Matthey, & Co., of Hatton Garden, have analysed two samples of the ore for the proprietor, and Mr. H. Friend, senior, of Gladstone, sends the following copy of their certificate:—

Available peroxide of manganese	74·84	57·00
Protoxide of manganese	8·20	9·30
Oxides of iron	8·60	3·80
Alumina	2·80	2·00
Carbonic acid	traces	
Sulphur	0·22	0·13
Water	3·80	2·70
Siliceous insoluble matter	1·10	25·00
Loss	0·44	0·07
	100·00	100·00

    8061 Dark marble
    8062   Do
    8063   Do   marked with ferric oxide
    8064   Do
    8065 Red marble

GLADSTONE ... ... *Coase's Hill*

    8066 White marble

GLADSTONE ... ... *Gatecombe Head, 9 miles above Calliope Crossing*

    8067 Pyrolusite   —*Exhibitor:* H. FRIEND, SEN., ESQ.

Gladstone Town Mine

    8068 Pyrolusite

CALLIOPE ... ... *John Bull United Gold Mining Company Limited*

    8079 Quartz from reef at 70ft, showing gold
    8080 Sample of reef from surface to 100ft
    8081 Foot-wall at 100ft
    8082 Country rock, main shaft
    8083   Do
    8084 Reef in shaft No 2, at 30ft

The reef runs east and west, dips north with an underlay of 1 in 10, and an average width of 12in. The old workings are being re-opened.

GLADSTONE ... ... *Mount Hetherington or Degalgil P.C.*

8090 Sample of reef; yield by assay over 20oz of gold per ton
The reef runs east and west, and is vertical.

CALLIOPE FIELD, SHEEP-STATION HILL ... *Hetherington and Fairfax P.C.*

8100 Auriferous ironstone, said to show gold

Harriet P.C. Gold Mining Company

8110 Sample of quartz, showing gold, at 17ft
The reef runs north and south, dips west, is nearly
vertical, and has an average thickness of 9in.

NORTON FIELD ... *No. 2 South Advance Gold Mining Company, Ltd*

8011* Samples of reef
8012* Country rock
8013* Calcspar and formation between the walls of the reef
The reef runs north-west and south-east, and is vertical.
The width between the walls is from 1½ft to 7ft. The
mundic is gold-bearing.

NORTON FIELD ... ... *Advance P.C. Gold Mining Company, Ltd.*

8018* Reef at about 270ft, showing blende, galena, and mundic
in calcite
8019* Country rock
8020* Tailings from about 300ft level, concentrated from stone
with 80 per cent mineral
The reef runs north-west and south-east, dips south-east,
and underlays 1 in 9; its width between the walls 9in to 7ft.

Little Wonder Gold Mining Company, Limited

8031* Mundic from 40ft level
8032* Formation between walls at 40ft
8033* Country rock
The reef runs east-south-east, and west-north-west, dipping south-south-west, with an underlay of 1 in 20, and
width of 4ft, 18in to 24in being solid mundic.

NORTON FIELD ... ... { *Couran's Gold Mining Company, Limited*
{ *(Frampton's Reef)*

8038* Mundic from shaft from 50ft to 240ft
8039* Do with mispickel from winze at 70ft
8040* Do with blende from 240ft
8041* Country rock, walls and formation
The reef runs north-west and south-east, dipping south-
west, and is almost vertical; its width is 1ft to 5ft of solid
mundic, and it also carries a very large mineralised formation. The usual return is about 3oz to 4oz per ton.

NORTON FIELD ... ... { *Couran's Gold Mining Company* *(Goody's Reef)*

8048* Mundic with blende and galena from 70ft level
8049* Country rock
8050* Cross-course running at right angles to reef
The reef runs north-west and south-east, dipping south-west and nearly vertical; its average thickness is 1ft to 2ft.

GLADSTONE ... *Griffith PC. Gold and Silver Mine.* (*Table Land*)

8051* Mundic and blende from reef 3ft to 4ft wide, containing about 20oz silver and 1oz gold per ton

ROCKHAMPTON DISTRICT.

MOUNT MORGAN.

8500 Cubes of rough-dressed limonite, showing stuff as quarried; average crushing
8501 Bulk sample of limonite, weight 100lbs, averaging 7oz gold per ton
8502 Sinter, dyke and auriferous limonite
85C3 Stalactitic sinter

ROCKHAMPTON FIELD ... . *Emerald Junction*

8561 Jasperoid rock with colloid silica filling crevices

Hibernia Claim

8562 Auriferous chalcopyrite and galena in quartz from 120ft level
The reef runs north-east and south-west, and dips about 1 in 3. The width is 18in and the yield by crushing has averaged 23dwts of gold per ton.

MOUNT WHEELER FIELD ... ... *Mount Wheeler*

8563 Asbestos adhering to country rock
8564 Do
8565 Sample
Mount Wheeler is 18 miles from Rockhampton. It is composed of serpentine, which is traversed by auriferous reefs within a radius of 1 mile from the Mountain.

ROSEWOOD FIELD ... ... *Golden Bar*

8566 Country rock at 95ft
8567 Auriferous calcite at 86ft
8568　　Do　　quartz
8569　　Do　　do　and calcite
The lode runs east and west.

ROCKHAMPTON FIELD, NEW ZEALAND GULLY   ...   *Keppel Bay View*

    85˙0   Mundic; yield by crushing 1oz per ton, the tailings assaying 10oz 14dwts 7grs gold and 1300oz silver

MORINISH FIELD   ...   .   *Welcome Gold Mining Company*

    8571   Auriferous mundic and galena in quartz from 310ft level
    8572   Auriferous mundic in quartz, No. 2 shaft, 50ft level
    8573* Dyke
    8574   Country rock

ROCKHAMPTON FIELD, NEW ZEALAND GULLY   ...   *Hidden Treasure*

    8575   Auriferous quartz from 54ft level; yield by crushing 2oz per ton
    8576   Auriferous quartz, surface; yield by crushing 3oz per ton
    The reef runs east and west and dips north 1 in 5.

Mary Florence

    8577   Blende, mundic and chalcopyrite in quartz from 75ft level
    8578   Auriferous mundic in quartz at 30ft
    8579   Auriferous quartz
    8580   Formation from 75ft level
    8581   Country rock
    8582   Auriferous mundic in quartz leader at 75ft

Salvation Army

    8583   Auriferous mundic in quartz at 32ft; yield by crushing 4oz gold per ton
    8584   Auriferous mundic in quartz at 15ft
    The stone from this claim yields on an average 2oz gold per ton.

Band of Hope

    8585   Auriferous quartz
    Keppel Bay, Hidden Treasure, and Band of Hope are claims on one reef, about half a mile from the North Star line of reef. The reef is over 12in thick, and the crushings have hitherto yielded nearly 2oz gold per ton.

ROSEWOOD FIELD   (60 miles west   ...   { *Caledonian Gold Mining*
    from Rockhampton)   }   { *Company's Lease*

    8586   Ironstone at surface
    8587   Hanging-wall at 10ft
    8588   Auriferous mundic, with quartz and calcite formation
    8589   Auriferous mundic, with quartz at 75ft
    8590   Foot-wall
    The reef is about 18in wide, runs east and west, and dips 85° north; depth of shaft, about 70ft. A crushing of 5 tons averaged 1oz 16dwt gold per ton.

CROCODILE CREEK FIELD ... *Windsor Gold Mining Company's Lease*

  8591 Auriferous mundic in quartz, with formation
  8592   Do   do   dyke, porphyry
  8593   Do   do   quartz
      Formation, 16ft wide at 130ft level; a drive of 60ft east from the foot of the shaft has been made. The dyke runs east and west. The average yield by crushing of 150 tons was 7dwt gold per ton. The clean mundic is said to assay 9oz gold per ton.

ROCKHAMPTON FIELD, NEW ZEALAND GULLY ... ... *North Star*

  8594 Auriferous mundic in quartz, adhering to country rock, from 40ft level
  8595 Quartz from 70ft level, with cavities left by decomposed pyrite
  8596 Mundic and quartz from 40ft level
  8597 Country rock at 50ft
  8598   Do   do 90ft

Union Gold Mining Company's Lease

  8599 Auriferous mundic in schorl and calcite from 152ft level
  8600   Do   do   do   do
  8601   Do   do   do   do
  8602 Country rock
  8603 Auriferous mundic and schorl in formation
  8604 Pyrite crystals in lode formation from 172ft level
  8605 Auriferous chalcopyrite
  8606 Auriferous mundic in granite, at 50ft, from Alabama shaft
      The average yield has been 7dwts gold per ton, but the quantity of stone makes up for its quality.

CROCODILE CREEK FIELD ... ... *Hit or Miss P.C.*

  8607 Auriferous mundic in quartz at 150ft
  8608 Country rock at 150ft
  8609 Casing or "dig"
      This reef runs north and south, and underlies easterly nearly 1 in 3. A crushing has yielded 30oz gold from 20 tons stone.

Greenvale Gold Mining Company's Lease

  8610 Auriferous rock at 133ft in underlie shaft
  8611 Sample
      There is no distinct lode formation in the ground; the underlie shaft dips 45°. 77 tons of stone have yielded by crushing 11dwts gold per ton, and 26 tons an average of 10dwts.

Union Gold Mining Company, Limited

  8610A Reef from 200ft level
  8611A Auriferous mundic

8612A Auriferous mundic at 265ft in calcite and quartz
8613A Country rock
The reef runs south 80° west, and north 80° east, with northerly dip, and 15° underlay; it has an average width of 4ft, and the average crushing yield is 11¼dwts per ton. An assay of the mundic, recently made, gave—gold, 10oz 14dwts 3grs; silver, 3oz 9dwts 10grs, per ton.

DEE RIVER ... ... *Champion Claim*

8612 Pyrite and chalcopyrite, the pyrite assaying 19oz gold per ton

CROCODILE FIELD ... ... *Niagara Falls Claim*

8613 Auriferous blende in quartz at 28ft
8614 Country rock

BLACKFELLOW'S GULLY ... ... *Homeward Bound*

8615 Auriferous quartz
8616 Auriferous mundic in quartz at about 150ft
8617 Hanging-wall
8618 Auriferous quartz at surface
8619 Foot-wall
The reef runs north and south. An adit has been driven into the side of the hill in the direction of the course of the reef.

CAWARRAL FIELD ... ... *Annie Claim*

8620 Auriferous mundic in country rock
8621 Auriferous galena and blende in quartz at 135ft level
The lode runs north-north-east and south-south-west, and dips east-south-east 1 in 3; depth of shaft, 135ft.

Block and Pillar Claim

8622 Auriferous mundic with calcite at 115ft
8623 Auriferous quartz at 100ft
8624 Country rock
The reef runs east and west and dips north at 45°; clean pyrites from this claim is said to have assayed as high as 30oz gold per ton.

Endeavour Claim

8625 Auriferous mundic in lode formation at 60ft

Stover's Claim

8626 Auriferous quartz from surface
8627 Do do at 10ft from mouth of tunnel
8628 Do do at 28ft from mouth of tunnel
8629 Do do and pyrites
8630 Do do

MOUNT MORGAN FIELD ...   . *Callan's Knob*

8631   French chalk
8632   Mundic from No. 2 tunnel
8633   Quartz   Do   do
8634   Quartzite Do   do
8635   Country rock from No. 1 tunnel face
8636   Do   do   do
8637   Quartz   do   No. 3   do

Tarangabah Gold Mining Company

8640   Sample of ore

MORINISH FIELD   ...   ... *Alliance Gold Mining Company, Limited*

8650   Auriferous quartz at 140ft; yield by crushing, 1½oz free
       gold per ton
8651   Auriferous quartz, with serpentine and chalcopyrite;
       yields an alloy of copper and gold at the rate of 50oz
       per ton = ⅙ per oz
8652   Quartz at 40ft; yields about 1½oz free gold per ton
8652* Crystalline quartz on chalcedony
8653   Foot-wall
8654   Hanging-wall
8655   Country rock, conglomerate
       The reef runs north and south, dips west, with an under-
       lay of about 18°; its width is from 1ft to 4ft.

CAWARRAL FIELD   ..   .. *Annie Gold Mining Company*

8660   Quartz and serpentine, showing gold
8661   Dolomite and serpentine, with mispickel
8662   Quartz, with serpentine and mundic
8663   Ironstone from surface of lode near Annie Reef
8664   Foot-wall and hanging-wall and country rock, serpentine
       The reef runs north and south, dipping east, with an
       underlay of 1 in 3. It has an average width of 12in to 18in,
       solid stone, crushing 1oz 12dwts to 5oz 15dwts per ton.
       Area of lease, 25 acres.

CAWARRAL FIELD   ... *Mount Dulzell Gold Mining Company, Limited*
8670   Quartz, showing gold

MORINISH FIELD   ... *Marie Louise Gold Mining Company, Limited*
8680   Quartz from tunnel

RIDGELANDS FIELD ... *Dawn of Hope Gold Mining Company, Limited*

8690   Ironstone from reef at 50ft
8691   Foot-wall
8692   Hanging-wall
       The reef runs north-east and south-west, dipping about
       north-west, with an underlay of 1 in 4; its average thickness

E

is 18in. Sixteen tons crushed with Chilian mill returned 55½oz gold; the tailings assayed 1¼oz on an average.

CAMBOON   ...   ...   *Camboon P.C. Gold Mining Company, Limited*

   8700   Hornblendic stone; trial by chlorinating process 1oz 12dwts

   8701   Mundic stone   Do   do   8dwts
      Width of each lode about 14ft.

CROCODILE CREEK FIELD   ...   *Homeward Bound Gold Mining Co. Ltd.*

   8710   Reef at 45ft
   8711   Hanging-wall, chlorite
   8712   Foot-wall
      This reef runs east and west, dips south, and underlays 1 in 4, with an average width of 8in.

MORINISH FIELD, BLACKFELLOW'S GULLY   ...   *Mary Florence Gold Mining Company, Limited*

   8720   Reef at 120ft
   8721   Do   50ft, showing copper carbonates
   8723   Rock in connection with reef
      The reef runs east and west, dips south, and underlays 1 in 4; the average width is 6in, and yield by crushing 4oz per ton.

MORINISH FIELD, BLACKFELLOW'S GULLY   ...   *Eddington P.C. Gold Mining Company, Limited*

   8730   Quartz at 12ft
   8731   Rubble, rich in gold, in connection with reef
   8732   Foot-wall
      The reef runs north and south, dips east, and underlays 1 in 4; its width is from 6in to 12in, and average crushing yield 2½oz.

CROCODILE FIELD   ...   *Mountain Maid Gold Mining Company, Limited*

   8740   Quartz at 40ft, with blende and mundic
   8741   Do   68ft
   8742   Do   100ft
   8743   Country rock

CAWARRAL FIELD, NEW ZEALAND GULLY   *Mount Chalmers Gold Mining Company, Limited*

   8750   Surface stone
   8751   Sample of reef near surface
   8752   Fahlerz, said to contain gold, silver, copper, iron, arsenic, antimony, zinc, nickel, cobalt
   8753   Auriferous quartz

8754   Ironstone, containing lead, gold, silver, and copper; 200,000 tons in sight; treated 14 years ago with defective machinery, gave from 4dwts to 15dwts gold per ton

8755   Auriferous stone, 4dwts to 15dwts gold per ton
This mine has recently been transferred to a Company, and is to be vigorously worked. The ore is refractory and in very large quantities.

CAWARRAL FIELD   ...   .   { *Westbrook Gold Mining Freehold, T. W. Dodgson, Proprietor*

8760   Quartz from near surface

CROCODILE FIELD   ...   *Block and Pillar Gold Mining Company, Ltd.*

8770   Reef-quartz showing auriferous mundic

MORINISH FIELD, BLACKFELLOW'S GULLY   ...   *No. 1 Mary Florence East*

8780   Reef from 60ft level, quartz showing copper carbonates
8781   Rock in connection with reef, shale

MORINISH FIELD, BLACKFELLOW'S GULLY   ...   ...   *Jubilee Reef*

8790   Reef at 20ft
8791   Auriferous quartz, containing copper pyrites
8792   Country rock also forming wall of reef
The reef runs north-west and south-east, dips south-west and underlays about 1 in 10; the wall well defined, and the average width 6in.

20 tons yielded by crushing 68oz 8dwts
31 tons   Do   do   123oz
42 tons   Do   do   150oz

Long Tunnel Gold Mine, W. K. Dalzell, Proprietor

8810   Quartz from tunnel with galena and chalcopyrite
The reef runs north 30° east and south 30° west; it is nearly vertical with a south-easterly dip; a tunnel has been put in about 700ft, of which 370ft are along line of reef.

MOUNT MORGAN FIELD   ...   { *South Mount Morgan Gold Mining Company, Limited*

8820   Core and diamond drill shoe

ST. LAWRENCE   ...   .   *West Hill Prospecting Association*

8830   Argentiferous ore from surface
—*Exhibitor :* MR. LAZARD

CROCODILE FIELD   ...   .   *Antonio's Mount Bischoff Mine*

8840   Ferruginous quartz
8841   Ferruginous quartz
8842   Chalcopyrite in quartz

8842* Ferruginous quartz from long cutting on south side of mountain

8843 Ferruginous quartz from lode on top of mountain 10ft wide

8844 Ferruginous quartz from No. 1 tunnel

8845 Mundic

8846 Diorite bar

8847 Gossan

RIDGELANDS FIELD   ...   .   *Moonlight, Nil Desperandum*

8850 Mundic

8851 Ferruginous quartz

RANNES FIELD   ...   ...   *Great Kauffman Gold Mining Company*

8860 Quartz

CAWARRAL FIELD, GARRY GULLY ... *Ethel Reef Prospecting Area No. 90*

8870 Ferruginous quartz

CROCODILE FIELD   ... *Old Hector Gold Mining Company, Limited.*

8880 Mundic and chalcopyrite from 245ft level

8881 Mundic and chalcopyrite from 145ft level

PEAK DOWNS DISTRICT.

COPPERFIELD...   ..   .. *Peak Downs Copper Mine*

9500 Native copper in quartz

9501 Mundic, fine grained

9502 Copper carbonates

9503 Native copper in quartz

9504 Country rocks

9505 Mundic and chalcopyrite

9506 Copper, black oxide

9506* Malachite, silky

9506** Malachite and azurite

9507 Conversions of oxides into carbonates

9507* Malachite

9507** Copper carbonates with mica on quartz

9508 Copper sulphides and oxides with quartz

—*Exhibitor :* H. SALMOND, Esq.

"Igneous and metamorphic rocks predominate; the country rocks of the 'Peak' being entirely composed of partially decomposed trachyte. An amygdaloidal dolerite sometimes contains patches of copper-ore, and some of the cupriferous traps are said to very closely resemble those of the Lake Superior Copper Mines. As early as 1870, 29,168 tons of 20 per cent. copper-ores had been raised from this property. About that period a lode, 2ft in width, running east and west was cut at a depth of 40 fathoms from the surface, and traced for a distance of 250 fathoms. This discovery was followed, in 1873, by that of another lode containing large quantities of black oxide of copper. In five years the dividends on a nominal capital of £100,000 reached the sum of £215,250, besides which £23,577 had been written off the value at the mine. The company, however, had to contend with serious difficulties—a land carriage of 250 miles to the port, and miners' wages ranging from £3 to £4 a week. A decline in the shipment of ore, or in the price of copper, very seriously affected the undertaking, which was eventually closed."[*] The company put up some scores of smelting furnaces (reverberatory).

THE SPRING FIELD ... ... *Cement Hill*

9509 Auriferous drift, yielding 10dwts gold

The plant consists (1886) merely of four stampers and riffles to catch the gold; no mercury is used. The proprietors intend putting up a complete plant now that the value of the deposit is proved.

The cement consists mainly of quartz pebbles of various sizes, very much waterworn, and carries coarse finely divided gold.

McDONALD'S FLAT ... ... *Somersetshire Reef*

9510 Surface quartz, yielded by crushing 1¼oz gold
9511 Auriferous quartz at 56ft
9512 Mundic in quartz at 100ft
9513 Auriferous quartz at 110ft
9514 Country rock

COPPERFIELD .. .. *Aylmery's Claim*

9515 Auriferous mundic in quartz
9516 Country rock, contorted by quartz leader

Cumberland Reef

9517 Auriferous quartz, yield by crushing 4oz gold

CLERMONT ... ... *Somersetshire Claim*

9604 Quartz showing mundic from 90ft level; assays 1oz 9dwts per ton

Star of Hope

9605 Auriferous mundic in quartz from lode at 135ft level

---

[*] "Ore Deposits," J. A. Phillips, 1884, p. 490.

Venus

9606   Gold in micaceous schist

COPPERFIELD.

9610   Malachite

—*Exhibitors :* TRUSTEES OF QUEENSLAND MUSEUM

NEBO DISTRICT.

NEBO FIELD   ...   . *Mount Orange Copper Mine*

9700   Specular iron ore and malachite
9701   Chalcopyrite, crystalline
9702   Specular iron ore with copper
9703   Azurite and atacamite
9704   Specular iron ore, cupriferous
9705   Tetrahedrite
9706   Chalcopyrite with pyrite crystals
9707   Hæmatite, cupriferous
9708   Hæmatite with copper carbonates
9709   Specular iron ore, cupriferous
9709* Black oxide and carbonates of copper
9710   Chrysocolla azurite and hæmatite
9711   Quartzite with chalcopyrite
9711* Copper carbonates and black oxide
9712   Chalcopyrite
9712* Samples for analysis

—*Exhibitor :* W. S. C. ADRIAN, ESQ.

MACKAY DISTRICT.

9713   Specular iron ore
9714   Do   do
9715   Quartz with liquid enclosure
9716   Amethysts
9717   Agates
9718   Do
9719   Chert and chalcedony
9720   Waterworn quartz
9721   Wolfram in quartz
9722   Molybdenite in quartz

—*Exhibitor :* Mr. G. FRANCAS

MOUNT BRITTEN   ...   *Mount Britten Gold Mining Company, Limited*

9800   Gold-bearing quartz from the Wanderer and Union reefs
         at depths varying from 40ft to 240ft

Edith May Reef

9801   Gold-bearing quartz

—*Exhibitors :* MESSRS RICKETT & MILLS

NORTH DIVISION.*

HERBERTON DISTRICT.

Herberton is the official and commercial centre of the district. It is 80 miles from Port Douglas, and 50 miles from Cairns, the two ports of the field. Herberton was opened out as a tinfield by Mr. Gold-Warden Mowbray, who issued the first mining licenses on the 30th October, 1880, the town having been laid out by the same official on 21st August, 1880.

Messrs. William Jack, John Newell, Thomas Brandon, and John Brown discovered the district. The Great Northern prospecting claim was taken possession of by these gentlemen in May, 1880.

Stream-tin was first found by Mr. John Newell in the gully of the Great Northern prospecting claim in November, 1879.

Mr. John Moffat, of Messrs. John Moffat and Co., introduced capital to the field; and that firm's private exhibit is a testimonial to their energy as well as to the great extent of their interest in the district.

There are several townships. The next in importance to Herberton is Watsonville. It was s'ated that the mills of Watsonville were turning out, more black tin than even Herberton. There are some very rich claims in the neighbourhood, notably the North Australian, owned by Messrs. O'Loan and Casey, which turned out £50,000 worth of black tin in $2\frac{1}{2}$ years, the mine only being worked by 6 men. The Great Western Company, who hold very important mines in the vicinity of Watsonville, was floated by Mr. John Moffat.

Coolgara is another township, 25 miles from Herberton, and is the centre of Return Creek claims.

Irvinebank is quite new and very important, the centre of the finest group of properties yet discovered. The dressing plant for tin is the most perfect plant that could be got together—members of the firm of Messrs. John Moffat and Co. visiting Germany, and Cornwall, and Swansea for the express purpose of getting the very latest improvements incorporated into their plant at Irvinebank. The black tin is smelted on the spot, and the tin ingots are exhibited among the firm's private trophies.

Scrubby Creek is an agricultural centre; it is about 10 miles from Herberton. Cedar trees grow in such great luxuriance here that it was found cheaper to send the Herberton minerals home in cedar cases.

Newelltown.—Silver galena and chalcopyrites occur here. The Silver Valley Mining Company have erected a Pacific smelter for smelting the galenas. It is 10 miles from Herberton.

---

* From $20\frac{1}{4}$ S. lat. to Northern boundary, and from 146 to 142 E. long.

Eureka Creek.—Discovered by Joss and party; is about 16 miles from Herberton, and 10 miles from Watsonville. The tin deposits appear to be very rich in the vicinity of the camp.

California Gully, Halpins Creek, and *Gregory's Gully* are mining centres and camps, within 9 miles of each other, and from 30 to 40 miles from Herberton.

The Tate River, 60 miles from Herberton, is the centre of a stream tin deposit.

Mount Garnet is a hill about 35 miles from Herberton, *via* Return Creek (Coolgara). There is a huge outcrop of carbonate of copper (estimated at 4,000 tons) in sight, samples from which are stated to assay 20 per cent. copper.

Silverfield is the latest and most valuable acquisition to the mineral discoveries of the district, and as Mount Albion deposits include horn-silver and gold, Herberton appears to possess in its minerals gold, silver, tin, copper, and bismuth. For smelting purposes there are deposits of hæmatite and limestone; fire-clay has been found in the neighbourhood of Messrs. Moffat's mines.

Mineral Exhibit of the Herberton Local Committee.

NEWELLTON FIELD ...   .   *Cacara, W. B. Stenhouse*

  11500 Calcite at 20ft, limestone used in conjunction with iron ores for smelting the silver ores of the field

North Queensland Silver Mining Company, R. Collins, Manager

11501	Silver lead at	10ft, yield	90oz per ton
11502	Do	20ft, do	105oz	do
11503	Do	40ft, do	105oz	do
11504	Do	60ft, do	117oz	do
11505	Do	70ft, do	43oz	do
11506	Do	80ft, do	123oz	do
11507	Do	100ft, do	151oz	do
11508	Do	150ft, do	120oz	do
11509	Do	200ft, do	201oz	do

Water jacket, furnace and all appliances on the ground ready for smelting silver ores.

W. B. Stenhouse

  11510 Compact limestone for smelting purposes

Goodall's, J. G. Goodall

  11511 Copper carbonates from different parts of the lode at 20ft

IRVINEBANK   ...   .   *John Moffatt & Co.*

  11512 Firebrick

NEWELLTON ... ... *Slumiker's, W. B. Stenhouse*

    11513   Copper sulphides at 60ft
    11514   Do   at 80ft
    11516   Do   at 100ft

                             Stenhouse's, W. B. Stenhouse

    11518   Iron ore at 20ft, used for smelting purposes at Newellton
           and Mount Albion

HERBERTON ... ... *Three Star, C. Hoare & Party*

    11519   Tinstone at 200ft
    11520   Country rock, foot-wall, at 200ft
    11521   Country rock, hanging-wall, at 200ft
    11522   Tinstone at 200ft

WATSONVILLE ... *North Australian 40 acre lease, O'Loan & Casey*

    11523   Tinstone at 100ft
    11524   Copper carbonates at 20ft
    11525   Tinstone samples from various parts of the mine which
           has yielded to five men in less than two years £50,000
           worth of tin

CALIFORNIAN CREEK.

    11526   Dolomite, surface

HERBERTON ... ... *Deep Lead, Masterson & Party*

    11527   Petrified wood at 20ft

EUREKA CREEK ... ... *Gladstone, John McKenzie*

    11528   Tinstone at 50ft

EMU CREEK ... ... *Fanny Parnell*

    11529   Tinstone at 20ft

                              Alexandra

    11530   Tinstone at 50ft

                            City of Bagdad

    11531   Tinstone at 50ft

COOLGARA.

    11532   Manganese ore

NEWELLTON ... ... *Stenhouse's, W. B. Stenhouse*

    11533   Tinstone at 25ft, near the ironstone reefs

HERBERTON ... ... *Lovely Nancy, G. S. Davis's 5 acre lease*

    11534   Tinstone at 40ft

NEWELLTON .. .. *Slumiker's, W. B. Stenhouse*

11534* Copper ores at 100ft

Stenhouse's, W. B. Stenhouse

11535 Tinstone (chlorite) at 10ft
11536   Do   do   15ft

WATSONVILLE ... ... *Try no More*

11537 Tinstone at 20ft
11538   Do   25ft

Great Wheel Busy, Allan Bros.

11539 Tinstone with galena and pyrite at 60ft

EUREKA CREEK ... ... *Black Rock, W. Seaman*

11540 Tinstone from a lode 16ft wide at 40ft

WATSONVILLE ... ... *Boundary Claim, Toy Bros.*

11541 Tinstone at 45ft
11542   Do   20ft

Great Western Tin Mining Company, John Munday

11543 Tinstone at 100ft
11544   Do

Rose of England, J. Pyle

11545 Tinstone at 120ft
11546   Do   100ft

Caledonia, J. Meehan

11547 Tinstone at 120ft

Glen Cairn, J. Watson

11548 Tinstone at 150ft
11549   Do   do

Boundary Claim, Toy Bros.

11550 Tinstone at 50ft

Caledonia, J. Meehan

11551 Tinstone at 100ft

Guldunda, J. Cassida

11552 Tinstone at 80ft
11553   Do   50ft

Bismarck, Petersen & Wright

11554 Tinstone at 80ft
11555   Do   90ft

COOLGARA ... ... *Spranklin's, J. Spranklin*

11556 Tinstone at 20ft

Victoria, Cross & Boldiki

11557	Tinstone at 100ft	
11559	Do	120ft

Lovely Ethel, S. de Lany

11560   Tin crystals at surface

Magdala, O'Hara Bros.

11561   Tinstone at 90ft

Austral, S. de Lany

11562	Tinstone at 12ft	
11563	Do	15ft

Butcher's Creek

11564   Surface specimen

Alhambra, S. de Lany & Co.

11565	Tinstone (chlorite), at 80ft		
11566	Do	do	90ft

Extended, John Moffat & Co.

11567   Tinstone at 73ft

Minerva, J. K. Tucker

11568	Tinstone at 20ft	
11569	Do	25ft

Recommended by the Committee as a safe investment for capitalists.

Koh-i-noor, Ranken & McManus

11570 ⎫
11571 ⎭ Silver ore, containing 90oz and 113oz per ton

"This lease adjoins the Minerva, and is considered by experts to be a valuable property."—*Committee's Report.*

CALIFORNIA CREEK   ...   .   *New Zealand, Ahearne Bros*

11572   Tinstone (chlorite) at 20ft

Far Downer, O'Hara Bros.

11573   Tinstone with blende at surface

Gladstone, Mulany & Roberts

11574   Tinstone (chlorite) at 40ft

Gladstone No. 1, Atkinson Bros.

11575	Tinstone (chlorite) at surface		
11576	Do	do	25ft

"The above four claims are all within two miles of each other, and considered by some to be the best investment in the Walsh and Tinaroo Districts. Over 500 tons of ore at surface, which will average 16 per cent. black tin, waiting machinery for treatment."—*Committee's Report.*

COOLGARA ... ... *Austral, S. de Lany*
     11577   Tinstone at surface

CALIFORNIA CREEK ... ... *Gladstone, Mulany & Roberts*
     11578   Tinstone at surface

EUREKA CREEK ... ... *Lass o' Gowrie, J. McKenzie*
     11579   Tinstone at 60ft

CALIFORNIA CREEK ... ... *Far Downer, O'Hara Bros*
     11580   Tinstone at 5ft

IRVINEBANK ... ... *J. Latham*
     11581   Copper carbonates at surface

IRVINEBANK ... ... *John Moffat & Co.*
     11582   Tin slag, refuse from smelting process

EUREKA CREEK ... ... *Gladstone, J. M'Kenzie*
     11583   Tinstone at 40ft

IRVINEBANK ... ... *Great Southern, W. Richards*
     11584   Tinstone (chlorite) faced with bismuth sulphide at 30ft

MOUNT GARNET ... ... *O'Loan & Party's 60 acre lease*
     11585   Copper carbonates
     11586   Copper oxides
     11587   Talc, impure, used in manufacture of fire brick
     11588   Copper carbonates at surface

COOLGARA ... ... *Bonny Dundee, S. de Lany*
     11589   Tinstone (chlorite) at 20ft
     11590   Country rock

                                   Beaconsfield, J. Field
     11591   Tinstone (chlorite) at 20ft
     11592   Do   do   27ft

EUREKA CREEK ... ... *Great Eastern, J M'Kenzie*
     11593   Tinstone (chlorite) at surface

COOLGARA ... ... *Victoria, Cross & Boldikey*
     11594   Quartz and arsenical pyrites

COOLGARA ... ... *Magdala, O'Hara Bros*
     11595   Tinstone at 70ft

COOLGARA ... ... *Rose of Denmark, S. de Lany*
    11596 Tinstone at 20ft

COOLGARA ... ... *Valentine, J. Moxam*
    11598 Tinstone at 20ft

COOLGARA .. .. *John Bull, J. Moxam*
    11599 Tinstone at 60ft
    11600   Do   90ft

HERBERTON ... ... *Republic, W. C. Ranson*
    11601 Tinstone at 20ft

GLEN LINEDALE ... ... *California, J. Cody*
    11602 Tinstone at 20ft
    11603   Do   surface

HERBERTON ... ... *St. Patrick, Dan Lavary*
    11604 Tinstone at 20ft
    11605   Do   40ft
    11606   Do   60ft
    11607   Do   80ft
    11608   Do   100ft
    11609 Country rock at 80ft
    Said to be the richest stone in this collection.

Great Northern Gully, W. M. Bonar
    11610 Tinstone at surface

EMU CREEK ... ... *Tasmania, T. Thompson*
    11611 Tinstone at 20ft

HERBERTON ... ... *Ly-ee-moon, Jas. Clark*
    11612 Tinstone at 100ft

EMU CREEK ... ... *Transatlantic*
    11613 Tinstone at 50ft

HERBERTON ... ... *Black King, T. Maguire, Manager*
    11614 Tinstone at 40ft
    11615 Tinstone at 60ft
    11616   Do at 80ft
    11617   Do at 120ft

WATSONVILLE ... ... *Chance, W. Lewis*
    11618 Tinstone at 20ft
    11619   Do at 60ft

Glencairn, J. Watson
    11620 Tinstone at 100ft

St. Patrick, S. de Lany

11620* Tinstone at 60ft
11621   Do   at 80ft
11622   Do   at 120ft

HERBERTON ... Monarch Tin Mining Company, J. Williams, Manager

11623 Tinstone at 200ft
11624   Do   do

Ironclad, St. Patrick's Hill

11625 Tinstone

Great Northern, W. M. Bonar

11626 Tinstone at 300ft

Scotchman, part of Phœnix Lease, J. Irwin

11627 Tinstone at 80ft

Poor Stroller

11628 Tinstone at 126ft

Big Ben

11629 Tinstone at 60ft

Bradlaugh, J. Manning

11630 Tinstone at 100ft

Parnell

11631 Tinstone at 20ft

Perseverance

11632 Tinstone and wolfram at 80ft

Union

11633 Tinstone at 20ft

Maori Chief

11634 Tinstone at 20ft
11635 Prophyry at surface

Crucible, F. J. Denny

11636 Tinstone at 20ft
11637 Copper carbonate at 10ft

London

11638 Tinstone at 62ft

WATSONVILLE   ...   . Dead Secret
11639 Tinstone at 50ft

HERBERTON ..   .. Silver King
11640 Tinstone at 80ft

Clan Ronald, J. Weate

11641· Copper carbonates at 10ft
11642   Do   do

EUREKA CREEK ... *Centennial (late discovery), J. Green & Party*
    11643 Tinstone on surface
    11644 Do   do

Black Rock, W. Seaman
    11645 Tinstone (chlorite) at 50ft

Clan Ronald, J. Weate
    11646 Tin and copper at 80ft

J. Green
    11647 Copper outcrop, near tin claim
    11648   Do   do
    11649 Wolfram on surface

EUREKA CREEK ... ... *Australian, J. McKenzie*
    11650 Tinstone at 20 ft

Eclipse, D. Montgomery
    11651 Tinstone (chlorite) at 30ft
    11652 Do   do   do

BAKER'S CAMP ... ... *Little Bischopf, Broad & Party*
    11653 Silver lead at 20ft

HERBERTON ... ... *Nancy's Daughter, G. S. Davis & Party*
    11654 Tinstone at 5ft
    11655   Do   20ft
    11656   Do   24ft

Ly-ee-moon, J. Clark
    11657 Tinstone at 20ft
    11658   Do   40ft
    11659   Do   60ft
    11660   Do   80ft

GLEN LINEDALE ... ... *Caledonia, J. Cody*
    11661 Tinstone at 20ft

DEEP LEAD ... ... *Masterson's, Masterson & Party*
    11662 Washdirt at 40ft
    11663   Do   do

Donovan's Claim (6 miles from Herberton), F. Donovan & Party
    11664 Washdirt

Phœnix, J. Irwin, Manager
    11665 No. 1 Tinstone at bottom of shaft
          2   Do 20ft from bottom of shaft
          3   Do 180ft Do   do
          4   Do 24ft Do   do

5	Tinstone at 170ft from bottom of shaft			
6	Do	30ft	Do	do
7	Do	118ft	Do	do
8	Do	20ft from shaft		
9	Do	182ft	Do	
10	Do	24ft	Do	
11	Do	24ft	Do	
12	Do	surface		

WATSONVILLE   ...   .   *Lass o' Gowrie, J. McKenzie*

11666   Tinstone at 80ft
11667   Country rock at 20ft

North Australian, O'Loan & Casey

11668   Various samples at 50ft

Rose of England, J Pyle

11669   Country rock at 50ft
11670   Various samples incapable of identification

Herberton Tin Company

11671   Dressed ore

Great Northern Tin Mining Company

11672   Felspathic rock with tin crystals occurring in longitudi-
        nal bands at 216ft, estimated yield 35 per cent black tin,
        from a block of about two tons
11673   Quartzite rock with slickenside joints at 180ft, estimated
        yield 40 per cent black tin
11674   Surface stone in soil under outcrop of east lode, estimated
        yield 20 per cent black tin
11675   Samples showing wolfram, associated with tin and quartz
        at 216ft
11676   Brown tinstone, extra quality, with quartz at 60ft,
        estimated yield 60 per cent black tin
11678   Quartzite and felspathic rock with tin crystals occurring
        in bands at 180ft, estimated yield 30 per cent black
        tin
11680   Felspathic and serpentinous rock at 250ft, estimated
        yield 25 per cent black tin
11681   Fine grained green chlorite from gully lode at 120ft,
        estimated yield 20 per cent black tin
11682   Fine grained green chlorite from gully lode at 120ft,
        estimated yield 20 per cent black tin

—*Exhibitors :* THE COMPANY *per* THE HERBERTON LOCAL COMMITTEE

Mineral Exhibits of the Mount Albion Silver Mining and Smelting Company, Limited, Mount Albion, near Herberton.

Albion Silver Mine

11700   1 Gossan ore containing 146oz silver per ton
          2 Lead ore containing 77oz silver per ton
          3 Seleniferous ore
         3A Species of bournonite sulph. antimonide and arsenide
              of copper and lead with selenium and zinc
          4 Iron cinder
          5 Green ore (seleniferous)
             Specimens of horn silver

This mine is situated on the eastern slope of a prominent conical hill about half a mile distant from the company's smelting works. The deposit occurs in a fissure formed in a country rock, consisting of more or less altered sandstone and slate. Work has been carried on continuously since January, 1885, and between that date and April, 1888 over 3000 tons of ore containing 289,000oz of silver have been raised.

Lady Jane Silver Mine

          6 Galena
          7 Galena
         7A Galena containing 408oz silver per ton
          8 Iridescent cinder

This mine, which is over 220ft in depth, opened in the form of an iron blow poor in silver. The first indications of rich deposits were the discovery of pockets of horn silver at about 70ft, since when the shoot has opened out into a large body of very rich galena. Over 30,000oz of silver contained in 660 tons of ore have been got from this mine.

Agnostic Cutting

          9 Galena and anglesite containing 100oz silver per ton

Silverhill Mine

         10 Galena and anglesite containing 60oz silver per ton

Silverfield Mine

         11 Galena and anglesite and large specimen of galena containing 72oz silver per ton

The Silverhill and Silverfield mines are situated about two miles south from the smelting works. The ore occurs in a definite lode through a slate formation. Both mines are

F

worked by means of tunnels driven along the lode, which averages 4ft 6in wide. The present monthly output of ore from these mines is about 200 tons, averaging 45oz silver per ton.

No. 1 Star Silver Mine

12   Scorodite ore, hydrated arseniate of iron

The following is the analysis of a characteristic specimen of ore from this mine:—

	PER CENT.
Arsenic acid	37·00
Peroxide of iron ...	30·75
Alumina	3·00
Sulphate of lead	3·35
Silica	7·75
Combined water	18·16
Moisture	0·12
	100·13

Silver averages 40oz per ton. Green ore occurs in bands alternating with a brown ore of similar composition and a gossan lead ore between walls of quartz porphyry.

13   Brown ore containing 32oz silver per ton
14   Irony ore containing 18oz silver per ton
14A Lead ore containing 46oz silver per ton

Nannam Mine

15   Gossan ore containing 22oz silver per ton

Blue Bell Mine

16   Gossan ore

Star South Mine

17   White ore

Callao Mine

18   Manganese silver ore

Jubilee Mine

19   Manganese silver ore

The foregoing six mines are members of the Orient group which is situated five miles to the east of the works. The deposits occur in a decomposed porphyry formation and show great signs of permanence. The output per month from this group is about 225 tons, averaging 40oz silver per ton.

Fluxes.—Ironstone, limestone, fluor spar

Furnace Products.—50 model bars silver-lead bullion, speiss, arsenide and antimonide of iron containing 7oz silver per ton, matte sulphide of iron

Litharge.—Oxide of lead, containing 3oz silver per ton

Slags.—Varying from ½oz to 1oz silver per ton

The object in smelting being to obtain the lead and silver in the ores in the state of base bullion, the ores are first mixed in such proportions as to contain a sufficient per centage of lead, say 25 per cent., to dissolve and carry as much of the silver as possible. The ores thus mixed consist of oxides of iron and lead with silica, clay, sulphur, arsenic and antimony. They are mixed with the fluxes in such proportions that the clay and lime and silica with a portion of the iron unite to form a fusible slag containing only traces of silver (½oz to 1oz) and lead, the sulphur combining with iron to form matte, and the arsenic and antimony combining with the remainder of the iron to form speiss, thus leaving the lead and silver in the metallic state as base bullion.

No. 11999.—Tin Ore Specimens from Walsh and Tinaroo Districts, Exhibited by Hammond & Denney, Watsonville.

No.	Name of Mine	Owners	Description of Mineral	Locality.
1	"Boundary"	Toy Bros.	Tin in quartz, 10 per cent. black tin	Watsonville
2	Specimens		Tin in felspar, 40 per cent. black tin	Eureka Creek
3	"Wild Irish Girl"	Allen Bros.	Tin in quartz and felspar	Watsonville
4	"Lass"	J. & G. McKenzie	Grey tin ore and felspar, 60 per cent. metal tin	Eureka Creek
5	Specimens		Tin and fluorspar	Thompson's Creek
6	Do		Do do 48 per cent. black tin	Do
7	"Silver Crown"	Dempster & Co.	Rosin tin, very rare, 74 per cent. metal tin	Watsonville
8	"Caledonian"	Company	Tin in quartz, 18 per cent. black tin	Do
9	Specimens		Solid tin ore, 68 per cent. metal tin	Do
10	Do		Goesan tin ore, 60 per cent. black tin	Do
11	Do		Tin in veins (stratified tin)	Irvine Bank
12	Do		Tin kaolin (and decomposed rock)	Do
13	Do		Tin and mundic, &c.	Watsonville
14	Do		Tin ore, 38 per cent. black tin	Do
15	Do		Grey tin ore, 20 per cent. black tin	Do
16	Do		Tin and tourmaline, 16 per cent. black tin	Eureka Creek
17	"Wild Irish Girl"	Allen Bros.	Tin in clear quartz, 54 per cent. black tin	Watsonville
18	"Croesus Mine"	Noonan &|Party	Fine tin in granite, porphyry, &c., 22 per cent. black tin	Thompson's Creek
19	Specimen		Tin ore, 60 per cent. metal tin	Do
20	Do		Tin and iron, 48 per cent. black tin	Cummins' Camp
21	Do		Crystal tin	Emu Creek
22	Do		Red tin and iron, 56 per cent. metal tin	Watsonville
23	"Glen Cairn"	Watson & Co.	Tin ore, 18 per cent. black tin	Do
24	Specimen		Tin and mica	Near Watsonville

No.	Name of Mine.	Owners.	Description of Mineral.	Locality;
25	Waterworn Specimen	...	Tin ore, 56 per cent. black tin ...	Watsonville
26	Specimen	...	Black tin in quartz, 25 per cent. black tin ...	Do
27	Do	...	Red tin ore, 22 per cent. black tin ...	Do
28	Do	...	Rich tin ore, 60 per cent. metal ...	Do
29	Do	...	Tin and iron, 20 per cent. black tin ...	Do
30	Do	...	Tin in porphyry, &c., 40 per cent. black tin...	Do
31	Do	...	Tin and mundic ...	Do
32	Do	...	Tin in decomposed rock, 32 per cent. black tin	Bakerville
33	Do	...	Grey tin ore, 60 per cent. black (dressed) tin	Watsonville
34	Do	...	Tin in quartz, 30 per cent. do	Do
35	Do	...	Solid tin, 68 per cent. metal tin	Do
36	Do	...	Tin in porphyry, 21 per cent. black tin ...	Do
37	Do	...	Tin in brown quartz, 15 per cent. black tin...	Do
38	Do	...	Tin in kaolin, mica, &c., 32 per cent. black tin	Do
39	Do	...	Crystal tin in quartz, &c. ...	Coolgarra
40	Do	...	Tin in quartz, 18 per cent. black tin...	Watsonville
41	"Jubilee"	...	Tin in chlorite, 10 do do ...	Cummins' Camp
42	Specimen	Hammond & Denney	Tin in dense quartz, 21 per cent. black tin...	Watsonville
43	Do	...	Tin ore, 30 per cent. black tin...	Do
44	Do	...	Crystal tin and iron, 50 per cent. black tin ...	Do
45	Do	...	Tin and wolfram in fluorspar, &c. ...	Eureka Creek
46	Do	...	Tin ore, 58 per cent. black tin ...	Watsonville
47	Do	...	Tin and mundic ...	
48	Black Rock	Mongomery, Seamen & Party	Tin in decomposed rock, 62 per cent. black tin	Eureka Creek
49	Specimen	...	Tin in chlorite, 20 per cent. black tin ...	Do
50	Do	...	Tin and garnets ...	Bakerville
51	"Gladstone"	Mellaney & Roberts	Tin and silicate of iron... ...	Eureka Creek
52	Do	Do	Crystal tin in chlorite, 15 per cent. black tin	Californian Gully
53	"Chance"	...	Crystal tin, 60 per cent. metal tin ...	Do
54	Specimen	Armuller & Lewis	Tin ore and zeolites ...	Watsonville
55	Specimen	...	Tin in chlorite, 25 per cent. black tin	Emu Creek

No.	Name of Mine.	Owners.	Description of Mineral.	Locality.
56	Specimen	...	Tin in felspar &c., 56 per cent. black tin, ...	Eureka Creek
57	Do	...	Tin in fluorspar and feldspar, 55 per cent. black tin	Return Creek
58	Do	...	Tin and arsenical pyrites, 20 per cent. black tin	Watsonville
59	Do	...	Crystal (massive) tin, 60 per cent. metal	Do
60	Do	...	Tin ore, 60 per cent. black tin	Do
61	Do	...	Massive tin ore, 55 per cent. metal	Do
62	"North Australian"	Casey & O'Loan	Tin ore, 20 per cent. black tin	Do
63	Specimen	...	Massive tin ore and quartz, 60 per cent. black tin	Do
64	Do	Petersen & Co.	Massive tin ore and quartz, 65 per cent. metal	Do
65	"Bismarck"	...	Tin ore in black killas (slate), 54 per cent. metal	Do
66	Do	Petersen & Co.	Tin ore in black killas (slate), 60 per cent. metal	Do
67	"Great Western"	Company	Tin in iron and chlorite, 60 per cent. metal	Do
68	Specimen	...	Tin ore, 70 per cent. black (dressed) tin	Do
69	Do	...	Tin in veins of quartz	Do
70	Do	...	Tin ore, 56 per cent. metal tin	Do
71	Do	...	Solid tin ore, 60 per cent. metal	Eureka Creek
72	Do	...	Crystal tin, 70 per cent. black tin	Watsonville
73	Do	...	Black tin ore, 66 per cent. black tin	Do
74	Do	...	Crystal tin ore, 43 per cent. metal tin	Do
75	Do	...	Solid tin ore, 65 per cent. metal tin	Do
76	Do	...	Red (speckled) tin ore, 50 per cent. black tin	Do
77	Do	...	Solid tin ore, 60 per cent. metal tin	Do
78	Do	...	Crystal tin, 65 per cent. black tin	Do
79	Do	...	Solid tin ore, 60 per cent. metal tin	Do
80	Do	...	Fine tin in micaceous rock	Irvine Bank
81	Do	...	Ruby tin ore, 50 per cent. metal tin	Emu Creek
82	Do	...	Solid tin ore, 75 per cent. metal tin	Watsonville

No.	Name of Mine.	Owners.	Description of Mineral.	Locality.
83	Specimen	...	Stratified tin ore	Irvine Bank
84	"Federation"	Hammond & Denney	Tin and 80 oz. silver per ton of mineral	Watsonville
85	Do	do	Tin and iron, 16 per cent. black tin ...	Do
86	Do	do	Tin and arsenic, 15 per cent black tin	Do
87	Do	do	Do do 25 do do ...	Do
88	Do	do	Tin in iron scoriæ	Do
89	Do	do	Tin and iron, 50 per cent. black tin ...	Do
90	Do	do	Good tin ore, 60 per cent. metal tin ...	Do
91	Specimen	...	Tin, copper, lead, and bismuth and silver	Do
92	Do	...	Tin and iron, 20 per cent. black tin ...	Do
93	"Maud and Mary"	Walsh Tin Co.	Do do do do ...	Walsh River
94	Do	do	Tin in chlorite, 18 per cent. black tin	Do
95	Do	do	Diamond tin ore, 20 per cent. black tin	Do
96	Specimen	...	Tin in chlorite do do	Watsonville
97	"Jubilee"	Hammond & Denny	Tin and arsenical pyrite,18 per cent. black tin ...	Eureka Creek
98	Specimen	...	Crystal red tin ore, 65 per cent. black tin	Do
99	Do	...	Crystal tin ore, 60 per cent. metal tin	Bakerville
100	Do	...	Crystal ruby and brown tin, 74 per cent. metal tin	Do
101	"Gladstone"	Mellaney & Roberts	Crystal tin and iron, 62 per cent. metal tin...	Californian Creek
102	Specimen	...	Tin ore in quartz, 32 per cent. black tin ...	Watsonville
103	Do	...	Tin in black quartz, 50 per cent. black tin	Cummins' Camp
104	Do	...	Crystal tin ore, 68 per cent. metal tin	
105	Do	...	Tin in micaceous (volcanic) rock, crystals ...	Walsh River
106	"Federation"	Hammond & Denney	Tin in gossany iron, 43 per cent. black tin ...	Watsonville
107	"Vulcan"	Mongomery & Seamen	Tin in chlorite, 10 per cent. black tin	Eureka Creek
108	"Black Rock"	Mongomery & Seamen	Tin ore and iron, 40 per cent. black tin	Do
109	"Federation"	Hammond & Denney	Tin ore, 20 per cent. black (dressed) tin	Watsonville
110	"Glen Cairn"	Watson & Co.	Do 50 do do do	Do
111	"Black Rock Extended"	Mongomery & Seamen	Tin in chlorite, 20 per cent. black (dressed) tin	Eureka Creek

No.	Name of Mine.	Owners.	Description of Mineral.	Locality.
112	Specimen	...	Tin ore, 20 per cent. black (dressed) tin ...	Thompson's Creek
113	A. Thompson's Claim	...	Tin ore in quartz, &c., 40 per cent. black (dressed) tin	Cummins' Camp
113*	"Nil Desperandum" Claim	...	...	
114	Specimen	...	Tin ore, 30 per cent. black tin...	Walsh River
115	"General Gordon" Claim	Moffat & Co.	Tin, speckled through micaceous rock	Do
116	"Comet"	Do	Tin ore	Glen Linedale
117	Specimen	...	Tin ore	Irvine Bank
118	"Red King"	Moffat & Co.	Tin ore	Do
119	"Great Southern"	Do	Tin in ferruginous rock	Do
120	Specimen	Moffat & Co.	Tin ore	Glen Linedale
121	"Oberlin"	...	Tin in quartz, 25 per cent. black tin	Do
122	Specimen	...	Tin ore, 20 per cent. black tin...	Watsonville
123	Do	...	Tin in quartz, 50 per cent. black tin...	Do
124	"Royal Standard"	R. Watson & Co.	Tin in decomposed rock, 6½ per cent. metal tin	Walsh River
125	Specimen	...	Surface specimen, 30 per cent. black tin	Watsonville
126	Do	...	Fine tin in (wall) rock	Do
127	Do	...	Tin in felspar, porphyry, &c., 15 per cent. black tin	
128	"Glen Cairn"	Watson & Co.	Solid tin, 50 per cent. metal tin	Do
129	Specimen	...	Tin (killas) slate, 45 per cent. metal tin	Do
130	Do	...	Tin in ferruginous chlorite, 10 per cent. black tin	Watsonville
131	Do	...	Tin and copper, 17 per cent. metal copper, 20 per cent. black tin	
132	Do	...	15 per cent. black tin, 20 per cent. metal copper	Do
133	Do	...	10 per cent. black tin, 16 per cent. metal copper	Do
134	Do	...	25 per cent. black tin, 4 per cent. metal copper	Do

No.	Name of Mine	Owners	Description of Mineral	Locality
135	"Ivanhoe"	Vandeleur & Co.	Tin with mundic, 30 per cent. black tin	Eureka Creek
136	Cummins & Co.'s claim	...	Tin in black killas (slate, etc.), 30 per cent. black tin	Cummins' Camp
137	"Gem"	R. Watson & Co.	Tin in quartzose rock, 28 per cent. black tin	Walsh River
138	A. Thompson's Claim	...	Tin and copper, black tin 19 per cent.	Cummins' Camp
139	Specimen	...	Tin and iron, 25 per cent. black (dressed) tin	Watsonville
140	Do	...	Surface specimen, 60 per cent. metal tin	Do
141	Do	...	Crystal tin ore	Do
142	Do	...	Arsenical pyrites and tin ore, 62 per cent. metal	
143	Do	...	Waterworn tin-stone, 20 per cent. black tin	Eureka Creek
144	Do	...	Black quartz, etc., and tin, 68 per cent. metal tin	Watsonville
145	"Eclipse"	Mongomery & Seamen	Fine tin in quartz rock, 25 per cent. black tin	Eureka Creek
146	"Cosmopolitan" claim	...	Tin ore in decomposed rock	Irvine Bank
147	Specimen	...	Blue and green carbonates and tin ore	Watsonville
148	"North Australian"	O'Loan & Casey	Tin and copper, 54 per cent. black tin, 3½ per cent. metal copper	Do
149	"Federation"	Hammond & Denney	Tin in quartz, etc., 30 per cent. black (dressed) tin	Do
150	"Chance Extended" Claim	Lewis & Armuller	Tin from 70ft level, 20 per cent. black (dressed) tin	Do
151	Do	Do do	Mundic and tin, 25 per cent. black (dressed) tin	Do
152	Do	Do do	Tin and carbonates of copper	Do
153	Specimen	...	Mica, near lode Spark's claim	Bakerville
154	Do	...	Tin ore, crystalised round quartz	Watsonville
155	Do	...	Fluorspar, Stenhouse Claim	Silver Valley
156	Do	...	Grey tin ore, 66 per cent. black tin	Eureka Creek

No.	Name of Mine.	Owners	Description of Mineral.	Locality.
157	"Bischoff"	Herberton Tin Co.	Mill-dressed brown coarse No. 1 tin, 68·5 per cent. metal	Watsonville
158	Do	Do	Mill-dressed black No. 1 tin, 71 per cent. metal	Do
159	Do	Do	Mill-dressed slimes tin, 72 per cent. metal	Do
160	Do	Do	Mill-dressed brown slimes tin, 70 per cent. metal	Do
161	...	...	Stream tin found in gullies and creeks near lodes, 73 per cent. metal	Do
162	...	...	Tin ore found near lodes in creeks—indicating lodes	Watsonville and District
163	"T Claim"	Stewart & Co.	Tin ore from 300 feet level, 46 per cent. black tin	Watsonville
164	"Caledonian"	Company	Tin ore from 180 feet level, 70 per cent. black tin	Do
165	McLelland and Green's Claim		Tin from large surface block, 48 per cent. black tin	Eureka Creek
166	"Gladstone"	Ellwood & Co.	Tin ore in quartz, &c., 66 per cent. black tin	Do
167	Specimen		Tin and carbonate of copper	Do
168	Do		Tin in chlorite (black), 20 per cent. black tin	Watsonville
169	Do		Grey tin ore, 60 per cent. metal tin	Eureka Creek
170	"North Australian"	O'Loan & Casey	Tin and copper, showing country rock	Watsonville
171	"Black Rock Extended"		Tin from 80 feet level, 42 per cent. black tin	Eureka Creek
172	"Lass o' Gowrie"	Mongomery & Seamen J. & G. McKenzie	Banded tin with quartz, 56 per cent. black tin	Do
173	Do	Do	Rich tin from deep workings, 65 per cent. metal	Do
174	Specimen		Crystal tin, found in Wild River	Near Herberton
175	Cummin and Party		Tin from deep workings	Cummin' Camp

MINERALS MISTAKEN FOR TIN BY PROSPECTORS.

A, Wolfram, B, Garnets and Mica, C, Mica, &c., D, Tourmaline, E, Tourmaline, F, Zinc Blende (Black Jack), G, Iron (crystals), H, Iron Crystals, I, Zeolite with Iron, J, Iron, K, Iron, L, Iron Crystals, M, Iron, N, Chromate Iron, O, Wolfram.

NOTE.—Specimens, name of claim not known, exhibited as showing different qualities of Tin and Gangue.

All specimens are from Walsh and Tinaroo Mining District.

HAMMOND & DENNEY,

Assayers,
Watsonville, North Queensland.

Tinaroo Section—Irvinebank.

Description of the field and list of exhibits furnished by Messrs. John Moffat & Co.

IRVINEBANK (Tinaroo District).

11998 About 85 miles south and west from Port Douglas, with which it is connected by a good waggon road.

The township is situated on the head waters of the Walsh river (western fall), in rugged broken country composed of schists, shales and greywackes principally. It is connected with Herberton, Watsonville, Newellton, and Montalbion by good roads.

The Great Southern, Comet, Tornado, and other lodes were discovered in 1883 by Gibbs and party, who sold their interests to John Moffat & Co.

Work was commenced by this company in the early part of 1884 by the construction of a large dam, the erection of a battery of five stamps with all necessary tin dressing machinery; also, smelting works for the reduction of the tin oxide to metal (the only tin reducing works in Queensland.)

An additional set of five stamps have been added to this plant since March, 1887.

The tinstone treated has been 12,000 tons, producing 1500 tons of black tin, and 900 tons of metallic tin have been despatched to port.

Population of Irvinebank and vicinity about 500, of whom 250 are employed on the works and mines owned by John Moffat & Co.

The township is laid off round the Loudoun mill and smelting works. There are four hotels, a school of arts and hall for public purposes, a provisional school and church. The climate of this district is cool and salubrious, perhaps due to its altitude above sea level.

GREAT SOUTHERN LEASE ...   . *John Moffat & Co.*

Situated about one mile from the Loudoun Battery.

Comprises a group of lodes known as the Prospector's, Red King, and Nos. 1, 2, 3, 4, 5 and 6, Great Southern shafts and extensions of what might prove to be one main or champion lode.

They occur in highly metamorphosed sedimentary rocks, greywackes and schists, at times so hard and silicious as to be quartzite, veined with dykes of schorlaceous quartz, ramifying in all directions, sometimes stanniferous.

The general strike of the lodes is roughly north 30° west, invariably dipping west. The gangue is chlorite and quartz carrying cassiterite, disseminated and massive, accompanied by small quantities of fluor spar, iron pyrites, wolfram, and blende.

This lease has been continuously worked since 1884, employing about 40 men.

Tinstone raised   ...   .   7500 tons
Black tin produced ..   ..   850 „

THE RED KING ...   . *John Moffat & Co.*

Originally a claim adjoining the Great Southern, now included in the foregoing lease.

Tinstone raised   .   ...   525 tons
Black tin produced ...   .   60 „

Characteristic specimens from last crushing.

Specimen of wolfram from No. 3, Great Southern shaft.

Specimen of surface tinstone from No. 6, Great Southern shaft.

EXCELSIOR LEASE   ...   . *Jonathan White*

About 500 yards west of the Great Southern Lease. A well-defined schorlaceous dyke in graywacke country. Characteristic specimens from last crushing, 20 tons, value £7 5s per ton, February, 1888, at present on tribute to Wilson and party.

HARD TAE GET CLAIM   ...   . *Wm. Alexander*

Situated about 500 yards south-east of the Great Southern Lease. A small rich vein in quartzite, yielding ore which was smelted without dressing, assaying 65 per cent. metallic tin. In this mine are occasionally vughs, which are lined with quartz crystals and cassiterite. Characteristic specimens exhibited.

Wm. Wilson

Characteristic specimens from last crushing in February, 1888, from mine situated about 200 yards north of the Excelsior Lease. Value of tinstone raised £10 15s per ton.

THE COMET LEASE ... ... *John Moffat & Co.*

Situated about 1¼ mile north-east from the Loudoun Battery. The country rock near the main fissures is of a highly silicious character, approaching hornstone, otherwise the usual local formations, greywackes and shales. The general strike of the lode is north-west dipping to the west. The gangue is quartz chlorite and schorl, with cassiterite disseminated, but often in solid ferruginous nodules, accompanied by small quantities of iron pyrites, traces of copper and wolfram. From this lease 1000 tons tin stone have been raised and crushed for a produce of 150 tons black tin.

Kehoe & Edge

Characteristic specimens from crushing, February, 1888; value, £19 10s. per ton. This lode is situated a quarter of a mile north-east of the Comet Lease.

BULL DOG CLAIM ... ... *Moffat & Hardman*

Characteristic specimens from an immense schorlaceous quartz dyke, carrying rich patches of cassiterite, situated half a mile north-east of Comet Lease.

Madigan & Wolstencroft

Characteristic specimen from crushing, February, 1888; value, £17 10s. per ton. Raised from chlorite lode, situated half a mile north-west from Comet Lease.

CHRISTMAS BOX CLAIM ... ... *Madigan & Wolstencroft*

Characteristic bulk specimen.

T. Cornish

Characteristic hand specimens from crushing, February, 1888. Value, £8 per ton.

Frame & Roberts

Characteristic hand specimens from crushing, February, 1888. Value, £7 5s. per ton.

JUMNA LEASE ... ... *John Moffat & Co.*

Characteristic specimens from schorlaceous dyke, opened 1884; situated about a mile and a half north-north-west from the Comet

PLANET CLAIM   ...   .   *Wm. Moss*
Characteristic bulk specimens; situated about two miles north-north-west from the Loudoun Mill. It is a schorlaceous quartz lode. The cassiterite is remarkable in the bulk specimens for the regularity with which it is formed in thin parallel streaks. Ore at grass 70 tons, estimated at 14 per cent. black tin.

LUCKY HIT CLAIM...   ...   .   *Robert Edge*
Characteristic hand specimens; situated near "The Bull Dog;" worked since 1884 with varying success.

Thomas Madigan
Characteristic specimens from last crushing in February, 1888, valued at £22 15s per ton.

Allesso Leoni
Characteristic specimens from last crushing in February, 1888. Value per ton, £14 5s.

James Gibbs
Characteristic bulk specimens recently discovered half-a-mile north-east of Great Southern, on the same hill, ore at grass about 70 tons, estimated to yield 15 per cent. black tin. Bulk specimens showing small patches of wolfram accompanying the disseminated binoxide of tin.

JUST IN TIME CLAIM   ...   .   *John Moffat & Co.*
Characteristic hand specimens from ore at grass, situated within the boundary of the Mill Lease.

TORNADO LEASES   ...   .   *John Moffat & Co.*
Characteristic specimens from Nos. 1, 2, 3, 4, 5, and 6 workings. Situated about one mile west from the mill, on the western fall of a ridge, trending north Composed of quartzite and greywackes, traversed by ferruginous dykes and outcrops, invariably carrying black tin. It is remarkable that the eastern fall of this ridge should be non-stanniferous, although the formations and outcrops are of the same general character as the western side. The general strike of this group of lodes is west 30° north, underlying south. Ore shoots dipping east, and are bunchy in character. Tinstone crushed at Loudoun mill, 1050 tons, producing black tin, 180 tons; ore at grass of average quality, 400 tons.

ADVENTURE LEASE ...   .   *John Moffat & Co.*
Characteristic bulk and hand specimens. Situated about four miles west from the Loudoun Mill. In greywackes and

shales. The most conspicuous feature of this lode is its regularity in width, strike and parellelism of the walls; it has an average width of 5ft., with occasional carbonas. Strike north-west, underlie 30° west. Deepest shaft, 180ft.; levels, 200ft. The ores have been raised from two well defined shoots, dipping to the south, and are of an argillaceous, friable character, carrying binoxide of tin in grains and small compact masses. Specimen marked in margin, from bottom level, carries 12 per cent. black tin, is of slightly brecciated character, accompanied by considerable quantities of iron pyrites. This lease has been worked since 1885, producing 1120 tons tinstone, yielding 190 tons black tin.

FAIRVIEW ... ... *John Guerin*

Characteristic specimens from last crushing, and ore at grass. Situated on the northern boundary of the Tornado, No. 2, the ore being of varied character, quartz, chlorite, clay, and at times highly ferruginous, carrying disseminated oxide of tin. The shaft is sunk to a depth of 80ft., on the junction of two veins, cutting each other diagonally.

COSMOPOLITAN ... ... *Thomson & Eales*

Characteristic hand specimens. This lease, situated about three miles west of the mill, has been worked since its discovery in 1885, with payable results, being the pioneer claim of this portion of the Irvinebank district. Specimens exhibited from crushing, February, 1888, of 32 tons tinstone. Value, £13 5s per ton.

WANDERER ... ... *John Pollard*

Characteristic specimens from last crushing, February, 1888; 30 tons, value £10 10s. per ton; adjoining Cosmopolitan; worked since 1885.

James Green

Characteristic hand specimens from last crushing, February, 1888; valued at £19 per ton. Situated about six miles west from Irvinebank.

. *David Howell*

Characteristic hand specimens from last crushing, February, 1888; value, £18 per ton; situated near James Green's claim.

GENERAL GORDON LEASE, }
Glen Linedale } ... ... *John Moffat & Co.*

Characteristic bulk specimens. Situated about nine miles south-south-east from Irvinebank. Country rock, schorlaceous, talcose schists and greywackes, probably a continua-

tion of the Irvinebank formations. The Gordon lode is of
immense size, but as yet undefined extent. The gangue is
composed of schorlaceous quartz. 2,000 tons of ore have
been raised from shallow open-cast workings, from which a
shaft has been continued on ore of a satisfactory character.
A tunnel has been driven to cut the lode at shaft bottom,
110ft. from the surface, disclosing quantities of ores similar
to upper level. A dam has been constructed, 10-stamp
battery, and all the necessary appliances for the treatment of
tin ores, which will be run direct from the workings into
stone-crusher attached to mill, which is expected to commence crushing immediately. Since the discovery of this
place by Edward Giblett in 1886, upwards of 30 men have
been employed in making roads, erecting machinery, and
carrying on the exploitations of the mine. Ore at grass,
3,000 tons.

OBERLIN LEASE.

Characteristic specimens, amalgamated with The General
Gordon.

CALEDONIAN CLAIM   ...   .   *Embleton, Codz & Co.*

Characteristic specimens from last crushing, February,
1888. Value, £23 per ton. Situated about one mile west
from the Gordon, Glen Linedale.

M. Hickey & Party.

Characteristic specimens from last crushing, February,
1888. Value, £23 per ton. Situated about six miles south-
east from Irvinebank, on Wooloman creek. Exhibit showing coloured fluor spar.

GREAT EXTENDED CLAIM, at Coolgarra ...   ...   *John Moffat & Co.*

Characteristic specimens. This mine has produced 160
tons black tin and a considerable quantity of tin lying at
grass. The lode is chlorite, in chloritoid country of a permanent character.

F. Tucker, Return Creek.

Characteristic specimens from last crushings, February,
1888. Value, £6 15s per ton. Situated near Coolgarra.

Harry Waz, Return Creek.

Characteristic specimens from a recently discovered lode.
Creek Boulder specimen obtained from a large mass found
by James Arbouin, Esq.

Patrick McCulloch.

Hand specimens from an undeveloped lode, Emu Creek.
Characteristic hand specimens from last crushing, February, 1888. Value £7 per ton.

Patrick O'Hara, California Creek

Characteristic specimens from last crushing, February, 1888, at Irvinebank. Value of ore, £14 10s per ton.

BANSHEE ... ... *Patrick McNamara, California Creek*

Characteristic specimens from last crushing, February, 1888, at Irvinebank. Value of ore, £10 10s per ton.

CALIFORNIAN KING ... ... *Great Western Tin Company*

Characteristic specimens from last crushing, at Loudoun Mill, Irvinebank, February, 1888.

GLADSTONE ... ... *Mullany & Roberts, California Creek*

Characteristic specimens from last crushing, February, 1888, at Irvinebank. Continuously worked since its discovery in 1885. Value of ore, £17 15s per ton.

Characteristic specimens from the Canadian Claim, discovered and worked by James Mullany, California Creek.

Harry Atkinson, California Creek

Characteristic specimens from last crushing, February, 1888, at Irvinebank. Value of ore, £29 5s per ton.

MAGNET LEASE TIN LODE,⎫ Newellton ⎭ ... ... *W. B. Stenhouse*

Characteristic specimens. Trial crushing, 90 tons tinstone, yielding 8¼ tons black tin.
Specimens of fluor spar (translucent).
Do   do   (greenish)
Specimens of hæmatite.
Specimens of magnetite.

CARRARA LEASE, Newellton ... *John Moffat and W. B. Stenhouse*

Specimens of blue massive limestone, used for flux and building purposes.
Specimens of calcspar (manganiferous)

IRVINEBANK ... ... *John Moffat & Co.*

Three samples of stream tin, found in the vicinity of Irvinebank. The black variety from Emu Creek assaying 74 per cent. metallic tin; the light coarse grain from Nettles Creek, assaying 73 per cent. metallic tin; the fine grain, assaying 73 per cent metallic tin.

A sample bag of lode tinstone from the "Hard tae Get" claim, smelted as raised, assaying 68 per cent. metallic tin.

Dressed tin ores from Loudoun Mill. Average sample from 40 lots tinstone; crushed and dressed at mill, February, 1888. Assaying 68 per cent. metallic tin.

G

Average sample of dressed tin oxide, produced from the Great Southern, Comet, Adventure, and Red King tinstones, during April, 1888, viz.:—Coarse jiggers, assaying 73 per cent metallic tin; fine jiggers, assaying 73 per cent. metallic tin; coarse slimes, assaying 71 per cent. metallic tin; fine slimes, assaying 71 per cent. metallic tin.

One bag mixed black tin and three small ingots of tin, representing the weight or quantity of binoxide of tin it would take to make the miniature ingots exhibited in glass vessel

Four fire bricks made at Irvinebank; the same as used at smelting works.

Tin slag from smelting works.

One test ingot, showing the usual mercantile test applied to a whole ingot.

Trophy of metallic tin ingots, and half a dozen 14lb. ingot moulds, for remoulding.

SILVERFIELD ...   .   *Mary Knot*

12000   Hanging-wall, from surface
12001   Country-rock
12002   Tinstone from near surface, showing occurrence in foot-wall

Barossa

12003   Country-rock at surface
12004   Do   40ft
12005   Argentiferous galena (silver-lead, silver ore)

Silverfield

12006   Argentiferous galena, showing decomposition from exterior inwards
12007   Country rock at surface
12008   Do   70ft
12009   Sample from same lode, from a cutting

Victoria

12010   Argentiferous galena, granular and cubical
12011   Stibnite and galena

Cumnor

12012   Country rock
12013   Decomposed argentiferous galena, from 40ft level
12014   Argentiferous galena, coated with ferric oxide and litharge, said to assay on the average 800oz. of silver per ton—the highest assay being 1400oz
12015   Impure malachite from 40ft level
12016   Hanging-wall

Mount Albion

12017 Hanging-wall, 30ft level
12018   Do   80ft   do
12019 Decomposed galena, with copper stained ferric oxide and litharge
12020 Ironstone
12021 Do
12022 Do
12023 Rich nodules from various depths, assaying from 1000oz per ton

Caledonia

12024 Tinstone in hæmatite

J. Liddle's Claim

12025 Galena, with litharge and ferric oxide, from 20ft level

Cuzco

12026 Fine-grained galena, assaying 100oz per ton, from 30ft level
12027 Country rock
       This lode is well defined, and the outcrop can be traced for two miles. The average yield is 65oz per ton

Wanderer

12028 Tinstone in hæmatite, from 60ft level
12029   Do   country rock at surface
12030 Country-rock at 40ft level
12031   Do   surface
12032 Tinstone in gangue, from 60ft level

Pinnacle Lease, Gregory's Gully

12032* Tinstone in orthoclase felspar

Adventure

12033 Tinstone in kaolin and quartz granules

Cosmopolitan

12034 Tinstone from 30ft level
12035   Do   in kaolin from 80ft level
12036 Country-rock

Tornado

12037 Hanging-wall at 170ft level
12038 Country rock

12039 Blende, chalcopyrite, mispickel and galena at 170ft, yielding on analysis :—

Zinc	13·42	per cent.
Copper	5·10	do
Lead	6·06	do
Arsenic	11·99	do
Iron	29·06	do
Sulphur	32·74	do
Silica	2·11	do

100·48 per cent.

By fire assay, 1oz 2dwt silver per ton.

—*A. W. Clarke*

12040 Tinstone in kaolin
12041 Hanging-wall at 30ft level
12042 Foot-wall

COOLGARA (Return Creek).

12043 Tinstone
12044 Tinstone in hæmatite, yielding on analysis :—

Moisture	1·50	per cent.
Water of combination	5·82	do
Peroxide iron... ...	49·20	do
Silica	4·36	do
Tin	28·30	do
Oxygen, by difference	8·72	do

100·00 per cent.

—*A. W. Clarke*

Great Republic

12045 Tinstone in crystallised quartz

Derwent Mine

12046 Hanging-wall
12047 Tinstone
12048 Tinstone with quartz and felspar
12049 Auriferous galena in limestone, midway between Mount Garnet and Coolgara

Grand Junction Line

12050 Tinstone in micaceous quartz

City Pompeii

12051 Tinstone

Return Creek

12052 Tinstone in boulders in creek

Blair's Claim

12053   Tinstone in hæmatite

Magdala

12054   Tinstone in quartz at 30ft level
12055   Do   at 50ft level
12056   Do   with quartz
12057   Do   in quartz

Nevada Claim

12058   Tinstone at surface

IRVINEBANK   ...   .   *Great Southern*

12059   Fine tinstone, disseminated through hæmatite, at 70ft
        level
12060   Hanging-wall at 70ft level
12061   Foot-wall at surface
12062   Foot-wall at 70ft level
12063   Tinstone
12064   Country rock at 35ft level

Red King

12065   Tinstone in hæmatite at surface
12066   Country rock

Claim adjoining Freethinker

12067   Tinstone in quartz
12067*   Do   nearly clean

Little Wonder

12068   Tinstone in hæmatite
12069   Country rock

Little Claim

12070   Tinstone in hæmatite
12071   Foot-wall
12072   Hanging-wall

Crœsus

12073   Tinstone, clean, at 80ft level
12074   Do   with fluor spar at 80ft level
12075   Do   at 80ft level

City of Bagdad

12076   Tinstone

Comet

12077   Tinstone, clean, at 80ft level, north lode
12078   Do   in hæmatite at surface
12079   Country rock at surface
12080   Tinstone at surface, south lode
12081   Hanging-wall, near surface
12082   Foot-wall, near surface, north lode

12083   Tinstone at 80ft level
12084   Quartzite rock with mispickel

Freethinker

12085   Country rock at 76ft
12086   Tinstone   do   30ft
12086*   Do   do   60ft

John Bull

12087   Tinstone, with quartz and felspar

John Bull, No. 1

12088   Tinstone in quartz

North Britain

12089   Mispickel in quartz at 30ft
12090   Tinstone in quartz and felspar at 30ft
12091   Do   at 30ft

Mount Garnet

12092   Malachite and azurite in gossan of lode
12093   Hæmatite at 40ft
12094   Country rock at 40ft
12095   Copper carbonates on hæmatite
12096   Outcrops of lode
12097   Copper carbonates permeating hæmatite
12098   Decomposed galena, showing copper carbonates and cerussite
12099   Copper carbonates at surface
    This mine is a freehold of 60 acres area, granted to Messrs. J. A. J. M'Leod and C. O'Loan as a prospecting claim. Galena, rich in silver, and cobalt ore are said to have been found on the property, and 3000 or 4000 tons of copper carbonates awaiting railway rates of freight are said to be in sight. Mount Garnet is 10 miles from Coolgara and 35 miles from Herberton.

NEWELLTON ...   ... *Target Mine, Silver Valley Smelting Company*

12100   Decomposing galena from an adit
12101   Fine-grained galena
12102   Do   do   with quartz and carbonates
12103   Galena decomposing into litharge and cerussite on quartz and felspar
12104   Galena decomposing into litharge and cerussite
12105   Galena
12106   Gossan
    The lode runs 10° south of east, and dips 60°.

Potosi Claim

12107   Limestone
12108   Hæmatite
    Fluxes employed in treating the Target and other silver ores

Rainbow

12109   Galena at 80ft level
12110   Do   decomposed; decomposition products
Strike of the lode north-west and south-east, nearly vertical. The lode is from 2ft to 4ft wide; the country rock is black slate.

Caledonia

12112   Galena
12113   Do   with ferric oxide and litharge
12114   Do   fine-grained
12115   Do   decomposition products
12116   Country rock near surface, acted upon by the decomposing lode stuff

Koh-i-noor

12117   Galena from 80ft level
A clean sample gave 12½oz 3dwts silver per ton.—*E. B. Lindon.*
12118   Mispickel
12119   Blende
A clean sample gave 22oz 1dwt of silver per ton.—*E. B. Lindon.*
12120   Mundic in "dig" or casing of lode
12121   Blende and fine-grained galena
12122   Country rock

Just in Time

12123   Tinstone at surface
12124   Do   20ft
12125   Country rock at 20ft

EUREKA CREEK ...   .   *Great Eastern*

12126   Cassiterite in kaolin
12127   Do   hæmatite
12128   Do   do   at 70ft

Clan Ronald

12129   Malachite on hæmatite at surface
12130   Tinstone in felspathic quartz
12131   Do   with felspar, at 20ft
12132   Do   do   argyrite do
12133   Do   do   do   and malachite, at 20ft
12134   Do   in quartz

Lass of Gowrie

12135   Tinstone at 60ft
12136   Do   in mica, at 60ft
12137   Country rock

Black Rock

12138   Tinstone at 30ft
12139   Do   in hæmatite at 70ft

12140   Tinstone at surface
12141   do   at 70ft

Eclipse

12142   Tinstone in quartzite

Ivanhoe

12143   Tinstone in quartz and felspar at 50ft
12144   Tinstone in quartz
12145   Mundic in quartz
12146   Tinstone in quartz and hæmatite at surface

Rose of England

12147   Mundic on quartz
12148   Tinstone on quartz, 100ft level
12149   Do   do   mica in the matrix
12150   Fluor spar
12151   Dyke through lode at 80ft level
12152   Country rock

NEWELLTON   ...   .   *Schlamelcher's Copper Claim*

12153   Copper ore
Mr. Schlamelcher raised several tons for the purpose of
concentrating the ore to a matte in a cupola furnace, as in
the Mansfield process. The experiment failed mainly on
account of the complex nature of the ore, and for other
reasons. It is an ore which could hardly be treated locally
at present.

WATSONVILLE FIELD   ...   .   *Union Claim*

12154   Tinstone in quartz at surface

GREAT WESTERN HILL   ...   .   *Stewart's Claim*

12155   Country rock, through which a tunnel has been driven
12156   Tinstone with mundic and copper trace
12157   Foot-wall
12158   Tinstone in quartz with mundic
The Government Geologist in 1883 reported that 'A shaft
65ft deep has been sunk near the southern boundary of the
ground, on a north-west and south-east quartz reef which
underlies slightly to the south-west. At the bottom of the
shaft the quartz continues as a narrow shoot, but for the last
12ft contains no tin ore, although it is still accompanied
by wolfram and pyrites. A sort of foot-wall with a serpentinous face continues all the way down. At the bottom a
hanging-wall of dark diorite is seen—probably a dyke with
which the quartz reef is connected. In the north-west
corner of the ground is a shaft 50ft deep on a ferruginous
and chloritic joint which underlies to the south-west. The
shaft is sunk through the joint, which has tin ore on the

under-side. In the corner, near the Queen of the West, is a north-east and south-west lode of arsenical pyrites and red peroxide of iron, with some blue and green carbonate of copper and red copper ore. On the south-east side of the lode is a coarse-grained diorite dyke with large quartz blebs, the quartz containing a little tin ore. A tunnel has been driven to the north-east for 255ft on the course of the dyke. Tin ore nearly 3ft wide is seen in a narrow horizontal floor. Other floors of ore further along the tunnel underlie to the north-east. At 200ft the tunnel is intersected by a shaft which reaches its bottom level at 70ft and is continued for 40ft below. At the surface the lode is about 1ft in width, and contains good tin ore. Thirty-five feet further along the tunnel a blind shaft has been sunk for 40ft below the level of the tunnel. At the bottom of the blind shaft the ore is in a vein a few inches to 2ft thick and 6ft wide, occurring in coarse-grained diorite, underlying at a high angle to south-south-east. The vein contains also much copper pyrites and some tin pyrites. Above this shaft the roof of the tunnel has been stoped out to the height of 18ft. The tin ore is said to have been 7ft wide in some places. The tunnel continues about 20ft beyond the blind shaft, through porphyry country below the pyritous foot-wall of the dyke, from which the water brings out hair-like crystals of copper sulphate."

HERBERTON FIELD ... ... *Great Northern Prospecting Claim*

12159 Tinstone in red chlorite and quartz from the Gully lode
12160 Do from 120ft level from the Gully lode
12161 Tinstone in red chlorite from 120ft level from the Gully lode
12162 Fluor spar from 216ft level
12163 Tinstone do
12164 Fluor spar on quartz from 216ft level
12165 Tinstone in quartz at surface
12166 Country rock
12167 Tinstone with quartz from 100ft level, No. 2 lode
12168 Do from 100ft level, No. 2 lode
12169 Do with quartz and steatite from 100ft level, No. 2 lode
12170 Tinstone with quartz and steatite from 216ft level, No. 2 lode
12171 Wolfram in quartz, No. 2 lode
12172 Lode formation, 216ft level, Gully lode

" The most conspicuous feature of the P.C. on the surface is a wide dyke of compact, highly silicated, yellowish or pinkish felsite or elvan with quartz blebs. The elvan sometimes passes into quartzite, and is sometimes veined with quartz. The quartz is sometimes charged with mispickel. A cavity in the elvan dyke, in shape and size like the interior of a coffin, has its sides coated with the blue carbonate of copper. The Gully lode has a general trend of north 20° east to south 20° west, and is nearly vertical. It is a dyke, probably once of quartzose diorite, but which has undergone much metamorphism. South of the principal shaft the dyke terminates, so far as the surface is concerned, against a vertical wall of porphyry running north-east and south-west; this wall stands about 10ft. above the level of a floor of puddled clay designed to keep the water of the gully out of the workings. The dyke and ore have been quarried up to this wall.

"Two chains south of the 60ft shaft, an elvan dyke is seen traversing the porphyry country from south-east to north-west. To the north-west it probably intersects a north-and-south quartz reef which is visible at intervals on the surface. To the south-east a wedge-shaped mass of red syenite (widening south-eastward) adjoins the elvan on its north-eastern side. More or less ore was obtained all the way down in sinking the 60ft shaft. The matrix of the ore is a dark-green chlorite rock with grains and kernels of quartz. Sometimes reef quartz replaces the chlorite. The chlorite rock is in all probability a dyke, originally erupted as a quartzose diorite, and which has subsequently undergone much alteration. The dyke was probably never continuous at the level of the present surface, but I have little doubt of its connection at some low level with the Erin-go-Bragh."[*]

Hibernian

12173	Tinstone with quartz crystals at 30ft	
12174	Do in hæmatite at 50ft	

Sunrise

12175	Tinstone with quartz crystals

Surprise

12176	Tinstone in quartz with talc

Mowbray

12177	Tinstone in felspathic quartz at 30ft

Three Star

12178	Country rock at surface
12179	Lode at surface, showing tinstone veins in matrix
12180	East-wall at surface
12181	West-wall at 50ft

---

* Abridged from "Report on the Tin Mines of Herberton, Western, and Thompson Creek Districts," by R. L. Jack.

12182 Tirstone in quartz at 50ft
12183 East-wall at 50ft
12184 West-wall at 150ft
12185 Tinstone do
12186 East-wall do

" This claim presents the peculiarity—almost without parallel on the field, although so common in Cornwall and elsewhere—of an elvan dyke containing payable tin ore. The elvan is of the usual type—a silicated felstone, with quartz blebs. Its western side is seen in the west shaft, with porphyry adjoining. The shaft is 150ft deep. The elvan runs north 20° west, and goes down vertically in the shaft. At about 10ft deep the elvan becomes mixed with vein-quartz, and the matrix becomes serpentinous, the quartz blebs still remaining distinct. Fair tin ore occurs in the shaft here.

" One chain to the east three shafts are sunk on the course of the dyke. The northmost is 12ft deep, the central and southern each 40ft. The elvan is much mixed here with vein-quartz. A little stone is left—quartz with tin ore. About 50 tons of stone were bought on the ground by the Herberton Tin Company for £16 10s. per ton.

" A shaft about 1½ chains to the east has been sunk 50ft. The eastern edge of the elvan is seen in a cutting at the surface. The width of the dyke is therefore about 100ft. In the shaft, at the depth of 40ft, is a 2ft quartz-vein with tin ore at the junction of the elvan with porphyry. A wedge-shaped diorite mass, partly decomposed and partly very hard and quartzose, comes in at the north end of the shaft."*

CALIFORNIA CREEK ... ... *Industry Rewarded*

12187 Tinstone in chloritic matrix

GREGORY GULLY.

12188 Tinstone in quartz-matrix, apparently micaceous
12189 Tinstone, mundic and chalcopyrite with quartz

Arbouin's Claim

12190 Tinstone in quartzite

WATSONVILLE ... ... *King of the Ranges*

12191 Tinstone in decomposing felspar
" The workings are mainly open-cast following two slips or lodes; the northern running north-north-east and under-lying west-north-west, and the southern running east-north-

---

* "Report on the Tin Mines of Herberton, Western, and Thompson Creek Districts," by R. L. Jack, Government Geologist, 1888.

east and underlying at 65° to north-north-west. On the upper or northern slip a 50ft shaft has been sunk. A band of quite unaltered slate, striking east and west, is seen at the mouth of the open-cast in contact with the porphyry of the country. A drive has been started to cut the deposit where the tin ore was lost, on a very fine-grained, hard, black diorite, running east-north-east and containing arsenical pyrites."—*Jack*, 1883.

Bismarck

12192   Tinstone in quartz

RETURN CREEK.

12193   Garnets in chloritic rock

NEWELLTON.

12194   Cerussite with litharge on galena

MOWBRAY.

12195   Tinstone and quartz, the first found on the **Mowbray** Claims

MOWBRAY   ...   . *Alexandra*

12196   Tinstone on quartz

RETURN CREEK   ...   . *Lovely Ethel*

12197   Tinstone on quartz
12198   Do   with hæmatite
12199   Do   with quartz
12200   Do

North Australian

12201   Hanging-wall at 51ft
12202   Foot-wall at 51ft
12203   Tinstone
12204   Lode formation at 40ft
12205   Tinstone surface
12206   Tinstone in quartz
12207   Sample said to contain bismuth arseniate, tinstone, **argentite**, mundic, chalcopyrite and cobalt
12208   Lode formation at 50ft level, carries a little tin in **the** quartz
12209   Mundic in lode formation from 65ft
12210   Azurite
12211   Tinstone with steatite

"This mine has proved hitherto a very valuable property, having yielded a large amount of ore in return for the simplest possible work. When first discovered the 'blow' or outcrop stood several feet above the ground. It has been worked down to the depth of 24ft in an open-cast 10ft to 20ft wide, and extending about 50ft north-north-west and south-south-east. The country is greywacke and shale, with a dip at 35° to the south-west. The tin ore occurs in 'heads' or joints, at right angles to the dip of the stratified rock. The ore has a distinct character of its own. It is fine-grained, grey, and friable, but occasionally finely crystalline on faces. The grey colour results from the presence of steatite in the interstices between particles of the ore. A few blocks of pure ore lying at the surface weigh some hundredweights each."—*Jack*, 1883.

Ironclad

12212   Black oxide of copper at 30ft level
12213   Hanging-wall at 30ft level
12214   Foot-wall at 30ft level
12215   Tinstone in felsite
12216   Sample of stone

"This claim adjoins the North Australian to the north-east, but differs widely from it in its characteristics. It extends about 11 chains north-westward and 5 chains north-eastward. Near the southern corner of the claim is the 'copper shaft.' It is 30ft deep, and is sunk on a deposit of carbonate of copper and ochres, which runs mainly east and west, and underlies to the south. The country is alternating shale and greywacke. In the latter the deposit is contracted, and in the former wide and diffuse. About 70ft up the hill (to the north) another lode is seen. Its cap has red gossan and green carbonate of copper. The lode has been followed in labyrinthine open-cast and other workings till it communicates with the bottom of the 'copper shaft.' Shortly below the cap the copper ore begins to be intimately and extensively mixed with tin ore in small grains. From the upper levels in the open cuttings about five tons of stone were taken, which realised £55 in Sydney. It is granular tin ore with a small proportion of tile ore (ferruginous red oxide of copper) and ochre, and a little green and blue carbonate of copper. At the very end of the claim is seen, on the north side of the Herberton road, the outcrop of a strong lode of copper carbonate, underlying to south 40° east at 30°."—*Jack*, 1883.

Christmas Eve

12217   Copper carbonates with quartz
12218   Tinstone with quartz
12219   Tinstone and quartz, foliated alternately

WATSONVILLE   ...   .   *Chance Mine*

12220   Country rock, copper stained, at about 25ft

12221   Tinstone with stellate groups of crystals
12222   Do   in chlorite and quartz
12223   Do   in quartzite
12224   Wolfram in ferruginous gangue, containing quartz and
           tinstone

"In the middle of the ground to the west of St.
Patrick's Day Claim, and south of the gully, a shaft has been
sunk to the depth of 88ft. On descending this I found for
the last 30ft a perpendicular joint trending north-north-east.
Against this there abuts a joint running west-north-west
and underlying at 70° to north-north-east. This latter
was followed on the bottom level for 18ft, and tin ore was
found underlying it all the way. At 18ft the tin ore shot to
south-south-east, and was followed by a drive in that direction for 12ft. It occurred mainly in joints and heads. Near
the surface a brecciated gangue is seen in the shaft, and
about half a ton of arsenical pyrites and copper pyrites,
coated with sulphate and green carbonate of copper, has
been raised from this place. The stone now being raised
from the bottom is a fine-grained bluish-black chlorite with
small and sparse quartz blebs and very fine-grained tin ore
interspersed. Up the hill from the present main shaft is a
short tunnel with a 40ft shaft sunk at the inner end on
something not now accessible for water, running south-
south-west and dipping east-south-east. The tunnel tra-
verses porphyry country. Ferruginous chlorite is seen at
the mouth of the shaft. There is at grass about a ton of
iron pyrites, marcasite and copper pyrites with a coating of
copper sulphate, and 19 tons mixed green and red chlorite
ore, with tin in crystals and finely disseminated, amounting
to, say, 5 per cent. Near the north end of the ground is a
shaft 38ft deep on a dyke of quartzose chlorite 12ft wide.
The dyke is well seen in the open cutting at the mouth of
the shaft, and runs to north-north-east. At the depth of 10
feet some carbonates and lumps of red oxide of copper are
seen. In the north-west corner of the ground is a shaft
48ft deep   At the bottom the shaft cuts the top of a dyke
(running north 15° west and underlying to east 15°
north) of soft decomposing diorite with green treacherous
steatite joints. On the top of the dyke is a ferruginous
gangue with a little quartz and tin ore, and a good deal of
wolfram. The tin ore, which may amount to 10 per cent.,
is mixed with quartz and a zeolite."—*Jack*, 1883.

Nigger Creek

12225   Sample of opal-like stone

WATSONVILLE....   ....   *Boundary Tribute*

12226   Tinstone in quartz and felsite

Australian Lease

12227 Tinstone with felspar and quartz at 50ft
12228   Do   locality doubtful

RETURN CREEK   ... ... *First Shot*

12229 Galena, with decomposition products
12230 Tinstone in chlorite
12231   Do   quartzite

Eureka Claim

12232 Tinstone at 20ft
12233   Do   with quartz and hæmatite
12234 Finely divided tinstone, with steatite and quartz

GLENCAIRN.

12235 Hanging-wall at 80ft
12236 Foot-wall   do
12237 Tinstone minutely disseminated in country rock
12238 Tinstone
12239   Do   with quartz and felspar
12240   Do   in ferruginous matrix

COOLGARA   .. .. *Bonnie Dundee*

12241 Hanging-wall
12242 Foot-wall
12243 Tinstone and mica in ferruginous matrix, from 20ft level
12244 Tinstone
12245   Do   in red chloritic matrix, 20ft level
12246   Do   and mica in ferruginous matrix, from 15ft level
12247   Do   in decomposed felspar
12249 Wolfram

COOLGARA ... ... *Claim*

12248 Bismuthite, from a claim once worked for bismuth

HERBERTON   ... ... *Prospect Gully*

12249 Tinstone, bulk samples

—*Exhibitor :* J. C. BAIRD, ESQ.

Mineral Exhibit of Messrs. John Moffat & Co., London, 1886.

Silver Hill Claim, George Young

12250* Galena, decomposing and forming concentric rings of carbonate, from surface
12251* Galena, decomposed, save a centre of fibrous galena, from upper tunnel

12252* Fine-grained galena, decomposing as in No. 12250, **from** shaft in upper tunnel

12253* Fine-grained galena, decomposing as in No. 12250, **from** 20ft in shaft

12254* Fine-grained galena, decomposing as in No. 12250, **from** 20ft in shaft

12255* Galena from surface cutting

12256*	Do	do	do
12257*	Do	do	do
12258*	Do	do	do
12259*	Do	do	do
12260*	Do	do	do

12261* Fine-grained galena—average assay, 65oz silver per ton

Silverfield Claim

12262*	Fibrous galena, No. 1 cutting					
12263*	Do	do	No. 2	do		
12264*	Do	do	do	do		
12265*	Do	do	do	shaft, at 20ft		
12266*	Granular	do	do	do	35ft, decomposing	
12267*	Do	do	do	cutting	do	do
12268*	Do	do	do	do	do	do
12269*	Do	do	do	do	do	do
12270*	Do	do	do	do	do	do	**average**

assay, 65 to 81oz silver per ton

Victoria Claim

12250A	Fibrous galena, No. 1 surface cutting				
12251A	Do	do	No. 2 cutting		
12252A	Do	do	do	do	
12253A	Do	do	do	do	
12254A	Do	do	do	do	assay from 65 to 114oz silver

per ton

Cusco Claim

12255A	Finely granular galena, from No. 1 surface cutting			
12256A	Do	do	do	30ft in shaft
12257A	Do	do	do	do	do
12258A	Samples from No. 2 cutting			
12259A	Do	do	do	average assay, 65oz silver per

ton

Hardman & Hoecastle's Claim

12260A	Fibrous galena from surface cutting	
12261A	Do	do
12262A	Do	from surface

Barossa Claim

12263A	Coarsely crystalline galena, No. 1 shaft, 30ft		
12264A	Do	do	46ft

12265ᴀ Coarsely granular galena, No. 1 shaft, 30ft
12266ᴀ   Do   do   do
12267ᴀ Galena and lead carbonate, No. 1 shaft, 60ft
12268ᴀ Coarsely crystalline galena,   do   20ft
12269ᴀ Galena decomposition results, coated with lead and iron
      oxides
12270ᴀ Galena from shaft, 20ft
12250ʙ   Do   do
12251ʙ Galena decomposing into grey ore, at 58ft
12252ʙ Friable lead carbonate from surface cutting
12253ʙ Galena decomposed from shaft, 60ft
12254ʙ Argentiferous ore, iron oxide with lead carbonate, from
      65ft
12255ʙ Argentiferous lead carbonate, at 40ft
12256ʙ   Do   from surface cutting ; assays
    from 30oz to 212oz per ton

Albion Claim

12257ʙ Decomposed galena at surface
12258ʙ Galena centres of boulders of decomposed ore, surface
      cutting
12259ʙ Agentiferous iron ore, at 20ft in shaft
12260ʙ Horn-silver, silver 75 per cent., surface cutting
12261ʙ Highly argentiferous iron ore, at centre a soft, friable,
      earthy red ochre rich in chloride
12262ʙ Argentiferous iron ores, 20ft in shaft
12263ʙ   Do   12ft   do
12264ʙ   Do   20ft in No. 2 shaft, Albion-Lady
    Jane Blow; 74oz silver per ton
12265ʙ Similar sample from same shaft at 30ft

Messrs. John Moffat & Co.'s Claims.

Great Southern Claim

12267ʙ Lode tin ore, No. 2 shaft, at 40ft
12268ʙ   Do   do   at 25ft
12269ʙ   Do   60ft level
12270ʙ   Do   do
12250ᴄ   Do   No. 3 face
12251ᴄ Tin ore on cap of lode
12252ᴄ Green chlorite, with finely disseminated tinstone from No.
    1 shaft

Red King Claim

12253ᴄ Tin ore in chlorite, from surface cutting

Tyrconnel Claim

12254ᴄ Tin ore, with quartz gangue
12255ᴄ   Do   with chlorite gangue

H

Tornado Claim

12256c Lode tin, surface cutting
12257c   Do   at 25ft
12258c   Do   at 34ft
12259c   Do   at 60ft, containing pyrites
12260c   Do   with quartz gangue

Freethinker Claim

12261c Tinstone in kaolin, shaft at 20ft
12262c Lode tinstone, shaft at 50ft
12263c Tinstone in quartz gangue, surface
12264c   Do   80ft in shaft

No Name Claim

12265c Tinstone in red chlorite, 30ft in shaft

Comet Claim

12266c Lode tinstone in red chlorite, surface cutting
12267c Quartz gangue with tin ore
12268c Samples from surface cutting
12269c Compact green country rock with tin ore

Luck Hill Claim

12270c Lode tin ore
12250d Lode tin ore in chlorite 20ft in shaft
12251d Water-worn samples containing tin ore, from Gibb's Creek

Johnson's Claim

12252d Lode tin, surface cutting

Little's New Improvement

12253d Tin-ore from surface cutting

Little Wonder Claim

12254d Chlorite with finely disseminated tin ore

J. White's Mary Claim

12255d Chlorite with tin

Gibblet's Columbia Lease

12256d Sample containing tin from cap of lode
12257d Tin ore at 10ft

IRVINEBANK ...   . *Thompson's Claim*
12257d* Tinstone

Day Dawn Claim

12258d Samples at surface, tourmaline, quartz and tinstone

Gibblet's Elizabeth Lease

12259d Surface samples containing tin ore
12259d*Sample from Halpin's, near Irvinebank, containing tinstone

	Watson's Royal Standard
12260D Tin ore	
	Fry's Pinnacle Claim
12261D Felspar and tinstone	
	Californian Claim
12262D Surface samples rich in tin	
CALIFORNIA CREEK	*Industry Rewarded Claim*
12263D Tin ore	
EUREKA CREEK	*Jose's Claim*
12263D* Tin ore	
EUREKA CREEK	*Ivanhoe*
12264D Lode tin	
EUREKA CREEK	*Arbouin's Claim*
12265D Tinstone	
MOWBRAY	*Alexandra Claim*
12266D Lode tin	
EMU CREEK	*Farley's Claim*
12267D Tinstone	
EMU CREEK	*Roma Claim*
12268D Tinstone	
EMU CREEK	*City of Bagdad Claim*
12269D Tinstone	
EMU CREEK	*Gibblet's Claim*
12270D Samples from cap of lode	
EMU CREEK	*Gibblet*
12250E Samples from cap of lode	
EMU CREEK	*Stenhouse's Claim*
12251E Tinstone	
EMU CREEK	*Normanby Claim*
12252E Tinstone	
EMU CREEK	*Crœsus Claim*
12253E Tinstone at 30ft	
EMU CREEK	*Curran's Claim*
12254E Tinstone in chlorite, from tunnel	

EMU CREEK   ...   .   *W. Miller's Claim*
  12255E Tinstone

EMU CREEK ...   .   *City of Pompeii Claim*
  12255E* Tinstone

WOOLOMAN'S CREEK.
  12256E Sample of lode

WOOLOMAN'S CREEK   ...   .   *Minnie Moxam's Claim*
  12257E Tinstone

WOOLOMAN'S CREEK.
  12258E Tinstone at surface

RETURN CREEK   ...   .   *Polson's Claim*
  12259E Tinstone

WOOLOMAN'S CREEK   ...   .   *Noel's Claim*
  12200E Tinstone

WOOLOMAN'S CREEK   ...   .   *John Liddell*
  12261E Tinstone

WOOLOMAN'S CREEK   ...   .   *The Two Friends*
  12262E Tinstone

RETURN CREEK   ...   .   *Never-can-tell Claim*
  12263E Tinstone

RETURN CREEK...   ...   .   *Magdala Claim*
  12048* Tinstone

RETURN CREEK   ...   .   *Victoria Claim*
  12264E Tinstone

RETURN CREEK   ...   .   *Morning Star*
  12265E Tinstone

RETURN CREEK   ...   .   *The Briton Claim*
  12266E Tinstone

                                        Great Southern Claim
      12052* Bulk sample of tinstone
                                        Comet Claim
      12053* Tinstone

IRVINEBANK   ...   .   *Happy Thought Claim*
  12267E Tinstone

IRVINEBANK ...   .   *Tornado Claim*
   12057* Bulk sample tinstone

IRVINEBANK   ...   .   *Great Southern Claim*
   12058* Bulk sample tinstone

IRVINEBANK ...   .   *Tornado Claim*
   12059* Bulk sample tinstone
   12060*   Do   do

IRVINEBANK   ...   .   *Great Southern Claim*
   12061* Bulk sample tinstone

IRVINEBANK ...   .   *... Comet Claim*
   12062* Bulk sample tinstone

IRVINEBANK   ...   .   *... Elizabeth Claim*
   12063* Bulk sample

Mineral Exhibit of the Herberton Local Committee, London, 1886.

Great Northern Tin Mining Company

12070** Tinstone in chlorite at 20ft, Gully lode, estimated 40 per cent.
12071* Tinstone, quartz, felspar and mundic at 120ft, Gully lode, 30 per cent. tin
12072* Tinstone, quartz, and chalcopyrite at 210ft; 50 per cent. tin
12073* Tinstone in quartz gangue, Eastern lode, at 30ft; 55 per cent tin
12074* Tinstone in black chlorite at 100ft; 40 per cent. tin
12075* Tinstone with quartz and felspar, Eastern lode, at 220ft
12076* Country rock, Gully lode
12268E   Do   Eastern lode

COOLGARA   ...   .   *Rose of Denmark Claim*
   12269E Tinstone at 80ft; lode, 4ft wide

THOMPSON CREEK   ...   .   *... Vesuvius Claim*
   12270E Tinstone, with granite and diorite walls, at 50ft; from lode 18in wide

COOLGARA   ...   .   *Tasmanian Claim*
   12250F Tinstone at surface
   12251F   Do   do

Vesuvius, No. 4 Claim

12252ᶠ Tinstone at surface; by crushing, yields 40 per cent. of black tin

COOLGARA ...   .   *Who'd a Thought It Claim*

12253ᶠ Tinstone at 37ft; lode, 18in wide

Lovely Ethel

12254ᶠ Tinstone at 70ft; lode, 4ft wide; formation, porphyry

Alexandra Claim

12255ᶠ Tinstone at 90ft; lode, 12in wide; averaging 50 per cent. black tin; formation granite, walls undefined

COOLGARA...   ...   .   *Bonnie Dundee Claim*

12256ᶠ Tinstone

Eclipse Claim

12257ᶠ Tinstone, No. 2 spar lode, at 20ft; lode 4ft wide

Black Rock Extended

12258ᶠ Tinstone from chlorite lode, worked by cutting and tunnel; width of lode unknown; trial crushing, 40 per cent. black tin; depth, 20ft

12259ᶠ Tinstone from chlorite lode, worked by cutting and tunnel; width of lode unknown; trial crushing, 30 per cent. black tin

12260ᶠ Tinstone from chlorite lode, worked by cutting and tunnel; width of lode unknown; trial crushing, 30 per cent. black tin

Bradlaugh

12262ᶠ Tinstone at 80ft
12263ᶠ   Do   50ft
12264ᶠ   Do   20ft

EUREKA CREEK   ...   .   *Clan Ronald*

12265ᶠ Tinstone at surface
12266ᶠ   Do   and wolfram at 10ft

WATSONVILLE ...   .*Glen Cairns*

12267ᶠ Tinstone in quartz at 50ft
12268ᶠ   Do   do ·   60ft

WATSONVILLE   ...   .   *Spear Claim*

12269ᶠ Tinstone in quartz at 80ft

Gregory's Gully

12270ᶠ Tinstone in hard granite, surface

WATSONVILLE ... ... *Chance*
  12250G Tinstone at 50ft; trial crushing yielded 35 per cent.

EUREKA CREEK ... ... *Black Rock*
  12251G Tinstone with wolfram at 10ft

EUREKA CREEK... ... ... *Clan Roland*
  12252G Tinstone in porphyry

WATSONVILLE ... ... *Oakey Creek*
  12253G Tinstone in felspar at 20ft

EUREKA CREEK.
  12254G Tinstone in quartz at 50ft

WATSONVILLE ... ... *King of Ranges*
  12255G Tinstone at bottom, 90ft
  12256G   Do   low class, at 60ft, same shaft

WATSONVILLE ... ... *Chinaman's Garden*
  12257G Tinstone, 50 tons yielded by crushing 41 per cent. black
      tin

EUREKA CREEK.
  12258G Tinstone at 70ft
  12259G   Do   20ft, 30 per cent. black tin

WATSONVILLE ... ... *Arbouin's Tin Mine*
  12260G Tinstone at 25ft, 32 per cent. black tin
  12261G   Do   60ft, 45   do   do

                              Perseverance Claim
  12262G Tinstone at 30ft

                              Industry Rewarded
  12263G Lode tin, near stream tin workings

COOLGARA... ... ... *Victoria Lease*
  12264G   Tinstone with country rock at 120ft

COOLGARA ... ... *Christmas Eve Claim*
  12265G Tinstone with quartz

                              First-shot Claim
  12266G Tinstone from 18in, lode at 30ft
  12267G   Do   do   do

WATSONVILLE ... ... *Bolton Folly*
  12267G* Tinstone with garnets at 30ft

WATSONVILLE ... ... *Ironclad Tin Mining Company*
12267a** Tinstone with a little copper from junction of slate and granite at 70ft

WATSONVILLE ... ... *Perseverance*
12268G Tinstone

City of Pompeii
12269G Tinstone in quartz at 30ft, lode 2ft wide

COOLGARA ... ... *Lovely Ethel*
12270G Tinstone in porphyry formation at 70ft, width of lode 4ft

THOMPSON'S CREEK ... ... *Alexandra*
12250H Tinstone averaging 50 per cent. black tin, from 12in, at 80ft

COOLGARA ... ... *Bonnie Dundee*
12251H Tinstone in chlorite
12252H   Do   do

EMU CREEK ... ... *Stars and Stripes*
12253H Tinstone, 50 per cent., lode 6in wide, at 25ft, granite country

Lovely Ethel
12254H Tinstone in quartz at 20ft

St. Patrick
12089   Tinstone at surface
12090   Do   bulk sample

Bakerville
12255H Tinstone at surface

North Australian
12093   Tinstone with greywacke and shale at 30ft
12094   Do   do   do   do

WATSONVILLE ... ... *Bismarck*
12095   Tinstone with felspar and quartz at 70ft

COOLGARA ... ... *Republic*
12256H Tinstone at 30ft

Koh-i-noor
12257H Galena at 60ft, assaying 187oz silver per ton
12258H   Do   70ft, assaying 187oz silver per ton; formation, slate and porphyry
12259H Galena at 70ft, assaying 187oz silver per ton; forma slate and porphyry
12260H Galena at 80ft, assaying 120oz

... .   *Republic*

12261H Decomposed galena, assaying 561oz silver, at 14ft

Mount Garnet

12262H Gossan with copper carbonates, cap of a large blow, traceable for miles
12263H Copper carbonates with silver
12264H Cupriferous galena partially decomposed
12264H*   Do   do   do

COOLGARA   ... ... *Magdala*

12265H Tinstone at 70ft, lode 7ft 6in wide

NEWELLTON ... .. *North Queensland Silver Mining Company*

12265H*Galena at 60ft, lode 5ft to 6ft; yield by assay, 64 per cent.
  lead, 147oz silver per ton
12265H**Galena at 65ft, lode 5ft; yield by assay, 78 per cent. lead,
  209oz silver per ton
12265H***Galena at 30ft, lode 6ft; yield by assay, 75 per cent.
  lead, 203oz silver per ton
12266H Galena at 30ft, lode 5ft; yield by assay, 56 per cent. lead,
  90oz silver per ton
12267H Galena at 60ft, lode 6ft; yield by assay, 75 per cent. lead,
  100oz silver per ton

NEWELLTON.

12115   Sulphides, copper ore at 30ft

Herberton Tin Smelting Company

12268H Tin slag

Tasmanian

12269H Tinstone in felspar at 20ft
12269H*   Do   at 25ft
12269H**   Do   at 30ft

Little Wonder

12270H Ferruginous tinstone in porphyry at 10ft
12250M Tinstone at 20ft

HERBERTON ... ... *Ly-ee-Moon*

12251M Tinstone in quartz, 25 per cent. black tin, returns £10
  per ton

Ironclad

12252M Tinstone with granite at 20ft
12253M   Do   do   do

Alexandra

12253M*Tinstone with quartz at 10ft
12254M   Do   do   at 25ft
12254M*   Do   do   at 15ft

GREGORY'S GULLY ...   . *Royal Standard*

 12255ᴍ Tinstone in gneiss at 10ft
 12256ᴍ Do do at 20ft
 12257ᴍ Do
 12258ᴍ Do
 12259ᴍ Do

              Stewart's T Claim

 12260ᴍ Country rock, foot wall, at 305ft
 12261ᴍ Do change at 305ft
 12262ᴍ Do   do at 310ft
 12263ᴍ Do with mispickel at 290ft

                 Chance

 12264ᴍ Tinstone and felspar at 20ft
 12265ᴍ Do mundic at 30ft
 12266ᴍ Do   do
 12267ᴍ Do arsenical pyrite on cap of lode

      North Australian Tin Mining Company

 12140* Tinstone, cupriferous, at 110ft

   Tin-ore to the value of £50,000 was taken from this mine
  in two years by six men; it is still one of the best paying
  mines in the district.

             North Britain

 12270ʜ* Tinstone with galena, chalcopyrite, cerussite, and quartz
   at 30ft; width of lode, 5ft 6in
 12270ʜ** Foot-wall

WATSONVILLE ...   . *Gl ncairn*

 12268ᴍ Tinstone at 50ft
 12269ᴍ Do 60ft
 12270ᴍ Do 70ft
 12250ɴ Hanging-wall, 80ft
 12251ɴ Foot-wall, 90ft

COOLGARA   ...   . *Bismarck*

 12151 Cupriferous gossan
 12252ɴ Copper carbonate at 10ft
 12253ɴ   Do surface

NEWELLTON   ...   . *Mulligan Freehold*

 12254ɴ Copper ore
 12155 Do
 12255ɴ Do

WATSONVILLE   ...   . *Baker's Claim*

 12256ɴ Tinstone

Ivanhoe

12256N* Tinstone ; trial crushing gave 22 per cent. black tin

Bolton's Folly

12257N Tinstone and garnets

EMU CREEK.
12258N Tinstone
12259N   Do

Stewart's T Claim

12260N Tinstone at 300ft

Clan Roland

12261N Tinstone, cupriferous

CALIFORNIA CREEK...   ...   .   *Industry Rewarded*
12262N Tinstone near stream works

EMU CREEK   ...   .   *Moran Brothers*
12263N Tinstone in quartz

WATSONVILLE ...   .   *Bismarck*
12264N Tinstone in quartz
12265N   Do   at 30ft

Eureka

12266N Tinstone and wolfram
12267N   Do

OAKEY CREEK.
12268N Tinstone and granite

Rose of England

12269N Wolfram with tinstone

Silver Crown

12270N Gossan with tinstone
12250P Cap of lode, 20oz silver per ton
12251P Tinstone at 10ft
12252P   Do
12253P   Do
12254P   Do   rich at 15ft
12255P   Do
12256P Country rock at 20ft

Stewart's T Claim

12257P High-class tin ore at 300ft

COOLGARA...   ...   .   *Christmas Eve*
12258P Tinstone at 30ft

EUREKA CREEK.

12259P Tinstone in country rock

Hodgkinson Field.

Marquis Reef

12250 Hanging-wall
12251 Auriferous quartz with mundic, 90ft level
12252   Do   do   galena   do
12253 Foot-wall
12253* Sample showing gold

—*Exhibitor :* MR. GOLD-WARDEN TOWNER

Macdonald's P.C.

12254 Auriferous quartz with galena
12255   Do   do
12256 Country rock
12257 Country rock

Victory

12258 Hanging-wall at 100ft
12259 Auriferous quartz from reef at 100ft, showing gold
12260   Do   do
12261 Foot-wall adjacent to lode
12262 Country rock

Hit or Miss

12263 Foot-wall at 100ft
12264 Auriferous quartz showing gold
12265   Do   do   with mundic and galena
12266 Country rock at 100ft

Black Ball

12267 Hanging-wall at 20ft
12268   Do   do   200ft
12269 Foot-wall at 20ft
12270 Quartz with galena and auriferous mundic
12271   Do   auriferous
12272 Do   do
12273 Do   do   showing gold on galena

Since March, 1887, 1,359 tons 12cwt quartz have been crushed for a yield of 1,672oz 12dwt., which averages 1oz 4dwt 14grs per ton. Mr. Jack says :—"At the 205ft level the reef is rather flatter than its general underlie. It is 2ft to 3ft in thickness at the end of the level. The quartz has its joints coated with carbonate of lime, which has a greenish tint from a minute quantity of carbonate of copper." The water pumped out of the mine must be very strongly charged with calcic carbonate, as the children of the neighbourhood put twigs and other trifles in the channel of the water, and in a few days they become " petrified."

The reef runs north and south, and dips west, and the laminated quartz contains specks of mispickel; the mispickel sticks close to the grey streaks.

Mark Twain

12274 Hanging-wall showing mundic at 250ft level
12275 Auriferous mundic in quartz   do
12276   Do   quartz at 250ft level
12277   Do   do   showing gold at 250ft level
12278 Foot-wall

The total crushings of stone to August, 1884, are 2,242 tons, which yielded 3,343oz 5dwt gold, equal to 1oz 9dwt 19grs per ton. The first transaction recorded is as follows:— 111tons 10cwt for a yield of 389oz 10dwt of gold ; price, £3 14s 10d per oz.

Cardigan

12279 Hanging-wall at 120ft level
12280 Auriferous quartz at 120ft level
12281 Foot-wall

Total crushings of stone to August, 1884, are 1,455 tons 2cwt, which yielded, 1,633oz 10dwt gold, equal to 1oz 2dwt 11grs per ton. The value of the gold appears to be low— only £2 11s 5d per oz.

Caledonia

12282 Country rock at 200ft
12283 Auriferous quartz with auriferous mundic

The total crushings are 2,301 tons 15 cwt, which yielded 3,044oz 11dwt gold, equal to 1oz 6dwts 10grs per ton. The highest value recorded is 56 tons, which yielded 123oz, at £3 13s 5d per oz.—*Jack.*

Going Home

12284 Auriferous quartz, yield by crushing about 1oz

Tyrconnel

12285 Hanging-wall
12286 Auriferous quartz at 490ft level
12287 Foot-wall

The total crushings are 10,875 tons 14cwt for a yield of 17,494oz 10dwts 18grs gold, an average of 1oz 12dwt 4grs per ton. The highest value recorded is :—40 tons for 107oz 5dwt, valued at £3 7s. 4d. per oz. The very large quantity of stone crushed from this claim shows its importance nearly £60,000 worth of gold has been taken out of the mine.

Bismarck

12288 Auriferous quartz

Hero P.C.

12289 Hanging-wall at 100ft
12290 Auriferous quartz
12291 Country rock
12292 Foot-wall

—*Exhibitor :* Mr. Gold-Warden Towner

Explorer

12293 Auriferous quartz at surface
12294 Country rock

Mr. Jack says of this reef:—"Strike north 6° east ; underlie west 6° north at 65° This may be taken as a type of the reefs, which do not coincide with the strike of the country rock. It was abandoned shortly after October, 1880. At 14ft the reef was 2ft thick at south end of shaft ; at 3ft north of north end of shaft the reef 'cut out,' but the gold continued in clay leaders ; at depth of 30ft the reef was 3¼ft thick, but was almost all shaly gangue. The engine shaft is 80ft vertical and 57ft on the underlie ; at 25ft down the underlie a drive has been carried 33ft north. Here the last payable quartz was obtained. A drive was made to the north from the foot of the underlie shaft ; but although it was carried 67ft—*i.e.,* beyond where the rich stone should have come— it was not met with. . . . . Quartz was obtained . . . carrying 2dwt to the ton."

The total crushings up to June, 1880, gave the following returns :—629 tons 5cwt yielded 2,804oz 18dwt gold, equal to an average of 4oz 9dwt 4grs per ton.

The only record of value of gold from this reef mentioned by Mr. Jack is :—60 tons yielded 401oz 17dwt ; value £3 3s. 5d. per oz.

It may be mentioned that in 1885 Mr. Nicholls, a miner, seeing gold in a lump of quartz weighing about 1cwt, which was lying on the surface at the Explorer mine, then abandoned, broke up the quartz and obtained about 5oz of gold therefrom. He has since obtained from the same place about 20oz more, and has 15 tons of good stone on grass awaiting crushing. A short time ago Mrs. Nicholls picked up, near the same place, a piece of quartz, weighing about a quarter of a pound, and containing ½oz of gold.

Pioneer

12295 Hanging-wall at 60ft
12296 Auriferous quartz
12297 Foot-wall

The total crushings are—1,865 tons 5cwt for a yield of 3,543oz 7dwt, equal to an average of 1oz 18dwt 1gr per ton.

Chance Tunnel

12298 Country rock
12299 Country rock

This tunnel is near the northern boundary of the township of Thornborough, and is being driven by Mr Murphy (single-handed), an experienced miner, who has worked at the tunnel for over three years; the object is to cut the Chance and other parallel reefs in the Pig Hill. "The locality is a mile south of the conglomerate in Glen Mowbray, and the strata cut occupy an horizon which may be estimated at 4,610ft below that of the conglomerate. They consist for the most part of dark-blue shales (commonly known as slates), with alternations of hard gritty grey-wackes and a few bands of fine conglomerate The fine-grained greywackes yielded a fossil which is in the "risbane Museum, having been pronounced by Mr. C. De Vis, the curator, to be *Lepidodendron*, probably *L. australe* of McCoy. I found among the shales numerous casts of crustacean or molluscan tracks, some reed-like plant impressions and a fragment of carbonised wood."—*Jack.*

This tunnel has been driven for 278ft, and is 6ft high by 3¼ broad.

Tichborne

12300 Hanging-wall at 230ft level
12301 Foot-wall at 230ft level
12302 Auriferous quartz, 60ft level

The total crushings are 926 tons for a yield of 1726oz 5dwt, equal to an average of 1oz 17dwt 6grs per ton.

Homeward Bound

12302**Country rock
12302* Auriferous quartz

Reef strikes east 20deg. north, and underlies to south 20deg. east, in dark shale country. The principal shaft is 210ft down; the best "stone" occurred in the hanging wall. In places the quartz was upwards of 6ft in thickness, but not rich. About 15ft west of the bottom of the shaft a wedge-like body of quartz appeared and widened westward, till about 35ft from the shaft it was 8ft to 10ft wide. Ten feet further the reef had thinned to 3ft, with 18 inches of quartz between two bands of black "mullock" or gangue; from this point up to the shaft at the surface the "shoot" of stone had been continuously worked, and it had averaged 1¼ oz to the ton. The "shoot" "dipped" to the west at an angle of about 1 in 4.

Union Reef

12302**Country rock at 250ft

12302***Auriferous quartz showing gold, galena, mispickel, and blende

The gold is very good, the highest value being—171 tons stone, 305oz gold, value £3 19s per oz. The total crushings are 9,051 tons 10 cwt, yielding 11,384oz 2dwt 12grs gold, equal to an average of 1oz 5dwt 3grs per ton.—*Jack.*

Monarch

12302*****Auriferous quartz

Crushings as follow :—5065 tons 14cwt yielded 6215oz 19dwt 19grs, of which one crushing of 100 tons gave 78oz 14dwt, valued at £3 11s 1d per oz.

—*Exhibitor :* MR. GOLD-WARDEN TOWNER

NORTHCOTE FIELD   ...   .   *Emily Lease Antimony Mine*

12303   Antimony sulphide (stibnite) at 76ft level
12304   Stibnite in quartz, from reef
12305   Country rock at 76ft
12306   Foot-wall at 26ft
12307   Foot-wall, adjacent to reef
12308   Foot-wall, with mundic

The reef is at present worked for stibnite, as the specimens show, but it was originally opened as a gold-bearing quartz-reef, but the crushings were poor, the total crushings being 382 tons 12cwt for a yield of 1315oz 3dwt of gold. From the Annual Report of the Department of Mines for 1881-82, it appears that Mr. J. A. Parker, the local assayer, drew attention to the rich deposits. Messrs. Denny and Co. commenced preparations for the erection of antimony smelting works, but the real work of erection of plant, etc., was carried out under the direction of Messrs. Field & Son, for the Northcote Antimony Smelting Works Company. Mr. E. R. Field has experience in the metallurgy of antimony, and the works appear to be well laid out. The output for 1884—the year the company started—was 145 tons crude antimony, which was disposed of in the English market at £19 1s. 3d. per ton ; 49 tons of white oxide were obtained from the chambers, which was reduced to 25 tons of regulus. The gross returns were about £3500. The capital sunk on the works is about £6000.

12309   Crude sulphide resulting from smelting of ore
12310   Crystals of white antimony oxide adhering to walls of chambers nearest to furnaces
12311   Slag containing antimony, produced in the preparation of the regulus

12312 Yellow glass of antimony found in the end of the flue nearest the furnace connecting chambers and furnace

12313 Regulus

Emily Lease Antimony Mine

12308* Antimony sulphide, from shaft at 80ft; assaying 60 per cent; lode, 6ft wide, composed of stibnite, producing 10 tons of ore per fathom

—*Exhibitor :* JOHN MUNDAY, Esq.

Minnie Moxham

12314 Auriferous quartz
12315   Do   do   at 350ft
12316   Do   do   at 450ft

The gold in this reef is very valuable. Mr. Jack's figures are—for the highest value, 123 tons, 282oz 16dwt gold, at £4 0s 1¾d per oz; and the lowest, 60oz 18dwt gold, sold for £3 19s 3¼d per oz. The quartz is heavily charged in parts with specks of stibnite. Total crushings to December, 1883, 1053 tons 10 cwt, yielding 2112oz 3dwt of gold, or an average of just over 2oz of gold per ton.

Craig's Lease

12317 Stibnite at 12ft
12318   Do   with quartz at 15ft
12319   Do   do   and slate

" This is a continuation of the Emily line of reef, distant about a mile and a half; the lode is about two feet wide; the strike is west 40° north."—*Jack.*

HODGKINSON FIELD ...   .   *Black Ball Mine*

12320 Auriferous quartz in bulk

Exhibited by W. BALS, Esq.

The owners' report is inserted at large.

The reef occurs near the head of Springs Creek, its strike is south 10deg. east, and its underlie at 65deg. to west 10deg. south. Annexed is a plan of the workings on the scale of 30ft to the inch.

The mine was opened in 1877 and has been productive ever since. It has been payable from the beginning, and the former owner cleared £4000 or £5000 out of it before he sold to the present owner, Mr. Wm. Bals.

Operations are principally carried on at the 250ft level, where enormous bodies of stone exist of the same character as that forwarded to the Exhibition, and which was taken from this level.

The mine carries a 8h.p. engine, and keeps employed upon an average about eight men.

I

Mr. Wm. Nicholas, F.G.S., Consulting Mining Engineer, Lecturer on Mining, University, Melbourne, reported upon the reef in October, 1886, as follows, viz:—

"The Black Ball reef has already been extensively worked and with such results as to indicate that here occurs valuable permanent quartz reef. The reef has been stoped out for over 300ft continuous length, and still at both ends, north and south, quartz exists from 3ft to 4ft in thickness, and from appearances it should be payable; certainly good prospects are in view at the northern extremities of the mine underground.

"In the reef the quartz forms in lenticular blocks which splice on to one another, or to put it in other words, where the blocks of quartz wedge out they overlap so that although it cannot be said that there is actually a continuous run of regular quartz between two walls yet there is a very near approach to such a mode of occurrence.

"The quartz in the reef is of a laminated character and contains galena, zinc blende, and arsenical pyrites   In fact it contains all the characteristics of the most permanent and rich quartz reefs of Australia, such as those that have proved remunerative down to 1000ft and 2000ft in depth.

"Already some 4000 tons of quartz have been raised and crushed from this reef for an average yield of over 1oz of gold to the ton; which, I take it, is simply indicative of future yields from depths below 200ft from the surface.

"The pyrites in the quartz presents the appearance of pyrites that yield many ounces of gold to the ton, and I feel confident that they will repay the necessary outlay of concentration and treatment and that they will prove to be a valuable addition to the auriferous resources of this property."

PALMER DISTRICT AND FIELD.

This field is situated in the Cape York Peninsula, north-east of Queensland, on the Palmer River.   It is the most northerly of all the mineral fields in Queensland.

Maytown, 76 miles south-south-west of Cooktown—the port—and 135 miles by the main coach road, the official and commercial centre, is built on the River Palmer.

The known auriferous belt covers 2,000 square miles.   Payable alluvial gold has been found in the bed of the Palmer and its tributary creeks for a distance of over 100 miles.   In Maytown and its vicinity, nuggets of gold have been found varying from 2oz or 3oz to 100oz and over.   They generally have adherent particles of quartz, showing the proximity of the quartz veins with which the gold was associated, and that have detrited away with the country rocks.

" Fifteen miles below Maytown, in the river bed, the gold is in a finer state of division ; and 70 miles down the river, at Lukinville, the gold is very minutely divided, but without deteriorating in value."

KINGSBOROUGH ... ... *Caledonia*

12321 Mundic ore in bulk
12322 Quartz in bulk

The shareholders report that the Caledonia is situated in Kingsborough, and was among the first lot of claims taken up on the Hodgkinson in the early part of 1876. On this line of reef there were the P.C. and numbers 1, 2, 3 west, and the same numbers on the east.

Good average crushings came from all the claims, but on account of the high price of carting and crushing, viz., 45s per ton, the greater number were abandoned for the newer fields of the Coen and Lukinville.

The P.C. and No. 1 west worked up to the beginning of 1883. During this time there were crushed from the whole line of the reef 2,000 tons of quartz for 3,000oz of gold, valued at from £3 9s 6d to £3 13s 5d. per oz.

During the latter portion of the time that the reef was being worked, the water-level was reached, and the P.C. and No. 1 west amalgamated. After sinking some depth they came on a reef heavily charged with mineral, from which they could not obtain any gold. They saved and crushed any stone they could get that was free from mineral, carefully picked and threw away the mineral stone among the mullock.

Herberton tin mines were opened about this time, and as the water was rather heavy for baling with a windlass, the mine was abandoned.

In October, 1887, some residents of Kingsborough sent ¼ ton of the mineral stone to Messrs. Parkes & Lacey, the proprietors of the Huntingdon Mill, Pyrmont, New South Wales The stone was crushed and concentrated by them, and valuing the gold at only 60s per oz, it yielded at the rate of £13 6s 10d per ton, on learning this the present owners immediately secured 800ft on the line of reef, purchased a winding engine, and have now raised a large lot of quartz and pyrites, but on account of the want of water they will not be able to crush until next wet season.

There are 5 shares in the claim, four-fifths being held by residents of Kingsborough.

Ida Reef

13000 Hanging-wall at 175ft
13001 Foot-wall at 200ft
13002 Do 250ft

The bearing of the reef is north 106deg. east, the underlay dipping south. The reef averages 18in to 24in wide, and consists of a dense white crystalline quartz, with blue, very regular, amorphous laminations; the specimens exhibit gold in the quartz and in the laminations. Two shafts have been sunk 250ft down.

Comet Reef

13003   Hanging-wall at 180ft
13004   Auriferous quartz, various levels
13005

Queen of the North

13006   Hanging-wall at 190ft
13007   Auriferous quartz at 190ft
13008   Foot-wall at 190ft
13009   Hanging-wall at 270ft
13010   Auriferous quartz at 270ft

Queen of the North

13010* Auriferous quartz at 270ft

—Exhibitor: MR. GOLD-WARDEN H. ST. GEORGE

The quartz in this claim is very similar to that in the Comet, except that the sulphur-yellow deposit between the laminations, which is held to be the best indication for gold throughout the field, is more strongly marked here. There is no sulphur in the yellow deposit. In the petition and report of the Deep Sinking Committee to the Legislature, dated 17th January, 1885, The Queen is reported to have crushed altogether 6,884 tons of quartz, yielding 18,849oz 8dwt 14grs gold, equal to 2oz 14dwt 18grs per ton.

Hart's Content

13011   Quartz showing gold

The country rock is slate, and the specimens come from a depth of 90ft. The shaft is 120ft down, and the Deep Sinking Committee give the total quantity of stone crushed as follows :—678 tons quartz, yielding 2,368oz 9dwt 10grs gold, equal to 3oz 9dwt 20grs per ton.

St. Patrick

13012   Auriferous quartz

The Deep Sinking Committee report on this mine :—Shaft 100ft down; quartz crushed, 977 tons, yielding 1,060oz 18dwt 12grs gold, equal to 1oz 1dwt 17grs per ton

NORMANBY FIELD ...   .   *Queen of the North*

13013   Auriferous quartz and mispickel

These specimens are from a division of the field called the Normanby, distant 75 miles east of Maytown. The Isabella has produced good stone, but the records are meagre; the last 100 tons quartz crushed 2oz 4dwt per ton, and the reef is from 16in to 3ft thick. The pyrites in the Queen of the North is very rich in gold. Some of the leading merchants of Cooktown are about to erect a plant for the treatment of the pyrites locally.

NORMANBY ... ... *Isabella*

13014　Auriferous quartz

This specimen was in the possession of Mr. Warden St. George, and shows gold very finely divided on each face and between the laminations.

Hit or Miss

13015　Hanging-wall
13016　Auriferous quartz
13017　Foot-wall

This mine is 175ft down, and, according to the report of the Deep Sinking Committee, has crushed 1,207 tons of quartz, yielding 3,572oz 8dwt 12grs gold, equal to 2oz 19dwt 4grs per ton. The reef is about 16in wide.

Hit or Miss

13017*　Auriferous quartz at 60ft

—*Exhibitor :* MR. GOLD-WARDEN ST. GEORGE

Viking

13018　Auriferous quartz
13019*　　Do　　do　　at 60ft

—*Exhibitor :* MR GOLD-WARDEN ST. GEORGE

Cannibal Creek

13019　Argentiferous galena, assaying 60oz silver per ton

Purdie's Reef

13020　Auriferous quartz, showing nuggety gold

Welcome Stranger

13021　Auriferous quartz
13022　Dyke, apparently diorite, bearing north-west and south-east and traceable for many miles

ANALYSIS :

Silica	46·80
Alkalies	7·30
Protoxides, iron and manganese ...	32·20
Loss on ignition	9·22
Lime	2·34
Magnesia	3·68

101.54

—*A. W. Clarke*

CANNIBAL CREEK, 16 miles from Maytown   ...   ...   *Phœnix Mine*

     13023   Lode tin

GRANITE CREEK, 9 miles from Cannibal Creek.

     13024   Stream tin

                                                  Queen of the North

     13025   Tailings weathered

                                                  Chance Mine

     13026   Hanging-wall, with calcite vein
     13027   Auriferous quartz

                                                  Queen of Beauty

     13028   Auriferous quartz

                                                  Mosman Creek

     13029   Sandstone, bed of creek, with trace of gold
     13030   Do   coarser   do   do
     13031   Do   top of range, desert sandstone

MAYTOWN FIELD   ...   .   *Ida*

     13032   Quartz showing gold
     13C33   Do   do
     13034   Do   do
     13035   Do   do

                                                  Comet

     13036   Gold-bearing quartz, 200ft level
     13037   Do   do   do
     18038   Black slaty rock
     13039   Silver-grey slate
     13040   Dark-grey slate, 250ft level

                                                  Queen of Beauty

     13041   Quartz showing gold

                                                  Blackbird

     13042   Quartz showing gold

                                              Maytown Township

     13043   Country rock, slate
     13044   Do   do
     13045   Quartz mixed with slate

LIMESTONE CREEK FIELD   ...   .   *Anglo-Saxon P.C.*

     13046   Quartz showing gold, 16ft level, water-shaft
     13047   Do   do   from 100ft level.
         The reef averages 2ft 9in in thickness, and yields 8½oz per ton without tailings and blankets.

13048 Quartz showing gold
13049   Do   do
13050   Do   do
13051   Do   do

Anglo-Saxon No. 1 West

13052 Gold-bearing quartz with slate ; average width of reef 2ft
13053   Do   do
13054 Crystallised quartz with black slate
13055 Black slate
13056 Sandstone
13057 Decomposed slate with quartz

Rosannah

13058 Quartz showing gold, chalcopyrite, and copper carbonates;
           average width of reef, 2ft 6in
13059 Quartz showing gold
13060   Do   do
13061   Do   do
13062   Do   do
13063   Do   do
13064 Country rock, also containing gold

North Cross

13065 Quartz showing gold
13066   Do   do
13067   Do   do
13068   Do   do
13069   Do   do
13070   Do   do
13071 Country rock, sandstone
13072   Do   slate

German Miner

13073 Quartz (honeycombed) with gold

WOOLGAR DISTRICT AND FIELD.

Soap Spar Gold Mine

13994 Quartz showing gold
13395 Galena in quartz showing gold
13996 Galena
13997 Heavy spar

WOOLGAR.

13998 Quartz showing gold

—*Exhibitor :* W. MOIR, ESQ.

MOUNT HOGAN.

13999 Mundic, galena and auriferous quartz from various mines
           in district

CROYDON DISTRICT.

MOUNTAIN MAID FIELD　　...　*Mountain Maid Nos 1 & 2 South United*

14000　Auriferous quartz in bulk, 4cwt

　　—*Exhibitor:* W. F. SMITH, ESQ., *per* MR. GOLD-WARDEN TOWNER

This claim lies about three miles to the north-east of Croydon. A portion of the claim No. 2 was taken up some three months ago (Feb , 1888), with a view of working a line of reef within two chains of, and almost running parallel with the Mountain Maid line. Good surface prospects having been obtained from this reef, a shaft was sunk to a depth of about 11ft when heavy rains flooding the shaft further work was prevented for the time being. That portion of the Mountain Maid line running through the claim was then prospected with the result that the sinking of a shaft was commenced at once. As sinking was gone on with, the reef widened, the stone from it often showing gold freely and always giving payable prospects. The stone now being forwarded to Melbourne was obtained at a depth of from 23ft to 26ft from the surface, the reef averaging in thickness 5½ft to 6ft. In February last a spare piece of ground immediately north of the claim and known as No. 1 South was applied for and added to the first taken up claim, so that the claim now contains 10 men's ground (500ft x 400ft). No. 1 South is the northern boundary of Nos. 1A and 2 south, and crushed 90 tons for 2oz 7dwts per ton. At present there are about 40 tons of stone at grass and in a few weeks a trial crushing will be obtained. It is also intended to continue sinking the shaft on the parallel line mentioned above and there is every indication of a second good solid reef soon being met with.—W. FAWCETT SMITH.

The stone exhibited is estimated to yield 1½oz per ton; gold valued at £3 5s 6d per oz. Width of reef at bottom of shaft, 2ft 6in.

MOUNTAIN MAID FIELD ... *Mountain Maid United Gold Mining Company*

14001　Auriferous quartz in bulk, 2cwt 1qr

　　　　　—*Exhibitor :* THE COMPANY, *per* THE MANAGER *and* MR. GOLD-WARDEN TOWNER

This claim comprises an area of 25 acres, having 1,400ft along the line of reef. The reef runs north and south through a fine-grained granite country, with a slight underlay to the east. The mine has been in work 2 years, and the reef opened out and sunk on by 7 shafts, varying in depth from

:30ft to 90ft; the reef has been driven on in Nos. 3 and 4 shafts by drives north and south 80ft. The stone sent has been obtained from No. 4 shaft in the south drive, at 60ft level, where the reef averages 5ft in thickness for the whole length of the drive.

In sinking the 7 shafts and driving 80ft, 1,050 tons of stone have been raised, 597 tons of which have been crushed for a yield of 707oz 16dwt of gold, thus averaging 1oz 3dwt 17grs per ton, the assay value of the gold being £3 2s 6d per oz. The balance of the stone, 457 tons, is now in the machine yards awaiting crushing.

The total output from the whole line of reef for the 2 years it has been working is 1,529 tons crushed, for a yield of 1,910oz 3dwt, and 870 tons now in the yards awaiting crushing on account of different owners.

The Mountain Maid line of reef for 2,200ft in length will average 4ft in width, and will crush about 1¼oz to the ton, stoped away indiscriminately. The only drawback to this line of reef is want of machinery to raise and crush the stone in order to make it one of the best paying lines of reef on Croydon Goldfield.

M. PENHALLURICK, Manager.

CROYDON FIELD ... ... *Croydon Queen Nos. 12 and 13 South*

14002   Auriferous quartz in bulk, 2cwt

– *Exhibitors :* THE SHAREHOLDERS, *per* MR. GOLD-WARDEN TOWNER

This stone is taken from different parts of the reef, and from a few feet to 40ft in depth, the width of reef between walls is from 1ft. to 2ft. 6in., the stone increasing going down, and the gold getting more plentiful. Reef proved right through Nos. 12 and 13 into No. 14, carrying gold all along. Shaft down on boundary of 12 and 13 about 40ft, following a rich shoot of gold on the underlay, also a shaft on the boundary of 12 and 13 on same line ; another shaft going down on No. 13 to strike Queen Reef at a greater depth. Have struck in this shaft a big body of quartz about 30ft from surface, carrying gold and rich silver gossan ; this apparently being a parallel reef to the Queen. Extent of ground 12 and 13 South, 500ft along the line of reef by 400ft. The shareholders wish 1cwt. of stone to be treated in Melbourne, and the result therefrom to be exhibited with the other hundredweight.

There are 18 claims at work on this line.

J. VAN DER HAYDEN.

HOMEWARD BOUND FIELD   ...   { *Croydon Homeward Bound Gold Mining Company*

14003   Auriferous quartz in bulk, 2½cwt

—*Exhibitor :* THE COMPANY, *per* E. B. FRAZER, MANAGER, *and* MR. GOLD-WARDEN TOWNER

GOLDEN VALLEY FIELD ...   . *Vasco de Gama P.C.*

14004   Auriferous quartz in bulk, 5cwt

—*Exhibitor :* J. W. STUART, *per* MR. GOLD-WARDEN TOWNER

GOLDEN VALLEY FIELD...   ...   . *Belfast United*

14005   Auriferous quartz in bulk, 5cwt

—*Exhibitor :* J. W. STUART, *per* MR. GOLD-WARDEN TOWNER

CROYDON FIELD   ... *The Content P.C. and No. 1 Amalgamated*

14006   Auriferous quartz in bulk, 1cwt

—*Exhibitors :* MESSRS. D. M'LAUGHLIN, G. TALBOT, J. BOWEN, *and* C. KEAN, *per* MR. GOLD-WARDEN TOWNER

Area of claim, 350ft by 400ft; situated on the True Blue and Iguana line of reef, about 1¼ mile west of Croydon. The sample is from the north shaft, 70ft in depth. The reef is between 3ft and 4ft in thickness, with well defined walls.

TABLETOP FIELD   ... *Croydon Mount Morgan Gold Mining Company*

14007   Auriferous quartz in bulk, 4cwt 1qr

—*Exhibitor :* THE COMPANY, *per* H. MACALLUM, MANAGER

CROYDON FIELD   ...   . *Black Snake P.C.*

14008   Gold and silver ore in bulk, 5cwt 2qr

—*Exhibitor :* R. H. ROWE, *for self and Party, per* MR. GOLD-WARDEN TOWNER

"The Black Snake is on the celebrated Croydon Queen line of reef, about half-a-mile south of the Croydon Queen P.C. On this line is also the No. 1 North Black Snake, now known as the Silver King, from which claim exceedingly rich stone is being raised, both for gold and silver. Immediately south are the Nos. 1 and 2 South Black Snake, who are sinking and expect daily to strike the reef. Adjoining No. 2 is a limited liability company called the Miner's Right, who have a large quantity of stone at grass of good quality. Further south on the same line is the Waratah, which has had several good crushings, some of which yielded over 12oz of gold per ton. By the foregoing you will note that this line of reef has been proved for a long distance—nearly two miles. The sample of stone exhibited contains a large amount of silver as well as gold. It was obtained from a depth of 40ft from the surface, where the reef is 18in thick. At this depth we have driven north towards the Silver King 35ft, the reef averaging 18in; and have also driven south 6ft, reef in south drive 15in. The reef runs north and south, with an eastern underlie of about 1ft in 4ft. The great want of this line is proper machinery for treating this class of ore, there being no machinery on the field for its treatment; and several claims have sent and some are now sending their stone to Footscray, Melbourne, for treatment, as all parcels so far treated at those works have proved to be very rich in gold and silver.

"R. H. Rowe, Mining Manager."

Area of ground, 4 acres, in lease.

LAYCOCK'S CAMP OR GOLDEN VALLEY FIELD ...　...　...　*Hercules*

14010　Gold-bearing quartz, 86ft level
14011　　Do　　do　with altered porphyry
14012　　Do　　do　with country rock (altered porphyry)
　　The reef is from 8ft to 15ft wide.*

Grace Leigh

14013　Quartz showing gold, 60ft level
14014　Country rock, altered porphyry
　　Reef 18in wide.

Monkland

14015　Quartz showing gold
14016　　Do　　do
　　A reef westward of the Grace Leigh. The owners are sinking and raising fair stone.

Australian Beauty No. 1 North

14017　Quartz showing gold

---

*For particulars respecting this and the following claims and fields of the Croydon District, see collector's report, appendix and map exhibited.

Australian Beauty P.C.

| 14018 | Quartz with gold |
| 14019 | Do   do   and country rock |

Vasco da Gama

| 14020 | Gold-bearing quartz with rock |
| 14021 | Do   do |

Vasco da Gama No 1 South

| 14022 | Gold-bearing quartz |

King of Wallabadah

14023	Gold-bearing quartz from reef 8ft in width
14024	Do do a leader
14025	Hanging-wall, altered porphyry
	Reef 8ft wide.

Queen of Sheba

14026	Gold-bearing quartz
14027	Do do
14028	Country rock, altered porphyry, sometimes showing gold
14029	Do do

Golden Rose, on the Carron

14030	Gold-bearing quartz
14031	Do do
14032	Do do
14033	Country rock, altered porphyry

TABLE TOP FIELD...   ...   . *No 1. North, Bobby Dazzler*

14034	Gold-bearing quartz
14035	Do do
14036	Do do
14037	Do do
	Average width of reef 9ft.

Great Eastern

14038	Honeycomb quartz, showing gold
14039	Quartz crystallised do
14040	Do with country rock (altered porphyry)
14041	Do do do
14042	Country rock decomposed, near surface
14043	Do do do

Ace of Hearts

14044	Gold-bearing quartz		
14045	Do	do	crystallised
14046	Do	do	

Width of reef, 3ft.

Comet

14047	Gold-bearing quartz, from reef 3ft in width		
14048	Do	do	do	do
14049	Do	do	from leader parallel with reef

Day Dawn

14050	Gold-bearing quartz		
14051	Do	do	
14052	Do	do	
14053	Do	do	
14054	Do	do	
14055	Do	do	
14056	Do	do	crystallised and honeycombed
14057	Do	do	do	do
15058	Do	do	honeycombed, with fine gold
14059	Do	do	and country rock (altered porphyry)

The reef averages 15ft in width.

Mount Morgan

14060	Gold-bearing quartz		
14061	Do	do	with galena

La Perouse

14062	Gold-bearing quartz		
14063	Do	do	and country rock
14064	Do	do	
14065	Do	do	
14066	Do	do	

TWELVE-MILE FIELD ... ... *Lady Lottie*

14067	Gold-bearing quartz	
14068	Do	do
14069	Do	do
14070	Do	do

The reef averages 2ft 6in in width, and crushes 2½oz per ton.

TWELVE-MILE FIELD ... ... *Apex*

14071	Gold-bearing quartz and blende with gold

TWELVE-MILE FIELD   ...   .   *Golden Spur*

    14072   Quartz showing gold freely

TWELVE-MILE FIELD ...   .   **President**

    14073   Gold-bearing quartz
            The reef averages 4ft 6in in width.

TWELVE-MILE FIELD   ...   .   *Golden Point or May Bell*

    14074   Quartz with gold
            Reef 2ft wide.

TWELVE-MILE FIELD   ...   .   *Rising Sun*

    14075   Quartz with mundic containing gold
    14076   Do   do

TWELVE-MILE FIELD   ...   .   *Orient*

    14077   Gold-bearing quartz
    14078   Do   do
    14079   Do   do   near the wall
    14080   Do   do   with formation
    14081   Do   do   do
    14082   Do   do   do
    14083   Do   do   honeycombed
    14084   Country rock
    14085   Do
    14086   Do
    14087   Do

MOUNTAIN MAID FIELD   ...   .   *Phœnix*

    14088   Quartz with gold
    14089   Do   do
    14090   Foot-wall
    14091   Do
    14092   Do
    14093   Hanging-wall over bend in reef, 30ft level
    14094   Gravel above No. 14093
    14095   Hanging-wall proper, light altered prophyry

MOUNTAIN MAID FIELD   ...   .   *Rainbow*

    14096   Gold-bearing quartz from surface to 50ft, crushed 2oz per
            ton
    14097   Gold-bearing quartz
    14098   Do   do

14099 Hanging-wall, country light altered porphyry
14100   Do
14101   Do
14102   Do
14103 Foot-wall, reddish altered porphyry
14104   Do
14105   Do

MOUNTAIN MAID FIELD   ...   .   *Babe P.C.*

14106 Gold-bearing quartz

Babe No. 1 North

14107 Gold-bearing quartz
14108   Do   do

Welcome P.C.

14109 Gold-bearing quartz, showing gold

MOUNTAIN MAID FIELD   ...   .   *Mountain Maid United*

14110 Gold-bearing quartz
14111 Quartz showing gold
14112   Do   crystals
14113   Do   do   loose on a blueish clay
14114 Decomposed porphyry with quartz carrying gold

MOUNTAIN MAID FIELD   ...   .   *St. Patrick*

14115 Gold-bearing quartz

HOMEWARD BOUND FIELD   ...   ...   *Pride of the Hills No. 3 South*

14116 Gold-bearing quartz with country rock, altered porphyry
14117   Do   do   do   do

HOMEWARD BOUND FIELD   ...   .   *Walhalla*

14118 Gold-bearing quartz
14119 Hanging rock, light altered porphyry
14120 Foot-wall, light altered porphyry

HOMEWARD BOUND FIELD   ...   ...   *Pride of the Hills No. 2 South*

14121 Country rock

HOMEWARD BOUND FIELD   ...   ...   *Pride of the Hills No. 1 South*

14122 Gold-bearing quartz

HOMEWARD BOUND FIELD   ...   .   *Pride of the Hills P.C.*

    14123   Gold-bearing quartz from surface
    14124   Do   do   do   15ft level

HOMEWARD BOUND FIELD   ...   ...   *Pride of the Hills No. 3 South*

    14125   Quartz and foot-wall

HOMEWARD BOUND FIELD   ...   .   *Waterfall No. 3 South*

    14126   Altered porphyry in layers

HOMEWARD BOUND FIELD   ...   .   *Waterfall P.C.*

    14127   Quartz with gold at 150ft
    14128   Ferruginous clay, rich in gold

HOMEWARD BOUND FIELD   ...   .   *Waterfall Block*

    14129   Country rock at 75ft level
    14130   Do   do
    14131   Do   at 90ft level
    14132   Do   at 130ft level

HOMEWARD BOUND FIELD   ...   ...   *Homeward Bound No. 2 South*

    14133   Gold-bearing quartz
    14134   Do   do   honeycombed, with hanging-wall

HOMEWARD BOUND FIELD   ...   ...   *Homeward Bound No. 1 South*

    14135   Gold-bearing quartz honeycombed

HOMEWARD BOUND FIELD   ...   .   *Ironclad*

    14136   Quartz and ironstone, both showing gold
    14137   Do   do   do
    14138   Do   do   do
    14139   Do   do   do
    14140   Foot-wall, altered porphyry
    14141   Hanging-wall, altered granulite

HOMEWARD BOUND FIELD...   ...   .   *Mark Twain*

    14142   Quartz showing gold
    14143   Do   do

South Croydon Field ... ... { *Waratah, Grant United P.C.,
or May Queen*

14144   Quartz with ironstone, showing gold freely
14145   Do   do   do   do
14146   Do   do   do   do
14147   Do   with hanging-wall
14148   Foot-wall
14149   Do
14150   Do

South Croydon Field... ... . *Rockton*

14151   Country rock at 50ft
14152   Do   at 55ft

South Croydon Field... ... ... *Mystery*

14153   Quartz and mundic carrying gold
14154   Do   do   do
14155   Do   do   altered by water
14156   Do   do
14157   Do   do
14158   Do   do

South Croydon Field ... ... *Harp of Erin P.C.*

14159   Gold-bearing quartz
14160   Do   do
14161   Do   do

South Croydon Field .. .. *Harp of Erin No. 2 South*

14162   Samples delayed in transit
14163   Do   do
14164   Do   do

South Croydon Field ... ... *Harp of Erin Block*

14167   Samples delayed in transit
14168   Do   do

South Croydon Field ... ... *King of Croydon Block*

14169   Country rock (altered granulite)
14170   Do   do   do

South Croydon Field ... ... *King of Croydon No. 7 North*

14171   Quartz showing gold
14172   Do   do
14173   Do   do
14174   Do   do
14175   Do   do

K

SOUTH CROYDON FIELD   ...   ... *King of Croydon No. 5 North*

14176 Quartz showing gold
14177 Do   do   do
14178 Do   do   do
14179 Do   do   do
14180 Country rock, quartz

SOUTH CROYDON FIELD... ... ... *Richmond P.C.*

14181 Quartz showing gold ⎫
14182 Do   do   ⎬ Lent by the Prospector
14183 Gold-bearing quartz
14184 Do   do
14185 Country rock, altered and decomposed granite
14186 Do   altered porphyry
14187 Do   do   do
14188 Do   whitish sandstone
14189 Do   reddish   do

SOUTH CROYDON FIELD   ... ... *Moonstone Block*

14190 Quartz showing gold freely
14191 Do   do   do   at 126ft
14192 Do   do   do   at 130ft
14193 Hanging-wall, altered granulite
14194 Foot-wall
14195 Formation between the walls
14196 Country rock at 75ft

SOUTH CROYDON FIELD ... ... *Archer P.C.*

14197 Quartz with gold
14198 Do   do and hanging-wall
14199 Do   do and foot-wall

Queen of Croydon No. 2 South

14200 Gold-bearing quartz
14201 Do   do
14202 Do   do
14203 Do   do

Queen of Croydon No. 4 South

14204 Gold-bearing quartz

Queen of Croydon No. 9 South

14205 Gold-bearing quartz

Queen of Croydon No. 10 South

14206 Gold-bearing quartz

Queen of Croydon No. 12 South

14207 Gold-bearing quartz
14208   Do   do

Queen of Croydon No. 13 South

14209 Gold-bearing quartz
14210   Do   do

SOUTH CROYDON FIELD ... ... *True Blue Nos. 3 and 4 South*

14211 Gold-bearing quartz

True Blue No. 2 South

14212 Gold-bearing quartz
14213   Do   do
14214 Country rock (altered porphyry) at 60ft
14215   Do   do   do
14216 Reddish sandstone from 22ft to 55ft level

True Blue No. 1 South

14217 Gold-bearing quartz
14218   Do   do
14219 Quartz with altered porphyry
14220   Do   do   foot-wall
14221 Country rock, light altered porphyry
14222   Do   do   do   hanging-wall

True Blue P.C.

14223 Gold-bearing quartz
14224   Do   do
14225   Do   do
14226 Altered porphyry
14227 Sandstone with fossils, surface

True Blue Block

14228 Altered porphyry, 100ft level

ETHERIDGE DISTRICT.

GILBERTON FIELD.

14750 Copper ore

    The lode runs east and west, and the width is 50ft. The lode has not been worked at all.

The analysis by Mr. K. T. Staiger, analyst, Brisbane, gives the following percentage composition :—

Oxides and carbonates of copper ...	71·163
Oxide of iron	19·709
Insoluble	9·128
	100·000
Metallic copper	58·091 per cent.

Cumberland Reef

14751   Auriferous mundic ore, from the 180ft level

The reef is 9ft wide. The sample weighs 185lb. The stone of this reef has assayed as high as 27oz of gold per ton. The company (the Cumberland No. 1 North Gold Mining Company) have extensive machinery on the way to the mine for the treatment of this ore

14752   Decomposed lead ore

Running east and west, about 100ft wide. It is stated some of the samples from this reef have assayed 125oz of silver to the ton; but when the sample arrived in Brisbane it was only found to contain a trace of silver and 1·17 per cent. of copper, with 5·12 per cent. of lead, the remainder principally consisting of oxide of iron and silicates.—(Abridged from Mr. K. T. Staiger's Report.)

Gilberton

14754   Silver galena

The lode is very large. The average assay of samples has given 155oz of silver per ton. No work has been done on the reef yet.

14755   Silver galena, from a neighbouring reef

Titania Reef No. 1

14756   Auriferous mundic ore from the 60ft level
Exhibit weighs 56lb.

Titania Reef No. 2

14757   Auriferous mundic

This reef is from 3ft to 5ft wide. The mundic is described as being rich, dark, and intractable. A quantity has been sent to England to be smelted. It is stated that the assays give 57oz of gold per ton of ore. Weight of sample, 90lb.

New Zealand P.C. Reef

14758   Auriferous mundic from 130ft below surface

The reef is nearly vertical, and is about 3ft. wide. The stone assays 15oz of gold per ton. There is good machinery on the reef, steam winding and pumping gear. The sample weighs 56lbs.

Cumberland P.C. Lease

14759   Auriferous mundic from 520ft below surface

The reef is at present 9ft to 10ft wide. The pyrites is described as dark free mundic which assays from 10oz to 15oz of gold per ton. The company (which is working with local capital—Messrs. O'Brien and Company) has powerful steam winding gear; also a fine crushing plant erected about half-a-mile from the mine, on a creek, across which a dam has been thrown to conserve the water. The underlie dips at about 45deg. The reef is about 13 miles west of Georgetown.

NORTH-WEST DIVISION.

NORMANTON DISTRICT.

Exhibits collected for the Commissioners (London, 1886) by Frank Hann, Esq.

18000   Lenticular concretions

In the broken specimen a kind of cone in cone structure can be traced, the centre and beginning of the formation being possibly determined by a fragment of wood or other minute decomposing vegetable product.

18002   Bulk hæmatite from surface
18003   Do specimen copper carbonates from surface
18004   Do   do   hæmatite, expected to carry gold, from surface
18005   Three specimens copper carbonates from surface
18006   Samples forwarded by Mr. Hann for analysis
18007   Do   do   do   do
18009   Galena
18010   Do

CLONCURRY DISTRICT AND FIELD.

Cloncurry Copper Smelting Company

18500 Auriferous hæmatite

—*Exhibitor :* R. H. SHEAFFE, ESQ.

MOUNT MANTONI.

18501 Copper oxides with native copper and malachite

DUGALD RIVER, 45 miles north-west of Cloncurry

18502 Native copper with oxides, malachite and calcite
18503   Do   do   do
18504 Copper oxides with malachite
18505 Copper oxides with native copper
18506 Native copper with oxides, malachite and calcite
18507 Copper oxides and malachite

—*Exhibitor :* CLONCURRY COPPER MINING COMPANY

VARIOUS LODES, south-west of Cloncurry

18508 Malachite with calcite
18509   Do   do copper oxide
18510   Do   do   do   red oxide
18511 Cuprite and native copper with carbonates
18515 Native copper with cuprite and malachite
18516   Do   do
18517 Cuprite and malachite
18517* Tetrahedrite
18519 Cuprite and carbonates
18520 Cuprite and malachite
18521 Native copper changing to cuprite
18522 Cuprite
18523 Cuprite and native copper
18524 Bismuthite containing gold
18525 Cuprite and malachite

—*Exhibitor :* CLONCURRY COPPER MINING COMPANY

SOLDIER'S CAP ...   . *Rose and Thistle P.C.*

18530 Quartz showing gold
       Width of reef, 6ft ; average yield, 2oz per ton ; value, £4
per oz. Depth of workings, 70ft.

—*Exhibitor :* MR. GOLD-WARDEN SAMWELL

Rose and Thistle United

18531 Auriferous quartz
       Width of reef, 3ft ; average yield, 1oz per ton. Depth of
workings, 40ft.

—*Exhibitor :* MR. GOLD-WARDEN SAMWELL

CLONCURRY ... ... *Eagle and Kangaroo Extended*

  18532 Auriferous quartz

      Width of reef, 2ft; depth of workings, 80ft. There are four reefs, carrying good gold, in the ground.

          —*Exhibitor :* MR. GOLD-WARDEN SAMWELL

CLONCURRY ... ... *Golden Star Extended*

  18533 Auriferous quartz

      Width of reef, 1ft 6in ; depth of workings, 30ft Three reefs, carrying good gold, in the ground.

          —*Exhibitor :* MR. GOLD-WARDEN SAMWELL

CLONCURRY ... ... *Comus P.C.*

  18534 Auriferous quartz

      Width of reef, 6ft; average yield, 2oz per ton; depth of workings, 30ft.

          —*Exhibitor :* MR. GOLD-WARDEN SAMWELL

CLONCURRY ... ... *Caledonian*

  18536 Auriferous quartz

          —*Exhibitor :* J. P. ORMOND, ESQ.

CLONCURRY . ... *The Victory*

  18537 Auriferous quartz

          —*Exhibitor :* J. P. ORMOND, ESQ.

CLONCURRY ... . *Great Australian Copper Mine*

  18538 Copper oxides and carbonates at 120ft level

          —*Exhibitor :* MR. GOLD-WARDEN SAMWELL

CLONCURRY.

  18538* Magnetic iron ore from a mountain of same

COAL AND COKE EXHIBITS.

IPSWICH COAL FIELD ... { *Waterstown Coal and Coke Company, Limited, Ipswich.*

  18539 Coal, coke, and smithy coal

      —*Exhibitor :* THE COMPANY, *per* J. JOHNSON, *Manager*

  18540 Coke and the article which it is made from by the Waterstown Coal and Coke Company, Eagle Street, Brisbane

      —*Exhibitor :* THE COMPANY, *per* G. K. MOFFAT

West Moreton Coal and Coke Company, Limited, Ipswich

18541   First-class steam coal

Depth of shaft, 646ft; thickness of seam from which exhibit was taken, 19ft; method of working, stoop and room.

Exhibitor : BRYDON, JONES, & CO., *Brisbane and Ipswich*

18542   Smelting coke

Exhibitor : THE COMPANY

New Ebbwvale Coal Company, Limited, Dinmore

18543   Coal

Exhibitor : THE COMPANY, *per* W. H MAPLESTON, *Secretary*

Queensland Collieries Company, Limited

18544   Coal with samples of roof and floor

Exhibitor : THE COMPANY

MARYBOROUGH COAL FIELD   ...   . *Torbanelea Colliery*

18545   Sample of a top lift of coal at about 350ft from surface ; a gas, coking and steam coal

Depth of shaft, 400ft ; thickness of seam—top coal, 3ft 6in to 3ft 9in; band, 3in to 1ft 6in; bottom coal, 1ft 6in ; total, 5ft 3in to 6ft 9in ; method of working, the long wall system.

Exhibitor : THE ISIS INVESTMENT COMPANY OF QUEENSLAND, *Maryborough*

ANALYSIS—

Carbon (fixed)	...	...	...	...	67·925
Gas, oils, tars, &c.	...	...	...	...	27·330
Ash ...	...	...	...	...	3·640
Sulphur	...	...	...	...	·460
Moisture	...	...	...	...	·645
					100·000
Coke ...	..	...	...	...	71·565
Heating power	...	...	...	...	95·255
Gas ...	...	...	...	...	8.987
Ash per ton ...	...	...	...	...	81lbs.

By MR. RANDS,

Assistant Government Geologist.

Mr. Charles C. Rawlins, 95 Collins Street, Melbourne, reports that this coal gives 10,280 cubic feet of 15 candle power.

The evaporative power, as tested with 2 tons of coal, under the auspices of Mr. D. M. Barry (of Munroe, Barry, & Co.) and Mr. John Blyth (of John Blyth & Co.), Melbourne, is as follows :—8¼lbs. of water per pound of coal.

RICHARD JOSEPH, *Secretary Isisford Investment Company*

BOWEN COAL FIELD.

18546   Sample of coal

Exhibitor : THE MUNICIPALITY OF BOWEN

APPENDIX.

Report on the Croydon District.

[By H. F. Wallmann.]

Surrounding the Gulf of Carpentaria is one vast alluvial flat, extending east, south and west, with little irregularities of surface, to relieve its monotony, until the different ranges bounding it in these directions are reached. This great plain probably conceals everywhere deposits of coal. The encircling high ground from its commencement at Cape York as far as is now known is everywhere auriferous. Gold is found on the Peninsula itself (and here the discovery bids shortly to be more amplified), on the Palmer, the Hodgkinson, the Etheridge, the Gilbert, the Woolgar and at Cloncurry. Moreover, everywhere the rocks in which these gold fields are found exhibit changes accountable only by the influence of the presence of water. Croydon gold field also is situated in this circle of ranges related to the plains at the head of the Gulf as the shores to an ocean. Its geographical situation may be roughly stated to be 18deg. south latitude and 142deg. longitude. It is distant 110 miles from Normanton, lying east by south-east from that town, across the above-mentioned featureless flat country. This distance may be traversed in two days. The township of Croydon itself is placed on level ground on the first spur of the ranges met with; and, since its foundation was owing to the discovery of gold in its vicinity, it is needless to remark, is but a few years old. In the immediate neighbourhood of the town and even within its boundaries, reefs are worked with very good results as far as the yield of gold is concerned. The formation, as is also all the country west of Croydon, is sandstone, containing fossils of apparently recent geological age, followed by decomposed granite which passes into granulite. The rocks in fact favour the presence of gold. As soon as one rises the hills porphyry takes the place of the sandstone, insomuch so that almost all the physical features of the field are due to the presence of this rock, exhibiting all those variations in the aggregation of its component elements, and so in appearance, which result from changes of a peculiar class. In some parts this porphyry is again overlaid by sandstone, as will be seen on inspection of the map.

The reefs around the Croydon township, such as the Post Hole, Sovereign, Come-at-Last, Norah, Sir Walter, Lady Mary, Silver King, Waratah United, Miner's Right, &c , all run nearly north and south, underlaying north-east at a low angle. The Queen of Croydon, however, runs west 30deg. north, underlying north-east, and the Iguana strikes north 40deg. west, underlying north-east. From all these reefs good returns of gold are won, as may be concluded from an inspection of the stone (quartz); near the surface, some of them proved very rich in silver also. This metal occurred in the condition of native silver, and as chloride of silver, also as an alloy of gold, determining by this last mode of association the varying price obtainable for Croydon gold.

To the south of the Croydon township there are also reefs which have proved rich in gold, and still maintain this character, such as the Caledonia, &c. This reef is about half a mile south-east of the township, and strikes east 10deg. north, underlying 71deg. south 10deg. east. The Bradlaugh is a continuation of the Caledonia Reef. To the south-west of the latter the Highland Mary is met with, which strikes nearly due north, and underlies 71deg. east 10deg. north. The mining properties known as Glengarry and Sir Garnet are also on this line of reef. The Archer, distant a quarter of a mile south-west by south from the Highland Mary, is a reef which has a semicircular course, north through west to south, and underlies 80deg. to the east

On the road leading from Croydon to Georgetown, also to the south-east by south, the following reefs are worked:—The Rockton, which strikes north underlying 10deg. to the west. The character of the formation at this spot is somewhat peculiar. A gravel extends downwards to nearly 50ft from the surface; at that level large boulders of somewhat worn granite are met with, and these are succeeded by the altered porphyry rock The Mystery is another reef, situated about half a mile south from this last one. It strikes north but underlays 45deg. to the east. Here the surface stone for a few feet downwards is ferruginous gravel, and this again covers the altered porphyry. The reef itself has an average thickness of 5ft, and the quartz composing it is heavily charged through and through with iron pyrites yielding a good return of gold. Distant two and a half miles from Croydon, and also along the Georgetown Road, which intersects it, is a reef named the Harp of Erin. This runs north, but has a very variable underlay in different parts of its course. At the Prospecting Claim it is 75deg. to the east; in No. 1 South the underlay is 45deg. to the east; in No. 2 South 70deg., and in No. 3 South 75deg.—in both also to the east. A change of this extent in the underlay of a reef is not an uncommon occurrence on the Croydon field. The Harp of Erin has yielded good results on crushing. At the block claim, to the east of the line of reef, the sinking is through granulite, but no doubt the reef will be met with in good country.

Along the Cork-tree Creek there are also several reefs which are fortunately situated within a short distance of the crushing mills. These reefs, as for instance the Baal Gammon and others, either strike north or east-north-east, which is the case with the Hidden Treasure At the spot where this Cork-tree Creek, after having passed through the Gorge, enters the flat, there are two crushing mills situated; and in their neighbourhood a prospecting area, 601 p.a., is worked, which has yielded 28oz of gold for 13 tons crushed. Another 3 miles south from the crossing of the creek, and to the west of the Georgetown road, we meet with the King of Croydon reef. This strikes north 10deg. west, and underlays about east 70deg., north 10deg., with the prospect of becoming more vertical on sinking. It has a foot-wall of decomposed and altered granite passing into granulite in the deeper levels, and a harging-wall of altered porphyry. The average thickness of the reef scarcely exceeds 1ft. The surface stone along the King of Croydon line was remarkably rich in gold. To the north of the prospecting claim are nine other claims, worked with good results. The prospecting claim itself crushed at different times—2 tons of ore, yielding 32oz 8dwts of gold; 10 tons, yielding 276oz; 8cwt, yielding 33oz; 10cwt (from the surface), yielding 25oz 7dwt; 12 tons (from the surface), yielding 25oz; 24 tons, yielding 240oz; 86 tons, yielding 630oz; and 10 tons, yielding 276oz. The nine other claims along the same line have exhibited the following returns:—No. 1 North gave 245oz from 10 tons, and 2,054oz from

590 tons; No. 2 North, 165oz from 10 tons, and 758oz 12dwt from 54 tons; No. 3 North, 731oz 19dwt from 41 tons, and 724oz from 60 tons; No. 4 North, 20½oz from 9½ tons; No. 5 North, 770oz from 200 tons; No. 6 North, 23oz from 16 tons; No. 7 North, 246oz from 52tons; No. 8 North, ... ; No. 9 North, ... The claims lying to the south of the prospecting claim did not turn out so well as those to the north of it, and when visited were registered, as was the case with the prospecting claim itself. Although in the block claims sinking had been prosecuted to a depth of 120ft, the reef had not been met with, which is evidence conclusive that the King of Croydon, as is the case probably with all the other reefs in the field, alters its underlay with the depth. The rock sunk through in the Block Claim is a hard granulite. The King reef has a leader striking north, named the Emperor; two crushings from it yielded respectively 2oz and 4oz to the ton. At a distance of a mile and a half to the east of the King reef, and nearly on the summit of a sandstone range, the Richmond reef is met with. This strikes north, and underlays 70deg. east. Sandstone and altered (decomposed) porphyry constitute the formation near the reef. It has a width of from 15in to 4ft, and carries gold all through. Operations along the Richmond line of reef have as yet been chiefly confined to surface workings, although two shafts have been sunk to a depth of 40ft, with the result of finding the country of a more settled nature and the reef more solid. The crushings from this reef have given good returns, the prospecting claim crushing 105 tons which yielded 273oz 16dwt of gold, and 1 ton which yielded 98oz. The No. 1 North gave 118oz 10dwt of gold from a single crushing of 37 tons of ore.

Four miles to the south of the King of Croydon, on the east side of the Moonlight Creek, is a reef named the Moonstone Reef. This on the Prospecting Claim strikes north-east, underlaying 70deg. north by west, and has an average thickness of about 15in. In the claims to the north of the Prospecting Claim, the reef, after taking a turn to the west, strikes nearly due north, underlaying west at 60deg. For a long distance along the surface the reef has been worked out. It carries gold visibly, a crushing of 211 tons yielded 425oz of it. The country rock is a light-coloured altered porphyry. In the Moonstone Block the reef was met with at a depth of 96ft, after passing through

60ft of a decomposed bluish-coloured granulite, and the same rock in a harder state for the remaining depth. Where found it had the same width and underlay as in the Prospecting Claim. Here also it showed gold freely, and gave 93oz 10dwts for 10 tons crushed.

To the north-west of the Croydon township and on the west side of the telegraph line is the True Blue reef. This strikes north-west by north and underlays 72deg. towards the north-east. The Prospecting Claim of this reef is situated on the northern slope of a hill; in it we find that the first 4ft beneath the surface are made up of loose ground to succeed altered porphyries. The reef in it has an average thickness of 22in ; 83 tons of it yielded 200oz of gold, and 34 tons 75oz. No. 1 south is on the top of the same hill, and the formation is for 10ft boulders, and these are succeeded by sandstone. The reef underlays, in this claim, 75deg., has an average thickness of 2ft 6in, and crushed 136oz from 54tons. The large block adjoining the No. 1 south and the prospecting claims, and all No. 8 south also, are owned by the same Company. The country in them is similar to that in No. 1 south. In No. 2 south the True Blue reef averages 2ft in thickness and underlays north-east 79deg. In this claim, from the surface to a depth of 22ft, rough boulders are gone through, and then the formation changes to a reddish sandstone. The foot-wall of the reef in it is a soft altered porphyry, and the hanging-wall hard rock of the same description. No. 2 south is on the southern fall of the hill. Good stone showing gold was being raised at the time of my visit. In No. 3 and No. 4 south the reef widens out to a thickness of 3ft 6in. These claims are on level ground, and the following are the conditions under which the True Blue is met with in them :—From the surface to a depth of 9ft reddish sandstone is gone through, and this passes into a sandstone with clay seams. The foot-wall of the reef is composed of a very soft altered and decomposed porphyry, and the hanging-wall is also soft. As in the previous claim, the quartz shows gold freely.

Situated to the north of the True Blue line are the Isabel and Content. These occur in a somewhat similar formation to that in which this reef occurs, but the returns from them are not so rich.

Following up the Station Creek, the Mountain Maid township, with Bibby's crushing mill, is arrived at. There are also numerous reefs in its neighbourhood. Of these the St. Patrick reef crushed 56 tons with a yield of 75oz of gold. The Babe yielded at the rate of a little over 1oz to the ton. The Mountain Maid has improved lately and gives good crushing stone. The Ironclad reef, so named from the abundance of iron contained in it, shows gold freely both in the quartz and ironstone. On treatment of a very secondary description the stone from it crushed at the rate of 3oz to the ton.

To the north of O'Brien's Creek occur the Rainbow, the stone from which averaged 2oz to the ton, the Phœnix which gave about the same return, and the Welcome which yielded 25oz from 20 tons. There are two reefs which run parallel one to the other and come from the Homeward Bound line. These are the Springs of Waterfall Creek. The Pride of the Hills reef is situated above the Homeward Bound and occurs on a range of about 100ft altitude. It strikes nearly due north and underlays 71deg. towards the east. The formation in which this reef occurs is porphyry altered throughout. Returns show from 2oz to 3oz of gold to the ton of ore crushed. On the west side are two east and west reefs, the Walhalla and the Surprise, both of which carry gold To the north of the latter of these occurs the Waterfall which is a continuation of the Pride of the Hills reef. Crushings from this yielded nearly 3oz of gold to the ton The Ayrshire and Homeward Bound are the same reef again north from the fall of Waterfall Creek. The last crushing from the latter, made at the Homeward Bound mill, showed a return of 3oz to the ton.

To the north of the Homeward Bound is the Twelve-Mile township with a perfect net of reefs in its vicinity. Amongst these may be mentioned the Lady Lottie, the Apex, the President, the May Bell, the Golden Point, the Jubilee Golden Spur, the Rough-and-Tumble, the New Chum, the Rosshire, &c. A large amount of quartz from these different reefs is on the ground awaiting treatment. All give an average yield of 2oz of gold to the ton and show gold freely. The reefs average in thickness from 2ft to 3ft and are situated in altered porphyry country. A detailed survey of this part of the field is very much wanted.

On the Lower Twelve-Mile Creek we have the Oriental and Gem reefs, situated in what appears to be an altered serpentine country of a slaty nature. A crushing from this made at a Georgetown mill yielded 6oz of gold to the ton.

Again, on the old main road to Table Top and to the north of its intersection of the Twelve-Mile Creek, we have the Rising Sun reef. This strikes north and underlays east, and can be traced along the surface for a considerable distance. The ore derived from the surface gave good returns of gold, and several different shafts were put down on the reef. The gold was associated in the ore with pyrites and galena and was itself visible. Returns showed the precious metal present at the rate of 3oz to the ton.

On the same, near Table Top, another reef is worked, named the Happy Jack, and from this a crushing of 4 tons yielded 15oz 16dwts of gold.

Table Top township, located on a creek of the same name, and situated also on high flat land, is surrounded by mines, the future of which bids to be as prosperous as that of any mining properties in the Croydon District. To the west of the township we have the Mount Morgan Mine—a large reef carrying good gold. South of the town we have a still larger reef, the Day Dawn, averaging in thickness about 11ft, and giving splendid returns. Again, to the east of the township we find the Bobby Dazzler; this is a reef having an average thickness of 9ft, and, although as yet it has not been fairly tested by crushing, carries good gold. Each of these three reefs is sufficient in extent and rich enough in gold to admit of a separate crushing plant being profitably employed upon it; and, moreover, the facilities for saving water in their vicinity are present. The Ace of Hearts, the Comet, and the Great Eastern are other reefs in the neighbourhood of Table Top; and these, as is known, would yield at least 3oz of gold for every ton of ore crushed. Besides these reefs mentioned, there are also numerous other ones close at hand which are worked, and yield richly auriferous quartz.

To the north-east of Table Top we have Golden Valley, or Laycock's Camp, on the Christmas Creek; and on the upper part of the same watercourse the Hercules, a perpendicular reef, having an average thickness of 8ft; and also the Venture.

The main reefs, however, lay to the west and south-west of the township; such are the Grace Leigh, the Monkland, the Australian

Beauty, the Belfast, or Vasco de Gama. All these produce richly-auriferous stone, the gold in which has an average value of £3 18s. per ounce.

The Queen of Sheba and King of Wallabadah are other reefs in the neighbourhood.

On the Carron River we have the Golden Rose, which has given splendid returns, and other claims also. Here good prospects have been procured for a long distance around, and the limits of auriferous country in this particular district are far from reached.

To the west of the Croydon township there is a considerable amount of work done, especially at a place named Mulligan's Camp. Here a good many mines are being developed, which in time will give good returns.

To the south of Mulligan's Camp are the Mark Twain and Alabama reefs, both of which have yielded to crushing 2oz of gold to the ton.

Still further to the south are the Ancient Briton, the Problem, the Crocodile on the Pyramids, all of which have yielded fair crushings.

Near Flanagan's Hotel, north of the Georgetown Road, and about 20 miles distant from Croydon, there is a line of reef continued for a considerable distance. Along this line several claims are located which have turned out very well, and prospecting is being prosecuted in its vicinity. Amongst these may be mentioned the Good Iron, which yielded over 3oz of gold to the ton of crushing stuff; the Eureka and the Duke, both of which yielded over 2oz; and amongst those whose yield reached 2oz, but did not exceed this amount, we have the Bismarck, the Star and Empress, the Duke, the Queen of Beauty and others. It must be borne in mind, however, that opportunities for fairly testing this line of reef have not yet occurred.

To the north of this line, known as the Duke line of reef, we have the Parnell and the Wanderer, from both of which good stone has been raised.

In conclusion, it may be remarked that prospecting parties are pushing further and further east in the direction of the Gilbert Gold-field, and everywhere we hear of the existence of auriferous reefs being brought to light. In fact it seems as if the area of the Croydon goldfield, at present an unknown quantity, will turn out to be an exceedingly large one.*

The following is a list of all crushings which have been made on the field since its opening. It is derived from the *Golden Age* newspaper, and has been furnished by Messrs. Barker & Frew :—

Name of Claim.	Tons.	oz. dwt.	Locality.	Mill.
Ace of Hearts	...	...	Tabletop	...
Alabama	34	61 18	Mulligan ...	Bibby
Alabama	329	25 0	Mulligan ...	Bibby
Alice P.C.	60	484 0	...	Company
Alice (surface)	41	57 0	...	Bibby
Alice, No. 1 (surface)	121	140 19	...	Bibby
Alice, No. 1 North	25	45 3	...	Company
Alice, No. 2 South	10	16 11	...	Company
Ancient Briton	...	...	East ...	...
Apex	...	...	12-Mile ...	...
Archer	18	39 5	Croydon ...	Company
Australian Beauty	...	...	Laycock's	...
Australian Beauty, No.1 North	61	104 14	Laycock's	..
Ayrshire...	8	2 0	Homeward Bound ...	...
Austr. Inv. Co. Claims... ...	?	290 0	Laycock ...	Clarthe
Baal Gammon	18½	238 2	Gorge ...	Georgetown
Baal Gammon	120	270 0	Gorge ...	B. Larkins
Babe P.C.	96	102 7	Mountain Maid ...	Bibby
Babe, No. 1 South	55	55 5	Mountain Maid ...	Bibby
Babe, No. 2 South	16	18 16	Mountain Maid ..	Bibby
Babe, No. 1 North	80	71 0	Mountain Maid ...	Spent
Banner of Freedom, P.C. ...	137	122 17	Croydon ...	Bibby
Banner of Freedom	33	41 0	Croydon ...	Bibby
Banner of Freedom, No.1 South	24	22 7	Croydon ...	Company
Belfast	...	...	...	...
Better Luck P.C.	46	160 0	...	Company
Better Luck, No. 1 East ...	55	55 18	...	Company
Black Diamond...	...	...	...	...
Black Snake	40	190 0	Croydon ...	Company
Bismarck	40	46 0	Flanagan	...
Bird-in-Hand	..	...	Tabletop ...	...

* It must be borne in mind that the present report on the Croydon Goldfield is the result of a visit of only six weeks duration, though in this period every opportunity for inspecting the district was availed of. As a guide to his work the reporter made use of a topographical map, prepared by Mr. S. Haig, Surveyor; this, though only a sketch map, and therefore requiring considerable alteration in its detail, was of much service to him.

Name of Claim.	Tons.	oz. dwt.	Locality.	Mill.
Bobby Dazzler	...	...	...	...
Bradlaugh	32	59 0	...	...
Break of Day	22½	81 0	Croydon ...	Spent
Brittania	...	...	King ...	...
Bulletin	...	...	Tabletop ...	...
Caledonia	154	1,073 0	Croydon ...	Company
Caledonia (surface) ...	9	26 12	Croydon ...	Bibby
Caledonia, No. 1 East	136	630 0	Croydon ...	Company
Carron P.A.	5	8 17	Carron ...	Duffy
Carron P.A.	8	13 18	Carron ...	Duffy
Carron P.A.	5	21 16	Carron ...	Duffy
Chance P.C.	28	28 0	Croydon ...	Bibby
Chance P.C.	18	21 0	Croydon ...	Spent
Chance P.C.	45	131 5	Croydon ...	Company
City of London	4	51 0	Moonstone	...
Clencoe	39	29 0	Tabletop ...	...
Come at Last	140	98 8	Croydon ...	Company
Comet	17	46 0	Tabletop ...	...
Content	30	27 0	Croydon ...	Company
Cooper's P.A.	36	77 0	...	Spent
Crocodile	6	39 10	East ...	Spent
Dan's P.A.	22	9 10	...	Spent
Dan's P.A.	37	22 0	...	Spent
Day Dawn	80½	51 0	Tabletop ...	Company
Devil's Own	57	73 5	...	Bibby
Duchess	74	77 15	Flanagan	Spent
Duke, No. 2	43	55 0	Flanagan...	Hale
Duke P.C.	38	55 11	Flanagan	Hale
Duke P.C.	15	20 5	Flanagan	Hale
Duke (Iron)	122	253 9	Flanagan	Bibby
Emperor P.C.	22½	81 10	King ...	Spent
Emperor P.C.	29	80 0	. .	B. Larkins
Emperor, No. 1 North... ...	40	79 2	King ...	Byce
Empress and Good Iron ...	46	48 0	Flanagan...	Hale
Eureka P.C.	60	153 0	Flanagan	Byce
Eureka P.C.	48	68 0	Flanagan	Hale
Eureka, No. 1 South	30	53 4	Flanagan	Byce
Eureka, No. 1 South	34	66 17	Flanagan	Hale
Federation	...	...	Tabletop ...	...
Floraville P.A.	6	11 0	...	Bibby
Fulton's P.A.	15	15 13	...	Spent
Frost's Claim	19	28 0	Flanagan	Company
Gem P.C.	43	75 0	12-Mile ...	Bibby
Glengarry	156	437 0	Croydon ...	Byce
Golden Butterfly	...	...	Croydon ...	...
Golden Crest	10	17 10	...	Bibby
Golden Gate P.C.	214	183 16	Croydon ...	Bibby
Golden Gate P.C.	8	34 9	Croydon ...	Georgetown
Golden Gate, No. 1 North ...	80	85 0	Croydon ...	Spent
Golden Point	...	...	12-Mile ...	...
Golden Rose	22	147 18	Carron ...	Duffy
Golden Spur	28	25 15	12-Mile ...	Bibby
Good Iron	25	88 17	Flanagan...	Hale

Name of Claim.	Tons.	oz. dwt.	Locality.	Mill.
Gorge Creek 601	13	28 0	Gorge ...	Spent
Grace Leigh	85	150 0	Laycock's...	Clarthe
Grace Darling P.C.	50	23 9		Bibby
Great Britain	...	...	Tabletop ...	...
Great Eastern	...	...	Tabletop ...	...
Great Western	...	...	Tabletop ...	...
Harp of Erin P.C.	96	586 19	Croydon ...	Company
Harp of Erin P.C.	21	125 0	Croydon ...	Byce
Harp of Erin, No. 1 South ...	14	17 14	Croydon ...	Spent
Happy Jack	4	15 16	Tabletop ...	Bibby
Haythorn's Surface	14	13 0		Bibby
Hercules	5	6 2	Laycock's...	...
Hero	...	..	Tabletop ...	...
Highland Mary...	183	460 0	Croydon ...	Company
Highland Mary, surface	300	268 10	Croydon ...	Spent
Highland Mary, No. 1 North...	69	103 0	Croydon ...	Company
Highland Mary, No. 1 North...	70	127 0	Croydon ...	B. Larkins
Highland Mary, No. 1 South...	153	328 0	Croydon ...	Company
Highland Mary, No. 2 South...	211	831 5	Croydon ...	Company
Highland Mary, No. 3 South...	94	98 0	Croydon ...	Bibby
Hidden Treasure	...	...	Croydon ...	...
Homeward Bound P.C. ...	58	171 0	Homeward Bound	Bibby
Homeward Bound P.C. ...	...	...	Homeward Bound	...
Homeward Bound, No. 2 South	95	262 9	Homeward Bound	Bibby
Iguana P.C.	254	685 8	Croydon ...	Company
Iguana, No. 1 East	65	196 16	Croydon ...	Company
Iguana, No. 1 East	71	193 16	Croydon ...	Company
Ironclad P.C.	95	254 0	Croydon ...	Spent
Ironclad P.C.	37	84 0	Croydon ...	Bibby
Ironclad P.C.	87	193 0	...	...
Ironclad, No. 1 North	55	72 0	Croydon ...	Bibby
Isabella P.C.	25	28 19	Croydon ...	Duffy
Isabella, No. 1 South	31	41 19	Croydon ...	Duffy
Jubilee (Hill)	12	8 10	Richmond	Byce
Jubilee (12m.)	...	...	12-Mile ...	...
Just in Time P.C.	104	228 0	...	Byce
Just in Time, No. 1 West ...	62	61 17	...	Company
Just in Time, No. 1 East ...	63	112 14	...	Company
Just in Time, No. 1 West ...	4½	3 10	...	...
Just in Time, No. 2 East ...	98	100 0	...	Company
Kelmer's	13	27 0	...	Spent
King of Croydon	8cwt.	33 0	King of Croydon	Charters Towers
King of Croydon, surface ...	12	25 0	King ...	Byce
King of Croydon, surface ...	½	25 17	King ...	Georgetown
King of Croydon	2	32 8	King ...	Georgetown
King of Croydon P.C.	10	276 0	King ...	Georgetown
King of Croydon P.C.	86	630 0	King ...	Byce
King of Croydon, Pogg surface	24	240 0	King ...	Byce
King of Croydon, No. 1 North	590	2,054 0	King ...	Byce
King of Croydon, No. 1 North	10	245 0	King ...	Georgetown

Name of Claim.	Tons.	oz. dwt.	Locality.	Mill.
King of Croydon, No. 2 North	10	165 0	King ...	Georgetown
King of Croydon, No. 2 North	54	758 12	King ...	Byce
King of Croydon, No. 2 North	125	251 2	King ...	Byce
King of Croydon, No. 3 North	41	731 19	King ...	Georgetown
King of Croydon, No. 3 North	60	724 0	King ...	Byce
King of Croydon, No. 4 North	9½	20 15	...	B. Larkins
King of Croydon, No. 5 North	200	770 0	King ...	Byce
King of Croydon, No. 6 North	16	23 7	...	B. Larkins
King of Croydon, No. 7 North	52	246 0	...	Bibby
King of Wallabadah	41	84 0	Laycock's	...
Kreg's P.A.	6	12 10	...	Spent
Lady Catherine	87	52 2	Mountain Maid	Bibby
Lady Isabel P.C.	23	68 10	...	Company
Lady Lottie			12-Mile ...	...
Lady Mary P.C.	164	824 0	Croydon ...	Company
Lady Mary, surface	83	47 19	Croydon ...	Company
Lady Mary P.C. ...	79	535 1	Croydon ...	Company
Lady Mary, No. 1 North ...	201	1180 0	Croydon ...	Company
Lady Mary, No. 1 North ...	24	48 18	Croydon ...	Company
Lady Mary, No. 1 North ...	72	347 0	Croydon ...	Spent
Lady Mary, No. 1 South ...	25	27 19	Croydon ...	Company
Lady Norah	12	37 1	...	Company
Lady Norah	19	42 15	...	Company
La Perouse	...	...	Tabletop ...	...
Little Wonder	11	14 0	Croydon ...	Company
London P.C.	22	24 0	East Croydon ...	Spent
Lord Clyde	33	17 15	Homeward Bound ...	Spent
L. M'Arthur	...	...	Mulligan ...	...
M'Intosh P.A.	11	33 0	12-Mile ...	Company
M'Ivoy	...	...	...	...
M'Laughlin's P.C.	5	10 0	...	Company
Magenta P.C.	41	55 0	East Croydon ...	Spent
Mark Twain P.C.	124	327 0	East Croydon ...	Spent
Mark Twain, No. 1 North ...	24½	26 9	East Croydon ...	Spent
May Bell, or Golden Point ...	...	...	12-Mile ...	...
May Queen	23	251 10	Croydon ...	Company
May Queen	15½	34 8	Croydon ...	Spent
Michael Davitt	15	?	Mulligan ...	...
Miner's Right P.C.	30	38 8	Croydon ...	Company
Miner's Right, No. 1	21½	29 3	Croydon ..	Company
Monkland	...	...	Laycock's	...
Moonstone P.C.	41	427 0	King ...	Byce
Moonstone Block ...	10	93 10	King ...	Byce
Moonstone, No. 1 North ...	45	159 0	King ...	...
Mountain Maid P.C.	187	245 0	Mountain Maid	Bibby
Mountain Maid, No. 1 South...	74	169 0	Mountain Maid	Bibby

Name of Claim.	Tons.	oz. dwt.	Locality.	Mill.
Mountain Maid, No. 1 West ...	107	177 12	Mountain Maid ...	Bibby
Mountain Maid, No. 3 North...	86	68 13	Mountain Maid	Bibby
Mountain Maid, No. 5 North...	115	156 5	Mountain Maid	Bibby
Mountain Maid United ...	172	163 7	...	...
Mount Morgan	...	...	Tabletop ...	...
Morgan's, surface	10	21 0	...	Company
Morning Light	52	133 0	...	Hale
Morning Star	45½	71 19	...	B. Larkins
Mulway's P.A.	...	...	Tabletop ...	...
Mystery	5	3 0	Croydon ...	B. Larkins
Nancy Lee P.C....	30	28 3	Croydon ...	Company
New Chum	8	7 2	12-Mile	...
North Clunes	10	21 18	...	Duffy
North Star	...	...	Croydon ...	...
Oriental	...	...	12-Mile	...
Parnell	33	75 0	East ...	Hale
Phœnix P.C.	54	106 5	Mountain Maid	Bibby
Phœnix P.C.	98	160 0	Mountain Maid	Bibby
Post Hole	36	227 17	Croydon ...	Company
Post Hole	6½	8 5	Croydon ...	Company
Post Hole	42	547 14	Croydon ...	Bibby
P. O'Shannasy	20	39 18	...	Hale
President	44	62 17	12-Mile ..	Bibby
Pride of the Hills	78	93 5	Homeward Bound	Bibby
Pride of the Hills	142	206 0	Homeward Bound	Bibby
Pride of the Hills, No. 1 ...	30	113 15	Homeward Bound	Bibby
Problem P.C.	108	300 0	East Croydon ...	Spent
Queen of Beauty, Nos. 1 and 2 South, surface	96	27 6	East Flanagan's	Hale
Queen of Croydon P.C. ...	200	787 3	Croydon ...	Company
Queen of Croydon blank. P.C.	6	30 0	Croydon ...	Byce
Queen of Croydon blank. P.C.	...	37 3	Croydon ...	Byce
Queen of Croydon, surface ...	26	30 0	Croydon ...	Company
Queen of Croydon line, surface	31	53 0	Croydon ...	Company
Queen of Croydon, No. 2 South	80	500 0	Croydon ...	Company
Queen of Croydon, No. 2 South	98	666 4	Croydon ...	Bibby
Queen of Croydon, No. 9 South	44	56 6	Croydon ...	Company
Queen of Croydon, No. 9 South	20	80 0	Croydon ...	Company
Queen of Croydon, Burns ...	15	61 19	Croydon ...	Company
Queen of Croydon, No. 1 South	29	118 0	Croydon ...	...
Queen of Sheba...	...	...	Laycock's	...
Queen of Valley	39	69 18	...	Duffy
Rainbow P.C.	18	13 15	Mountain Maid ...	Bibby

Name of Claim.		Tons.	oz. dwt.	Locality.	Mill.
Rainbow, No. 1 North	...	104	101 1	Mountain Maid ...	Bibby
Rainbow, No. 3 ...	... ...	8	5 5	Mountain Maid ...	Bibby
Rainbow, No. 3 ...	... ...	20	15 19	Mountain Maid ...	Bibby
Rainbow, No. 5 ...	... ...	35	27 7	Mountain Maid ...	Bibby
Republic	... ...	...	...	Tabletop ...	...
Richmond P.C. ...	... ...	105	273 16	King ...	Company
Richmond P.C. ...	... ...	1	98 0	King ...	Company
Richmond, No. 1 North	...	37	118 10	King ...	Company
Richmond P.C. ...	... ...	121	354 0	...	Byce
Rising Sun P.C.	... ...	26	63 0	12-Mile ...	Spent
River's P.A. ...	... ...	11½	18 14	...	Spent
Rocton ...	... ...	...	...	Croydon ...	...
Ross-shire P.C. ...	... ...	66	183 7	12-Mile ...	Company
Ross-shire P.C. ...	... ...	23	51 10	12-Mile ...	Bibby
Rough-and-Tumble	... ...	...	...	12-Mile ...	...
Salamander	... ...	40	31 0	Croydon ...	Company
Sir Garnet	... ...	176	525 0	Croydon ...	Company
Sir Garnet	... ...	150	348 18	Croydon ...	Company
Sir Garnet	... ...	83	319 0	Croydon ...	Company
Sir Garnet	... ...	40	223 0	Croydon ...	Company
Sir Walter	... ...	100	673 5	Croydon ...	Bibby
Sovereign P C. ...	...	58	214 7	Croydon ...	Bibby
Sovereign, No. 1 West	...	74	628 0	Croydon ...	Byce
Spillaine's P.A. ...	...	40	74 11	...	Bibby
Stephen's Surface	...	16	62 17	...	Bibby
Star	... ...	...	...	East Flana-gan's ...	...
Star and Empress	... ...	...	...	East Flana-gan's ...	...
Stars and Stripes	... ...	...	..	Carron ...	...
St. Patrick P.C. ...	... ...	56	75 0	Mountain Maid ...	Bibby
St. Patrick P.C.	... ..	41	43 0	Mountain Maid ...	Bibby
Sunburst	... ...	...	...	Tabletop ...	
Sunset P.C.	... ...	162	125 0	...	Bibby
Surprise ...	... ...	28	61 9	Homeward Bound ...	Bibby
Surprise ...	... ...	...	...	Tabletop ...	...
Surrey Hills	... ...	20	13 0	...	B. Larkins
Taylor's P.A. ...	... ...	6	3 5	...	Spent
Telegraph	... ...	58	80 0	Croydon ...	Company
True Blue P.C. ...	...	34	75 0	Croydon ...	Company
True Blue P.C. ...	...	53	77 5	Croydon ...	Bibby
True Blue P.C. ...	...	83	200 18	Croydon ...	Bibby
True Blue, No. 1 South	...	54	136 0	Croydon ...	Bibby
True Blue, No. 1 South	...	35½	88 0	...	...
Vasco de Gama, No. 1 North	...	36	60 0	Laycock's ...	Carron
Venture	...	178	60 12	Laycock's	...

Name f Claim.			Tons.	oz. dwt.	Locality.	Mill.
Walhalla...	...	...	24	55 17	Homeward Bound ...	Bibby
Wanderer	...	...	30	91 11	East ...	Carron
Waratah United		...	23	118 12	Croydon ...	B. Larkins·
Ward's P.A.	...	...	13	49 0	...	Spent
Waterfall P.C. ...	...	...	85	335 15	Homeward Bound ...	Bibby
Welcome P.C. ...	...	...	20	25 0	Mountain Maid ...	Bibby
Welcome United	...	...	12	34 1	Mountain Maid ...	Bibby
Wherman's P.A.	...	...	6¼	14 8	...	Spent
Woldt's P.A.	...	...	3	6 0	...	Spent
Yellow Jacket ...	...	...	20	34 0	...	Spent